Cognitive and Behavioral Treatment
Methods and Applications

Cognitive and Behavioral Treatment
Methods and Applications

Edited by Donald K. Granvold
University of Texas, Arlington

Brooks/Cole Publishing Company
Pacific Grove, California

I(T)P ™
The trademark ITP is used under license.

 A CLAIREMONT BOOK

Brooks/Cole Publishing Company
A Division of Wadsworth, Inc.

Printed in the United States of America
10   9   8   7   6   5   4   3   2   1

Library of Congress Cataloging-in-Publication Data

Cognitive and behavioral treatment : methods and
    application / [edited by] Donald K. Granvold.
            p.   cm.
        Includes bibliographical references and index.
        ISBN 0-534-19194-0
        1. Cognitive therapy.   2. Behavior therapy.
    I. Granvold, Donald K.,
        [DNLM: 1. Behavior Therapy—methods. 2.
    Behavior Therapy— organization &
    administration.   WM 425 C6755 1993]
    RC489.C63C623   1993
    616.89′142—dc20
    DNLM/DLC
    for Library of Congress   93-24064
                                                                         CIP

Sponsoring Editor: *Claire Verduin*
Editorial Associate: *Gay C. Bond*
Production Editor: *Penelope Sky*
Production Assistant: *Chelsea Haga*
Manuscript Editor: *William Waller*
Permissions Editor: *Karen Wootten*
Interior and Cover Design: *Sharon L. Kinghan*
Art Coordinator: *Lisa Torri*
Interior Illustration: *Graphics Arts*
Typesetting: *Weimer Graphics, Inc.*
Cover Printing: *Phoenix Color Corporation*
Printing and Binding: *R. R. Donnelley & Sons Company*

Dedicated to the memory of my father, Colburn Granvold, who by personal example taught humility, unconditional regard for others, and dedication to hard work. Although our work worlds were divergent, his supportiveness and appreciation of my career were always obvious. Thanks, Dad.

Preface

Mental health practitioners are continually challenged to provide efficient, effective, and resilient treatment. Behavioral methods have long been established as psychotherapeutic procedures that are effective in treating a wide range of problems and populations. A recent shift in focus has shown that cognitive therapy is also effective in the treatment of various psychological disorders. Integrating these methodologies produces powerful therapeutic approaches to various clinical phenomena, including cognitive, behavioral, emotional, physical, physiological, and environmental factors.

This book is useful across disciplines and is appropriate not only for graduate students but also for experienced clinicians in the rapidly expanding field of cognitive-behavioral therapy. The contributions cover conceptual bases, intervention methods, and methods applied to selected populations and problems.

In Chapters 1 and 2, current cognitive and behavioral theory and methods are fully described. In the next fourteen chapters, collaborators from diverse backgrounds discuss applying cognitive and behavioral methods to an array of traditional and nontraditional populations. The final chapter is devoted to

such critical practice issues for effective cognitive-behavioral treatment as current information on cognitive assessment, the transfer of treatment effects to the client's natural environment, and relapse prevention.

The application chapters contain highly practical, skills-oriented methods for intervention. The diversity of the authors' practice orientations is reflected in their methods and in how they are combined. The application of methods to selected populations and problems is uniquely tailored to emphasize the flexibility of cognitive-behavioral treatment. Current procedures are presented practically, with empirical support. Case examples throughout the text clearly display intervention procedures.

ACKNOWLEDGMENTS

Many people deserve recognition for their contributions to this book. First, I acknowledge the tremendous contributions to the field by Albert Ellis, Aaron Beck, B. F. Skinner, Albert Bandura, Michael Mahoney, and Arthur Freeman. Although countless others have produced noteworthy work, these scholar-clinicians have most influenced my practice orientation and clinical skills, and I am sure that the effects of their influence are highly visible throughout this volume. I am also deeply grateful to the contributors for the time and energy it took them to share their expertise. All have thoughtfully and in great detail demonstrated the versatility of their approaches to cognitive-behavioral treatment. Sincere thanks go to Jo Ann Stevenson, who went above and beyond the call of duty in preparing the manuscript, and to Peggy Adams, for her early support and encouragement. Working with the staff at Brooks/Cole has been a great pleasure: thank you, Claire Verduin, Gay Bond, Penelope Sky, Bill Waller, Karen Wootten, and Sharon Kinghan.

I appreciate the efforts of the following people who provided constructive reviews of various parts of the manuscript: Frank Clark, University of Montana; Cynthia Franklin, University of Texas; Craig LeCroy, Arizona State University; Rona Levy, University of Washington; Lambert Maguire, University of Pittsburgh; Diane Harrison Montgomery, Florida State University; and A. Ali Syed, Paine College.

I thank my family and the friends who have felt the sacrifices that are required by a project such as this. And I am grateful to the graduate students at the University of Texas at Arlington who have challenged me and offered support, and to my clients who, during the past 25 years, have allowed me to learn the actual practice of cognitive-behavioral therapy.

Donald K. Granvold

About the Authors

Sharon Berlin is Associate Dean for Academic Affairs in the School of Social Service Administration at the University of Chicago. Professor Berlin received her M.S.W. and Ph.D. degrees from the University of Wisconsin. Her research focuses on women and depression, mental health services, and cognitive perspectives for social work practice. The co-author of *Informing Practice Decisions,* Professor Berlin recently investigated how depressed women improve within the context of cognitive therapy. She maintains a private psychotherapy practice in addition to her academic responsibilities.

Pamela Birsinger is a clinical social worker at CPC Parkwood Hospital in Atlanta. She received her M.S.W. from the University of Georgia. As director of Psychiatric Assessment Services, Ms. Bersinger specializes in crisis assessment of children, adolescents, and adults, and provides continuing education training programs for emergency room hospital staff.

William H. Butterfield is an associate professor at the George Warren Brown School of Social Work at Washington University. Professor Butterfield received his M.S.W. from the University of Michigan, and his Ph.D. from the Horace H. Rackham School of Graduate Studies. His principal teaching and practice interests are in behavior therapy, administration and organizational theory, research methodology, rural social work, and computer applications in social work. The author of numerous reviews and articles, Professor Butterfield has also served on a variety of editorial boards.

Norman H. Cobb is an assistant professor of social work at the University of Texas at Arlington. He received his M.S.S.W. from the University of Texas at Arlington and his Ph.D. from the University of California at Berkeley. His publications reflect his research interests in the areas of cognitive-behavioral interventions with children and the treatment of dual-career couples. Professor Cobb also maintains a private clinical practice.

Richard F. Dangel is a professor of social work and director of the M.S.S.W. program at the University of Texas at Arlington School of Social Work. His research interests include cross-cultural parent training, residential treatment of emotionally disturbed children, child abuse, and program evaluation. He has published three books and numerous articles. His current work involves the development of treatment packages to address gang involvement and the absence of caring in abused adolescents. He serves on the National Advisory Board of Father Flanagan's Boys' Town in Nebraska and on the editorial boards of several journals. He has two books forthcoming: *User Friendly Program Evaluation* and *Investigative Methods for Child Protective Service Workers*.

Wayne D. Duehn is a professor of social work at the University of Texas at Arlington, and he maintains a private clinical practice. He received his M.S.W. from Loyola University, and his Ph.D. from Washington University in St. Louis. A recognized authority and educator in the intervention and treatment of sexually abusive families, his current clinical research is on sexually abusive parents and juvenile sexual offenders. Professor Duehn lectures and conducts training throughout the United States and abroad. Most recently, Professor Duehn developed a child abuse prevention program for the Department of Defense Dependents School that has been implemented worldwide.

Gary Fashimpar is an associate professor of social work at Midwestern State University in Wichita Falls, Texas. He received his M.S.S.W. and Ph.D. from the University of Texas at Arlington. He teaches undergraduate courses in clinical practice, policy, and research. In his private practice he focuses on family and parenting issues. Professor Fashimpar has received a variety of grants and has numerous publications.

Eileen Gambrill is a professor of social welfare at the University of California at Berkeley, where she teaches clinical practice and research. Her areas of greatest interest include clinical decision making, the application of behavioral methods to personal and social problems, and social skills training. She has published widely in professional journals; her

books include *Critical Thinking in Clinical Practice, Controversial Issues in Social Welfare* (with Robert Pruger), *Controversial Issues in Child Welfare* (with T.J. Stein), and *Taking Charge of Your Social Life* (with Cheryl Richey).

Donald K. Granvold is a professor of social work at the University of Texas at Arlington; he also maintains a private clinical practice in individual, marital, and family treatment. Professor Granvold earned his M.S.W. and Ph.D. degrees from the University of Iowa. He has published numerous articles and book chapters on the application of cognitive-behavioral methods to the treatment of marital distress and divorce. He is a clinical member and approved supervisor of the American Association for Marriage and Family Therapy.

Vanessa G. Hodges is an associate professor at the University of Washington School of Social Work, where she teaches research and evaluation, practice methods with children and families, home-based services, and intervention with families of color. Professor Hodges received her M.S.W. from Morgan State University in Baltimore, and her Ph.D. from the University of Illinois. Her research interests include intervention development, social support systems of minority families, culturally relevant home-based services, families preservation practice, and risk and protective factors of at-risk children of color. Her publications include articles in professional journals and book chapters on child welfare, social support, adolescent maltreatment, and culturally sensitive practice.

Catheleen Jordan is an associate professor of social work at the University of Texas at Arlington and clinical director of the campus-based Community Service Clinic. She received her M.S.S.W. from the University of Texas at Arlington and her Ph.D. from the University of California at Berkeley. She has published primarily in the areas of child and family treatment and clinical assessment.

With Cynthia Franklin she is co-author of *Clinical Assessment and Measurement for Social Workers* and *Family Treatment: Intervention and Integration.*

Carlton E. Munson is a professor of social work and the director of the doctoral program at the University of Maryland School of Social Work. He received his M.S.W. and D.S.W. degrees from the University of Maryland. Professor Munson has studied clinical supervision and family intervention for more than twenty years, publishing a great many articles in journals and four books: *Social Work Supervision, An Introduction to Clinical Social Work Supervision, Family of Origin Applications in Clinical Supervision,* and *Clinical Social Work Supervision.* Professor Munson has a part-time practice in a child and adolescent clinic and directs the Washington Area Supervision Institute. He is currently conducting reasearch on family therapy and treatment of children who have suffered trauma and loss.

Paula S. Nurius is an associate professor at the University of Washington School of Social Work, where she directs the doctoral program and teaches research and practice courses. She received her M.S.W. from the University of Hawaii and her Ph.D. from the University of Michigan. Her publications include dozens of articles and chapters, and three books: *Human Services Practice, Evaluation, and Computers: A Practical Guide for Today and Beyond; Controversies in Social Work Research;* and *Cognitive-Ecological Practice: A Theory and Model for Practice.* In her research she has studied the role of cognitive appraisal in stress and coping (particularly with respect to self-concept change), violence against women, and critical thinking in practice judgment.

Cheryl A. Richey is a professor of social work and director of the doctoral program in social welfare at the University of Washington. She earned her master's and doctoral degrees at the University of California at Berkeley. Many of Professor Richey's articles focus on social skills assessment and intervention, especially group work strategies; clinical research utilization by social service providers; gender issues in practice and research; and social support and culturally diverse populations. Her practice activities emphasize group work, especially social skills training with shy or nonassertive women; staff development for agency-based social service providers; and clinical supervision of graduate social work interns in field practica.

Steven P. Schinke is a professor in the School of Social Work at Columbia University, where he teaches doctoral research methods. He received his Ph.D. from the University of Wisconsin. His research interests center on prevention training, with a special focus on substance abuse and minority culture. Professor Schinke has published more than 150 articles on preventive interventions and skills training for adolescents, is a consulting editor to numerous journals, and heads an AIDS minority research center.

Coleen Shannon is an associate professor in the School of Social Work at the University of Texas at Arlington. She received her M.S.W. from Tulane University and her Ph.D. from Texas Women's University. Professor Shannon is an expert on self-regulation methods, biofeedback, and stress management, and has published extensively on these topics. She has conducted many stress management workshops for widely diverse groups. Professor Shannon's credentials include certification by the Biofeedback Certification Association of America.

Clayton T. Shorkey is the Cullen Trust Centennial Professor of Alcohol Study and Education at the University of Texas School of Social Work. He earned his M.S.W. and Ph.D from the University of Michigan. For more than twenty-five years, Professor Shorkey has taught courses in social work methods, mental health, and chemical dependency at the undergraduate and graduate levels. He has contributed chapters, articles, and research reports in the areas of chemical dependence, mental health, culturally sensitive counseling, child abuse, behavior therapy, and rational-emotive therapy. Professor Shorkey currently chairs the Mental Health and Chemical Dependence Concentration.

Beverly Singer is a staff associate at Columbia University School of Social Work and project manager of a National Cancer Institute Study to reduce cancer risks among Native American youth in the northeast. She received her masters degree in sociology from the University of Chicago and is a doctoral student of American studies at the University of New Mexico. Ms. Singer has contributed papers and products on Native American education, cultural traditions, history, arts and crafts, ceremonies, and environmental protection.

N. Wim Slot is Director of Research at the Paedologisch Instituut in Amsterdam. His research and practice interests include adolescent development, parent training, and behavior modification. He is the author of numerous books and articles, and lectures extensively in the United States and Europe.

Edwin J. Thomas is Fedele F. Fauri Professor of Social Work and professor of psychology at the University of Michigan. He received his M.S.W. from Wayne State University and his Ph.D. from the University of Michigan. A founding faculty member of the University of Michigan doctoral program in social work and social science, Professor Thomas has been head of the program and chair of the supervising committee, and directed its postdoctoral training program in intervention research. He has been a senior Fulbright scholar and visiting professor abroad, and is widely known for his published contributions to behavioral science and social work. Other areas of interest include marital and family therapy, empirical practice, alcohol abuse, and assessment and research methods. As director of the Marital Treatment Project, Professor Thomas has conducted research to develop and evaluate unilateral family therapy for alcohol abuse.

Bruce A. Thyer is a professor of social work and an adjunct professor of psychology at the University of Georgia, and an associate clinical professor of psychiatry and health behavior at the Medical College of Georgia. The editor of the quarterly *Research on Social Work Practice,* Professor Thyer has published widely in social work, psychology, and psychiatric journals, and written or edited six books, including *Treating Anxiety Disorders.*

John S. Wodarski is a professor of social work and associate director of the Center for Family Studies at the University of Akron. He received his M.S.S.W. from the University of Tennessee and his Ph.D. from Washington University. Professor Wodarski's research has emphasized such critical social problems as poverty, violence, health, substance abuse, unemployment, and discrimination. His teaching and scholarly interests include clinical practice, research methods, and macro-level interventions. The latest of many publications are *Curriculums and Practical Aspects of Implementation: Preventive Health Services for Adolescents, Cultural Diversity and Social Work Practice,* and *The University Research Enterprise.*

Muriel Yu is an assistant professor at the School of Social Work at the University of Texas at Arlington. She received her M.S.W. and Ph.D. degrees from the University of Oklahoma. Professor Yu teaches courses in direct social work practice, and women and minorities. In her research and writing, she focuses on the treatment of children, family therapy methods, and cross-cultural and women's issues.

Contents

Cognitive and Behavioral Treatment
Methods and Applications

FOUNDATIONS OF COGNITIVE AND BEHAVIORAL TREATMENT

C H A P T E R

Concepts and Methods of Cognitive Treatment

Donald K. Granvold

The shift in clinical social work, clinical psychology, and other human-services disciplines from a strong behavioral perspective to a cognitive one has been identified as revolutionary (Baars, 1986; Dember, 1974; Mahoney, 1977). Many consider the revolution to be past, however, and the cognitive and behavioral perspectives have come to be viewed as compatible (Arkowitz & Hannah, 1989; Bandura, 1985; Ingram & Kendall, 1986; Kendall, 1981; LeDoux & Hirst, 1986; Mahoney, 1984, 1991; Wolpe, 1980). Nevertheless, much remains to be accomplished in the integration of cognitivism and behaviorism. This situation is due, in part, to the fact that cognitivism is in an early stage of its development. Ingram and Kendall (1986) aptly note that despite the strong infusion of cognitive concepts into clinical and research practice, cognitivism suffers from an overall lack of guiding conceptual perspectives. The development of conceptual knowledge about cognition and the clinical application of cognitive and cognitive-behavioral intervention strategies will probably be rapid, however, based on the strong orientation toward research and empirical practice predominant among cognitive-behaviorists.

The cognitive perspective owes its emergence primarily to the efforts of clinical, experimental, and social psychologists who became intrigued by cognition as a structure, as

*See Mahoney (1991) for a tracing of selected remarkable events in the evolution of cognitivism.

a process, and as a means of psychotherapeutic change. Albert Ellis is widely recognized as the leading pioneer in cognitive therapy from the discipline of clinical psychology. In the field of psychiatry, Aaron T. Beck is the prominent figure. Professionals from these fields and other human service disciplines, including clinical social work, have also made sound contributions, primarily in applying cognitive methods to practice and in empirically validating their efficacy.

This book is intended to expose the reader to a collection of works focused on the integrated application of cognitive and behavioral methods of intervention to an array of populations and problems. In this chapter, a presentation of cognitive treatment principles and methods will be preceded by a brief overview of mediational theory and an explication of concepts essential for understanding the literature on cognitive methods.

THE MEDIATIONAL MODEL AND RECIPROCAL DETERMINISM

The initial shift from radical behaviorism was the *mediational model,* a departure from the stimulus-response paradigm to the stimulus-organism-response one. The response to a given stimulus is assumed to be the product of a mediational process, with perception being the first covert activity. According to this model, a stimulus, rather than being pure, is a stimulus as *perceived*. Perceptual factors involve screening stimuli in or out, assigning a strength of meaning (weighing a stimulus along a continuum from minimal to strong), and applying various idiosyncratic factors (for example, values or self-interest) that may result in distortion. Other mediational processes following perception include the attachment of meaning to the stimulus (covert response) and a mental transaction (information processing) that results in a covert stimulus. The process of assigning meaning to the stimulus takes into account such factors as the social/environmental context, past experience with the same or a similar stimulus, and the emotional significance of the stimulus. After assigning meaning, the individual internally prepares to overtly respond (covert stimulus). This preparation involves the review and appraisal of competing responses from a stored matrix of response options. The overt response, then, is ultimately the product of a complex series of mediational activities beginning with perception. Early evidence in support of the mediational model was presented by Ellis (1973). He exposed the roles of perception and mediation in relation to classical conditioning:

> Even Pavlov's famous dog, when he heard the sound of a bell presented in connection with his being fed, did not become conditioned to salivating *only* because he had an inborn tendency to respond to food. He also, surely, had an inborn tendency to hear bells and to connect their sound with other stimuli that were presented to him. If he were born deaf or if he had no innate capacity to connect the hearing of the bell with the smelling of the food, he would hardly have served Pavlov very well [p. 33].

Recent conceptualizations of human behavior have taken on systemic qualities, viewing behavior as the product of an array of interacting variables and processes. This model is a departure from a perspective of "one-sided determinism" that explained human behavior as the product of either environmental forces or internal dispositions (Bandura, 1985). In this current model, behavior, cognition, and personal factors (emotion, motivation, physiology, and physical factors) and social/environmental factors are considered to be interactive, overlapping, and mutually influential. Bandura (1978b) refers to this conceptualization as *reciprocal determinism*; Lazarus (1989) uses the term *transaction*. The stimulus in this model becomes ambiguous and exists "buried in a person-environment transaction" (Lazarus, 1989, p. 100). The constant flux of the system and its recursive nature result in the potential of any variable to be antecedent, mediating process, or outcome. From this perspective there is no single *cause* of human behavior. To search for singular causation would both violate the interactional view and ignore the complexity of human functioning.

Agreement with this reciprocal, or interactional, view obligates the practitioner to identify and isolate cognitive variables along with behavioral, personal, and environmental factors, both in assessing human functioning and in constructing intervention strategies to treat human disturbance and distress. Bandura (1985) notes that "the reciprocal relationship between behavior and environmental events has received the greatest attention" (p. 84), and he contends that full understanding of this relationship requires the exploration of cognitive determinants. This exploration is no small challenge, given the complexity of cognition, the difficulty in accessing cognitive phenomena, and the embryonic state of current knowledge. The rewards of such efforts, however, lie in the extreme significance of cognitive factors in human functioning and change. Lazarus (1989) identifies cognition as the key to functioning and change and notes that "it provides motivational direction, emotional significance and the justification of action, and it connects action to the environmental context by the principle of feedback" (p. 99). In like support of the centrality of cognitive content in the human condition, Mahoney (1985) argues that "the problem of meaning is fundamental to our understanding of human experience"

(p. 11). In the following sections of this chapter, the variable meanings of cognition will be explored, the targeting of cognitive phenomena for change will be discussed, and select methods of cognitive intervention will be presented.

CONSTRUCTIVISM

Constructivism is a philosophy to which many cognitive and cognitive-behavioral therapists subscribe. *Constructivism* is the view that people are active participants in the construction of their own reality. Guidano and Liotti (1985) write that the constructivist framework, resting on a background of evolutionary epistemology, stems from a set of basic assumptions, as follows. Knowledge is an evolutionary result; knowledge is an interactive process; and knowledge development is biased by the self-organizing abilities of human mental processing. Knowledge of self and the world evolves through the organism's ongoing information gathering and processing in the context of "environmental pressures":

> Knowledge itself appears to be very far from a mere sensorial copy of reality (empiricism), as well as far from a mere unfolding of schemata already performed in the individual (innatism). On the contrary, knowledge appears to be a progressive hierarchic construction of models of reality where, step by step, the furniture is moulded inside knowledge structures by ordering activity carried out by the knowing subject [Guidano & Liotti, 1985, p. 102].

Constructivism is a shift away from conventional *sensory theories,* which hold that information from the external world flows inward through the senses to the mind, where it is maintained. Popper (1972) refers to this view as "the bucket theory of the mind." Both behaviorism and information-processing psychology have been described as sensory-theory-based (Weimer, 1977). In behaviorism the focus is on the response of the organism to environmental events, whereas the focus of information-processing psychology is on the cognitive processing of environmental information (Dowd & Pace, 1989).

The constructivist view is a *motor theory* of the mind in which "the mind appears as an active, constructive system, capable of producing not only its output but also to a large extent the input it receives, including sensations that lie at the base of its own constructions" (Guidano, 1988, p. 309). Thus, the mind not only receives and processes sensory data but also functions as a creative, knowledge-generating organism. Mahoney (1991) writes that a "major feature of psychological constructivism is the assertion that learning and knowing necessarily involve predominantly tacit (beyond awareness) processes that constrain (but do not specify) the contents of conscious experience" (p. 104). A two-level model of knowledge processing is thus defined. In this tacit/explicit duality, unconscious processes are accorded a central role in the formulation of cognitive structures necessary for the ordering of everyday experience. Hayek (1978), in referring to the existence of an abstract order, writes:

> All the conscious experience that we regard as relatively concrete and primary, in particular all sensations, perceptions, and images, are the product of a superimposition of many "classifications" of the events perceived. . . . What I contend, in short, is that the mind must be capable of performing abstract operations in order to be able to perceive particulars, and that this capacity appears long before we can speak of a conscious awareness of particulars [pp. 36–37].

The contention, as noted by Mahoney (1991), is that the contents of knowledge gained through sensory experience "are necessarily created through fundamental figure/ground classification processes operative at levels far removed from the 'experience of the experience'" (p. 106).

Constructivism is a developing philosophy in competition with empiricism. Its pro-

TABLE 1.1   Components of the Cognitive Taxonomic System, with Representative Constructs

Schema			
Structure	Propositions	Operations	Products
Short-term memory	Episodic knowledge	Spreading activation	Attributions
		Attention	Decisions
Long-term memory	Semantic knowledge	Cognitive elaboration	Images
Iconic/sensory storage	Internally generated information	Encoding	Thoughts
Cognitive networks/ associative linkages	Beliefs (stored)	Retrieval	Beliefs (accessed)
Memory nodes		Speed of information transfer	Recognition/detection of stimuli

NOTE: From "Cognitive Clinical Psychology: Implications of an Information Processing Perspective" by R. E. Ingram and P. C. Kendall. In *Information Processing Approaches to Clinical Psychology* by R. E. Ingram (Ed.). Copyright © 1986 by Academic Press. Reprinted by permission.

ponents are growing in numbers within the cognitive scientific and psychotherapeutic communities. Given this growth and the professional stature of those who have assumed prominence in the constructivist movement (for example, Beck, Ellis,* Frank, Guidano, and Mahoney), constructivism will no doubt be increasingly influential in the shaping of cognitive and cognitive-behavioral approaches to treatment.

A DEFINITION OF COGNITION

The formulation of a comprehensive definition of cognition is a formidable task due to the diversity of the cognitive concepts and the apparent independence and lack of cohesiveness of many of these concepts (Ingram & Kendall, 1986). Seiler (1984) notes that although the term *cognitive* is prevalent in the literature, it "is probably just as ambiguous as it is popular" (p. 11). An inherent difficulty arises from the fact that the term *cognition* is

*Rational-emotive therapy (RET) has come under some challenge as being "rationalistic." See Ellis (1990) for a discussion of the many respects in which RET is not only nonrationalistic but also highly constructivistic.

used variably as a label for an intrapsychic structure, a process, or an outcome. It includes such phenomena as perception; deployment of attention; labeling, coding, and categorizing stimuli; memory and retrieval; thinking, reasoning, judging, and problem solving; values, philosophies, beliefs, standards, rules, and expectations; imaging; and conditioned linkages between stimuli both stored and conscious.

In an effort to provide an organizing framework for the various cognitive constructs, Ingram (1983) has devised a useful taxonomic system in which cognition is divided into four interrelated but conceptually distinct major elements: (1) cognitive structure, (2) cognitive propositions, (3) cognitive operations, and (4) cognitive products. A list of constructs representative of each element is presented in Table 1.1.

Cognitive structure refers to the way in which information is organized and internally represented. It is the psychological mechanism that functions to store information. Seiler (1984) writes that cognitive structure "can be regarded as a plan stored in memory for perceiving, acting, and thinking which has been acquired over a long period of time and can be called forth again in comparable situations"

(p. 18). *Cognitive propositions* refer to the content stored in the cognitive structures. Stored content may be knowledge either received from external sources or internally generated, and it may exist in such forms as beliefs or philosophies (maintained at an implicit level). *Cognitive operations* serve as the mechanism for information processing and involve selective attention to available stimuli, perception, encoding, storage, and retrieval. In short, "cognitive operations (or processes) are the processes by which the system operates to input, transform, and output information" (Kendall & Ingram, 1987, p. 90). *Cognitive products* are the results of information processing and exists as thoughts, self-verbalizations, and explicitly held outcomes such as beliefs, opinions, attitudes, values, judgments, and conclusions.

Schemata

Although the definitions of *schemata* vary considerably, Kendall and Ingram (1987) note that the concepts of cognitive structure and cognitive propositions are together usually termed schemata. Schemata are inflexible, general rules or silent assumptions (beliefs, attitudes, concepts) that (1) develop as enduring concepts from past (early) experiences; (2) form the basis for screening, discriminating, weighing, and coding stimuli; and (3) form the basis for categorizing, evaluating experiences, and making judgments and distorting reality situations (Rush & Beck, 1978). The individual's perceptual filters, views of self, others, and the world, and cohesive factors that form the bases of appraising and judging are all based on schemata. Schemata, as memory structures, fulfill the functions of matching objects or situations to previous knowledge (stored prior knowledge) and guiding the search for more information when there is no match (Winfrey & Goldfried, 1986). Questions such as "What should I buy her for her birthday?" "What is that?" or "Should I wash my car?" result in matching current contemplations with previous experience. Hence, making the connection between current stimuli and one's unique psychosocial history involves schemata. In this manner, current phenomena become integrated into a stored matrix of associations.

Schemata can be identified as etiologically accountable for such problems as (1) distortions in thought processing, (2) maladaptive emotional episodes, and (3) faulty, exaggerated, or unrealistic expectations of self, others, or environmental conditions. Improvements in these problem areas can be achieved by targeting underlying schemata for change and effectively modifying them.

COGNITIVE TREATMENT PRINCIPLES

A number of principles form the underpinnings of cognitive treatment. In the following presentation several tenets will be isolated and discussed. Although there is general agreement regarding key concepts, as with any methodology the emphasis placed on foundation elements varies. Each principle is a significant component of cognitive treatment, and the order of presentation is not intended to imply greater or lesser importance. The degree of importance is variable and subject to the unique interests and applications of cognitive practitioners.

Unconditional
Regard for Self and Others

A cornerstone of the philosophy of cognitive therapy is unconditional regard for self and others. Early in his work, Ellis identified negative self-rating as a major cause of human disturbance. Ellis (1977b) discusses innumerable problems that result when people fail to value themselves very highly. Among the consequences are their diminished appraisal of their successes, a strong demand to prove themselves, intense seeking of approval, self-sabotage of their potential achievements, obsessive comparisons with others, intense performance anxiety, short-range hedonism, a lack of self-discipline, defensiveness, hostility, depression, withdrawal, lack of self-confidence, and self-berating. Ellis makes a profound distinction between self-esteem and self-acceptance when he writes that self-esteem "means that the individual values himself because he has behaved intelligently, correctly, or competently" (1977b, p. 101). Hence, *conditions* are placed on self-esteem that evolve from an appraisal of performance. Obvious flaws in this process result from such characteristics as the imperfect nature of human functioning; changes in skill level over time; extreme, unrealistic performance standards; and the unrealistic expectation that one can exert control over uncontrollable factors.

In addressing the unconditional acceptance of self, Ellis and Dryden (1987) write that "the person accepts herself and others as fallible human beings who do not have to act other than they do and as too complex and fluid to be given any legitimate or global rating" (p. 18). Self-acceptance, or unconditional self-regard, involves the acknowledgment and acceptance of one's strengths *and* limitations. One's knowledge, talent, skills, and aptitudes are counterbalanced by one's ignorance, incompetence, ineptness, and lack of potential in specific areas. Inasmuch as all humans possess a ledger of strengths and limitations, it is unrealistic to expect to perform with exceeding competence in all areas of life. In short, accepting oneself with one's flaws and limitations is tantamount to the psychologically healthy acceptance of self as *human.*

The association between low self-regard and self-rating is well established (Beck, 1976; Beck, Rush, Shaw, & Emery, 1979; Ellis, 1976, 1977c; Grieger & Grieger, 1982; Wessler & Wessler, 1980). Grieger and Grieger (1982) describe the self-rating of individuals who create and sustain low self-esteem and its accompanying emotional disturbances as

the tendency to rate one's acts, behaviors and performances as good or bad, and to generalize this evaluation to one's entire worth. It is a habitual tendency that may occur without the individual's awareness, and can exist in episodic bursts or as a chronic and continuous stream of meaning which may monopolize one's mind [p. 118].

Although, as Ellis (1977b) contends, all humans may be predisposed to self-rating, the objective in cognitive treatment is to minimize the degree of self-rating and control the manner in which it is engaged.

Just as unconditional self-regard is critical in healthy psychological functioning, the unconditional acceptance of others is equally important. Rating others as worthy or unworthy on the basis of action and deed is as flawed as rating one's own worth on the basis of performance. Judgment and condemnation of others based on selected characteristics, behavior, affiliation, or other extraneous factors represents a leap from trait to total essence. The pejorative labeling of others with such terms as jerk, bitch, wimp, ass, and the like is representative of faulty generalization. One trait does not a person make. These total evaluations ignore the complexity of human functioning, fail to acknowledge human fallibility, make unidimensional and single-event judgments representative of the entire individual, and make the action equal to the person. A view of others as worthy *with* their flaws, foibles, fallibilities, shortcomings, and undesirable traits (in the view of the appraiser) promotes healthy, rational, logical interpersonal regard. This way of thinking and appraising is compatible with the philosophy of cognitive therapy.

Acceptance of oneself as worthwhile with humanly inherent flaws and imperfections is not meant to imply resigning oneself to mediocre performance and low-level achievement. This stance does not promote a disappreciation of excellence, a lack of interest in competence, or a lack of enthusiasm for achievement and developing of skills. It is healthy to work toward goals and objectives, to cultivate and hone skills, to limit ignorance through study, and to unleash creativity through experimentation and practice. These activities, however, are in no way measures of self-worth or personal value. The joy, sense of accomplishment, and stimulation derived from such successes are ends in and of themselves. The appraisal of such outcomes as meaningful in establishing "OK-ness" is faulty and makes self-regard once again conditional.

The Continuity Assumption

The presumption that covert behaviors are subject to the same rules of learning as overt behaviors is termed the continuity assumption. In support of this assumption, Mahoney (1974) provides evidence indicating that there is justification to presume some degree of correspondence. Thus, cognitions can be taught much as overt behavior is. Modeling, coaching, rehearsing, and vicarious methods of learning can be applied to cognitive phenomena. Complex cognitive transactions can be broken down into incremental parts for step-by-step learning just as overt behaviors can be shaped. Cognitions are subject to reinforcement and can be strategically strengthened, weakened, or extinguished. Furthermore, cognitions can variably function as stimulus, response, or consequence (Mahoney, 1974). Self-generated actions result from cognitive stimuli. A cognition may be elicited in response to an overt event or a covert activity, as in a chain of thoughts. Third, covert events can serve as consequences of behavior wherein images and symbolic events reinforce or punish overt or covert behavior. As an example of this latter function, on a difficult day jogging, I use the image of downhill skiing and the associated exhilaration as a reinforcer for incremental achievement. I "image the scene" at 1 mile, 2 miles, and so forth. By covertly reinforcing the jogging completed, I increase the likelihood of jogging farther rather than walking or stopping altogether.

Conditioning

It would be short-sighted to ignore the strength of social learning in the human condition. The effects of past conditioning on current emotional responses and corresponding overt behavior are particularly noteworthy. Schindler and Vollmer (1984) note that "the process of anticipation, selection and decision making in a given situation is determined by the individual learning history and associated attitudes" (p. 312). Some years ago my wife and children and I went to the train depot in Chicago to meet my parents, who were arriving on the Great Northern Railway from Seattle. Entering the depot with joy in anticipation of their arrival, I heard the train designations being given over the public-address system. In response to the reverberating sound distinctive of depots, I felt a strong wave of melancholy and an unexplainable sense of loss. This response clearly did not fit the circumstances. I dismissed the emotional response—as much as I could at the time—only to have it return in response to the strong smell of creosote as we entered the track area. Again, I recognized that this melancholy did not logically belong. It was only several weeks later, after a series of contemplations of my past, that I clearly understood my responses. When I was a child growing up in a suburb of Seattle, for several consecutive years my father took my mother and me to the station in Everett, Washington, where my mother and I, leaving my father behind, boarded the train for extended summer visits to relatives in eastern Montana. What I had experienced at the Chicago depot was historic conditioning, a paired association between depots and separation anxiety (object-loss trauma) in relation to my father. The echoing sound of the PA system and the smell of creosote were the discriminative stimuli for the melancholy feelings. The strength of that paired association was so great that the *meaning* of the current event failed to prevent the unpleasant emotional response on such a joyous occasion. Although I was able to develop a clear understanding of the conditioning operative in this example, we have all experienced thousands of conditioned responses that remain stored in memory, some of them possibly inaccessible. Traumatic past experiences such as sexual abuse as a child have long-lasting ill effects as a consequence of this conditioning process.

Another phenomenon germane to this consideration of conditioning is automaticity. Kendall (1981) notes that "there is a negative correlation between the amount of practice on a cognitive learning task and the subject's awareness of the intermediate stages of the learning process. That is, with extended practice, awareness is reduced and automaticity sets in" (p. 6). There is a resulting decrease in mediational activity, which produces responses without the benefit of such mediation. In such situations, change will be more difficult to bring about, because there is less mediational activity available for modification.

Conditioned responses may continue, somewhat intractably, without conscious awareness and long after there is a logical "fit" with the immediate stimulus conditions. Although current and cumulative experience foster change in the individual's historic emotive and behavioral responses, the conditioned stimulus-response association may predominate. Isolating these associations and targeting them for counterconditioning procedures may result in a more adaptive and situationally relevant response pattern.

Self-Responsibility

A sign of psychological health is the acceptance of responsibility for one's own emotional disturbance and maladaptive behavior. Blaming others or social conditions for one's own emotional upset and corresponding dysfunctional behavior places the control over one's well-being outside rather than within. Although circumstances, social conditions, and others' actions realistically do have a bearing on the individual, the way the individual chooses to react is variable and, viewed rationally, is within his or her control. The client is taught to distinguish between contribution and cause. Although others may *contribute* to an individual's distress through misdeed and wrongdoing, ultimate *responsibility* for emotional distress and behavioral consequences resides with the individual. The belief system of the individual is the *cause* of the disturbance rather than the activating event. For example: Joe failed to call Mary to tell her that he would be arriving home from work late. When he got home, she said, "Joe, you make me so mad when you don't call to tell me you'll be late." Mary is assigning the responsibility for her anger to Joe. Although he *is* responsible for having failed to call, he cannot logically be held accountable for her anger. Her anger is her responsibility and it is her *view* of his failure to call that causes the anger. Although many spouses would be angry if their mate failed to call, some spouses would not be angry. They might feel only concerned, disappointed, or unhappy. If it is possible to respond to a given situation with an array of optional emotions, by logical extension the only person who can be held accountable for the emotion expressed is the responding individual. Assuming a stance of self-responsibility for emotional and behavioral responses is highly compatible with an internal locus of control (Rotter, 1966) and a strong sense of self-efficacy (Bandura, 1977, 1978a). Although intervention efforts may well focus on environmental factors and the conduct of others as they have an internal impact on the client, appraisal of the client's response patterns is critical for determining the extent to which emotional and behavioral self-responsibility is being assumed.

Questioning and the Socratic Method

Cognitive therapists use Socratic methods to promote desired changes. There are many important reasons for the use of questioning techniques. Because covert phenomena are being sought for modification, their discovery inherently involves client self-reporting. Although these data can be gathered through paper/pencil measures, during the interview oral questioning is necessary. The use of questioning stimulates the client's development of self-awareness and self-observation. Questions allow strategic exploration of problem areas so that vague, ill-defined concerns can be clarified and molded into more focused understanding. A line of questioning may be designed to elicit feelings and to promote an understanding in both client and therapist of the association between various feelings and cognitions.

In cognitive therapy it is critical to gain access to the client's cognitive operations. Through questioning, the therapist can gain insight into the client's characteristic patterns of perceiving, reasoning, information processing, and problem solving. Knowledge of the client's idiosyncratic ways of appraising self, others, and the world is essential to cognitive treatment and can likewise be gained through questioning. Furthermore, insight into schematic operations is important. How, for example, do particular beliefs bear on the client's attachment of meaning and significance to specific events and situations, patterns of emotions, and patterns of behavioral response? Additional cognitive functions sought through questioning include "the patient's coping mechanisms, stress tolerance, functional level and capacity for introspection and self objectivity" (Beck et al., 1979, p. 67).

Another valuable purpose of questioning is therapist modeling. By asking questions, the therapist guides clients in identifying the bases of certain conclusions they have reached, prompts their reasoning process, and exposes the appraisals they are making regarding themselves, others, and the world. Questions can be used to promote effective problem solving and to challenge irrational beliefs, information processing errors, unrealistic expectations, and the like. By directing clients through single challenging questions or a series of questions, the therapist teaches a cognitive activity they can call on later when confronted with a similar emotional episode, maladaptive thought or thought pattern, or undesirable behavioral response. Emery notes the use of questions to model coping strategies with anxious clients, including such questions as "Where is the logic?" . . . "What would be the worst thing that could happen?" "What can I learn from this experience?" (Beck & Emery, 1985, p. 178).

Following are examples of questions to accomplish various objectives. To challenge ill-founded conclusions, the therapist might ask: "Where is the evidence to support that view?" "What other explanations can you identify?" To expose an ill-founded premise or standard, the therapist might ask, "What kind of people would have to exist in order to guarantee that no mistakes would be made?" To expose an undesirable emotional consequence flowing from a negative self-statement, a therapist might ask a question such as "How do you feel when you think 'I'm stupid'?" To prompt clients' judgment of their behavior as undesirable and to challenge them to make a commitment to change, the therapist might ask, "Do you like feeling angry?" Assuming a client's response was no, the therapist's second question might be, "Do you want to learn to control your anger?" The challenging of irrational beliefs or unrealistic expectations can be accomplished through a question like "Who would you have to be to wield that kind of influence over others?" Questioning techniques are useful in establishing baseline readings and in registering reduction in the strength of specific beliefs held by the client. "On a ten-point scale, with zero as the low score, how strongly do you believe that approval from others is necessary to feel good about yourself?"

As indicated, a wide range of objectives can be achieved through questions. Beck and his colleagues (1979) note:

> In fact a single question may simultaneously attempt to draw the patient's attention to a particular area, assess his responses to this new subject of inquiry, obtain direct information regarding this problem, generate methods for solving problems that had been regarded as insoluble, and, finally, raise doubts in the patient's mind regarding previously distorted conclusions [p. 66].

Enlisting the client's active participation in the generation of a comprehensive understanding of the problem(s) and in the problem-solving process is dependent, in part, on effective questioning. The therapist's skilled, strategic use of questions can be expected to be measurably more effective than extensive explanation or indoctrination.

The therapist's use of Socratic questioning allows the client to be guided through a process of reasoning. The unique meanings of environmental circumstances and the actions of self and others are explicated and connected with past and current views and beliefs. Thought-processing functions and basic beliefs are exposed, clarified, and analyzed. Logical/empirical evidence is sought to substantiate or refute these thoughts and beliefs. Given the complexity of the human condition and the human tendency to simplify meanings, clients are encouraged through rhetorical questioning to expand their thought processing to consider an array of meanings, feelings, and behavioral responses in given situations. They are guided in identifying their appraisals of stimulus conditions and response patterns in order to expose their value judgments and the extent to which they are placing conditions on self-regard and regard for others. The therapist also seeks the consequences of the client's cognitions, emotions, and behavior as a means both to promote the awareness of short- and long-term effects and to stimulate problem solving to avoid undesirable outcomes.

Socratic questioning brings about the active participation of clients in their own problem solving and avoids authoritarian instruction that can discount their role in the treatment experience. Beck, Freeman, and Associates (1990) note that telling clients what their problems are and what needs to be done to change them prompts dependency rather than autonomy. Although active guidance and practical suggestions are appropriate at times, helping clients reach their own solutions is most desirable.

COGNITION AS A TARGET FOR CHANGE

As noted earlier, there is no single cause of human distress. Cognitions, emotions, and behavior are viewed as interactive within a social/environmental context. Although cognitions do not *cause* dysfunction in the sense of singular causation, they are an intrinsic part of it (Beck & Weishaar, 1989). The focus of cognitive therapy is the modification of mediational factors that are identified as operative in the client's personal and interpersonal distress. Targets for change include both cognitive outcomes and processing. Beliefs, expectations, and meanings attached to life events may be the objects of exploration and change. Alternatively, process variables may be isolated, including the selection of stimuli to which to respond, memory and retrieval, and cognitive transactions operative in arriving at meanings and responses (thought patterns).

Several interrelated cognitive variables can be targeted for change, including perception, expectancies, attributions, information processing, and beliefs. Although each of these factors will be presented individually, the isolation of these variables is for the purpose of clarity of expression. They function as interrelated, overlapping, and mutually influential phenomena.

Perception

Many theorists have identified perception as an active process rather than the passive receptivity of stimuli (Baucom & Epstein, 1990; Guidano, 1987; Juola, 1986; Neisser, 1967; Shulman, 1985). Prior knowledge stored within the individual converges with external sensation in the construction of perception (Neisser, 1967; Roth & Tucker, 1986). This stored information, schemata, influences perception with regard to selective attention, meaning of stimuli, and memory. Shulman (1985) has identified this perceptual selectivity as influencing such cognitive functions as memory (composed of attention, registration, and retrieval), learning, expectancy, fantasy, and symbol creation. Perceptual selectivity may account for maladaptive functioning. Beck and his colleagues (1979) identify the selective attention of depressed individuals to stimuli that support, reinforce, and promote depression. Stimuli that would promote a sense of emotional well-being are screened out, whereas stimuli supportive of depression receive attention. In essence, negative input is screened in, and positive input is screened out. Beck and Emery (1985) likewise indicate that highly anxious individuals tend to focus on symptoms of anxiety and that this focus ultimately serves to exacerbate the anxiety. Selective attention has also been identified as significant in marital distress (Baucom & Epstein, 1990).

Perceptual error may also arise from evaluative beliefs, values, and stored prior experience, which serve to bias the perceptual process. For example, individuals who have experienced physical abuse and other forms of aggressive behavior may be less reactive (both emotionally and behaviorally) to aggression than those who have experienced passivity. They may be so desensitized to aggression that they actually unconsciously ignore (screen out) specific acts of aggression. Alternatively, individuals may be sensitized to a given category of stimuli and function

with hypervigilance and supersensitivity in relation to it. In this case, they would be "on the lookout" for evidence to support their bias and would react strongly when target stimuli were experienced.

Perceptual error may also result from factors related to the individual's current physical and emotional state. Fatigue and emotional arousal frequently influence perception. One who is in an extreme emotional state is strongly predisposed to perceptual error.

Expectancies

People's subjective expectancies that they can significantly influence life events (outcomes) have been the focus of several authors. Baucom and Epstein (1990) identify the functions of expectancies as giving individuals a belief in their capacity to understand, predict, and control life events. These expectancies are considered to fulfill an active role in decision making in which the individual selects among response options those viewed as most likely to produce the most desirable effects. Hence, motivation, the selection of behavior to exhibit, and coping efforts are all profoundly influenced by self-expectations. Expectancies evolve over time from life experiences in which events are viewed either as greatly self-controlled or as greatly controlled by outside, environmental forces. Rotter (1954, 1966) identifies the concept of locus of control as the degree to which people view themselves as capable of producing a specific outcome. The view that an event is contingent on one's own behavior is termed internal locus of control, and the view that life events are controlled by outside forces (not contingent on one's own behavior) is termed external locus of control. Individuals with a greater sense of internality (internal locus of control) are more likely to see themselves as having more choice in decision making and tend to seek more information relevant to the problem solving process. Such individuals take an active role in their world, whereas those with a sense of external locus of control can be characterized as passive responders to their world. A sense of internal locus of control tempered with a rational, realistic view of the appropriate responsivity one is to have to others and life events appears to characterize well-adjusted, achieving people, whereas a sense of externality (control by others, situations, and events) appears to coincide with maladjustment and disturbance.

Seligman (1975) identifies the concept of learned helplessness as characteristic of depressed persons—an expectation of self as inept, helpless, and failing. Consistent with Rotter's external locus of control, such clients see themselves as unable to control significant life events. They view success and failure as independent of their own skill and influence. They lack aggressiveness and competitiveness. They meet trauma with passivity and tend to display a retarded response pattern to reduce trauma.

Schulz and Hanusa (1988) note that the learned-helplessness model has been reformulated to include attributional processes and, as a result, has been relabeled the hopelessness model. According to the reformulated model, people's conclusions about their control over outcomes can be evaluated on three dimensions: internal-external, stable-unstable, and global-specific. People can attribute an outcome to self (internal) or to outside causal factors (external); to conditions that are long standing, repetitive, and highly unchangeable (stable) or that are short term, infrequently intermittent, and highly changeable (unstable); and to factors that have a *global* effect across many situations and conditions or to a *specific,* narrowly focused cause. Noting that "each type of attribution has specific consequences for the individual," Schulz and Hanusa (1988) write that "attributions to internal-external factors should affect self-esteem; attributions to stable-unstable factors should determine the long-term consequences of a particular experience; and attributions to global-specific factors

should determine the extent to which individuals will generalize a particular experience to other situations" (p. 98).

Bandura's self-efficacy model (1977, 1978a) is a third conceptualization of self-expectation as a significant mechanism in the regulation of human behavior and the motivation to perform. He identifies two types of expectancies, outcome expectancies and efficacy expectancies. An outcome expectancy is the view that a given behavior will produce a specific outcome, and an efficacy expectancy is the conviction that one can effectively behave in a manner to produce the desired outcome. This dichotomy establishes the independence between the judgments of *what* behavior is necessary to produce the desired outcome (as perceived by the individual) and the belief (or lack thereof) in one's *ability* to behave successfully. In applying the concept of self-efficacy to coping, Bandura notes that "the strength of people's convictions in their own effectiveness is likely to affect whether they will even try to cope with given situations" (1977, p. 193). People's sense of self-efficacy is considered to directly influence both their willingness to approach certain situations and the level of assurance they display in the face of demanding, challenging, or threatening situations. Bandura goes on to say that self-efficacy not only influences people's choice of activities and settings but also affects their coping effort once it is initiated. Their expectation of effective coping will translate into how much effort they are willing to expend and the persistence they display. Efficacy expectations differ in magnitude, generality, and strength. The greater the magnitude of people's sense of efficacy, the more difficult are the tasks they are prepared to address. Generality relates to the breadth or narrowness of the sense of efficacy. Finally, the stronger the sense of efficacy, the greater the perseverance in the face of disconfirming experiences. Bandura contends that an adequate assessment of efficacy expectations requires consideration of these three dimensions.

Self-efficacy is considered to have a circular effect, to the extent that the successes that people derive from persistent, focused coping will reinforce their sense of efficacy. Successful performance that they attribute to personal factors (such as skill or perseverance) establishes and strengthens their efficacy expectations. Although expectancy is of critical importance, Bandura (1977) cautions that it is not a replacement for skill or necessary incentives for performance. He identifies the major sources of efficacy expectancies as performance accomplishments, vicarious experience, verbal persuasion, and physiological states. The development of efficacy expectations may evolve from experiences in any of these categories, and the design of a treatment strategy may thus combine several sources in the promotion of self-efficacy.

In developing a treatment strategy to address expectancy deficiencies, it is critical to make the aforementioned distinction between outcome and efficacy expectancies. Should clients possess performance skill and a sense of self-efficacy but fail to act, they may view environmental contingencies as unresponsive to their efforts. In such a situation the intervention is best focused on a change in environmental contingencies in order that a client's existing competencies can be effective. Alternatively, the treatment of efficacy-based futility should focus on the individual and the development of competencies along with expectations of personal effectiveness (Bandura, 1977).

Causal Attributions

People's views about the causes of life events, including their own behavior and that of others, have been increasingly recognized as influential in the promotion of psychological well-being (Metalsky & Abramson, 1981). This important information processing function is referred to as attribution. Simply stated, attribution means implied causality. At-tributions are the beliefs or statements a person uses to explain why a behavior, condition, or event has occurred. To resolve causal ambiguity, people tend to seek singular, definitive, simplistic explanations drawing on contextual information or beliefs held regarding self, others, and the world. Such explanations may be fraught with error and may result in negative views and conclusions and corresponding maladaptive emotional responses.

In the previous section, we examined people's views about their control over life events. Locus of control, learned hopelessness, and self-efficacy can be expected to have an influence on people's attributional beliefs. People with a greater sense of internality, hopefulness, and self-efficacy will tend to view outcomes as the products of their own efforts, whereas "externals" will tend to view outcomes as *caused* by such factors as luck, chance, or fate and not by their own influence (Metalsky & Abramson, 1981). Analysis of attributions on the internal-external dimension may provide useful insight into the affect, cognition, and behavior of the client and present a viable intervention point for the practitioner.

Negative attributions take many forms. Blaming is an attributional statement in which the client places responsibility for feelings and other outcomes on another: "You make me mad." "You make me feel guilty." Hurvitz (1975) identifies "terminal hypotheses" as interpretations of behavior, meanings, or feelings in such a way that nothing can be done to change the existing situation. Included are such determinants of behavior as psychological classifications ("You're a manic depressive"); pseudoscientific labels ("You're a Leo; that's why you act as you do"); and inappropriate generalizations about innate qualities or traits that cannot be changed ("He has no willpower—he was born that way. That's why he's so fat").

In addressing the interactions of marital couples, Epstein (1982) identifies several forms of faulty attribution. Attributing a change in behavior to coercion or impression management results in a negative and possibly suspicious view of the change ("You've become more involved with the children because you're afraid you'll lose them if you don't"). Another form of negative attribution is that of malevolent intent ("You went to lunch with your boss just to make me jealous." "You deliberately kept from telling me about that large commission check just to make me worry about our finances"). Misattributions may result from thought distortions described by Beck (1976), including personalization, dichotomous thinking, selective abstraction, arbitrary inference, and overgeneralization. For example, personalization may result in attributing the responsibility for a mate's behavior to oneself ("I caused her depression." "I failed to put his lunch by his briefcase, so I caused him to go hungry all day"). Other thought distortions and examples will be provided in the section that follows.

Abramson, Seligman, and Teasdale (1978), drawing on the work of Doherty, categorize attributions into three dimensions: stable-unstable, internal-external, and specific-global. Outcomes may be attributed to factors that are more changeable (unstable) or less changeable (stable) ("I lost the game because I don't have the capacity to play it well" [stable], as opposed to "I lost the game because I had an 'off' day" [unstable]). The former view would result in the individual's resignation to playing poorly forever, whereas the latter view would allow a sense of optimism about performing with greater skill in the future. Internal-external dimensions, addressed earlier in this section, involve the attribution of outcomes to oneself or to outside factors—other people or environmental conditions. Negative outcomes may be attributed to oneself, whereas positive potential outcomes are attributed to outside forces. Global versus specific attributions refer to the representativeness of the causal explanation concluded. A negative attribution with global meaning has more far-reaching implications and is correspondingly less responsive to change than a more specific negative attribution. For example, students who struggle to perform marginally in the sciences may take the view that they do not have academic abilities (global), or they may hold the view that the sciences are uncharacteristically difficult for them (specific).

Attributional style is associated with a range of psychological problems and conditions. Attributional error and bias have been identified in depressed individuals (Abramson, Metalsky, & Alloy, 1988; Abramson et al., 1978; Cutrona, 1983; Mukherji, Abramson, & Martin, 1982; Seligman, Abramson, Semmel, & von Baeyer, 1979). An association has been identified between low self-esteem and causal attributions (Ickes, 1988; Ickes & Layden, 1978). Those with low self-esteem attribute negative, undesirable outcomes to internal factors, whereas they tend to attribute positive, desirable outcomes to external factors. Research with victims of disease, crime, and accidents supports the meaningful role of attribution in relation to coping (Bulman & Wortman, 1977; Janoff-Bulman & Lang-Gunn, 1988; Wortman, 1976; Wortman & Silver, 1979). For example, victims who blamed themselves for an accident resulting in permanent paralysis coped better than those who blamed others. Attributional style has also been found to be associated with interpersonal conflict (Newman & Langer, 1988). Furthermore, studies of distressed and nondistressed couples have exposed significant differences in attributional styles. For example, distressed spouses tend to view negative partner behavior as caused by more global and stable factors than do nondistressed spouses, whereas nondistressed spouses tend to view positive partner behavior as caused by more global and stable factors than do distressed spouses (Baucom & Epstein, 1990; Jacobson, McDonald, Follette, & Berley, 1985).

Although there is ample evidence to support the contention that certain attributional styles promote vulnerability to various psychological and interpersonal problems, there is much to be learned about the process of attribution and its measurement. Despite this incomplete state of knowledge, in those situations in which attributional style is identified as deleterious, therapeutic interventions aimed at attributional change should be an integral part of the treatment effort.

Information Processing

Information processing has been identified as "the cognitive scientist's central dogma: Stimulation received at the periphery is *coded* by receptors, *represented* in some spatiotemporal set of brain activities, and then *processed, transformed,* and perhaps *stored* in the service of specific ends" (Tataryn, Nadel, & Jacobs, 1989, p. 86). There is evidence that errors in information processing partially cause, or at least sustain, many forms of psychological dysfunction (Miller & Porter, 1988). Distortions in this process can occur in many ways. The following is an incomplete list of typical distortions drawn heavily from the work of Beck and his colleagues in the treatment of depression (Beck, 1976; Beck et al., 1979). Although insight into common information processing errors arose from work with depressed patients, these distortions are evident to some degree in those evidencing other forms of psychological disturbance and in the psychosocially adjusted as well! As noted by Freeman (1990), these distortions occur in many combinations and permutations and are presented individually for the purpose of clarity. Much of the following is abstracted from Granvold (1988).

Absolutistic Thinking.   Some people have a tendency to view experiences, objects, and situations in a polarized manner as good/bad, right/wrong, or strong/weak ("I am a com-

plete incompetent." "Life's a bitch"). This tendency is known as absolutistic, or dichotomous, thinking (all-or-nothing thinking).

Absolutistic thinking simplifies and distorts the meaning of life events. It is illogical because a given condition can rarely, if ever, be rated objectively as totally to one extreme or another. Concomitant negative emotions tend to be evident with negative absolutistic thinking. Exposing and modifying the cognitive distortion may begin the process of eroding the associated maladaptive emotions.

Overgeneralization.   People who overgeneralize draw a general rule or conclusion on the basis of one or more isolated incidents and apply the concept across the board to related and unrelated situations (Beck et al., 1979) ("I do poorly at Trivial Pursuit. I'm just no good at table games of any kind." "Stores *never* have my size. I don't know why I even bother to go shopping at all").

Selective Abstraction.   The distortion of selective abstraction involves focusing on the negative in a situation, ignoring other positive (sometimes more salient) features, and viewing the entire experience as negative based on the selective view. For example, Bart and Jane are at Jane's company cocktail party. They are attentive to each other throughout the evening. Jane's boss, Arlene, asks to speak with her privately for 15 minutes, during which time Bart is left to socialize on his own. Lacking well-developed social skills, he feels insecure and awkward while Jane is away. Upon her return, he acts coldly toward her and asks to leave the party immediately. He thinks, "This whole night has been unpleasant" and tells her, "I really don't appreciate being left alone all night." Bart is overlooking the pleasant part of the evening before Jane talked with her boss and the fact that she left for only 15 minutes of the three hours they were at the party. Were Bart to say to Jane, "I had a terrible time at your company party, and I'm *never* going to another because they will *all* be terrible for me," this would be an overgeneralization.

Arbitrary Inference.   Some people reach an arbitrary negative conclusion when there is no evidence to support it, when the evidence is circumstantial, vague, or unclear, or when there is evidence to the contrary. Freeman (1983) describes two types of arbitrary inference as mind reading and negative prediction:

1. *Mind reading*: "She thinks I'm weak, I just know it." "The boss doesn't like me, I'm certain."
2. *Negative prediction*: This type of arbitrary inference involves imagining or anticipating that something bad or unpleasant is going to happen without adequate or realistic support for the prediction. "I just know there will be problems with this vacation." This individual will probably be hypervigilant during his or her vacation and, should something problematical develop, will probably either become upset or feel content, smug, or relieved because the "prediction" was accurate. The sense of hopelessness and futility an individual feels may be based on a negative prediction ("I will never gain the confidence to date. I might as well resign myself to living alone for the rest of my life"). Such beliefs not only promote feelings as noted but can be expected to affect people's behavior. Beliefs, feelings, and behavioral tendencies combine to promote the predicted outcome—a self-fulfilling prophecy.

Magnification and Minimization.   The thought disorders of magnification and minimization involve errors in evaluating the significance or extent of a behavior, condition, or event that are so extreme as to constitute a distortion. People magnify imperfections in themselves and others and minimize talents, knowledge, and skill. Magnification may result in a client's becoming extremely emo-

tional and critical over the misdeeds or human errors of others. Ann forgets to take the dog to the veterinarian for a routine vaccination visit. When Del finds out, he becomes extremely angry and chastises Ann. Perceptual blinders may serve to filter the meaning of one's own and others' talents, positive qualities, and performances. After 12 years with her law firm, Mary Ann becomes one of the 15% promoted to partner. She believes and says that "anyone could have done it."

Personalization.   Personalization is the act of relating a negative event or situation to oneself without the adequate causal evidence to make the connection. There are two forms of personalization. In the first instance people reach an arbitrary conclusion that they have caused a negative event ("If I had been home with Dad, I don't believe he would have had a heart attack"). In the second form of personalization, people reach an arbitrary conclusion that they are the object of a negative event and are therefore causally connected to it ("They stopped the scholarship program just because I'm ready to go to college." "They're working on the road because I'm running late for the meeting with my boss").

Cognitive distortions such as those detailed above develop as habits of the mind as a result of "normal" socialization. It is highly likely that such clients have a lengthy history of faulty information processing in relation to themselves, others, events, and life situations. The result of these repeated distortions is that personal awareness moves from an explicit to a tacit level, and clients perform automatically (Mahoney, 1991). They apply habituated distortions in thinking with little awareness, and if there is a degree of awareness, they may not be skilled at identifying specific errors in a given situation. The practitioner seeks to uncover and guide clients' awareness of the content and process of their distorted transactions. Clients are challenged to appraise their degree of belief in the statements they make mentally, to appraise and judge their concomitant behavioral and emotional responses, and to define their goals for change.

The discovery and modification of information processing errors is an important and viable process in and of itself. However, the content, trends, style, and themes uncovered at this level may also be highly useful in the determination of significant deeper content. Freeman (1990) notes that "cognitive distortions become the thematic directional signs that point to the underlying cognitive schema" (p. 66).

Beliefs, Schemata, or Deep Structures

Whereas information processing variables can be rather readily discerned, underlying beliefs are more difficult to access and are more resistant to modification once they are explicated. Various terms are used to identify the rules, principles, beliefs, and philosophies that guide human behavior. The most common, comprehensive term is *schemata*. Alternative terms found in the literature include *personal constructs* (Kelly, 1955), *irrational beliefs* (Ellis, 1973, 1977a), and *deep structures* (Guidano, 1987, 1988; Guidano & Liotti, 1983, 1985). The concept of a schema as originally described (Bartlett, 1932, 1958; Piaget, 1926) related to the process of attaching meaning to events and the integration of meaning within the individual. Although many writers have expanded and developed the concept, Beck and his colleagues have been the most visible and influential (Beck, 1964, 1967; Beck & Emery, 1985; Beck et al., 1990; Freeman, 1990; Rush & Beck, 1978).

Schemata are initially formed during childhood and are maintained as relatively stable and durable despite being in a constant state of change (Freeman, 1990). As products of socialization they are influenced by a variety of cultural, social, familial, religious, ethnic, and gender-based factors. A schema may be rigid or flexible, durable or fragile, concrete or abstract, active or dormant, broad or narrow, prominent in the cognitive structure (highly likely to influence behavior) or relatively inconsequential, and maintained explicitly or tacitly. This latter characteristic is particularly significant. Schemata at the explicit level exist within the awareness of the individual, can be verbalized, and are available for debate, disputation, and direct influence. Explicit schemata (expectations, beliefs, standards, rules, and the like), however, are considered to be, at least in part, a function of tacitly held schemata (Airenti, Bara, & Colombetti, 1982a, 1982b; Guidano, 1988; Tulving, 1972; Weimer, 1975). Tacit schemata are unconscious mental structures and processes that underpin explicit schemata and other conscious information processing. The relationship between the tacit and explicit levels is clarified by Polanyi (1958): "We can know more than we can tell and we tell nothing without relying on our awareness of things we may not be able to tell" (p. x). Tacitly maintained schemata bear upon human functioning and, in their tacit state, can be accessed through such means as introspection, deductive reasoning, and testable inference. Freeman (1990) notes that the

> extent of a schema's effect on an individual's life depends on several factors: (a) How strongly held is the schema? (b) How essential does the individual perceive that schema to be for personal safety, well-being, or existence? (c) Does the individual engage in any disputation of the particular schema when it is activated? (d) What was learned previously regarding the importance and essential nature of a particular schema? (e) How early was a particular schema internalized? and (f) How powerfully, and by whom was the schema reinforced? [p. 67].

Schemata that promote maladaptive cognitive, emotional, and behavioral consequences may be oriented toward self, others, the world, or life experiences. Dormant maladaptive schemata may become activated at times of stress and emotional disturbance. It has been suggested that when they are highly active, idiosyncratic or maladaptive schemata displace and probably inhibit other more adaptive or situationally appropriate schemata and, as a consequence, "introduce a systematic bias into information processing" (Beck et al., 1990, p. 32). In this active state, little stimulation is required to trigger maladaptive schemata. The associated negative effects include (1) negatively biased perceptual error; (2) the attachment of negative meanings to situations, interactions, and events (cognitive distortion, mislabeling, and misinterpretation); (3) an increase in erroneous information processing; (4) an erosion in the individual's sense of self-efficacy; (5) more extreme negative emotions; and (6) behavioral tendencies that sustain, reinforce, and promote further dysfunction.

COGNITIVE INTERVENTION METHODS

An early objective in treatment is to develop clients' awareness of the cognitive model and of the impact that their cognitive processes are having on their current functioning. This goal can be accomplished through didactic presentation or through the use of written material. Clear understanding can best be achieved, however, through applying cognitive methods to a client's current issue, problem, or concern.

The therapeutic alliance is formed as the client and practitioner explore cognitive, emotional, behavioral, and social/environmental factors that they consider relevant to the client's problem or dysfunction. Cognitive variables addressed include thoughts, perception, attributions, information processing, expectancies, beliefs, and motivation. Emotion is assessed in terms of frequency, intensity, and duration, and factors associated with the emotional episodes are explored (trigger events, contextual factors, and reinforcing conse-

quences). Behavioral competencies and skills, excesses (such as alcohol consumption), and deficits (such as a lack of social skills) are identified. Social/environmental factors such as opportunity, resource limitations and availability, and the like are considered. This assessment should include the use of relevant tests and measures along with interviews. The outcome of this exploration is the collaborative formulation of a treatment plan, which includes a series of "testable" hypotheses generated by the client and practitioner. Beck and his colleagues (1979) introduce the term *collaborative empiricism* to denote this cooperative process. The focus is on an empirical investigation of the client's functioning in which hypotheses regarding current and future functioning are formulated and their validity is tested in a systematic way.

The testing process requires that clients perform homework. They may be expected to track their thoughts or thought patterns, record the restructuring of their dysfunctional thinking, track their negative emotions and corresponding cognitive, behavioral, and environmental factors, and perform and record the performance of targeted behaviors or tasks. The homework is used in treatment sessions to validate hypotheses, to modify existing strategies, and to generate new directions in treatment.

Cognitive Restructuring

Cognitive restructuring is an intervention method in which dysfunctional schemata and thinking patterns are identified. Then they are appraised as both ill-formed (having little or no logical support or evidence) and as interfering with the pursuit and attainment of goals (producing undesirable emotional or behavioral consequences). Finally, methods are applied to modify them. The exposure, challenge, and disputation of faulty cognitions is accomplished through the implementation of a logico-empirical method of scientific questioning (Ellis, 1977a) in which supportive evidence is sought to validate or invalidate them. The restructuring of faulty perceptions, faulty attributions, information processing errors, and schematic errors can be accomplished through exposing the distortion (client awareness) and guiding the client in observing, evaluating, disputing, and modifying the cognitive distortion. Homework assignments are employed to promote the application and habituation of adaptive thinking and speaking. An example of the cognitive restructuring of a negative attribution is described below:

Client: My stepdaughter tried to manipulate me yesterday. Boy, did I get angry with her! I could see right through her sly efforts. I confronted her with it. She denied it, but I know I'm right. We argued, and Janie screamed and cried, ran to her room, and slammed the door.

Practitioner: What specifically did Janie do that you consider to be manipulative?

Client: She came right in from school, did her chores, studied for about an hour, and then came out and asked me if there was anything I needed done—that she had finished her homework and was bored. Can you believe it?!

Practitioner: What is it about Janie's behavior that you consider to be manipulative?

Client: That she did her chores and homework without being asked. And secondly, that she asked to help me.

Practitioner: So it's your view that the specific reason that Janie did her chores and homework was to manipulate you?

Client: Yes.

Practitioner: How do you feel toward Janie when you think of her as being manipulative?

Client: I feel hostile, and I don't like her.

Practitioner: Do you like feeling this way toward your stepdaughter?

Client: Of course not; it goes against what we've been trying to accomplish with you—to improve our relationship.

Practitioner: So the conclusions you've reached about the motives for Janie's behavior are negative. They lead to negative feelings toward her and, in this case, resulted in an argument that was upsetting to you both. You've also experienced a setback in your goal of an improved relationship with Janie.

Client: Yes.

Practitioner: Where is the evidence that Janie's motive was to manipulate you?

Client: Well, that's what kids do, don't they?

Practitioner: Yes, some children at times do act manipulatively. But in the examples you've given, is there any evidence to support your conclusion?

Client: No, not really.

Practitioner: Has Janie acted in a manipulative way any other times lately, since we last discussed it in family therapy?

Client: No, she hasn't.

Practitioner: So in this case there was no evidence to support the conclusion [negative attribution] that you reached. Can you think of an alternative, more positive motivation behind Janie's behavior?

Client: I guess I could think that Janie was trying to follow through better on things. Putting off her chores and doing her homework have been issues, you'll recall. And you've asked that each family member make more efforts to be helpful. Maybe that's what Janie was doing when she asked if she could help me.

This exploration achieved the following: (1) gained specific information regarding the attribution reached, (2) established the consequences emotionally, (3) exposed a value judgment about the emotional consequences, (4) produced awareness of the effects of the negative attribution and confrontation on the relationship between the client and her stepdaughter, (5) exposed a lack of evidence to support the negative attribution, and (6) led the client to generate an alternative, positive causal explanation for her stepdaughter's behavior. Following this interchange, the practitioner might choose to review (or introduce to the client) the notions of faulty attribution and information processing errors. The client would be invited to see that a greater improvement in her relationship might result if cognitive distortions such as those in the current episode were minimized. She would later be asked if her restructured views of Janie's motives had resulted in improved feelings toward Janie. Homework would be assigned in which the client would be challenged to catch and revise her faulty attributions (either before or after they were overtly expressed) and to record her effort for review at the next session.

In the foregoing scenario the information-processing error (negative attribution) was challenged and ultimately modified. An alternative approach using cognitive restructuring would involve modifying the client's underlying beliefs supporting her negative emotional responses and dysfunctional behavior. Using the same scenario, the following is an example of a rational-emotive approach to cognitive restructuring:

Client: My stepdaughter tried to manipulate me yesterday. Boy, did I get angry with her! I could see right through her sly efforts. I confronted her with it. She denied it, but I know I'm right. We argued, and Janie screamed and cried, ran to her room, and slammed the door.

Practitioner: Assume that Janie *was* trying to manipulate you. This assumption may or may not be accurate, but assume that on that occasion she really was trying to manipulate you. Why *must* Janie not attempt to manipulate you?

Client: Well, it's wrong.

Practitioner: OK, so you think it's wrong. Why must Janie only act *rightly* or appropriately at all times?

Client: Because she should . . . She just should. She knows better.

Practitioner: How do you feel when you think Janie must not act manipulatively in light

of your view that she was acting manipulatively the other day?

Client: I feel angry . . . really upset with her.

Practitioner: Now, where is the evidence to support your belief that Janie should not act manipulatively?

Client: I just don't like it when she acts that way.

Practitioner: So there really isn't any evidence, then, to support your belief, other than that you don't like it. Who says that others should do *only* what you like?

Client: I guess *I* do [smiling].

Practitioner: Do you *only* get what you like from everyone in your world?

Client: Of course not.

Practitioner: Do you get upset with virtually *everyone* on *every* occasion that you don't get from them what you want?

Client: No.

Practitioner: What determines whether you will be upset when you don't get what you think you "should" get from others?

Client: I guess I just decide not to get upset, or I make some excuse for them.

Practitioner: So if you don't *demand* to get what you want, you act with tolerance. Then you don't get so upset.

Client: That's right.

Practitioner: So it's the *demand* that results in your getting upset, not necessarily what others do or don't do. Rather than saying that Janie *must* not act manipulatively, suppose you were to say that you *prefer* that she not act manipulatively. Now how do you feel?

Client: I guess disappointed and somewhat frustrated with her.

Practitioner: But not angry . . . or not intensely angry?

Client: No, maybe a little angry . . . but really just bothered by it.

Practitioner: So by changing from the *demand* that Janie not act manipulatively to only preferring it, you feel better. Do you like feeling better toward Janie?

Client: Yes, I do. I really do want to have a better relationship with her.

Practitioner: So in this case, we can conclude that your anger toward Janie came from the *demand* that she *never* act manipulatively, and that by changing your demand to only a preference you don't feel as upset with her.

After this interchange, the practitioner would discuss with the client the major irrational derivatives evolving from her absolutistic demand: "awfulizing," "I-can't-stand-it-itis," and "damnation" (Ellis & Dryden, 1987). Awful, in RET terms, is a condition that is 100% bad, and 100% bad cannot exist. Something worse could always happen (Wessler & Wessler, 1980). The rational view is that it is unpleasant, undesirable, or unappealing. To conclude that one cannnot stand it (the condition or event) is blatantly irrational because the client *is* standing it. The rational view is "I don't like it." Damnation involves the client's evaluation of self and others as unworthy or no good on the basis of a given action or failure to act. The rational view is that the individual (or self) is fallible, flawed, and error-prone—but not without redemption. The client would be given homework in which she would practice identifying and disputing irrational beliefs and would record the corresponding changes in her emotional reactions and behavior.

The cognitive restructuring of distorted schemata, as opposed to more superficial cognitive distortions, requires greater persistence (repeated bombardment) due to their stronger resistance to change. Although there is variability among cognitive therapists regarding the specific procedures of cognitive restructuring, the following guidelines are offered for use in the formulation of an intervention strategy:

- Expose the belief or beliefs that are hypothesized to be operative in a given situation.
- Gain the historical meaning of the belief.
- Determine the strength of the belief now and in the past.
- Determine the ways in which the belief has been used and the perceived consequences of maintaining the belief, both past and present.
- Determine the matrix of beliefs associated with the target belief.
- Establish the cognitive, emotional, behavioral, and social consequences of maintaining the belief.
- Guide the client in a search for the evidence to support the belief.
- Guide the client in a search for evidence that may compete with or refute the target belief.
- Train the client to monitor and record (1) faulty thinking associated with the belief and (2) emotional, behavioral, and social consequences of the faulty thinking.
- Assign homework to transfer this training to the client's daily life.
- Check the client's homework and guide the repetitious challenging of faulty schemata.

Cognitive restructuring can be used in conjunction with other cognitive methods (thought stopping, covert sensitization, guided imagery) and behavioral methods (behavior rehearsal, skill training, deep-muscle relaxation). It is highly desirable to promote specific behavior change along with cognitive restructuring assignments. (For example, the depressed client can be assigned to increase the performance of pleasurable activities or those involving mastery.) The combined changes in both cognitive dysfunction and behavior can be expected to produce a positive interactive effect that presumably yields more effective change than would result from the isolated use of either methodology.

Problem Solving

Problem solving has been classified alternatively as a behavioral procedure and a cognitive-behavioral procedure. D'Zurilla and Goldfried (1971) define problem solving as "a behavioral process, whether overt or covert in nature, which (a) makes available a variety of potentially effective response alternatives for dealing with the problematic situation and (b) increases the probability of selecting the most effective response from among these various alternatives" (p. 108). D'Zurilla (1988) has modified this definition, specifying problem solving as "a cognitive-affective-behavioral process through which an individual (or group) attempts to identify, discover, or invent effective or adaptive means of coping with problems encountered in everyday living" (p. 86). Problem-solving deficiencies have been found to be associated with a variety of personal and interpersonal problems (Dobson & Dobson, 1981; Jacob, Ritchey, Cvitkovic, & Blane, 1981; Kazdin, Esveldt-Dawson, French, & Unis, 1987; Nezu & Carnevale, 1987; Vincent, Weiss, & Birchler, 1976; Weisz, Weiss, Wasserman, & Rintoul, 1987), and training in problem solving has been found to improve the functioning of various clinical populations (Bedell, Archer, & Marlow, 1980; Chaney, O'Leary, & Marlatt, 1978; Ewart, Burnett, & Taylor, 1983; Jannoun, Munby, Catalan, & Gelder, 1980; Nezu, 1986).

Problem-solving training has been used effectively with both children and adults, and it can be used alone or in conjunction with other methods. There are several approaches to problem solving, but the most widely accepted is the five-step model of D'Zurilla and Goldfried (1971): (1) problem orientation, (2) problem definition and formulation, (3) generation of alternative solutions, (4) decision making, and (5) implementation and verification of solutions. Problem orientation relates to the cognitive "set" of the individual in relation to problem solving and coping with life situations. D'Zurilla (1988) identifies the significant problem-orientation factors as follows: "problem perception, causal attributions, problem appraisals, beliefs about personal control, and values concerning the commitment of time and effort to problem solving"

(p. 89). Step 2, problem definition and formulation, involves an assessment of the problem and the establishment of an achievable goal. The third step involves "brainstorming" to generate alternative solutions to the problem. At step 4 the alternatives are evaluated, and a solution is selected for implementation. The final component of the process is designed to determine the effectiveness of the problem-solving effort and, if the solution is found to be lacking, to promote modification of the original solution or a return to step 3 to select another promising alternative solution.

The goal of problem solving is to treat life problems that are antecedents of maladaptive responses and are considered to be causally related to these responses. Only when these antecedent problems are difficult to define or change is the approach to be applied to the maladaptive responses (D'Zurilla, 1988). Examples of problem-solving issues are as follows:

- How can I make better use of my time?
- How can my husband and I do more novel activities?
- How can I reduce the disruptive behavior of my children at the table?
- How can I get my aging father to take better care of himself?
- How can I reduce the stress of my job?

The effectiveness of problem solving can be extended through the use of such adjuncts as cognitive restructuring and training in social skills, assertiveness, self-control techniques, and coping skills.

Self-Instruction Training

Self-instruction involves the use of self-verbalizations to guide the performance of a task, skill, or problem-solving process. Drawing on the work of Luria (1959, 1961) and Vygotsky (1962), Meichenbaum and Goodman (1971) developed the method to treat hyperactive, impulsive children. Before performing tasks automatically, young children verbalize instructions. As they develop skill and begin to act automatically, the verbalizations become subvocalized.

Meichenbaum (1975) recognized that verbal mediation could be inserted between a stimulus and response to prevent maladaptive behavior and performance deficiency. In this manner, the stimulus/response chain can be interrupted, and the maladaptive response can be inhibited. The anticipated result is an increased likelihood that an adaptive response will follow a given stimulus.

Self-instruction training provides the client with step-by-step self-statements (including verbal self-reinforcement and coping statements) for the development of competency in the performance of targeted tasks and skills. A five-step procedure is used to instruct the client (Meichenbaum, 1977):

1. The practitioner models performance of the task while talking to himself or herself out loud (cognitive modeling).
2. Clients perform the same task while receiving verbal guidance from the practitioner (overt, external guidance).
3. Clients perform the task while instructing themselves out loud (overt self-guidance).
4. Clients perform the task while whispering instructions to themselves (faded, overt self-guidance).
5. Clients perform the task while instructing themselves privately (covert self-instruction).

The self-statements modeled by the practitioner and rehearsed by the client may incorporate error correction, self-praise, and coping statements. Initial self-instruction training should begin with simple tasks, followed by more complex skills such as problem solving. In like fashion, complex tasks should be broken down into manageable incremental steps to allow for response chaining and successive approximation. Homework may be assigned in which the client is to practice the rehearsal of self-instruction while performing tasks.

The verbalizations modeled by the practitioner and rehearsed by the client include several performance-relevant skills:

- *Problem definition:* "What is it that I'm trying to do?"
- *Statements regarding task completion:* "I'm going to ask her for a date."
- *Guidance of performance by self-instruction:* "Relax, approach her comfortably, and make the invitation."
- *Coping self-statements and error-correcting options:* "I can still approach her even if I feel some anxiety—that's OK."
- *Self-reinforcement:* "There, I did it!"

Self-instruction has been used to treat a wide range of academic and clinical problems in various populations. Effective results have been reported in improving the self-control of hyperactive, impulsive children; reducing children's aggressiveness; developing social skill in social isolates; enhancing memory recall in children; improving creativity in college students; reducing test anxiety; improving problem-solving skills in the elderly; and reducing psychotic speech in adult schizophrenics. It has been modified to include such components as operant procedures (for example, social and token reinforcement), relaxation training, stimulus-modeling films and tapes, and covert modeling procedures.

Other Cognitive Methods

Although cognitive restructuring, problem solving and self-instruction are the most widely used cognitive intervention methods, several others have been found to be effective. Covert-conditioning methods—including systematic desensitization (Wolpe, 1958), thought stopping (Wolpe, 1958, 1969; Wolpe & Lazarus, 1966), "coverant" control (Homme, 1965), covert sensitization (Cautela, 1966, 1967), and covert modeling (Cautela, 1971)—have been used with variable efficacy in treating a wide range of disorders. Cognitive therapies—including coping-skills training (Goldfried, 1971, 1973), stress-inoculation training (Jaremko, 1980; Meichenbaum, 1977; Novaco, 1975, 1977), and guided imagery (Beck, 1970; Edwards, 1989; Leuner, 1984)—likewise have been found to be effective in changing cognitive processes, patterns, and behaviors.

CONCLUSION

The cognitive sciences have been described by an admittedly biased authority as representing "one of the most powerful developments of the twentieth century" (Mahoney, 1991, p. 67). The cognitive revolution has given way to cognitive evolution, and the promise for the cognitive sciences in the next century is great. Some of the challenging issues for exploration and discovery include the relationship between sensory reception and cognitive processing; the relationship between emotion and cognition; the mechanisms by which tacit knowledge influences explicit knowledge, emotion, and overt behavior; the relationship between creativity and cognitive structural integrity; and the general development of psychological constructivism.

A correspondingly formidable challenge is the translation and application of cognitive scientific knowledge into strategic efforts toward human change. Although there is mounting empirical support for the efficacy of cognitive methods in the treatment of various emotional disorders (for example, depression, anxiety, anger), behavioral problems (substance abuse, eating disorders), and interpersonal problems (marital distress), additional controlled explorations are needed to offer further validation, to further refine specific treatment procedures, and to modify and expand the application of the methods to special populations (particularly the at-risk

and disadvantaged). It is the collective responsibility of the human service disciplines to develop, demonstrate, and promote increasingly effective, efficient, and enduring interventions. Cognitive methods hold great promise in the advancement of these goals.

REFERENCES

Abramson, L. Y., Metalsky, G. I., & Alloy, L. B. (1988). The hopelessness theory of depression: Does the research test the theory? In L. Y. Abramson (Ed.), *Social cognition and clinical psychology.* New York: Guilford Press.

Abramson, L. Y., Seligman, M. E. P., & Teasdale, J. D. (1978). Learned helplessness in humans: Critique and reformulation. *Journal of Abnormal Psychology, 87,* 49–74.

Airenti, G., Bara, B., & Colombetti, M. (1982a). Semantic network representation of conceptual and episodic knowledge. In R. Trappl (Ed.), *Advances in cybernetics and system research* (Vol. 2). Washington, DC: Hemisphere.

Airenti, G., Bara, B., & Colombetti, M. (1982b). A two level model of knowledge and belief. In R. Trappl (Ed.), *Proceedings of 6th E.M.C.S.R.* Amsterdam: North Holland.

Arkowitz, H., & Hannah, M. T. (1989). Cognitive, behavioral, and psychodynamic therapies: Converging or diverging pathways to change? In A. Freeman, K. M. Simon, L. E. Beutler, & H. Arkowitz (Eds.), *Comprehensive handbook of cognitive therapy.* New York: Plenum.

Baars, B. J. (1986). *The cognitive revolution in psychology.* New York: Guilford Press.

Bandura, A. (1977). Self-efficacy: Toward a unifying theory of behavior change. *Psychological Review, 84,* 191–215.

Bandura, A. (1978a). Reflections on self-efficacy. *Advances in Behavior Research and Therapy, 1,* 237–269.

Bandura, A. (1978b). The self system in reciprocal determinism. *American Psychologist, 33,* 344–358.

Bandura, A. (1985). Model of causality in social learning theory. In M. J. Mahoney & A. Freeman (Eds.), *Cognition and psychotherapy.* New York: Plenum.

Bartlett, F. C. (1932). *Remembering*. New York: Columbia University Press.

Bartlett, F. C. (1958). *Thinking: An experimental and social study*. New York: Basic Books.

Baucom, D., & Epstein, N. (1990). *Cognitive-behavioral marital therapy*. New York: Brunner/Mazel.

Beck, A. T. (1964). Thinking and depression: II. Theory and therapy. *Archives of General Psychiatry, 10,* 561–571.

Beck, A. T. (1967). *Depression: Clinical, experimental, and theoretical aspects*. New York: Harper & Row. (Republished as *Depression: Causes and treatment*. Philadelphia: University of Pennsylvania Press, 1972.)

Beck, A. T. (1970). The role of fantasies in psychotherapy and psychopathology. *Journal of Nervous and Mental Disease, 150,* 3–17.

Beck, A. T. (1976). *Cognitive therapy and the emotional disorders*. New York: International Universities Press.

Beck, A. T. (1985). Cognitive therapy, behavior therapy, psychoanalysis, and pharmacotherapy: A cognitive continuum. In M. J. Mahoney & A. Freeman (Eds.), *Cognition and psychotherapy*. New York: Plenum.

Beck, A. T., & Emery, G. (1985). *Anxiety disorders and phobias*. New York: Basic Books.

Beck, A. T., Freeman, A., & Associates. (1990). *Cognitive therapy of personality disorders*. New York: Guilford Press.

Beck, A. T., Rush, A. J., Shaw, B. F., & Emery, G. (1979). *Cognitive therapy of depression*. New York: Guilford Press.

Beck, A. T., & Weishaar, M. (1989). Cognitive therapy. In A. Freeman, K. M. Simon, L. E. Beutler, & H. Arkowitz (Eds.), *Comprehensive handbook of cognitive therapy*. New York: Plenum.

Bedell, J. R., Archer, R. P., & Marlow, H. A., Jr. (1980). A description and evaluation of a problem solving skills training program. In D. Upper & S. M. Ross (Eds.), *Behavioral group therapy: An annual review*. Champaign, IL: Research Press.

Bulman, R. J., & Wortman, C. B. (1977). Attributions of blame and coping in the "real world": Severe accident victims react to their lot. *Journal of Personality and Social Psychology, 35,* 351–363.

Cautela, J. R. (1966). Treatment of compulsive behavior by covert sensitization. *Psychological Record, 16,* 33–41.

Cautela, J. R. (1967). Covert sensitization. *Psychological Reports, 20,* 459–468.

Cautela, J. R. (1971). *Covert modeling*. Paper presented at the meeting of the Association for the Advancement of Behavior Therapy, Washington, DC.

Chaney, E. F., O'Leary, M. R., & Marlatt, G. A. (1978). Skill training with alcoholics. *Journal of Consulting and Clinical Psychology, 46,* 1092–1104.

Cutrona, C. (1983). Causal attributions and perinatal depression. *Journal of Abnormal Psychology, 92,* 161–172.

Dember, W. N. (1974). Motivation and the cognitive revolution. *American Psychologist, 29,* 161–168.

Dobson, D. J., & Dobson, K. S. (1981). Problem-solving strategies in depressed and nondepressed college students. *Cognitive Therapy and Research, 5,* 237–249.

Dowd, E. T., & Pace, T. M. (1989). The relativity of reality: Second-order change in psychotherapy. In A. Freeman, K. M. Simon, L. E. Beutler, & H. Arkowitz (Eds.), *Comprehensive handbook of cognitive therapy*. New York: Plenum.

D'Zurilla, T. J. (1988). Problem-solving therapies. In K. S. Dobson (Ed.), *Handbook of cognitive-behavioral therapies*. New York: Guilford Press.

D'Zurilla, T. J., & Goldfried, M. R. (1971). Problem solving and behavior modification. *Journal of Abnormal Psychology, 78,* 107–126.

Edwards, D. J. A. (1989). Cognitive restructuring through guided imagery. In A. Freeman, K. M. Simon, L. E. Beutler, & H. Arkowitz (Eds.), *Comprehensive handbook of cognitive therapy*. New York: Plenum.

Ellis, A. (1973). *Humanistic psychotherapy*. New York: McGraw-Hill.

Ellis, A. (1976). RET abolishes most of the human ego. *Psychotherapy: Theory, Research and Practice, 13,* 343–348.

Ellis, A. (1977a). The basic clinical theory of rational-emotive therapy. In A. Ellis & R. Grieger (Eds.), *Handbook of rational-emotive therapy*. New York: Springer.

Ellis, A. (1977b). Psychotherapy and the value of a human being. In A. Ellis & R. Grieger (Eds.), *Handbook of rational-emotive therapy*. New York: Springer.

Ellis, A. (1977c). Rational-emotive therapy: Research data that supports the clinical and personality hypotheses of RET and other modes of cognitive-behavior therapy. *The Counseling Psychologist, 7*(1), 2–42.

Ellis, A. (1990). Is rational-emotive therapy (RET) "rationalist" or "constructivist"? In W. Dryden (Ed.), *The essential Albert Ellis: Seminal writings on psychotherapy.* New York: Springer.

Ellis, A., & Dryden, W. (1987). *The practice of rational-emotive therapy.* New York: Springer.

Epstein, N. (1982). Cognitive therapy with couples. *American Journal of Family Therapy, 10,* 5–16.

Ewart, C. K., Burnett, K. F., & Taylor, C. B. (1983). Communication behaviors that affect blood pressure: An A-B-A-B analysis of marital interaction. *Behavior Modification, 7,* 331–344.

Freeman, A. (1983). Cognitive therapy: An overview. In A. Freeman (Ed.), *Cognitive therapy with couples and groups.* New York: Plenum.

Freeman, A. (1990). Cognitive therapy. In A. S. Bellack & M. Hersen (Eds.), *Handbook of comparative treatments for adult disorders.* New York: Wiley.

Goldfried, M. R. (1971). Systematic desensitization as training in self-control. *Journal of Consulting and Clinical Psychology, 37,* 228–234.

Goldfried, M. R. (1973). Reduction of generalized anxiety through a variant of systematic desensitization. In M. R. Goldfried & M. Merbaum (Eds.), *Behavior change through self-control.* New York: Holt, Rinehart & Winston.

Granvold, D. K. (1988). Treating marital couples in conflict and transition. In J. S. McNeil & S. E. Weinstein (Eds.), *Innovations in health care practice.* Silver Spring, MD: National Association of Social Workers.

Grieger, R., & Grieger, I. Z. (1982). *Cognition and emotional disturbance.* New York: Human Sciences Press.

Guidano, V. F. (1987). *Complexity of the self.* New York: Guilford Press.

Guidano, V. F. (1988). A systems, process-oriented approach to cognitive therapy. In K. S. Dobson (Ed.), *Handbook of cognitive-behavioral therapies.* New York: Guilford Press.

Guidano, V. F., & Liotti, G. (1983). *Cognitive processes and emotional disorders.* New York: Guilford Press.

Guidano, V. F., & Liotti, G. (1985). A construc-

tivistic foundation for cognitive therapy. In M. J. Mahoney & A. Freeman (Eds.), *Cognition and psychotherapy.* New York: Plenum.

Hayek, F. A. (1978). *New studies in philosophy, politics, economics, and the history of ideas.* Chicago: University of Chicago Press.

Homme, L. E. (1965). Perspectives in psychology: XXIV. Control of coverants, the operants of the mind. *Psychological Record, 15,* 501–511.

Hurvitz, N. (1975). Interaction of hypotheses in marriage counseling. In A. S. Gurman & D. G. Rice (Eds.), *Couples in conflict.* New York: Aronson.

Ickes, W. (1988). Attributional styles and the self-concept. In L. Y. Abramson (Ed.), *Social cognition and clinical psychology.* New York: Guilford Press.

Ickes, W., & Layden, M. A. (1978). Attributional styles. In J. Harvey, W. Ickes, & R. Kidd (Eds.), *New directions in attributional research* (Vol. 2). Hillsdale, NJ: Erlbaum.

Ingram, R. E. (1983). Content and process distinctions in depressive self-schemata. In L. B. Alloy (Chair), *Depression and schemata.* Symposium presented at the meeting of the American Psychological Association, Anaheim, CA.

Ingram, R. E., & Kendall, P. C. (1986). Cognitive clinical psychology: Implications of an information processing perspective. In R. E. Ingram (Ed.), *Information processing approaches to clinical psychology.* New York: Academic Press.

Jacob, T., Ritchey, D., Cvitkovic, J., & Blane, H. (1981). Communication styles of alcoholic and nonalcoholic families when drinking and not drinking. *Journal of Studies on Alcohol, 42,* 466–482.

Jacobson, N. S., McDonald, D. W., Follette, W. C., & Berley, R. A. (1985). Attribution processes in distressed and nondistressed married couples. *Cognitive Therapy and Research, 9,* 35–50.

Jannoun, L., Munby, M., Catalan, J., & Gelder, M. (1980). A home-based treatment program for agoraphobia: Replication and controlled evaluation. *Behavior Therapy, 11,* 294–305.

Janoff-Bulman, R., & Lang-Gunn, L. (1988). Coping with disease, crime, and accidents: The role of self-blame attributions. In L. Abramson (Ed.), *Social cognition and clinical psychology.* New York: Guilford Press.

Jaremko, M. E. (1980). The use of stress inoculation training in the reduction of public speaking anxiety. *Journal of Clinical Psychology, 36,* 735–738.

Juola, J. (1986). Cognitive psychology and information processing: Content and process analysis for a psychology of mind. In R. Ingram (Ed.), *Information processing approaches to clinical psychology.* New York: Academic Press.

Kazdin, A. E., Esveldt-Dawson, K., French, N. H., & Unis, A. S. (1987). Problem-solving skills training and relationship therapy in the treatment of antisocial child behavior. *Journal of Consulting and Clinical Psychology, 55,* 76–85.

Kelly, G. (1955). *The psychology of personal constructs* (Vols. 1 & 2). New York: Norton.

Kendall, P. C. (1981). Assessment and cognitive-behavioral interventions: Purposes, proposals and problems. In P. C. Kendall & S. D. Hollon (Eds.), *Assessment strategies for cognitive-behavioral intervention.* New York: Academic Press.

Kendall, P. C., & Ingram, R. (1987). The future for cognitive assessment of anxiety: Let's get specific. In L. Michelson & L. M. Ascher (Eds.), *Anxiety and stress disorders.* New York: Guilford Press.

Lazarus, R. S. (1989). Constructs of the mind in mental health and psychotherapy. In A. Freeman, K. M. Simon, L. E. Beutler, and H. Arkowitz (Eds.), *Comprehensive handbook of cognitive therapy.* New York: Plenum.

LeDoux, J. E., & Hirst, W. (Eds.). (1986). *Mind and brain: Dialogues in cognitive neuroscience.* Cambridge, England: Cambridge University Press.

Leuner, H. (1984). *Guided affective imagery: Mental imagery in short term psychotherapy.* New York: Thieme-Stratton.

Luria, A. (1959). The directive function of speech in development. *Word, 18,* 341–352.

Luria, A. (1961). *The role of speech in the regulation of normal and abnormal behaviors.* New York: Liveright.

Mahoney, M. J. (1974). *Cognition and behavior modification.* Cambridge, MA: Ballinger.

Mahoney, M. J. (1977). Reflections on the cognitive-learning trend in psychotherapy. *American Psychologist, 32,* 5–13.

Mahoney, M. J. (1984). Behaviorism, cognitivism, and human change processes. In M. A. Reda & M. J. Mahoney (Eds.), *Cognitive psychotherapies: Recent developments in theory, research, and practice.* Cambridge, MA: Ballinger.

Mahoney, M. J. (1985). Psychotherapy and human change processes. In M. J. Mahoney & A. Freeman (Eds.), *Cognition and psychotherapy.* New York: Plenum.

Mahoney, M. J. (1991). *Human change processes.* New York: Basic Books.

Meichenbaum, D. (1975). Theoretical and treatment implications of developmental research on verbal control of behavior. *Canadian Psychological Review, 16,* 22–27.

Meichenbaum, D. (1977). *Cognitive-behavior modification: An integrative approach.* New York: Plenum.

Meichenbaum, D., & Goodman, J. (1971). Training impulsive children to talk to themselves: A means of developing self-control. *Journal of Abnormal Psychology, 77,* 115–126.

Metalsky, G. I., & Abramson, L. Y. (1981). Attributional styles: Toward a framework for conceptualization and assessment. In P. C. Kendall & S. D. Hollon (Eds.), *Assessment strategies for cognitive-behavioral interventions.* New York: Academic Press.

Miller, D. T., & Porter, C. A. (1988). Errors and biases in the attribution process. In L. Y. Abramson (Ed.), *Social cognition and clinical psychology.* New York: Guilford Press.

Mukherji, B. R., Abramson, L. Y., & Martin, D. J. (1982). Induced depressive mood and attributional patterns. *Cognitive Therapy and Research, 6,* 15–22.

Neisser, U. (1967). *Cognitive psychology.* New York: Appleton-Century-Crofts.

Newman, H. M., & Langer, E. J. (1988). Investigating the development and courses of intimate relationships. In L. Y. Abramson (Ed.), *Social cognition and clinical psychology: A synthesis.* New York: Guilford Press.

Nezu, A. M. (1986). Efficacy of a social problem solving therapy approach for unipolar depression. *Journal of Consulting and Clinical Psychology, 54,* 196–202.

Nezu, A. M., & Carnevale, G. J. (1987). Interpersonal problem solving and coping reactions of Vietnam veterans with posttraumatic stress syndrome. *Journal of Abnormal Psychology, 96,* 155–157.

Novaco, R. (1975). *Anger control: The development and evaluation of an experimental treatment.* Lexington, MA: D. C. Heath.

Novaco, R. (1977). A stress inoculation approach

to anger management in the training of law enforcement officers. *American Journal of Community Psychiatry, 5,* 327–346.

Piaget, J. (1926). *The language and thought of the child.* New York: Harcourt, Brace.

Polanyi, M. (1958). *Personal knowledge: Towards a post-critical philosophy.* Chicago: University of Chicago Press.

Popper, K. R. (1972). *Objective knowledge: An evolutionary approach.* London: Oxford University Press.

Roth, D. L., & Tucker, D. M. (1986). Neural systems in the emotional control of information processing. In R. E. Ingram (Ed.), *Information processing approaches to clinical psychology.* New York: Academic Press.

Rotter, J. B. (1954). *Social learning and clinical psychology.* Englewood Cliffs, NJ: Prentice-Hall.

Rotter, J. B. (1966). Generalized expectancies for internal versus external control of reinforcement. *Psychological Monographs, 80* (1, Whole No. 609).

Rush, A. J., & Beck, A. T. (1978). Adults with affective disorders. In M. Hersen & A. S. Bellack (Eds.), *Behavioral therapy in the psychiatric setting.* Baltimore: Williams & Wilkins.

Schindler, L., & Vollmer, M. (1984). Cognitive perspectives in behavioral marital therapy: Some proposals for bridging theory, research, and practice. In K. Halweg & N. S. Jacobson (Eds.), *Marital interaction: Analysis and modification.* New York: Guilford Press.

Schulz, R., & Hanusa, B. H. (1988). Information-seeking, self-esteem, and helplessness. In L. Y. Abramson (Ed.), *Social cognition and clinical psychology.* New York: Guilford Press.

Seiler, T. B. (1984). Developmental cognitive therapy, personality and therapy. In N. Hoffman (Ed.), *Foundations of cognitive therapy: Theoretical methods and practical applications.* New York: Plenum.

Seligman, M. E. P. (1975). *Helplessness: On depression, development, and death.* San Francisco: W. H. Freeman.

Seligman, M. E. P., Abramson, L. Y., Semmel, A., & von Baeyer, C. (1979). Depressive attributional style. *Journal of Abnormal Psychology, 88,* 242–247.

Shulman, B. H. (1985). Cognitive therapy and the individual psychology of Alfred Adler. In M. J. Mahoney & A. Freeman (Eds.), *Cognition and psychotherapy.* New York: Plenum.

Tataryn, D. J., Nadel, L., & Jacobs, W. J. (1989). Cognitive therapy and cognitive science. In A. Freeman, K. M. Simon, L. E. Beutler & H. Arkowitz (Eds.), *Comprehensive handbook of cognitive therapy.* New York: Plenum.

Tulving, E. (1972). Episodic and semantic memory. In E. Tulving & W. Donaldson (Eds.), *Organization of memory.* New York: Academic Press.

Vincent, J., Weiss, R., & Birchler, G. (1976). A behavioral analysis of problem solving in distressed and nondistressed married and stranger dyads. *Behavior Therapy, 6,* 475–487.

Vygotsky, L. (1962). *Thought and language.* New York: Wiley.

Weimer, W. B. (1975). The psychology of inference and expectation: Some preliminary remarks. In G. Maxwell & R. M. Anderson (Eds.), *Induction, probability and confirmation* (Minnesota Studies in the Philosophy of Science, Vol. 6). Minneapolis: University of Minnesota Press.

Weimer, W. B. (1977). A conceptual framework for cognitive psychology: Motor theories of the mind. In R. Shaw & J. Bransford (Eds.), *Perceiving, acting, and knowing: Toward an ecological psychology.* Hillsdale, NJ: Erlbaum.

Weisz, J. R., Weiss, B., Wasserman, A. A., & Rintoul, B. (1987). Control-related beliefs and depression among clinic-referred children and adolescents. *Journal of Abnormal Psychology, 96,* 58–63.

Wessler, R. A., & Wessler, R. L. (1980). *The principles and practice of rational-emotive therapy.* San Francisco: Jossey-Bass.

Winfrey, L. L., & Goldfried, M. R. (1986). Information processing and the human change process. In R. Ingram (Ed.), *Information processing approaches to clinical psychology.* New York: Academic Press.

Wolpe, J. (1958). *Psychotherapy by reciprocal inhibition.* Stanford, CA: Stanford University Press.

Wolpe, J. (1969). *The practice of behavior therapy.* New York: Pergamon Press.

Wolpe, J. (1980). Cognitive behavior and its roles in psychotherapy: An integrative account. In M. J. Mahoney (Ed.), *Psychotherapy process.* New York: Plenum.

Wolpe, J., & Lazarus, A. A. (1966). *Behavior therapy techniques.* New York: Pergamon Press.

Wortman, C. B. (1976). Causal attributions and perceived control. In J. Harvey, W. Ickes, & R. Kidd (Eds.), *New directions in attribution research* (Vol. 1). Hillsdale, NJ: Erlbaum.

Wortman, C. B., & Silver, R. (1979). Coping with undesirable life events. In M. E. P. Seligman & J. Garber (Eds.), *Human helplessness: Theory and applications.* New York: Academic Press.

Concepts and Methods of Behavioral Treatment

Eileen D. Gambrill

Behavioral practice involves an empirical approach to personal and social problems in which the selection of assessment and intervention methods is based whenever possible on related research. In applied behavior analysis the principles of behavior form the basis of contingency management (rearranging the relationships between behavior and the environment to attain socially valid outcomes). As Krasner says, "The unifying factor in behavior-therapy is its basis in derivation from experimentally established procedures and principles" (1971, p. 487). The terms *behavior modification* and *behavior therapy* are often used synonymously. Initially, behavioral methods drew primarily on relevant research on respondent and operant conditioning. Applied efforts now draw on a wider range of related research, including data and theory from social psychology and ethology. A rich empirical literature describes the application of behavioral principles to a broad range of problems that directly concern practitioners (Bellack, Hersen, & Kazdin, 1990; Gambrill, 1977; Pinkston, Levitt, Green, Linsk, & Rzepnicki, 1982; Pinkston & Linsk, 1984; Thyer, 1983). New fields of application, such as behavioral medicine, have been developed. Behavioral community psychology offers a rich source of guidelines for practitioners.

Variations in behavioral practice reflect different, often conflicting approaches to understanding behavior. These approaches include applied behavior analysis, which focuses attention on environmental factors related to clients' concerns; neobehavioral models, focusing on the application of principles of classical conditioning; and cognitive-behavioral methods, which draw on social-learning theory. Differences involve the relative influence of different causes of behavior (for example, thoughts versus environmental histories and changes) and the preferred focus for intervention (Kazdin, 1978). One of the key differences concerns the role of thoughts and feelings: do they have a causal role? Another relates to preferred methodology (intensive, process-oriented study of single individuals in contrast to actuarial methods, in which the average response of a group of individuals is correlated with environmental events).

Some models of behavioral practice (such as applied behavior analysis) involve a contextual approach, which devotes attention to individual, family, community, and societal factors to understand the causes of personal and social problems. In Patterson's work with antisocial youths, variables related to delinquency include social disadvantage, academic failure, low self-esteem, parental rejection, peer rejection, conduct problems, lack of parental supervision, involvement in a deviant peer group, and parents' ineffective disciplinary practices (Patterson, Reid, & Dishion, 1992). Guidelines are offered for discovering the relationships between behaviors, feelings, or thoughts and environmental factors, for identifying the system levels that require change (individual, family, community, or society), and for rearranging environmental conditions in order to attain desired outcomes. These guidelines are helpful in distinguishing when it is possible to "change the system" and when trying to do so would be a waste of time because there is no way to influence key contingencies. This is not to say that these guidelines are complete; that is far from the case. The development of a science of behavior and the successful use of it to attain socially valid outcomes is a slow process. The more complex the levels involved, the more planning and time may be required to achieve valued outcomes (Fawcett, 1991). Guidelines that are available are not always followed. A focus on altering the behavior of the individual with a problem (for example, a battered wife) may result in ignoring environmental factors (lack of money, transportation, and child care) required to escape an unwanted situation (Davis & Hagen, 1992). All that is called behavioral practice is not. Over the past decade the term *behavior therapy* has been loosely applied to many practices that in fact are not behavior therapy (Wolpe, 1986).

Behavioral methods that focus on rearranging contingencies are often combined with cognitive methods such as cognitive restructuring. The term *cognitive-behavioral methods* is used to refer to such combinations. Cognitive therapies differ in the extent to which they draw on behavioral principles, methods, and terms. Terms are often inappropriately used. An example would be calling "cognitive" a treatment of depression that involves increasing pleasant activities through rearranging contingencies. Lively debates can be found in the professional literature about different kinds of practice (Wolpe, 1989). Behavior analysts would argue that cognitive methods often include rearrangement of cues and consequences and that these changes (not changing expectations, for example) are related to successful outcome.

In this chapter, a description of applied behavior analysis and the philosophy on which it is based is first presented. The differences between radical behaviorism and social learning theory are discussed, and what has been termed "neobehaviorism" is described. Basic terms and concepts are then reviewed, and characteristics of behavioral practice are presented. Guidelines for assessment, intervention, and evaluation are described, and some common misconceptions are addressed.

APPLIED BEHAVIOR ANALYSIS

Behavior analysis and its applied branch involve the study of functional relationships between behavior and the environment, with a focus on variables that have strong effects; they permit the prediction and influence of behavior. Single case studies are used to evaluate outcomes and explore relationships between environmental factors and behaviors of interest. This approach has been applied to a broad range of behaviors and settings, including industry, classrooms, residential settings, environmental problems such as littering, health concerns, job finding, delinquency, depression, and parent/child and marital communication, to name but a few. (See, for example, the section in the Winter 1991 issue of the *Journal of Applied Behavior Analysis* on behavioral community intervention.) A number of approaches help low-income, minority clients acquire skills that will be of value in attaining resources (Fawcett & Miller, 1975). "The behavior analytic view is a contextualist world view that emphasizes prediction and influence as the criteria for the truth of statements; explanation is considered to be achieved to the extent that statements lead to successful prediction and control" (Biglan, 1987, p. 4). It is assumed that behavior is orderly, predictable, and controllable and that this underlying order can be discovered through systematic exploration. These assumptions are basic to a scientific approach that is analytical, questioning, skeptical, and experimental.

"Applied" refers to the extent to which a response is socially important: "The applied criterion of behavior analysis focuses attention on the relevant behaviors of people actually experiencing problems in real-world contexts" (Fawcett, 1991, p. 622). "Behavior" refers to what people do, not to what they say they do (Baer, Wolf, & Risley, 1968, 1987). Behavior and the translation of personal and societal problems into behaviors are the central subject. "Analysis" requires "a believable demonstration of the events that can be responsible for the occurrence or non-occurrence of that behavior" (Baer et al., 1968, p. 94)—a demonstration of experimental control by altering presumed causes. According to Baer, "The analytic challenges for anyone who deserves to be called an 'applied behavior analyst' are (1) to restate the complained-of problem in behavioral terms; (2) to change the behaviors indicated by that restatement; and then (3) to see whether changing them has decreased the complaining response" (1982, p. 284). Personal and social problems are translated into observable behaviors that, when altered, remove complaints. There is a focus on altering the patterns of behavior associated with original complaints so that these complaints no longer occur. (Many other perspectives entail a remarkable lack of interest in exploring what people actually do in specific situations and the environmental factors related to behavior.) Other characteristics identified by Baer and his colleagues (1968) include the requirements that applied behavior analysis be technological (attentive to modifiable features of the social and physical environment), conceptually systematic, effective, and display generalization and longevity of effects.

There is a focus on altering the relationship between observable behaviors and related environmental factors, which often consist of social consequences. This approach emphasizes the importance of a functional analysis of behavior in which environmental factors related to behaviors of concern are identified through rearranging contingencies (altering what happens before and after behavior). The effects of altering a given variable are tracked on an ongoing basis. Contributors to this approach have taken a leading role in developing and evaluating programs of benefit to a wide range of clients, including students at all levels of education, youths labeled delinquent, mental patients, those with developmental disabilities, people experiencing chronic pain, the unemployed, the elderly, parents, and children.

Applied behavior analysis is process-oriented, functional, and analytic rather than actuarial (correlating the average responses of a group of people with environmental events). A determination that the methods used or the environmental events altered are responsible for changes observed is usually made by using single-case experimental designs. There is an interest in strong rather than weak correlations between behavior and environmental events discovered through experimental procedures. The problem with correlational data is that a wide range of quite varied cause/effect relationships is possible in most nonexperimental correlations. Explanations of behavior are considered to be complete only when they relate behavior to contingencies adequate to account for it (Baer, 1982). That is, the analysis of behavior has been achieved if one can exercise influence over it. Private as well as public events are assumed to be subject to environmental influence. It is assumed that private events such as thoughts and feelings "operate as elements in chains that begin with observable environmental events and end with observable responses; thus, their analysis is environmental and empirical, as is the analysis of observable behavior" (Baer, 1982, p. 178).

Various other terms that have been used to describe applied behavior analysis include ecobehavioral intervention and contextualism. A radical behavioral perspective is contextual; it is ecobehavioral in terms of attending to factors that influence behaviors of concern. A proliferation of unnecessary terms is confusing rather than helpful.

Radical Behaviorism

Radical behaviorism is the philosophy related to applied behavior analysis. It "is the attempt to account for behavior solely in terms of natural contingencies—either contingencies of survival, contingencies of reinforcement, or contingencies of social evolution" (Day, 1983, p. 101). The belief in a "science of behavior" is a basic premise of radical behaviorism—the belief that behavior is knowable and that knowledge can be discovered through empirical inquiry. It is not claimed that a radical-behavioral perspective is the only scientific psychology. It is believed that this approach is the one most likely to yield knowledge about behavior and how it can be altered. There are perhaps more misunderstandings about this view and more objections to it than any other perspective in psychology. Many writers have discussed the misinformation and distortions of radical behaviorism that have been presented in the mass media as well as in the professional literature (Todd & Morris, 1983). It is important to address and correct misconceptions that interfere with the use of a framework that offers information about how to help clients. Radical behaviorism does not embrace associationism, operationism, positivism, or environmental determinism (Day, 1980). It "does *not* deny the possibility of self-observation and self-knowledge or its possible usefulness, but does question the nature of what is felt or observed and hence known" (Skinner, 1974, p. 16). "It does not call these [private] events unobservable and it does not dismiss them as subjective. It simply questions the nature of the object observed and the reliability of the observations" (p. 17).

Behaviorism defines the study of psychology as "the study of behavior via a reasonable

and pragmatic level of objectivity and verifiability" (Levis, 1990b, p. 4). Different kinds of behaviorism are often confused. *Radical behaviorism* received its name because it represented a radical break with earlier forms of behaviorism such as Watsonian and methodological behaviorism. There is no insistence on truth by agreement in radical behaviorism as there is in *methodological behaviorism,* in which self-observation and self-knowledge are denied and attention is confined to external events. B. F. Skinner's radical behaviorism explicitly rejects the methodological behaviorist's form of operationism and instead embraces a nonmediational, environmentally based account (that is, a focus on the direct relationship between environmental events and behavior):

> [Radical behaviorism] does not insist upon truth by agreement and can therefore consider events taking place in the private world within the skin. It does not call these events unobservable and it does not dismiss them as subjective [Skinner, 1974, p. 16].

> Methodological behaviorism also viewed publicly observable behavior as the only appropriate data of psychology, but this data was to be used to infer inner processes and underlying structures that were given special explanatory status. Although S-R [stimulus/reponse] links were considered to be important, these links had to be mediated by processes within the organism to account for variability in behavior. Skinner's radical behaviorism explicitly rejected the methodological behaviorist's form of operationalism and instead embraced a nonmediational, environmentally based account (i.e., a focus on the direct relationships between environmental events and behavior). Also, Skinner explicitly included private events in his behavioristic account; however, private events were distinguished by their inaccessibility to an observer or interpreter of behavior, not by any special causal role [Lonigan, 1990, p. 1180].

A radical-behavioral perspective is also very different from Watsonian associationism. According to Lonigan (1990), "Watsonian behaviorism insisted that the only acceptable area of inquiry in psychology was the study of behavior (as in the publicly observable responses of an organism). In this version of behaviorism, thoughts, feelings, and other internal states either did not exist or were considered epiphenomenal" (p. 1180). What is radical about radical behaviorism is not only that private events such as thoughts and feelings are *not* dismissed but also that they are considered to lie in the behavioral domain. They are viewed as behaviors that themselves require an explanation (traced to their environmental, evolutionary, or physiological origins). (See Hayes & Brownstein, 1987, for a further discussion.) Thoughts and feelings are assumed to have the same functions as public stimuli and responses. They can serve as eliciting events for emotional reactions, as discriminative stimuli for operant behavior, or as responses in their own right. The advantage of viewing thoughts and feelings as behaviors is that they cannot as readily be inaccurately presumed to be the causes of behavior.

Private events such as thoughts and feelings are not considered to be the causes of behavior. Feelings are considered to be collateral effects, or by-products, of reinforcement contingencies (relationships between behavior and the environment) (Skinner, 1971). That is, rather than a feeling causing a certain behavior, the feeling itself is considered to be a product of what we have experienced. For example, punishment for a behavior generates certain feelings. We may feel guilt, shame, or anger. "We do not cry *because* we are sad or feel sad *because* we cry, we cry *and* feel sad because something has happened" (Skinner, 1988, p. 172). Feelings are vivid. It is thus easy to assume that they cause our behavior. What are introspectively observed are viewed as collateral products of genetic and environmental histories. The difference between private and public behaviors lies in their observability. Cognitive psychologists,

in contrast to radical behaviorists, "view their subject matter as mental events and processes (in addition to public behavior) that are, or may be, essentially different from overt behavior" (Wyatt, 1990, p. 1181). Publicly observed behavior is used to infer inner processes and underlying structures that are alleged to have a special explanatory status.

In a radical-behavioral perspective, to reiterate, the causes of behavior are sought in the relationships between behavior and environmental changes, not in the feelings and thoughts, which are considered to be collateral effects, or by-products of these contingencies.

> The origination of behavior is sought in natural selection, operant conditioning, and the evolution of cultural practices [Skinner, 1984].

> Troublesome behavior is due to troublesome contingencies of reinforcement, not to troublesome feelings or states of mind, and to correct the trouble we should correct the contingencies [1988, p. 172].

Thus, private events can be called causes, but they are not initiating causes. Culture is viewed "as a social environment that shapes the behavior of new members of a group. . . . Variations occur in the individual, but it is the culture with its practices that survives" (Skinner, 1984, p. 718). Expectations and feelings are viewed as "surrogates" of histories of reinforcement. It is not assumed that contingencies cause any behavior. To assign causal power to contingencies is what is meant by *radical environmentalism*. Radical behaviorism does *not* advocate this. Behavior is not endlessly malleable.

The experimental analysis of behavior shows that contingencies of reinforcement influence behavior. This is not to say that they are the only influence. Genetic and biological factors also affect behavior. At first glance, attributing such an influential role to the environment seems to take away freedom. However, it can be argued that only if one understands the causes of behavior, as shown by effectively altering behavior, can one be free and that acceptance of mentalistic causes that do not offer intervention guidelines for effective behavior change compromises freedom:

> In its search for internal explanations supported by the false sense of cause associated with feelings and introspective observations, mentalism has obscured the environmental antecedents which would have led to a much more effective analysis. . . . The objection to the inner workings of the mind is not that they are not open to inspection but that they have stood in the way of the inspection of more important things [Skinner, 1974, p. 165].

Radical Behaviorism and Social Learning Theory

Social learning theory provides the underlying theory for cognitive-behavioral methods (Bandura, 1977, 1986). It gives thoughts a causal initiating and explanatory role, in contrast to radical behaviorism, which views private events such as thoughts and feelings as covert behaviors that may be part of chains of behavior but do not have an initiating role. Consider the definition of cognitive-behavioral therapy given by Ingram and Scott (1990): "Specifically, cognitive-behavioral therapy is defined as those sets of therapeutic procedures that (1) embody theoretical conceptualizations of change that place primary importance on cognitive process, and that (2) procedurally target at least some therapeutic maneuvers specially at altering aspects of cognition" (p. 55). Radical behaviorists view thoughts (and feelings) as behaviors in need of explanation rather than as events providing explanations. Both perspectives assume that thoughts and feelings influence behavior as eliciting, discriminative, and reinforcing events. Thoughts and feelings may function as eliciting events for emotional reactions, discriminative cues for operant behaviors, responses in their own right, or negative or positive consequences.

Social learning theory assumes that thoughts play an important role in the complex processes that influence attention. It is assumed that we present an important part of our environment via our expectations, goals, and standards (Bandura, 1986). Social learning theory involves an information processing view in which verbal and classical conditioning, social influence, incentive effects, and self-referent mediation are addressed in cognitive terms (Rosenthal, 1982). Thus, it relies on cognitive explanations in contrast to applied behavior analysis and behavioral approaches, which invoke changes in conditioning as explanatory (Wolpe, 1990). It considers thoughts to play a critical role in the degree to which different interventions are effective in altering "self-efficacy," which in turn is assumed to influence behavior (Bandura, 1986). *Performance efficacy* refers to expectations that a behavior can be carried out; *outcome efficacy* refers to expectations that the behavior will be effective if it is carried out. Social-learning theory assumes that it is the extent to which different kinds of interventions alter self-efficacy that determines their effectiveness. Observational learning, the acquisition of new behavior via exposure to modeled behavior, is given a key role. Bandura (1986) argues that cognitive mediation is required for delayed performance of observed behavior. Radical behaviorists do not think that recourse to symbolic causes is required to account for the experimental data in this area (Deguchi, 1984). Rather than attributing similar behaviors on the part of many people in a situation to "imitation effects" all individuals involved may have experienced similar contingencies in that situation (whether this be leaving a church, entering a restaurant, sitting in a movie, or starting a conversation at a party).

Radical behaviorists argue that cognitive-behavioral procedures can be conceptualized within the framework of applied behavior analysis—that is, without reliance on unobservable events such as thoughts (Ledwidge, 1978). They contend that cognitive-behavioral methods involve the rearrangement of environmental cues and consequences and that it is these changes rather than the alteration of cognitive events that are responsible for change. Applied behavior analysts argue that key explanatory concepts in social learning theory such as self-efficacy are not explanatory, do not account for research data, and are superfluous constructs (Biglan, 1987; Lee, 1989). They argue that judgments of self-efficacy are covert behaviors that themselves require an explanation. Efficacy expectations are viewed as the product of environmental contingencies. Many procedures developed early in the history of the use of behavioral methods, such as systematic desensitization, depended heavily on changing unobservable events such as thoughts and images. Conceptually, however, the explanatory focus was on conditioning and changes in conditioned reactions (Wolpe, 1958). The key question from a scientific perspective is whether assumptions are testable. If, for example, it is assumed that behavior can be changed by verbal instructions, this assumption can be tested with an appropriate research design focusing on changes in behavior. Excessive focus on cognitive constructs obscures the role of contingencies of reinforcement. As Skinner points out, expectancy "is a gratuitous and dangerous assumption if nothing more than a history of reinforcement has been observed" (1969, p. 147). To enhance "efficacy" in a given situation, positive contingencies allowing successful experiences should be arranged.

Thus, social learning theory differs considerably from radical behaviorism. The difference lies in the initiating role attributed to thoughts. Both views assume a reciprocal interaction between individuals and their environments (we both influence and are influenced by our environment). But social learning theory views this mutual interaction as more bidirectional than does radical behaviorism. The latter gives the influence of contingencies of reinforcement a preeminent role. Both applied behavior analysis and cognitive-behavioral approaches emphasize evaluation of results, relying on observable outcomes.

NEOBEHAVIORISM

Levis (1990a) uses the term *neobehaviorism* to refer to the accumulation of evidence about behavior and how it can be altered. This term is popular with investigators who focus on the treatment of stress and anxiety disorders. Emotional reactions are altered through respondent conditioning (altering the relationship between stimulus events). For example, anxiety is viewed as a conditioned response acquired via unique learning histories. Change in such reactions can be made by arranging new conditioning experiences (Levis, 1990b; Wolpe, 1958, 1990). Intervention methods include systematic desensitization and flooding. Here, too, conditioning principles are emphasized, but there is a greater emphasis on respondent conditioning (rearrangement of antecedents) than in applied behavior analysis, which stresses operant conditioning and its effects (Eysenck, 1982; Wolpe, 1989). As with other kinds of behaviorism, there is an interest in discovering the lawful processes involved in developing, maintaining, and altering behavior. The principle of contiguity (the association between events) and the importance of respondent extinction and counterconditioning (for example, associating a feared event with a positive reaction) are emphasized in contrast with the law of effect. Eysenck highlights the role of genetically determined personality factors such as introversion and extroversion in relation to understanding the ease of conditioning. Advocates of neobehaviorism believe that cognitive approaches disregard accumulated findings in psychology, appealing instead to ill-defined and unverifiable entities.

Other varieties of behaviorism include paradigmatic behaviorism (Staats, 1990), ecobehavioral practice (Lutzker, 1984), and contextualism. Although these terms may be more "user-friendly" in communicating with the general public, they are misleading if meant to connote that radical behaviorism and applied behavior analysis do not involve a broad contextual approach. Paradigmatic behaviorism attempts to unify psychology, including all current theories of learning and conditioning. The conceptual richness of radical behaviorism is underestimated in descriptions of what is claimed to be unique to paradigmatic behaviorism.

BASIC TERMS AND CONCEPTS

Effective behavioral practice requires a thorough understanding of basic behavioral principles and skills in applying this knowledge to real-life problems. Behavioral principles describe relationships between behavior and environmental events. Key principles and procedures include reinforcement, punishment, establishing operations, extinction, differential reinforcement, shaping, conditioned reinforcement, and discrimination training and fading. Contingencies (associations between behavior and consequences), such as positive reinforcement, are defined not only by a certain procedure but also by the effect they have on behavior. Some contingencies, such as punishment and response cost, decrease behavior, whereas others, such as positive reinforcement and negative reinforcement, make it more likely on future occasions. Factors influencing the patterns of behavior that are established include the interval between a behavior and reinforcer as well as the schedule, frequency, and amount of reinforcement. Schedules of reinforcement influence the pattern and rate of behavior. (For further detail

see Martin and Pear, 1988, and Sulzer-Azaroff and Mayer, 1991.) Although there are relatively few behavioral principles, behavioral analysis of a given problem can become quite complex in terms of identifying current, delayed, and remote contingencies related to behaviors of concern.

Operant Behavior

The term *operant* refers to a class of behaviors all of which have the same effect on the environment. A child may gain his mother's attention by yelling, by tugging on her clothes, or by hitting his brother. The consequences of a behavior increase or decrease its future probability. That is, depending on what happens after a certain behavior, we may be more or less likely to perform it on similar occasions in the future. Thus, operant conditioning involves selection by consequences. The environment selects adaptive behaviors (what is beneficial for the individual or culture may not necessarily benefit the species): "Behavior is the joint product of (i) the contingencies of survival responsible for the natural selection of the species and (ii) the contingencies of reinforcement responsible for the repertoires acquired by its members, including (iii) the special contingencies maintained by an evolved social environment" (Skinner, 1981, p. 502). Both current and past environments (the individual's history in a given situation) influence behavior, as do certain other factors (such as physiological changes, genetic differences, and drugs). The concept of the *operant* highlights the fact that different forms of behavior can have the same function as well as the futility of punishing only one behavior included in an operant. The components of an operant are influenced by cultural practices. In Japan, for example, carrying any other kind of school bag but the one other children carry may be punished (Lock, 1988).

Behavior may be established or maintained by either positive or negative reinforcement. Reinforcement is a key principle in behavior analysis. The term *positive reinforcement* refers to a procedure in which an event (a reinforcer) is presented following a behavior and there is an increase in the future likelihood of that behavior. The definition involves two parts: *a procedure* (behavior is followed by the presentation of an event) and *an effect on behavior* (the probability that the behavior will occur in the future on similar occasions is increased). If you do a favor for a friend and she thanks you, you may be more likely to do her another favor in the future. The definition of negative reinforcement also involves two parts. *Negative reinforcement* is a procedure in which an event is removed, reduced, postponed, or prevented following a behavior and there is a subsequent increase in behavior. Crossing the street to avoid meeting someone and throwing a tantrum to get rid of an unwanted demand are examples. Much of our behavior is maintained by negative reinforcement. Reinforce*ment* refers to a procedure, whereas reinforc*er* refers to an event that, when presented or removed contingent on a behavior, increases the future likelihood of that behavior. As with positive reinforcers, the classification of an event as a negative reinforcer depends on its effects on behavior. We cannot tell for sure whether an event will function as a negative reinforcer until we arrange its removal following a behavior and see whether there is a future increase in behavior. Just as there are many different positive reinforcers, there are many different negative reinforcers, including social ones (disapproval, criticism), undesired tasks (cleaning), and negative self-statements ("I'm really stupid"). Most are conditioned reinforcers; that is, they acquire their reinforcing effects through learning.

Most reinforcers are *conditioned* or *secondary reinforcers,* in contrast to *primary reinforcers,* such as food, which function as reinforcers without any prior learning history. Conditioned reinforcers are often events that consistently precede other reinforcers. An

event may assume a reinforcing function by being associated with the removal of negative events. Conditioned reinforcers such as money and approval that are paired with a variety of reinforcers become *generalized reinforcers,* capable of maintaining a range of behaviors independent of particular states of deprivation. Token and point programs involve the use of conditioned reinforcers (Ayllon & Azrin, 1968; Kazdin, 1977). Because of people's different learning histories, current situations, and biological characteristics, an event that functions as a reinforcer for one person may not do so for another. Likewise, an event that functions as a reinforcer for an individual in one situation may not do so in another. Each person has a unique reinforcer profile—that list of events that function as reinforcers. Thus, reinforcers are known not by their physical characteristics but by their functional effects. Consequences may also decrease behavior. If behavior is followed by an aversive event (punishment), is followed by the removal of a positive reinforcer (response cost), or is no longer followed by reinforcing events (operant extinction), it will decrease in frequency. Aversive events are defined as those that decrease behaviors they follow and increase behaviors that succeed in preventing, delaying, decreasing, or removing them. Thus, aversive events are involved in punishment and response cost as well as negative reinforcement. The mix of positive reinforcement for desirable behaviors and extinction (withholding of reinforcement) of undesired behaviors is known as differential reinforcement.

Most of our behavior consists of *discriminated operants*—behaviors that occur only in certain situations (those in which they are reinforced). Antecedent events acquire influence over behavior through their association with reinforcement or its absence. We are likely to perform a behavior in situations in which it was reinforced in the past and unlikely to perform a behavior in situations in which it was punished in the past. An antecedent event that increases the probability of a behavior is called a *discriminative stimulus* (S^D). An event that signals that behavior will probably not be reinforced is called an *s delta* (S^Δ). A discrimination can be established by reinforcing a behavior in one situation and not reinforcing it in other situations (by differential reinforcement). Establishing appropriate discriminations is a critical aspect of developing effective repertoires. Stimulus control involves the rearrangement of antecedents to alter behavior. Setting events also influence behavior; these events are removed in time from a behavior and affect its rate (Wahler & Fox, 1981). An example would be a fight at home between a parent and child that affects the child's behavior at school. Antecedent events that are similar to those present during conditioning will elicit or occasion similar behaviors. This process is known as *stimulus generalization*. The term *response generalization* refers to the fact that behaviors similar to a behavior that is reinforced will also tend to increase in the future. If a child is reinforced for telling a particular type of joke, he may tend to tell similar jokes. That is, he may display and expand his "joke repertoire."

What is reinforcing or punishing varies from time to time, dependent on the individual's learning history and biological characteristics as well as the particular setting, including competing contingencies. The term *establishing operations* is used to refer to conditions that increase or decrease the strength of reinforcing and punishing events. Motivation can be viewed as a relationship between a set of operations (such as increasing deprivation) and the effects of these operations on behavior (such as increased persistence in overcoming obstructions and increased resistance to extinction) (Millenson & Leslie, 1979). Operations involved in motivation are deprivation and satiation. Malott (1989) argues that behavior analysts often mistake motivating operations (for example, placing a note on a calendar as a reminder to complete a task) for cues and discriminative stimuli. Emotion can also be viewed as a relationship between a set of operations (abrupt stimulus change, such as receiving an intense aversive or positive stimulus) and the effects of these operations on behavior. Here, too, the reinforcing value of events and general activity level are altered. Large changes in the schedule or amount of reinforcement or punishment are usually accompanied by emotional reactions and a disruption in ongoing behavior (Millenson & Leslie, 1979). Emotional reactions provide information about what consequences might occur (or have occurred) in a situation. For example, anxiety when thinking about a visit home may be due to a past history of unpleasant exchanges with family members. Feelings thus serve as clues to relationships between behavior and environmental consequences. Reframing and paradoxical instructions may be used to increase motivation. For example, Kolko and Milan (1983) used these methods to increase school attendance by three predelinquent youths.

Respondent Behavior

Respondent behaviors include those that involve the autonomic nervous system, such as heart rate and blood pressure, whereas operants (behaviors that "operate" on or affect the environment) involve the skeletal muscles. Examples of respondent reactions include an increased heart rate before taking the stage to give a speech, sweaty palms before a test, and goose pimples on a chilly day. Both respondents and operants are involved in almost any reaction or chain of behavior. Anxiety not only involves respondent components (for example, increases in heart rate or "butterflies" in the stomach) but may also occasion avoidance or escape responses. In the past, a wide separation was made between these two classes in terms of their controlling variables. Respondent behavior was thought to be influenced mainly by what happened before the behavior, and operant behavior by what happened after it. We now know that the separation between these two types of reactions, in terms of whether they can be influenced by their consequences, has been exaggerated (Rescorla, 1987). Heart rate, blood pressure, and a range of other responses can be brought under operant control; that is, they can be influenced by what happens after they occur. Some events elicit behavior without any previous learning (unconditioned stimuli); others elicit behavior only after learning (conditioned stimuli). Most respondent behavior of clinical import, such as stage fright and social anxiety, is learned. Only after an experience of painful drilling at a dentist's office may a patient's approach to the office cause discomfort. Thus, respondent conditioning involves the pairing of neutral events with cues that already elicit a given reaction. Neutral events that are paired with aversive stimuli become conditioned aversive stimuli. Avoidance of such events will be reinforcing just as the presentation of conditioned positive events will be reinforcing.

Close contiguity between two events is not required to achieve conditioning (Gormezano & Kehoe, 1981). Even backward conditioning (presentation of the unconditioned event before the neutral one) may be effective with humans. With conditioned responses, the degree of similarity of an event to the one present during conditioning influences the likelihood of a reaction, as well as its magnitude and latency. Thoughts about feared events influence the effects of the described relationships. Respondent extinction involves repeated presentation of an event without pairing it with stimuli with which it has typically been associated in the past. Repeated nonpunishing exposure to feared events is thought to be the major effective factor in methods designed to decrease anxiety, such as systematic desensitization (Barlow, 1988; Marks, 1987). Counterconditioning involves pairing an event with a response that is incompatible with the reaction typically elicited. In systematic desensitization based on relaxation, for example, feared events are presented in a context of relaxation. It is often important in practice to distinguish between problems that involve a deficit in respondent conditioning and those that involve an incentive deficit (desired behaviors are available but are not reinforced)—for example, in the problem of bed-wetting.

Verbal Behavior

Human beings are unique in the development of complex verbal repertoires that have a variety of effects on behavior—their own as well as that of others. We talk to ourselves as well as to other people. Verbal behavior includes talking, thinking, imaging, and writing. Because reinforcement for verbal behavior is typically mediated by other people, verbal behavior is social behavior. It acquires an influence over our actions because of its past association with certain consequences. One function of verbal behavior is to describe contingencies; these descriptions may not be accurate. The influence of verbal statements will thus partly depend on the extent to which they accurately describe what happened on past occasions.

Lately, a great deal of attention has been devoted to rule-governed behavior, in which behavior is influenced by descriptions of contingencies (in a book or lecture, for example). This kind of learning differs from contingency-shaped behavior involving direct experience (Skinner, 1969). Reading the descriptions of a contingency in this book ("If you do x, y will occur") will generally not be as effective in developing effective behavior as will learning experiences in which direct feedback is used to shape behavior. Rule-governed behavior is more variable. Often rules are incomplete—neither the required behaviors, the consequence, nor the S^D may be described. Ineffective self-statements can be viewed as rule pathologies (Poppen, 1989). Examples include overgeneralization and attending to only part of a situation (focusing on negative outcomes and ignoring positive outcomes). Excessive following of rules that decreases sensitivity to actual contingencies is a common side effect of verbal influence (Hayes, Kohlenberg, & Melancon, 1989). Altering verbal behavior is a common goal in marital counseling and teacher/student interaction. Altering self-instructions (covert verbal behavior) is a component of many kinds of intervention programs, including those designed to decrease anxiety, depression, and aggression and those designed to increase effective performance of tasks.

CHARACTERISTICS OF BEHAVIORAL PRACTICE

A number of characteristics distinguish a behavioral approach from other models of practice:

A. *What will be found*
   1. focus on altering real-life complaints of clients or significant others
   2. translation of complaints into behaviors that if altered would remove the complaints (Baer, 1982)
   3. use of multiple sources of assessment information including observation in real-life settings whenever feasible and ethical
   4. descriptive analysis based on observation: clear description of behaviors related to complaints as well as related environmental factors (setting events, antecedents, and consequences)
   5. functional analysis: rearrangement of environmental factors based on descriptive analyses (identification of

antecedents and consequences that influence behaviors of interest)
   6. involvement of significant others (those who interact with clients and influence their behavior) in assessment and intervention
   7. selection of assessment and intervention methods based on what clients find acceptable and (whenever possible) on applied or basic research that suggests what will be effective
   8. ongoing evaluation of progress using both subjective and objective measures, comparing outcomes with baseline data whenever feasible
   9. a concern for social validity, ensuring that procedures used are acceptable to clients and that outcomes are of value to clients and significant others
   10. clear description of assessment, intervention, and evaluation methods
   11. graphs depicting the frequency or rate of key outcomes over different phases
B. *What will not be found*
   1. appeals to mentalistic causes (thoughts, feelings, dispositions, states, expectations, anticipations) as causes of behavior
   2. uninformative diagnostic labels
   3. reliance on self-report alone for assessment and/or evaluation
   4. vague statements of problems, procedures, and outcomes
   5. blaming clients for resistance

Many of these characteristics are directly related to ethical practice: selection of procedures based on the empirical literature, building on client assets, avoiding uninformative, negative labels, increasing clients' options through increasing their skills and knowledge, use of positive methods to bring about change, clear identification of desired outcomes, careful tracking of progress, and clear description of procedures. Practice is based on empirical research, both in applied and in laboratory settings, that describes associations between behavior and environmental factors. If research demonstrates that the observation of behavior in the natural environment offers valuable information that can complement and correct impressions given by self-reports, such data will be used if feasible and ethical. If one kind of intervention has been found to be more effective than another, then within ethical and practical limits, behavioral practitioners will suggest this approach. Certainly, in practice, extensions of knowledge are made, and it would be untrue to say that the application of behavioral principles is always empirically based. In areas in which research is sparse, behavioral theory and principles are used to guide decisions.

A behavioral perspective encourages the view that people are doing the best they can at any given moment under current contingencies. This view reduces the likelihood and relevance of personal blame and criticism—as well as personal praise (Skinner, 1969)—and increases the likelihood of exploring how environmental factors limit or expand opportunities for reinforcement. If clients are reluctant to participate in helping efforts, rather than blaming them for a lack of motivation, a behavioral practitioner will explore how contingencies can be arranged so that participation will be worthwhile. Many characteristics of the behavioral approach are compatible with formats preferred by minority-group clients, such as an emphasis on achieving concrete goals, clarifying expectations, and the use of a structured approach (Sue & Sue, 1990). Inclusion of significant others, a hallmark of some behavioral approaches such as applied behavior analysis, meshes nicely with the importance of relatives and friends in many ethnic groups.

ASSESSMENT

One characteristic of behavioral assessment is the use of multiple sources of information, including, when feasible and ethical, the observation of clients and significant others in relevant environments (O'Neil, Horner, Albin, Storey, & Sprague, 1990). If the observation of behavior in real-life settings is not feasible, an alternative is the observation of behavior in simulated situations designed to be as similar as possible to real life. The objective is to observe a sample of relevant behaviors and to identify setting events, antecedents, and consequences. Self-monitoring—in which the client or significant others keep track of behaviors, feelings, thoughts, or outcomes of concern—is another source that can be used with many clients (Bornstein, Hamilton, & Bornstein, 1986). Other sources include physiological measures such as muscle tension and blood pressure (Haynes, Falkin, & Sexton-Radek, 1989) and self-reports including behavioral interviews, self-anchored scales, and standardized questionnaires (Jensen & Haynes, 1986). There is a focus on present concerns and current factors related to them. The purpose of assessment is to identify desired outcomes and to discover how they can be attained. It requires attention to individual, family, and community concerns and includes attention to remote and delayed as well as current contingencies. For example, some studies have found that parents are more punitive to their children on days when they have few contacts with friends (Wahler, 1980). A change in parental behavior may therefore require attention to the parents' social networks (a distal antecedent) as well as to parent/child interaction, in which proximal antecedents and consequences affect behavior.

The products of assessment include (1) specific objectives that must be achieved to address presenting problems, (2) baseline information regarding behaviors or outcomes of concern, (3) related intermediate steps, (4) personal and environmental resources that can be drawn on to achieve objectives, (5) significant others who could be involved and a plan for their involvement, (6) specific intervention methods that are likely to be useful in achieving desired outcomes, (7) progress indicators that will be used to assess outcomes, (8) obstacles that must be overcome and a plan to address them, and (9) a sense of optimism by clients and significant others and their readiness to participate in plans. There is a deemphasis on labeling. Diagnostic labels are helpful if they have treatment implications (if they are of value in selecting intervention methods). Often, however, psychiatric labels are difficult to define explicitly, are used inconsistently, and do not offer intervention guidelines (information about what to do about a problem). Although some progress has been made in increasing the clarity and usefulness of such labels, significant problems remain (Kirk & Kutchins, 1992; McReynolds, 1989). Behavioral approaches stress clear description of both assessment and intervention methods. This practice fulfills one of the conditions for informed consent and increases the likelihood that clients will carry out agreed-on tasks. If the methods being used are clearly described, colleagues will be able to duplicate successful methods, and supervisors will be able to offer more refined feedback.

Helping skills, such as developing rapport and putting clients at ease, are important in behavioral practice. The relevance of social-influence variables in working with clients is clearly shown by research in interpersonal helping (Patterson & Forgatch, 1985; Snyder & Thomsen, 1988; Wills, 1982). Ignoring such influences allows their use in an unsystematic or undercover way (Jurjevich, 1974). The emphasis on contingencies (relationships between behaviors and environmental consequences) highlights the mutual influence between clients and helpers. This perspective reduces the tendency to blame clients for resistance (not doing what practitioners want them to do). Relationship factors are, however, not considered the sole or main effective ingredient in achieving desired outcomes. Rather, they are viewed as the interpersonal context in which intervention is most likely to be successful. An understanding of and competence in providing conditions associated with these variables are important skills of the behavioral practitioner.

For example, enhancing positive expectations, clarifying mutual roles, providing empathy and warmth, and offering supportive feedback increase the likelihood of client participation and positive outcome.

Emphasis on Individualized Assessment

The behavioral model assumes that factors related to presenting problems can be identified only through individually tailored assessment. Each individual has a unique learning history as well as unique genetic and physiological characteristics. Consider a client who complains of panic attacks. Nothing informative can be said about factors related to this concern until assessment data are collected about the exact nature of these "attacks," the situations in which they do and do not occur, and related life circumstances such as reactions from significant others. So when students ask, "I have a client who has panic attacks. What's the cause of these?" behavioral practitioners would suggest the need to collect assessment data to answer this question. They would not speculate about possible causes, because the form of the behavior (which is not yet clearly described) may not reflect the functions it serves. An individualized assessment requires consideration of cultural and ethnic differences in relation to selection of assessment formats and tools. For example, norms for standardized tests may not be available for many ethnic groups. The tests themselves may contain items that are irrelevant or puzzling to members of some groups.

Translation of Problems into Observable Behaviors

One of the hallmarks of applied behavior analysis is the translation of personal and social problems "into observable behaviors that, if changed, would constitute a solution to the problems" (Baer, 1982, p. 281). This translation is a key initial step in assessment. The aim is to translate problems such as loneliness, depression, anxiety, or marital discord, ". . . into a set of behaviors which, once changed, satisfies the complaint" (p. 287). The development of systematic guidelines for translating problems into such behaviors is a key challenge in the field (Baer, 1982). The challenge is "(1) to restate the complained of problem in behavioral terms; (2) to change the behaviors indicated by that restatement; and then, (3) to see whether changing them has decreased the complaining response" (p. 284). Consider the example of loneliness on the part of residents of a retirement home. Behavioral questioning revealed that one of the indicators of this complaint was receiving few letters. The next question was "What behaviors of whom were responsible for that low rate?" (p. 285). Examination of letters written by residents revealed that residents who had complained of receiving few letters had reproached correspondents for not writing. Thus, it seems that the residents were actually punishing letter writing. The next step was to determine if this contingency was functional by altering letter-writing behavior on the part of the residents and determining whether more letters were received and fewer complaints of loneliness were voiced (Goldstein & Baer, 1976):

> That change was a very easy one, requiring only the slightest application of any behavioral technology—a nonreproachful letter that asked at least one question meriting an answer was modeled, and the next several letters written by the elderly complainers were read and commented on, approvingly or disapprovingly according to their content, before they were mailed. A few early ones needed rewriting; the complainers always agreed readily to do so. The analyst then prompted the complainers to write to relatives or old friends who rarely or never wrote to them. Within a very few tries, the complainers were now writing totally nonreproachful, nonaccusatory letters to everyone. Perhaps to fill the space formerly occupied by that reproachful

kind of content, they now wrote about their daily lives, happenings of interest, and memories of their past experiences with their correspondents, which probably made it easy for their correspondents to reply responsively and may well have reinforced rather than punished the correspondents' letter writing. Furthermore, the complainers were taught to include self-addressed, stamped envelopes in their letters, with comments explaining that they wanted to make a reply easy—their correspondents shouldn't have to "hunt up" their address.

> These changes in the complainers' letter writing were made in a multiple-baseline design, across three complainers. In perfect response to the staggered timing of that design, the three complainers began to receive prompt replies to their letters, almost tripling their average rate of receiving letters. Furthermore, presumably in part because of gratified communication among their pool of potential correspondents, and in part by their prompted writing to some long-silent people, they began to receive letters from new correspondents. This led them to begin other potential correspondence and to receive prompt answers, accomplishing still higher rates of letters received—and letters to answer. All this activity filled time in otherwise often empty days. The behavior change and its snowballing effects were accompanied by a thorough absence of complaints about loneliness [pp. 285–286].

The client is an active participant in the selection of outcomes. The behavioral approach's emphasis on the role of environmental factors in maintaining behavior and its rejection of a disease model of mental illness decrease the likelihood of imposing negative labels on clients. For examples of the application of behavioral principles to quite different system levels see Lamal (1991), Kunkel (1970), and Redmon and Dickinson (1990).

Within a behavioral model, the behaviors, thoughts, feelings, or other outcomes selected for change must be countable as well as relevant to presenting problems. For example, a depressed client could count the number of pleasant events in which she engages each day and could rate her mood daily. Trying to achieve vague outcomes may prevent discovery of the consequences that maintain relevant behaviors. Observation of behavior in relevant settings may be required to clearly identify behaviors of concern and related setting events, antecedents, and consequences (O'Neil et al., 1990). If behavior is only vaguely described (for example, if a teacher does not identify the behavioral referents for "aggressiveness"), it will be difficult to identify environmental antecedents and consequences related to these behaviors. Lack of clarity may therefore prohibit effective intervention. If the maintaining conditions are not identified, intervention may be misdirected. If desired outcomes are not clearly described, it will be difficult to find out how often a behavior occurred prior to intervention and so will be difficult to assess progress. Clear description of desired outcomes precludes the pursuit of hidden objectives that may not be in the clients' best interests. Because objectives are clearly stated, clients are in a better position to raise questions if actions are recommended or areas are explored that seem to bear no relation to original complaints. (See also the prior discussion of translating problems into observable behaviors.)

Rejection of Special Causative Factors Related to "Problematic" Behavior

Many theories of psychopathology infer processes to exist that are not inferred when "normal" behavior is considered (Ullman & Krasner, 1969). In the behavioral model, no such sharp distinction is made about the controlling conditions of behavior labeled as normal and behavior labeled as abnormal. All behavior is considered to be influenced by the same principles of behavior, although varied social and genetic histories result in a wide range of behavior. In addition, there are unique "biological boundaries" on learning in different species (Wood, 1988) and unique genetic influences. Physiological processes may differ, resulting in individual variations. However, it is

not assumed that because a behavior is bizarre or there are profound behavior deficits, unique causative factors are involved. A behavioral approach requires exploration of the role of environmental consequences (or their lack) in relation to concerns. Such a search has often resulted in success with problems previously considered unchangeable. Behavior that may seem quite bizarre typically serves adaptive functions, but only when contingencies of reinforcement are clarified may these become apparent (Goldiamond, 1984; Layng & Andronis, 1984). Behavior always "makes sense" in this manner.

A Preference for Observation and Exploration and a Rejection of Mentalistic Causes

Beliefs about why people act as they do and how behavior can be changed can be reached in a variety of ways. Some people prefer "empathic explanations" (Nettler, 1970). They rely on what "feels right." Empathic explanations tend to refer to unobservable entities such as thoughts, feelings, or personality traits that deflect attention from environmental causes. Thinking that you have arrived at an explanation, you do not go on to explore environmental contingencies of reinforcement related to behaviors of concern. Someone may say, "He hit her because he was angry" (referring to an abusive spouse). Both the behavior (hitting his wife) and the emotion (anger) may be the result of environmental contingencies that have yet to be described. Let's say that a practitioner writes in the record, "Mrs. Jones tried to kill herself because she felt lonely and believed that no one cared about her." Why did she feel lonely? What is going on in her life that resulted in her feelings, thoughts, and suicide attempt? These examples illustrate that such accounts stop too soon, without identifying the contingencies (relationships between behavior and the environment) that caused both the feelings (or thoughts) and the behavior. In the behavioral approach there is a preference for exploring the accuracy of beliefs by altering presumed causative variables and determining the effects on outcomes of interest. A belief that things happen by chance discourages systematic exploration (looking and seeing). This is not to say that random variability does not occur. It is to say that unexamined assumptions of random occurrence may prevent identification of environmental contingencies. For example, a practitioner who believes that the behavior of clients labeled "mentally ill" is random might not explore possible relationships between behaviors of concern and biological and environmental events and, as a result, might overlook maintaining conditions that can be altered. Similarly, if a biological cause is prematurely accepted, options to alter the behavior through rearrangement of the environment may be overlooked. In applied behavior analysis, there "is a reluctance to impose on individuals unproven limitations that are said to be inherent in actual or hypothesized biological factors. Instead, behavior analysts allow individuals to define their own limits by working with them to achieve all that can be achieved" (Milan, 1990, p. 69). A variety of tools has been developed to assist in the collection of valuable observational data (Hartmann & Wood, 1990; O'Neil et al., 1990).

Emphasis on Contingency Analysis

The behavioral approach focuses on the relationship between behavior and the current antecedent and consequent environmental events that influence it. Assessment includes a careful search for factors related to complaints. Drinking alcohol, for example, may be related to the unavailability of friends, lack of assertive behavior, marital discord, or work-related problems. If the maintaining conditions are not discovered and altered, a recurrence of drinking or a failure to change

drinking patterns may take place. A behavioral analysis consists of identifying the setting events, antecedents, and consequences that influence behaviors of concern. (For further detail see Alberto and Troutman, 1990, Martin and Pear, 1988; and Malott, Whaley, & Malott, 1993; and Sulzer-Azaroff and Mayer, 1991.) Explanations for behavior that do not include a description of relevant contingencies of reinforcement are considered to be inadequate and incomplete. Such accounts often interfere with the discovery of explanations that do describe contingencies (Moore, 1990). There is an interest in functional as well as descriptive analyses of behavior. In a functional analysis, environmental events are rearranged to determine their influence on behavior. This process is in contrast to an account that may merely label a behavior or appeal to unobservable entities as causative agents (such as expectations). Use of a behavioral model requires identification of the environmental events that occasion and maintain behavior. Attention is often directed toward the changing of "deviant" environments rather than toward the changing of clients' "deviant" behaviors. Past histories of reinforcement are considered to be reflected in present behavior, and information about a person's past may provide valuable information about possible reinforcers or unusual social histories that may be related to presenting problems. However, current maintaining conditions may be quite different from those present when a behavior was initially established.

Behavior surfeits such as temper tantrums, lying, drinking, and stealing may be maintained because of the contingent presentation of positive reinforcers or because of the contingent avoidance or removal of aversive events. Behavior deficits may be related to an absence of required skills, or there may be a lack of cues and adequate schedules of reinforcement to maintain behaviors of interest. Competing contingencies may interfere with desired reactions. Desired behaviors may be punished, or various obstacles that decrease opportunities for reinforcement may exist, such as physical limitations. Both antecedents and consequences must be carefully examined in each situation to identify how desired changes could be attained. For example, if staff members complain about apathetic residents who just sit around a nursing home all day, contingency analysis would be used to identify how prompts and incentives could be rearranged to increase residents' participation in social activities.

Emphasis on Identifying
Personal and Environmental Assets

Behavioral practice involves a constructional approach in which the skills and resources of the client are identified and used to advantage (Schwartz & Goldiamond, 1975). This process requires identifying the personal assets of the client, such as useful problem-solving or social skills. Intervention programs can build on these available skills. Environmental resources include both informal ones (neighbors, relatives) as well as formal ones (recreation centers, day care, vocational-training programs).

INTERVENTION AND EVALUATION

Assessment and selection of intervention methods are closely related in the behavioral approach. What is found during assessment directly informs the selection of intervention methods. Assessment will yield information about promising options. Behavioral methods are not focused on the presenting problem, or "symptom," but on altering contingencies related to it. Symptom substitution does not occur if important related antecedent and maintaining conditions are addressed. In fact, removing a problem is typically followed by positive changes in how

clients feel and think about themselves and others as well as by an increase in positive feelings on the part of significant others (Wahler & Pollio, 1968). A decrease in bedwetting that has been a problem for months or years is usually a relief to parents and encourages them to respond more positively toward their children. Behavioral practice involves a constructional approach (Pinkston et al., 1982; Schwartz & Goldiamond, 1975). It emphasizes helping clients acquire knowledge and skills that they can use to attain valued outcomes and create more positive environments.

Quantitative data regarding the effects of intervention are collected. The frequency, magnitude, or duration of a behavior, thought, feeling, or other outcome before intervention is compared with the frequency, magnitude, or duration afterward. Other progress indicators such as behavior products may also be used (Gambrill, 1977). A clear definition of desired outcomes and ongoing monitoring of progress offers feedback to clients, significant others, and practitioners and permits timely alteration of plans. Evaluation about degree of progress offers practitioners and clients a built-in self-corrective function in terms of countering behavioral confirmation tendencies (Gambrill, 1990; Snyder & Thomsen, 1988). Clients often gather data needed for evaluation. The behavioral literature shows the wide variety of presenting problems that can be clearly defined and evaluated using multiple indicators of progress. Examples include depression, child abuse and neglect, marital discord, and communication problems. Many outcomes, such as maintenance of full-time employment, can be readily defined. Single-case studies are widely used (Barlow, Hayes, & Nelson, 1991; Bloom & Fischer, 1982; Jayaratne & Levy, 1979).

The behavioral model emphasizes the use of positive methods (LaVigna & Donnellan, 1986; Meyer & Evans, 1989). Clients are encouraged to "catch" others doing something good (rather than to catch them doing something bad), and the same applies to their own behavior. Behavioral clinicians and researchers have taken a leading role in designing intervention methods that use only positive or low-level aversive procedures (for example, response cost) even with very difficult behaviors and in advocating against the use of high-level aversive methods, such as prolonged social isolation, or any other method that inflicts unnecessary stress or physical discomfort (LaVigna & Donnellan, 1986; Meyer & Evans, 1989).

Many behavioral programs, such as the job-finding program developed by Azrin and Besalel (1980), include a variety of intervention methods consistent with the complexity of the circumstances related to a desired outcome. Programs designed to decrease depression may include rearrangement of consequences offered by significant others, enhancement of social skills, and alteration of material circumstances related to depression. Weight-reduction programs may consist of many components, including procedures to increase exercise, alter eating patterns, and gain support from significant others.

Developing New Behaviors

Desired outcomes often involve learning new behaviors. New behaviors can be established through shaping, chaining, model presentation, rehearsal, or fading and prompting. (For more detail, see Alberto and Troutman, 1990, and Martin and Pear, 1988.) Social-skills training is often used to develop new behaviors. It includes a number of components, such as clear identification of required skills, model presentation, rehearsal, feedback, coaching, and homework assignments.

Shaping. The procedure known as shaping involves the differential reinforcement of approximations to a desired behavior. It takes advantage of the variability of behavior, selecting variations that are closest to

desired behavior to reinforce, and ignoring others. Thus, two procedures are used: positive reinforcement for successive approximations and operant extinction for other behaviors. (In the latter procedure, reinforcement is withheld; that is, the behavior occurs but is no longer reinforced.) Shaping was used to increase verbal behavior of a catatonic schizophrenic who had not spoken for 19 years prior to training (Isaacs, Thomas, & Goldiamond, 1960). Gum was used as a reinforcer. Behaviors reinforced included looking toward the gum, facial movements, mouth movements, lip movements, vocalizations, and words spoken. Shaping can be used when instructions and model presentation cannot be relied on alone. For example, it is used with children with severe behavior deficits. Shaping can be used to change the form of a behavior, to increase a behavior, to shorten the time between a cue and a behavior, or to alter the intensity of a behavior. It requires clear identification of objectives as well as approximations to these. Prompts (verbal instructions, gestures, physical guidance, or environmental changes) may be used to encourage closer approximations. Behavioral training programs for caregivers such as staff and parents often include training in the use of behavior shaping (McClannaghan, Krantz, McGee & MacDuff, 1984). Caregivers are encouraged to take advantage of informal teaching opportunities that arise in the course of daily activities (Chock & Glahn, 1984).

Chaining. Most behavior consists of complex chains, such as answering a telephone and putting on a sweater. Chains of behavior are joined by cues (discriminative stimuli) and reinforcers. Shaping, model presentation, stimulus control, and reinforcement can be used in establishing a chain of behavior such as ordering at a fast-food restaurant. The sequence of behaviors involved in a chain of behavior can be identified by a task analysis (observation of relevant behaviors in real-life contexts and identification of component behaviors). Thirty-one steps were identified in the task of putting on hearing aids by multi-handicapped children (Tucker & Berry, 1980). The chain began with sight of the hearing-aid container, which was a cue for opening the container. The final reinforcer was assisted hearing. Some chains of behavior can most readily be established by starting from the last component, as when teaching a child how to put on a pair of slacks.

Model presentation. Another method of developing new behaviors is for clients to observe someone else performing a sequence of behaviors. Model presentation is an important part of parent-training programs and is used in social-skills training (L'Abate & Milan, 1985) and in fear-reduction procedures. For example, videotape presentations of problem situations and demonstrations of parents successfully handling them were shown to parents who had abused their children as one part of a program to enhance positive parenting skills (Denicola & Sandler, 1980). Model presentation is more efficient than shaping because an entire sequence of behaviors can be presented and the client can be asked to imitate it, instead of waiting for each approximation to occur before reinforcing it. Drawing attention to important response components through verbal prompts will facilitate learning (Bandura, 1986). A client may be coached to notice the model's eye contact and body orientation. Helpful self-statements can also be modeled during role plays if negative thoughts are interfering with success. They can first be spoken out loud by the client when imitating the model's behavior and then, by instruction, moved to a covert level. Components involved in the effective use of modeling include:

- Identification of specific behaviors to be altered
- Presentation of a model

- Arranging for the observer to attend to the model
- Imitation of modeled behaviors
- Reinforcement for imitation

Model presentation, rehearsal, prompts, and feedback are repeated as needed until desired skills and comfort levels are demonstrated. The more extensive the behavior deficits, the more likely that model presentation, rehearsal, feedback, and instructions will be necessary to develop needed skills. If deficits are less pronounced, practice or instructions alone may be sufficient to achieve desired outcomes. As skills are acquired, prompts and guidance should be phased out. Models can be presented in many different ways, including written scripts, audiotape, videotape film, or live models.

Behavioral rehearsal. The simulation of social exchanges is known as behavioral rehearsal. For example, a client who has difficulty during job interviews can practice effective ways of acting after watching a model. Analogue situations include those in which clients interact with significant others in an artificial environment such as the office, as well as situations in which a client participates in role plays with someone other than a real-life significant other, such as a practitioner. An explain/demonstrate/practice/feedback model is used, in which the practitioner first explains why certain skills are of value and then identifies situations in which these can be used. Practice should be preceded by model presentation of effective responses and identification of *specific* verbal and nonverbal behaviors to be increased, decreased, or varied. Coaching or prompting can be used during rehearsal to encourage desired reactions. For example, Liberman, King, DeRisi, and McCann (1975) developed a series of hand signals to coach clients during role plays. Programming of change (identifying initial skill levels and building on these in a step-by-step manner, in accord with degree of mastery) is an important component of behavioral rehearsal. Constructive feedback should be offered following each role play.

Prompting and fading.

Desired behaviors can be *prompted* by self-instructions or by environmental cues. For example, teachers' rate of praise was increased by use of an audio cuing system (Van Houten & Sullivan, 1975). Written or verbal instructions may be sufficient to alter behavior. If a client forgets to ask the doctor important questions, she can write these down and refer to her notes during appointments. *Fading* involves the gradual change in the conditions that control a behavior so that the behavior occurs in the presence of a new event. The level of prompts that is required to obtain a desired reaction can be discovered either by first presenting the stimulus without the prompt and then introducing prompts as needed or by using prompts from the start and then fading them. Fading is often used to increase the verbal skills of severely retarded and autistic children. Take the example of teaching a child to respond with his name when asked, "What's your name?" rather than repeating the question (Martin & Pear, 1988). The child was asked, "What's your name?" and immediately the trainer loudly said, "Peter." The boy imitated "Peter" and was reinforced. Over a number of trials, the question "What's your name?" was asked more loudly, and the answer "Peter" was given more softly. One of the last steps consisted of just mouthing the word "Peter," and the boy still answered the question with "Peter." In time-delay fading, the period between the presentation of a stimulus and a prompt is gradually increased.

Increasing Behavior

There are many ways to increase behavior. Some are easier to arrange than others. Low-cost methods such as modeling and rearranging antecedents take advantage of existing repertoires. Positive or negative reinforcement may also be used to increase behavior.

Rearranging antecedents.

Altering behavior by rearranging antecedents is known as stimulus control. Rearranging antecedent events is often as important as rearranging the consequences of relevant behaviors, feelings, or thoughts. Enhancement of positive parenting skills often requires alteration of parental instructions and rules as well as the consequences parents offer to their children (Dangel & Polster, 1988). Stimulus control involves developing a strong relationship between a stimulus and a particular response that takes place when the situation is present. This is accomplished by discrimination training. Cues for desired behaviors are strengthened, and cues that encourage undesired reactions are removed or reduced. Discrimination training involves reinforcing behavior in one situation and not reinforcing it in other situations. One response is involved, and two or more stimulus situations. A discrimination has been established when there is a high rate of response in one situation and a low rate in others.

Antecedents can be altered by environmental programming in which aspects of the environment are changed (for example, removing fattening foods from the house) and by behavioral programming in which behaviors that alter the likelihood of behaviors of interest are planned (for example, relaxing before an interview). Serving food family style (in bowls) rather than on individual plates increased the conversation of elderly people in a nursing home (Risley, Gottula, & Edwards, 1978). Stimulus enhancement may be used in which the intensity or contrast value of a stimulus is increased to facilitate desired stimulus control. Stimulus-enhancement methods include prompting and area definition, in which behaviors are prompted and reinforced in a particular context. For example, social interactions could be prompted; medication could be given to elderly residents in a certain room. Artificial prompts should be faded as quickly as possible and should not be distracting.

Positive reinforcement. Both behavior surfeits (the presence of unwanted behavior) and behavior deficits (the absence of expected behavior) may call for the rearrangement of contingencies. Positive reinforcers are defined by their effect on behavior (their functions). Thus, we cannot know for sure whether an event will function as a positive reinforcer (increase behavior it follows) until a contingency is arranged and the results are observed. Reinforcers are relative. What will function as a positive reinforcer for an individual on one occasion might not on another, for a number of reasons such as deprivation/satiation and competing contingencies. Rules for the effective use of positive reinforcement include the following (Ayllon & Azrin, 1968; Homme, Csanyi, Gonzales, & Rechs, 1969):

- Reinforce specific behaviors.
- Reinforce accomplishment rather than obedience.
- Reinforce immediately after desired behaviors occur.
- Reinforce consistently.
- Do not mix criticism with praise.
- Use a variety of reinforcers.
- Use multiple sources of reinforcement (for example, teachers and parents).
- Prompt desired behavior so that reinforcement can be given often.

Positive reinforcement has been successfully used to increase a wide range of behaviors, including following of instructions; wearing of seat belts; providing of institutionalized residents with appropriate care; communication skills such as initiating conversations; and self-help, vocational, and community survival skills for developmentally disabled individuals.

Frequent reinforcement can be provided by reinforcing approximations. Positive reinforcement of desired behavior is often combined with extinction (ignoring) of undesired behaviors. This combination of procedures is known as *differential reinforcement* and is probably the most widely used procedure to alter behavior. Group contingencies can be of value when peers reinforce inappropriate behavior. For example, a reward could be offered to class members contingent on a certain level of performance on the part of one student.

Some people object to the emphasis within the behavioral approach on the use of positive reinforcement on the ground that it is bribery. The term *bribery,* however, refers to giving someone something for carrying out an unethical action. Thus, the use of positive reinforcement to increase desired behaviors could not accurately be considered bribery. Another concern is that if positive incentives are offered for desired behavior, people will become dependent on them. The term *dependency* may refer either to continued expectation of reinforcement or to loss of intrinsic interest in an activity. Functionally superfluous rewards (those that are not required to maintain behavior) do decrease intrinsic motivation. External reinforcers that are not functionally superfluous can be used to *increase* intrinsic motivation (Dickinson, 1989; Lepper & Hodell, 1989). External reinforcers should not be introduced when intrinsic ones are present unless intrinsic reinforcers result in injury to self or others. Incentives that are not already part of the natural environment are avoided when possible. If it is necessary to introduce artificial reinforcers such as tokens or points, removal should be planned so that behavior is maintained under natural conditions.

Negative reinforcement. Here too, as with positive reinforcement, there is an emphasis on function rather than form or structure. "Any stimulus change, regardless of its form, that weakens behavior it follows or whose termination, reduction or postponement maintains responding is, by definition, an aversive stimulus" (Starin, 1991, p. 207). Problematic behaviors are often maintained by negative reinforcement. For example, unpleasant demands or tasks may result in escape behavior—such as tantrums, hitting others, or destroying materials—that removes those demands. Techniques that have been successfully used to decrease behavior and increase desired alternatives include embedding demands in a positive context, using errorless training methods in which task difficulty is gradually decreased, and providing alternative escape responses (Iwata, 1987). Children who are nonverbal can learn to use request cards or can be trained to use manual signals to indicate a "time-out" from learning tasks. These behaviors provide alternatives to disruptive escape behaviors. A prime advantage of such methods is that they place control in the hands of learners, who can indicate when they want a time-out from a task.

Decreasing Behavior

A variety of short-cut methods can be used to decrease behavior, including modeling, role playing, physical guidance, removing the early components of a chain of behavior, rearranging antecedents, and prompted or reinforcing alternative behaviors. Other procedures include extinction, differential reinforcement, response cost, time-out, overcorrection, satiation, and punishment. (For further detail, see Martin and Pear, 1988, and Matson and DiLorenzo, 1984.)

Behaviors can be decreased by establishing new *stimulus control*. A teacher could use a sign saying "work time" to indicate when students should work on their own and not ask questions. Cues for undesired behaviors should be eliminated or suppressed, and cues for desired behaviors should be enhanced

and increased. If losing weight is a goal, high-calorie food could be removed from the house, only a certain amount of food could be placed on plates, and serving dishes could be kept in the kitchen (Stuart & Davis, 1972). Programs for increasing studying attend closely to rearranging antecedents, including removing cues for competing responses such as writing letters, talking on the telephone, or daydreaming. The stimulus situation is "purified" by allowing desired behaviors to occur only in a particular setting; cues are removed for undesired reactions and strengthened for desired ones. Shorkey and Taylor (1973) decreased a child's generalized crying that was related to the painful changing of bandages by suggesting that personnel who changed the dressings wear a particular color of gown and that all others, including the parents, wear other colors. Crying decreased in the presence of others not involved in this painful procedure. In *differential reinforcement of other behaviors* (DRO), reinforcement is offered if a certain time passes in which a behavior does *not* occur. A child may receive a reinforcer if she is not accused of stealing for an entire day. Reinforcement can be offered contingent on a specific low rate of behavior (DRL). For example, a student may receive points if he talks out of turn only once every hour. Unlike the differential reinforcement of low rates of behavior (DRL), which encourages a gradual reduction in behavior, only zero occurrence is reinforced in DRO schedules. In the differential reinforcement of incompatible behaviors (DRI), behavior that is incompatible in form is reinforced, and reinforcement is no longer provided for undesired behaviors (operant extinction).

Response cost involves loss of a positive event contingent on a behavior. Examples include losing access to toys for a day when they are left out and not being permitted to play pool for 15 minutes contingent on arguing with peers. Exclusionary time-out involves removal of an individual to a less reinforcing environment for a brief period contingent on undesired behavior or lack of a desired behavior. In nonexclusionary time-out the individual is denied temporary access to certain reinforcers but is not physically removed from a situation. Time-out should be combined with positive reinforcement of desired behavior; duration of time-out should be brief (for example, 5 to 15 minutes). *Overcorrection* can be used to decrease inappropriate behaviors and to offer practice in desired alternatives. In *restitutional overcorrection,* the person is required to correct the consequences of his misbehavior by restoring the situation to a vastly improved condition. A youth who spits on the floor may be required to wash the entire floor, for example. *Positive-practice overcorrection* involves the practicing of correct behaviors. For example, a youth who throws trash around could practice placing trash in wastebaskets.

Response cost, time-out, and overcorrection all involve punishment (behavior decreases when followed by a certain event). Many procedures that are described as nonaversive in fact involve punishment (Starin, 1991).

Planning for Generalization and Maintenance

Behavioral practice involves planning for the generalization and durability of change in real-life settings both during assessment (e.g., involving significant others) as well as intervention (fading out any artificial procedures) (see prior definition of stimulus and response generalization). Maintenance (sometimes referred to as generalization over time) refers to the durability of behavior over time. Skills developed in the office must occur in real-life settings if positive outcomes are to be achieved. Behavioral researchers have taken a leading role in exploring how to encourage generalization and maintenance (Horner, Dunlap, & Koegel, 1988; Stokes & Osnes,

1989; Wahler & Dumas, 1984). A problem-solving approach in which participants used rules (such as asking "What's happening?" or "What might happen if . . . ?") have been found to enhance generalization and maintenance with mentally retarded youths (Park & Gaylord-Ross, 1989).

COMMON MISCONCEPTIONS ABOUT RADICAL BEHAVIORISM AND APPLIED BEHAVIOR ANALYSIS

A lack of understanding of applied behavior analysis and the philosophy on which it is based (radical behaviorism) is common (Catania & Harnad, 1988; Thompson, 1988). Skinner addresses many popular misconceptions in *About Behaviorism* (1974). This approach is a radical departure from commonly accepted accounts of behavior as well as from Watsonian and methodological behaviorism, with which it is often confused. Accurate understanding of this approach should be of special interest to practitioners because of the guidelines it offers for altering environmental conditions that are often directly related to personal and social problems. Many case examples can be found in applied behavior analysis that focus on empowering clients— for example, by enhancing advocacy skills and increasing voter registration (Balcazar, Seekins, Fawcett, & Hopkins, 1990; Fawcett, Seekins, & Silber, 1988).

Accurate understanding of radical behaviorism as well as knowledge of behavioral principles and acquisition of skill in applying these to real-life problems require time and effort. Superficial knowledge encourages rejection on philosophical grounds. It may be assumed (incorrectly) that thoughts and feelings play no role in influencing behavior, that we are controlled by stimulus/response connections, or that individual values and meanings should be ignored. Practice based on a superficial knowledge is likely to result in selection of weak or ineffective intervention methods of little value to clients. As behavioral methods have become more popular, some practitioners have "rechristened" themselves as behavioral without acquiring necessary knowledge, values, and skills (Levis, 1990a). Misunderstandings about the scientific method and selection of knowledge based on entertainment value, popularity, or simple authority contribute to a rejection of behavioral methods (Gambrill, 1991). Behavioral terminology has encouraged some myths, particularly terms such as *behavior modification,* which seems to connote a cold, mechanistic, inhumane approach.

Mislabeling of interventions such as lockups and long time-outs as *behavioral* also contributes to misunderstandings. Some people believe that the term *behavior modification* refers to any attempt to alter behavior, including chemotherapy, brain surgery, and electroshock procedures. This is not an accurate use of this term. People have been trying to alter the behavior of their fellows since the beginning of time, but only in select instances could we say that a behavioral approach was used. It is the *systematicness* and inclusiveness with which contingencies are analyzed and altered in relation to specific objectives and the concern for evaluation and social validity (achieving outcomes that make a real difference in enhancing the quality of life for clients) that characterize a behavioral approach. Occasional unevaluated use of positive incentives to change vaguely defined or even well-defined behaviors is not a behavioral approach. It is sometimes said that the contingencies that already exist are "more natural," meaning that no one has arranged them to attain given ends. Actually, many contingencies that influence our behavior are arranged by governmental agencies and businesses (Skinner, 1953).

Behavioral methods, if effective, increase clients' skills in influencing their environment (a large part of which may be provided by other people), but they do not teach them to manipulate this environment in an insidious or unfair way. A good example is social skills training, in which clients acquire more effective interpersonal skills that offer benefits both to themselves and others (L'Abate & Milan, 1985; O'Donahue & Krasner, in press). Clients are encouraged to involve significant others and to pursue changes from which all parties will benefit. There may be occasions when an ethical argument could be made for showing one group how to change the behavior of another group without the awareness of the latter. Students aged 12 to 15 were taught how to increase their teachers' positive statements and to decrease their negative statements (Graubard, Rosenberg, & Miller, 1971). If students have no other way to alter the teachers' behavior, is it not unethical to withhold such skills from them? Those who are active in behavioral community change efforts encourage practitioners to involve participants actively in all stages of programs (Fawcett, 1991).

CONCLUSION

Varieties of behavioral practice include applied behavior analysis and cognitive-behavioral therapy. The former rests on radical behaviorism; the latter rests on social-learning theory. Radical behaviorism is a contextual perspective that requires the translation of personal and social problems of concern into observable behaviors that, if altered, will remove complaints. Radical behaviorism does not embrace a radical environmentalism in which the environment is assumed to have total control over behavior. Thoughts and feelings are recognized, and efforts are made to offer clients skills that increase their influence over their environment. It is believed that the best way to guard against or alter unwanted influences is to recognize sources of influence. A prime difference between radical behaviorism and social-learning theory is in the role attributed to private events. Thoughts are given an initiating and explanatory status in social learning theory. In a radical behavioral perspective thoughts and feelings are viewed as behaviors in need of explanation.

Major hallmarks of behavioral practice include the selection of assessment and intervention methods based on practice-related research and translation of problems into observable behaviors. There is an emphasis on describing and altering the contingencies between behaviors of concern and environmental events. Positive reinforcement, negative reinforcement, punishment, and response cost all involve contingencies (associations between behavior and changes in the environment). They are defined not only in terms of a procedure but also in terms of an effect on behavior. The function of behavior and environmental cues and consequences are focused on rather than their form or structure. The focus is on current problems as well as on current factors related to them. Presenting problems and related outcomes, as well as progress indicators, are described in specific terms that require a minimum of interpretation. There is an emphasis on the use of positive methods of change, arranging for generalization and maintenance of gains, evaluation of progress, building on personal assets, and increasing clients' skills and knowledge. Special causative factors related to most problematic behavior are rejected, as is the use of labels that are stigmatizing and uninformative in terms of how to remove complaints.

Applied behavior analysis should be of special interest to practitioners because of its attentiveness to environmental factors that are often directly related to personal and social problems and its attentiveness to social validity (attaining real-world outcomes that clients and significant others value). Lack of understanding of radical behaviorism and thorough knowledge of behavioral principles contribute to misconceptions about behavioral practice. These myths include the belief that heavy use is made of aversive control and bribery, that interpersonal helping skills such as warmth and empathy are not needed, and that feelings and thoughts are ignored. Critics of radical behaviorism often confuse it with Watsonian stimulus/response behaviorism or with methodological behaviorism. Accurate understanding of this approach as well as thorough training in its application will help practitioners take maximum advantage of the assessment, intervention, and evaluation guidelines provided.

REFERENCES

Alberto, P. A., & Troutman, A. C. (1990). *Applied behavior analysis for teachers* (2nd ed.) Columbus, OH: Merrill.

Ayllon, T., & Azrin, N. H. (1968). *The token economy: A motivational system for therapy and rehabilitation.* New York: Appleton-Century-Crofts.

Azrin, N. H., & Besalel, V. A. (1980). *Job club counselor's manual: A behavioral approach to vocational counseling.* Baltimore: University Park Press.

Arzin, N. H., & Holz, W. L. (1966). Punishment. In W. K. Honig (Ed.), *Operant behavior: Areas of research and application.* New York: Appleton-Century-Crofts.

Baer, D. M. (1982). Applied behavior analysis. In G. T. Wilson & C. M. Franks (Eds.). *Contemporary behavior therapy: Conceptual and empirical foundations.* New York: Guilford Press.

Baer, D. M., Wolf, M. M., & Risley, T. R. (1968). Some current dimensions of applied behavior analysis. *Journal of Applied Behavior Analysis, 1,* 91–97.

Baer, D. M., Wolf, M. M., & Risley, T. R. (1987). Some still current dimensions of applied behavior analysis. *Journal of Applied Behavior Analysis, 20,* 313–327.

Balcazar, F. E., Seekins, T., Fawcett, S. B., & Hopkins, B. L. (1990). Empowering people with physical disabilities through advocacy skills training. *American Journal of Community Psychology, 18,* 281–295.

Bandura, A. (1977). *Social learning theory.* Englewood Cliffs, NJ: Prentice-Hall.

Bandura, A. (1986). *Social foundations of thought and action.* Englewood Cliffs, NJ: Prentice-Hall.

Barlow, D. H. (1988). *Anxiety and its disorders: The nature and treatment of anxiety and panic.* New York: Guilford Press.

Barlow D. H., Hayes, S. C., & Nelson, R. O. (1984). *The scientist practitioner: Research and accountability in clinical and educational settings.* New York: Pergamon Press.

Bellack, A. S., Hersen, M., & Kazdin, A. E. (Eds.). (1990). *International handbook of behavior modification and behavior therapy* (2nd ed.). New York: Plenum.

Biglan, A. (1987). A behavior-analytic critique of Bandura's self-efficacy theory. *The Behavior Analyst, 10,* 1–15.

Bloom, M., & Fischer, J. (1982). *Evaluating practice: Guidelines for the accountable professional.* Englewood Cliffs, NJ: Prentice-Hall.

Bornstein, P. H., Hamilton, S. B., & Bornstein, M. T. (1986). Self-monitoring procedures. In A. R. Ciminero, C. S. Calhoun, & H. E. Adams (Eds.), *Handbook of behavioral assessment.* New York: Wiley.

Catania, A. C., & Harnad, S. (Eds.). (1988). *The selection of behavior: The operant behaviorism of B. F. Skinner: Comments and consequences.* New York: Cambridge University Press.

Chock, P. N., & Glahn, T. J. (1984). Care providers and respite care services. In W. P. Christian, G. T. Hannah, & T. J. Glahn (Eds.), *Programming effective human service: Strategies for institutional change and client transition.* New York: Plenum.

Dangel, R. F., & Polster, R. A. (1988). *Teaching child management skills.* New York: Pergamon Press.

Davis, L. V., & Hagen, J. L. (1992). The problem of wife abuse: The interrelationships of social policy and social work practice. *Social Work, 37,* 15–20.

Day, W. F. (1976). Contemporary behaviorism and the concept of intention. In W. J. Arnold (Ed.), *Nebraska symposium on motivation.* Lincoln: University of Nebraska Press.

Day, W. F. (1980). The historical antecedents of contemporary behaviorism. In R. W. Rieber & K. Salzinger (Eds.), *Psychology: Theoretical-historical perspectives.* New York: Academic Press.

Day, W. F. (1983). On the difference between radical and methodological behaviorism. *Behaviorism, 11,* 89–102.

Deguchi, H. (1984). Observational learning from a radical-behavioristic viewpoint. *The Behavior Analyst, 7,* 83–95.

Denicola, J., & Sandler, J. (1980). Training abusive parents in cognitive-behavioral techniques. *Behavior Therapy, 11,* 263–270.

Dickinson, A. M. (1989). The detrimental effects of extrinsic reinforcement on "intrinsic motivation." *The Behavior Analyst, 12,* 1–15.

Eysenck, H. J. (1982). Neobehavioristic (S-R) theory. In G. T. Wilson & C. M. Franks (Eds.), *Contemporary behavior theory: Conceptual and empirical foundations.* New York: Guilford Press.

Fawcett, S. B. (1991). Some values guiding community research and action. *Journal of Applied Behavior Analysis, 24,* 621–636.

Fawcett, S. B., & Miller, L. K. (1975). Training public speaking behavior: An experimental analysis and social validation. *Journal of Applied Behavior Analysis, 8,* 125–136.

Fawcett, S. B., Seekins, T., & Silber, L. (1988). Low-income voter registration: A small-scale evaluation of an agency-based voter registration strategy. *American Journal of Community Psychology, 16,* 751–758.

Gambrill, E. D. (1977). *Behavior modification: Handbook of assessment, intervention and evaluation.* San Francisco: Jossey-Bass.

Gambrill, E. D. (1990). *Critical thinking in clinical practice.* San Francisco: Jossey-Bass.

Gambrill, E. D. (1991, August). *Science and mentalism: Different paths with different goals.* Address given at the annual conference of the American Psychological Association, San Francisco.

Goldiamond, I. (1984). Training parent trainers and ethicists in nonlinear analysis of behavior. In R. F. Dangel & R. A. Polster (Eds.), *Parent training: Foundations of research and practice.* New York: Guilford Press.

Goldstein, R. S., & Baer, D. M. (1976). R.S.V.P.: A procedure to increase the personal mail and number of correspondents for nursing home residents. *Behavior Therapy, 17,* 348–354.

Gormezano, I., & Kehoe, E. J. (1981). Classical conditioning and the law of contiguity. In P. Harzem & M. D. Zeiler (Eds.), *Predictability,* correlation and contiguity (Vol. 2). New York: Wiley.

Graubard, P. S., Rosenberg, H., & Miller, M. B. (1971). Student applications of behavior modification to teachers and environments or ecological approaches to social deviancy. In E. A. Ramp & B. L. Hopkins (Eds.), A new direction for education: Behavior analysis (Vol. 1). Lawrence: University of Kansas, Department of Human Development.

Hartmann, D. P., & Wood, D. D. (1990). Observational methods. In A. S. Bellack, M. Hersen, & A. E. Kazdin (Eds.), International handbook of behavior modification and therapy. New York: Plenum.

Hayes, S. C., & Brownstein, A. J. (1987). Mentalism, private events, and scientific explanation. In S. Modgil & C. Modgil (Eds.), B. F. Skinner: Consensus and controversy. New York: Falmer Press.

Hayes, S. C., Kohlenberg, B. S., & Melancon, S. M. (1989). Avoiding and altering rule-control as a strategy of clinical intervention. In S. C. Hayes (Ed.), Rule-governed behavior: Cognition, contingencies, and instructional control. New York: Plenum.

Haynes, S. N., Falkin, S., & Sexton-Radek, R. (1989). Psychophysiological measurement in behavior therapy. In G. Turpin (Ed.), Handbook of clinical psychophysiology. London: Wiley.

Homme, L. E., Csanyi, A., Gonzales, M., & Rechs, J. (1969). How to use contingency contracting in the classroom. Champaign, IL: Research Press.

Horner, R., Dunlap, G., & Koegel, R. (1988). Generalization and maintenance: Lifestyle changes in applied settings. Baltimore: Paul H. Brookes.

Ingram, R. E., & Scott, W. D. (1990). Cognitive behavior therapy. In A. S. Bellack, M. Hersen, & A. E. Kazdin (Eds.), International handbook of behavior modification and behavior therapy (2nd ed.). New York: Plenum.

Isaacs, W., Thomas, J., & Goldiamond, I. (1960). Application of operant conditioning to reinstate verbal behavior in psychotics. Journal of Speech and Hearing Disorders, 25, 8–12.

Iwata, B. (1987). Negative reinforcement in applied behavior analysis: An emerging technology. Journal of Applied Behavior Analysis, 20, 361–378.

Jayaratne, S., & Levy, R. L. (1979). Empirical clinical practice. New York: Columbia University Press.

Jensen, B. J., & Haynes, S. N. (1986). Self-report questionnaires. In A. R. Ciminero, C. S. Calhoun, & H. E. Adams (Eds.), Handbook of behavioral assessment (2nd ed). New York: Wiley.

Jurjevich, R. M. (1974). The hoax of Freudism: A study of brainwashing the American professionals and laymen. Philadelphia: Dorrance.

Kazdin, A. E. (1977). The token economy: A review and evaluation. New York: Plenum.

Kazdin, A. E. (1978). History of behavior modification: Experimental foundations of contemporary research. Baltimore: University Park Press.

Kirk, S., & Kutchins, H. (1992). The selling of the DSM: The rhetoric of science in psychiatry. Hawthorne, NY: Aldine de Gruyter.

Kolko, D. J., & Milan, M. A. (1983). Reframing and paradoxical instruction to overcome "resistance" in the treatment of delinquent youths: A multiple baseline analysis. Journal of Consulting and Clinical Psychology, 51, 655–660.

Krasner, L. (1971). Behavior therapy. In P. H. Mussen (Ed.), Annual Review of Psychology (Vol. 22). Palo Alto, CA: Annual Reviews.

Krasner, L. (1990). History of behavior modification. In A. S. Bellack, M. Hersen, & A. E. Kazdin (Eds.), International handbook of behavior modification and therapy (2nd ed.). New York: Plenum.

Kunkel, J. (1970). Society and economic growth: A behavioral perspective of social change. New York: Oxford University Press.

L'Abate, L., & Milan, M. A. (1985). Handbook of social skills training and research. New York: Wiley.

Lamal, P. A. (Ed.). (1991). Behavior analysis of societies and cultural practices. New York: Hemisphere.

LaVigna, G. W., & Donnellan, A. M. (1986). Alternatives to punishment: Solving behavior problems with nonaversive strategies. New York: Irvington.

Layng, T. V. J., & Andronis, T. (1984). Toward a functional analysis of delusional speech and hallucinatory behavior. The Behavior Analyst, 7, 139–156.

Ledwidge, B. (1978). Cognition-behavior modification: A step in the wrong direction? Psychological Bulletin, 85, 353–375.

Lee, C. (1989). Theoretical weaknesses lead to

practical problems: The example of self-efficacy theory. *Journal of Behavior Therapy and Experimental Psychiatry, 20,* 115–123.

Lepper, M. R., & Hodell, M. (1989). Intrinsic motivation in the classroom. In C. Ames & R. Ames (Eds.), *Research on motivation in education: Vol. 3. Goals and cognitions.* New York: Academic Press.

Levis, D. J. (1990a, November). *Behaviorism and cognitivism in behavior therapy.* Paper presented at the 24th annual convention of the Association for Advancement of Behavior Therapy, San Francisco.

Levis, D. J. (1990b). The experimental and theoretical foundations of behavior modification. In A. S. Bellack, M. Hersen, & A. E. Kazdin (Eds.), *International handbook of behavior modification and therapy* (2nd ed.). New York: Plenum.

Liberman, R. P., King, L. W., DeRisi, W. J., & McCann, M. (1975). *Personal effectiveness: Guiding people to assert themselves and improve their social skills.* Champaign, IL: Research Press.

Lock, M. (1988). A nation at risk: Interpretations of school refusal in Japan. In M. Lock & D. Gordon (Eds.), *Biomedicine examined.* Boston: Kilmer Academic.

Lonigan, C. J. (1990). Which behaviorism? A reply to Mahoney. *American Psychologist, 1,* 1179–1181.

Lutzker, J. R. (1984). Project 12-Ways: Treating child abuse and neglect from an ecobehavioral perspective. In R. F. Dangel & R. A. Polster (Eds.), *Parent training: Foundations of research and practice.* New York: Guilford Press.

Malott, R. W. (1989). The achievement of evasive goals: Control by rules describing contingencies that are not direct acting. In S. C. Hayes (Ed.), *Rule-governed behavior: Cognition, contingencies, and instructional control.* New York: Plenum.

Malott, R. W., Whaley D. L., & Malott, M. E. (1993). *Elementary principles of behavior* (2nd ed.) Englewood Cliffs, NJ: Prentice-Hall.

Marks, I. M. (1987). *Fears, phobias, and rituals.* New York: Oxford.

Martin, G., & Pear, J. (1988). *Behavior modification: What it is and how to do it* (3rd ed.). Englewood Cliffs, NJ: Prentice-Hall.

Matson, J. L., & DiLorenzo, J. M. (1984). *Punishment and its alternatives.* New York: Springer.

McClannahan, L. E., Krantz, P. J., McGee, G. G., & MacDuff, G. S. (1984). Teaching-family model for autistic children. In W. P. Christian, G. T. Hannah, & T. J. Glahn (Eds.), *Programming effective human service: Strategies for institutional change and client transition.* New York: Plenum.

McReynolds, P. (1989). Diagnosis and clinical assessment: Current status and major issues. In M. R. Rosenzweig & L. W. Porter (Eds.), *Annual Review of Psychology, 40,* 83–108.

Meyer, L. H., & Evans, I. M. (1989). *Nonaversive intervention for behavior problems: A manual for home and community.* Baltimore: Paul H. Brookes.

Milan, M. A. (1990). Applied behavior analysis. In A. S. Bellack, M. Hersen, & A. E. Kazdin (Eds.), *International handbook of behavior modification and therapy* (2nd ed.). New York: Plenum.

Millenson, J. R., & Leslie, J. L. (1979). *Principles of behavioral analysis* (2nd ed.). New York: Macmillan.

Moore, J. (1990). On mentalism, privacy and behaviorism. *Journal of Mind and Behavior, 11,* 19–36.

Morris, E. K. (1990). What Mahoney "knows." *American Psychologist, 45,* 1178–1179.

Nettler, G. (1970). *Explanations.* New York: McGraw-Hill.

O'Donohue, W., & Krasner, L. (Eds.). (in press). *Handbook of Psychological Skills.* Boston: Allyn & Bacon.

O'Neil, R. E., Horner, R. H., Albin, R. W., Storey, K., & Sprague, J. R. (1990). *Functional analysis of behavior: A practical assessment guide.* Sycamore, IL: Sycamore Publishing Co.

Park, H. S., & Gaylord-Ross, R. (1989). A problem-solving approach with social skills training in employment settings with mentally retarded youth. *Journal of Applied Behavior Analysis, 22,* 373–380.

Patterson, G. R., & Forgatch, M. S. (1985). Therapist behavior as a determinant for client noncompliance: A paradox for the behavior modifier. *Journal of Consulting and Clinical Psychology, 53,* 846–851.

Patterson, G. R., Reid, J., & Dishion, T. (1992). *A social interactional approach: Vol. 4. Antisocial boys.* Eugene, OR: Castalia.

Pinkston, E. M., Levitt, J. L., Green, G. R., Linsk, N. L., & Rzepnicki, T. L. (1982). *Effective social work practice: Advanced techniques for behavioral intervention with individuals, families, and institutional staff.* San Francisco: Jossey-Bass.

Pinkston, E. M., & Linsk, N. L. (1984). *Care of the elderly: A family approach.* New York: Pergamon Press.

Poppen, R. L. (1989). Some clinical implications of rule-governed behavior. In S. C. Hayes (Ed.), *Rule governed behavior: Cognition, contingencies and instructional control.* New York: Plenum.

Redmon, W. K., & Dickinson, A. (1990). *Promoting excellence through performance management.* New York: Haworth Press.

Rescorla, R. A. (1987). A Pavlovian analysis of goal-directed behavior. *American Psychologist, 42,* 119–129.

Risley, T. R., Gottula, P., & Edwards, K. (1978, January). *Social interaction during family and institutional style meal service in a nursing home dining room.* Paper presented at the Nova Behavioral Conference on Aging, Port St. Luce, FL.

Rosenthal, T. L. (1982). Social learning theory. In G. T. Wilson & C. M. Franks (Eds.), *Contemporary behavior therapy.* New York: Guilford Press.

Schwartz, A., & Goldiamond, I. (1975). *Social casework: A behavioral approach.* New York: Columbia University Press.

Shorkey, C. T., & Taylor, J. (1973). Management of maladaptive behavior of a severely burned child. *Child Welfare, 52.* 543–547.

Skinner, B. F. (1953). *Science and human behavior.* New York: Macmillan.

Skinner, B. F. (1969). *Contingencies of reinforcement.* New York: Appleton-Century-Crofts.

Skinner, B. F. (1971). *Beyond freedom and dignity.* New York: Knopf.

Skinner, B. F. (1974). *About behaviorism.* New York: Knopf.

Skinner, B. F. (1981). Selection by consequences. *Science, 213,* 501–504.

Skinner, B. F. (1984). The operational analysis of psychological terms. *The Behavioral and Brain Sciences, 7,* 547–581.

Skinner, B. F. (1988). The operant side of behavior therapy. *Journal of Behavior Therapy and Experimental Psychiatry, 19,* 171–179.

Snyder, M., & Thomsen, C. J. (1988). Interactions between therapists and clients: Hypothesis testing and behavioral confirmation. In D. C. Turk & P. Salovey (Eds.), *Reasoning, inference, and judgement in clinical psychology.* New York: Free Press.

Staats, A. W. (1990). Paradigmatic behavior therapy: A unified framework for theory, research and practice. In G. H. Eifert & I. M. Evans (Eds.), *Unifying behavior therapy: Contributions of paradigmatic behaviorism.* New York: Springer.

Starin, S. (1991). "Nonaversive" behavior management: A misnomer. *The Behavior Analyst, 14,* 207–209.

Stokes, T. F., & Osnes, P. G. (1989). An operant pursuit of generalization. *Behavior Therapy, 20,* 327–356.

Stuart, R. B., & Davis, B. (1972). *Slim chance in a fat world: Behavioral control of obesity.* Champaign, IL: Research Press.

Sue, D. W., & Sue, D. (1990). *Counseling the culturally different: Theory and practice* (2nd ed.). New York: Wiley.

Sulzer-Azaroff, B., & Mayer, G. R. (1991). *Behavior analysis for lasting change.* Fort Worth, TX: Holt, Rinehart & Winston.

Thompson, T. (1988). Retrospective review: Benedictus behavior analysis: B. F. Skinner's Magnum Opus at Fifty. *Contemporary Psychology, 33,* 397–402.

Thyer, B. A. (1983). Behavior modification in social work practice. In M. Hersen, R. M. Eisler, & P. Miller (Eds.), *Progress in behavior modification* (Vol. 15). New York: Plenum.

Todd, J. T., & Morris, E. K. (1983). Misconception and miseducation: Presentations of radical behaviorism in psychology textbooks. *The Behavior Analyst, 96,* 153–160.

Tucker, D. J., & Berry, G. W. (1980). Teaching severely multihandicapped students to put on their own hearing aids. *Journal of Applied Behavior Analysis, 13,* 65–75.

Ullman, L. P., & Krasner, L. (1969). *A psychological approach to abnormal behavior.* Englewood Cliffs, NJ: Prentice-Hall.

Van Houten, R., & Sullivan, K. (1975). Effects of an audio cuing system on the rate of teacher praise. *Journal of Applied Behavior Analysis, 8,* 197–201.

Wahler, R. G. (1980). The insular mother: Her problems in parent–child treatment. *Journal of Applied Behavior Analysis, 13,* 207–219.

Wahler, R. G., & Dumas, J. E. (1984). Changing the observational coding styles of insular and

noninsular mothers: A step toward mainte-
nance of parent training effects. In R. F.
Dangel & R. A. Polster (Eds.), *Parent training:
Foundations of research and practice.* New
York: Guilford Press.

Wahler, R. G., & Fox, J. J. (1981). Setting events
in applied behavior analysis: Toward a conceptual and methodological expansion. *Journal of
Applied Behavior Analysis, 14,* 327–338.

Wahler, R. G., & Pollio, H. R. (1968). Behavior
and insight: A case study in behavior therapy.
*Journal of Experimental Research in Personali-
ty, 3,* 45–56.

Wills, T. A. (1982). Nonspecific factors in helping
relationships. In T. A. Wills (Ed.), *Basic processes in helping relationships.* New York: Academic Press.

Wolf, M. M. (1978). Social validity: The case for
subjective measurement or how applied behavior analysis is finding its heart. *Journal of Applied Behavior Analysis, 11,* 203–214.

Wolpe, J. (1958). *Psychotherapy by reciprocal inhibition.* Stanford, CA: Stanford University
Press.

Wolpe, J. (1986). Misrepresentation and underem-
ployment of behavior therapy. *Comprehensive
Psychiatry, 27,* 192–200.

Wolpe, J. (1989). The derailment of behavior
therapy: A tale of conceptual misdirection.
*Journal of Behavior Therapy and Experimental
Psychiatry, 20,* 3–15.

Wolpe, J. (Ed.). (1990). *The practice of behavior
therapy.* Elmsford, NY: Pergamon Press.

Wood, R. (1988). Clinical constraints affecting human conditioning. In G. Davey & C. Cullen
(Eds.), *Human operant conditioning and behavior modification.* New York: Wiley.

Wyatt, W. J. (1990). Radical behaviorism misrep-
resented: A response to Mahoney. *American
Psychologist, 45,* 1181–1184.

INTERVENTIONS WITH CHILDREN AND YOUTHS

Cognitive-Behavioral Treatment of Children and Adolescents

William H. Butterfield
Norman H. Cobb

Cognitive-behavioral methods with children are relatively new compared with conventional behavioral interventions. Strictly behavioral methods have been successfully applied to children, and their successful outcomes have overshadowed the development and use of cognitive-behavioral interventions. In the last ten years, however, numerous chapters and books and well over 500 journal articles have appeared on cognitive-behavioral therapy with children.* Practitioners and other social scientists have integrated the newest information on child and adolescent development and have effectively developed cognitive-behavioral methods for children. These methods, therefore, deserve attention from and possible adoption by modern practitioners who work with children and adolescents.

Cognitive-behavioral therapy is clearly problem focused. Problems are specified in children's and adolescents' behavior, values or belief systems, personal interactions, and environments. Because few problems can be treated successfully in isolation, assessments and interventions usually occur on several levels (Franks, 1990). This approach represents a maturing of the field, because problems are no longer viewed in isolation but as part of a matrix of interactions. Stated another way, complex problems usually require

complex interventions. Good examples are found in Lutzker and Rice's (1987) writing on child abuse and neglect, Patterson's (1982) work with conflicted families, and Schinke and Gilchrist's (1984) experience with preventing teenage pregnancy.

THEORETICAL FOUNDATION

The cognitive-behavioral model is primarily a training, or teaching, model. Through gaining new knowledge and skills, children change cognitions, behaviors, moods, or motivation (Persons, 1989). Whereas strictly behavioral assessments focus on overt behavior, cognitive-behavioral assessments focus on cognitive mediation in the form of covert behaviors or mechanisms that are learned and maintained by various contingencies. These cognitions, while interacting with other behavioral determinants, may activate and control behavior. With adults, cognitive-behavioral methods focus primarily on cognitive errors (Kendall & Braswell, 1985). With children, however, cognitive absences or deficiencies and cognitive errors are likely areas for assessment and treatment.

Two different, yet similar, theoretical perspectives on children's cognitive-behavioral treatment focus on the presence of cognitive errors or the absence of helpful cognitions (DiGiuseppe, 1989). The first perspective emphasizes irrational thoughts as the source

*We want to thank Marilyn Coleman, of the George Warren Brown School of Social Work, for the many hours she devoted to collecting and organizing the research articles and the bibliographies used to write this chapter.

of emotional disruptions and problematic behavior (Beck, 1976; Ellis 1962). The model contends that internal errors in thinking (or information processing) guide children's emotions and actions. Cognitive distortions are the cause of most childhood phobias, depression, and social withdrawal (Braswell & Kendall, 1988). When children are exposed to the fallacy of their logic or thinking, they can correct their erroneous mediations. As a result, their behavior and emotions change.

The second theoretical view explains problematic behavior and emotional difficulties as the result of cognitive deficits. Children can get into emotional and behavioral difficulties because they lack the ability to successfully cope with their world. They demonstrate poor problem-solving skills and poor self-management skills (Braswell & Kendall, 1988). Children, therefore, should be taught how to solve problems, take the perspective of others, establish rapport with others, and so forth.

The preceding theoretical perspectives would suggest slightly different yet congruent interventions. For example, a child of one of the authors reported that everyone at school hated her. Following the first perspective, she could have been told that she was "catastrophizing" and making an irrational judgment. Following the second view, the rational perspective would emphasize that some people might not like her but that other people liked her very much. The second approach, however, would suggest enacting the problem-solving approach by defining the problem and generating alternative solutions to her dilemma. Consequently, she was asked to operationally define the problem by listing the children at school whom she believed did not like her and those who liked her. Then, she was asked to generate a list of reasons why certain children at school did not like her and others liked her. Her list included such alternatives as "I can be a little bossy," "They don't like anybody except each other," and "They're monkeys."

The first perspective addresses the irrationality of her current thoughts and may or may not generalize to future events. With the second approach, the operationalization of the problem (naming the children who like you and those who don't) requires a change in the irrational labeling "All the kids at school hate me." The problem-solving task of generating alternative solutions assumes the correctness of her list and teaches a skill for solving present and future occurrences of a common childhood problem. The distinction of irrational belief systems or cognitive skill training is a function of the nature of the child's problem and his or her developmental readiness.

Child Development

Franks (1982) asserts that developmental issues distinguish cognitive-behavioral interventions with children and adolescents from interventions with adults. Clinicians must carefully assess the nature and role of children's cognitive development, because development is an interaction of several factors, such as inheritance, children's social world, and their physical environments. Children's biological inheritance predisposes them to develop in certain ways and according to a certain timetable. The timetable is not fixed but differs from child to child. Environments affect children's growth, because some settings provide ample nutrition and resources, whereas other environments lack essential elements. For example, low-income children may suffer from the effects of malnutrition, including lack of energy, stunted growth, and so forth. Children's social relationships also alter their rate of development.

Many theories equate specific ages with developmental levels, but "significant behavior changes are not synchronized simply with the ticking of a clock" (Bijou & Baer, 1961a, p. 23). In the early 1960s many undergraduates were told that children did not have the visual acuity or cognitive development to profit from reading instruction until they were 5 or 6 years of age. Also, violin instruction was delayed until children were nearing adolescence. In each of these cases the limits were imposed by the training methods rather than by empirically validated knowledge of children's developmental stages.

On the other hand, a 1-year-old would not be likely to have the motor skills to hold and bow a violin or the cognitive skills to learn to read. For most children, an additional year or two of development would significantly reduce the effort and time needed to accomplish such tasks. By age 4, for example, most children can easily learn to read. Furthermore, at least in the case of reading, a substantial amount of research shows that 6- or 7-year-olds who were earlier taught to read at 2 years of age do not have an advantage over children who learned at 4 or 5. Children, however, learn spoken language much better if they are exposed to adult speakers of the language earlier in life rather than later.

Furthermore, children's development is not uniform. Some children's language skills develop quickly, whereas their motor skills develop more slowly; in other children the reverse is true. Consequently, careful assessment of children's specific developmental skills may be needed for different interventions. Wasserman (1984) related cognitive levels with specific cognitive-behavioral interventions such as modeling, environmental manipulation, verbal mediation, visual imagery, and semantic-based interventions.

Modeling. Perhaps the most pervasive method of learning for children or adults is through modeling. Children would never survive their early years if they were limited to learning only through direct experience. All people learn vicariously by watching others, hearing about them, reading descriptions of behavior, and so forth:

Modeling does not require children to have formal language ability: A child merely has to reproduce . . . images in the form originally presented. . . . A child need not classify events, articulate concepts, serialize objects according to quantifiable dimension, or reason simultaneously about part-whole relationships. . . . The only requirement is that the child understands that some reinforcement would be obtained [Wasserman, 1984, p. 40].

Some might even question the need for understanding. The experimental literature clearly shows that awareness (the ability to identify when a contingency exists) is not necessary for reinforcement contingencies to be effective (Nisbett & Ross, 1980).

Environmental Manipulation. Although not mentioned by Wasserman, environmental contingencies control behavior with children who lack language ability. Many interventions with children are behavioral rather than cognitive-behavioral. They emphasize reinforcement, punishment, and alteration of stimulus conditions rather than verbal or cognitive mediation. Appropriate levels of cognitive development are not present in many children under the age of 8. Fortunately, strictly behavioral methods work well with children. By middle to late adolescence, reinforcers, punishers, and stimulus events are less effective at controlling behavior. The loss of effectiveness is not due to a breakdown in the basic laws of behavior change but, rather, to the fact that the sources of environmental influence have become much more complex. Traditional reinforcers and punishers, therefore, lose some potency because other competing sources of reinforcement appear, and older children gain more ability to escape or avoid punishers.

Verbal Mediation of Overt Behavior. According to Wasserman, self-instructional techniques, such as those of Meichenbaum and Goodman (1971), by which children are taught to talk to themselves as a means of reducing their impulsivity, may not be effective with children 6 and below for any but highly specific tasks. Young children lack the ability to generalize from specific situations to other situations. For example, Grody (1982) showed that the ability to delay impulsive behavior was largely unaffected by training but improved as children matured.

Visual Imagery.   Clients are often asked to form mental images and then associate them with some event or state. In systematic desensitization, for example, clients are asked to imagine pleasant scenes. They are taught to relax and visualize the situation. Piaget (1967, 1972) and others report that children cannot process and relate imagery to overt behavior until the period of formal operational thought: "Complex images that contain sequences of actions would be precluded for use with young children [and] . . . limited in [their] clinical application to acquisition of specific behavioral skills . . . or for use in simple desensitization paradigms" (Wasserman, 1984, pp. 43–44). Consequently, some methods like visual imagery require clinicians to assess children's cognitive age or capacity to perform prerequisite cognitive skills.

Semantic-Based Interventions.   Cognitive-behavioral techniques that require higher language skills are the most complex and require the most sophisticated cognitive skills. For this reason they are used primarily with adolescents. Selman, Beardslee, Schultz, Krupa, & Podorefsky (1986) report that most children pass through four stages in their ability to process the values and opinions of others:

Level 0. Children lack social perspective and do not consider others' points of view. The major way of handling disagreements is with impulsive fight-or-flight behavior.
Level 1. Children recognize others' ideas as different from their own but have little un-

derstanding of them. The major ways of dealing with issues at this level are "one-way commands and assertions and, conversely, simple and unchallenging accommodation . . . to the perceived needs and requests of significant others" (p. 451).
Level 2. Children or adolescents consider different views one at a time and then compare the different views with their own. At this level the major means of interaction are reciprocal exchanges and include such things as trades, exchanges, and verbal persuasion that protect the interests or rights of children or adolescents.
Level 3. Children or adolescents can simultaneously consider two or more views and evaluate them independently of their own perspective. Strategies used at this level include "compromise, dialogue, process analysis, and the development of shared goals. They indicate an understanding that concern for the relationship's continuity over time relates to the solution of any immediate problem" (p. 451).

An example from the clinical practice of one of the authors illustrates this point. A teenage boy was referred by his single mother for oppositional behavior. The boy was expected to be home by 4:00 P.M. so that when the younger children got home from school, he would be there to supervise them. His mother reported that he "routinely" was not home when she arrived at 6:00 P.M. The boy responded that she was never home when she promised either and that he got stuck with the kids until she came "meandering in sometime between 6:30 and 7:00." The mother tried to persuade the boy that she would make it up to him when she had to be late. He was not willing to negotiate on the basis of long-term promises but, rather, demanded a concrete, short-term consequence that he felt protected his rights. He demanded that his mother agree that for every minute she was late, he could stay a minute longer at the Saturday night dance that same week. After she finally agreed to this proposal, the issue of the afternoon baby-sitting was quickly resolved. This Level 2 exchange and contingency were easily understood and accepted by the boy. (Indeed, he no longer complained about her being late but gleefully marked it on the weekly tally sheet.)

Not only does the level of thinking change as children develop, children increasingly question adults' ideas and rules (Olinger & Epstein, 1991). Many adults perceive this questioning as a violation of long-held norms that give them the right to exert unquestioned authority over children. Unfortunately, they do not realize that maturing is the healthy product of their own parenting and that in the future the increase in their children's cognitive complexity will require that authority-by-assertion be replaced with authority-by-reason.

With increased thinking skills, children's maturity enhances the processing of emotions. Donaldson and Westerman (1986) identify several stages of emotional growth: In the first stage, feeling is based on external events. Gradually, feelings shift to internal evaluations of thoughts, attitudes, and memories. As evidence of this phenomenon, depression is manifested differently in children of different ages (Garber, 1984; Webb & VanDever, 1985).

To summarize, ignoring developmental readiness can lead to interventions not suited for specific children. Wasserman (1984) reports that strictly rational procedures such as rational-emotive procedures and interventions are of limited usefulness with children younger than 10 to 12. On the other hand, overreliance on age norms can lead to labeling children as not developmentally ready when, in fact, they are. Developmental norms represent the average or most common way groups of people behave in given environments at a given age. Reliance on the average or norm guarantees that clinicians will underestimate up to half of the children in their care. Norms should be viewed only as guidelines to be balanced with clinicians' assessment of specific children.

Other Issues in Treating Children

Thus far we have focused on the relationship between development and cognitive abilities. Other issues affecting therapy are changing referent groups, changing language and values, relative power differences, selective communication, lack of experience, limited expectations, and rapport.

Changing Referent Groups. Children's referent groups change over time. In the beginning, most of children's experiences are with their family. Thus, families largely control information, reinforcers, and punishers that shape children's behavior and understanding. By the time children reach adolescence, their families are only one of many sources of information and control. The implications for treatment are readily apparent. The propensity of adults to influence their children is reduced. The strength, or valence, of many previous reinforcers declines. Specifically, the value of praise and other adult-mediated reinforcers is reduced relative to the same reinforcers mediated by peers. Therapists, therefore, must work with families and children to carefully determine the reinforcement value of any contingencies that might be developed.

Changing Language and Values. Adolescents' language and values begin to diverge from those of their parents and other adults. Differences in language (for example, "bad" meaning good) increase the probability of miscommunication. Furthermore, as children's exposure to the outside world grows, the likelihood increases that they will be exposed to information that violates family norms and values. Thus, practitioners must also spend time learning how value conflicts influence people's perceptions of problems and solutions.

Relative Power Differences.   The relative power differences between adults and children also influence the treatment process. In most societies parents or other adults presume the right to regulate the behavior of children. Even when adults' rules are questionable, cultural norms and the law give wide discretion to them. Practitioners cannot apply absolute standards for defining problematic behaviors but, rather, must evaluate them in each context. The context helps practitioners decide whether intervention should consist of relabeling behaviors (so that caregivers no longer consider them as problems), changing behaviors of children, or changing behaviors of the people who originally defined the behaviors as problematic. Practitioners may have to act as children's advocates so that reasonably "normal" behaviors do not get labeled as deviant due to the views and values of adults who have power over them. When clients are younger and, therefore, less powerful, the practitioner must be more active in advocating their interests.

Selective Communication.   As children grow, they learn that information is power and thus become selective about what information they share. By the time they become adolescents, many of them have learned that the best way to keep out of trouble is to share as little information as possible with the people who have control over them. In treatment an important task is to encourage children and parents to increase their exchange of information, to enhance the quality of their interchanges, and to demonstrate that shared information will be helpful to everyone and not be used against anyone.

Lack of Experience.   Children lack experience; therefore, many situations are new to them. Consequently, prior experience does not always give them the tools needed to evaluate novel situations. Schug and Birkey (1985), for example, found that children's economic reasoning was greatly influenced by prior experience. They may not have learned many important tasks, skills, and contingencies that would enable them to respond appropriately. To satisfy deficiencies of inexperience, practitioners may provide specific skill training to better socially equip their clients.

Limited Expectations.   Unfortunately, children's parents rarely prepare them for the experience of talking to therapists (DiGiuseppe, 1989). Children have little knowledge about therapy or practitioners. This critical oversight is partially due to parents' lack of understanding about the therapeutic process. For example, most experienced clinicians have had a parent directly or indirectly give the message "Fix him [or her], and I'll wait outside."

Children learn about therapists through television or school counselors. A situation comedy on television does not perpare them to be "good clients." Therapists must take an active role to educate them and refute their fears of possibly being "crazy." Children's level of development dictates the nature of this task. With adolescents and older children, therapists must define the limits of confidentially and the responsibility of each person to contribute to the discussions and decision making. With children in lower elementary grades, the relationship between therapists and clients must be described in concrete terms. For example, "From right now until the clock points to the 9, we can talk about you and what you think about Mommy having a new baby. You can say anything you want, and I'll listen. I may ask some questions if I don't understand something. But, before we run out of time, we'll see if there is something you and I can do to make things better for you." Preschool children require rather brief explanations. They are more influenced by therapists' warmth, calmness, and caring.

Rapport. Younger children do not understand descriptions of the client/therapist relationship. They do, however, respond to the warmth and nonjudgmental attitudes of experienced child therapists. Rapport, however, is not just for young clients; older children and adolescents require an atmosphere of nondefensiveness and nonreactivity. They are normally reluctant to discuss feelings and behavior that, in most instances, have previously earned them rejection and criticism. Finally, because children are very reluctant to believe therapists' promises of confidentiality, good rapport may be therapists' only means of persuasion. For these reasons and many others, therapists with a warm sense of humor may be very effective. They may be able to replace an atmosphere of judgment and hostility with a sense of acceptance that allows clients and therapists to laugh or at least smile over past mistakes.

Our emphasis thus far has been on the need to assess children's developmental levels rather than assuming that children of a particular age possess certain developmentally related skills or abilities. The research literature identifies many ways in which children and adolescents differ from one another as well as from adults. No matter what differences are identified, they are normative generalities rather than specific guides to children's levels of development. In essence, for every child who exhibits developmentally relevant behaviors at a given age, another child does not. Effective treatment must incorporate approaches that are appropriate for clients' developmental levels. See the developmental-psychology text by Hoffman, Paris, Hall, & Schell (1988) for an overview of various theories.

ASSESSMENT

Assessment is the initial stage for clarifying and defining children's problems and setting goals. Cognitive-behavioral assessment requires the analysis of cognitions, behavior, and any confounding variable such as the level of cognitive development.

Functional analysis is a key to effective assessment and subsequent treatment. The functional aspect of behavior and cognitions is contained in the final assessment stage, of problem specification and treatment planning, which will be discussed following the two earlier assessment stages, identifying the problems and setting priorities.

Jordan and Franklin's text (in press) on assessment and measurement thoroughly describes five assumptions about assessment:

1. that practice is empirically based
2. that assessment must be from a systems perspective
3. that measurement is essential
4. that ethical practitioners evaluate their clinical work
5. that well-qualified practitioners are knowledgeable about numerous assessment methods in developing assessments

These assumptions are incorporated into the three stages of assessment discussed below.

Problem Identification

Problem identification establishes the broad areas of functioning that are problematic. Three major types of assessment tools are commonly used:

1. checklists, questionnaires, surveys, and scales
2. structured interviews
3. unstructured interviews

Checklists, Questionnaires, Surveys, and Scales. Checklists, questionnaires, surveys, and scales can be quite specific and focus on a single problem, such as depression. When used in this manner, they give clinicians an empirically based measure of the overall functioning of clients and their environment.

Numerous rapid-assessment instruments measure almost every conceivable problem (Corcoran & Fischer, 1987). Areas usually included are behavioral problems, emotional problems, social problems, developmental problems, and medical problems. For example, the Child Behavior Checklist (Achenbach & Edelbrock, 1983) is commonly used for assessing children's behavior and their ability to focus attention. The Children's Depression Inventory (Kovacs, 1983) is a revision of the Beck Depression Inventory (Beck, 1967) and is designed to assess depression in children between the ages of 8 and 17. The Clinical Measurement Package (Hudson, 1982) is very inclusive and covers individual and relationship issues. A subset of the scales assesses family interactions and beliefs such as attitudes of children toward their parents and vice versa.

Assessment of cognitive development is particularly important to help clinicians match interventions with children's developmental readiness. Corcoran and Fischer (1987) describe numerous assessment tools for children and adolescent's cognitive functioning: the Children's Cognitive Assessment Questionnaire (Asher, Hymel, & Renshaw, 1984), the Common Belief Inventory for Students (Hooper & Layne, 1987), the Children's Perceived Self-Control Scale (Humphrey, 1982), the Hopelessness Scale for Children (Kazdin, French, Unis, Esveldt-Dawson, & Sherick, 1983; Kazdin, Rodgers, & Colbus, 1986), the Young Children's Social Desirability Scale (Ford & Rubin, 1970), and the Children's Cognitive Assessment Questionnaire (Zatz & Chassin, 1983).

Hughes (1988) describes two of the most common performance measures that indirectly measure cognitive abilities. The Matching Familiar Figures Test (Kagan, Rosman, Day, Albert, & Phillips, 1964) consists of 12 items and requires children to match familiar pictures to variations of the picture. The latency and error scores are helpful in evaluating impulsivity. The test has often been used for measuring outcomes of treatment. Hughes mentions the Cairns and Cammock (1978) variation of Kagan's scale as possibly superior. The Means-End Problem Solving Scale (Shure & Spivack, 1972) is typical of similar tests (Lochman & Lampron, 1986). The test provides children with the beginning and end to a series of stories, and the task is to fill in the middle portion. Children's responses suggest to clinicians the level of cognitive development and problem-solving skills.

The most widely used tests of cognitive functioning of school-age children are the Wechsler Scales (Wechsler, 1974). They consist of the Wechsler Preschool and Primary Scale of Intelligence (WPPSI) and the Wechsler Intelligence Scale for Children—Revised (WISC-R).

Because some children's dysfunctional behavior is based on cognitive errors in reasoning, clinicians may find the Children's Negative Cognitive Error Questionnaire helpful (Leitenberg, Yost, & Carroll-Wilson, 1986). As an assessment tool or evaluative measure of treatment, the scale's 24 items evaluate children on their level of catastrophizing, overgeneralizing, personalizing, and selective abstraction (Hughes, 1988). These four categories of cognitive responses indicate children's level of rational or irrational thoughts about various situations.

Therapists can help children construct scales or measures to take home and record their cognitions. Self-anchored rating scales are generally simple questions with two to seven Likert-style anchoring points that children can define for themselves. For example, children can create a five-point scale to measure pain. In preparing the scale, a child would identify a simple question to be answered, such as "How much pain do I feel right now?" The child and therapist would relate words to the numbers on the scale. The child might label "1" to mean "feel no pain, free as a bird"; "3" might be labeled "it hurts but I can take it"; and "5" might be described as "hurts like a pin in the eye." At specified times during the day, the child could write down or circle the number that best described the pain.

Structured Interviews and Unstructured Interviews.

Some structured interviews are created for gathering a comprehensive set of information. Unfortunately, the great bulk of information is seldom used. More important, in many cases the majority of the information is not necessary to address problems of most clients. The third approach, unstructured interviews, takes a very different tack and asks clients to identify their own specific problems. Unstructured interviews are assumed to focus on information that is more relevant to clients' problems. They also presume that problem specification is an ongoing process, because as new issues surface, they are added to the problem list.

Practitioners supporting comprehensive approaches such as structured interviews argue that problems cannot be adequately treated without understanding the overall context of children's lives. Although comprehensiveness is desirable, most therapists do not have the time or ability to deal with all of the complexities of clients' lives. Consequently, they tend to focus on smaller areas that have a significant impact on clients' functioning. The differences between comprehensive or specific approaches in assessment have been extensively debated in the treatment literature, and they do lead to different interventions. In the final analysis, however, no clear evidence supports the superiority of one approach over the other.

The broad-ranging problems treated by clinicians differ in degree of difficulty. Some problems are quite specific—for example, temper tantrums—whereas others, such as depression or child neglect, involve many response systems. Where problems have been successfully treated without resorting to multiple interventions, therapists are usually on safe ground in attempting treatment without a comprehensive assessment of clients. This approach always increases the risk of making wrong assumptions. Some argue that the costs of failed interventions are too high. Others argue that the risk is acceptable because it is often more efficient (it takes less time and less effort) to collect new information as needed. The facts about what information is used by effective clinicians are open to debate. Even though numerous approaches exist, all involve planning and goal setting. They differ on when and how the necessary assessment information is collected rather than their ultimate purposes of assessment. A list of assessment tools at the end of the chapter contains several sources of structured interviews and developmental and behavioral screening instruments that are helpful in identifying problems.

Disagreements between Children and Parents.

Regardless of the method used to develop a list of problems, children and their referring agents are likely to differ. Numerous studies have shown that children and parents identify different problems (Costello, 1986; Kashani, Orvaschel, Burk, & Reid, 1985). The differences are due, in part, to the developmental phases of children. Edelbrock (1986) found that parent/child agreement increased sharply with age. Systematic investigations of the differences between the perceptions of children and other caregivers show similar results. Face-to-face discussions with parents and children are recommended to clarify the differences in each participant's view of reality and of the issues involved in specific problems. Often, parents and children, particularly adolescents, possess different information. For example, a father had no idea that his daughter was contemplating suicide until she revealed to a therapist that she was a regular user of the suicide hot line. The participants may also be using different labels and words to describe the same situation. For example, in a dialogue recorded by Schinke

(1984), a teenager reported that the problem with her mother was that she "dumped on" the girl's boyfriend whenever he came over late in the evening. As discussion continued, she and her mother both clearly preferred that the friend come over earlier. The teenager, however, did not know how to ask her boyfriend to change his pattern. So instead she labeled her mother as the problem.

Sometimes the differences are not over facts but values. Some adolescents, for example, believe that they have the right to set their own hours, but their parents have the opposite view. When values are involved, the conflict-resolution procedures developed by Fisher and Ury (1983) are very helpful. Clarifying differences in problem lists serves an assessment and diagnostic function. Unrealistic values and expectations as well as maladaptive cognitions or interaction patterns are often revealed.

Priority Setting

With many clients the ultimate treatment goal of developing problem-solving skills is initiated during the assessment phase of setting priorities. From the beginning, clients are encouraged to make their own decisions. To paraphrase Weatherhead (1965), clients will again and again clamor to be told what to do. They want shortcuts. They want decisions made for them. Wise therapists spread the whole situation before their clients and help them see their problems in a new way. They refuse to be infallible directors. The choices people make for themselves have far greater authority and power than directions imposed on them by others, however distinguished.

Once the list of problems is identified, therapists should help clients set treatment priorities with the awareness that not all child-behavior problems require treatment. Many behaviors that adults define as problems occur frequently in childhood and adolescence and thus are probably within the expected limits of "normal" behavior. For example, fears, social withdrawal, temper tantrums, aggression, and noncompliance are common (Schwartz & Johnson, 1985). According to Lapouse and Monk (1985) over 40% of children aged 6 to 12 have fears sufficiently strong to be reported by their mothers. Unfortunately, during the initial stages of assessment, the seriousness of problems may be difficult to determine. If so, treatment may be advisable. LeCroy and Ashford (1992), for example, recommended that children with common developmental problems receive brief treatment and extended follow-up. Brief intervention would ensure that the problem was alleviated within the expected developmental period.

Clients are usually the best at determining the consequences of treating or overlooking a problem. They should, therefore, be allowed or encouraged to take the lead in determining treatment priorities. Therapists may find that giving clients some rules for setting priorities is useful. (See Gambrill, 1983, pp. 102–104, for a suggested list of priorities.) When clients guide the selection of problems, they often reveal their values and priorities. Typical themes used or invoked in priority setting include socially sanctioned rights (for example, parents' rights to make decisions for their children), equity, fairness, time, cost, efficiency, pain, potential for harm, and so forth. The process also reveals the participants' patterns of communication and affect.

Some practitioners question the ability of children to participate competently in the decision-making process of problem selection. The empirical evidence, however, suggests the opposite. Weithorn and Campbell (1982), for example, found that 9-year-olds were able to make informed decisions about treatment and that 14-year-olds were as competent as adults in their reasoning and understanding. Their study was handicapped by their inability to generalize results to children who were younger than 9, but younger children can be helped to make informed decisions. In fact, many 7-year-olds' cognitive development is probably adequate for them to participate in selecting and prioritizing problems for treatment (Ollendick & Cerny, 1981). (See DiGiuseppe, 1989, for a further discussion of age as a treatment consideration.)

Problem Specification and Treatment Planning

In problem specification, information is gathered to treat selected problems. Three major tasks are generally involved:

1. the collection of information to decide whether children and other participants possess the knowledge necessary for change efforts to be successful
2. an analysis of the current level of all participants' skills
3. a functional analysis of the selected targets for intervention

The first two tasks are fairly clear and straightforward; however, the third, functional analysis, needs more discussion. Functional analysis is an important element of assessment, because it is a major key to successful intervention and evaluation. Regrettably, many practitioners fail to conduct a careful functional analysis. Practitioners who focus on cognitive interventions often seem to revert to an old, discredited view of stimuli that considers the effect of a stimulus as invariant. The cognitive literature is full of examples assuming that irrational thoughts always lead to "bad" outcomes. Arnkoff and Glass (1982) maintain that cognitive therapists

> must not fall prey to the menace of careless inference. It is dangerous to assume the thought "I'm going to fail" has the same meaning for everyone. One person may be discouraged and give up after such a thought while another may counter the thought, become encouraged, and try harder (Kendall & Hollon, 1981). We are most likely to err in our inferences about meaning if we extrapolate from the content of a cognitive "snapshot" taken at one point in time.

> We must consider the shifting interconnections and the threads of experience . . . and the function that a thought process plays [p. 7].

They also point out that self-statements and thoughts that are "maladaptive for one individual at time X may also serve a more adaptive function for that same person at time Y. The same may be said for different settings or situations" (p. 16).

A special issue of *Behavioral Assessment* (Vol. 13, No. 1, 1991) contains several articles affirming how attitudes and behaviors differ in their adaptiveness over time. A functional analysis provides a way of understanding how behavior and the environment interact. It helps explain many situations that otherwise would be unclear or incomprehensible. If the mother of a preadolescent boy puts her arm around his shoulders in the privacy of the family den, for example, the boy's response is likely to be positive. But if she walks onto the school playground where he is playing with his schoolmates and does the same thing, his response will probably be very different. Because the stimulus is the same (a mother's hug), we might be puzzled by the difference in response. A functional analysis might show that, in the latter case, the hug functioned as a setting event that, after his mother left, led to his playmates teasing and embarrassing him. In the first case the hug strengthened a relationship (with his mother), and in the second it weakened his relationships with both his mother and his playmates. As Bijou and Baer (1961a) point out, the significance of a stimulus lies less in its physical makeup than in its stimulus function.

A functional analysis of behavior is necessary to determine why behaviors decrease or increase. Behaviors are, at the same time, responses and stimuli. Functional analysis is a relationship analysis, because behaviors are not analyzed in isolation but as part of an ongoing social exchange. The interaction may involve a single individual, a family, or some other grouping.

In summary, assessment is both an information-gathering process and a planning process. The gathering of information is followed by an analysis of which problems must be addressed. As these problems are evaluated, treatment goals or outcomes are identified that lead to the development of a treatment plan.

TREATMENT

In this section we present cognitive-behavioral interventions and report relevant research efforts. Unfortunately, space prohibits a comprehensive or exhaustive listing of treatment approaches. Five interventions are briefly described because they represent many of the principles underlying cognitive-behavioral interventions with children. Then, we provide two treatment examples to demonstrate additional interventions. In the first example, the treatment of pain is used to illustrate how a wide variety of interventions with a relatively specific problem can lead to clinically useful outcomes. The second example of a common adolescent difficulty illustrates that complex problems require extensive and comprehensive interventions. We begin by briefly describing modeling because it is frequently used to communicate and teach various skills. Furthermore, modeling does not require specific levels of developmental readiness.

Modeling

Training children and adolescents is a complex process. They need the opportunity to observe and describe verbal and nonverbal communication (Schinke & Gilchrist, 1984). The major instructional tool to teach skills is modeling. In the modeling sequence, the behavior or skill is performed in view of the clients. The model's performance is analyzed by those involved, and finally, the participants replicate the model's behavior.

For example, Camp and Bash (1981) used modeling to present the skill of relaxation to adolescents. Their group approach involves the leader modeling how someone would sit down in a chair if he or she were completely relaxed. The children are positively reinforced for rehearsing or reenacting the leader's relaxed behavior.

A significant amount of evidence supports the importance of using models that can adequately but not superlatively perform the behaviors. When teenagers or children view and analyze a modeled skill and they believe it is within their abilities, they learn rather quickly. The findings of Schinke and Gilchrist are congruent with those of Braswell and Kendall (1988), who found that when a "model succeeds but experiences some difficulties and expresses some emotion" (p. 195), children and youths gain the skill more readily than when the model has no difficulty.

Five Common Interventions

Problem-Solving Training. Several versions of the problem-solving approach have grown out of the cognitive-behavioral literature. D'Zurilla and Goldfried (1971) are often recognized as the instigators of the approach in clinical settings. Spivack and Shure (1974) applied the problem-solving method to normal children and children with behavioral disorders. Sarason and Sarason (1981) successfully applied the general format to adolescents in the classroom. As a result of problem-solving training, children and adolescents improve in social functioning. The sequential problem-solving steps are (1) defining the problem, (2) generating alternatives, (3) weighing and selecting alternatives to apply to the problem, (4) evaluating the success of the solution and, perhaps, returning to earlier stages for a redefinition of the problem or a selection of another alternative solution.

The turtle technique uses problem solving in the context of a temporary withdrawal from a threatening situation (Robin, Schneider, & Dolnick, 1976). By shaping their body like a turtle, children apply relaxation responses and problem-solve alternative solutions to the situation.

Self-Instructional Training. Children can be taught to say words or phrases to themselves that either (1) guide them through difficult procedures or tasks, (2) allow them to substitute words or phrases for troublesome thoughts (see thought stopping, discussed below), or (3) reinforce themselves for appropriate behavior. In the first instance, clinicians model the performance of a task while thinking out loud using self-instructional words (Bandura, 1977b; Meichenbaum, 1977). The modeling provides a visual picture of how to perform the cognitive and behavioral task. For example, children can imitate clinicians' actions and repeat the steps of problem solving while performing similar tasks. Children might repeat a catchy phrase designed to lead to problem-solving activities, such as "Say it, list it, do it," which represents the stages of define the problem, list alternatives, and select and solve the problem. In the second case, an easily distracted child can be taught to internally repeat a particular phrase like "Watch [the teacher] and listen [to her words]." The third use of self-instruction may involve repeating words or phrases designed to increase children's self-esteem (Pope, McHale, & Craighead, 1988) or self-efficacy (Anderson, 1981; Bandura, 1977a), such as the classic "I think I can, I think I can."

Rational-Emotive Therapy. DiGiuseppe, Miller, and Trexler (1977) reviewed studies that had applied rational-emotive therapy to children. They surmised that rational-emotive approaches were largely preventive and were highly effective at enhancing self-esteem. With the rational-emotive approach, children are taught to recognize their emotions and to realize that their emotions vary in intensity. They are taught to see the connection between feelings and cognitions. For example, they are asked to describe their thoughts while they are feeling or acting emotionally. They are taught that some thoughts are rational and some are irrational. For example, Anderson (1981) translated Ellis's (1962) 11 irrational beliefs into children's terms. The irrational beliefs were shared with the children, who proceeded to evaluate emotions and thoughts in terms of rational versus irrational thoughts. Bernard and Joyce (1984) concluded this approach with a procedure in which children listed their good and their negative qualities. The children were taught to limit their self-criticism by emphasizing that although their negatives might be real, they were not the dominant forces in their identities. In actuality, their negatives were offset by their positives.

Thought Stopping. Thought stopping is a cognitive skill to which children can readily relate. When they are taught to yell "Stop!" "inside their heads," most children quickly develop the ability to control many of their thoughts. One of the authors of this chapter suspects that permission to yell such a familiar word as "Stop" *inside their heads* is so fundamentally attractive that it is self-reinforcing.

Campbell (1974) revised thought stopping to help a 12-year-old boy cease negative thoughts about his sister's violent death. He taught the child to begin a negative thought and shift his attention to counting backwards from 10 to 1. Afterward, he switched his thinking to pleasant thoughts. Consequently, the child changed from 15 ruminations per day to no obsessional thoughts at a three-year follow-up.

Reattribution Training. When children attribute the cause of their failures to themselves, such as "I'm no good. I always screw up," their self-image and sense of self-efficacy are affected. Fincham (1983) taught children that their failures were due to lack of skill rather than to some persistent, internal characteristic. When the children were taught the needed skill, they were much more certain and positive about their self-esteem.

The preceding list of interventions is by no means inclusive of all cognitive-behavioral methods. It was presented to introduce common, general themes. Although many other methods are frequently used in treatment, they all require clinicians to adapt them to fit specific children, problems, and treatment situations. The remainder of the chapter briefly describes how various methods are adapted for the treatment of pain, teenage sexuality, and family conflict.

Treatment of Pain in Children

Significant numbers of children and adolescents experience high levels of acute and chronic pain. The reduction or elimination of pain improves the quality of clients' lives and reduces the need to use medications that may have long-term harmful effects or that may be addictive (Dolgin & Jay, 1989, p. 384). The following discussion focuses on Dolgin and Jay's contributions to pain treatment and illustrates how cognitive-behavioral interventions have been used for pain alleviation.

Assessment.   The assessment of pain focuses on clients' reports of their pain experiences. Several methods are used to evaluate pain:

- pain "thermometers," on which clients estimate the level of pain on a scale of 0 (no hurt) to 100 (the worst hurt possible)
- pain questionnaires, which ask children about the intensity and location of pain
- projective techniques, by which children are shown pictures depicting painful situations and are asked to relate the intensity, duration, and causation of pain

- using the outline of a person on which children can locate their pain centers and color painful areas according to the intensity (Eland, 1982)
- pain diaries, or logs, which are used to record data such as time of pain onset, intensity, duration, and a wide variety of other variables

Attempts are made to assess the behavioral impact of pain. Measures include medication used, change in activities, and checklists or inventories of behavior. For example, the Observational Scale of Behavioral Distress is used to record clients' responses to pain (Dolgin & Jay, 1989). From the physiological perspective, measures of muscle tension, blood flow, or joint temperatures (using biofeedback devices) are used to assess variables associated with pain.

Treatment.   Dolgin and Jay (1989) identify numerous treatment interventions with children and adolescents:

A. relaxation training
B. breathing exercises
C. hypnosis
D. biofeedback
E. guided imagery training
F. attention distraction
G. operant management
   1. differential reinforcement of other behavior
   2. extinction of pain-related behaviors
   3. shaping
H. Modeling

Three studies illustrate some of these treatment approaches. Varni (1981) treated five children with hemophilia who were experiencing arthritic pain. Treatment consisted of the following:

- self-regulation training: progressive muscle relaxation and controlled breathing
- modeling by a therapist of warmth, freedom from discomfort, and increased blood flow

• patient imitation of the behavior modeled by the therapist

The children showed significant relief from arthritic pain and improvements in mobility, sleep, overall functioning, and reductions in analgesic consumption. With biofeedback instruments, a clinician was able to record an average decrease in arthritic joint temperatures of 4.1° F (Dolgin & Jay, 1989).

Varni, Bessman, Russo, and Cataldo (1980) used operant approaches to control pain in a 3-year-old. They treated the behavior by differential reinforcement of other behavior. These procedures reduced the pain and increased other nonpain behaviors.

A third approach (Melamed & Siegel, 1975) addressed the management of anxiety associated with the anticipation of pain. Children who were experiencing painful medical procedures or who anticipated that a medical procedure would be painful engaged in a variety of emotional, escape, or avoidance behaviors. These included screaming, crying, flinching, hitting caregivers, leaving the treatment area, and so forth. Melamed and Siegel used a film to manage the anxiety of children scheduled for surgery. The film used a 7-year-old boy to model appropriate behavior with several events leading up to surgery. Included were "admissions, meeting the surgeon and anesthesiologist, having a blood test, exposure to equipment, separation from mother and scenes in the operating and recovery rooms. The child in the film narrates his feelings and thoughts as he copes with anxiety-provoking situations" (Dolgin & Jay, 1989, p. 396). Children exposed to the film showed less anxiety and fewer behavioral problems after treatment than did children in the control group.

The remarkable aspect of the pain literature is that all of the procedures illustrated worked. Whether the treatment was primarily cognitive or used operant or respondent procedures, reductions occurred in pain-related behaviors or in the levels of pain reported by the children. Future research should assess how children's subjective experience of pain differs from objectively measured pain. Tursky and his colleagues found that cultural factors influenced adults' verbal reports of pain but not their nonverbal perception of pain (Tursky & O'Connel, 1972; Tursky & Sternbach, 1987; Tursky & Watson, 1964). They found that people of different cultural backgrounds responded differently even though they had experienced the same level of electric shock. Some cultural groups showed almost no reaction, whereas other groups wept and screamed. The same subjects, however, made similar estimates when estimating pain level by squeezing a hand dynometer. Until such comparisons are carried out, the question will remain unanswered whether children experience less pain after treatment or simply learn to behave differently in the presence of pain.

The results reported for the treatment of pain are consistent with the results obtained with many other disorders. With younger children, a wide variety of techniques has been successfully used to treat a wide range of problems. A good source for detailed descriptions of interventions with children is Hersen and Van Hasselt (1987).

Treatment of Adolescent Problems

The focus in this section is on adolescent problems. The following studies were selected because treatment manuals outlining the interventions are available and because the treatments appear to be effective with at least some adolescents.

About 80% of adolescents grow into adulthood without experiencing major behavioral or emotional problems, and of the remaining 20%, many of the problems are transitory. By their early 20s, most adolescents will have left behind the problems that were painful for themselves and others. Nevertheless, the treatment of many of these problems is probably desirable because "aggressiveness, achievement patterns, and social skill development in children are generally established before adolescence, and childhood problems in these areas frequently persist into adulthood (Robins, 1979). Antisocial behavior in childhood increases vulnerability to a variety of mental disorders, alcoholism, and other problems in adult life" (Mechanic, 1989, p. 67). In the two following subsections we will review adolescent problems with sexuality and problems with their parents, and we will describe successful cognitive and behavioral interventions.

Teenage Sexuality.   Schinke and Gilchrist (1984) developed Life Skills Counseling, a comprehensive training program for adolescents. Although this program has been used with a variety of adolescent problems, the following material focuses on teenage sexuality because the area is so troublesome for adolescents and their parents and because the complex nature of sexuality is intriguing to most clinicians.

Adolescents give birth to 16.1% of the children born in the United States. Although not all of these children are born to single mothers, teenage pregnancy is an enormous problem. Schinke (1984) reports that cognitive-behavioral techniques have been successfully used with this population.

Assessment includes four primary methods. Information is collected through:

1. self-reports of somatic responses, thoughts, information processing, and a variety of other self-report procedures
2. role playing tests, often videotaped, in which adolescents respond to a contrived situation with someone who acts in a predetermined manner
3. naturalistic observation, in which trained observers observe the adolescent engaging in everyday activities
4. reports from others who are asked to provide relevant information from memory or direct observation

The information is used to assess teenagers in the following domains: somatic, cognitive, behavioral, and functional analysis. In each domain three basic questions are helpful to the analysis (Schinke & Gilchrist, 1984):

1. What does the problematic or target social situation require?
2. How does the adolescent client react when in that situation?
3. What is going on when the adolescent is performing poorly in that situation?

In planning *treatment,* "counselors must decide whether to work with adolescents individually, with whole family units, or with groups of adolescents. . . . Usually, the circumstances under which counseling occurs dictate one format as best" (Schinke & Gilchrist, 1984, p. 13). Whatever the format, programs to enhance interpersonal skills are generally organized around seven phases:

1. *Information giving:* Whatever its focus, life-skills training communicates information with instant meaning. "As an example, sexual counseling for 10-year-olds ought to cover physiology, hormonal vagaries, nocturnal emissions, menarche, and the role of sex in human functioning. With 14-year-olds, such counseling should highlight same gender relationships, love, and contraception" (Schinke & Gilchrist, 1984, p. 13).
2. *Problem-solving:* Adolescents are taught to identify recurring problems by learning to ask a series of questions: "What is the problem? Who has the problem? What will happen if the problem continues? How did you get into trouble? Who can get you out of trouble?" (p. 14). Brainstorming procedures are used to teach the adolescents how to generate solutions.
3. *Self-instruction:* Adolescents are taught to attend to their private thoughts that accompany daily experiences. They are taught that they have control over their thoughts. Therefore, they can manage

these thoughts to develop control in the problematic areas of their lives (Meichenbaum & Goodman, 1971).

4. *Coping:* Schinke and Gilchrist emphasize that youths can learn to cope with stressful life events. Training teaches covert and overt mechanisms. Overt coping enables adolescents to tangibly reward themselves. Similarly, with covert methods they can learn to relax, use meditation, or simply say constructive and rewarding messages to themselves.

5. *Communication:* Teaching adolescents to communicate involves numerous skills. Clinicians must teach or model appropriate "postures, facial mannerisms, gestures, voice inflections, and words that unambiguously express personal resolve" (Schinke, 1984, p. 18). The training frequently takes place in small groups where participants role play, coach each other, offer helpful feedback, and, most important, affirm and reinforce each other. In this setting adolescents are less apt to feel insulted that they need to learn a behavior, such as communication, that most people assume develops "naturally."

6. *Support systems:* Schinke and Gilchrist are not very clear about what is involved. Generally, they trained adolescents to program reinforcement and other positive elements into their lives so that their newly learned behaviors were supported in their everyday environments.

7. *Evaluation:* Schinke, Gilchrist, and Small (1979) found that training students to use new interpersonal skills, by themselves, was not effective. They reported that effective pregnancy prevention must combine (a) the presentation of information, (b) behavioral change, and (c) changes in the cognitive processing of decision making. In the most effective groups, reproductive and contraceptive information as well as problem-solving and decision-making skills were used. They also modeled interactional skills such as eye contact, voice inflection, and volume, and physical gestures, which the subjects then practiced. In addition, the adolescents made written contracts that included "anticipated forthcoming problems, specified youths' responses to problems and planned backup contingencies. . . . These combined techniques were effective in altering the subjects' behavior. At follow-up the subjects reported fewer occasions of unprotected intercourse, greater habitual use of birth control, and more positive attitudes toward delaying pregnancy" (Schinke, 1984, p. 51).

Family Conflict.   Family conflict has received a significant amount of attention in the treatment literature. Foster and Robin (1989), Robin and Koepke (1990), and Patterson (1982) extensively discuss the processes that occur in conflicted families. Their recommendations for assessment and treatment cover such areas as problem-solving, communication skills, and the functional analysis of behavior in the family context.

Another approach to adolescent conflict was developed by Brigham (1989). He asserts that adolescents learn to discriminate stimuli when a response leads to reinforcement from others. Self-management, therefore, requires not only the ability to emit a particular response or set of responses but also the ability to discriminate which set of responses is appropriate for particular situations. Self-management training focuses on directing adolescents in general concepts rather than teaching them how to deal with isolated problems. Once the concepts have been learned, adolescents learn to apply them in specific situations. The conceptual framework is largely built on the work of Skinner (1966), Becker (1986), and Becker and Engelmann (1978).

Adolescents need to learn what reinforcers control their behavior and the behavior of others. Consequently, they learn how to reinforce themselves and also how to affect the behavior of others. Additionally, adolescents gain significant skills when they learn the reciprocal nature of behavioral exchanges. They are better prepared to have an impact on the interaction between environmental events and private feelings. As a result they are better able to analyze their own behavior/environment interactions (Brigham, 1989).

Modification consists of developing the skills in reinforcement, extinction, and shaping others' behaviors that are appropriate to the specific situation. Also, adolescents must learn to structure the environment so that it reduces the probability of inappropriate behaviors and maximizes the occurrence of more appropriate behaviors.

Even a cursory review of the literature on cognitive-behavioral intervention with adolescents confirms the conclusion that the techniques work well with specific and clearly delimited problems. Attempts to intervene with adolescents who exhibit more generalized problematic behaviors have been moderately successful. The procedures are less successful with adolescents who have more severe behavioral disorders. These outcomes are surprising considering the elaborate and extensive interventions that have been developed.

CONCLUSION

In this chapter we have addressed the issues of how developmental factors impinge on interventions with children and adolescents. Cognitive-behavioral assessment and intervention processes have demonstrated their effectiveness with adolescents and children. We have not attempted to review the extensive literature on the use of cognitive-behavioral interventions, instead using typical interventions to demonstrate the variety of treatments.

Although children and adolescents differ from adults, many studies of interventions

make no mention of alterations to accommodate younger clients. Behavioral strategies predominate with younger children, but cognitive-behavioral interventions are increasingly being employed. Not surprisingly, modeling is the primary vehicle. "Virtually all effective cognitive-behavioral interventions with children involve some form of active modeling as a means of conveying the coping methods the therapist wishes to train" (Braswell & Kendall, 1988).

Young children are often seen as targets of change rather than as active participants in the change process. Although they may lack some developmentally related skills, practitioners must strive to involve children to the greatest extent possible. Children can actively participate in many aspects of the treatment process, and adolescents possess many of the abilities of adults. Brigham (1989) writes:

In the case of the younger child, it can be (and has been) reasonably assumed that the child's parents and teachers control a significant portion of his/her environment. The strategy typically adopted in such a situation is to teach the parents and teachers how to modify the child's behavior. . . . On the other hand, a number of investigators have ruefully found that such a strategy has little chance of success with an adolescent. . . . As a consequence, the intervention strategy must change from a behavior modification focus . . . to one of changing behavior to modify the broad patterns of behavior-environment interactions [p. 41].

We conclude this chapter by addressing the question of effectiveness. Each of the examples we have reviewed included some information on the effectiveness of the intervention. These few examples, however, cannot tell us about the overall effectiveness of cognitive-behavioral interventions. These interventions appear to be effective with many of the problems of childhood and adolescence (Craighead, Meyers, & Craighead, 1985; DiGiuseppe, 1989; LeCroy & Ashford, 1992; Mash & Barkley, 1989; Meador & Ollendick,

1984; Olinger & Epstein, 1991; Weisz, Weiss, Alicke, & Klotz, 1987).

Generally, therapy is more effective with children than with adolescents (Brigham, 1989), although as the studies reviewed in this chapter show, some programs are quite effective with some adolescents. The Achilles heel of much research is the short duration of follow-up. The fact is, long-term follow-up is a rarity. Weisz and her colleagues (1987) concluded a meta-analysis of the impact of a variety of therapies on children and adolescents. They found that after treatment, across multiple measures of adjustment, the average treated youngster was functioning better than 79% of those not treated. In summary, the evidence supports cautious optimism about the use of cognitive-behavioral techniques with children and adolescents. However, the interaction between development and such interventions requires more research and application.

ASSESSMENT TOOLS

Behavioral Coding Systems

Behavioral Coding System (Forehand & McMahon, 1981)

Checklists, Questionnaires, Behavioral Surveys, and Data-Recording Forms

Assertiveness Self-Statement Test (Schwartz & Gottman, 1976)

Attentional Deficits Assessment (Blondis, Accardo, & Snow, 1989)

Automatic Thoughts Questionnaire (Hollon & Kendall, 1980)

Beck Depression Inventory (Beck, 1967)

Behavioral Interpersonal Problem Solving Test (Vaughn, Ridley, & Bullock, 1984)

Child Behavior Checklist (Achenbach, & Edelbrock, 1983)

Child Behavior Rating Scale (Hudson, 1990)

Children's Cognitive Assessment Questionnaire (Asher, Hymel, & Renshaw, 1984; Zatz & Chassin, 1983)

Children's Depression Inventory (Kovacs, 1983)

Children's Negative Cognitive Error Questionnaire (Leitenberg & Yost, 1986)

Children's Perceived Self-Control Scale (Humphrey, 1982)

Child's Attitude toward Father (Hudson, 1990)

Child's Attitude toward Mother (Hudson, 1990)

Client Report of Session Form (Freeman, Pretzer, Fleming, & Simon, 1990)

Clinical Anxiety Scale (Hudson, 1990)

Clinical Measurement Package (Hudson, 1981)

Cognitive Assessment of Social Anxiety Scale (Glass, Merluzzi, Biever, & Larsen, 1982)

Cognitive Therapy Scale (Freeman et al., 1990)

Common Belief Inventory for Students (Hooper & Layne, 1983)

Fear of Negative Evaluation Scale (Watson & Friend, 1969)

Five-Scale Test of Self-Esteem for Children (Pope, 1988)

General Screening Inventory (Hudson, 1990)

Generalized Contentment Scale (Hudson, 1990)

Hare Self-Esteem Scale (Hare, 1985)

Hopelessness Scale for Children (Kazdin, French, Unis, Esveldt-Dawson, & Sherick, 1983)

Index of Alcohol Involvement (Hudson, 1990)

Index of Brother Relations (Hudson, 1990)

Index of Clinical Stress (Hudson, 1990)

Index of Family Relations (Hudson, 1990)

Index of Peer Relations (Hudson, 1990)

Index of Self-Esteem (Hudson, 1990)

Index of Sister Relations (Hudson, 1990)

Interpersonal Reactivity (Empathy) Index (Davis, 1983)

Irrational Beliefs About Assertion Scale (Craighead, 1989)

Issues Checklist (Foster & Robin, 1988)

Loneliness Scale (Russell, Peplau, & Freeman, 1978)

Matching Familiar Figures Test (Kagan, Rosman, Day, Albert, & Phillips, 1964)

Means-End Problem Solving Scale (Shure & Spivack, 1972)

Parent Consumer Satisfaction Questionnaire (Forehand & McMahon, 1981)

Parent Record Sheet (Forehand & McMahon, 1981)

Piers-Harris Children's Self-Concept Scale (Piers, 1984)

Preschool Interpersonal Problem Solving Test (Shure & Spivack, 1974)

Problem Behavior Identification Checklist (Mash & Terdal, 1989)

Problem-Solving Measure for Conflict (Lochman & Lampron, 1986)

Scale for Suicide Ideation (Freeman, Pretzer, Fleming, & Simon, 1990)

Self-Concept Scale for Children (Lipsitt, 1958)

Sexual Attitude Scale (Hudson, 1990)

Social Anxiety and Distress Scale (Watson & Friend, 1969)

Wechsler Intelligence Scale for Children—Revised (WISC-R) (Wechsler, 1974)

Wechsler Preschool and Primary Scale of Intelligence (WPPSI) (Wechsler, 1974)

Young Children's Social Desirability Scale (Ford & Rubin, 1970)

Structured Interviews

Child Assessment Schedule (Hodges, Kline, Stern, Cytryn, & McKnew, 1982)

Diagnostic Interview for Children and Adolescents (Herjanic & Campbell, 1977; Reich, Herjanic, Welner, & Gandhy, 1982)

Disability Assessment Schedule (Holmes, Shah, & Wing, 1982)

First Interview: Family Therapy (Bryant, 1984)

Interpersonal Negotiation Strategies (Selman, Beardslee, Schultz, Krupa, & Podorefsky, 1986)

Review of Five Interview Formats (Paget, 1984)

Structured Interview for Adolescents. (Mathews & Jennings, 1984)

Other Sources, Reviews, and Listings of Assessment Devices

Assessment Strategies for Cognitive and Behavioral Interventions: Bierman & Schwartz, 1986; Cone & Hawkins, 1977; Haynes & Wilson, 1979; Keefe, Kopel, & Gordon, 1978; Kendall, & Hollon, 1981; Mash & Terdal, 1988; Merluzzi, Glass, & Genest, 1981)

Assessment/Treatment Strategies for a Variety of Cognitions (Persons, 1989)

Behavior Analysis Forms (Cautela, 1979, 1981; Cautela, Cautela, & Esonis, 1983; Corcoran & Fisher, 1987)

A Detailed Guide for Developing a Treatment Program (Kozloff, 1979)

Review of Irrationality Scales (Sutton-Simon 1981)

REFERENCES

Achenbach, T. M., & Edelbrock, L. (1983). *Manual for the Child Behavior Checklist and revised child behavior profile.* Burlington, VA: Queen City Printers.

Anderson, J. (1981). *Thinking, changing, rearranging.* Eugene, OR: Timberline Press.

Arnkoff, D. B., & Glass, C. R. (1982). Clinical cognition constructs: Examination, evaluation and elaboration. In P. C. Kendall (Ed.), *Advances in cognitive-behavioral research and therapy.* New York: Academic Press.

Asher, D. R., Hymel, S., & Renshaw, P. D. (1984). Loneliness in children. *Child Development, 55,* 1457–1464.

Bandura, A. (1977a). Self-efficacy: Toward a unifying theory of behavior change. *Psychological Review, 84,* 191–215.

Bandura, A. (1977b). *Social learning theory.* Englewood Cliffs, NJ: Prentice-Hall.

Barkley, R. A. (1981). *Hyperactive children: A handbook of diagnosis and treatment.* New York: Guilford Press.

Barkley, R. A. (1987). *Defiant children: A clinician's manual for parent training.* New York: Guilford Press.

Beck, A. T. (1967). *The Beck Depression Inventory.* San Antonio: Psychological Corp.

Beck, A. T. (1976). *Cognitive therapy and the emotional disorders.* New York: International Universities Press.

Becker, W. (1986). *Applied psychology for teachers: A behavioral cognitive approach.* Chicago: Science Research Associates.

Becker, W., & Engelmann, S. (1978). Systems for basic instruction: Theory and application. In A. C. Catania & T. A. Brigham (Eds.), *Handbook of applied behavior analysis.* New York: Irvington.

Bernard, M. E., & Joyce, M. R. (1984). *Rational-emotive therapy with children and adolescents:*

Theory, treatment strategies, preventative methods. New York: Wiley.

Bierman, K. L., & Schwartz, L. A. (1986). Clinical child interviews: Approaches and developmental considerations. *Journal of Child and Adolescent Psychotherapy, 3,* 267–278.

Bijou, S. W., & Baer, D. M. (1961a). *Child development: Vol. 1. A systematic and empirical theory.* Englewood Cliffs, NJ: Prentice-Hall.

Bijou, S. W., & Baer, D. M. (1961b). *Child development: Vol. 2. Universal stage of infancy.* Englewood Cliffs, NJ: Prentice-Hall.

Blondis, T. A., Accardo, P. J., & Snow, J. H. (1989). Measures of attention deficit: Questionnaires. *Clinical Pediatrics, 28,* 222–228.

Braswell, L., & Kendall, P. C. (1988). Cognitive-behavioral methods with children. In K. S. Dobson (Ed.), *Handbook of cognitive-behavioral therapies.* New York: Guilford Press.

Brigham, T. A. (1989). *Self-management for adolescents: A skills training program.* New York: Guilford Press.

Bryant, C. (1984). Working for families with dysfunctional children: An approach and structure for the first interview. *Child and Adolescent Social Work Journal, 1,* 102–117.

Cairns, E., & Cammock, T. (1978). Development of a more reliable version of Matching Familiar Figures Test. *Developmental Psychology, 5,* 555–560.

Camp, B. W., & Bash, M. A. (1981). *Think aloud.* Champaign, IL: Research Press.

Campbell, L. M. (1974). A variation of thought-stopping in a twelve-year-old boy: A case report. *Journal of Behavior Therapy and Experimental Psychiatry, 4,* 69–70.

Catania, A. C. (1975). The myth of self-reinforcement. *Behaviorism, 3,* 192–199.

Cautela, J. R. (1979). *Behavior analysis forms for clinical intervention* (Vol. 1). Champaign, IL: Research Press.

Cautela, J. R. (1981). *Behavior analysis forms for clinical intervention* (Vol. 2). Champaign, IL: Research Press.

Cautela, J. R., Cautela, J., & Esonis, S. (1983). *Forms for behavior analysis with children.* Champaign, IL: Research Press.

Cone, J. D., & Hawkins, R. P. (Eds.). (1977). *Behavioral assessment: New directions in clinical psychology.* New York: Brunner/Mazel.

Corcoran, K., & Fisher, J. (1987). *Measures for clinical practice: A source book.* New York: Free Press.

Costello, A. J. (1986). Assessment of affective disorders in children. *Journal of Child Psychology and Psychiatry and Allied Disciplines, 27,* 565–574.

Craighead, W. E. (1979). Self instructional training for assertive refusal behavior. *Behavior Therapy, 10,* 529–546.

Craighead, W. E., Meyers, A. W., & Craighead, L. W. (1985). A conceptual model for cognitive-behavior therapy with children. *Journal of Abnormal Child Psychology, 13*(3), 331–342.

Davis, M. H. (1983). Measuring individual differences in empathy: Evidence for a multidimensional approach. *Journal of Personality and Social Psychology, 44,* 113–126.

DiGiuseppe, R. (1989). Cognitive therapy with children. In A. Freeman, K. M. Simon, L. E. Beutler, & H. Arkowitz (Eds.), *Comprehensive handbook of cognitive therapy.* New York: Plenum.

DiGiuseppe, R., Miller, N., & Trexler, L. (1977). A review of rational-emotive psychotherapy outcome studies. *Counseling Psychologist, 7*(1), 64–72.

Dolgin, M. J., & Jay, S. M. (1989). Pain management in children. In E. J. Mash & R. A. Barkley (Eds.), *Treatment of childhood disorders.* New York: Guilford Press.

Donaldson, S. K., & Westerman, M. A. (1986). Development of children's understanding of ambivalence and causal theories of emotions. *Developmental Psychology, 22,* 655–662.

D'Zurilla, T. J., & Goldfried, M. R. (1971). Problem solving and behavior modification. *Journal of Abnormal Psychology, 78,* 107–126.

Edelbrock, C. S. (1986). The parent-child agreement on psychiatric symptoms assessed via a structured interview. *Journal of Child Psychology and Psychiatry and Allied Disciplines, 27,* 181–190.

Eland, J. M. (1982). Pain. In L. Hart, J. Reese, & M. Fearing (Eds.), *Concepts common to acute illness.* St. Louis: C. V. Mosby.

Ellis, A. (1962). *Reason and emotion in psychotherapy.* New York: Stuart.

Ellis, A. (1980). Rational-emotive therapy: Similarities and differences. *Cognitive Therapy and Research, 4,* 325–340.

Epstein, M. H. (1982). Special education programs for the handicapped adolescent. *School Psychology Review, 11,* 384–390.

Epstein, M. H., & Cullinan, D. (1979). Education of handicapped adolescents: An overview. In D. Cullinan & M. H. Epstein (Eds.), *Special education for adolescents: Issues and perspectives.* Columbus, OH: Merrill.

Fincham, F. D. (1983). Clinical applications of attribution theory: Problems and prospects. In M. Hewstone (Ed.), *Attribution theory: Social and functional extensions.* Oxford: Blackwells.

Fisher, R., & Ury, W. (1983). *Getting to yes: Negotiating agreement without giving in.* New York: Penguin.

Ford, L. H., & Rubin, B. M. (1970). A social desirability questionnaire for young children. *Journal of Consulting and Clinical Psychology, 35,* 195–204.

Forehand, R. L. (1986). Parental positive reinforcement with deviant children: Does it make a difference? *Child and Family Behavior Therapy, 8,* 15–21.

Forehand, R. L., & McMahon, R. J. (1981). *Helping the non-compliant child.* New York: Guilford Press.

Foster, S. L., & Robin, A. L. (1989). Parent-adolescent conflict. In E. J. Mash & R. A. Barkley (Eds.), *Treatment of childhood disorders.* New York: Guilford Press.

Franks, C. M. (1982). *Contemporary behavior therapy: Conceptual and empirical foundations.* New York: Guilford Press.

Franks, C. M. (1989). Review of D. H. Ruben & D. J. Delprato (Eds.), *New ideas in therapy: Introduction to an interdisciplinary approach. Child and Family Therapy, 11,* 79–81.

Franks, C. M. (1990). Behavior therapy with children and adolescents. In C. M. Franks, G. T. Wilson, P. C. Kendall, & J. B. Foreyt (Eds.), *Review of behavior therapy: Theory and practice.* New York: Guilford Press.

Franks, C. M., Wilson, G. T., Kendall, P. C., & Brownell, K. D. (Eds.). (1982). *Annual review of behavior therapy.* New York: Guilford Press.

Freeman, A., Pretzer, J., Fleming, B., & Simon, K. M. (1990). *Clinical applications of cognitive therapy.* New York: Plenum.

Gambrill, E. (1983). *Casework: A competency-based approach.* Englewood Cliffs, NJ: Prentice-Hall.

Garber J. (1984). The developmental progression of depression in female children. *New Directions for Child Development, 26,* 29–58.

Glass, C. R., & Arnkoff, D. B. (1982). Issues in cognitive assessment and therapy. In P. C. Kendall (Ed.), *Advances in cognitive-behavioral research and therapy.* New York: Academic Press.

Glass, C. R., Merluzzi, T. V., Biever, J. L., & Larsen, K. H. (1982). Cognitive assessment of social anxiety: Development and validation of self-statement questionnaire. *Cognitive Therapy and Research, 6,* 55–67.

Goldiamond, I. (1976). Self-reinforcement. *Journal of Applied Behavior Analysis, 9,* 509–514.

Grody, D. (1982). *Effects of cognitive strategies and cognitive levels of development on delay of gratification in children and adolescents.* Unpublished doctoral dissertation, Hofstra University.

Group for the Advancement of Psychiatry. (1968). *Normal adolescence.* New York: Scribner's.

Hare, B. R. (1985). *The Hare general and area-specific self-esteem scale.* Unpublished manuscript, State University of New York at Stony Brook, Department of Sociology.

Haynes, D. N., & Wilson, C. C. (1979). *Behavioral assessment.* San Francisco: Jossey-Bass.

Herjanic, B., & Campbell, W. (1977). Differentiating psychiatrically disturbed children on the basis of a structured interview. *Journal of Abnormal Child Psychology, 5,* 127–134.

Hersen, M. & Van Hasselt, V. B. (Eds.). (1987). *Behavior therapy with children and adolescents.* New York: Wiley.

Hodges, K., Kline, J., Stern, L., Cytryn, L., & McKnew, D. (1982). Child assessment schedule. *Journal of Abnormal Child Psychology, 10,* 173–189.

Hoffman L., Paris, S., Hall, E., & Schell, R. (1988). *Developmental psychology today.* New York: Random House.

Hollon, S. D., & Kendall, P. C. (1980). Cognitive self statements in depression: Development of an automatic thoughts questionnaire. *Cognitive Therapy and Research, 4,* 383–395.

Holmes, N., Shah, A., & Wing, L. (1982). The disability assessment schedule: A brief screening device for use with the mentally retarded. *Psychological Medicine, 12,* 879–890.

Hooper, S. R., & Layne, C. C. (1987). Common belief inventory for students: A measure of rationality in children. *Journal of Personality Assessment, 47,* 85–90.

Hudson, W. W. (1982). *The Clinical Measurement Package.* Homewood, IL: Dorsey Press.

Hudson, W. W. (1990). *The Walmyr assessment scales scoring manual.* Tempe, AZ: Walmyr Publishing Co.

Hughes, J. (1988). *Cognitive behavior therapy with children in schools.* New York: Pergamon Press.

Humphrey, L. L. (1982). Children's and teachers' perspectives on children's self-control: The development of two rating scales. *Journal of Consulting and Clinical Psychology, 50,* 624–633.

Jordan, C., & Franklin, C. (in press). *Clinical assessment for social workers.* Chicago: Lyceum.

Kagan, J., Rosman, B. L., Day, D., Albert, J., & Phillips, W. (1964). Information processing in the child: Significance of analytic and reflective attitudes. *Psychological Monographs, 78*(1), 1–37.

Kashani, J. H., Orvaschel, H., Burk, J. P., & Reid, J. C. (1985). Informant variance: The issue of parent-child disagreement. *Journal of the American Academy of Child Psychiatry, 24,* 437–441.

Kazdin, A. E., French, N. H., Unis, A. S., Esveldt-Dawson, K., & Sherick, R. B. (1983). Hopelessness, depression, and suicidal intent among psychiatrically disturbed inpatient children. *Journal of Consulting and Clinical Psychology, 51,* 504–510.

Kazdin, A. E., Rodgers, A., & Colbus, D. (1986). The Hopelessness Scale for Children: Psychometric characteristics and concurrent validity. *Journal of Consulting and Clinical Psychology, 54,* 241–245.

Keefe, F. J., Kopel, S. A., & Gordon, S. B. (1978). *A practical guide to behavioral assessment.* New York: Springer.

Kendall, P. C. (Ed.). (1982). *Advances in cognitive-behavioral research and therapy.* New York: Academic Press.

Kendall, P. C., & Braswell, L. (1982). Cognitive-behavioral self control therapy for children: A components analysis. *Journal of Consulting and Clinical Psychology, 44,* 852–857.

Kendall, P. C., & Braswell, L. (1985). *Cognitive-behavioral therapy for impulsive children.* New York: Guilford Press.

Kendall, P. C., & Hollon, S. D. (1981). Assessing self-referent speech: Methods in measurement of self-statements. In P. C. Kendall & S. D. Hollon (Eds.), *Assessment strategies for cognitive-behavioral interventions.* New York: Academic Press.

Kovacs, M. (1983). *Children's Depression Inventory.* Pittsburgh: University of Pittsburgh School of Medicine—Western Psychiatric Institute.

Kozloff, M. (1979). *A program for families of children with learning and behavioral problems.* New York: Wiley.

Lapouse, R., & Monk, M. A. (1959). Fears and worries in a representative sample of children. *American Journal of Orthopsychiatry, 29,* 803–818.

LeCroy, C. W., & Ashford, J. B. (1992). Children's mental health: Current findings and research. *Social Work Research and Abstracts, 28*(1), 13–20.

Leitenberg, H., Yost, L. W., & Carroll-Wilson, M. (1986). Negative cognitive errors in children: Questionnaire development, normative data, and comparisons between children with and without self-reported symptoms of depression, low self-esteem, and evaluation anxiety. *Journal of Consulting and Clinical Psychology, 54,* 528–536.

Lipsett, L. P. (1958). A self-concept scale for children and its relationship to the children's form of the Manifest Anxiety Scale. *Child Development, 29*(4), 463–472.

Lochman, J. E., & Lampron, L. B. (1986). Situational social problem-solving skills and self-esteem of aggressive and non aggressive boys. *Journal of Abnormal Child Psychology, 13,* 527–538.

Lutzker, J. R., & Rice, J. M. (1987). Using recidivism data to evaluate Project 12 Ways: An ecobehavioral approach to treatment and prevention of child abuse and neglect. *Journal of Family Violence, 2,* 283–290.

Mash, E. J., & Barkley, R. A. (Eds.). (1989). *Treatment of childhood disorders.* New York: Guilford Press.

Mash, E., & Terdal, L. (1988). *Behavioral assessment of childhood disorders* (2nd ed.). New York: Guilford Press.

Mathews, K. A., & Jennings, J. R. (1984). Cardiovascular response of boys exhibiting the type A behavior pattern. *Psychosomatic Medicine, 46,* 484–497.

Meador, A. E., & Ollendick, T. H. (1984). Cognitive-behavior therapy with children: An evaluation of its efficacy and clinical utility. *Child and Family Behavior Therapy, 6,* 25–44.

Mechanic, D. (1989). *Mental health and social policy* (4th ed.). Englewood Cliffs, NJ: Prentice-Hall.

Meichenbaum, D. H. (1977). *Cognitive-behavior modification.* New York: Plenum.

Meichenbaum, D., & Goodman, J. (1971). Training impulsive children to talk to themselves. *Journal of Abnormal Psychology, 77,* 115–126.

Melamed, B., & Siegel, L. (1975). Reduction of anxiety in children facing hospitalization and surgery by use of filmed modeling. *Journal of Consulting and Clinical Psychology, 43,* 511–521.

Merluzzi, T. V., Glass, C. R., & Genest, M. (Eds.). (1981). *Cognitive assessment.* New York: Guilford Press.

Nisbett, R. E., & Ross, L. (1980). *Human inference: Strategies and shortcomings of social judgment.* Englewood Cliffs, NJ: Prentice-Hall.

Olinger, E., & Epstein, M. H. (1991). The behavioral model and adolescents with behavior disorders: A review of selected treatment studies. In M. Hersen, R. Eisler, & P. Miller (Eds.), *Progress in behavior modification.* Newbury Park, CA: Sage.

Ollendick, T. H., & Cerny, J. A. (1981). *Clinical behavior therapy with children.* New York: Plenum.

Paget, K. D. (1984). The structured assessment interview: A psychometric review. *Journal of School Psychology, 22,* 415–427.

Patterson, G. R. (1982). *Coercive family process.* Eugene, OR: Castalia.

Persons, J. B. (1989). *Cognitive therapy in practice: A case formulation approach.* New York: Norton.

Persons, J. B. (1991). Psychotherapy outcome studies do not accurately represent current models of psychotherapy. *American Psychologist, 46,* 99–106.

Piaget, J. (1967). *Six psychological studies.* New York: Vantage Press.

Piaget, J. (1972). Intellectual evolution from adolescence to adulthood. *Human Development, 15,* 1–12.

Piers, E. V. (1984). *Piers-Harris Children's Self-Concept Scale—Revised manual.* Los Angeles: Western Psychological Services.

Pope, A. W., McHale, S. M., & Craighead, W. E. (1988). *Self-esteem enhancement with children and adolescents.* New York: Pergamon Press.

Reich, W., Herjanic, B., Welner, Z., & Gandhy, P. R. (1982). Development of a structured psychiatric interview for children: Agreement on diagnosis comparing child and parent interviews. *Journal of Abnormal Child Psychology, 10,* 325–336.

Robin, A. L., & Koepke, T. (1990). Behavioral assessment and treatment of parent-adolescent conflict. In M. Hersen, R. M. Eisler, & P. M. Miller (Eds.), *Progress in behavior modification* (Vol. 25). Orlando, FL: Academic Press.

Robin, A. L., Schneider, M., & Dolnick, M. (1976). The turtle technique: An extended case study of self-control in the classroom. *Psychology in the Schools, 13,* 449–453.

Robins, L. N. (1979). Follow-up studies of behavior disorders in children. In H. C. Quay & J. S. Werry (Eds.), *Psychopathological disorders of childhood* (2nd ed.). New York: Wiley.

Russell, D., Peplau, L. A., & Freeman, M. L. (1978). Developing a measure of loneliness. *Journal of Personality Assessment, 42,* 290–294.

Sarason, I. G., & Sarason, B. R. (1981). Teaching cognitive and social skills to high school students. *Journal of Consulting and Clinical Psychology, 49,* 908–918.

Schinke, S. P. (1984). Preventing teenage pregnancy. In M. Hersen, R. M. Eisler, & P. M. Miller (Eds.), *Progress in behavior modification* (Vol. 18). Orlando, FL: Academic Press.

Schinke, S. P., & Gilchrist, L. D. (1984). *Life Skills Counseling with adolescents.* Baltimore: University Park Press.

Schinke, S. P., Gilchrist, L. D., & Small, R. W. (1979). Preventing unwanted adolescent pregnancy: A cognitive-behavioral approach. *American Journal of Orthopsychiatry, 49,* 81–88.

Schug, M. C., & Birkey, C. J. (1985). The development of children's economic reasoning. *Theory and Research in Social Education, 13*(1), 31–49.

Schwartz, F., & Johnson, J. H. (1985). *Psychopathology of children.* New York: Pergamon Press.

Schwartz, R. M., & Gottman, J. M. (1976). Toward a task analysis of assertive behavior. *Journal of Consulting and Clinical Psychology, 44,* 910–920.

Selman, R. L. (1980). *The growth of interpersonal understanding: Developmental and clinical analysis.* New York: Academic Press.

Selman, R. L., Beardslee, W., Schultz, L. H., Krupa, M., & Podorefsky, D. (1986). Assessing adolescent interpersonal negotiation strategies: Toward the integration of structural and functional models. *Developmental Psychology, 22,* 450–459.

Shure, M. B., & Spivack, G. (1972). Means-ends thinking, adjustment and social class among elementary school-age children. *Journal of Consulting and Clinical Psychology, 38,* 348–353.

Shure, M. B., & Spivack, G. (1978). *Problem-solving techniques in child rearing.* San Francisco: Jossey-Bass.

Skinner, B. F. (1966). An operant analysis of problem solving. In B. Kleinmuntz (Ed.), *Problem solving: Research, method and theory.* New York: Wiley.

Spivack, G., Platt, J. J., & Shure, M. B. (1976). *The problem-solving approach to adjustment.* San Francisco: Jossey-Bass.

Spivack, G., & Shure, M. (1974). *Social adjustment of young children: A cognitive approach to solving real-life problems.* San Francisco: Jossey-Bass.

Stokes, T., & Baer, D. (1977). An implicit technology of generalization. *Journal of Applied Behavior Analysis, 10,* 349–358.

Sutton-Simon, K. (1981). Assessing belief systems concepts and strategies. In P. C. Kendall & S. D. Hollon (Eds.), *Assessment strategies for cognitive-behavioral interventions.* New York: Academic Press.

Tursky, B., & O'Connel, D. (1972). Reliability and interjudgement predictability of subjective judgements of electrocutaneous stimulation. *Psychophysiology, 9,* 290–295.

Tursky, B., & Sternbach, R. (1967). Further physiological correlates of ethnic differences in response to shock. *Psychophysiology, 4,* 67–74.

Tursky, B., & Watson, P. D. (1964). Controlled physical and subjective intensities of electric shock. *Psychophysiology 1,* 151–162.

Varni, J. W. (1981). Self-regulation techniques in the management of chronic arthritic pain in hemophilia. *Behavior Therapy, 12*(2), 185–194.

Varni, J. W., Bessman, C. A., Russo, D. C., & Cataldo, M. F. (1980). Behavioral management of chronic pain in children: Case study. *Archives of Physical Medicine and Rehabilitation, 61,* 375–379.

Vaughn, S. R., Ridley, C. A., & Bullock, D. D. (1984). Interpersonal problem-solving skills training for aggressive young children. *Journal of Applied Developmental Psychology, 5,* 213–223.

Wasserman, T. H. (1984). The effects of cognitive development on the use of cognitive-behavioral techniques with children. *Child and Family Behavior Therapy, 5,* 37–50.

Watson, K. W., & Friend, R. (1969). Measurement of social-evaluative anxiety. *Journal of Consulting and Clinical Psychology, 33,* 448–457.

Weatherhead, L. D. (1965). *The Christian agnostic.* Nashville, TN: Abingdon Press.

Webb, T. E., & VanDever, C. A. (1985). Sex differences in the expression of depression: A developmental interaction effect. *Sex Roles, 12,* 91–95.

Wechsler, D. (1974). *Manual for the Wechsler Intelligence Scale for Children—Revised.* New York: Psychological Corp.

Weisz, J. R., Weiss, B., Alicke, M. D., & Klotz, M. L. (1987). Effectiveness of psychotherapy with children and adolescents: A meta-analysis for clinicians. *Journal of Consulting and Clinical Psychology, 4,* 542–549.

Weithorn, L. A., & Campbell, S. B. (1982). The competency of children and adolescents to make informed treatment decisions. *Child Development, 53,* 1589–1598.

Zatz, S., & Chassin, L. (1983). Cognitions of test-anxious children. *Journal of Consulting and Clinical Psychology, 51,* 526–534.

Home-Based Behavioral Intervention with Children and Families

Vanessa G. Hodges

Behavioral intervention in the home has tremendous potential for effectively treating family crises, particularly when the problems relate to parent/child conflict. In some instances, progress is greater when home-based intervention is used than when residential or outpatient treatment is utilized (Mueller & Leviton, 1986; Sherman, Barker, Lorimer, Swinson, & Factor, 1988). Home-based behavioral technology has been successfully employed with a variety of target problems, including child maltreatment (Kowal et al., 1989), marital problems (Rabin, Rosenbaum, & Sens, 1982), child-behavior problems (Bunyan, 1987; Cipani, 1984; Fox & Savelle, 1987; Rowland, Taplin, & Holt, 1983; Sanders, 1982), child neglect (Lutzker, 1990), juvenile delinquency (Barton & Butts, 1990; Gordon, Arbuthnot, Gustafson, & Mc-Green, 1988), autism (Avery, DiPietro, & Glynnis, 1987), temper tantrums (Ralph, 1987), aggression (Frankel & Simmons, 1985), behavioral problems of developmentally disabled children (Mueller & Leviton, 1986), children with severe emotional problems (Heying, 1985), and disruptive school behavior (Leach & Ralph, 1986; Rosen, Gabardi, Miller, & Miller, 1990). Safe and effective use of behavioral techniques and methods in the home requires a thorough understanding of the theory and philosophy underlying home-based practice as well as a knowledge of fundamental behavioral principles. The home as the primary location for providing services to families has a long and rich history, particularly in the field of social work (Richmond, 1917). The influence of the ecological model in social work (Bronfenbrenner, 1979; Greene, 1991) supports practitioners using the home and natural environment for service delivery.

The first part of this chapter is devoted to a discussion of the importance of home-based intervention. Information is presented on the underlying value base, attitudes, and personal attributes that characterize well-rounded home-based practitioners. The next section highlights relationship development and assessment techniques in the home. The final section addresses home-based intervention techniques.

HOME-BASED PRACTICE: BASIC PRINCIPLES

Home-based practice is defined as that which uses the home environment as the primary location of service delivery (CASSP Technical Center, 1988). Interventions are designed to preserve and strengthen the family. These services for children and families have gained renewed popularity in recent years (Aaronson, 1989; Bryce & Lloyd, 1981; Maybanks & Bryce, 1979). Child-welfare reforms, permanency-planning movements, and enabling legislation have contributed to the increase of home-based programs for children. These services have been described variously in the literature as home visiting, family-centered practice, family-focused practice, family-based services, and family-preservation services. Although individual programs vary depending on the purpose of the service, level of intensity, public or private auspices, intervention modality, and duration of services, most of them share the following basic principles (Cole & Duva, 1990; Tracy, Haapala, Kinney, & Pecora, 1991; Whittaker, Kinney, Tracy, & Booth, 1990):

The Family Is the Unit of Service.
Home-based services involve the entire family as opposed to singling out any member as the "identified patient." Each family member is guided to examine his or her own unique contribution to the crisis, and consequently each member is involved in the solution.

Family composition and membership varies from culture to culture and subculture to subculture. Practitioners serving families of color are reminded that extended and fictive kin are important family members and therefore are included as part of the intervention (Gray & Nybell, 1990; Hodges, 1991; Hodges & Blythe, 1992; Turner & Jones, 1982).

The Focus Is on Family Empowerment.
Home-based practitioners strive to empower families. It is assumed that family members have the desire and power to change; they possess potential insight into their problems and the capacity to learn and apply skills to ameliorate them. The practitioner's role is to facilitate, offer resources, advocate, and teach skills that aid families in resolving their problems. Practitioners try to draw heavily on the individual and collective efforts of family members in making change through hard work and perseverance.

Families Are Partners in the Change Process.
Family members are enlisted as partners in the change process. Partnership implies equality. Family members are equal partners in planning and implementing change. Goals and intervention plans are collaboratively negotiated. Parents, as equal partners, have the right to reject plans that are the sole agenda of the practitioner. Families know when they are in trouble, and they generally know the desired outcomes. The practitioner serves as a resource, teacher, and enabler to help the family reach their objectives. Practitioners make a focused effort to reduce the difference in status that often exists between helper and client.

Home-Based Practitioners Serve Families Holistically.
Home-based practitioners help families in meeting their basic needs, learning new skills, and resolving interpersonal conflict. They also refer families to other social, financial, and health services to maintain and improve functioning in those areas.

Child Safety Is First.
Child protection is the most important goal in child welfare programs. Home-based practitioners strive to preserve and strengthen families so that children are able to remain with them in a safe environment. As a result of the frequency of contact with the family and the length of time spent in the home, practitioners are in an excellent position to monitor safety issues while working with the family to develop a stable environment for the child.

Children Should Be Reared by Their Own Families.
Families are not perfect, yet home-based practitioners believe that the family is the best place to rear a child. Out-of-home placement severely disrupts family functioning. If removed, children may not clearly understand why, may suffer uncertainty and its corresponding emotions, and may feel responsible for the removal. While the child is out of the home, families rarely receive the intensity of treatment needed to resolve the crisis that precipitated the placement. Children may be returned to a home situation where little change has taken place

since their removal. Gains they have made may be quickly lost when the dynamics of the family remain unchanged. With home-based services, families remain together and work toward resolving the crisis *together*. The responsibility for change lies within the entire family rather than with any one member.

Practitioners Are Responsible for Offering Hope to Families.   Families oppressed by poverty, family violence, racism, or other discrimination typically feel overwhelmed, frustrated, and hopeless with regard to change. Practitioners offer the hope that life experiences can be different and that families can be instrumental in the change process. Practitioners help motivate families by facilitating change.

Home-Based Services Offer Environmental Advantages.   Home-based practitioners intervene where problems are most likely to occur. Services are provided on the client's turf, and the practitioner promotes change within the context of house rules and norms of the family. Parents and children practice new behaviors in the natural environment in which they occur. Simple environmental modifications are easily assessed and altered to improve the success of the intervention. Practitioners have an opportunity to observe the natural environment and to conduct assessments and interventions that include altering behaviors as well as environmental obstacles. They can observe parental interaction, model appropriate behavior, and coach parents as they attempt to implement new interventions.

HOME-BASED
PRACTICE TECHNIQUES

Practicing in the natural environment requires skills and knowledge beyond the application of theory, techniques, and methods. In fact,

home-based practitioners are often challenged to engage involuntary families (Balgopal, Patchner, & Henderson, 1988) or isolated families (Dudzinski & Peters, 1977; Hodges & Blythe, 1992). The relationship between the home-based practitioner and the family is critical to a successful outcome (Halpern, 1986). Practitioners need to develop relationships with families in the midst of a crisis, often in a limited amount of time. Therefore, they must be skilled at developing these relationships quickly and communicating to the family the value of participating in treatment. This section offers guidelines and outlines steps in the family-engagement process. It also describes the conducting of a comprehensive assessment of problems and strengths in the home.

Developing a Positive
Working Relationship with the Family

The therapeutic relationship begins with the practitioner's first contact with the family. Often, this initial contact is over the telephone. Although the primary purpose of the call is to set up the initial appointment, many families are in the midst of the crisis and are angry, hurt, pressured, or irritable, to name a few of the range of emotions. Therapists in the Homebuilders program, a pioneering home-based treatment program, encourage family members to express their feelings during the telephone conversation (Kinney, Haapala, & Booth, 1991). This allows the practitioner an opportunity to get more information about the situation; it gives the family member a chance to vent feelings and frustration and lays the groundwork for a positive relationship. At Homebuilders, it is not unusual to talk to several family members during this initial phone contact or to talk for more than an hour (Kinney et al., 1991).

It is wise to spend an extended period with the family on the initial home visit. This time allows the practitioner to accomplish a number of goals, including explaining the service and the practitioner's role, clarifying expectations, and completing agency releases and paperwork (CASSP Technical Center, 1988). It also gives the family members an opportunity to get to know the practitioner and to define problems from their perspective. The extra time gives the practitioner an opportunity to begin a comprehensive assessment of family history, current dynamics, motivation to participate in counseling, and strengths and limitations in family functioning.

Be willing to listen without judging or rationalizing a family's dilemma. Active listening can be the practitioner's greatest tool during the initial engagement period. Active listening involves an intense concentration on what is being shared by the client and then a reflection of meaning and feeling back to the client (Ivey, 1983). This simple but important interviewing skill acknowledges that you are hearing what the client is telling and experiencing. Active listening also encourages clients to continue to share their perspective on the problem without feeling constrained by a lot of structured questions.

Use the initial home session to make informal observations about the home, neighborhood, and community (Hodges & Blythe, 1992; Woods, 1988). For example, during the initial visit the practitioner has the opportunity to observe and develop an awareness of family norms and rules. The family and practitioner will bond more quickly if the practitioner is respectful of these norms during following visits. A drive through the neighborhood can give insight into safety issues; the availability of mass transportation; retail, public, and social services; schools; and recreational facilities.

Finally, in keeping with the empowerment perspective, practitioners can use the initial session to identify clients' strengths. It will be important to incorporate these strengths into the intervention plan. Highlighting family limitations and weaknesses does little to offer encouragement and hope. However, building on strengths gives families pride, dignity, and a level of confidence in their capacity to change. It offers family members hope that they can build from the strengths rather than suffer sustained dysfunction and deterioration.

The Home-Based Behavioral Assessment Process

Using behavioral techniques in the home is dependent on conducting a comprehensive assessment. Because home-based practitioners serve families holistically, it is important to identify family strengths and resources, as mentioned above, as well as those concerns that are amenable to change through specific behavioral intervention and those that are best addressed through other types of intervention such as advocacy, referral, or mediation.

The first task in home-based assessment is to develop and prioritize the problem inventory. For the target behaviors that are amenable to behavioral intervention, practitioners also need to operationally define the target behavior, develop an ABC matrix, develop goals and contracts, and collect baseline data. The home-based practitioner should also develop assessment and intervention plans to meet other needs identified in the problem inventory. For purposes of this chapter, however, examples will focus on planning, developing, and using behavioral assessment and interventions.

Developing a Problem Inventory.   After actively listening to the family members share their perspective on the problem, the home-based practitioner is ready to begin the assessment process by developing a problem inventory. The inventory is a comprehensive list of the concerns the family is experiencing. The list is developed from data gathered during pretreatment observations and interviews. The problem inventory for the Johnson family lists issues that the members believe cause, maintain, or contribute to their problems:

Problem Inventory for Johnson Family

1. Sandra and Tina are fighting.
2. Reggie is flunking out of high school.
3. Mom is drinking on weekends.
4. Reggie is disobeying his mother and not being respectful.
5. Housing is inadequate.
6. Sandra has asthma.
7. Reggie has gang "wannabe" friends.
8. Mom is losing her job.

It is also important for the practitioner and the family to represent the concerns of referring agencies in the problem inventory. This is particularly significant when Child Protective Services (CPS) is involved. Problem inventories are enhanced by encouraging family members to be specific and provide concrete examples of each item on the inventory.

Setting priorities for intervention is an essential step in breaking the assessment process into manageable parts. The home-based practitioner guides the family in determining the most important item on the problem inventory. Families generally identify items that are the most troublesome or painful for family members or concerns raised by the referring agency that, if not resolved, would result in a negative consequence—for example, placement in foster care or loss of funding or services for one member or the entire family. For example, the Johnson family decided that learning to play cooperatively was the most important inventory item because Sandra, age 12, and Tina, age 10, were "constantly" fighting. The arguing, bickering, and fighting were a source of irritation and aggravation for Mom. In addition, Mrs. Johnson was more likely to be physically abusive when she was tense, upset, or irritated by the girls' fighting.

Defining Target Behaviors.   After the home-based practitioner and family have selected a limited number of inventory items as the focus of change, the practitioner then assists the family in defining the desired outcome behavior. Defining target behaviors is probably one of the most difficult tasks for family members. Descriptions must be specific, vivid, and couched in language that family members understand. When identifying problem behaviors, it is helpful for family members to give examples. Practitioners can help families find appropriate words to describe behaviors, particularly when they have observed the behavior during a home session.

Developing an ABC Matrix.   In addition to defining the target behavior, it is helpful to develop an ABC (antecedents/behavior/consequences) matrix. This matrix puts the target behavior into a context. Antecedents are events, people, places, language, or objects that precede, signal, or trigger the target behavior. Consequences are reinforcing events that follow the behavior and serve to maintain or strengthen it and increase the chances that it will occur again (Sundel & Sundel, 1982). Identifying the antecedents and consequences of behaviors is highly important, because it expands the nature of the intervention. The focus is not merely on the targeted problem behavior. The intervention may be focused on altering antecedents or modifying consequences in addition to changing specific problem behaviors. In the following example, the Johnson family is assisted in developing an ABC matrix around Sandra and Tina's fighting:

ABC Matrix for Sandra and Tina's Fighting

A. *Antecedents*
   1. Mom asks Sandra to play with Tina while she relaxes.
   2. Sandra finds Tina and tells her that Mom wants them to play.
   3. Sandra forces Tina to play "doctor"; Sandra is usually the doctor, and Tina generally plays the patient.

4. Sandra starts yelling if Tina refuses to play doctor or wants to play a different game.
5. Sandra begins to whine and runs to tell her mother.
6. Mom tells Sandra: "Get out of here. I'm tired and I want to relax."
7. Sandra returns to Tina and begins to yell and call Tina names.
8. Tina begins to cry.
9. Sandra tells her to shut up and continues to call her names.

B. *Behavior*
1. Tina begins the fight by hitting Sandra. Her eyes are closed and her arms are flailing. She is not landing very many hits.
2. Sandra hits her back, laughs at her, and calls her names.
3. Tina begins to cry and flails her arms even faster. She lands more hits but still not very hard.
4. Sandra continues to hit Tina with more deliberate and harder blows. She continues to call Tina names but stops laughing at her.
5. Tina runs off to tell her mother.

C. *Consequences*
1. Mom yells at the girls: "Please stop! I'm trying to relax."
2. Mom becomes angry when the girls disrupt her rest time. She goes to them and begins to spank with a ruler, stick, brush, or her bare hands.

With the Johnson family, the practitioner and family have several intervention points to consider in altering the target behavior. For example, if the family members decided they wanted to intervene in the antecedents, Sandra and Tina could learn to alternate selecting a game when they were asked to play. To intervene in the behavior portion of the matrix, the girls could be taught how to play cooperatively. To intervene in the consequences, Mom might be instructed in alternative ways

of disciplining Sandra and Tina when they began to fight.

Developing Goals and Contracts.   Once the target behavior has been operationally defined, the family is ready to begin setting goals. These goals and objectives will be used to measure the progress of the intervention. Goal setting has a number of components that guide the process. First, goals should be stated in measurable terms (increase, decrease, acquire, extinguish, maintain, display). These measures will be used to determine change in relation to targeted outcomes. Whenever possible, goals should be stated in positive terms. For example, rather than to decrease the number of tantrums, the goal might be to teach Sandra and Tina to share, or to teach them alternative ways of disagreeing. Both these goals would eventually serve to decrease the tantrums, but in the latter example, Sandra and Tina would learn new behaviors to aid them when they played together as well as when they interacted with others.

One helpful approach in goal setting is developing a contract. The contract is an explicit agreement between the family and the practitioner regarding the goals of intervention, the tasks involved in achieving them, the person(s) responsible for respective tasks or implementation steps, the ultimate outcome or criteria for determining accomplishment of the goals, timelines, and a consent statement (Goodyear & Bradley, 1980). Contracts can be written or verbal. Written contracts are preferable, and they are particularly helpful because they are constant and visible reminders of the intervention goals. Practitioners may recommend that families post the contract on the refrigerator door or alternate space where it can be easily seen or read. It should be noted that contracts, as well as assessment in general, should be constantly reviewed and updated. As family needs and situations change, the priority or necessity of certain goals may likewise

FIGURE 4.1   Contingency Contract for Sandra Johnson

March 9, 1992

Purpose: This is a contract between Sandra, Mrs. Johnson, and Ms. Robinson (a child-welfare worker) to specify Sandra's responsibilities. It is in effect Monday morning through Friday evening.

Mrs. Johnson will give Sandra 25 cents each time she completes one of her daily responsibilities:

1. She will come to the kitchen dressed and ready for breakfast by 7:15 A.M.
2. She will clear the dinner table and wash, dry, and put away the dishes.
3. She will help Tina with her bath and read her one story at bedtime.
4. She will read at least 25 pages herself. Sandra can select the book but must finish it before she begins a new one.

Sandra will receive a bonus of $1 on Saturday morning if she completes all of her responsibilities for five consecutive days.

Sandra will lose telephone privileges for one day if she fails or refuses to complete one or more of her responsibilities.

_____   _____

Sandra Johnson   *Mrs. Johnson*

_____

Ms. Robinson

---

change. A regular review and renegotiation of the contract promotes the appropriate focus of family members on the designated goals of change.

Families might also opt to develop a contingency contract. A contingency contract is an agreement that explicates the bonuses for performing the desired behaviors and the consequences or sanctions for failing to perform the behavior (Framer & Sanders, 1980; Stuart, 1971). Contingency contracts stipulate what the client expects to gain, the target behavior, the consequences for failing to meet the terms of the contract, bonuses for meeting or exceeding the agreed-upon terms, and a system for monitoring the rewards and consequences (Stuart, 1971). Contingency

contracts are especially helpful with young children and adolescents (Framer & Sanders, 1980) who can be highly motivated to earn rewards for meeting the terms of the contract. Figure 4.1 shows a sample contract for Sandra.

Obtaining Baseline Data.   The next step in home-based behavioral assessment is obtaining a baseline, or a standard for measuring the existence, frequency, intensity, and duration of target behaviors. Baseline data serve as the benchmark against which progress is measured. For example, do Sandra and Tina already know alternative ways of resolving disagreements that don't result in fights and tantrums (existence of alternative behavior)?

How often do Sandra and Tina fight (frequency)? How long do the fights last (duration)? How loud do the girls yell, or how hard do they hit when they begin to fight (intensity)? The type of data collected will depend on the behavior that is being measured. Baseline data can be collected through a number of different resources, including interviews, direct observation, checklists and questionnaires, rating scales, clients' logs, permanent agency records, verbal reports from significant others, and physiological measures. Families have choices when collecting data. It is important that practitioners provide them with several available alternatives and allow them to select the method considered to be the most appropriate. Various methods have advantages and disadvantages depending on the nature of the problem, the intervention focus, the capabilities of family members, and other factors. Practitioners can aid the decision-making process by providing insight into the advantages or disadvantages of various options. In addition, they can provide information to families on how often and how long data should be collected depending on the measurement approach. When possible, it is highly advisable to use multiple measurement methods (Bloom & Fischer, 1982). Multiple measures provide practitioners with more confidence in the effectiveness of their intervention measurements and may detect change in other aspects of functioning. This latter effect is significant in that behavior change can be multidimensional. A change in one specific targeted behavior may result in changes in associated behaviors and capabilities. This "ripple effect" may be detectable through the use of more comprehensive outcome measures. For example, Sandra might begin to share and play more cooperatively with Tina at home and display more cooperative behavior at school as well.

Obtaining an accurate measure of the target behavior is a crucial step in behavioral assessment. Two cautions are especially important when collecting measures in the home.

The first caution is that after the practitioner has provided information and consultation on the range of data-collection strategies, the family may not select the method or methods the practitioner considers to be the best. It is important to remember that family members must consider their own needs and habits. If they are responsible for selecting the data-collection method, it may increase the likelihood that they will collect the information accurately and consistently. Directing the family to choose a procedure that appears more accurate but is, in fact, more time consuming or tedious might result in ineffective data collection.

Second, behaviors that are self-injurious or dangerous to others should *not* be allowed to continue simply in order to collect baseline data. In such instances, the practitioner should intervene immediately and measure change on the basis of retrospective baseline. Another instance when baseline data are not needed is when a behavior does not yet exist in a client's repertoire of skills. For example, if a child does not possess the skills for making her bed, recording data over a two-week period on the frequency that she makes her bed will not yield useful information. Data on the existence of a skill can be obtained by observing the family member or interviewing a caregiver who is familiar with the child and able to give accurate information.

Identifying Reinforcers. Before implementing the intervention plan, it is critical for practitioners and family members to identify activities, tangible items (food, toys), and social gestures (praise, smiles, touch) that can be used as reinforcers for each member participating in an intervention program. One of the basic underpinnings of behavioral theory is the view that individuals are motivated to change behaviors based on reinforcing consequences or on avoidance of punishing or aversive consequences. Therefore, it is important that the practitioner and family members spend time identifying reinforcers. Parents are generally readily aware of the items and privileges that are reinforcing to their children. Food such as candy, fruit, ice cream, or cookies may be appropriate choices, depending on specific client characteristics (for example, candy would be inappropriate for a diabetic child). Activities such as having the parent's undivided attention, getting to hear a story read, or playing sports or board games are additional reinforcers. Finally, social gestures such as praise, hugs, and touching are also good reinforcers. It is imperative that reinforcers be individualized to maximize effectiveness. What is reinforcing to one individual may not be reinforcing to another. Similarly, what is punishing to one person may not be punishing or as strongly punishing to another.

BEHAVIORAL INTERVENTION

Once baseline data have been collected, the family and the home-based practitioner are ready to develop the intervention plan. The intervention plan includes specific techniques for altering target behaviors and achieving client goals. Social learning theory (Bandura, 1977) offers several tools, which are broadly categorized as interventions for increasing behaviors, interventions for decreasing behaviors, and interventions for developing new behaviors. They include such techniques as reinforcement, punishment, extinction, modeling, and shaping. Definitions and examples of techniques in each of these major categories are discussed below.

Interventions for Increasing Behaviors

Positive and negative reinforcement are two procedures utilized for increasing target behaviors. These procedures are based on the principles of reinforcement, which assert that the frequency of a target behavior will increase if the desired response is followed immediately by the presentation or removal of certain consequences. In positive reinforcement, rewards are delivered immediately after the display of the desired response is performed (Kazdin, 1989). Both positive and negative reinforcement assume that the client possesses the active skills necessary to perform the desired behavior(s). The assumption is that the individual has the capacity to behave appropriately but is failing to do so.

Positive Reinforcement. The primary technique for increasing target behaviors is implemented by delivering a reward after the display of the desired target behavior. The reward increases the likelihood that the target behavior will be displayed again. We have many examples of positive reinforcement in everyday life. Employees receive raises as rewards for hard work at the job. A smile or hello is the response to your greeting to a neighbor or friend. The smile or good word is your reward for speaking and increases the likelihood that you will speak again. This same principle of rewarding the target behavior immediately after it is displayed can be applied to increase behaviors in the home. For example, praising a child immediately after she picks up her toys will increase the likelihood that she will pick them up the next time she plays with them. It is imperative that the practitioner make a determination whether a given reward is actually reinforcing. It has been found in controlled studies of human behavior that rewards given immediately after a desired behavior has been displayed are stronger than rewards following a time lapse. The individual makes a stronger association between the behavioral performance and the reward if the reward follows the behavior immediately.

Negative Reinforcement. Though seldom used, negative reinforcement is also designed to increase a target behavior. It involves removing an aversive consequence following the display of the target behavior. For example, a mother nags her teenage son for leaving the bathroom a mess after he showers. The teenager begins to tidy the bathroom after every shower. Mom stops nagging. In this example, the target behavior is cleaning the bathroom after showering. The aversive consequence is the mother's nagging. The mother removes the negative reinforcer (nagging) when the son leaves the bathroom tidy. The son is motivated to leave the bathroom clean to avoid his mother's nagging, and this motivation will increase the frequency of his leaving the bathroom tidy. It is important to remember that negative reinforcement is different from punishment. In negative reinforcement, when an individual displays compliance with desired expectations, the aversive consequence that was displayed when there was noncompliance is withheld. The result is an increase in the likelihood that the target behavior will occur. In punishment, an aversive consequence is delivered following the display of an undesirable behavior. The aversive consequence, if meaningful to the individual, will decrease the likelihood that the undesirable behavior will occur.

Interventions for Decreasing Behaviors

Interventions that decrease the frequency of the target behavior are based on the principles of punishment. Target behaviors are reduced when an aversive stimulus is presented (verbal reprimand), the client is removed from a positive event (time-out), or extra effort is required following the display of the target behavior (overcorrection) (Kazdin, 1989).

Although interventions based on punishment can rapidly decrease the target behavior, home-based practitioners should use great caution when utilizing these interventions. Intervention utilizing punishment is appropriate when a family member's behavior is dangerous to the person or other family members. However, interventions based on punishment have the potential for producing undesirable negative side effects. These effects include emotional reactions such as crying or increased anger, and an increase in the likelihood that the punished child will react aggressively toward the person delivering the punishment. Furthermore, using punishing interventions in isolation does little to teach the client appropriate responses. When interventions are chosen based on punishment, therefore, they should be paired with interventions that reinforce positive behaviors that are incompatible with the punished response.

Overcorrection. Another intervention involves having a child overcompensate for displaying a maladaptive behavior by returning the environment to a condition better than it was before the behavior was displayed (Carey & Bucher, 1986). If a child throws toys during a temper tantrum, for example, overcorrection requires that the child not only return all the toys to their original places but also clean the entire room: make the beds, fold and hang clothes, and dust and sweep. The overcorrection procedure involves two components, restitution and positive practice. Restitution refers to reversing the results of the target behavior. In the above example, the restitution component would involve having the child return all the toys to the toy box. Positive practice, the second component of overcorrection, consists of practicing the appropriate behavior repeatedly. In this case, positive practice would require the child to clean the entire room. The primary objective in overcorrection is to make the consequences of displaying the negative behavior aversive enough that the child will avoid displaying the behavior. Overcorrection is a viable alternative to punishment because it also involves teaching the child new skills (Carey & Bucher, 1986). One of the major limitations to overcorrection is that the family member enforcing the consequence must remain with the child during the procedure. Parents supervising the overcorrection procedure can use that opportunity to model and coach correct behavior and provide positive feedback on the quality of the child's performance.

Extinction.   Another approach for decreasing behaviors involves removing all reinforcement when the maladaptive behavior is displayed. Many troublesome behaviors in children are reinforced, or maintained, because they receive attention from parents or adults, often inadvertent. Extinction is achieved by ignoring the target behavior. It is an alternative to punishment and gradually reduces or eliminates a target behavior. It can be used when the reinforcer is easily identified and can be withdrawn. For example, a child who gets his parents' attention each time he interrupts their conversation will continue to do so as long as he is being rewarded (with parents' attention) for his interruptions.

Extinction is extremely effective, particularly when it is paired with positive reinforcers for behaviors that are inconsistent with the targeted negative behavior. However, extinction should not be used when the target behavior is dangerous to the child or to others, because behavioral change is gradual using this technique. Furthermore, children tend to have extinction bursts—or increases in the frequency or intensity of the target behavior—when the extinction procedure is initiated. Basically, some children cannot believe that their parents are really ignoring them and believe that if they display the target behavior more frequently or with more intensity, their parents will give in. It is extremely difficult for some parents to ignore the targeted behavior when it is irritating or embarrassing. For example, Sandra's mother may have a goal of extinguishing her tantrum behavior. If she decides to use extinction, she will need to ignore the behavior each time it occurs. Initially, Sandra's tantrums can be expected to get worse. They may come more often, may be more intense, or may last longer.

Sandra's mother, as well as other members of the family, will need to ignore her tantrums each time they occur. This might present problems if the tantrums take place in public places such as a store, church, or playground. Also, if the tantrum includes screaming and kicking, the behaviors may be too destructive to ignore.

Home-based practitioners considering extinction as an intervention will want to raise some important points with family members. First, extinction is a difficult procedure to implement because change is slow. Parents must be prepared to ignore the behavior each time it occurs, because attending to the behavior periodically will strengthen it rather than having the intended effect of eliminating the behavior. Parents will need to ensure that all of the important figures in the child's life also agree to this intervention. The target behavior will not cease if one parent ignores the behavior while a grandparent or child-care provider attends to it. Second, family members need to be aware of the initial increase of the target behavior and resist the temptation to react. The effect of intermittent reinforcement will actually cause the behavior to be stronger than if the parent had continuously reacted.

Differential Reinforcement of Other Behavior (DRO).   Another alternative to punishment involves a combination of positive reinforcement and extinction. Desirable or appropriate behaviors are reinforced, and undesirable target behaviors are ignored. The practitioner and parent first decide on the behavioral goal—for example, putting toys away. Any behaviors that the child engages in related to getting toys from the floor to the toy box are reinforced. Conversely, any behaviors that are not related to putting toys away are ignored. The child soon learns to discriminate that she is reinforced when targeted behaviors are displayed and ignored when they are not. Practitioners and parents must clearly articulate the targeted behavior goal and communicate this goal to the child.

Time-Out (TO).   A popular procedure based on the principles of punishment, time-out involves physically removing children from the source of reinforcement and placing them in a quiet area where they remain for a specified period. While being placed in time-out, the child is typically given a very brief explanation, such as "You threw a toy at your sister, so you must go to time-out." The child is essentially removed, or "timed-out," from the reinforcement. This quiet time is intended to help children calm down so that they can return to the activity and continue participation. Time-out is frequently used in a school or group-care setting and, as a result of the increased number of parent-training programs, is also being used in the home. In addition to identifying maladaptive behaviors that qualify for time-out, parents and practitioners must also identify and prepare a space where the child can be placed during time-out. This space should be free of alternate forms of stimulation. For example, children could be placed at the end of a hallway, under a stairwell, or in another area of the home relatively free of external stimulation. Because time-out is based on removing children from reinforcement, it would be unwise to place them in front of a television set, in a room full of toys, in front of a window, or in a place that affords them access to other reinforcers.

Time-out procedures can be highly effective in rather rapidly reducing maladaptive behavior. However, it is important for the parent or home-based practitioner to be consistent in the delivery of time-out. This requires a clear identification of behaviors that would qualify for time-out and an explanation of the behaviors and the procedure to the child. It is also important to decide on the number of minutes the child will remain in time-out. Research has demonstrated that brief periods (1 to 5 minutes) work as well as longer periods (20 to 30 minutes) (Kazdin,

1989). The briefer period appears to be less punitive. A kitchen timer near the time-out site helps to ensure that the child does not remain in time-out beyond the designated period.

Response Cost.   Another procedure that can be used to reduce maladaptive behavior, response cost, involves the removal of a reward or reinforcer for displaying maladaptive behaviors. Examples include removing car keys from a teenager who arrives home late or removing telephone privileges from adolescents for talking back to their parents. When using response cost, it is important that the target behavior be well specified and that reinforcers be present and therefore available for removal. Additionally, it is important to determine the reinforcement value of the privilege or reward. For example, a home-based practitioner and parent may decide to remove television-watching privileges from a child for failing to complete his homework. If the child maintains an indifferent attitude about watching television, the removal of TV watching as a privilege will probably be ineffective in influencing the targeted undesirable behavior. It is important to remember that the reinforcer must be potent to the child and must be available for removal.

Interventions for Developing New Behaviors

Home-based practitioners often find that family members lack specific skills and are therefore unable to display desired adaptive behaviors. Modeling and shaping are two techniques that are helpful in developing new skills.

Modeling and Rehearsal.   New behaviors can be taught through demonstrating (modeling) the desired target behavior and having the client practice it. Learning through observation is an established and viable means of developing new skills (Bandura, 1977). Children already learn new behaviors vicariously by imitating the behavior of television characters, sports and movie stars, peers, parents, and siblings. Presumably, the new behavior is acquired through cognitive coding of the observed event and rehearsing, or practicing, the new behavior (Bandura, 1977). The use of modeling as an intervention captures some of the vicarious learning that is already occuring through observation and attempts to focus that learning on a specific behavior.

This method of teaching new behavior has four major components: providing clients with a rationale, providing modeling, guiding their rehearsal, and assigning homework (Bandura, 1969; Cormier & Cormier, 1990). The first component is providing the client with a rationale. The rationale should include the reasons why the behavior is important and an overview of the procedure (Kazdin & Krouse, 1983). The rationale establishes the purpose of the intervention and prompts the child to look for certain components in the model. The next step, modeling, involves a demonstration of the desired behavior. Models can be live (parents, siblings, counselor, teacher) or symbolic (videotapes, magazines, drawings). Clients are more likely to identify with models who possess similar characteristics in gender, age, ethnicity, and lifestyle (Rosenthal & Bandura, 1978). The third step is rehearsal, or practice. Rehearsal gives clients an opportunity to practice the behavior they have just observed in the model. Rehearsal, sometimes referred to as role playing, involves developing a scenario (situation and context) in which the client acts out the target behavior. Just before the rehearsal, it is helpful for the client to review the specific steps of the behavior. The practitioner can also serve as a coach during the rehearsal if the client becomes stuck or forgets the steps. The coach can give suggestions verbally or by using cues in the environment. If the client continues to have difficulty rehearsing the behavior, it might be necessary to go back to the previous

step and model the behavior again. An important part of practice is providing clients with feedback on their performance of the skill. Feedback helps them understand what parts of the procedure they did well and what parts need additional practice. It serves as a mechanism to improve their performance and mastery of the target behavior. The final step is homework, or transferring the learning to the natural environment. Clients are given specific assignments to practice the newly acquired skill in the natural setting. Following is an example that highlights the four components of learning new skills through modeling and rehearsal: providing a rationale, modeling, rehearsal, and feedback.

The home-based practitioner is working with Sandra and Tina on playing cooperatively and sharing. A common area of intense conflict between the sisters is watching television. Sandra usually enters the room and changes the channel despite the fact that Tina is watching another program. When the girls can't arrive at an agreement on the show to watch, they usually end up fighting. The practitioner could use modeling to teach them how to negotiate television viewing. The first step would be to identify the skill that is being taught (asking politely to change the TV channel) and to provide a rationale for why it is important. The next step would be to model the behavior. Because it is important that the model be as similar to the client as possible, it might be helpful to enlist a peer or child relative to model the behavior. The model would demonstrate how to ask to change the channel when another person is looking at a program. Sandra and Tina would be instructed to observe the model very carefully. After the demonstration, they would be encouraged to ask questions about the demonstration. Next, the practitioner would ask Sandra to "imagine that you just entered the living room and Tina is already there looking at a cartoon." If possible, they would continue their session in the living room to make the setting and context as realistic as possible. The practitioner would instruct Sandra to remember how the model negotiated the TV watching: "Practice how you would ask Tina if you could change the channel." If Sandra got stuck or forgot what she had observed, the practitioner could employ the coaching technique by reminding her of the steps. After the rehearsal, the practitioner would offer Sandra and Tina feedback on what aspects of the negotiation they had done well and what they could do to improve their performance. After providing feedback, the practitioner could go through the rehearsal and feedback again to reinforce the newly acquired skills or could assign a homework assignment that required them both to practice the new skills.

It should be noted that all modeling is not so systematic. Children constantly learn behaviors through observation. Some behaviors may be immediately displayed, and others may be "filed away" until later. Just as positive behaviors can be observed and learned through modeling, so can negative or inappropriate behaviors.

Shaping.   A shaping intervention to teach a new behavior is accomplished by positively rewarding small steps or approximations of the desired target behavior (Kazdin, 1989). For example, rather than requiring that a toddler be fully dressed before giving a compliment as a reinforcer, a parent would compliment her for putting one leg in her pants, because this is an important step in the sequence of actions needed to eventually be fully dressed. Shaping is employed when modeling or verbal instructions fail to teach the new behavior. To shape a behavior, the practitioner must first identify the desired behavior and then break it down into small, incremental steps. Initially, the parent reinforces any behavior that approximates the first step. Once the first step has been mastered, the reinforcers are delivered only for behaviors that approximate the second step. The practitioner proceeds through each of the respective steps until the family member reaches the desired

outcome. Shaping might be used to teach Sandra how to make her bed. The desired outcome is a bed with the sheets pulled to the top and the pillow tucked under. The incremental steps might include:

1. straightening the bottom sheet
2. pulling the top sheet to the top of the bed
3. straightening the top sheet
4. pulling the cover to the top of the bed
5. straightening the cover
6. folding the cover back one-third
7. placing the pillow at the top of the bed
8. tucking the top cover over the pillow

The treatment effort initially focuses on the task of straightening the bottom sheet. The practitioner or family member begins by reinforcing any behavior that approximates straightening the bottom sheet. After Sandra masters that step, she moves on to pulling the top sheet up to the top of the bed. She must master each intermediate step until she has reached the desired level of competency. It should be noted that verbal instruction and coaching or manual guidance may be required as each subsequent step is begun. They should be withdrawn when the family member begins to grasp the skills to complete the task independently.

CONCLUSION

Behavioral intervention can be effectively used in home-based practice with children and families if careful assessment and planning takes place. A number of interventions can be used to increase or decrease target behaviors as well as develop new behaviors. Perhaps the most exciting aspect of behavioral treatment is that intervention plans are individualized and are designed to meet the unique needs of family members. This chapter concludes with some general guidelines for developing intervention programs for home-based practice.

The most important guideline for parents and practitioners is to apply behavioral interventions consistently. *Consistency* is the key to learning and maintaining newly acquired behaviors. Parents who are lax in delivering consequences or rewards will find that the child's behavior does not change and, in fact, maladaptive behaviors may become more resistant to change. Family members need to understand that beginning a behavioral program requires dedication and commitment to consistency.

A second overarching principle is to develop plans and guidelines for generalizing the learning. *Generalization* refers to the utilization of skills, originally learned, rewarded, and practiced in one setting, to other similar settings. For example, Fellbaum, Daly, Forrest, and Holland (1985) studied the extent to which children transferred to the school skills to manage noncompliance, aggression, defiance, temper tantrums, and other problem behaviors originally learned through a behavioral program in the home. Although many behavioral programs fail to assess for maintenance of treatment following termination or generalizability (Keeley, Shemberg, & Carbonell, 1976), Fellbaum and colleagues found that teachers rated children participating in a home behavioral program as having significantly improved their acting out, distractibility, and total scores on a pretest/posttest measure. Behavioral programs are sometimes criticized for being too narrow. That is, the change is displayed only in limited settings or for specific people. Generalization is an important and necessary component in all behavioral programs. For example, if you are teaching a young child to put toys away to keep her room clean, it is also important to generalize the learning to other settings where play occurs—grandparents' and aunts' and uncles' homes, day care, and school. Learning to transfer the effects of the behavioral program to other settings should be a systematic and deliberate component of the program design. The family might need to enlist the assistance of others (teachers, neighbors, and relatives) to ensure that targeted behavior change is being generalized.

Assuring that interventions are in keeping with the development age of the child is another important general guideline (Azar & Siegel, 1990). This *developmental appropriateness* may require some prior intervention from the home-based practitioner, because parents often have unrealistic expectations about age-appropriate competencies. For example, a parent of a toddler should not expect that the child will be able to make his or her bed perfectly or wash and dry dishes. The practitioner can serve as a resource in establishing appropriate, realistic expectations of performance.

Details of intervention programs need to be shared among all family members who will be participating in the program by delivering consequences or rewards. This *information sharing* is particularly important for contingency contracts or interventions that call for immediate reinforcement or punishment. Family members can unknowingly undermine interventions as a result of being ill-informed. This information sharing also applies to extended family members who visit the home frequently. Undermining by uninformed family members of the focused effort to change behavior can be highly frustrating to the parents. Inconsistency also is upsetting and confusing for the child. An astute child will quickly learn which adults require appropriate behavior and which can be manipulated.

Finally, it is important for the home-based practitioner to provide *support* to families frequently and in sufficient quantity so that parents do not feel alone in the effort to improve family functioning. Because escalation in the targeted problem behavior typically immediately follows the initiation of many interventions, parents need to be both prepared for and supported in enduring the initial acting out. Furthermore, initial intervention plans might need altering, and the practitioner's expertise and knowledge will be needed as a resource.

The future of home-based practice with children and families is very promising. Over the last ten years, there has been an explosion of programs for families that are delivered in the home and that address problems in child-behavior management and parenting skills. Home-based practice offers many advantages over agency-based child and family interventions. First, family members often feel more comfortable in a familiar setting. Second, problematic behaviors are more likely to be observed in the home than the artificial surroundings of agency offices. Additionally, obstacles to intervention are more easily identified and modified when home-based practitioners and parents work on the details of implementing procedures in the environment where they will be employed. Finally, home-based practice seeks to identify and intervene in all the needs of the family. For some families this includes resources to meet basic needs such as clothing, food, and shelter, while other families' needs are primarily in interpersonal or child-behavior management. Whatever the needs, however, families are in a much better position to stabilize and change when efforts have been directed at assuring that all needs are addressed.

REFERENCES

Aaronson, M. (1989). The case manager-home visitor. *Child Welfare, 68*(3), 339–346.

Avery, S. R., DiPietro, E. K., & Glynnis, E. L. (1987). Intensive home based early intervention with autistic children. *Education and Treatment of Children, 10*(4), 356–366.

Azar, S., & Siegel, B. (1990). Behavioral treatment of child abuse: A developmental perspective. *Behavior Modification, 14,* 279–300.

Balgopal, P., Patchner, M., & Henderson, C. (1988). Home visits: An effective strategy for engaging the involuntary client. *Child and Youth Services, 11*(1), 65–76.

Bandura, A. (1969). *Principles of behavior modification.* New York: Holt, Rinehart & Winston.

Bandura, A. (1977). *Social learning theory.* Englewood Cliffs, NJ: Prentice-Hall.

Barton, W., & Butts, J. (1990). Viable options: Intensive supervision programs for juvenile delinquents. *Crime and Delinquency, 36*(2), 238–256.

Bloom, M., & Fischer, J. (1982). *Evaluating practice: Guidelines for the accountable professional.* Englewood Cliffs, NJ: Prentice-Hall.

Bronfenbrenner, U. (1979). *The ecology of human development.* Cambridge, MA: Harvard University Press.

Bryce, M., & Lloyd, J. C. (1981). *Treating families in the home.* Springfield, IL: Charles C Thomas.

Bunyan, A. (1987). "Help, I can't cope with my child": A behavioral approach to the treatment of a conduct disordered child within the natural home setting. *British Journal of Social Work, 17*(3) 237–256.

Carey, R. G., & Bucher, B. B. (1986). Positive practice overcorrection: Effects of reinforcing correct performance. *Behavior Modification, 10,* 73–92.

CASSP Technical Center. (1988). *Home-based services.* Washington, DC: Georgetown University Child Development Center.

Cipani, E. (1984). A behavioral model for the delivery of technical assistance in the home. *Child Care Quarterly, 13*(3), 177–192.

Cole, E., & Duva, J. (1990). *Family preservation: An orientation for administrators and practitioners.* Washington, DC: Child Welfare League of America.

Cormier, W., & Cormier L. (1990). *Interviewing strategies for helpers: Fundamental skills and cognitive behavioral interventions* (3rd ed.). Pacific Grove, CA: Brooks/Cole.

Dudzinski, D., & Peters, D. (1977). Home-based programs: A growing alternative. *Child Care Quarterly, 6*(1), 61–71.

Fellbaum, G. A., Daly, R. M., Forrest, P., & Holland, C. (1985). Community implications of a home based change program for children. *Journal of Community Psychology, 13*(1), 67–74.

Fox, J., & Savelle, S. (1987). Social interaction research and families of behaviorally disordered children: A critical review and forward look. *Behavioral Disorders, 12*(4), 276–291.

Framer, E. M., & Sanders, S. H. (1980). The effects of family contingency contracting on disturbed sleeping behaviors of a male adolescent. *Jour-*

nal of Behavior Therapy and Experimental Psychiatry, 11,* 235–237.

Frankel, F., & Simmons, J. Q. (1985). Behavioral treatment approaches to pathological unsocialized, physical aggression in young children. *Journal of Child Psychology and Psychiatry and Allied Disciplines, 26*(4), 525–551.

Goodyear, R. K., & Bradley, F. O. (1980). The helping process as contractual. *Personnel and Guidance Journal, 58,* 512–515.

Gordon, D. A., Arbuthnot, J., Gustafson, K. E., & McGreen, P. (1988). Home-based behavioral-systems family therapy with disadvantaged juvenile delinquents. *American Journal of Family Therapy, 16*(3), 243–255.

Gray, S. S., & Nybell, L. M. (1990). Issues in African-American family preservation. *Child Welfare, 6,* 513–523.

Greene, R. R. (1991). The ecological perspective: An eclectic theoretical framework for social work practice. In R. R. Greene & P. H. Ephross (Eds.), *Human behavior theory and social work practice.* New York: Aldine de Gruyter.

Halpern, R. (1986). Home based early intervention: Dimensions of current practice. *Child Welfare, 65*(4), 387–398.

Heying, K. (1985). Family based, in-home services for the severely emotionally disturbed child. *Child Welfare, 5,* 519–527.

Hodges, V. G. (1991). Providing culturally sensitive family preservation services to ethnic minority families. In E. Tracy, D. Haapala, J. Kinney, & P. Pecora, (Eds.), *Intensive family preservation services: An instructional sourcebook.* Cleveland: Case Western Reserve University, Mandel School of Applied Social Sciences.

Hodges, V. G., & Blythe, B. J. (1992). Improving service delivery to high-risk families: The case for home-based practice. *Families in Society, 73,* 259–265.

Ivey, A. E. (1983). *Intentional interviewing and counseling.* Pacific Grove, CA: Brooks/Cole.

Kazdin, A. E. (1989). *Behavior modification in applied settings.* Pacific Grove, CA: Brooks/Cole.

Kazdin, A. E., & Krouse, R. (1983). The impact of variations in treatment rationales on expectancies for therapeutic change. *Behavior Therapy, 14,* 657–671.

Keely, S. M., Shemberg, K. M., & Carbonell, J. (1976). Operant clinical intervention: Behavior management or beyond? Where are the data? *Behavior Therapy, 7,* 292–305.

Kinney, J., Haapala, D., & Booth, C. (1991). *Keeping families together: The homebuilders model.* New York: Aldine de Gruyter.

Kowal, L., Kottmeier, C. P., Ayoub, C. C., Komives, J. A., Robinson, D. S., & Allen, J. P. (1989). Characteristics of families at risk of problems in parenting: Findings of a home-based secondary prevention program. *Child Welfare, 68*(5), 529–538.

Leach, D. J., & Ralph, A. (1986). Home-school reinforcement: A case study. *Behavior Change, 3*(1), 58–62.

Lutzker, J. (1990). Behavioral treatment of child neglect. *Behavior Modification, 14*(3), 301–315.

Maybanks, S., & Bryce, M. (1979). *Home-based services for children and families.* Springfield, IL: Charles C Thomas.

Mueller, M., & Leviton, A. (1986). In-home versus clinic-based services for the developmentally disabled child: Who is the primary client—parent or child? *Social Work in Health Care, 11*(3), 75–88.

Rabin, C., Rosenbaum, H., & Sens, M. (1982). Home-based marital therapy for multiproblem families. *Journal of Marital and Family Therapy, 16*(4), 451–461.

Ralph, A. (1987). Utilizing family resources to manage tantrum behavior: A home based single subject study. *Behavior Change, 4*(4), 30–35.

Richmond, M. (1917). *Social diagnosis.* New York: Russell Sage Foundation.

Rosen, L., Gabardi, L., Miller, C., & Miller, L. (1990). Home-based treatment of disruptive junior high school students: An analysis of the differential effects of positive and negative consequences. *Behavioral Disorders, 15*(4), 227–232.

Rosenthal, T. L., & Bandura, A. (1978). Psychological modeling: Theory and practice. In S. L. Garfield & A. E. Bergin (Eds.), *Handbook of psychotherapy and behavior change* (2nd ed.). New York: Wiley.

Rowland, C., Taplin, J., & Holt, A. (1983, August). *Home-based crisis therapy: A comparative study.* Paper presented at the 91st annual convention of the American Psychological Association, Anaheim, CA.

Sanders, M. R. (1982). The effects of instruction, feedback, and cueing procedures in behavioral parent training. *Australian Journal of Psychology, 34*(1), 53–69.

Sherman, J., Barker, P., Lorimer, P., Swinson, R., & Factor, D. C. (1988). Treatment of autistic children: Relative effectiveness of residential, out-patient and home-based interventions. *Child Psychiatry and Human Development, 19*(2), 109–125.

Stuart, R. B. (1971). Behavioral contracting within the families of delinquents. *Journal of Behavior Therapy and Experimental Psychiatry, 2,* 1–11.

Sturmey, P., & Crisp, A. G. (1986). Portage guide to early education: A review of research. *Educational Psychology, 6*(2), 139–157.

Sundel, M., & Sundel, S. S. (1982). *Behavior modification in the human services* (2nd ed.). Englewood Cliffs, NJ: Prentice-Hall.

Tracy, E., Haapala, D., Kinney, J., & Pecora, P. (Eds.). (1991). *Intensive family preservation services: An instructional sourcebook.* Cleveland: Case Western Reserve University, Mandel School of Applied Social Sciences.

Turner, S., & Jones, R. (Eds.). (1982). *Behavior modification in black populations: Psychological issues and empirical findings.* New York: Plenum.

Whittaker, J., Kinney, J., Tracy, E., & Booth, C. (1990). *Reaching high-risk families: Intensive family preservation in human services.* New York: Aldine de Gruyter.

Woods, L. J. (1988). Home-based family therapy. *Social Work, 33,* 211–214.

5

Behavioral Parent Training

Richard F. Dangel
Muriel Yu
N. Wim Slot
Gary Fashimpar

Behavioral parent training began in the late 1950s with the work of Williams (1959), who taught two parents to use an extinction procedure to eliminate the bedtime tantrums of their 21-month-old son. Although the procedure worked, the child's well-meaning aunt inadvertently reinforced an emotional outbreak on one occasion, and the procedure had to be reimplemented, thus providing an excellent demonstration of both the strength (quick results) and weakness (temporary results) of the procedure. In another pioneering study, Hawkins, Peterson, Schweid, and Bijou (1966) successfully taught a mother to contingently apply differential consequences to reduce the aggressive and disobedient behavior of her 4-year-old son. Since these studies, the field of behavioral parent training has burgeoned, with dozens of books and hundreds of articles appearing in such diverse sources as the *Journal of Applied Behavior Analysis* and the *National Enquirer.*

Even the most cynical critics recognize the effectiveness of behavioral procedures in child management. Virtually all agencies that serve children, including schools, orthodontic offices, recreational centers, pediatric clinics, sports teams, and so on, commonly employ reward systems to encourage "good" behavior. Although the mechanics of these systems range from simple to complex and from correct to incorrect, all can trace their parentage to behaviorism. Similarly, most parenting programs, regardless of their theoretical orientation, integrate some behavioral parenting

practices, although sometimes under different labels. For example, one program that crested in popularity a few years ago, *Systematic Training for Effective Parenting* (STEP), instructed parents to use encouragement, considered to be Adlerian, rather than praise, considered to be behavioral (Dinkmeyer & McKay, 1976). In real life, however, a verbal statement of encouragement sounded identical to a verbal statement of praise.

In *Parent Training: Foundations of Research and Practice,* Dangel and Polster (1984) present descriptions of the major empirically oriented behavioral parenting research projects operational in the United States. The book dramatically illustrates the depth, breadth, and effectiveness of the parent training work done over the previous two decades. Programs focused on serving parents from different cultural, ethnic, and socioeconomic backgrounds; parents whose children had severe developmental disabilities; parents in a wide variety of settings, ranging from schools to government-subsidized housing projects to pediatric offices; and adults serving as surrogate parents in residential treatment facilities.

A number of excellent reviews of the behavioral parent training literature exist (for example, Berkowitz & Graziano, 1972; Dembo, Sweitzer, & Lauritzen, 1985; Graziano & Diament, 1992; Johnson & Katz, 1973; Krebs, 1986; McAuley, 1982; Moreland, Schwebel, Beck, & Wells, 1982; O'Dell, 1974; Weise & Kramer, 1988). Rather than duplicating the information in these reviews, we aim in this chapter to illustrate what *problems* parents have been trained to address, the *skills* that parents have been trained to use, and the *methods* that have been used to train parents. We also describe two alternative parent training intervention models and suggest directions for future research and practice.

PROBLEMS THAT PARENTS HAVE BEEN TRAINED TO ADDRESS

Parents have been trained to modify a tremendous variety of child behaviors, including noncompliance with parental requests (Forehand & McMahon, 1981), chore completion (Dangel & Polster, 1984), enuresis (Azrin, Sneed, & Foxx, 1974), hyperactivity (Barkley, 1981), self-help (Allen, Bryant, & Bailey, 1986), overeating and exercise (Israel, Silverman, & Solotar, 1988), table manners (Greene, Hardison, & Greene, 1984), interrupting (Sloane, Endo, Hawkes, & Jenson, 1991), sleep problems and bedtime fears (Graziano & Mooney, 1982), fire setting (Kolko, 1983), and child perception of pain during medical procedures (Jay, Elliott, Katz, & Siegel, 1987), to name a few.

Dangel and Polster (1984) trained parents to increase their children's rates of completing chores by using a chore chart and tangible reinforcers. A videotaped lesson gave the parents precise instructions on how to chart chores and showed vignettes of parents describing to their own children what chores were to be done, by what time of the day they were to be finished, and what consequences the children would receive for completed chores. In one experimental group, 11 of the 15 parents established chore charts and reported 57% increases in the rates of chore completion.

Numerous studies document the effectiveness of training to help parents modify enuresis (Bollard, Nettlebeck, & Roxbee, 1982;

Fincham & Spettell, 1984) and to teach toilet training (Arzin & Foxx, 1976). To modify enuresis, parents are typically trained to change antecedent conditions by giving verbal prompts to the child ("Do you have to go to the bathroom?"), by intermittently waking the child at night to use the toilet, and by systematically applying positive consequences for dry periods or for using the toilet and mildly negative consequences, such as changing the sheets on the bed or washing out wet underpants, for accidents. For toilet training, similar procedures are followed, with the parent providing abundant liquids to increase opportunities for reinforcing correct use of the toilet.

Noncompliance with parent requests is the most widely researched category of children's problem behavior, perhaps because most parents who seek treatment identify noncompliance as a concern (Taplin & Reed, 1976). (For an excellent review of the compliance literature, see Houlihan, Sloane, Jones, and Patten, 1992.) Noncompliance is usually defined as the failure of the child to follow a parent's request. Some researchers have added other components to the definition, such as failure to respond to a request within a specific number of seconds (Roberts & Hatzenbuehler, 1981) or failure to complete a specific behavior within a specific number of seconds after the parent request (Parrish, Cataldo, Kolko, Neef, & Egel, 1986). Researchers have shown that parents can increase the rate of compliance to their requests by giving clear commands that require a specific motor behavior ("Take your dishes to the counter" compared with "Settle down"); by making the requests at times when the child is not engaged in a strongly competing behavior (such as watching television); by making the requests when the child is already engaged in appropriate behavior rather than disruptive behavior; by not asking too often; by using physical or eye contact with the request; and by following compliance with positive consequences, such as parental attention, and noncompliance with negative consequences, such as time-out. Generally, the research indicates that parents can be successfully trained to increase child compliance. However, whether they maintain their use of skills over time and whether they use them with other children and in other circumstances have not been well documented. No studies have been published that examine compliance training for parents of teenagers, perhaps suggesting that parents may need to be trained in different procedures to elicit adolescent compliance.

To date, behavioral training appears to have been quite effective in helping parents change a wide variety of significant problem behaviors in their children. For the most part, these efforts have focused on discrete observable events, such as temper tantrums and chore completion, rather than on more global categories of children's problems, such as depression, poor self-concept, or lack of friends, that practitioners must often help parents address, and the preponderance of research has been with parents of preadolescent children.

SKILLS THAT PARENTS HAVE BEEN TRAINED TO USE

Most behavioral parent training programs aim to teach parents to use basic behavioral procedures, including contingent positive attention, usually verbal praise, physical contact, or tangible rewards; punishment, usually removal of rewards or privileges, spanking, or time-out; extinction, usually withholding attention; shaping; and differential reinforcement of other behavior (DRO). They have also been trained in more specialized skills such as improving home safety (Barone, Greene, & Lutzker, 1986), managing parental anger (Barth, Blythe, Schinke, & Schilling, 1983), contingency contracting (Patterson & Forgatch, 1987), and using various types of instructions (Burke & Herron, 1992; Forehand & McMahon, 1981).

Recent expansions of traditional behavioral approaches to parent training have yielded promising findings. Kazdin, Siegel, and Bass (1992) compared the relative effectiveness of behavioral parent training, cognitive problem-solving training, and the two methods combined to modify antisocial behavior in young children. They found that although all three interventions produced measurable results, the combined package produced greater results than either intervention alone and that the effects maintained over the one-year follow-up.

In a brilliant analysis of over a decade of research, Patterson and his colleagues generated substantial support for the conclusion that parents should closely monitor their children's whereabouts (Patterson, Reid, & Dishion, 1992). They found that parents of antisocial children had little information about where their children were, who they were with, what they were doing, or when they would return home. Patterson and Forgatch (1987) have translated these findings into practical procedures for parents. The trend toward expanding the list of methods that have been demonstrated to be effective in modifying complex classes of child behavior should produce exciting results.

METHODS THAT HAVE BEEN USED TO TRAIN PARENTS

Parents have been trained individually and in groups by television, by lectures, by printed materials, by computer software, by role playing, by using videotaped models to provide demonstrations, and by using bug-in-the-ear devices to provide verbal instructions and prompts. Each of these training formats has been shown to be effective, at least to some extent with some parents, in increasing parental skills and knowledge of behavioral principles, changing children's behavior, or changing parental attitudes or perceptions.

Training Individual Parents

Early parent training paralleled the development of applied behavior analysis. Early applied behavior analysis involved an experiment using a single procedure to modify a single behavior of a single subject. Subsequent studies looked at modifying classes or collections of behaviors in a single subject, progressing to classes or collections of behaviors in small groups of subjects. From these efforts, applied behavior analysis moved to the development of procedures for replicating and exporting entire service delivery systems (Wolf, 1992). The development of the Achievement Place Model of residential care for children typifies this progression (Willner, Braukmann, Kirigin, & Wolf, 1978).

Similarly, early behavioral parent training involved a therapist instructing one parent how to apply a single technique with a single child to solve a single problem. As behavior-change technology developed, interventions moved toward helping one parent change classes or groups of behavior and, eventually, toward helping groups of parents change classes or groups of behaviors.

Training Groups of Parents

Professionally led group parent training in the United States started as early as 1888 with the Child Study Association of America (Auerbach, 1968). Small, psychodynamic groups encouraged parents to share their parenting problems with one another. A professional leader offered reflections and interpretations. Consistent with the underpinnings of psychodynamic theory, parents were led to believe that people, including their children, could change.

This same basic structure is widely used today by parent trainers across theoretical orientations. A group of parents whose children have problems meet with a professional leader to discuss their difficulties, offer explanations and suggestions, and gain a promise of

hope. What distinguishes behavioral parenting programs is not so much the basic group structure but, rather, the inclusion of content related to the application of behavioral principles to solve child-management problems. Group parent training is not, however, standardized in terms of what principles and practices are covered, how they are covered, or what emphasis is placed on changes in parent skills, changes in parent attitudes and perceptions, or changes in child behaviors.

No definitive conclusions can be drawn regarding the relative efficacy of group as opposed to individual parent training (Brightman, Baker, Clark, & Ambrose, 1982; Hornby & Singh, 1983; Webster-Stratton, 1984). Group participants typically report decreased feelings of isolation and increased feelings of understanding and support. What contribution, if any, these feelings make to this acquisition of skills or to changes in the behavior of their children remains unclear. Group training is considered to be more cost effective because a single group leader can distribute the same content to many parents simultaneously. On the other hand, individual training affords parents more privacy, more individualized assessment, and a program specifically designed to meet their needs. Parents do not spend time listening to the problems of others or acquiring skills or information that may have little applicability to their own circumstances. The trainer can also devote more time to the parent, which may facilitate change and permit the detection of other family problems that impede the effectiveness of the training.

Television

Several television series, such as *What Every Baby Knows* and *Mother's Day,* aim to distribute parenting information. Experts offer advice on everything from how to handle night terrors to the effects of birth order on child personality. Some of the information is derived from behavioral theory and from research findings; some is derived from everyone's Aunt Martha. The effectiveness of broadcast television in imparting parenting information has not been determined. Nevertheless, television as a delivery medium should not be overlooked; the number of parents reached by television dramatically exceeds the number of those served in parenting classes.

Videotaped Models

An array of programs that use videotaped models to show examples of particular parenting skills is on the market. Most of the commercially available programs have not undergone sufficient experimental evaluation to determine their effects. Nevertheless, they are used worldwide. One of the earliest programs, *Parents and Children: A Positive Approach to Child Management* (Baxley & Baxley, 1979), uses short vignettes to model the use of reward and punishment to shape child behavior. The *Nurturing Program* (Bavolek & Bavolek, 1988), originally issued with a filmstrip, now uses videotapes to teach behavioral and Adlerian parenting techniques to distressed and abusive parents. *Active Parenting* (Popkin, 1983) draws heavily from Dreikurs and Soltz (1964) in its videotaped presentations of concepts like democratic decision making within families, using "I" messages in communication, and listening for feelings. *Winning!* (Dangel & Polster, 1981), designed for parents of 3- to 12-year-olds, consists of 8 basic videotaped lessons, each devoted to a single behavioral parenting skill such as praise, and 14 advanced videotaped lessons, each devoted to the application of the basic skills to a specific child-management problem such as temper tantrums.

One approach widely used in the Netherlands, called Hometraining (Van den Bogaast & Wintels, 1988), involves videotaping parents interacting with their own children in the home. Parents and trainers subsequently view the videotapes together, and the parents receive detailed feedback about each of their interactions with their children. Although the theoretical assumptions underlying the feedback given to parents tend to be predominantly psychodynamic, in practice the actual training methods employed are predominantly behavioral. Evaluation of Hometraining has been limited, and the results are unconvincing, perhaps because the model includes few safeguards to ensure the nature or quality of the trainer feedback.

Videotaped models have been shown to be effective in teaching complex behaviors (Webster-Stratton, Kolpacoff, & Hollinsworth, 1988) and to be more effective than live models (Kashima, Baker, & Landen, 1988). Videotaped models have several advantages. The first is consistency. A live demonstration is likely to differ with every performance and across trainers. Videotaped models also allow demonstrations of small components of an entire skill and the use of narration to help viewers focus on important points. Finally, videotaped demonstrations allow the use of multiple, diverse examples, which helps parents identify with what they see and promotes generalization (Stokes & Baer, 1977). For stimulus-modeling videotapes to be the most effective, they must show numerous variations of the same skill. Sometimes this makes for a videotape that differs dramatically from what people are used to viewing, in which a concept may be shown only once very briefly. Repetition is crucial because the salient cues in each example may vary across viewers. One example may "hit home" with one viewer because the child is the same age as hers. Another example may ring true to a different viewer because he had precisely the same problem with his child the previous week. Unless the videotape includes a sufficient number of diverse examples, many viewers will not be engaged. Most commercially available videotaped programs underuse the stimulus-modeling contribution that examples make in an attempt to teach too much and to entertain rather than to provide multiple demonstrations of the skills.

Computer Software

Computer software is the most recent technology to be used in parent training. *Mind over Minors* (1988) gives parents custom-designed advice about their children. Parents select adjectives that best describe their child, and the software generates a prescription. The prescription provides guidelines for the parents about how to understand their child, how to improve communication, how to increase performance, effective discipline, and learning activities. This software is among the first of its kind, and it has not been experimentally evaluated. As more sophisticated software becomes available, however, computer technology is likely to provide a convenient way to reach parents. Likewise, interactive video technology should permit parents to receive very precise parenting information with demonstrations.

Written Materials

Books that describe the application of behavioral procedures to solve child-management problems provided one of the first efforts at disseminating standardized information for parents and parent trainers. *Living with Children* (Patterson & Guillon, 1968) (over 400,000 copies in print) and *Parents Are Teachers* (Becker, 1971) set the early standards both in terms of content and style. Later books, such as *Helping the Noncompliant Child* (Forehand & McMahon, 1981) and *Teaching Child Management Skills* (Dangel & Polster, 1988), added to the original content and provided more specific guidelines for trainers to follow when working with parents. All of these books were designed for parents of younger children.

Parents and Adolescents Living Together, Part 1 (Patterson & Forgatch, 1987) and *Part 2* (Forgatch & Patterson, 1989), represent two of the few examples of textbooks written for parents of young teenagers. Part 1 covers compli-

ance training, monitoring and tracking, encouragement, point charts, and negative consequences. Part 2 covers problem-solving methods and how to use them with complex adolescent problems such as sexual behavior and drug and alcohol use. The authors claim to have evaluated most of the procedures in the text, but the text itself has not been evaluated.

Bauman, Reiss, Rogers, and Bailey (1983) developed and tested a brief advice package designed to assist parents in the management of their children in restaurants. The package advised parents to follow a variety of procedures, including separating children, removing silverware before arrival of the meal, and providing the children with toys and crackers. Troublesome and inappropriate behavior decreased, and the improved behavior generalized to a second restaurant.

Dangel (1991) developed an instructional flyer that was to be distributed to parents at a large outdoor water park. The flyer outlined eight steps from the literature on behavioral training for parents to follow to ensure a safe park visit (clearly state rules, have children stay within sight, have children check back, take rest periods, do not allow running, give frequent praise and snacks for compliance, enforce sit-and-watch for noncompliance, and grant an extended stay for no violations). Evaluation by parent focus groups indicated that the instructions were clear, easy to understand, easy to follow, and appealing. Last-minute legal concerns over insurance liability prohibited the park from distributing the flyer, so no evaluation of its effectiveness was conducted.

Parent and Child Characteristics

Parent characteristics—such as socioeconomic status, ethnicity, voluntary or court-ordered status, maternal depression, and intellectual functioning—and child characteristics—such as gender, degree and type of disturbance, and intellectual functioning—interact with training methods and program content to influence outcome to an extent and in ways that are not fully understood. For example, Patterson (1974) found that low social class was negatively correlated with successful outcomes for parents of behavior-disordered boys. Strom, Griswold, and Slaughter (1981) found that white mothers responded more in keeping with child-development research than did African-American mothers. Wahler (1980) found that parent training effects were influenced by the social contacts of low-income mothers. Knapp and Deluty (1989) found that middle-income parents learned from both didactic and modeling training methods, whereas low-income parents did not benefit from the didactic model. Other researchers have corroborated these findings (Israel, Silverman, & Solotar, 1986; Webster-Stratton, 1985). However, Mischley, Stacy, Mischley, and Dush (1985) found that low-income families responded well to treatment that included flexible schedules and financial incentives for program completion. Dangel and Polster (1984) found that parents who had been ordered by a court to complete an eight-week, skill-based parenting program had the same dropout rate, weekly attendance, and lesson mastery and the same level of satisfaction with the program as voluntary parents.

Child characteristics, as they influence treatment outcomes, have been researched considerably less than parent characteristics. Holden, Lavigne, and Cameron (1990) found that the number of presenting problems, the child's age, and the child's initial level of compliance related to positive outcomes with preschool children. It seems reasonable to assume that the greater the level of disturbance, the more resistant to treatment effects the behaviors will be and the more powerful the training methods required to show effects. Until more studies investigate behavioral parent training with parents of adolescents (and of adolescents with varying levels of disturbance), comparisons of overall effectiveness by age of child cannot be made.

Diverse methods—including individual and group didactic instruction, television, computer software, role-playing exercises, videotaped models, and printed materials, including books, manuals, and self-instructional flyers—have been used to train parents, with varying degrees of success. It seems clear that treatment outcome reflects an interaction between the training methods used, the content of the program, and parent and child characteristics. Research findings are not definitive with regard to matching particular training methods with particular types of parents. Baer (1984) has suggested that the search for such a match may be premature until a consistently effective intervention package has been assembled. Taking what is known about modifying behavior in general, however, a more active approach to training, including behavioral rehearsal, practice, role playing, and feedback, is more likely to yield consistent positive results than methods that rely exclusively on classroomlike instruction or printed materials to promote cognitive understanding.

ALTERNATIVE INTERVENTION MODELS

Over the past two decades of research into parent training, two basic intervention models have emerged, a problem-focused model and a skill-building model. This section of the chapter describes each of these models and delineates the components of effective skill-based training for parents.

Problem-Focused Model

A commonly used approach in parent training requires the parent, in this example, Ms. Foster, to identify one or more specific problems she is having with her nine-year-old child, Cecil. Usually, the parent and practitioner discuss the problems and, in collaboration, identify the most pressing one. For instance, Ms. Foster and the practitioner decide to first address Cecil's problem of arguing. Ms. Foster reports that he argues all the time with everybody. The practitioner helps her define what she means when she says "arguing."

Once a clear definition has been constructed, the practitioner asks Ms. Foster to keep track of how often Cecil argues. He constructs a simple recording form for her to post on the refrigerator door. She records how often Cecil argues, with whom, and how the argument ends. After two weeks of recording, she returns to the practitioner, and together they review the information she has collected. He is profuse in his praise of her data-collection efforts. The data show that Cecil argues with his mother on the average four times per day. The arguments end when she gets frustrated and gives him what he wants or when she loses her temper, yells, curses, and sends him to his room for the rest of the evening.

The practitioner and Ms. Foster devise a plan to stop Cecil's arguing. Over the next six weeks, the practitioner teaches her to tell Cecil that, from now on, when he argues, he will go to his room for five minutes and when he answers politely and doesn't argue, he will earn an extra five minutes of television time.

Ms. Foster continues to record Cecil's arguing as well as her own application of the procedures she has learned from the practitioner. During the first two weeks, when she rewards Cecil for answering politely and for not arguing, he continues to argue. During the third and fourth weeks, when she adds sending him to his room for arguing, his arguing decreases from four times per day to four times in the entire week. She continues to use the procedures, and by the end of two months, he is arguing only one time per week. She and the practitioner decide that the intervention procedures have been successful and the case is closed.

In this approach to the delivery of parent training services, the client and the practitioner meet weekly to address a particular behavior problem the client has sought help in correcting. In the example, the client defined the target problem, arguing, and collected baseline and treatment data on frequency, antecedents, and consequences. The treatment focused on the practitioner helping the parent learn and apply new skills selected to modify the target problem.

Practitioners and parents find this approach appealing, for at least two reasons. First, this approach allows the practitioner to devise a program specifically for the parent requesting services. The practitioner can consider the parent's motivation, educational level, family circumstances, and so on to determine the amount and nature of the service to be offered. The practitioner may determine, for example, that Cecil's arguing is related to the unpredictable visitation schedule he has with his father and that before Ms. Foster addresses Cecil's arguing, she should clarify her joint-custody agreement.

Secondly, parents typically seek help because of a specific source of discomfort; that is, their child displays some characteristic that is of concern either to them or to someone in the community, such as a relative or teacher. Their motivation is not generally to become "better parents." To draw a parallel situation, if an adult visited his physician for relief from backache pain, only to receive instead an offer of eight weeks of training about healthy lifestyles, he would probably seek another physician. This problem-focused approach may more immediately address the parents' needs.

This model has two main disadvantages. First, it assumes that the parent will learn from applying specific skills to a single problem how to apply those skills to subsequent problems. There is limited evidence to support this assumption. More evidence suggests that parents do not generalize when there is an absence of multiple examples in the training (Stokes & Baer, 1977). If this is the case, the practitioner would expect Ms. Foster to return for help with the next problem presented by Cecil, even though the application of the same set of skills might be sufficient to address the problem.

Secondly, the model is not cost effective in that it requires extensive individual assessment, which may not influence the actual intervention. There are a finite number of basic behavioral parenting skills, and many of the same skills are prescribed regardless of the particular child problem.

Skill-building Model

The second intervention model to emerge in the literature on parent training can be conceptualized as the skill-training model. In this model, parents receive training in a standardized package of skills, usually simple behavior-management practices such as using descriptive praise, following appropriate behavior with tangible consequences, and using time-out. Every parent receives the same instruction in the same set of skills in the same order regardless of the presenting concern. In this approach, the primary focus of the intervention is on the acquisition of a set of skills that can be used to address a wide range of child problems across children, across settings such as school and home, and over time. The parent may, however, receive intermittent feedback on how to apply the skills to a particular problem.

This model has three main advantages. First, it generally emphasizes *skill acquisition* more than the transmission of information or knowledge. A focus on skills is likely to yield greater behavioral change in parents. Secondly, the focus on the acquisition and mastery of skills, rather than on the resolution of a particular problem, increases the likelihood that parents will be able to apply the skills to other existing problems or to problems that occur in the future or with other children. Finally, the model is cost effective in that less time is required for assessment and the development

of an intervention plan because the treatment is standardized.

Parents sometimes find this approach unsatisfactory because they may not see the immediate relevance of the skills in the program for their presenting problem. For example, many behavioral parent training programs offer as a first skill the use of praise. Distressed parents often report that their children do nothing praiseworthy. Consequently, they question the applicability of praise to helping them to stop their children's behavior problems. Usually, however, solid rationales, such as *"Please be patient. Remember, your children's behavior problems did not start in a day, nor will they vanish in a day. What you are learning now will help you with the challenges you are facing now and the challenges you will face tomorrow,"* can help maintain parents' interest and involvement.

The literature suggests that most parent-training programs spend considerably more time providing information and concepts than they do teaching skills, with the hope that parenting skills will emerge as a result. Certainly, some parents can learn skills from verbal descriptions. And not all parents who participate in training classes have skill deficits. Some parents may fail to use skills that they are capable of demonstrating. Others may insist on using certain practices, such as physical punishment, because of belief systems or religious doctrine (Fugate, 1980). However, for those programs that aim to equip parents with observable skills to use with their children, the training literature identifies at least nine methods that are associated with successful skill acquisition. These practices have been described in detail elsewhere (Dangel & Polster, 1984, 1988), so they are only briefly described here:

1. *Outcome objectives are clearly stated.* Clear outcome objectives facilitate both parents' performance and evaluation of the program (Sundel & Sundel, 1975). If the objectives are clearly articulated, parent

needs can be matched against the aims of the program.

2. *Objectives are analyzed according to task.* Every outcome objective should be analyzed to determine that prerequisite skills are taught first and that easy skills are taught before difficult skills, to promote learner confidence (Markle, 1969).

3. *Objectives are taught in short units.* Short training units avoid tiring learners, facilitate understanding and mastery, and allow time between skills for practice. Parents will typically retain only a few main ideas from each unit. Too much material or too many objectives presented each time dilute what they will retain.

4. *Criteria are established to demonstrate mastery.* Several researchers have suggested the use of performance criteria as a way to ensure skill mastery (Forehand & King, 1977; Saudergas, 1972). Mastery criteria allow parents and trainers to determine whether parents are ready to advance to the next skill or whether additional training is necessary. Criteria should be quantitative and qualitative to allow for complex or subtle skill characteristics—for example, sincere voice tone when making a statement of approval.

5. *Skills are modeled using videotapes.* Videotaped demonstrations allow the parents repeated opportunities to see each skill used by a variety of parents in a variety of settings. Skill nuances that may not be otherwise easily communicated can be shown repeatedly to facilitate acquisition of skills.

6. *Opportunities to practice are given.* As with any new skill acquisition, practice makes perfect. Parents should be given ample opportunities to practice each new skill under training conditions and in the home. Their reports of competence in the skill are not accepted as substitutes for demonstrations.

7. *Practice homework is assigned and monitored.* Transfer of skill acquisition from the training setting to the home can be facilitated by giving parents specific assignments that require them to practice each skill a specified number of times between each session. Homework must be monitored, and parents must receive recognition to encourage compliance with assignments.

8. *Parent receives precise feedback.* Parents should be given specific feedback about their mastery of each skill. The feedback should be primarily positive to provide encouragement, and suggestions for improvement should be carefully selected to contribute to the intended outcome objectives. Feedback should also indicate whether the parent has demonstrated mastery of the skill according to the mastery criteria and what changes are required to reach mastery.

9. *Program is self-paced.* A self-paced program enhances motivation by allowing parents who demonstrate mastery to advance quickly while allowing other parents to receive additional training, practice, and feedback so they can ultimately master each skill and feel successful.

FUTURE DIRECTIONS IN BEHAVIORAL PARENT TRAINING

The research literature on behavioral parent training and the number of behaviorally oriented programs continue to grow. Despite these efforts, practitioners face many daily examples of poor, sometimes abusive, parenting, and the challenges that today's parents face are staggering. The need for effective parent training is unquestionable.

Training Methods

The research findings suggest that a variety of training methods will produce some results with some parents. Future research is needed to assemble a systematic, state-of-the-art package of training methods, independent of particular skills or parent populations. Once this goal has been accomplished, skills that have been demonstrated to be valuable to parents could be taught using these methods, with new skills added as they are discovered. The long-term aim should be to develop stand-alone, expandable training packages that require minimal professional intervention for the largest and most diverse group of parents possible. This strategy will increase the overall impact of parent training by making it available and effective without depending on expensive professionals. After a comprehensive set of training methods has been assembled and experimentally evaluated, subsequent research could investigate what modifications in the package are required to effectively reach parent and child populations with particular characteristics. Some parents may require a less comprehensive training package; others may require the full package plus additional individualized interventions. Differences may be found, for example, between parents who participate for self-improvement and those who participate because of child-management or child mental-health problems.

Skills to Be Taught

Most of the parent training research has focused on teaching discrete skills or general information, for the most part drawn from the principles of behavior, to parents of young children. These studies have demonstrated that parents can learn information about applying behavioral principles to child management and can learn to use the skills under certain conditions. Fewer studies, however, have demonstrated that the application of behavioral principles results in the long-term modification of children's behaviors. Additional research is needed to more closely examine and document the relationship between parents' use of behavioral skills and changes in

specific, targeted child behaviors. In addition, future applied research should draw from the basic child-development research to determine what parenting behaviors influence broader classes of child behavior. For example, what particular classes of parent behavior mitigate adolescent substance use, academic underachievement, teenage pregnancy, or gang involvement? Once these classes of parent behavior are identified, they can be defined as skills and incorporated into a stand-alone parent training package.

Target Behaviors of Children

Research has demonstrated that parents can modify a variety of problem behaviors in children. For the most part, however, these behaviors have been discrete and specific, and few studies demonstrate long-term effects. Additional research is necessary to determine what classes of child behaviors are amenable to modification by parents, to what extent, and for how long and to determine their relationship to other classes of behavior as the child develops. For example, what behaviors should be, or could be, modified by parents when the presenting problem is that the child is depressed, suffering from a low self-concept, easily misled by peers, in a gang, and so on? Or, if young children are taught by their parents to be compliant to requests from adults, will these same children as teenagers be more likely to be misled by peers?

Target Populations

The majority of the research into behavioral parent training has been with parents of young children, mostly middle-class and predominantly white. Certainly this population benefits from parent training. However, ethnic and cultural minorities, families from lower socioeconomic groups, homosexual families, multiproblem families, and parents of teenagers also need services. Future research should identify technologies to reach these populations. The training methods used, the applicability of the content, the consumer acceptability of the content, the location of services, and the characteristics of the trainer can each present obstacles to reaching certain populations. Each can be modified, however, and each can influence program outcomes. Financial incentives, aggressive recruitment, court mandates, the use of paraprofessional and community leaders as trainers, parent support groups, and providing time off from work are just a few interventions that can extend the reach of parent training programs and that warrant further experimental investigation.

CONCLUSION

Most people agree that rearing healthy, happy, well-adjusted, productive children in today's society presents a challenge for even the most competent parents. The decline in national and worldwide economic conditions, decaying urban areas, the prevalence of illegal substances, and the breakdown of the extended family with its attendant loss of social support and of informal sources of parenting information contribute to the challenge. Yet more and more responsibility is placed on parents. They are told that they are responsible for their children's success or failure in school, out-of-wedlock pregnancy, participation in gangs, and use of drugs. Whether or not these allegations are true, parents face an awesome task.

Parent training stands to influence the lives of more parents and children than any other social service program. Behavioral parent training, including programs that teach parents behavioral skills and those that use behavioral principles to teach other parenting skills, has made significant contributions to parents in the past two decades. Large-scale

parent training interventions that combine state-of-the-art training technologies with empirically derived parenting skills cannot be far away.

REFERENCES

Allen, L. D., Bryant, M. C., & Bailey, J. C. (1986). Facilitating generalization: The effectiveness of improved parental report procedures. *Behavior Modification, 10*, 415–434.

Auerbach, A. B. (1968). *Parents learn through discussion.* New York: Wiley.

Azrin, N. H., & Foxx, R. M. (1976). *Toilet training in less than a day.* New York: Pocket Books.

Azrin, N. H., Sneed, T. J., & Foxx, R. M. (1974). Dry-bed training: A rapid method of eliminating bedwetting (enuresis) of the retarded. *Behavior Research and Therapy, 11,* 427–434.

Baer, D. M. (1984). Future directions?: Or, is it useful to ask, "Where did we go wrong?" before we go? In R. F. Dangel & R. A. Polster (Eds.), *Parent training: Foundations of research and practice.* New York: Guilford Press.

Barkley, R. A. (1981). *Hyperactive children: A handbook for diagnosis and treatment.* New York: Guilford Press.

Barone, V. J., Greene, B. F., & Lutzker, J. R. (1986). Home safety with families being treated for child abuse and neglect. *Behavior Modification, 10,* 93–114.

Barth, R. P., Blythe, B. J., Schinke, S. P., & Schilling, R. F. (1983). Self-control training with maltreating parents. *Child Welfare, 62,* 313–324.

Bauman, K. E., Reiss, M. L., Rogers, R. W., & Bailey, J. S. (1983). Dining out with children: Effectiveness of a parent advice package on pre-meal inappropriate behavior. *Journal of Applied Behavior Analysis, 16,* 55–68.

Bavolek, S. J., & Bavolek, J. D. (1988). *Nurturing program for teenage parents and their families.* Park City, UT: Family Development Resources.

Baxley, N. B. (Producer), & Baxley, G. B. (Director). 1979. *Parents and children: A positive approach to child management* [Film]. Champaign, IL: Research Press.

Becker, W. C. (1981). *Parents are teachers.* Champaign, IL: Research Press.

Berkowitz, B. P., & Graziano, A. M. (1972). Training parents as behavior therapists: A review. *Behavior Research and Therapy, 10,* 297–317.

Bollard, J., Nettlebeck, T., & Roxbee, L. (1982). Dry-bed training for childhood bedwetting: A comparison of group with individually administered parent instruction. *Behavior Research and Therapy, 20,* 209–217.

Brightman, R. P., Baker, B. L., Clark, D. B., & Ambrose, S. A. (1982). Effectiveness of alternative parent training formats. *Journal of Behavior Therapy and Experimental Psychiatry, 13,* 113–117.

Burke, R. V., & Herron, R. W. (Eds.). (1992). *Common sense parenting: A practical approach from Boys Town.* Omaha, NE: Boys Town Press.

Dangel, R. F. (1991). *Water park safety: Guidelines for parents.* Unpublished flyer.

Dangel, R. F., & Polster, R. A. (1981). *Winning! Parent specialist handbook.* Arlington, TX: American Children's Foundation.

Dangel, R. F., & Polster, R. A. (Eds.). (1984). *Parent training: Foundations of research and practice.* New York: Guilford Press.

Dangel, R. F., & Polster, R. A. (1988). *Teaching child management skills.* New York: Pergamon Press.

Dembo, M. H., Sweitzer, M., & Lauritzen, P. (1985). An evaluation of group parent education: Behavioral, PET, and Adlerian programs. *Review of Educational Research, 55,* 155–200.

Dinkmeyer, D., & McKay, G. (1976). *Systematic Training for Effective Parenting: Parent's handbook and leader's manual.* Circle Pines, MN: American Guidance Service.

Dreikurs, R., & Soltz, V. (1964). *Children: The challenge.* New York: Hawthorn Books.

Fincham, F. D., & Spettell, C. (1984). The acceptability of dry bed training and urine alarm training treatments of nocturnal enuresis. *Behavior Therapy, 15,* 388–394.

Forehand, R., & King, H. E. (1977). Noncompliant children: Effects of parent training on behavior and attitude change. *Behavior Modification, 1,* 93–108.

Forehand, R., & McMahon, R. J. (1981). *Helping the non-compliant child.* New York: Guilford Press.

Forgatch, M. S., & Patterson, G. R. (1989). *Parents and adolescents living together: Part 2. Family problem solving.* Eugene, OR: Castalia.

Fugate, R. J. (1980). *What the Bible says about child training.* Garland, TX: Aletheia Publishers.

Graziano, A. M., & Diament, D. M. (1992). Parent behavioral training: An examination of the paradigm. *Behavior Modification, 16,* 3–38.

Graziano, A. M., & Mooney, K. C. (1982). Behavioral treatment of children's "nightfear": A 3-year follow-up. *Journal of Consulting and Clinical Psychology, 50,* 598–599.

Greene, R. B., Hardison, W. L., & Greene, B. F. (1984). Turning the table on advice programs for parents: Using placemats to enhance family interaction at restaurants. *Journal of Applied Behavior Analysis, 17,* 497–508.

Hawkins, R. P., Peterson, R. F., Schweid, E., & Bijou, S. W. (1966). Behavior therapy in the home: Amelioration of problem parent-child relations with the parent in a therapeutic role. *Journal of Experimental Child Psychology, 4,* 99–107.

Holden, G. W., Lavigne, V. V., & Cameron, A. M. (1990). Probing the continuum of effectiveness in parent training: Characteristics of parents and preschoolers. *Journal of Clinical Child Psychology, 19*(1), 2–8.

Hornby, G., & Singh, N. N. (1984). Behavioral group training with parents of mentally retarded children. *Journal of Mental Deficiency Research, 28,* 43–52.

Houlihan, D., Sloane, H. N., Jones, R. N., & Patten, C. (1992). A review of behavioral conceptualizations and treatments of child noncompliance. *Education and Treatment of Children, 15,* 56–77.

Israel, A. C., Silverman, W. K., & Solotar, L. C. (1986). An investigation of family influences on initial weight status, attrition, and treatment outcome in a childhood obesity program. *Behavior Therapy, 17,* 131–143.

Israel, A. C., Silverman, W. K., & Solotar, L. C. (1988). The relationship between adherence and weight loss in a behavioral weight loss program for children. *Behavior Therapy, 16,* 169–180.

Jay, S. M., Elliott, C. H., Katz, E., & Siegel, S. E. (1987). Cognitive behavioral and pharmacologic interventions for children's distress during painful medical procedures. *Journal of Consulting and Clinical Psychology, 55,* 860–865.

Johnson, C. A., & Katz, C. (1973). Using parents as change agents for their children: A review. *Journal of Child Psychology and Psychiatry, 14,* 181–200.

Kashima, K. J., Baker, B. L., & Landen, S. J. (1988). Media-based versus professionally-led training for parents of mentally retarded children. *American Journal of Mental Retardation, 93,* 209–217.

Kazdin, A. E., Siegel, T. C., & Bass, D. (1992). Cognitive problem-solving skills training and parent management training in the treatment of antisocial behavior in children. *Journal of Consulting and Clinical Psychology, 60*(5), 733–747.

Knapp, P. A., & Deluty, R. H. (1989). Relative effectiveness of two behavioral parent training programs. *Journal of Clinical Child Psychology, 18,* 314–322.

Kolko, D. J. (1983). Multicomponent parental treatment of firesetting in a six-year-old boy. *Journal of Behavior Therapy and Experimental Psychiatry, 14,* 349–353.

Krebs, L. L. (1986). Current research on theoretically based parenting programs. *Individual Psychology, 42,* 375–387.

Markle, S. M. (1969). *Good frames and bad: A grammar of frame writing* (2nd ed.). New York: Wiley.

McAuley, R. (1982). Training parents to modify conduct problems in their children. *Journal of Child Psychology and Psychiatry, 23,* 335–342.

Mind over Minors. (1988). [Computer program]. Human Edge Software Corp., 2445 Faber Place, Palo Alto, CA 94303.

Mischley, M., Stacy, E. W., Mischley, L., & Dush, D. (1985). A parent education project for low income families. *Prevention in Human Service, 3,* 45–57.

Moreland, J. R., Schwebel, A. I., Beck, S., & Wells, R. (1982). Parents as therapists: A review of the behavioral parent training literature—1975–1981. *Behavior Modification, 6,* 250–276.

Mother's Day, with Joan Lunden. [Television series]. Lifetime, 1211 Avenue of the Americas, Department A, New York, NY 10036.

O'Dell, S. L. (1974). Training parents in behavior modification: A review. *Psychological Bulletin, 81,* 418–433.

Parrish, J. M., Cataldo, M. F., Kolko, D. J., Neef, N. A., & Egel, A. L. (1986). Experimental analysis of response covariation among compliant and inappropriate behaviors. *Journal of Applied Behavior Analysis, 19,* 241–254.

Patterson, G. R. (1974). Interventions for boys with conduct problems: Multiple settings, treatments, and criteria. *Journal of Consulting and Clinical Psychology, 42,* 471–481.

Patterson, G. R., & Forgatch, M. S. (1987). *Parents and adolescents living together: Part 1. The basics.* Eugene, OR: Castalia.

Patterson, G. R., & Guillon, M. E. (1968). *Living with children: New methods for parents and teachers.* Champaign, IL: Research Press.

Patterson, G. R., Reid, J. B., & Dishion, T. J. (1992). *Antisocial boys.* Eugene, OR: Castalia.

Popkin, M. H. (1983). *Active parenting.* Atlanta: Active Parenting.

Roberts, M. W., & Hatzenbuehler, L. C. (1981). Parent treatment of command-elicited negative verbalizations: A question of persistence. *Journal of Clinical Child Psychology, 15,* 107–112.

Saudergas, R. A. (1972). *Setting criterion rates of teacher praise: The effects of videotape in a behavior analysis Follow-Through classroom.* Unpublished doctoral dissertation, University of Kansas.

Sloane, H. N., Endo, G. T., Hawkes, T. W., & Jenson, W. R. (1991). Reducing children's interrupting through self-instructional parent training materials. *Education and Treatment of Children, 14,* 38–52.

Stokes, T. F., & Baer, D. M. (1977). An implicit technology of generalization. *Journal of Applied Behavior Analysis, 10,* 349–367.

Strom, R., Griswold, D., & Slaughter, H. (1981). Parental background: Does it matter in parent education? *Child Study Journal, 10,* 243–260.

Sundel, M., & Sundel, S. S. (1975). *Behavior modification in the human services.* New York: Wiley.

Taplin, P. S., & Reid, J. B. (1977). Changes in parent consequation as a function of family intervention. *Journal of Consulting and Clinical Psychology, 45,* 973–981.

Van den Bogaast, P. H. M., & Wintels, P. M. A. E. (1988). *Evaluatie van intensieve thuisbegeleiding* [Hometraining]. Leiden: Ryksuniversiteit.

Wahler, R. G. (1980). The insular mother: Her problems in parent-child treatment. *Journal of Applied Behavior Analysis, 13,* 207–219.

Webster-Stratton, C. (1984). Randomized trial of two parent-training programs with conduct-disordered children. *Journal of Consulting and Clinical Psychology, 52,* 666–678.

Webster-Stratton, C. (1985). Predictors of treatment outcome in parent training for conduct disordered children. *Behavior Therapy, 16,* 223–243.

Webster-Stratton, C., Kolpacoff, M., & Hollinsworth, T. (1988). Self-administered videotape therapy for families with conduct-problem children: Comparison with two cost effective treatments and a control group. *Journal of Consulting and Clinical Psychology, 56,* 558–566.

Weise, M. R., & Kramer, J. J. (1988). Parent training research: An analysis of the empirical literature, 1975–1985. *Psychology in the Schools, 25,* 325–330.

What Every Baby Knows, with Dr. Berry Brazelton. [Television series]. Lifetime, 1211 Avenue of the Americas, Department A, New York, NY 10036.

Williams, C. D. (1959). The elimination of tantrum behavior by extinction procedures. *Journal of Abnormal and Social Psychology, 59,* 269.

Willner, A. G., Braukmann, C. J., Kirigin, K. A., & Wolf, M. M. (1978). Achievement Place: A community model for youths in trouble. In D. Marholin (Ed.), *Child behavior therapy.* New York: Gardner Press.

Wolf, M. M. (1992, November). *Hamburgers, Hondas, hippopotamuses, and responsible dissemination of behavioral programs.* Address given at Father Flanagan's Boys' Home 75th Anniversary Conference, Boys Town, NE.

3

COGNITIVE AND BEHAVIORAL TREATMENT WITH ADULTS

Cognitive-Behavioral Approaches in the Treatment of the Child Sex Offender

Wayne D. Duehn

The treatment of the child sex offender has only recently evolved into a specialized field of practice. This evolution has been spurred by two factors: the increasingly widespread acknowledgment of the extent of the problem and the increasing acceptance of the fact that traditional forms of treatment are not effective with this population. Sex offenders rarely voluntarily pursue treatment (James & Nasjleti, 1989) because they do not want to give up their sexual preferences. Generally, the motivation to seek treatment is the avoidance of incarceration (Langevin & Lang, 1985). Sex offenders are notoriously difficult to treat. They do not admit either the extent or the frequency of their abusive behavior. They are manipulative, exploitive, and secretive. They are narcissistic and therefore experience little if any guilt or awareness of the impact that their abusive behavior has on children (Langevin & Lang, 1985).

This chapter will address the problems of assessing and treating the child sex offender utilizing a cognitive-behavioral approach. Topics to be covered include criteria for determining client selection, designing a comprehensive assessment package, selected cognitive-behavioral approaches, sex offenders' therapy groups, couples and family therapy, social and dating skill-building groups and follow-up treatment strategies. This approach also recognizes the necessity of incorporating regular surveillance-type evaluative measures such as penile plethysmography, polygraphy, interagency staffings, and outside informants to ensure treatment compliance and to appraise treatment and efficacy.

EVALUATION OF THE CHILD SEX OFFENDER

There has been a recent explosion in the literature attempting to define what child sexual abuse is, what characteristics the sex offender exhibits, and how this problem can best be addressed (Finkelhor, 1986; Hindman, 1989; Hollin & Howells, 1991; MacFarlane & Waterman, 1986; Maletzky, 1991; Salter, 1988; Sgroi, 1982). In this chapter child sexual abuse is defined as any sexual behavior with children with the intent to sexually arouse or control them. It is an act of sexual aggression by an adult against a child. The act originates from a clear and specific focus of sexual arousal that the adult has for the child and for the behavior. It is the adult who is always responsible for the act regardless of situational circumstances. The definition labels the sexual behavior as aggression by the adult even in the absence of blood or bruises or with the cooperation or learned conditioned initiative response by the child victim.

The treatment literature on child sexual abuse has been sparse, and the research methods are often inadequate. Explanations of sexual anomalies often lack controlled research data and, therefore, lack empirical support (Langevin & Lang, 1985). Case studies are often unsystematic and are generally so confusing that the factors operative in treatment outcome remain unclear (Langevin, 1983).

In evaluating treatment programs for sex offenders Hollin and Howells (1991) found limitations in the following areas: "the adequacy of sample sizes and subject matching, the inclusion of control groups, the types of outcome measures, the lengths of follow-up, and the statistical evaluation carried out" (p. 173). Travin, Bluestone, Coleman, Cullen, and Melella (1985) report that varying criteria for improvement and minimal follow-up data after five years made it difficult to assess the efficacy of treatment programs. In addition, interventions are often not completed (Hollin & Howells, 1991). Further, it is difficult to examine the pedophile's response to treatment because the outcome study must evaluate a population that has the opportunity to reoffend (Abel, Mittelman, Becker, Rathner, & Rouleau, 1988). Considerable underreporting of sexual offenses makes it difficult to establish recidivism rates (Hollin & Howells, 1991).

To date, the clinical literature consistently suggests that child sex offenders are evenly distributed across all demographic, socioeconomic, ethnic, cultural, social, and religious categories. Although more than 99% of offenders reported in the literature have been male, clinical evidence from sex offenders in treatment and from male and female adult survivors of childhood abuse suggests that sexual offenses by women in general, and child sex abuse in particular, are seriously underreported.

In the clinical findings from agencies conducting evaluation and treatment, the character of the child sexual abuser most often presents a curious mixture of prosocial activity in community or religious organizations and involvement in a pattern of sexual abuse of other individuals. The profile as assessed by personality instruments such as the Minnesota Multiphasic Personality Inventory (MMPI) indicates a high level of narcissism and self-confidence, along with little understanding or empathy for how other people might feel or be affected by one's behavior. The child sexual offender also "tends to be an impulsive individual who, as a defense against the discomfort which his thoughts and actions cause, projects responsibility for his behavior onto other people or forces" (Wolf, 1984, p. 3). Most importantly, he is also an individual who is aroused by his deviant behavior. In terms of physical and emotional arousal, he is excited by his deviance. Marshall and Barbaree (1990) and Quinsey (1979), using psychophysiological measures such as the penile plethysmograph, have shown a consistent and measurable pattern of this sexual arousal.

Wolf (1984) notes that although offenders may despise their deviance and be frightened by its consequences on an intellectual level, they learn to mentally protect themselves through a variety of intellectual gymnastics and cognitive distortions. In the cycle or pattern that he describes, following the completion of an abusive sexual act offenders are filled with guilt and remorse and promise "never to do it again." It is a promise that they believe at that moment. But it is a promise that they have made many times in the past. Child abusers usually have a history of sexually abusive behaviors dating back many years, leaving a trail of multiple victims. This pattern of attraction, arousal, abuse, guilt, promises to terminate the behavior, and back to attraction is predictably present in nearly all child sexual abusers. Individual components may vary, but the central cyclical structure remains and can usually be graphically charted as a reoffense cycle. In short, child sex offenders usually protect themselves from emotional discomfort by cognitively distorting or projecting responsibility for their abusive actions. They are individuals who are attracted to and enjoy their deviance. They are addicted to it. At the time of disclosure, as noted above, they have probably already experienced a long history of sexually abusive activities and victimized multiple children.

From this discussion, it is clear that much information is necessary if the child sex offender is going to be adequately treated. Furthermore, based on current research and clinical experience, some offenders will be assessed as not treatable within the community and may be seen as requiring long-term inpatient treatment or permanent incarceration. These individuals demonstrate histories of escalating violence, sadistic assaults, or repeated offenses without recognition that the behavior is wrong.

Prior to evaluation, a team should collect and review all pertinent police reports, victim statements, and collateral information. It goes without saying that assessment of the child sex offender requires the necessity of a well-coordinated team approach. Teamwork maximizes the sources of information. It is not recommended that a clinician work alone with a child sex offender, regardless of his or her skill level. Ideally, the team should include probation and parole officers, Child Protective Services workers, polygraphers, and clinicians who are seeing other members of the sex offender's family.

A comprehensive clinical interview should gather the following information:

- referral information
- background information
- educational history
- marital history: strengths and problems
- employment history
- military history
- medical history
- drug and alcohol history
- criminal history: extent to which sexual acting out is part of an overall pattern of criminal or psychopathic behavior
- sexual history, of fantasies as well as behaviors

- arousal pattern: if deviant, with what age and sex of child combined with what degree of force
- attitudes and knowledge regarding sexuality
- chain of events leading to sexual acting out
- cognitive distortions regarding sexually deviant behavior
- particulars of the offense
- degree of denial
- degree of responsibility taken
- degree of empathy for victim
- attitudes toward women
- social skills
- assertiveness
- aggressiveness
- family problems
- family-of-origin issues

The following is a list of recommended psychological tests that address issues relevant to understanding and treating child sex offenders. Salter (1988) maintains that the only means absolutely necessary is the plethysmograph, because it is the only objective one. Jensen and Jewell (1991) require polygraph examinations. All other tests rely on self-reports. They measure either sexual deviance or issues relevant to treatment—for example, social skills, empathy, and cognitive distortions.

- Million Clinical Multiaxial Inventory (MCMI)
- Multiphasic Sex Inventory (MSI)
- Able and Becker's Cognitions Scale
- Duss-Durkee Hostility Inventory
- Burt Rape Myth Acceptance Scale
- Penile plethysmograph
- Polygraph examination
- Minnesota Multiphasic Personality Inventory (MMPI)
- Family Adaptability and Cohesion Scale (FACES)

Salter (1988) notes that obtaining information from a complete assessment package is a lengthy process, with the bulk of the time being spent filling out the tests. She adds that although the offender may object to its length, sexual abuse of children is a crime for which individuals do some lengthy prison terms; several hours spent in testing cannot be considered cruel and unusual punishment. Finally, the compelling argument for using these tests, despite the lack of norms, is that no tests are available that address relevant issues and that have been empirically standardized.

TREATMENT TECHNIQUES

Effective treatments for child sex offenders are generally cognitive-behavioral in orientation. There is now an array of good programs to treat these offenders (Greer & Stuart, 1983; Hollin & Howells, 1991; Horton, Johnson, Roundy, & Williams, 1990; Jensen & Jewell, 1991; Laws, 1989; Salter, 1988; Sgroi, 1989). Although each program has its own integrity and coherence, there is little reason why clinicians working together cannot take the best of each. Within such a perspective, specific techniques are viewed as complementary rather than contradictory. Programs that specialize in treating child sexual offenders tend to favor cognitive-behavioral techniques delivered within individual and group treatment modalities. Contrary to the traditional assumption that treatment goals are attainable and time-limited is the notion that there is no cure for the child sex offender and that the task of relapse prevention is lifelong. Successful treatment of recovering child sex offenders involves training them in a variety of self-management techniques for ongoing, regular use. The clinician's task is to train offenders to be their own therapist. The methods must be unintrusive, easily learned, and applicable throughout the individual's lifetime. The treatment protocol should be designed so that the client is able to apply and carry out the procedures without the assistance of a clinician. Furthermore, clinical experience has shown that effective programs for child sex

offenders impart skills. They model prosocial behaviors and attitudes. They are directive, not punitive. They focus on modifying antecedents to deviant behavior, and they all include a provision for monitoring by someone in the community. Finally, and perhaps most important of all, they must be easily understood by the child sex offender. For example, many past efforts to control deviant sexual behaviors and arousal patterns by the application of aversion techniques have failed. The client has not understood the procedure, has not been motivated, and has not had the apparatus required to self-administer the aversive stimuli. Although it is known that arousal control is a lifelong process, if the client cannot do the procedure simply and easily five years from now, it will not be done.

Arousal Control

Arousal control is a most difficult task and is frequently misunderstood. One reason for this misunderstanding is that researchers have not given sufficient attention to the problem. Jensen and Jewell (1991), for example, found that covert sensitization, although once highly regarded as an effective means for controlling sexual arousal, had a negligible effect on very high arousal levels of sex offenders imprisoned in the Oregon State Hospital. They conclude that efficacy may be limited to select offenders or to very minor levels of sexual arousal. Similarly, masturbatory reconditioning techniques have been criticized for being too intrusive. Although they may be effective for the 40-year-old man who takes longer to regenerate sexual arousal, for the younger offender who can regenerate arousal very quickly, they may in fact be serving to reinforce the deviant sexuality imagery. Similarly, aversive behavioral rehearsal techniques employed in therapy sessions in which clients act out their deviant sexuality explicitly (usually with a mannequin), resulting in inherent aversive consequences (feelings of shame, embarrassment), have limitations. These techniques have been found to be extremely intrusive and unlikely to be used outside of the session.

To avoid these limitations and provide a potent procedure that clients can easily learn to control urges, fantasies, and arousal to inappropriate sexual stimuli, Jensen and Jewell (1991) developed the procedure of minimal arousal conditioning (MAC). They found that an inappropriate behavior was more effectively reduced and controlled if the punishment was powerful enough to inhibit the undesirable behavior (arousal) after a few trials. Basically, the procedure is as follows: Clients are asked to write a brief scenario or series of scenarios describing one of their most arousing deviant experiences or an extremely powerful fantasy. This two- to three-page scenario includes the following: a specific account of the client's approach to the child, detailed and vivid descriptions of sexual behaviors imposed on the child, what was said, how the child responded, an exact accounting of the progression of the sexually abusive encounter, the offender's thoughts throughout the offense, and a description of how the abusive event was terminated. If there are multiple scenarios, multiple summaries are constructed. All summaries are revised by the clinician to ensure sufficient vivid detail and to eliminate existing cognitive distortions that would continue to support deviant thinking.

The client is assessed on a penile plethysmograph while he is reading his description out loud to determine where in his description significant arousal begins. Jensen and Jewell (1991) define significant arousal as 5% to 10% of full erection. After the assessment the client and clinician identify the point in the description where significant arousal was first detected. This is the point at which aversion will be applied. The client places this segment onto an audio tape or reads the written description, whichever produces the most arousal.

The client is then instructed to practice daily minimal arousal conditioning. In a private, comfortable setting, the client reads or listens to the tape version of his sexual scenario. He is instructed to read only up to the point of significant arousal and then to immediately punish this arousal by inhaling spirits of ammonia. Reading of this description and punishment are repeated ten times in succession. The client is told to log estimates of arousal and to estimate the effectiveness of punishment on an aversion chart. This procedure is repeated daily, reviewed by the clinician every two weeks, and continued until the arousal pattern has been reduced. This same procedure continues to be used with each description until arousal to all descriptions is below the 5% level.

When the client demonstrates at least four weeks of deviant arousal below the 5% level and has low responses to similar stimulus material, he moves to the second stage of arousal control, which is controlled maintenance. The maintenance phase involves application of the same basic technique but utilizes self-administered covert aversion cognitions in place of inhaling ammonia spirits. As the client demonstrates continued control over his undesirable arousal, he is instructed to diminish the frequency of his daily aversion program. The client is cautioned that deviant arousal will return and should not be viewed as a relapse. He should be prepared to use the ammonia spirits on a daily schedule to again reduce arousal.

It has been found that aversion techniques lead to response suppression but not to elimination. Jensen and Jewell (1991) write that if an alternative sexual response is not rewarded, the suppressed response will quickly return. Furthermore, punishment is most effective when it is introduced early in the arousal response to deviant stimuli. Also, when the client experiences intermittent reinforcement of arousal to deviant stimuli with no associated punishing consequences, there is an erosion effect.

Minimization of Stimulus

Child sex offenders must be taught to minimize stimuli. This most often means a change in lifestyle, learning to avoid situations and places where they are likely to come in contact with children. Along this line, Salter (1988) recommends the application of straightforward strategies such as avoidance of shopping malls, fast-food establishments, parks, and playgrounds and avoidance of dating women who have children.

Control of Desire, Fantasies, and Arousal

It is unlikely if not impossible that a client will be able to avoid all cues and situations that might evoke a deviant response. When the client inadvertently finds himself in a situation with a child he finds attractive, he is required to (1) immediately remove himself from the situation, (2) punish the arousal fantasy by inhaling ammonia spirits within ten seconds, and (3) report to a support person what happened and how he handled the situation. Every child sex offender is required to carry ammonia capsules on his person at all times. This specific instruction may often be made an explicit part of conditions for probation.

Cognitive Restructuring

A significant barrier to recognizing and neutralizing sexual deviancy is the extent to which offenders rationalize and defend their behavior. Such cognitive distortions increase and decrease with the strength of the deviant urges. For example, offenders might say that the child seduced them or even enjoyed the act (Langevin & Lang, 1985). They may believe that it is allowable to sexually involve oneself with a child if no force is used. It is common for offenders to rationalize that

their sexual offenses are educational for the child, that the child receives sexual pleasure from them, or that the child was sexually provocative (American Psychiatric Association, 1987). They do not seek to validate their beliefs with adults and portray their sexual abuse of children as impromptu (Langevin & Lang, 1985). Murphy (1990) refers to Yochelson and Samenow's criminal model of the personality, which states that these distortions "refer to self statements made by offenders that allow them to deny, minimize, justify, and rationalize their behavior" (p. 332). Elaborating further on this model, Murphy adds that the modification of these thinking errors is a major aspect of treatment in which faulty perceptions and cognitive distortions are restructured with the ultimate objective of altering the meaning attached to environmental cues. Environmental information is processed through these distortions, and they have a substantial effect on the way individuals evaluate or misevaluate their behavior and its consequences. Based on this information, Murphy presents examples such as those in Table 6.1 that demonstrate this distortion process. According to Murphy's (1990) literature survey, scales that assess cognitive distortions show that child molesters perceive the offense to be more beneficial to the child, perceive the child as being more responsible for the abuse, and perceive themselves as having less responsibility than do either rapists or a variety of other nonsex offenders.

Salter (1988) identifies such distortions as "releasers," in that they allow the deviant impulses to be acted on. Without such rationalizations, offenders may have some capacity to resist their deviant attraction and to seek help when their own coping mechanisms fail. An effective treatment program, therefore, must pay considerable attention to the offender's use of cognitive distortions.

Offenders must first identify all the specific self-statements of distortions that they have used to excuse, rationalize, and justify

TABLE 6.1   Cognitive Distortions Used by Offenders

General Category and Specific Process	Specific Child-Offender Statements
Justifying reprehensible conduct	
Moral justifications	"It was sex education."
Psychological justifications	"My offense occurred as a result of my wife's lack of understanding [my drinking] [my drug abuse]."
Palliative comparisons	"But I never had intercourse with the child."
Euphemistic labeling	"I was only fooling around." "I was only playing."
Misperceiving consequences	
Minimizing the consequence	"The child didn't suffer."
Ignoring the consequence	"I don't care."
Misattributing the consequence	"If the parents [Child Protective Services] [the police] had been more sensitive, the victim wouldn't have so many problems."
Devaluing and attributing blame to the victim	
Dehumanization	"She was a little whore anyway."
Attribution of blame	"She wanted me to fondle her."

their sexually abusive behaviors with children. Sexual offenses are not isolated but are the culmination of a chain of internal cognitive events (Laws, 1989). This chain is identified by the offender, promoting the recognition of the antecedents that set the stage for the sexual offense. The importance of each event is evaluated by the offender, and it is determined whether the event increased, decreased, or had no effect on the probability that the offense would occur. The events that had no effect or decreased the likelihood of occurrence are eliminated, and the cognitions and affects that represent the offender's interpretation of the events are recorded (Laws, 1989).

The completed cognitive-behavioral offense chain therefore explicates the internal phenomena and behavior that led the offender toward the offense. Specific, high-risk elements are highlighted, and the offender's responsibility for the past offense is emphasized. Effective coping responses are implemented when offenders are able to perceive where events may be leading and when they experience a sense of responsibility for the outcome (Laws, 1989).

A critical step in the process of behavioral change is the development of new thoughts and behaviors that are incongruous with the prior maladaptive ones (Laws, 1989). Thus, it is imperative that perpetrators realize that they have a range of options from which to respond to any situation and that they develop adequate coping responses to elements in the cognitive-behavior offense chain (Laws, 1989).

Offenders are taught that events can be construed in various ways, and their cognitive distortions are then challenged. When they consider other people's views, they evaluate the way in which their interpretations are influenced by their needs, desires, and personal history (Laws, 1989). Additionally, assessment of cognitive distortions may be done, in part, through the use of cognitive-distortion scales. They can also be listened for and recorded during the course of treatment. The use of groups and peers has been shown to be most effective in challenging rationalizations. Another exercise is to ask clients to list each distortion or rationalization and to provide a counterthought. Offenders may be instructed to convey their own "personalized" list of distortions and to read them at stressful moments or when they find themselves recognizing a cognitive distortion.

Building Social and Sexual Skills

Without appropriate social and sexual skills, the child sex offender will make inappropriate advances toward and continue to be involved with children, with whom appropriate social skills are less necessary. Barlow (1973) and Marshall and Barbaree (1990) maintain that enhancing social functioning is a crucial element in treating sex offenders, because it improves their access to appropriate partners and reduces stress, which in turn decrease the probability that offensive behavior will occur. Examples of social skills that should be taught include conversing, asking open-ended questions, gauging self-disclosure, listening actively to others, maintaining eye contact, and giving or receiving compliments. Learning responsible assertive behavior will help reduce the stress that results from constant passivity (Schwartz & Masters, 1983). The offenders should be taught, for example, to verbalize their positive and negative emotions, openly represent their needs, and negotiate differences.

While the above areas of focus assist offenders in reducing stress as well as improving their social skills, other stress management techniques should be taught as well. These include relaxation exercises (Sgroi, 1982) and physical exercise (Schwartz & Masters, 1983).

Sex education includes teaching offenders basic physiological and behavioral knowledge about sex (Enright, 1989), as well as exploring and modifying their beliefs about sexuality. Schwartz and Masters (1983) have noted how negative feedback and parental punishment related to sexuality and the instilling of sexual taboos by family or peers usually disrupt the normal development of sexuality in offenders and interfere with the ability to relate to either sex. Offenders frequently have grotesque misconceptions about women and about female sexuality. Thus, sex education and desensitization are important components in treatment.

Promoting constructive use of leisure time is another important element in the treatment of child sex offenders (Enright, 1989; Marshall & Barbaree, 1990; Schwartz & Masters, 1983). Spending a lot of time alone often leads to high-risk stimulus situations for offenders. Thus, they are encouraged to participate in activities outside the home that will bring them in contact with other adults. Joining new social organizations or starting to participate in group sports is not only encouraged but often mandated.

If the offender is a parent, instruction in parenting skills is included in treatment (Sgroi, 1982). Emphasis is placed on providing knowledge about setting appropriate boundaries between adults and children.

The use of group therapy for the life-skills portion of treatment provides offenders with the opportunity to establish comfort in social interaction with peers. It also provides the context for role playing, modeling, obtaining feedback from others, and support. Role-rehearsal procedures allow the offender to learn appropriate social skills from others practicing those skills in his real world. Social skill training packages are readily available, and some have been created especially for sex offenders. Because many offenders are either self-effacing or aggressive, assertiveness training is also a component of social skills training. Unless child sexual abusers are able to develop caring, intimate, and appropriate sexual relationships, they will probably return to inappropriate sources of sexual satisfaction. This necessitates sexual education, dating and social/sexual skill-building exercises, and resolution of any primary or secondary sexual dysfunction.

It goes without saying that during assessment and treatment it must be determined whether the offender abuses alcohol or other drugs or has a high frequency of aggressive, deviant sexual behavior. Alcohol frequently causes a decrease in the ability to control paraphilic urges, or deviant arousal patterns. Therefore, it is imperative that treatment include a strategy that will make the offender less likely to drink. Deviant arousal may also be associated with use of illicit drugs. Treatment must include random drug screens. A positive screen can be viewed as a failure of outpatient treatment and thus to necessitate inpatient treatment.

CONCLUSION

This chapter has focused on the assessment and treatment of the child sex offender. Providing sex offenders with a simple and effective strategy for arousal control allows them to maintain lifelong control over sexually deviant behavior. This treatment assumes that the client is able to acquire an understanding of antecedent behaviors and predisposing situations, and can learn coping strategies and social and sexual skills.

Sexual assaults on children represent a serious problem in our society. They occur all too often and have severe and long-lasting effects on their victims. The treatment of the sex offender is, relatively speaking, a new frontier. Although much attention has recently been focused on this area, what is needed is much more empirical research into the successes and failures of various specific therapeutic applications. There is growing evidence that cognitive-behavioral treatment of the offender can be very effective in controlling deviant behavior. However, much more research needs to be done to empirically sub-

stantiate the long-term effectiveness of these applications.

REFERENCES

Abel, G. G., Mittelman, M., Becker, J. V., Rathner, J., & Rouleau, J. L. (1988). Predicting child molesters' response to treatment. *Annals of the New York Academy of Sciences, 528,* 223–234.

American Psychiatric Association. (1987). *Diagnostic and statistical manual of mental disorders* (3rd ed. rev.). Washington, DC: Author.

Barlow, D. H. (1973). Increasing heterosexual responsiveness in the treatment of sexual deviation: A review of the clinical and experimental evidence. *Behavior Therapy, 4,* 655–671.

Enright, S. J. (1989). Paedophilia: A cognitive/behavioral approach in a single case. *Journal of Psychiatry, 155,* 399–401.

Finkelhor, D. (1986). *A sourcebook on child sexual abuse.* Beverly Hills, CA: Sage.

Greer, J. G., & Stuart, I. R. (1983). *The sexual aggressor: Current perspectives on treatment.* New York: Van Nostrand Reinhold.

Hindman, J. (1989). *Just before dawn.* Ontario, OR: Alexandria.

Hollin, C. R., & Howells, K. (1991). *Clinical approaches to sex offenders and their victims.* New York: Wiley.

Horton, A. L., Johnson, B. L., Roundy, L. M., & Williams, D. (1990). *The incest perpetrator: A family member no one wants to treat.* Newbury Park, CA: Sage.

James, B., & Nasjleti, M. (1989). *Treating sexually abused children and their families.* Palo Alto, CA: Consulting Psychologists Press.

Jensen, S. H., & Jewell, C. (1991, November). *Advanced training on comprehensive outpatient treatment with sex offenders and their families.* Workshop presented at the 10th annual Research and Treatment Conference of the Association for the Treatment of Sexual Abusers, Fort Worth, TX.

Langevin, R. (1983). *Sexual strands: Understanding and treating sexual anomalies in men.* Hillsdale, NJ: Erlbaum.

Langevin, R., & Lang, R. A. (1985). Psychological

treatment of pedophilias. *Behavioral Sciences and the Law, 3,* 403–419.

Laws, D. R. (1989). *Relapse prevention with sex offenders.* New York: Guilford Press.

MacFarlane, K., & Waterman, J. (1986). *Sexual abuse of young children: Evaluation and treatment.* New York: Guilford Press.

Maletzky, B. M. (1991). *Treating the sexual offender.* Newbury Park, CA: Sage.

Marshall, W. L., & Barbaree, H. E. (1990). Outcome of comprehensive cognitive-behavioral treatment programs. In W. L. Marshall, D. R. Laws, & H. E. Barbaree (Eds.), *Handbook of sexual assault.* New York: Plenum.

Murphy, L. D. (1990). Assessment and modification of cognitive distortions in sex offenders. In W. L. Marshall, D. R. Laws, & H. E. Barbaree (Eds.), *Handbook of sexual assault.* New York: Plenum.

Quinsey, V. (1979). Sexual preferences among incestuous and nonincestuous child molesters. *Behavior Therapy, 10,* 562–565.

Salter, A. C. (1988). *Treating child sex offenders and victims: A practical guide.* Beverly Hills, CA: Sage.

Schwartz, M. F., & Masters, W. H. (1983). Conceptual factors in the treatment of paraphilias: A preliminary report. *Journal of Sex and Marital Therapy, 9,* 3–18.

Sgroi, S. M. (1982). *Handbook of clinical intervention in child sexual abuse.* Lexington, MA: Lexington Books.

Sgroi, S. M. (1989). *Sexual abuse treatment for children, adult survivors, offenders and persons with mental retardation: Vol. 2. Vulnerable populations.* Lexington, MA: Lexington.

Travin, S., Bluestone, H., Coleman, E., Cullen, K., & Melella, J. (1985). Pedophilia: An update on theory and practice. *Psychiatric Quarterly, 57,* 89–103.

Wolf, S. E. (1984). *Evaluation and treatment of the sex offender.* Seattle, WA: Harborview Sexual Assault Center.

7 C H A P T E R

Use of Behavioral Methods with Individuals Recovering from Substance Dependence

Clayton T. Shorkey

Over the past decade many schools of social work have begun to provide part of a required course, a required or an elective course, or even a specialized sequence of course work and field training in chemical dependency as part of their curricula (Burt & Kerekes, 1987; King & Lorenson, 1989). As increasing numbers of helping professionals take jobs in primary chemical-dependency treatment programs, other professionals are recognizing that their jobs in more traditional human service organizations or in private practice necessitate an understanding of the dynamics of substance dependency and its treatment. This growing emphasis on education related to chemical dependency in graduate programs in social work, psychology, and counseling reflects the realization that substance abuse is a critical problem in all aspects of our society. Because no single agency carries out research into prevalence, demographics, and social problems related to alcohol and other substances, there is a lack of consistent data. The 1990 *Seventh Special Report to the U.S. Congress on Alcohol and Health* states that "alcohol abuse and dependence are serious problems that affect about 10% of the American population" (National Institute on Alcohol and Alcoholism [NIAAA], 1990, p. 7). It adds that "cirrhosis mortality was the ninth leading cause of death in the U.S. in 1986" (p. xxiii) and that "alcohol has been implicated as the leading cause of accidental death in the United States" (p. xxiv). The National Center for Health Statistics (Schoenborn,

1991), estimates that 43% of U.S. adults, or about 76 million people, have been exposed to alcoholism in the family. Alcohol abuse is related to a wide range of family and societal problems, including family violence, child abuse and neglect, incest, spouse and elder battering, loss of income and productivity, accidental death and injury, and crime. Limited information is available on the specific role of alcohol or other drugs in family violence. "Methodological weaknesses in much of the applied research preclude firm conclusions about alcohol's role in specific types of violence" (NIAAA, 1990, p. 171). Individual studies and estimates of alcohol-related child abuse and neglect range as high as 90% (Schiff & Cavaiola, 1991), and estimates for incest range from 20% to 50% (Meiselman, 1979). A special study on alcohol and trauma (NIAAA, 1989) reports that 20% to 37% of all emergency room trauma cases are alcohol related, as are 20% to 25% of all the injuries requiring hospitalization. The third *Triennial Report to Congress on Drug Abuse and Drug Abuse Research* from the U.S. Department of Health and Human Services (1991) reports that in 1988, "7.3% of the population 12 years and older were current users of illicit drugs" (p. 15) and that "75% of individuals arrested for serious crimes in 14 major urban areas tested positive for illicit drugs" (p. 3). "As of January 1990, 21 percent of the more than 117,000 cumulative cases of AIDS among adults were intravenous drug users (IVDAs), and another 7 percent were IVDAs who also reported homosexual or bisexual involvement" (p. 87). Despite the incomplete data on the impact of substance abuse on individuals, families, and society, it is clear that the problems associated with alcohol and other drugs are many and extreme.

Knowledge and skill related to substance abuse treatment are highly desirable as preparation for providing effective service in a wide range of practice settings. Child welfare and family service agencies, mental health clinics, public assistance and probation programs, and medical services are some of the settings where social workers and practitioners from other disciplines are providing services to clients whose chemical dependence is an important part of their problem.

Helping professionals may be involved in assessment, diagnosis, intervention, and referral of clients with substance abuse problems to local treatment programs (Corrigan, 1972; Ehline & Tighe, 1977). Others provide services to these individuals and their families after they have completed primary treatment (Mueller, 1972). Clients completing primary chemical-dependency treatment are expected to continue recovery in local self-help organizations such as Alcoholics Anonymous (AA), Narcotics Anonymous (NA), and Cocaine Anonymous or to participate in weekly, group-oriented aftercare programs. Because successful recovery from dependence on a psychoactive substance is a long and complex process, clients can benefit greatly from ongoing professional help from their therapist in maintaining sobriety. Efforts to stay drug-free are often intertwined with other difficulties the clients are experiencing. In order to work effectively with clients recovering from chemical dependence, practitioners need to be familiar with the philosophy, goals, and strategies of conventional treatment programs and the AA 12 Step Program of recovery. Those who lack knowledge related to the dynamics and treatment of chemical dependence may become professional enablers who are helping

chemically dependent clients deny their problem. Attempts to help clients and their families with other social and emotional problems without addressing the primary disease process allow chemically dependent individuals the opportunity to avoid taking responsibility for their addiction (Koppel, Stimmler, & Perone, 1980; Levinson & Straussner, 1978).

In addressing behavioral methods related to alcohol and illicit drugs, I have organized this chapter into three sections. The first section includes a review of assessment criteria for substance dependence and an overview of conventional treatment programs that utilize the 12 Step Program. In the second section I review selected studies on behavioral methods used as adjunctive procedures with individuals completing conventional treatment programs. The final section of the chapter contains suggestions for the use of behavioral methods to support the ongoing recovery of clients using the 12 Step Program. Social learning theory and behavioral methods provide a comprehensive framework and a broad range of techniques useful in helping the recovering clients who have completed treatment to utilize community self-help resources and work on individualized recovery programs to achieve a stable sobriety.

Some behaviorally oriented researchers and clinicians working in the field of chemical dependency prefer *cognitive-behavioral* as the generic term for techniques derived from learning theory. Nathan (1985) expresses the view that *cognitive-behavioral* is preferred to *behavioral* partially due to the bad name the latter term has acquired in the field of alcoholism because of controversial studies on controlled drinking. However, I will use the generic term *behavioral* throughout the chapter for all techniques and procedures based on learning theory. Behavioral methods are used to develop or change knowledge, thinking, emotions, or behavior patterns. Behavioral methods based on cognitive learning include didactics, reading, listening to or viewing recordings, modeling, and others. They also incorporate physiological techniques such as progressive muscle exercises and deep-breathing exercises to produce relaxation responses. A broad range of behavioral techniques and procedures is based on operant and respondent conditioning paradigms. Complex procedures may include cognitive and physiological aspects as well as operant or respondent conditioning techniques. As an example, a systematic desensitization procedure based on the respondent counterconditioning paradigm may incorporate the physiological technique of progressive muscle relaxation and utilize the cognitive technique of mental imagery to represent the anxiety-producing stimuli. This variation of desensitization should, perhaps, be called a "physiological-cognitive-behavioral" technique. Another frequently used method, cognitive restructuring, uses verbal referents of beliefs and ideas as a key component of the process, but it is put into operation through the use of the operant conditioning paradigms of discrimination training, positive reinforcement, punishment, and so forth. Because it would be awkward to use accurate individual labels to describe many complex procedures, the generic term *behavior* is preferred.

SUBSTANCE DEPENDENCE

Dependence on psychoactive substances is defined by the *Diagnostic and Statistical Manual of Mental Disorders* (DSM-III-R) (American Psychiatric Association, 1987) as a mental disorder that includes physiological, cognitive, and behavioral components. The disorder is diagnosed from observable behaviors that indicate impaired control of the use of one or more psychoactive substances, despite adverse consequences. Ten classes of psychoactive substances are associated with this disorder: alcohol; cannabis; cocaine; amphetamines; hallucinogens; opioids;

inhalants; sedatives, hypnotics, or anxiolytics; nicotine; and PCP or similarly acting arylcyclohexylamine substances. The diagnostic criteria for substance dependence include the presence of at least three symptoms that have persisted for at least a month or have occurred repeatedly over a longer time period. Six of the symptoms are related to the pattern of substance use or negative consequences of their use (American Psychiatric Association, 1987):

1. Substance often taken in larger amounts or over a longer period than the person intended.
2. Persistent desire or one or more unsuccessful attempts to cut down or control substance use.
3. A great deal of time spent in activities necessary to get the substance . . . [and in] taking the substance . . . or recovering from its effects.
4. Frequent intoxication or withdrawal symptoms when expected to fulfill major role obligations at work, school or home . . . or when substance use is physically hazardous. . . .
5. Important social, occupational, or recreational activities given up or reduced because of substance use.
6. Continued use despite knowledge of having a persistent or recurrent social, psychological, or physical problem that is caused or exacerbated by using the substance.

Two additional criteria relate to withdrawal from the substance but may not apply to cannabis, hallucinogens, or PCP. These symptoms are withdrawal reactions upon cessation of drug use and the use of the substance to relieve or avoid withdrawal reactions. Finally, one criterion relates to tolerance of the chemical, indicated by either need for increased amounts of the substance over time or a diminished effect with continued use of the same amount. Although symptoms of tolerance and withdrawal are included in the diagnostic criteria, specific information on quantities of the chemical used over time or the opportunity to observe withdrawal reactions of clients is not necessary to diagnose the disorder.

Individuals who do not meet or have never met the criteria for substance *dependence* may be diagnosed using the residual category of substance *abuse* if their pattern of use has lasted at least a month and includes either (1) continued use despite knowledge of having a persistent or recurrent social, occupational, psychological, or physical problem that is caused or exacerbated by the use of the substance or (2) recurrent use in hazardous situations. This diagnosis is related to the length of time the individual has used the substance and to the active potential of the substance. Chemically dependent clients often deny their disease; therefore, practitioners should specifically include a chemical-use history as part of the psychosocial study (Leikin, 1986; Morehouse, 1978). Numerous assessment tools are available to practitioners to assist in assessing the nature, degree, and impact of the client's disorder. The four-item CAGE questionnaire has been demonstrated to be highly reliable in identifying alcoholic clients (Mayfield, McLeod, & Hall, 1974). The Michigan Alcoholism Screening Test (MAST) is a widely used instrument with 25 items that measure signs and symptoms of alcoholism (Selzer, 1971). The Diagnostic Interview Schedule (DIS) includes items related to alcoholism and abuse of other drugs. The items are keyed to the diagnostic criteria of the DSM-III-R (Robins, 1981; Robins, Helzer, Croghan, Williams, & Spitzer, 1981).

Recent research data indicate that substance dependence is related to the genetic and biochemical characteristics of the neurotransmitters in the brain that produce craving responses in the individual (Blum & Payne, 1991). An important variable in the potential of a drug to produce addiction is the positive and negative reinforcement qualities of the chemical. Both positive and negative reinforcement are associated with initial substance use and abuse. After dependence occurs, negative reinforcement to avoid the symptoms of craving appears to provide the major motivation to continue substance use (Lewis, 1990). Current research related to the reinforcing effects of psychoactive substances provides initial support for the theory that chemicals such as alcohol, cocaine, and opiates have common biological determinants (George, 1991). Erickson, Javors, and Morgan (1990) reviewed available research related to the addiction potential of major classes of psychoactive substances, including strength as a reinforcer, and presented a tentative ranking of these substances according to addiction potential. Their ranking, in order of decreasing addiction potential, is stimulants (amphetamines), opiates, alcohol, sedatives/hypnotics, nicotine, anxiolytics, cannabis, inhalants and anesthetics, and PCP and hallucinogens. In addition to genetics and biochemical characteristics, chemical dependence is also influenced by factors in the natural environment, including the access to and constraints on the use of the chemical and the access to and restraints on the sources of alternative reinforcers (Vuchinich & Tucker, 1988).

Contemporary Treatment

The most frequently used approach to the treatment of drug and alcohol dependence is the Minnesota model. It has been reported that 95% of the inpatient treatment centers in the United States follow this model (Desmond, 1987; Kelley, 1991). This model was developed between 1948 and 1950 at three treatment centers in Minnesota: Pioneer House, a municipally funded public program; Hazelden, a private nonprofit program; and Willmer State Hospital (Anderson, 1981). The model is consistent with the diagnostic criteria of the DSM-III-R and views chemical dependence as an illness in its own right, not as merely a symptom of another disorder. The core features of the disease are "loss of control" over specific substances and vulnerability to loss of control over other mood-altering chemicals. The major treatment goals summarized by Cook (1988) include abstinence from all mood-altering chemicals and improvements in lifestyle. The main principles for recovery are derived from Alcoholics Anonymous. Treatment includes lectures and groups on the 12 Steps and 12 Traditions of AA and the medical, social, and psychological aspects of dependency. Group treatment examines the individual's current functioning, use of denial and other defenses, and positive and negative personality characteristics. Clients are advised or required to tell their life stories, work on the first 5 steps of the 12 Step Program, and complete reading and written assignments. Participation in AA or NA meetings is mandatory, and individuals are often expected to find a sponsor before leaving treatment. More recently, family counseling and family programs have been incorporated into this model. Following treatment, patients are encouraged to continue the 12 Step Program of recovery in the community and participate in aftercare groups. Homeless clients, those from dysfunctional families, and those with a high risk of relapse may be referred to halfway houses for a continuation of treatment and supervised living. Most programs are standardized and provide similar treatment for clients regardless of factors such as patterns of substance use, previous treatment attempts, and level of acceptance or denial of the problem of chemical dependency (Kelley, 1991).

The 12 Step Program of Recovery

Because the 12 Step approach to recovery is the central feature of conventional treatment for substance abuse, practitioners providing service to chemically dependent clients need a basic understanding and appreciation of its fundamental assumptions, process, and application. AA is a systematic process that was developed by recovering alcoholics as a self-help approach for achieving and maintaining sobriety. It includes both a program of recovery and a fellowship of chemically dependent individuals. This approach includes a number of fundamental principles to help alcoholics recover and function effectively. Chemical dependence is viewed as an illness of the body and mind that is chronic, progressive, and fatal if not treated. The key characteristic of the illness is powerlessness, or loss of control over the use of chemicals. Individuals with this illness can never safely use chemicals in any form. This loss of control is produced by physical and psychological craving for the chemical. "We believe . . . that the action of alcohol is a manifestation of an allergy; that the phenomenon of craving is limited to this class and never occurs in the average temperate drinker" (Alcoholics Anonymous World Services [AA], 1976, p. xxvi). Termination of chemical use is viewed as merely a beginning in the recovery process.

An important assumption of the 12 Step Program of recovery is that the solution to chemical dependency requires an essential psychic transformation through a vital spiritual experience. This change includes "huge emotional displacements and rearrangements," (AA, 1976, p. 27). It allows for major changes in attitudes, ideas, emotions, and behaviors. This important experience is achieved through accepting a belief in a power greater than oneself. The final conception of a higher power is left up to the individual and may be a traditional religious conception of God or an alternative personal conception of spirituality. For agnostics, an acceptance of the possibility of a higher power is considered an adequate starting point. The willingness to believe in a power greater than oneself is intimately connected to the concept of the elimination of egocentricity, narcissism, grandiosity, and associated character defects such as resentments and fears. The 12 Steps of AA have been modified slightly by NA (Narcotics

Anonymous World Service Office, 1976) to include a broad range of chemicals as follows:

1. We admitted that we were powerless over our addiction, that our lives had become unmanageable.
2. We came to believe that a power greater than ourselves could restore us to sanity.
3. We made a decision to turn our will and our lives over to the care of God *as we understood Him.*
4. We made a searching and fearless moral inventory of ourselves.
5. We admitted to God, to ourselves, and to another human being the exact nature of our wrongs.
6. We were entirely ready to have God remove all these defects of character.
7. We humbly asked Him to remove our shortcomings.
8. We made a list of all persons we had harmed, and became willing to make amends to them all.
9. We made direct amends to such people wherever possible, except when to do so would injure them or others.
10. We continued to take personal inventory, and when we were wrong promptly admitted it.
11. We sought through prayer and meditation to improve our conscious contact with God, *as we understood Him,* praying only for knowledge of His will for us, and the power to carry that out.
12. Having had a spiritual awakening as a result of these steps, we tried to carry this message to addicts and to practice these principles in all our affairs.*

Clients in conventional treatment programs are generally required to complete work through step 5 and are expected to continue working on the steps through participation in AA or NA meetings in the community

*Twelve Steps of Narcotics Anonymous reprinted by permission of World Services Office, Inc., Narcotics Anonymous. Twelve Steps adapted by permission of Alcoholics Anonymous World Services, Inc.

and by working with a sponsor. The role of the sponsor is important in helping an individual make the transition from treatment to participation in the 12 Step programs in the community. Sponsors are people who are successfully working through the steps and have maintained continuous sobriety for at least a year. This work of being a sponsor or of contributing in other ways to helping newly recovering individuals is an important part of the AA program. An understanding of the role of the sponsor in the 12 Step recovery process is an important ingredient in effective concurrent treatment. A practitioner who is providing service to a recovering individual who does not have a sponsor may help improve the client's chances for successful recovery by supporting the client's efforts to secure one.

Despite misconceptions, AA and other 12 Step groups support the notion that recovering individuals may need help outside the program in dealing with other life issues (Wallace, 1984). The 1989 AA membership survey indicates that after coming to the group, 60% of the members received some type of other treatment or counseling. Of those, 85% said that it was an important part of their recovery (AA, 1990).

The spiritual component of AA reflects the belief of the majority of American citizens, including counselors, in the importance of the spiritual and religious aspects of life. Gallup polls report that the percentage of Americans who believe in God or a universal spirit has remained remarkably constant throughout four decades of polling. The most recent survey data, from 1986, indicate that 94% of Americans polled (18 and older) believed in God or a universal spirit (Gallup, 1987). A 1990 poll reports that 85% of surveyed adults indicated that religion was a very important or fairly important part of their lives (Gallup, 1990; Gallup & Newport, 1990). In a survey of psychiatrists, clinical psychologists, marriage and family therapists, and clinical social workers, Bergin (1991) found that 80% of these therapists maintained a religious preference. Of the 106 social workers included in the sample, all identified a religious preference. Hence, the spiritual component of the 12 Step process is compatible with the beliefs of the majority of both chemically dependent clients and the human service professionals who assist them.

Behavioral Methods in the Treatment of Alcohol and Drug Dependence

In a review of outcome studies on behavioral techniques for treating alcoholism, Litman and Topham (1983) comment that it is surprising that behavior therapy has not affected the mainstream of alcoholism treatment to any great extent. The use of behavioral methods in chemical-dependency treatment continues to be limited, and it is clear why this is so. The authors of many early publications in which social learning theory was applied to alcohol dependence rejected the concept of substance dependence as a disease and explained it as a product of social learning. Alcoholism was viewed as a learned, maladaptive pattern of behavior that could be modified through social learning techniques. Treatment emphasized changes in drinking behavior and a reduction in quantity of alcohol consumed as the criteria of success. It is interesting to note that in the early to mid-1970s, although much of the experimental and clinical research employing behavioral methods in alcoholism treatment focused on the development of controlled drinking, concurrent research employing behavioral methods in the treatment of dependence on illicit drugs focused on the goal of abstinence. Therefore, legal issues as well as the theoretical conception of chemical dependence influenced the early goals of behavioral treatment.

In the late 1970s, the emphasis on the use of behavioral methods to develop controlled drinking began to wane due to disappointing

results in research studies and increased support for the disease concept of substance dependence. Since the 1980s, most research and case studies employing behavioral methods with alcohol-dependent clients as well as with individuals dependent on illicit drugs have incorporated these techniques as part of broader conventional treatment programs. Behavioral techniques used in recent studies have included positive reinforcement, self-monitoring, behavior rehearsal, desensitization, covert sensitization, and complex procedures such as cognitive restructuring, stress management, assertiveness and social skills training, and problem-solving training. The need for a change in focus regarding the use of behavioral methods in the substance-abuse field is summarized by Nathan and McCrady (1987):

> We would suggest that, instead of devoting time and energy to defending belief systems, behavior therapists and traditional alcoholism workers alike attempt to identify ways in which the approaches could be integrated. . . . Behavior therapists could more broadly influence the field, and learn more about alcohol abuse, by looking for points of interaction [pp. 127–128].

EXAMPLES OF BEHAVIORAL METHODS AS ADJUNCTS TO CONVENTIONAL TREATMENT

In this section of the chapter I review selected studies related to a broad range of behavioral techniques and procedures. These studies illustrate techniques that could be incorporated into service plans for recovering clients in a wide range of social agencies. Although most of the techniques reflect supplemental use of behavioral methods as a part of inpatient or outpatient treatment, they can be selectively used in individualized service plans for recovering clients to foster their maintenance of sobriety.

Positive Reinforcement, Contracting, and Self-Monitoring

Positive reinforcement—presentation of primary or secondary satisfying stimuli, including social approval or the opportunity to engage in pleasurable activities contingent on the performance of a desired response—is a major intervention technique to increase the performance of a broad range of behaviors associated with successful recovery. Often some form of behavioral contracting and self-monitoring, using a written record of compliance with the treatment contract, has been combined with this technique.

Polakow and Doctor (1973) report an early study related to the use of behavioral contracting and positive reinforcement. The program involved increasing non-drug-related behaviors and maintenance of abstinence from marijuana and barbiturates for a young married couple who were on probation for drug possession. The clients were seen for one hour each week over a 9-month period. A series of contracts with contingent reinforcement for performing non-drug-related social behaviors, job-finding behaviors, and job-maintenance behaviors was negotiated. During the first 6 sessions the probation officer assessed the clients' history of drug use, identified alternative non-drug social activities that the clients enjoyed, and identified relevant reinforcers for the couple. The clients were reinforced by having one week deducted from their probation period for each week that they performed the behaviors included in the contract for that week. In addition, the wife contracted to provide social reinforcement to the husband for verbalizations related to job-finding, job-maintenance, and non-drug-related behaviors. During the 7th through the 14th sessions, contracting focused on job-seeking behaviors. Once the husband obtained employment, reinforcement was contingent on his job attendance. Over the first 20 weeks, the number of selected non-drug-related social behaviors in-

cluded in the contracts increased from one to seven per week. After 20 weeks, reinforcement was contingent on maintenance of employment by the husband and completion of mutually agreed-on contracts negotiated by the couple. After 9 months, the couple were dismissed from attending probation meetings. A follow-up study at 12 months revealed that the husband was still employed and that the couple reported no drug use or marital difficulties. Examination of police and court records on the couple showed no drug-related activities, and their probation was ended.

Keane, Foy, Nunn, and Rychtarik (1984) compared compliance rates for three groups of Veterans Administration patients who had completed inpatient treatment and were then required to take daily Antabuse for a three-month period. Two experimental groups and a control group were included in the study. Eight patients in group 1 signed a contract to monitor and record their use of Antabuse daily and mail in their records monthly. Eight patients in group 2 signed a contract to monitor and record their use of Antabuse daily, mail in their records monthly, and self-administer reinforcement each Sunday for completing their week's medication. A control group of nine patients received only instructions on daily use of Antabuse. Using follow-up interviews with the patients' significant others, the researchers determined that seven of the nine patients in the control group and seven of the eight patients in both the self-monitoring and self-monitoring-plus-reinforcement groups had met the criterion of taking Antabuse daily for three months. Overall compliance of patients in this study was considered high by the authors, who concluded that both self-monitoring and monitoring plus reinforcement contributed to treatment compliance.

The effectiveness of behavioral contracts, reinforcement, and calendar prompts to increase attendance at aftercare sessions for patients who had completed treatment for alcoholism at a VA hospital was studied by Ossip-

Klein, Vanlandingham, Prue, and Rychtarik (1984). Twenty-five patients received a calendar, with eight circled aftercare appointments spread over a six-month period, and a contract to attend the aftercare sessions or to reschedule appointments if they could not attend a specific session. These patients also agreed to post the calendar prominently in their home. The patients' significant other agreed to provide reinforcement with a selected incentive such as a special meal or activity following attendance at each aftercare session. Twenty-five patients served as controls and received standard instructions stressing the importance of attending aftercare sessions. The attendance rate of subjects in the contract/prompt/reinforcement group was approximately double the attendance rate for patients receiving the standard instructions to attend the aftercare sessions.

Systematic Desensitization

Systematic desensitization uses the respondent counterconditioning paradigm to inhibit anxiety responses to selected stimuli and replace anxiety with conditioned relaxation. Relaxation responses may be produced using progressive muscle exercises, relaxation imagery, or hypnosis. The anxiety-producing stimuli selected for desensitization are graded into a hierarchy from low to high according to their anxiety-producing potential. Counterconditioning is completed by association of relaxation responses with items in the stimulus hierarchy beginning with the items with the lowest anxiety-producing potential. There have been a few limited studies on the use of desensitization to assist chemically dependent clients in dealing with anxiety interfering with maintenance of their recovery goals. Lanyon, Primo, Terrell, and Wener (1972) reviewed the effectiveness of a supplementary program including desensitization for patients being treated for alcoholism at May View State Hospital in Pennsylvania. All pa-

tients received 11 sessions over three weeks using a procedure designated as "aversion" therapy, in which two therapists used aversive verbal statements in the patients' group sessions related to their drinking and to their life due to drinking. Eight clients received a combination of aversion and desensitization treatment, and seven clients received aversion and counseling. Immediately following the aversion sessions, the eight clients in the aversion/desensitization group received 30 minutes of systematic desensitization related to drinking-related anxiety situations. The seven patients in the aversion/counseling group spent an additional half-hour in the group verbalizing anxiety problems. Six patients were assigned to a control group and received counseling-only sessions in which they were allowed to verbalize their anxiety. Eighteen patients were located for follow-up from six to nine months after their release from the hospital. Information on abstinence was obtained either by phone or personal interview. Five of the seven patients from the aversion/desensitization group reported that they were abstinent. One of the seven patients from the aversion/counseling group reported maintaining abstinence, and one of the four clients from the control group reported continued abstinence. The researchers concluded that the greater success in maintaining abstinence by the patients who had received desensitization plus aversion was due to the patients' reduced anxiety related to fearful situations that led to their drinking.

A very interesting use of systematic desensitization with a patient recovering from LSD addiction is reported by Matefy (1973). Systematic desensitization was used to reduce anxiety related to interpersonal interactions that triggered frightening flashbacks to bad trips. The treatment included eight sessions of training in deep-muscle relaxation followed by nine sessions of systematic desensitization. Several hierarchies were used related to interpersonal interactions. Three aspects of interpersonal interactions were varied in each hierarchy: familiarity with the other people, the number of people involved, and the intensity of the interaction. Following desensitization, the client was provided supportive therapy. One- and two-year follow-up interviews revealed no recurrence of the flashbacks.

Covert Sensitization

Covert sensitization is the only behavioral procedure from the class of aversive techniques that could be practically employed by practitioners with clients in traditional human-services settings. The use of covert sensitization related to alcoholism is described by Cautela (1970) as a technique to reduce the probability of drinking by alcoholics. Covert sensitization involves replacing excitement or other pleasurable responses to chemical use with anxiety responses through counterconditioning. "Sensitization" utilizes electric shock or the smell of nauseous substances to produce aversive responses. Covert sensitization employs imagery of unpleasant stimuli to elicit the aversive responses needed to accomplish the counterconditioning. Polakow (1975) reports successful use of the technique in fostering abstinence for 18 months with a 24-year-old barbiturate addict who was on three years' probation for possession of drugs. The first six meetings with the client were used to assess contingencies involved in her drug use and possible non-drug-related activities. Weekly covert sensitization sessions were held for 10 weeks focusing on all aspects of barbiturate use. The aversive imagery used was an attack by hordes of sewer rats. Also during these 10 weeks, she agreed in a bahavioral contract to engage in one non-drug-related activity per week. The probationer was also reinforced for completing her weekly contract and covert sensitization session by having one week deducted from her probation time. Weekly sessions of covert sensitiza-

tion continued for 20 more weeks, and the client was instructed to practice the procedure at home. The behavioral contract to perform non-drug-related activities was gradually increased to five activities during these 20 weeks. She was dismissed from probation at 15 months. Follow-up contact at 18 months indicated that she had had no arrests or drug usage.

Smith and Gregory (1976) also used this technique with a 51-year-old alcoholic patient who completed several months of treatment at a VA hospital. Eight sessions of covert sensitization were included as a part of his program toward the end of his treatment. The imagery associated with alcohol and alcohol use in the treatment procedure included the scenarios of killing a child while driving drunk and being homosexually abused in jail following arrest for manslaughter. The patient was also given homework assignments to practice the procedure between sessions. The client was interviewed six months after completion of treatment and reported no desire to drink. His self-report was corroborated by relatives and friends.

Stress Management Procedures

Stress management procedures often incorporate a variety of behavioral techniques to replace anxiety with a relaxation response—such as progressive muscle relaxation, relaxation imagery, or deep-breathing exercises—or reduce anxiety through cognitive restructuring methods. Several specially designed stress management programs have been developed to teach chemically dependent clients methods useful in maintaining their recovery. Examples of these programs include the SOBER program developed at St. Luke's Roosevelt Hospital in New York City (Brody, 1982) and a similar program at St. Vincent's Hospital, also in New York City (Kutner & Zahourek, 1989). Both programs utilize deep-muscle relaxation and deep-breathing exercises. The SOBER model also uses cognitive restructuring to reduce anxiety-producing self-talk related to stressful situations. The program at St. Vincent's Hospital includes the use of relaxation imagery, relaxing music, and relaxation tapes for patients between treatment sessions.

Parker, Gilbert, and Thoreson (1978) studied the comparative effectiveness of three types of stress-reduction techniques in a VA hospital. Thirty alcoholic patients who had scored above 30 on the State Trait Anxiety Inventory (STAI) were selected for the study. Patients were randomly assigned to one of the three treatment groups: deep-muscle relaxation, meditation, or quiet rest. In addition to STAI scores, researchers used several pretest and posttest measures of autonomic arousal, including heart rate, skin conductance, and systolic and diastolic blood pressure. Scores on the STAI and heart rates fell significantly from the beginning of session 1 to the end of session 3 for patients in all groups, although there were no significant differences between treatment groups. No significant differences were found between sessions 1 and 3 using the skin-conductance measure. A significant difference was found in the deep-muscle-relaxation and meditation groups compared with the quiet-rest group for mean diastolic blood pressure from session 1 to the end of session 3. All groups attained a significant decrease in systolic blood pressure from the first to the third treatment sessions. A significant difference between groups was found on systolic blood pressure, with the meditation group significantly lower at the end of the final training session than either the deep-muscle relaxation or quiet rest group. All the procedures were judged to be generally effective in reducing client anxiety and arousal over the brief period of their use.

Spoth (1983) investigated the effectiveness of two variations of the deep-muscle-relaxation technique with 55 alcoholics being treated at a VA hospital. This study was designed to test the hypothesis that cue-controlled relaxation is enhanced by matching training procedures with clients' locus of control of reinforcement. Patients were tested using Mirels's personal control scale, which estimates the extent to which clients choose internal reinforcement or reinforcement from others as the major determinant of their behavior. Based on median scores, subjects were split into internals ($n = 28$) and externals ($n = 27$). Subjects were then assigned to either a matched or unmatched stress-reduction group (internal or external). All four treatment groups used the deep-muscle relaxation followed by the association of the relaxed state with the word "relax." Patients in the externally oriented treatment groups were instructed to practice the procedure every day for ten minutes, focusing on their body tension. Patients in the internally oriented stress reduction groups were instructed to practice the procedure related to specific stressful situations outside of the group. All patients were tested prior to the first treatment and retested one hour after completion of the third and final session using four measures of anxiety: the S-R Inventory of General Trait Anxiousness, the State and Trait forms of the (STAI), and the IPAT Anxiety Scale. Patients also completed a digit symbol task and were monitored for pulse rate. Multivariate analysis of pretest-to-posttest changes on the experimental measures demonstrated that the individuals identified as internal locus of control patients performed significantly better on all measures than external locus of control patients. No significant effects were found for treatment conditions. A significant interaction effect was found for internal locus of control patients matched with the internal locus of control treatment variation.

Cognitive Restructuring

Cognitive restructuring employs teaching, reading assignments, audiovisual presentations, discrimination training, positive reinforcement, behavioral rehearsal, and other techniques to teach clients to modify maladaptive beliefs, attitudes, and ideas that produce undesirable emotional responses and behaviors. The procedure uses behavioral referents of the maladaptive self-talk of clients to produce cognitive and behavioral changes. Hindman (1976) reports on the early use of cognitive restructuring with alcoholics at three treatment centers: Sinai Hospital in Detroit, Mountain Manor Rehabilitation Center in Maryland, and the University of Kentucky Medical Center. Patients in all of these programs were taught to identify and replace irrational self-talk with more rational alternatives to reduce self-generated emotional and behavioral disturbances. Identification of rational and irrational beliefs and ideas represented in patient self-talk followed the theoretical formulation of rational-emotive therapy (RET) (Ellis, 1962; Ellis & Grieger, 1977; Ellis & Harper, 1975; Ellis, McInerney, DiGiuseppe, & Yeager, 1988). Irrational beliefs emphasized in the treatment programs included: irrational commands such as "shoulds," "musts," and "oughts"; "awfulizing" and "catastrophizing" the seriousness of unpleasant events; irrational needs for perfection, approval, and caring; and the belief that people must have perfect control over things that happen to them in life. Behavioral techniques used to implement the cognitive-restructuring procedures included instructions, model presentation, practice in discriminating between rational and irrational beliefs and emotions, practicing of alternative rational self-talk using behavioral rehearsal or homework assignments, self-monitoring, self-administered reinforcements, and penalties. No outcome data were presented related to the use of cognitive restructuring at any of the three programs, but all were considered generally successful.

Although there is limited research related to the use of cognitive restructuring procedures with chemically dependent clients, a study completed at the VA Medical Center in Providence, Rhode Island, provides some interesting initial data (Rohsenow et al., 1989; Monti et al., 1990). The researchers compared the effectiveness of deep-muscle relaxation and cognitive restructuring with two variations of communication skills training. Each of the communication skills training groups received training modules on listening skills, initiating conversations, giving and receiving compliments and criticism, enhancing close relationships, and assertiveness. One of the communication skills training conditions included only the patients, whereas the patient and one significant other were included in the second condition. All patients also completed the standard treatment program provided by the hospital. Each of the three treatment conditions included 12 hours of training over a three-week period. Every four weeks, a new cohort of clients would begin one of the treatment groups. Over the course of one year, 23 patients completed each of the three treatment procedures. Drinking rates for each patient were obtained for the 180 days prior to hospitalization using the Time Line Follow Back Interview (TLFB) devised by Sobell and Sobell. In addition, clients completed the Alcohol Dependence Scale (ADS), the STAI, and the Irrational Beliefs Test (IBT). The IBT was scored for a total score and nine factor scores: approval need, competence need, blame others, problem avoidance, rely on others, doomed by the past, need for precise solutions, external causes, and dwelling on negatives. In addition, all subjects completed an Alcohol Specific Role Play Test (ASRPT) of ten common drinking situations. Each role-playing situation was rated by judges for patients' skill and anxiety and was rated by clients concerning their urge to drink, anxiety level, and scene difficulty. Seventy-seven percent of the patients were located and interviewed, using the TLFB, six months after discharge from the program. Comparisons of pretreatment and follow-up using the TLFB data revealed no differences among the treatment conditions related to relapse or speed of relapse. The IBT did not discriminate between clients who were abstinent or who relapsed over the six-month follow-up period. Scores on the IBT subscale "doomed by the past" significantly correlated with the number of drinks per day and percentage of abstinence days for patients who relapsed. Correlations among measures, using pretest scores, yielded interesting results between subscales of the ADS and the IBT. The subscale "loss of behavioral control" on the ADS was significantly correlated with scores on the IBT subscales of "dwelling on negatives," "problem avoidance," and "need for competence." The authors concluded that although the IBT total scale did not predict whether alcoholics would start drinking again, it did predict how much and how often they would drink after relapse.

Assertiveness and Social Skills Training

It is difficult to differentiate between studies of behavioral procedures labeled assertiveness training and social skills training. Despite labeling differences, studies of this type include the use of modeling, didactics, coaching, behavior rehearsal, positive reinforcement, and punishment to develop a range of effective social skills, which often includes assertive behavior. A study by Adinolfi, McCourt, and Geoghegan (1976) used modeling, role playing, behavioral rehearsal, and social reinforcement to develop assertiveness with six patients at a VA hospital. Discussion of rejection and self-esteem issues related to situations selected for training was incorporated into the procedure. Patients attended from 5 to 15 sessions of training, with an average of 12 sessions. The researchers report that they initially planned to work with the clients on a limited set of situations in which they were unable to act assertively. The actual range of social problems identified by patients was very great and included intense fear, expectations of rejection, frustration of sexual and

companionship needs, job loss, self-deprecation, and others. Follow-up for 11 months following discharge revealed that three patients had maintained abstinence, one patient had had a three-day slip, one patient had had four one-day slips, and the final patient had had two binges lasting several weeks. The researchers reviewed case material related to relapse factors for these six patients and concluded that in addition to the importance of a stable residence (one's own home or a halfway house), employment and satisfying social relationships appeared to be the primary determinants of maintaining abstinence. The researchers, therefore, recommended that assertiveness training focus on developing skills needed by the patients for success in their social and occupational life.

Nelson and Howell (1982–1983) focused on development of skill areas using assertiveness training—making and refusing requests and expressing feelings—with 33 patients at a VA hospital. Patients were randomly assigned to one of three treatment conditions: behavior rehearsal, modeling, or an unstructured-discussion control group. Each group received five daily, one-hour training sessions and an additional booster session one week later. Researchers attempted to contact each patient and one collateral person per patient at approximately two months following discharge. They located and interviewed 82% of the patients and 81% of the collaterals. Fifty percent of the patients who participated in the control group were abstinent, whereas 70% of the subjects receiving assertiveness training using either behavioral rehearsal or modeling were abstinent.

An evaluation of a social skills program with drug abusers in a community residential program provided interesting information related to effective development and maintenance of these skills (Hawkins, Catalano, Gillmore, & Wells, 1989; Hawkins, Catalano, & Wells, 1986). Seventy patients received the behavioral-skills training, and 60 patients served as controls. Ninety-three percent of the patients receiving the special treatment and 88% of the addicts in the control group were assessed using pretreatment and post-treatment performance on the Problem Situation Inventory (PSI), a role-playing test to evaluate five categories of social skills. The skills training group met twice a week for two hours of training for four weeks, followed by one session per week for six weeks. Skills training included instruction, modeling, role playing, structured feedback, videotaped feedback, and group discussion. During weeks 6–10, addicts in the special treatment program also spent one session per week with community sponsors planning and evaluating community networking activities. Forty-seven of the patients in the treatment group completed the full treatment program. Comparison of treatment and control patients on scores of the PSI revealed that addicts in the treatment group (including those who had partially completed the program) obtained significantly better scores on social skills on all subscales of the test: avoidance of drug use, coping with relapse, social interaction, interpersonal problem solving, and coping with stress. The researchers reassessed 92% of the original total sample at a six-month follow-up. Addicts receiving complete or partial treatment continued to score significantly higher on the PSI than controls. A comparison of abstinence rates of addicts completing the specialized treatment program with controls receiving only the standard treatment program revealed no significant differences between the groups. Twenty-two percent of addicts receiving all or part of the special treatment remained abstinent, compared with 18% of control clients. Fully treated clients, however, maintained significantly higher scores on the social skills measures than controls, but their high relapse rate suggests that initial learning and later performance of social skills may require separate procedures. Continued successful use of skills developed during treatment for chronic drug abusers appears to require maintenance training after discharge.

Problem-Solving Training

Problem-solving training is a complex behavioral procedure that includes didactics, modeling, positive reinforcement, punishment, and behavioral rehearsal and practice to develop the skills to effectively problem-solve. Intagliata (1978) studied the effectiveness of problem-solving training with alcoholics being treated at a VA hospital, using the means-ends problem-solving (MEPS) story completion test and discharge plans of patients. Thirty-two patients received a ten-session program over a four-week period; an equal number of patients in a control group received only the standard treatment at the hospital. Comparison of pretest and posttest measures revealed that patients receiving the problem-solving training identified a significantly greater number of solutions to the MEPS stories. The patients receiving problem-solving training and the controls were also compared on the quality and comprehension of their discharge plans at the end of their treatment. The authors reported that patients receiving the special training were more likely to plan for problems than controls. Anecdotal evidence was obtained through follow-up contact with patients one month after discharge. Fourteen of the 72 patients interviewed reported that they had made practical use of knowledge obtained in their training program in dealing with real-life problems. The researchers also reported evidence in the follow-up interviews that the majority of patients contacted had forgotten significant portions of the training material. The researchers concluded that "refresher" sessions in problem-solving skills should be used to increase the long-term impact of the training.

Chaney, O'Leary, and Marlatt (1978) compared the effectiveness of problem-solving training, problem-discussion treatment, and a no-additional-treatment control group for 40 alcoholics receiving treatment at a VA hospital. Problem-solving skill was assessed using a verbal role-playing test, the Situational Competency Test (SCT). Responses to the SCT situations were scored on four measures: latency, duration, compliance, and specification of new behavior. Patients in the problem-solving training group received two 90-minute training sessions each week for four weeks, based on the steps in effective problem solving identified by D'Zurilla and Goldfried (1971). Instructions, modeling, behavioral rehearsal, and coaching techniques were employed to teach problem-solving skills related to situations that exposed the patients to a high risk of relapse. Patients in the discussion group received the same amount of training time to express and discuss their feelings related to problem situations with high relapse potential. Precomparison and postcomparison of scores in the three groups on the four measures of the SCT indicated that patients in the training group achieved higher scores than patients in the other two groups on measures of direction and specification of new problem-solving behaviors. There were no significant differences among the groups on scores on the latency or noncompliance measures of the SCT. A comparison among the three groups at three-month follow-up indicated that patients receiving problem-solving training performed significantly better on three measures of post-drinking behavior: days drunk, total number of drinks, and average length of drinking period. A one-year follow-up indicated that patients in the training group had shorter and less severe relapses than patients in the other two groups. The researchers concluded that their research data provided preliminary evidence that training based on effective problem solving related to high-risk drinking situations could improve the relapse rate of recovering patients.

Other Procedures

Several techniques and procedures (biofeedback, electrical or chemical aversion techniques, and cue exposure) have been omitted from this review because they require special equipment, medical support, special simulus environments, or the use of simulated drugs or drug paraphernalia. Requirements for use of these techniques make it unlikely that practitioners could practically employ them in most agency settings.

BEHAVIORAL METHODS TO FOSTER ONGOING RECOVERY

The remainder of the chapter is devoted to the use of behavioral methods to support ongoing recovery of chemically dependent clients through the 12 Step Program of recovery. Diminution of marital problems, resolution of family violence, remission from psychiatric or medical disorders, and successful completion of the conditions of probation are examples of the goals pursued by practitioners in community agencies that are directly associated with long-term abstinence from psychoactive substances. Behavioral methods may be incorporated into the primary service plan for recovering clients obtaining services at a broad range of social agencies to: (1) promote their attendance at and participation in community 12 Step groups and (2) encourage their individual recovery work using the 12 Step Program.

Promoting Participation in Community Self-Help Groups

The major resource contributing to long-term recovery for clients completing conventional treatment for chemical dependence is community 12 Step groups. Clients are introduced to the concepts and process of the 12 Step Program in treatment, but they are generally on their own in dealing with problems related to participation in these groups in the

community. The 12 Step Program was originally developed by highly educated, chemically dependent individuals who possessed a
broad range of interpersonal and social skills.
Many patients seeking treatment lack the
skills necessary for effective participation in
self-help groups and therefore fail to attend or
are unable to relate within these groups in
ways that address their personal concerns. Assisting clients in comfortable and appropriate
use of community self-help groups is an important role of the practitioner.

The following is a list of typical problems
that interfere with clients' attendance at and
participation in self-help groups. Suggestions
for the use of behavioral techniques to overcome these problems are presented.

Inadequate Motivation to Support Regular Group Attendance.

A *behavioral con-
tract* may be negotiated with the chemically
dependent client alone or may include members of the client's family or significant others. The frequency, time, place, and type of
meetings can be negotiated in a behavioral
contract and be renegotiated over time. For
chemically dependent clients attending self-
help groups, the number of meetings and
their times and places can be agreed on using
a weekly schedule. Special considerations are
necessary to accommodate the days and
hours that the client may be working, regular
days off from work, holidays, or such special
time constraints on nonworking clients as
child care responsibilities. Behavioral contracts may include other aspects of an individual's daily schedule in addition to attending self-help meetings, depending on the
client's need to follow a structured routine.
Individuals in early stages of recovery or
those who have recently experienced a relapse
may choose to follow a structured daily
schedule that includes sleep, work, meals, alternative nonchemical leisure activities, and
self-help meetings.

Demonstrated success over a selected
period using systematic *self-monitoring* of
group attendance may act as reinforcement
for clients to sustain their behavior. Initial
contracts may require testing out and revision. Lack of success in meeting group-
attendance goals identified through a self-
monitoring process provides valuable information needed to revise the initial contracts
to achieve a better fit between the goals selected and other aspects of the clients' life situation. Information from behavorial monitoring helps both clients and the practitioner
achieve a realistic, attainable plan.

Behavioral contracts may include an agreement that provides for contingent *positive reinforcement* for group attendance administered by the client, members of the client's
family, or significant others. Reinforcement
should immediately follow the behavior and
may include social approval from significant
others, a satisfying meal, or the opportunity
to engage in some other desirable behavior.
Generalized reinforcers such as points or tokens may be used for immediate reinforcement and applied toward the future choices
from a menu of reinforcers. *Punishment* may
be incorporated into a behavioral contract
contingent on any activities substituted for
meeting attendance. Because it is not possible
to punish the absence of the performance of a
desired behavior, punishment must be contingent on the substitute behavior. Performance of an undesirable activity may be
made contingent on the performance of an incompatible behavior or a response-cost system employing a token or point system associated with attendance at meetings. The
stimuli or activities selected to reinforce attendance at meetings may need to be varied
over time to avoid satiation with the
reinforcer, which would diminish its effect.
Because some chemically dependent clients
may lack self-reinforcement skills and possess
a limited repertoire of satisfying reinforcers
or activities, experimentation with possible
reinforcers may be useful to expand the range
of choices in the contracts. Discriminative
stimuli may be added to the use of positive

reinforcement in the form of cues or prompts. Prompts may include notes on a calendar, reminder notes in the car, home, or workplace, and telephone calls or verbal reminders from significant others. In order to function as discriminative stimuli, cues must signal the opportunity to obtain agreed-on positive reinforcement for performing the selected behavior. Care should be taken in selecting cues that will consistently be a part of the person's environment before the time comes to perform the desired response.

Obstacles That Interfere with Group Attendance.

Clients should be encouraged to maintain a log of the dates, times, and circumstances surrounding missed meetings, such as transportation problems, child-care responsibilities, or competing family activities. This information is useful in characterizing the obstacles and their sources (self, others, environment) that impede performance. Lack of performance of agreed-on behaviors provides the opportunity to teach the client the components of an effective *problem-solving process,* including a positive orientation to solving problems, definition and formulation of problems, generation of alternatives, decision making, and verification. Practice in performing behaviors that are needed to complete the process of effective problem solving may initially focus on difficulties in attending meetings. Skills in effective problem solving may later be applied to a broad range of personal, interpersonal, and resource problems. Because problem-solving effectiveness is enhanced in groups, significant others should be included in the training when possible.

Anxiety Related to Participation in Interpersonal Groups.

Recovering clients who experience moderate levels of anxiety in anticipation of self-help meetings or during their participation in these groups may be provided training and practice in the use of *anxiety-reduction procedures,* such as progressive muscle relaxation, deep-breathing exercises, relaxation imagery, relaxation audio tapes, meditation, positive affirmations, prayer (such as the AA serenity prayer), and relaxation-producing self-talk. Stress-reduction skills initially developed by clients related to anticipation and attendance at group meetings may be later transferred to other stressful life situations through additional training.

Systematic desensitization provides an effective procedure for use with recovering clients who experience anxiety that is elicited by stimuli associated with participation in small groups. Anxiety may be elicited by the physical characteristics of the group members, the number of members of the group, the size or characteristics of the room, or such aspects of group activities as reading aloud, being asked a question, holding hands with other group members in a circle, being given positive or negative feedback, or expectations about having to disclose personal or family problems. The reduction of maladaptive conditioned anxiety to group cues may be a major factor that determines whether the client continues to use self-help groups as a recovery resource.

Deficits in Communication or Assertiveness Skills.

A lack of skills needed for active and comfortable participation in self-help groups is an important factor that discourages many recovering clients from utilizing available community resources. Instruction and practice in the development of *communication skills* needed for participation in these small groups may reduce anxiety and increase participation. Furthermore, the reinforcement value of the group experience itself can be expected to strengthen along with increased social competency and concomitant interpersonal comfort. Clients may practice a broad range of social skills such as greeting others, saying goodbye, developing and maintaining eye contact, asking questions, expressing opinions, and giving feedback to other members. They may be given homework assignments to practice specific skills in groups.

A positive sense of personal control and self-determination is important for clients participating in self-help groups. A general axiom of anonymous groups is to "take the best and leave the rest." Supporting clients' exercise of personal choice regarding the dogma, goals, and activities of self-help groups is an important role of the practitioner. Clients who believe themselves to be deprived of self-determination or who lack the skills to actualize their choices through their behavior may resist participation in self-help groups. *Assertiveness training* can be used to provide the support that the client needs for personal values and choices, whether related to participation in group meetings or to informal interactions outside the meetings. Practitioners can help clients identify what they would like to gain from attendance at groups and the range of behaviors acceptable to them in the groups. A constant review of such choices provides the client with an ongoing opportunity to examine personal values and goals. Assertion training has the dual purpose of developing behaviors needed for attaining desired goals and for refusing unwelcome requests or activities. The importance of effective assertiveness skills is especially relevant to relations with other recovering individuals outside the group.

Skills Related to Group Attendance and Participation

The fellowship component of community self-help groups provides a living laboratory in which clients can develop and practice a broad range of important life skills. Support of clients' efforts to understand and effectively utilize this resource may be the most important determinant in helping them avoid relapse to chemical use. Many skills related to attendance and participation in self-help groups can be transferred to other areas of cli-

ents' activities and help solve other interpersonal, emotional, legal, and resource problems.

Supporting Individualized 12 Step Recovery Work

The 12 Step Program offers a systematic process for individuals recovering from chemical dependence to structure their efforts to stay clean and sober. The fellowship component offers ongoing positive role models, social reinforcement for successful efforts to maintain sobriety, hope, and encouragement despite possible slips or relapses. Practitioners providing services to recovering clients may use various conceptions of the 12 Step process for integration with traditional treatment methods. To maximize integration of behavioral treatment methods with the 12 Step Program, this program can be viewed as having four interacting components.

Component 1.   The first component of the 12 Step process of recovery is expressed by the first step, which identifies the problem and its consequences: that the individual is suffering from a chronic and progressive disease that directly results in a broad range of negative life situations, including the possibility of premature death. Step 1 also signifies a movement away from guilt and shame connected with having this disease and a movement toward a realistic understanding of this illness. Finally, it signifies a decision to stop using the substance and to begin the process of recovery.

Increasing knowledge of chemical dependence: Reading material, lectures, audiotapes, and videotapes can be assigned to clients to increase their knowledge about the nature of their disease and its consequences. Assignments should be selected and organized into a series of smaller components in line with the needs and abilities of the client. They should be designed to ensure the likelihood that the client will complete them. Written exercises may also be provided, and clients should be encouraged to write down questions about the material for later discussion with their practitioner. Self-monitoring of the completion of assignments and a system for reinforcement of task completion may be used to support the client's efforts.

Reducing shame and guilt: Cognitive restructuring can be used to reduce shame and guilt by teaching the client to differentiate between values placed on the characteristics and/or behaviors of individuals and values placed on the individuals themselves. The values associated with the illness and the negative consequences to the individual and others are uniformly bad, but these negative values need not be applied to the value of the clients themselves. Clients learn to differentiate between ascribing a negative evaluation to their disease and choosing to accept themselves as a person with intrinsic worth, despite their undesirable condition.

Increasing avoidance of chemical use: Covert sensitization can be used to increase clients' avoidance of the chemical(s) on which they are dependent. Initial training in covert sensitization should be carried out by the practitioner with the client. Following initial training, the client can be given homework assignments. The client can periodically practice the procedure to maintain a conditioned aversive response to chemical use, especially when faced with the possibility of situations that may threaten to undermine sobriety.

Strengthening alternative behaviors: Positive reinforcement and practice in the performance of alternative activities to replace substance use are important techniques. Clients can use substitutes for chemical use such as drinking fruit juice instead of beer, enjoying a movie instead of visiting a club, attending a 12 Step meeting, or calling another recovering person instead of using the chemical. Clients can be instructed to monitor the frequency of performance of alternative activities. Self-reinforcement or reinforcement by

significant others for performing substitute behaviors increases the client's performance as well as good intentions related to this goal.

Component 2. The second component of the 12 Step Program of recovery is the spiritual solution represented by steps 2, 3, 5, 6, 7, and 11. These steps reinforce the individual's belief in care and protection through God or an alternate, nontheistic conception of spirituality. The spiritual component of the recovery process encourages clients to accept their humanness and discourages grandiosity, egocentrism, and self-righteousness. It provides hope for the future, forgiveness for shortcomings and poor behavior, and faith in the client's ability to achieve self-improvement goals. This component emphasizes patience, serenity, and a fuller enjoyment of life. This philosophy is exemplified by 12 Step slogans such as "Easy does it" and "Let go and let God" and by the serenity prayer: "God grant me the serenity to accept the things I cannot change, the courage to change the things I can, and the wisdom to know the difference."

Personal development: Personal goals relevant to the spiritual component of recovery include sleep schedule, diet, exercise, work, and leisure activities. Self-management goals may include increased participation in religious services in the client's faith of choice. Development of a daily or weekly plan for living can help clients prioritize among competing goals given time limitations. An important aspect of prioritizing and selecting life goals is to take control of the use of a limited amount of time and energy. Goals for rest, relaxation, enjoyable activities, and quality time with family members and significant others are viewed as equally as important as goals related to producing income or fulfilling responsibilities.

Stress reduction: Deep-muscle relaxation exercises, relaxation imagery, meditation, and the use of audio or video recordings can be used to reduce stress and to foster serenity and contentment. Initial development of stress-reduction techniques involves instruction and practice to achieve the desired effects. Proactive planning and rehearsal of stress-management techniques for use in potentially stressful future situations are helpful.

Reducing grandiosity: Cognitive restructuring can be used to teach clients that they do not control the universe. A key aspect of this process is teaching them to discriminate between desires and preferences and demands and commands. Grandiosity is expressed by demands and commands that other people always behave perfectly well and that they and the world always operate in ways that are desirable for the client. Acceptance of one's fallibility as a human being, the fallibility and humanness of others, and the reality of good and bad aspects of the world are important beliefs to foster in the goal of reducing grandiosity. Through cognitive restructuring, the client can learn that demanding will not increase control over oneself, others, or the world and that work and effort to achieve one's goals will greatly increase, but not guarantee, the probability of their attainment.

Component 3.   The third component of the 12 Step Program focuses on personal work to identify and change dysfunctional thinking, emotional responses, and behavior patterns. Steps 4, 5, 8, 9, and 10 focus on self-improvement and personal growth. This component is linked with the spiritual solution by the belief that faith without works is dead (AA, 1976). Problems identified through completion of a personal inventory may reflect any aspect of intrapersonal or interpersonal life. Clients may choose to focus on work to change disturbed or irrational thinking; maladaptive emotional responses such as anxiety, anger, and resentment; or personal traits such as laziness, pride, envy, or procrastination. Many types of goals may also be identified related to overcoming problems in interpersonal relationships to foster more satisfying interactions with significant others, family members, and co-workers.

Reducing anxiety: A broad range of behavioral methods previously discussed is applicable to reducing anxiety. Systematic desensitization is appropriate for stimulus-specific anxiety responses. Progressive relaxation exercises, relaxation imagery, and deep-breathing exercises as well as relaxing music can be used to elicit responses incompatible with anxiety in anxiety-arousing situations and as preparation for situations that have a high probability of anxiety arousal. Cognitive restructuring can be used to replace anxiety-producing self-talk such as awfulizing and catastrophizing unpleasant situations. Clients can also be trained to change beliefs related to the dire necessity to behave perfectly in all situations and to be approved of by everyone. Clients can be taught to differentiate between their desires and demands and wants and needs for perfection and approval.

Improving interpersonal relationships: In addition to using basic social skills training procedures, practitioners can assist clients in identifying individual goals related to improving their relationships with significant others. Goals may include spending more time with family members, displaying increased interest in the concerns of others, and reducing the amount of verbal interactions that focus on their own issues. Basic operant techniques can be applied toward the goals of improved marital communication, conflict resolutions, and parenting skills. A broad range of clinical and research literature on improving relationships is available in books and journals to supplement the practitioner's knowledge of basic behavioral techniques.

Reducing resentment: Cognitive restructuring provides the most useful method for reducing vengeful resentment. Clients can be instructed to differentiate between demands and preferences related to the behavior of others. Reinforcement of statements of desires and preference is used to replace "shoulds," "musts," and "oughts." Learning also includes an understanding and acceptance of the fallibility of other individuals as well as oneself. Clients can be taught that demandingness produces anger and grandiosity, resulting in the view that others should be punished for behaviors that are not in line with our demands and extreme expectations.

Component 4. The fourth component of the 12 Step Program includes continued personal work toward self-development and spiritual growth through helping other chemically dependent individuals work on their recovery. Recovering clients are expected to draw on the knowledge and skills they have learned through their recovery and share them through acting as group leaders or sponsors or through supportive interactions outside of group meetings with other members. Practitioners can contribute to clients' 12 Step work by fostering their continued personal growth through encouragement and social reinforcement.

Behavioral Methods Applied to Alternative Recovery Programs

It must be recognized that not all clients will choose to pursue the 12 Step Program of recovery from substance dependence. Several new programs are gaining popularity, such as Women for Sobriety (Kaskutas, 1989; Kirkpatrick, 1990, n.d.), Rational Recovery (Trimpey, 1989, 1992), and Secular Organization for Sobriety (Christopher, 1988, 1989). Each of these newer programs has unique assumptions related to successful ingredients for recovery, and each approach utilizes a systematic step-by-step process for recovery combined with social support of members in self-help groups. Modifications in the 12 Step Program have also been developed for use with individuals having dual psychiatric disorders (Evans & Sullivan, 1990), and a generic model of recovery, Total Aspects of Re-

covery Anonymous (TARA), addresses all aspects of recovery in one system (Reah, 1992). Practitioners need to become familiar with the fundamental assumptions and recovery process of newer programs that may be selected by their clients. Behavioral techniques can be employed to support clients and work toward maintaining their recovery using any of the systems. Appropriate and effective utilization of behavioral methods is largely determined by the practitioner's skill in these techniques and understanding of the recovery program selected by the client. Although a detailed review of alternative or modified 12 Step methods is beyond the scope of this chapter, information on these approaches is readily available.*

CONCLUSION

The field of chemical dependence has experienced dramatic changes in recent years. Chemical dependence is now generally viewed as a complex biological and psychosocial disease. Persuasive research studies have documented the genetic and biochemical bases of the illness. There is also a growing recognition of the significance of social and environmental factors that contribute to initial substance use and work against individual efforts to recover. The dynamic influences of poverty, dysfunctional family systems, and the illegal drug industry cannot be underestimated. Greater humility about the effectiveness of current treatment methods available to chemically dependent individuals has begun to develop. As suggested by Tucker (1992), the focus of treatment utilizing the

*Information on alternate recovery methods can be obtained from the following sources: Secular Organization for Sobriety (SOS), P.O. Box 5, Central Park Station, Buffalo, NY 14215; Rational Recovery System, Box 800, Lotus, CA 95651; Total Aspects of Recovery Anonymous (TARA), 21736 Saddlebrook Drive, Parker, CO 80134; Women for Sobriety (WFS), P.O. Box 618, Quakertown, PA 18951.

technology of social learning theory requires a shift in emphasis from the expectation of rapid, permanent solutions to an extended sequence of short-term interventions to provide support to the recovering client living in a dynamic and changing environment.

Helping professionals have important roles to fill in the chemical dependency field, whether they work in primary treatment programs, work in private practice, or provide services in the diverse range of human service agencies that count substance-dependent clients as a large part of their caseloads. Practitioners in community agencies who have a basic knowledge of chemical dependence and its treatment are an invaluable resource to support the recovery efforts of their clients. Practitioners can bridge the gap between the short-term services offered by alcohol and drug-abuse treatment agencies and the needs experienced by clients for a lifelong recovery process utilizing self-help resources. Integration of behavioral methods with the process and support provided by self-help groups will no doubt strengthen the desired effects of both.

REFERENCES

Adinolfi, A. A., McCourt, W. F., & Geoghegan, S. (1976). Group assertiveness training for alcoholics. *Journal of Studies on Alcohol, 37,* 311–320.

Alcoholics Anonymous World Services. (1976). *Alcoholics Anonymous.* New York: Author.

Alcoholics Anonymous World Services. (1990). *1989 Membership Survey.* New York: Author.

American Psychiatric Association. (1987). *Diagnostic and statistical manual of mental disorders* (3rd ed. rev.) Washington, DC: Author.

Anderson, D. J. (1981). *Perspectives on treatment.* Center City, Minnesota: Hazelden Foundation.

Bergin, A. E. (1991). Values and religious issues in psychotherapy and mental health. *American Psychologist, 46,* 394–403.

Blum, K., & Payne, J. E. (1991). *Alcohol and the addictive brain.* New York: Free Press.

Brody, A. (1982). S.O.B.E.R.: A stress management program for recovering alcoholics. *Social Work with Groups, 5*(1), 15–24.

Burt, W., & Kerekes, M. (1987). *Survey results: The study of alcoholism in the social work curriculum.* Unpublished manuscript, Norfolk State University, School of Social Work, Norfolk, VA.

Cautela, J. R. (1970). The treatment of alcoholism by covert sensitization. *Psychotherapy: Theory, Research and Practice, 7,* 86–90.

Chaney, E. F., O'Leary, M. R., & Marlatt, G. A. (1978). Skill training with alcoholics. *Journal of Consulting and Clinical Psychology, 46,* 1092–1104.

Christopher, J. (1988). *How to stay sober: Recovery without religion.* Buffalo, NY: Prometheus Books.

Christopher, J. (1989). *Unhooked: Staying sober and drug free.* Buffalo, NY: Prometheus Books.

Cook, C. C. H. (1988). The Minnesota model in the management of drug and alcohol dependency: Miracle, method or myth? Part I. The philosophy and the programme. *British Journal of Addiction, 83,* 625–634.

Corrigan, E. M. (1972). Linking the problem drinker with treatment. *Social Work, 17,* 54–60.

Desmond, E. W. (1987, November 30). Out in the open. *Time,* pp. 80–90.

DiGiuseppe, R. A., Robin, M. W., & Dryden, W. (1990). On the compatibility of rational-emotive therapy and Judeo-Christian philosophy: A focus on clinical strategies. *Journal of Cognitive Psychotherapy, 4,* 355–367.

D'Zurilla, T. J., & Goldfried, M. R. (1971). Problem solving and behavior modification. *Journal of Abnormal Psychology, 78,* 107–126.

Ehline, D., & Tighe, P. O. (1977). Alcoholism: Early identification and intervention in the social service agency. *Child Welfare, 56,* 584–592.

Ellis, A. (1962). *Reason and emotion in psychotherapy,* Secaucus, NJ: Citadel Press.

Ellis, A., & Grieger, R. (1977). *Handbook of rational-emotive therapy,* New York: Springer.

Ellis, A., & Harper, R. A. (1975). *A new guide to rational living.* Englewood Cliffs, NJ: Prentice-Hall.

Ellis, A., McInerney, J. F., DiGiuseppe, R., & Yeager, R. J. (1988). *Rational-emotive therapy with alcoholics and substance abusers.* New York: Pergamon Press.

Erickson, C. K., Javors, M. A., & Morgan, W. W.

(Eds.). (1990). *Addiction potential of abused drugs and drug classes.* New York: Haworth Press.

Evans, K., & Sullivan, J. M. (1990). *Dual diagnosis: Counseling the mentally ill substance abuser.* New York: Guilford Press.

Gallup, G., Jr. (1987). *The Gallup poll.* Wilmington, DE: Scholarly Resources.

Gallup, G., Jr. (1990). *The Gallup poll.* Wilmington, DE: Scholarly Resources.

Gallup, G., Jr., & Newport, F. (1990, June). More Americans now believe in a power outside themselves. *The Gallup Poll Monthly,* pp. 33–35.

George, F. R. (1991). Is there a common biological basis for reinforcement from alcohol and other drugs? *Journal of Addictive Diseases, 10*(1/2), 127–139.

Hall, S. M., Bass, A., Hargreaves, W. A., & Loeb, P. (1979). Contingence management and information feedback in outpatient heroin detoxification. *Behavior Therapy, 10,* 443–451.

Hawkins, J. D., Catalano, R. F., Jr., Gillmore, M. R., & Wells, E. A. (1989). Skills training for drug abusers: Generalization, maintenance, and effects on drug use. *Journal of Consulting and Clinical Psychology, 57,* 559–563.

Hawkins, J. D., Catalano, R. F., Jr., & Wells, E. A. (1986). Measuring effects of a skills training intervention for drug abusers, *Journal of Consulting and Clinical Psychology, 54,* 661–664.

Hindman, M. (1976). Rational-emotive therapy in alcoholism treatment. *Alcohol Health and Research World, 1,* 13–17.

Intagliata, J. C. (1978). Increasing the interpersonal problem-solving skills of an alcoholic population. *Journal of Consulting and Clinical Psychology, 46,* 489–498.

Jones, S. L., & Lanyon, R. I. (1981). Relationship between adaptive skills and outcome of alcoholism treatment. *Journal of Studies on Alcohol, 42,* 521–525.

Kaskutas, L. (1989). Women for sobriety. *Contemporary Drug Problems, 16*(2), 177–200.

Keane, T. M., Foy, D. W., Nunn, B., & Rychtarik, R. G. (1984). Spouse contracting to increase Antabuse compliance in alcoholic veterans. *Journal of Clinical Psychology, 40,* 340–344.

Kelley, J. M. (1991). Extended stabilization: The future of inpatient treatment. *Addiction and Recovery, 2*(3), 40–43.

King, G., & Lorenson, J. (1989). Alcoholism training for social workers. *Social Casework, 70,* 375–382.

Kirkpatrick, J. (1990). *Turnabout: New help for the woman alcoholic.* New York: Bantam Books.

Kirkpatrick, J. (no date). *Women for Sobriety and A.A.* Quakerstown, PA: Women for Sobriety.

Koppel, F., Stimmler, L., & Perone, F. (1980). The enabler: A motivational tool in treating the alcoholic. *Social Casework, 61,* 577–583.

Kutner, G., & Zahourek, R. P. (1989). Relaxation and imagery groups for alcoholics. *Advances, 6*(3), 57–64.

Lanyon, R. I., Primo, R. V., Terrell, F., & Wener, A. (1972). An aversion-desensitization treatment for alcoholism. *Journal of Consulting and Clinical Psychology, 38,* 394–398.

Leikin, C. (1986). Identifying and treating the alcoholic client. *Social Casework, 67,* 67–73.

Levinson, V. R., & Straussner, S. L. A. (1978). Social workers as "enablers" in the treatment of alcoholics. *Social Casework, 59,* 14–20.

Lewis, M. J. (1990). Alcohol: Mechanisms of addiction and reinforcement. In C. K. Erickson, M. A. Javors, & W. W. Morgan (Eds.), *Addiction potential of abused drugs and drug classes.* New York: Haworth Press.

Litman, G. K., & Topham, A. (1983). Outcome studies on techniques in alcoholism treatment. *Recent Developments in Alcoholism, 1,* 169–194.

Matefy, R. E. (1973). Behavior therapy to extinguish spontaneous recurrences of LSD effects: A case study. *Journal of Nervous and Mental Disease, 156,* 226–231.

Mayfield, D., McLeod, G., & Hall, P. (1974). The CAGE questionnaire: Validation of a new alcoholism screening instrument. *American Journal of Psychiatry, 131,* 1121–1123.

Meiselman, K. C. (1979). *Incest.* San Francisco: Jossey-Bass.

Monti, P. M., Abrams, D. B., Binkoff, J. A., Zwick, W. R., Liepman, M. R., Nirenberg, T. D., & Rohsenow, D. J. (1990). Communication skills training with family and cognitive behavioral mood management training for alcoholics. *Journal of Studies on Alcohol, 51,* 263–270.

Morehouse, E. R. (1978). Treating the alcoholic on public assistance. *Social Casework, 59,* 36–41.

Mueller, J. F. (1972). Casework with the family of the alcoholic. *Social Work, 17,* 79–84.

Narcotics Anonymous World Services. *Narcotics anonymous: Who, what, how, and why* [Pamphlet]. (1976). Van Nuys, CA: Author.

Nathan, P. E. (1985). Alcoholism: A cognitive social learning approach. *Journal of Substance Abuse Treatment, 2,* 169–173.

Nathan, P. E., & McCrady, B. S. (1987). Bases for the use of abstinence as a goal in the behavioral treatment of alcohol abusers. *Drugs and Society, 1*(2/3), 109–131.

National Institute on Alcohol Abuse and Alcoholism. (1980). *Alcohol and the Family.* Rockville, MD: Author.

National Institute on Alcohol Abuse and Alcoholism. (1989, January). Alcohol and trauma. *Alcohol Alert,* pp. 2–3.

National Institute on Alcohol Abuse and Alcoholism. (1990). *Alcohol and health* (DHHS Publication No. ADM-281-88-0002). Washington, DC: U.S. Government Printing Office.

National Institute on Drug Abuse. (1991). *Drug abuse and drug abuse research* (DHHS Publication No. ADM-91-1704). Washington, DC: U.S. Government Printing Office.

Nelson, J. E., & Howell, R. J. (1982–1983). Assertiveness training using rehearsal and modeling with male alcoholics. *American Journal of Drug and Alcohol Abuse, 9,* 309–323.

Ossip-Klein, D. J., Vanlandingham, W., Prue, D. M., & Rychtarik, R. G. (1984). Increasing attendance and alcohol aftercare using calendar prompts and home based contracting. *Addictive Behaviors, 9,* 85–89.

Parker, J. C., Gilbert, G. S., & Thoreson, R. W. (1978). Reduction of autonomic arousal in alcoholics: A comparison of relaxation and meditation techniques. *Journal of Consulting and Clinical Psychology, 46,* 879–886.

Polakow, R. L. (1975). Covert sensitization treatment of a probationed barbiturate addict. *Journal of Behavior Therapy and Experimental Psychiatry, 6,* 53–54.

Polakow, R. L., & Doctor, R. M. (1973). Treatment of marijuana and barbiturate dependency by contingency contracting. *Journal of Behavior Therapy and Experimental Psychiatry, 4,* 375–377.

Reah, H. (1992). Total aspects of recovery anonymous. *The Counselor, 10*(1), 16–17.

Robins, L. N. (1981). *NIMH Diagnostic Interview Schedule: Version III: Instructions for use.* Rockville, MD: National Institute of Mental Health.

Robins, L. N., Helzer, J. E., Croughan, J., Williams, J. B. W., & Spitzer, R. L. (1981). *NIMH Diagnostic Interview Schedule: Version III.* Rockville, MD: National Institute of Mental Health.

Rohsenow, D. J., Monti, P. M., Zwick, W. R., Nirenberg, T. D., Liepman, M. R., Binkoff, J. A., & Abrams, D. B. (1989). Irrational beliefs, urges to drink and drinking among alcoholics. *Journal of Studies on Alcohol. 50,* 461–464.

Schiff, M. M., & Cavaiola, A. A. (1991). The education of the adolescent chemical dependence worker in the field of child abuse. *Journal of Adolescent Chemical Dependency, 1*(3), 3–10.

Schoenborn, C. A. (1991). Exposure to alcoholism in the family: United States, 1988. In *Advance Data,* No. 205 (pp. 1–13). Hyattsville, MD: National Center for Health Statistics.

Selzer, M. L. (1971). The Michigan alcoholism screening test: The quest for a new diagnostic instrument. *American Journal of Psychiatry, 127,* 1653–1658.

Smith, R. E., & Gregory, P. B. (1976). Covert sensitization by induced anxiety in the treatment of an alcoholic. *Journal of Behavior Therapy and Experimental Psychiatry, 7,* 31–33.

Snowden, L. R. (1978). Personality tailored covert sensitization of heroin abuse. *Addictive Behaviors, 3,* 43–49.

Spoth, R. (1983). Differential stress reduction: Preliminary application to an alcohol-abusing population. *International Journal of the Addictions, 18,* 835–849.

Trimpey, J. (1989). *Rational recovery from alcoholism: The small book.* Lotus, CA: Lotus Press.

Trimpey, J. (1992). Rational recovery: Twelve Step counterpoint. *The Counselor, 10*(1), 8–11.

Tucker, J. A. (1992). Clinical research on addictive behaviors in the 1980's: Shifting focus from treatment outcome evaluations to studies of behavioral process. *The Behavior Therapist, 15* 4–5.

U.S. Department of Health and Human Services. (1991). *Triennial report to congress on drug abuse and drug abuse research.* Washington, DC: U.S. Government Printing Office.

Vuchinich, R. E., & Tucker, J. A. (1988). Contributions from behavioral theories of choice to an analysis of alcohol abuse. *Journal of Abnormal Psychology, 97,* 181–195.

Wallace, J. (1984, Spring). Myths and misconceptions about Alcoholics Anonymous: An alcoholism counselor's view. *About AA,* pp. 1–2.

8

The Spouse as a Positive Rehabilitative Influence in Reaching the Uncooperative Alcohol Abuser*

Edwin J. Thomas

Through excessive drinking, alcohol abusers harm themselves and many others, particularly those in their family. Alcohol abuse is a major personal, social, health, and economic problem, as has been well documented. The refusal of the alcohol abuser to enter treatment makes an already difficult problem worse. Unfortunately, the majority of alcohol abusers are hard to reach. It has been estimated, for example, that 85% of excessive drinkers are "hidden" and untreated (Thomas, Santa, Bronson, & Oyserman, 1987). In being hard to reach, they either do not recognize that they have a problem or are unwilling to seek help. Most conventional methods of treatment are inadequate to the task of reaching and assisting the uncooperative alcohol abuser, and new methods need to be developed.

As a vital and potentially crucial source of influence, the abuser's spouse may be the main or only rehabilitative agent accessible to the practitioner. There is increasing evidence that spouses can be used productively in rehabilitative efforts with alcohol-abusing partners. For example, the involvement of nonalcoholic wives in the treatment of their alcoholic husbands has been found in some studies to be associated with selected positive outcomes (Cadogan, 1973; Corder, Corder, & Laidlaw, 1972; Ewing, Long, & Wenzel, 1961; Gliedman, 1957; Hedberg & Campbell, 1974; McCrady, Paolino, Longabaugh, & Rossi, 1979). Clinical reports have suggested the effectiveness of family confrontive interventions in influencing the drinker to enter treatment (Howard & Howard, 1978; Johnson, 1973; Maxwell, 1976; Thorne, 1983; Zimberg, 1982), as have several nonexperimental studies (Liepman, Nirenberg, & Begin, 1989; Logan, 1983).

Pilot research on unilateral family therapy—that is, involving only one partner—for alcohol abuse has indicated the feasibility and desirability of helping spouses increase their skills in coping with some of the personal distress and marital dysfunction associated with living with an uncooperative alcohol abuser and, more generally, of inducing the unmotivated drinker to begin recovery (Thomas, 1989; Thomas & Yoshioka, 1989; Thomas et al., 1987). My associates and I recently completed a four-year clinical experiment to evaluate a unilateral treatment program in which spouses of alcohol abusers unmotivated for treatment were assisted in influencing the drinker to enter treatment, reduce drinking (with abstinence preferred), or both. Positive changes for spouses included a reduction of dysfunctional drink-related behaviors, such as "enabling," and increases in personal and marital adjustment. Positive changes for abusers associated with spousal treatment consisted of

*The research reported in this chapter was supported in part by grants from the National Institute on Alcohol Abuse and Alcoholism. I wish to acknowledge the contributions of Denise Bronson, Cathleen Santa, Joanne Yaffe, and Daphna Oyserman in the pilot phase of the research and of Richard D. Ager, Marianne Yoshioka, Kathryn Betts Adams, and David Moxley in the evaluation phase.

a greater likelihood of entering treatment or re-ducing their drinking or becoming abstinent (Thomas, Yoshioka, Ager, & Adams, 1993). It was concluded that spouses could be taught to exert a positive rehabilitative influence on an uncooperative alcohol abuser.

This chapter presents the conception of the spouse as a positive rehabilitative influence along with illustrative treatment procedures drawn from the unilateral family therapy pro-gram. Enhancing the positive rehabilitative influence of spouses is an important step in preparing them to function as effective treat-ment mediators with their alcohol-abusing partners. In the context of the unilateral ap-proach, six distinguishing characteristics of this influence are highlighted. Also presented are relevant procedures, case illustrations, practice issues, client and therapist considera-tions, and other applications.

THE SPOUSE IN UNILATERAL FAMILY THERAPY FOR ALCOHOL ABUSE

As already suggested, in the unilateral ap-proach a spouse or other cooperative family member is trained to mediate change in an uncooperative family member (Thomas & Santa, 1982). There are three distinctive foci of intervention: (1) to assist the spouse alone with his or her coping (the individual focus), (2) to change aspects of the marital or family functioning through inductions mediated by the influence of the spouse (the interactional focus), and (3) to change the behavior of the uncooperative family member—that is, to fa-cilitate sobriety (the third-party focus). An important assumption is that inducing partic-ular changes in an individual can lead to changes in the system of which that person is a part, an assumption that has precedents in selected innovative clinical programs (Szapocznik, Kurtines, Foote, Perez-Vidal, &

Hervis, 1983), systems theory (Bowen, 1974; Carter & Orfanidis, 1976), and other concep-tions of addressing marital problems through one spouse (Bennun, 1984). This approach does not assume that the cooperative family member is to blame for the difficulties. As in-dicated, however, the spouse is viewed as a vital and potentially crucial source of influ-ence.

The spouse's potential, however, cannot automatically be realized. Spouses are typi-cally not ready at the beginning of treatment to serve as effective mediators of change. This, of course, is most understandable. Such spouses typically (1) experience considerable marital distress (Jacob & Krahn, 1988), often accompanied by marital and family disorga-nization (Bailey, 1961; Ghodse, 1982; Paoli-no & McCrady, 1977); (2) have made many accommodations and adjustments to try to adapt to the drinking (Jackson, 1954; Orford et al., 1975); (3) enable the drinking (Johnson, 1973; Orford et al., 1975); (4) have adopted a variety of home remedies that typically have been unsuccessful (Homila, 1985; Wiseman, 1980); (5) are overinvolved in the problem (Burnett, 1984; Cermak, 1986); (6) have mis-conceptions and faulty knowledge of alcohol abuse, despite being personally familiar with its effects; and (7) lack understanding of what to do about the problem.

COMPONENTS OF THE SPOUSE'S REHABILITATIVE INFLUENCE

If spouses are to assume a positive rehabilita-tive role, they need to make six changes: (1) adopt an appropriate role conception as a treatment mediator; (2) increase further their understanding of the alcohol problem; (3) re-duce their customary and generally dysfunc-tional efforts to exercise control over the drinking; (4) increase their positive therapeutic influences; (5) engage in abuser-directed interventions; and (6) continue sobriety support to maintain the gains achieved.

Selected elements of the unilateral treatment program are drawn on below to highlight these six generic aspects of the spouse's role. The order in which the categories are presented corresponds in general to the order in which treatment efforts should be carried out.

Changing the Spouse's Role Conception

In the initial session, an orientation is given in recognition that the treatment program is new and differs considerably from most others. In regard to the nature of the treatment itself, the following are among the points explained by the therapist: (1) the three foci of intervention (spouse coping, family functioning, and sobriety facilitation); (2) the right of the spouse to receive treatment and, likewise, the right of the abuser to refuse treatment; (3) the importance of keeping matters discussed in treatment in confidence, including especially not disclosing to the abuser what transpires in treatment; (4) an overview of the treatment program's components, to be carried out prior to conducting an active intervention with the abuser.

In regard to the role of the spouse, the orientation also covers (5) the assumption that the spouse is not to be blamed for the excessive drinking of the partner; (6) the potential of the spouse to become a positive rehabilitative influence; (7) the responsibilities of the spouse in treatment to provide needed information as frankly as possible, to cooperate in gathering data and formulating the intervention plan, to avoid premature or ad hoc initiatives with the abuser and intervene only as planned with the therapist at the agreed on time; and (8) assurance that although some of the treatment methods are new and further research is needed to validate the approach, results to date have indicated that the approach has been generally successful in the majority of cases and that no adverse effects have been found.

The spouse's role conception is also shaped in a step-by-step fashion by the brief introductory explanations given before carrying out each treatment component and by the spouse's experience in carrying out the program components. As things progress, spouses learn further that this is not conventional talk therapy, that their coping is handled largely through gains made by their participation in each of the role-induction models (for example, disenabling), that the primary focus is on working with them to reach the drinker, and that this is done through careful planning and problem solving with the therapist.

Increasing the Spouse's Understanding of the Problem

Although the spouses are those who have recognized that their marital partners have a drinking problem about which something must be done, most spouses still underestimate the seriousness of the problem, are poorly informed about the nature and effects of alcohol abuse, and hold various misconceptions. It is therefore necessary in most cases to provide spouses with some individualized education concerning aspects of alcohol abuse.

Topics include the characteristic behavior of alcohol abusers; the effects of alcohol; the seriousness of alcohol abuse for health, work performance, and family and psychological functioning; the role of learning and family factors in excessive drinking; and the nature and promise of contemporary treatment for alcohol abuse. In addition to information given in the orientation and at other relevant points by the therapist, a variety of booklets, pamphlets, and books can be given to spouses to read, depending on their educational needs. Literature, such as *I'll Quit Tomorrow* (Johnson, 1973), *Black Outs and Alcoholism* and *Chemical Dependence and Recovery: A Family Affair,* published by the Johnson Institute in Minneapolis, are particularly useful.*

The spouse's understanding of the abuser's problem is also increased through recording the abuser's daily alcohol consumption that is easily observable, using a monitoring form. Information is recorded concerning the amount of alcohol consumed, the type of drink, and the percentage of alcohol involved, with space for other relevant data and comments. This information provided by the spouse is generally sufficient for the therapist to determine the amount consumed.† In addition to providing the therapist with data about the abuser's level and pattern of alcohol consumption, such monitoring sensitizes the spouse to the amounts consumed and serves to make the level of the abuser's drinking and its effects more vivid.

The therapist also obtains a brief alcoholic history of the abuser from the spouse in an early session. The alcoholic history is additional "reality amplification" that can serve to further highlight the seriousness of the problem and the need for change (Thomas, 1989).

Reducing the Spouse's Customary Alcohol Influence with the Abuser

Spouses with partners who drink too much commonly try to exercise control of the drinking through such means as nagging and complaining, withdrawing from the drinker, or threatening the drinker with consequences if he or she doesn't stop. Drinking-control efforts are characteristic of the family's interaction patterns and are part of the customary alcohol-influence system that is in operation prior to treatment for the spouse or family member. Pretreatment efforts to bring about change in the abuser's drinking are typically carried out on an occasional, intermittent, and nonsystematic basis. Even so, they commonly consist of strongly ingrained responses that are ineffective or, worse, produce negative reactions that perpetuate existing patterns of marital conflict. The above description and the clinical results reported below were taken from Yoshioka, Thomas, and Ager (1992), where additional details are presented.

The Program to Reduce Spouse Drinking Control.

The purpose of changing the spouse's attempts to control the drinking is to reduce or eliminate the possible aversiveness of these efforts, to interrupt or eliminate old interaction and influence patterns that otherwise could interfere with intervention, and to create an atmosphere more conducive to active interventions to be introduced later. In an early session, the therapist initiates assessment to identify drinking-control behaviors by interviewing the spouse or through use of the Spouse Sobriety Influence Inventory (SSII), which contains the Spouse Drinking Control subscale. The SSII consists of 52 items relating to attempts by spouses of alcohol abusers to control or change the abuser's drinking behavior.* Each item (for example, "expressed disapproval of the drinking") is rated from "never" to "always" for the period of the previous six months on a five-point Likert-type scale. Items endorsed at the level of "occasionally" or more are listed separate-

---

*Among the many sources of alcohol-education materials in addition to the Johnson Institute are the Al-Anon Family Group Headquarters, Alateen, the Hazelden Foundation, the National Clearing House for Alcohol/Drug Information, the National Council on Alcoholism, and the National Institute on Alcohol Abuse and Alcoholism.

†Obviously, some abusers drink outside of the home, and in any case, not all drinking can be readily observed by the spouse. In these instances, the spouse can record whether alcohol was consumed and, if so, whether the abuser drank in moderation or was drunk.

*The Spouse Sobriety Influence Inventory, by Edwin J. Thomas, Marianne Yoshioka, and Richard D. Ager, © 1988 by these authors and the University of Michigan. A copy of this instrument along with an abstract of descriptive and psychometric details can be found in Thomas, Yoshioka, and Ager (in press-b).

ly by the therapist as candidate areas for possible intervention. After the list has been reviewed with the spouse, the therapist provides a description of the concept of drinking control as an aspect of the spouse's "old influence system." It is indicated that at this point the "old system" needs to be reduced. Frequently occurring drinking control behaviors are then screened for interventional feasibility and specified, and alternative noncontrolling responses are identified.

Case Example.   Steve and Gail were professionals in their late 30s with three young children. A Vietnam veteran, Steve had had a long history of excessive drinking before Gail's involvement in spouse treatment. During the course of the first few sessions, she described her intense frustration with and anger toward her husband and his drinking, attributing her frequent headaches to the stress that the drinking created. Following her completion of the SSII, four items were selected from the Spouse Drinking Control subscale as indicative of behaviors appropriate for drinking-control modification: (1) refusing to talk to the drinker because of the drinking, (2) ignoring the drinker to get back at him, (3) saying that if the drinker loved her or the children, he'd stop, and (4) having arguments about problems relating to the drinking. The first three were introduced for intervention in the first week, with the fourth added the week following.

After introducing the program, Gail reported that she felt more in control of herself and in a better emotional state. Over the weeks, there was some variation in her ability to refrain from the control behaviors. Overall, however, she was able to sustain a reduction and reported a more pleasant home environment, fewer physical symptoms, and less stress. Her scores on the Spouse Drinking Control subscale went from 3.75 at pretreatment to 3.25 at posttreatment 6 months later, were reduced further to 1.00 at the 12-month

follow-up, and were 2.50 at the 18-month assessment.

Case A was the first case in a pair of spouses of a crossover experimental dyad. A series of such dyads was employed in the experimental evaluation, in which the first spouse in each successive dyad was assigned at random to receive immediate treatment, given for 6 months, and the second to receive delayed treatment, given in the subsequent 6 months. Then there were two additional assessments, 6 and 12 months later.

The results for Case B, assigned to the delayed-treatment condition of the above dyad, also indicated successful change. Scores on the Spouse Drinking Control subscale of the SSII were 3.67 and 4.00 for the time 1 and time 2 assessments given prior to treatment for this case and were 1.00 at the time 3 and time 4 follow-up assessments 6 and 12 months later. (Although not necessarily because of their spouse's reduced drinking control, the abusers in both cases subsequently entered treatment.) Positive results were also found in both cases for drinking-control behaviors that were not targeted and for total drinking-control scores. The results for this crossover dyad were directly comparable to those found for the aggregate of spouses who received unilateral treatment in the evaluation phase of the research (Thomas, Yoshioka, Ager, & Adams, 1993).

Reducing Spouse Enabling.   As is well recognized in the field of alcohol treatment, most spouses and others associated with the drinker help make the abuser's drinking possible—that is, "enable" it. It is not at all uncommon, for example, to find that a spouse drinks with the abuser, buys alcohol for the abuser, delays meals while the abuser drinks, and gives cocktail parties and other engagements where the abuser characteristically drinks too much. Like drinking control, enabling is part of the customary alcohol-influence system; and, like drinking control, enabling needs to be reduced to make way for more beneficial spouse behaviors such as sobriety support, to be described below.

With emphasis on the major areas in which the spouse has enabled the abuser's drinking, a tailor-made program of "disenabling" is embarked on to counter the ways in which the spouse has enabled the abuser's drinking. Based on results obtained with the Spouse Enabling Inventory,* enabling may range from several identifiable behaviors to as many as 20 or more. More so than the reduction of drinking control, the reduction of enabling behaviors has the potential of producing negative reactions from the abuser and disrupting the marital relationship otherwise. Disenabling should therefore be carefully planned and implemented to avoid these risks (Thomas, Yoshioka, & Ager, 1993).

Increasing the Spouse's Positive Therapeutic Influence

Although many aspects of the unilateral treatment program involve increasing the spouse's positive therapeutic influence, broadly conceived, two treatment modules address this question directly, relationship enhancement and sobriety support.

Unilateral Relationship Enhancement. Relationships in alcoholic marriages are frequently strained and discordant and characterized by conflict, anger, mistrust, resentment, and poor communication and decision making. Discordant relationships provide a poor basis for spousal mediation. Enhancing the marital relationship is an important step in the preparation of the spouse to function as a posi-

*The Spouse Enabling Inventory, by Edwin J. Thomas, Marianne Yoshioka, and Richard D. Ager, © 1987 by these authors and the University of Michigan, consists of 47 items that ask the respondent to indicate how often he or she has engaged in that behavior over the previous six months (e.g., arranged parties where alcohol was served). A copy of this instrument along with an abstract of descriptive and psychometric details can be found in Thomas, Yoshioka, and Ager (in press-a).

tive rehabilitative influence. Because the program is necessarily implemented only through the cooperative spouse, it is called unilateral relationship enhancement (URE) to distinguish it from the relationship-enhancement programs that are bilateral between spouses.

The purpose of URE is, first, to reduce the conflict, distress, and alienation between the partners. In URE, the spouse independently initiates or discontinues behaviors with the intention of "calming" the marital system. The second purpose is to increase the reinforcement value of the relationship by enhancing its socioemotional and instrumental aspects. This, in turn, is intended to increase the ability of the cooperative spouse subsequently to influence the nonparticipating marital partner.

These changes are achieved by helping the participating spouse to select and increase behaviors that are potentially pleasing to the nonparticipating partner or to select and reduce behaviors that are potentially displeasing. It is critical that the URE behaviors be those the cooperative spouse is willing and able to carry out. The therapist can describe these behaviors to spouses as an "investment" made now to be realized later in beneficial changes that URE and the other aspects of the treatment may produce.

The intention in enhancing the relationship is not to bring about changes in other aspects of the marriage or to correct major marital problems. However, such outcomes may be facilitated in some instances. There is no expectation that URE alone will necessarily change the abuser's drinking, but it should facilitate positive marital interaction, which has been shown to be relevant in recovery and in maintaining sobriety (McCrady, 1989; O'Farrell, 1986).

The above description and the clinical results presented below were taken from Thomas, Adams, Yoshioka, and Ager (1990), where further details are given.

Case Example.   Margaret was a middle-aged part-time secretary whose husband, Ed, was a machine operator and a longtime heavy drinker unmotivated for treatment. Margaret was asked to briefly review a list of illustrative pleasers and displeasers we prepared for this purpose (Thomas, Adams, Yoshioka, & Ager [1989]).* She identified several items in her second session that survived the screening and were selected for her URE program. She had not been initiating much physical affection with her husband in recent years, and the other behaviors she chose as pleasers had stopped because of her anger about his drinking.

As shown in Table 8.1, the therapist obtained a retrospective baseline from Margaret for each behavior in the program. Prior to treatment, most of the pleasers were at the rate of zero times per month, and the two displeasers were carried out about once daily.

Margaret was forewarned not to expect responses from her husband and not to anticipate a decrease in drinking due to these efforts alone. Adopting a positive attitude about URE from the start, she began to carry out the behaviors right away and reported that her feelings toward the marriage had improved, although there were few positive reactions from Ed.

As she continued URE activities and monitoring throughout the course of treatment, the frequency with which she engaged in behaviors varied somewhat from week to week. Her pleasers increased markedly, and her displeasers decreased to levels well below her respective baseline, as shown in Table 8.1. She began to show more affection (through hugs and kisses), and reduced conflictual interactions such as nagging, criticism, and sarcasm. Her husband agreed to stop drinking and did so when she actively intervened later in the course of the spouse treatment. Although many factors were no doubt contributing to the abuser's abstinence, Margaret

*Copies of the list are available from the author at the School of Social Work, University of Michigan, Ann Arbor, MI 48109-1285.

performed the tasks of URE consistently to help establish conditions in the marital system that would favor achieving change in her husband's drinking.

In the analysis of the clinical results for the URE program, it was found, overall, that the program had been readily implemented and that most of the spouses had been able to continue the program during treatment at a level above baseline. Although relationship enhancement would ideally be undertaken bilaterally between marital partners, it is important to remember that this is not possible in the unilateral case, at least in the early stages prior to the unmotivated drinker's entering treatment. Again, in working with the cooperative spouse of an unmotivated drinker, it is essential that the therapist not impose a URE program on an unwilling spouse or one who does not have the requisite enhancing behaviors in his or her repertoire.

Sobriety Support.   Most spouses do not respond to the drinker so as to support sobriety, or if they do, their supporting responses tend to be occasional or otherwise nonsystematic. Sobriety support consists of behaviors by the spouse that serve to strengthen nondrinking responses by the abuser, to weaken the abuser's inducements to drinking, or both. For example, the spouse may endeavor to initiate a non-alcohol-related activity before the abuser can start a session of drinking. Such activities could include attending a movie, going to a restaurant that does not serve alcohol, or consuming a nonalcoholic beverage. During a session of the abuser's drinking, the spouse may take action to shorten the session or otherwise reduce the amount of alcohol consumed. Further, following periods of reduced drinking or abstinence, the spouse may reinforce the moderated drinking, be pleasant company, and not respond negatively or punish the sobriety-related behavior. Because of the variations in the amount consumed and the periods of drinking and nondrinking characteristic of the drinking patterns of most al-

TABLE 8.1   Frequency of Relationship-Enhancement Behaviors Before and During Treatment for Margaret

	Monthly Mean	
Areas of Behavior	Retrospective Baseline	Treatment Phase
Pleasers		
Going out alone with Ed	0	4.4
Initiating hugs, kisses, and touching	0	13.6
Bringing coffee or a snack	0	2.5
Discussing future plans	0	6.7
"Special things": meals, gifts	1	5.1
Expressing affection or approval	3	4.0
Displeasers		
Critical or sarcastic remarks	30	7.1
Nagging about smoking or chores	35	3.5

NOTE: The mean for the retrospective baseline is the client's estimated frequency for the month before treatment began, and for the treatment phase it is the monthly mean of the behaviors during 5.5 months of treatment. From "Unilateral Relationship Enhancement in the Treatment of Spouses of Uncooperative Alcohol Abusers" by E. J. Thomas, K. B. Adams, M. R. Yoshioka, and R. D. Ager. In the *American Journal of Family Therapy, 18,* p. 340. Copyright 1990 by Brunner/Mazel, Inc. Reprinted by permission.

cohol abusers, there are many opportunities to instigate or reinforce reduced drinking or abstinence prior to the unmotivated drinker's recovery.

To initiate sobriety support, the practitioner works with the spouse to identify appropriate opportunities to reinforce the drinker's sobriety and to plan how and when the spouse will reinforce the nondrinking behaviors. The isolation of potential reinforcers can be tricky, inasmuch as the drinking has often become so affectively charged between the partners that some comments by the spouse that are intended to be positive backfire, are interpreted as drinking control, and produce negative reactions. In consequence, indirect or subtle comments may be called for, or even saying nothing but still being pleasant and agreeable during periods of sobriety. An occasional verbal response may be enough, such as "I enjoy your company when you haven't been drinking," mentioned at an appropriate

time following periods of sobriety. Because it is intended to replace the old influence system, sobriety support should not be implemented until progress has been made in reducing customary drinking control. Although discussed here as it relates to the period when the abuser is continuing to drink excessively, sobriety support also applies in periods of moderated drinking or abstinence, described more fully below.

Engaging the Spouse in Giving Abuser-Directed Interventions

Abuser-directed interventions, being largely confrontational to penetrate the abuser's resistance, tend to be stronger and more intrusive than most conventional interventions. The purpose, then, is to induce abusers to enter treatment, to reduce their drinking, or both. (Ideally, the reduced drinking should take the form of abstinence, but in some cases moderated drinking short of abstaining is the best outcome that can be achieved at the time, with abstinence being the ultimate goal.) Such interventions should be undertaken only after sufficient progress has been made in otherwise preparing the spouse to assume a positive rehabilitative role.

Confrontive Interventions by the Spouse. With the aim of influencing the drinker to enter treatment, the *programmed confrontation* entails training the spouse either alone or with other family members to confront the abuser firmly but compassionately in the presence of a therapist. A programmed confrontation should not be carried out if other less intrusive interventions would be appropriate or if the spouse is unwilling to follow through with a strong contingent consequence if the abuser does not take the action recommended for treatment. Possible contingent consequences include the willingness of the spouse to separate, divorce, develop a separate life within the marriage, or alter domestic arrangements for household work if the recommendation is not followed. The confrontation is a powerful induction that can be successful if it is used with care and if selected conditions, such as those indicated here, are met.

The programmed confrontation bears some similarity to other confrontive interventions, including the "intervention" of the Johnson approach (Johnson, 1973, 1986). In the unilateral approach, however, the programmed confrontation is one of several possible abuser-directed interventions that are part of more comprehensive treatment, as presented here, in which spouses are also taught to increase their skills in coping with some of the personal distress and marital dysfunction associated with living with an uncooperative alcohol abuser and are helped more generally to assume a positive rehabilitative role.

Also confrontive, the *programmed request* consists of a carefully timed, staged, and delivered request to have the abuser carry out a rec-ommended action, usually to enter treatment for excessive drinking. Although generally weaker than the programmed confrontation, the programmed request, when appropriately made, can be strong enough to accomplish its objective. Because it is not just any old request of the drinker, this intervention, like the programmed confrontation, requires careful planning and rehearsal. Among the conditions that need to be met are evidence of some readiness by the abuser to respond favorably to the request and, in general, unwillingness of the spouse to carry out a strong consequence if the abuser fails to comply with the request.

Other abuser-directed interventions include programmed self-control for the abuser and programmed decision making and contingency contracting for the marital partners. These interventions also have particular conditions that make them the appropriate courses of treatment. The above material and the clinical application below are taken from Thomas and Yoshioka (1989), where additional details are presented.

Case Examples. Two cases from the same crossover experimental dyad of the pilot research are briefly summarized below. Programmed confrontation was employed in the first case, assigned to receive immediate treatment, and programmed request is illustrated in the second case, which was assigned to receive delayed treatment. Following the steps recommended for the development of either a programmed confrontation or a programmed request (see Box 8.1), selected details are summarized below.

Case A: Gene and Nancy, in their second marriage, were a professional couple in their 50s who had been married for 12 years and who had one child, a 15-year-old, still living at home. Gene had been a heavy drinker since before their marriage and was drinking approximately a fifth of 80-proof spirits every evening.

Assessment disclosed that in the *determination of suitability* Gene was strong-willed and stubbornly resistant to Nancy's efforts to change his drinking habits. She was dissatisfied with the marriage, given her husband's level of drinking, and believed that a very strong intervention was required to bring about any change. She was seriously considering separation or divorce if he did not receive help for his drinking. The risk of violence was assessed to be low.

In the *determination of feasibility,* it was judged that Nancy was fully capable of carrying out a confrontation and of following through with contingent consequences if Gene refused treatment.

In the *preparation of the spouse's script,* four striking factual events, difficult to dispute, which illustrated the effects of the drinking, were selected for scripting. Before the examples were made sufficiently specific to highlight the reality of the events without blame, guilt inducement, or use of language from the spouse's old influence system, several revisions were required. In the introduction, Nancy was helped to draft a statement of her strong concern about Gene's drinking and her avowal that she cared very much about him. She documented his drinking behavior and alcohol consumption on the basis of careful records she had kept during the alcohol monitoring. A summary of the more general problems associated with the drinking and their effects was drafted next. It was to be recommended that Gene enter treatment for alcohol abuse. If he refused, the consequences would be twofold: first, Nancy would organize and carry out a second confrontation involving family members and friends; second, she would state that she would take a further serious but unspecified action. (As earlier indicated, she was about ready to separate or initiate divorce.)

In *rehearsal of the presentation,* several sessions were called for during which Nancy practiced the script, with the therapist playing the role of Gene. Feedback was provided through audio recordings, and selective refinements were made in the script.

Then, careful attention was given to *staging the confrontation* and to *postconfrontation planning* prior to the *conduct of the confrontation.* In the confrontation, Gene interrupted his wife several times, but she was well prepared, was not diverted, and continued on with the delivery as planned. He was visibly uncomfortable and angry and refused to accept any alcohol-related treatment. He indi-

---

BOX 8.1   *Selected Steps in Programmed Confrontation and Programmed Request*

1. Determination of suitability
2. Determination of feasibility
3. Preparation of spouse's script
   A. Declaration of affection
   B. Statement of concern about the abuser's drinking and its effects
   C. Specification of drinking level and severity
   D. Itemization of drinking-related incidents, problems, and their effects
   E. Specification of action recommendations (such as to enter treatment)
   F. Specification of consequences if action is not taken

4. Rehearsal of presentation
5. Staging of confrontation
6. Postconfrontation planning
7. Conduct of confrontation
8. Postconfrontation monitoring and follow-through
9. Stabilization and maintenance

NOTE: From "Unilateral family therapy to reach the uncooperative alcohol abuser" by E. J. Thomas in B. A. Thyer (Ed.), *Behavioral family intervention,* 1989. Courtesy of Charles C Thomas, Publisher, Springfield, Illinois.

cated firmly that, instead, he would gradually reduce his alcohol consumption by 2 oz per week until he was at the level of 6 to 8 oz per day.* The therapist closed the session, encouraging both spouses not to discuss the matter further at this point.

In *postconfrontation monitoring and follow-through,* the graduated-reduction plan proposed by Gene was discussed with Nancy in light of the fact that he had already implemented the plan and steadfastly refused to enter treatment. Because he did all of his drinking at home and she was a good observer of the amount of alcohol consumed, it was agreed that she would go along with the graduated-reduction plan. She was to indicate that if he failed to follow through with the plan, she would invoke the contingencies.

Gene reduced his drinking as planned over a period of nine weeks; his alcohol consumption leveled off at approximately 6 oz per day, where it remained to the end of treatment. Nancy reported that her husband stayed up later in the evenings, was more pleasant, was able to awaken on his own in the mornings, and was in better moods during the day.

With regard to *maintenance,* Nancy was helped to identify and avoid possible high-risk situations, to initiate alternate activities not related to alcohol, to praise reduction efforts and the resulting improvements in his behavior, and to continue the new behaviors she had developed through the course of treatment. She agreed to carry out the contingency actions developed earlier in the event that Gene resumed his previous level of drinking. Follow-up at 6 and 12 months indicated that he was continuing to drink at the moderate level of 6 to 8 oz per day. Although abstinence is the preferred outcome, this case illustrates that in working with the unmotivated alcohol abuser, it is sometimes necessary to settle for less.

*When the abusers insist on trying to reduce their drinking on their own, a "what-if" agreement can be signed in which they agree to enter treatment if they cannot do it on their own.

Case B: Both in their 40s, David and Jan had been married for 18 years and had two children. A longtime heavy drinker, David characteristically began drinking on arriving home from work at approximately 11 P.M. and generally drank a dozen 12-oz cans of beer before going to bed about 4 A.M. During the period of delay before treatment for Jan, when treatment was being given to Nancy, David continued to drink at the same high level.

The steps indicated in Box 8.1 were also followed in the preparation of the programmed request. This intervention was chosen instead of a programmed confrontation because Jan was not prepared to make any major changes in her life or marriage in the event that David refused to stop drinking. She also indicated that if the request was properly presented, he might be receptive and enter alcohol treatment. If he refused to obtain help, she was prepared to say that the marital relationship would continue to deteriorate and that distance between her and David would increase (a "dire prognostication").

Following careful scripting, rehearsal, and planning, the request was delivered on David's day off in a familiar restaurant instead of in the project office. He agreed to the request but insisted on finding his own therapist, following which he entered inpatient treatment as that therapist recommended. Work by Jan's therapist on maintenance was cut short because the couple entered family treatment as part of David's inpatient program. He was abstinent following treatment and continued to be abstinent at the 6- and 12-month follow-ups.

Maintenance through Continuing Spouse Sobriety Support

The spouse can help maintain the abuser's sobriety by not reverting to dysfunctional pretreatment ways of interacting with the abuser and by providing active support for maintaining the abuser's sobriety. If spouse-initiated intervention is successful and the abuser enters treatment with the therapist, relapse-prevention training can be provided for the couple with both partners attending sessions together. Such training can then be provided following methods previously described by such writers as Gorski and Miller (1986), Marlatt (1982), Marlatt and Gordon (1980), McGrady (1989), and O'Farrell (1986).

It is frequently the case, however, that the abuser enters treatment without the spouse or does not enter treatment but does drink less or become abstinent. In these instances, assistance with sobriety support would need to be provided unilaterally for the cooperative spouse. Support would be provided for the abuser through the spouse by such means as the following: (1) identification with the spouse of high-risk situations for drinking; (2) training the spouse to help the abuser resist temptation; (3) helping the spouse accelerate nondrinking behaviors with the abuser; (4) teaching the spouse how to prevent and handle relapses; (5) educating the spouse about the nature of relapses and how they can be prevented; and (6) helping the spouse restore a balance in lifestyle with the recovering partner. The spouse needs to be trained to change his or her own behavior in regard to these areas and to be prepared to assist the recovering drinker in carrying out the desired behaviors (Adams, Thomas, Ager, & Yoshioka, 1990).

SOME SPECIAL CONSIDERATIONS

Selection of Clients

Criteria employed in the research also have relevance for the selection of clients. To be labeled as uncooperative, abusers had to have a drinking problem and be unmotivated to receive treatment, as reported by their spouses. These criteria were confirmed in research and clinical assessments conducted early on with

the spouses. Criteria for the spouse included recognition that the partner had a drinking problem, willingness to receive help to try to do something about the partner's drinking, and absence of a drinking problem for that spouse. Additional criteria for both partners were absence of domestic violence, no other drug abuse, no history of severe emotional disorder, no immediate plans for marital dissolution, and no current professional counseling. In addition to their clinical relevance in the research, these criteria served to keep the design and development of the research feasible and manageable.* In most instances, the use of confrontive interventions in cases in which criteria such as these are not met could increase the risk of failure and precipitate such adverse complications as domestic violence, marital estrangement, and self-destructive acts.†

In functioning as an intermediary in change, the spouse should ideally have capabilities to be a good treatment mediator. The following are among some of the important characteristics that good mediators should possess: (1) motivation to participate in the treatment program; (2) accuracy in remembering, observing, recording, and reporting; (3) willingness to be open in disclosing relevant information about themselves and the alcohol abuser; (4) compliance with the treatment regimen; and (5) willingness to give the requirements of mediation and treatment a very high priority in the face of other needs and demands on their time and effort. In addition, research by Ager (1991) has indicated that spouse psychopathology and marital con-

---

*In addition, there were human subjects criteria that required abusers to consent to allow their spouse to disclose information about them and to intervene with them in matters that could influence their drinking. Despite these criteria for abusers, all abusers were unwilling to enter treatment at the onset of provision of treatment for their spouses, and most did not acknowledge that they had an alcohol problem.

†An exception might be the abuse of other drugs in addition to alcohol, in which case the treatment methods described here could be appropriate and sufficient, with minor adaptations.

flict conspire against good treatment mediation as this was measured by scores on the Spouse Treatment Mediation Inventory.* It is important to realize, however, that even the most skilled mediator will be unsuccessful if the therapist is unskilled or if the alcohol abuser is sufficiently intransigent. For a review of other variables that could affect the success of treatment mediation and other aspects of treatment mediation, see Thomas and Ager (1991).

The Therapist

Therapists should be highly motivated to assist the cooperative family member and be well disciplined and organized in their professional work. Among the main activities of the therapist in working with a mediator are (1) to establish an effective relationship with the spouse in which the primary focus is on working toward change in the alcohol abuser; (2) to make appropriate use of the spouse's capabilities as a mediator; (3) to help the spouse become an effective source of influence, using careful preparation and training, as necessary; and (4) to structure planned interventions designed to change the targeted person (Thomas & Ager, in press). In carrying out treatment mediation, the therapist should become very familiar with relevant treatment procedures, such as those described here, follow them carefully, and be prepared to engage in further planning and problem solving with the mediator to address any unexpected problems. It is well to remember that even a very skilled therapist can be successful in mediation only if there is at least adequate spouse mediation, providing, of course, that the abuser changes as programmed.

*The Spouse Treatment Mediation Inventory, by Richard D. Ager and Edwin J. Thomas, © 1987 by the authors and the University of Michigan. A copy of this instrument along with an abstract of descriptive and psychometric details can be found in Ager and Thomas (in press).

Use of Other Family Members

Although the treatment methods described here were developed for the spouse as the cooperative family member, some of the abuser-directed interventions employed the abuser's parents or children in addition to the spouse. The methods described here should also be applicable in work with other family members than the spouse in trying to reach an unmotivated drinker. Other people, of course, such as physicians and employers, may also be employed as mediators and agents of change to reach the alcohol abuser, using methods much as those described elsewhere (Heyman, 1976; Johnson, 1973, 1987, 1990; Rosenberg & Liftik, 1976).

CONCLUSION

In addition to reaching the drinker, the use of the spouse as a positive rehabilitative influence should have many applications, particularly with other family members and in other areas, such as abuse of other substances and a host of marital, parent/child, and family problems. The particular means by which the rehabilitative role would be implemented could differ from one type of mediator (spouse) to another (parent or child) and from alcohol abuse to other problem areas. However, the six areas of the positive rehabilitative role described here and the principles relating to that role should be directly relevant in many areas of interpersonal helping and human services.

REFERENCES

Adams, K. B., Thomas, E. J., Ager, R. D., & Yoshioka, M. R. (1990). *A program of spouse sobriety support for the recovering alcoholic.* Unpublished manuscript, University of Michigan School of Social Work, Ann Arbor.

Ager, R. D. (1991). *A validation study of the spouse treatment mediation inventory.* Unpublished doctoral dissertation, University of Michigan, Ann Arbor.

Ager, R. D., & Thomas, E. J. (in press). The Spouse Treatment Mediation Inventory (STMI). In K. Corcoran & J. Fischer (Eds.), *Measures for clinical practice: A source book* (2nd ed.). New York: Free Press.

Bailey, M. B. (1961). Alcoholism and marriage (a review of research and professional literature). *Quarterly Journal of Studies on Alcohol, 22,* 81–97.

Bennun, I. (1984). Marital therapy with one spouse. In K. Hahlweg & N. S. Jacobson (Eds.), *Marital interaction: Analysis and modification.* New York: Guilford Press.

Bowen, M. (1974). Alcoholism as viewed through family systems theory and family psychotherapy. *Annals of the New York Academy of Science, 223,* 115–122.

Burnett, M. M. (1984). Toward a model for counseling the wives of alcoholics: A feminist approach. *Alcoholism Treatment Quarterly, 1,* 51–60.

Cadogan, D. A. (1973). Marital group therapy in the treatment of alcoholism. *Quarterly Journal of Studies in Alcohol, 34,* 1187–1194.

Carter, E., & Orfanidis, M. M. (1976). Family therapy with one person and the family therapist's own family. In P. J. Guerin (Ed.), *Family therapy: Theory and practice.* New York: Gardner Press.

Cermak, T. L. (1986). Diagnostic criteria for codependency. *Journal of Psychoactive Drugs, 18,* 15–20.

Corder, B. F., Corder, R. F., & Laidlaw, N. L. (1972). An intensive treatment program for alcoholics and their wives. *Quarterly Journal of Studies on Alcohol, 33,* 1144–1146.

Ewing, J. A., Long, V., & Wenzel, G. G. (1961). Concurrent group psychiatric treatment of alcoholic patients and their wives. *International Journal of Group Psychotherapy, 11,* 329–338.

Ghodse, A. M. (1982). Living with an alcoholic. *Postgraduate Medical Journal, 58,* 636–640.

Gliedman, L. H. (1957). Concurrent and combined group therapy of chronic alcoholics and their wives. *International Journal of Group Psychotherapy, 7,* 414–424.

Gorski, T. (1986). Relapse prevention planning: A new recovery tool. *Alcohol Health and Research World, 11,* 6–11.

Gorski, T. T., & Miller, M. (1986). *Staying sober: A guide for relapse prevention.* Independence, MO: Independence Press.

Hedberg, A. G., & Campbell, L. (1974). A comparison of four behavioral treatments of alcoholism. *Journal of Behavioral Therapy and Experimental Psychiatry, 5,* 251–257.

Heyman, M. M. (1976). Referral to alcoholism programs in industry: Coercion, confrontation and choice. *Journal of Studies on Alcohol, 37,* 900–907.

Homila, M. (1985). *Wives, husbands and alcohol: A study of informal drinking control within the family.* Helsinki: Finnish Foundation for Alcohol Studies.

Howard, D. P., & Howard, N. T. (1978). Treatment of the significant other. In S. Zimberg, J. Wallace, & S. B. Blume (Eds.), *Practical approaches to alcoholism psychotherapy.* New York: Plenum.

Jackson, J. K. (1954). The adjustment of the family to the crisis of alcoholism. *Quarterly Journal of Studies on Alcohol, 4,* 562–586.

Jacob, T. (1986). Alcoholism: A family interaction perspective. In P. C. Rivers (Ed.), *Nebraska Symposium on Motivation* (Vol. 34). Lincoln: University of Nebraska Press.

Jacob, T., & Krahn, G. L. (1988). Marital interaction of alcoholic couples: Comparison with depressed and nondepressed couples. *Journal of Consulting and Clinical Psychology, 56,* 73–79.

Johnson, V. E. (1973). *I'll quit tomorrow.* New York: Harper.

Johnson, V. E. (1986). *Intervention: How to help someone who doesn't want help.* Minneapolis: Johnson Institute Books.

Johnson, V. E. (1987). *How to use intervention in your professional practice.* Minneapolis: Johnson Institute Books.

Johnson, V. E. (1990). *Everything you need to know about chemical dependence.* Minneapolis: Johnson Institute Books.

Liepman, M. R., Nirenberg, T. D., & Begin, A. M. (1989). Evaluation of a program designed to help family and significant others to motivate resistant alcoholics into recovery. *American Journal of Drug and Alcohol Abuse, 15,* 209–211.

Logan, D. G. (1983). Getting alcoholics to treatment by social network intervention. *Hospital and Community Psychiatry, 34,* 360–361.

Marlatt, G. A. (1982). Relapse prevention: A self-control program for the treatment of addictive behaviors. In R. B. Stuart (Ed.), *Adherence, compliance and generalization in behavioral medicine.* New York: Brunner/Mazel.

Marlatt, G. A., & Gordon, J. R. (1980). Determinants of relapse: Implications for the maintenance of behavior change. In P. O. Davidson & S. N. Davidson (Eds.), *Behavioral medicine: Changing health lifestyles.* New York: Brunner/Mazel.

Maxwell, R. (1976). *The booze battle.* New York: Ballantine.

McCrady, B. (1989). Extending relapse prevention models to couples. *Addictive Behaviors, 14,* 69–74.

McCrady, B. S., Paolino, T. J., Longabaugh, R., & Rossi, J. (1979). Effects of joint hospital admission and couple's treatment for hospitalized alcoholics: A pilot study. *Addictive Behaviors, 4,* 155–167.

O'Farrell, T. J. (1986). Marital therapy in the treatment of alcoholism. In N. S. Jacobson & A. S. Gurman (Eds.), *Clinical handbook of marital therapy.* New York: Guilford Press.

Orford, J., Guthrie, S., Nicholls, P., Oppenheimer, E., Egert, S., & Hensman, C. (1975). Self-reported coping behavior of wives of alcoholics and association with drinking outcome. *Journal of Studies on Alcohol, 36,* 1254–1267.

Paolino, T. J., & McCrady, B. S. (1977). *The alcoholic marriage: Alternative perspectives.* New York: Grune & Stratton.

Rosenberg, C. M., & Liftik, J. (1976). Use of coercion in outpatient treatment of alcoholism. *Journal of Studies on Alcohol, 37,* 58–65.

Szapocznik, J., Kurtines, W. M., Foote, F. H., Perez-Vidal, A., & Hervis, O. (1983). Conjoint vs. one-person family therapy: Some evidence for the effectiveness of conducting family therapy through one person. *Journal of Consulting and Clinical Psychology, 51,* 889–899.

Thomas, E. J. (1989). Unilateral family therapy to reach the uncooperative alcohol abuser. In B. A. Thyer (Ed.), *Behavioral Family Therapy.* Springfield, IL: Charles C Thomas.

Thomas, E. J., Adams, K. B., Yoshioka, M. R., & Ager, R. D. (1989). *Illustrative pleasers and displeasers.* Unpublished manuscript, University of Michigan, School of Social Work, Ann Arbor.

Thomas, E. J., Adams, K. B., Yoshioka, M. R., & Ager, R. D. (1990). Unilateral relationship enhancement in the treatment of spouses of uncooperative alcohol abusers. *American Journal of Family Therapy, 18,* 334–344.

Thomas, E. J., & Ager, R. D. (1991). Treatment mediation and the spouse as treatment mediator. *American Journal of Family Therapy, 19,* 315–326.

Thomas, E. J., & Santa, C. A. (1982). Unilateral family therapy for alcohol abuse: A working conception. *American Journal of Family Therapy, 10,* 49–60.

Thomas, E. J., Santa, C. A., Bronson, D., & Oyserman, D. (1987). Unilateral family therapy with the spouses of alcoholics. *Journal of Social Service Research, 10,* 149–162.

Thomas, E. J., & Yoshioka, M. R. (1989). Spouse interventive confrontations in unilateral family therapy for alcohol abuse. *Social Casework, 70,* 340–347.

Thomas, E. J., Yoshioka, M. R., & Ager, R. D. (1993). *Drinking enabling of spouses of uncooperative alcohol abusers: Assessment and modification.* Manuscript submitted for publication.

Thomas, E. J., Yoshioka, M. R., & Ager, R. D. (in press-a). The Spouse Enabling Inventory (SEI). In K. Corcoran & J. Fischer (Eds.), *Measures for clinical practice: A source book* (2nd ed.). New York: Free Press.

Thomas, E. J., Yoshioka, M. R., & Ager, R. D. (in press-b). The Spouse Sobriety Influence Inventory (SSII). In K. Corcoran & J. Fischer (Eds.), *Measures for clinical practice: A source book* (2nd ed.). New York: Free Press.

Thomas, E. J., Yoshioka, M. R., Ager, R. D., & Adams, K. B. (1993). *Experimental outcomes of spouse intervention to reach the uncooperative alcohol abuser: Preliminary report.* Manuscript submitted for publication.

Thorne, D. R. (1983). Techniques for use in intervention. *Journal of Alcohol and Drug Education, 28,* 46–50.

Wiseman, J. P. (1980). The "home treatment": The first steps in trying to cope with an alcoholic husband. *Family Relations, 29,* 541–549.

Yoshioka, M. R., Thomas, E. J., & Ager, R. D. (1991). Nagging and other drinking control efforts of spouses of uncooperative alcohol abusers: Assessment and modification. *Journal of Substance Abuse, 4,* 309–318.

Zimberg, S. (1982). *The clinical management of alcoholism.* New York: Brunner/Mazel.

9

The Cognitive-Behavioral Treatment of Marital Distress

Donald K. Granvold
Catheleen Jordan

The treatment of marital distress from a cognitive-behavioral perspective involves intervention with both the interpersonal and the intrapsychic aspects of functioning. Cognitive, behavioral, and emotional factors are considered to be interactive and to contribute mutually to marital dysfunction. Marital unhappiness may predominantly result from a problem in one area of functioning (for example, the problem drinking of one spouse), but the likelihood is that problems in all three areas by each spouse significantly contribute to personal and interpersonal dissatisfaction. The practitioner therefore is obligated to assess the couple's cognitive, behavioral, and emotional functioning and to develop intervention strategies accordingly. In this chapter we address assessment and intervention methods consistent with this interactive perspective.

THEORETICAL FOUNDATIONS

Cognitive-behavioral marital therapy is founded on several theoretical models, including social learning theory, social exchange theory, and cognitive psychology. These theoretical models provide both an understanding of the nature of couple interaction and a guide to the intervention process. Couple interaction is viewed as reciprocally determined. Behavior is both a response to and an action toward the mate. The com-

plexity of a given behavior is evident as one considers the individual psychosocial development of each partner prior to coupling, the history of their relationship, and the current status of the union. Environmental factors and life-cycle dimensions further influence and complicate the couple's interaction.

Social Learning Theory

Social learning theory explains behavior in terms of the principles of operant and respondent conditioning, modeling, and cognitive mediation (Bandura, 1969, 1977b). Operant conditioning explains relationships in terms of their reinforcing or punishing consequences. If a wife yells at her husband each time he attempts to tell her how he feels, for example, he will be less likely in the future to attempt to tell her how he feels. Conversely, he will be more likely to continue to express himself to her if she is empathic when he tells her how he feels.

Respondent conditioning describes how behavior is elicited by antecedent discriminative stimuli. For instance, a husband may have learned to avoid his wife (response) when he sees her crying (antecedent discriminative stimulus); he has learned from previous experience that she will be likely to blame him for her unhappiness.

In addition to showing how environmental controlling conditions strongly influence individuals' behavior, social learning theory also describes behavior as being learned vicariously through observation of models and through cognitive mediational processes. Vicarious learning has been found to be highly influential on the subsequent behavior of the observer. For example, it has been found that those who are physically abusive with their mates are far more likely to have come from homes where they observed physical violence or were themselves physically abused than are those who are not abusive (Rosenbaum & O'Leary, 1981; Straus, Gelles, & Steinmetz, 1980). Members of a mate's family of origin may serve as powerful models of interaction in close relationships. Cognitive mediational processes that may influence how an individual behaves toward a mate include such factors as negative interpretations of the mate's behavior, faulty beliefs or unrealistic expectations, attributions, and erroneous information processing.

The patterns of interaction that develop in intimate relationships can be better understood and changes in those patterns can be effectively made by the application of social learning theory. There is evidence that spouses' behaviors that are rewarded by the partner will increase or continue, whereas those behaviors that go unrewarded or are punished will be decreased or discontinued (Jacobson & Dallas, 1981). Each spouse operates with a degree of reward power in relation to the mate; in essence, reinforcement contingencies are held by each in relation to the other. This interdependence exists as a powerful dynamic. At times it can produce a reinforcing, albeit negative, exchange pattern. For example, a wife who stops studying her college coursework and pays attention to her husband in response to his nagging will effectively reinforce the husband's nagging. She receives negative reinforcement for shifting her attention to him (the nagging stops). He is positively reinforced for nagging because it is followed by the rewards of her attention (Baucom & Epstein, 1990). Although there are significant negative components to this interchange (the aversiveness of his nagging; the potential undesirable consequences of not studying), there is a high likelihood that this pattern will continue due to the reinforcement each spouse receives.

Many significant factors differentiating distressed from nondistressed couples have meaningful implications from a social learning perspective. In their extensive review of the research on distressed and nondistressed couples, Weiss and Heyman (1990) report that satisfied couples use more (1) assent, (2) approval and caring, (3) empathy, (4) agreement, (5) humor, (6) smiling and laughing, (7) positive physical touch, (8) problem description, (9) problem solutions, (10) involvement, (11) positive verbal and nonverbal behaviors, (12) negative verbal behaviors, and (13) normative movements. Dissatisfied couples were found to (1) emit a higher level of global negativity, (2) criticize, (3) use hostility and displeasure, (4) use put-downs, (5) make excuses, (6) deny responsibility, (7) give no response, (8) not track, (9) use negative nonverbal behavior, and (10) complain more, make more complaints about personal characteristics, and pair complaints with negative affect. These behavioral patterns have been characteristically shaped in their respective relationships and continue to receive effective reinforcement for their continuance. The behavioral excesses and deficits reported above would be appropriate considerations as targets for behavioral intervention.

Social Exchange Theory

Whether you marry or whether you don't, you'll regret it (Kierkegaard, 1959). This paraphrase captures a significant component of social exchange theory, that there are costs (and benefits) associated with any social relationship. There is a down side to either social condition—being married or single—and there are moments when that down side is predominant in the mind of the individual. Social exchange theory, originally conceptualized by Homans (1958, 1974) and Thibaut and Kelley (1959), has been used to describe the dynamics of intimate relationships in which patterns of interdependency can be identified. Couple interaction is viewed, using economic theory, as an exchange of rewards and costs. *Rewards* are defined as "pleasures, satisfactions, and gratifications the person enjoys," and *costs* are defined as "factors which operate to inhibit or deter the performance of a sequence of behavior" (Thibaut & Kelley, 1959, p. 12). The behavior a spouse displays is both a response to the mate's behavior and an action toward the mate. Hence, the outcome sought by individuals depends on both their own actions and those of their partner. Their behavior is significantly influenced by the anticipated response from their mate. Past behavioral exchanges compose a collective cost/benefit ratio that serves several functions. One function is the promotion of rewarding or punishing behavior toward the mate. The likelihood that a given behavior will be displayed is regulated by the perceived rewards of the behavior relative to the perceived costs. For example, if a spouse anticipates that a display of affection will lead to a rewarding response, he or she will be more inclined to be affectionate. Likewise, if the spouse anticipates that a display of affection will go unrewarded or perhaps be punished, he or she will be less inclined to be affectionate. By virtue of the anticipated response from the mate, the mate wields influence and control over the spouse. The degree of control is assumed to be a product of the nature of the interdependent relationship. Where there is significant asymmetry in dependence, the less dependent person is in a position to exercise more influence in the relationship (Kelley, 1979).

The cost/benefit ratio described above as promoting further behavioral exchanges serves two other significant purposes. The level of satisfaction with the marriage and the commitment to stay in or leave the relationship can be viewed in the context of perceived rewards relative to costs. A primary concept of social exchange theory is that of comparison level (CL)—the tendency of individuals to compare the rewards they are receiving with what they believe they deserve from the relationship. This comparison is a complex process involving interrelated cognitive phenomena, including perception, labeling, and expectations. Behavior that has accrued to form the comparison level is subject to perceptual influence. Some behaviors may be selectively screened in or out of the subjective judgment process, thereby biasing the outcome. Likewise, the outcome may be biased as a result of labeling behavior in an irrational or distorted manner. An abused spouse may think a thought such as "He didn't hit me *that* hard" and fail to appraise a significant cost in the exchange. The person's expectations of appropriate, desirable, and acceptable behavior form the standard against which the mate's behavior is measured. These expectations derive from the individual's sense of self, personal value system, and past social experience. A person with low self-regard may evaluate a mate's behavior as appropriate, desirable, and acceptable where an individual with higher self-regard would not. Failure to share major financial decisions may be of little consequence for the individual who does not value that behavior as meaningful in coupling. A person whose past social experiences have included strong expressions of anger may be desensitized to such behavior and attach little or no cost value to it. It is in these and other ways that the establishment of comparison level is highly subjective. Careful attention to these and other variables is necessary in the determination of comparison level when analyzing couple satisfaction.

Coordination of Rewards.   A key aspect of interdependency is the degree to which one seeks rewards in the relationship (dependency) rather than seeking rewards independently or outside the union. Kelley (1979) has expressed discomfort on the part of Thibaut and himself with their theory of intimate interdependence being labeled an "exchange" theory, writing that "it is equally a 'coordination' theory" (p. 31). The coordination of the couple's efforts to contribute to each other's objectives is necessitated by the variability in the ways and extent to which they seek to satisfy specific expectations within the relationship. For example, the need to clean the couple's domicile obligates a coordination of effort in which one or both contribute to the outcome by actually cleaning or mobilize resources to have the cleaning accomplished by an outside source.

Although a couple may function with a significant level of interdependency, one or both members may desire to have some outcomes met independently or outside the marriage. For example, a spouse may seek to satisfy a creative interest and rely on the intrinsic meaning of the experience as the reward. The mate's social reinforcement of such an effort would, of course, bring the activity back into a level of interdependency. The involvement of an individual outside the partnership in the effort to satisfy a creative outcome, while excluding the mate, would exemplify independence in which rewards are sought through alternative relationship means (for example, a wife takes an art class from a talented instructor).

It is obvious that there will be ongoing shifts in how and to what extent the couple seek to satisfy their outcomes in the relationship. And conflict potentially exists in several ways: (1) mutuality of dependence—mutual interdependence in an outcome area or unilateral dependency; (2) degree of dependence—the higher the dependency, the greater the intensity; (3) correspondence of outcomes—commonality versus conflict of interests; and (4) basis of dependence—how each person's outcomes depend on his or her own actions, the partner's actions, or a combination of the two (Kelley, 1979).

The usefulness of this analytic model of interdependency is to expose patterns of interaction. Hence, rather than merely viewing an exchange of costs and rewards in the union, users of this model seek insight into the variety of ways in which partners behave interdependently with respect to their rewards and costs. Ultimately, each person's outcomes depend, in various ways, on his or her own actions and the partner's actions.

Comparison Level for Alternatives. Another significant concept is comparison level for alternatives—the perceived rewards and costs of single life or life with another partner. If a person views divorce as resulting in severe economic hardship or strongly believes that divorce is morally wrong, the perceived costs of the alternative to the marriage, even though the marriage may be very low in rewards, would be considered comparatively undesirable. Theoretically, the individual makes a comparison of two cost/benefit ratios. Comparison level (rewards to costs in the marriage) is evaluated against the comparison level for alternatives (rewards to costs outside the marriage), with the net result promoting a greater or lesser commitment to the marriage or alternatively to divorce.

Kelley (1979) notes that "divorce tends to occur when the rewards from the dyad are low, the costs of leaving the marriage are low, and rewards from outside alternatives are high" (p. 48). In treating marriage, the practitioner may encounter situations that appear confounding. Why would a physically abused spouse remain committed to the marriage? Using social exchange theory as a model, one may determine that the client is highly dependent on her mate, resulting in high tolerance for low rewards in the union. Coupled with this condition, she may have a strong view that marriage should be maintained at all costs, anticipate great economic hardship after divorce, fear the emotional insecurity of life "alone," and consider divorce as destroying her family. In sum, her extreme dependency and concomitant low reward expectancy in the marriage in conjunction with the high costs of leaving (comparison level for alternatives) incline her to remain in the relationship. A shift in the interdependency pattern in the marriage in which she functions less dependently, a change in the perceived negativity of the factors associated with divorce, or changes in both dimensions may result in her decision to divorce and seek her rewards outside the marriage.

Satisfaction and Commitment. Satisfaction with a relationship and commitment to it are mutually exclusive variables. The tendency is to view commitment as correlated with satisfaction. Although this is the case in most relationships, there are exceptions. As noted earlier, a low rate of rewards in the marriage may not result in a weak commitment if the consequences of divorce are viewed as more greatly punishing relative to the costs of the marriage. Furthermore, an individual may consider the marriage to be highly satisfactory but be disinclined to remain married: "As marriages go, it's fine. I just don't want to be married." Here the perceived rewards alternative to the marriage are so strong that the individual becomes uncommitted to the marriage. This stance would typify those individuals who almost exclusively seek to satisfy personal outcomes independently of the marriage. They may view the marriage as interfering with the development of their sense of self and the realization of their personal goals.

Reciprocity. The extent to which couples exercise reciprocity in their exchanges of rewarding and punishing behavior has been the focus of much exploration. Reciprocity is the concept that as one gives, so shall one receive. Weiss (1978) provides the operational definition of reciprocity as "providing reinforcement for reinforcing behavior" (p. 188). Studies have produced some significant findings. First, with regard to frequency of exchanges, it has been found that nondistressed couples exchange higher rates of rewarding behavior and lower rates of punishing behavior than do distressed couples (Birchler, Weiss, & Vincent, 1975; Gottman, 1979; Jacobson, Follette, & McDonald, 1982; Margolin, 1981; Margolin & Wampold, 1981; Vincent, Friedman, Nugent, & Messerley, 1979).

Differences between these two groups are apparent not only in frequency rate of exchange but also in reciprocity of exchange. Nondistressed couples are characterized by a reciprocal exchange of rewarding behavior. A positive action can be anticipated to beget a positive response from the mate. Distressed couples, likewise, appear to reciprocate positive behaviors, although at a much lower frequency rate, as noted above. The difference in reciprocity between these two groups is evident in negative behavior exchange. Distressed couples tend to reciprocate negative behavior, whereas nondistressed couples do not (Alberts, 1988; Gottman, 1979; Hooley & Hahlweg, 1989; Margolin & Wampold, 1981; Schaap, 1984; Ting-Toomey, 1983). Distressed couples have been described as "reactive" to each other as evidenced by the high likelihood that the negative behavior of a distressed mate will result in the partner reciprocating with a negative behavior (Jacobson et al., 1982; Jacobson & Holtzworth-Munroe, 1986). Once begun, this negative interchange may continue, putting the couple at risk of escalation. Jacobson and his associates note that both rewarding and punishing relationship events have an immediate impact on distressed couples and that they are consequently reactive to rewarding behavior as well (Jacobson et al., 1982).

In contrast, nondistressed couples appear to possess a nonreactive quality in relation to negative behavior in which punishing behavior is "absorbed" without a response. This failure to immediately reciprocate prevents the couple from escalating into an increasingly intense chain of negative exchanges. It has been theorized that this nonreactive quality is the product of an ongoing high rate of positive exchanges between nondistressed couples. Gottman and his colleagues describe such relationships as following a "bank-account" model of marital exchange in which the positive investments made over time sustain the couple through situational nonreciprocity (Gottman et al., 1976). Negative behavior, rather than being exchanged, is not reciprocated, presumably as a function of the accumulation of positive behavior exchanges. These findings serve as a meaningful rationale in encouraging couples to increase their rate of positive exchange while decreasing negative behavior exchange.

Baucom and Epstein (1990) suggest that when applying the social exchange model of marriage, clinicians

> take into account (a) rates of behaviors exchanged by a couple, (b) each spouse's subjective appraisal of how desirable or pleasant each of the partner's behaviors is, (c) the spouses' standards for what constitutes an equitable exchange, (d) their attributions about *why* the partner gives what he or she does give (e.g., "She only gives to me out of a sense of duty, not because she cares"), and (e) their expectancies about future exchanges (e.g., "If I request any further changes, he'll stop giving me anything") [p. 24].

Cognitive Psychology and Marital Treatment

Cognitive psychology gives mediation a central role in human functioning. Between stimulus and response, the individual privately processes data through the use of unique cognitive structures. Given this founding proposition, four basic tenets of cognitive psychology can be identified:

1. Cognitions, emotions, and behavior are interactive in a social/environmental context.

2. Learning principles apply equally to covert as well as overt behavior (the continuity assumption).

3. Cognitions and cognitive processes can be accessed and changed.

4. Cognitive change can produce changes in emotion, overt behavior, and cognitive functioning.

In the interactive view of human functioning, cognition, emotion, and behavior are experienced collectively and, where there is psychological disturbance, significantly overlap (Ellis & Dryden, 1987). Cognitive processes are afforded a central role in the stimulus-response sequence in several ways. First, there is awareness of the event, whether an overt or covert event. Second, selection takes place from among the available stimuli. Some stimuli will be screened out or ignored, and others will prompt a response. Third, a cognitive appraisal will be made of the stimulus in which meaning, significance, and value (positive, negative, neutral) are determined followed by, fourth, a cognitive decision-making process culminating in a response (selected from an array of alternatives). The response may be covert or both covert and overt. An emotional meaning may be a part of this process. The response, whether cognitive, emotional, behavioral, or a combination, is a stimulus for the subsequent stimulus-response sequence.

There is evidence to support the continuity assumption, the assumption that private phenomena follow the same rules of learning as overt behavior (Mahoney, 1974). This correspondence rule has significance with regard both to the development of cognitive structures and the design of methods for cognitive change. Cognitions can be learned by "observation," modeled, shaped, reinforced, conditioned, extinguished, and so forth. Many cognitive change strategies have been extrapolated from these overt learning phenomena.

The third tenet, that cognitions and cognitive processes can be accessed and changed, has amassed extensive support. Empirical methods have been applied to overt behavior "in order to make inferences about underlying factors that can explain the behavior" (Baars, 1986, p. 7). And direct access to cognitive structures has been sought through client self-report for the purposes of assessment (Merluzzi, Glass, & Genest, 1981) and promotion of change (Beck, 1976; Ellis, 1962; Meichenbaum, 1977).

The contention that cognitive change can produce change in emotion, overt behavior, and cognition likewise has extensive support. Bandura (1985) refers to reciprocal determinism as a conception of interaction in which "behavior, cognitive and other personal factors [emotion, motivation, and physical and physiological variables], and environmental influences all operate as interlocking determinants that affect each other bidirectionally" (p. 83). Lazarus (1989) likewise notes a shift from structural S-R and S-O-R formulations toward a systems approach. He uses the term *transaction* where Bandura uses *reciprocal determinism*. Both contend that change in one variable will influence other variables.

One objective of cognitive psychology is to explore the relationship between cognition and behavior and to determine the ways in which information processing, belief systems, perceptions, expectations, and other cognitive variables influence and bring about behavior. Mahoney (1985) has asserted that "unless we appreciate the patterns by which individuals order their realities, we are unlikely to understand fully their requests for help" (p. 9). Explorations into individuals' private worlds may expose the significance and meaning of personal experience, provide greater understanding of the various motives behind idiosyncratic behavior, and reveal cognitive errors ripe for modification. The reader is referred to Chapter 1 of this volume for more detailed information on cognitive psychology.

Cognitive methods of intervention have been effectively applied to a broad range of psychological problems. Only recently have they been specifically applied to couple interaction (Abrahms, 1983; Baucom & Epstein, 1990; Beck, 1988; Ellis, 1977b; Ellis, Sichel, Yeager, DiMattia, & DiGiuseppe, 1989; Epstein, 1982; Epstein & Baucom, 1989; Granvold, 1988, 1992; Jacobson & Holtzworth-Munroe, 1986; Margolin, 1987; Schindler & Vollmer, 1984; Weiss, 1984b). The shift in behavioral marital therapy to include cognitive variables as targets for change and the use of cognitive intervention strategies to promote change is both an acknowledgment of the significance that cognitive factors play in marital interaction and an expression of confidence in cognitive change methods. Couple interaction has been described behaviorally as "a process of circular and reciprocal sequences of behavior and consequences, where each person's behavior is at once being affected by and influencing the other" (Jacobson & Margolin, 1979, p. 13). Various cognitive factors have been identified as active ingredients in this interchange (Baucom, Epstein, Sayers, & Sher, 1989). Couples do not approach their interactions with a *tabula rasa* but, rather, with a recent and long-term relationship history, an individual developmental history, personal competencies and liabilities, and an array of resources. These preexisting factors, referred to by Weiss (1984a) as "context" variables will influence the actual interaction. Weiss identifies "process" variables as "behavioral data generated by the interaction itself" (p. 233). The spouses' preexisting ideas, attitudes, feelings, and the like will have a bearing on perception, labeling, interpretation, and value appraisal of interaction. Global feelings held by a spouse toward his or her mate may frequently predominate over the actual valence of the current interaction, producing an effect that Weiss (1980) refers to as "sentiment override." Alternatively, a spouse may attach a representative meaning, either consciously or subconsciously, to the behavioral variables of an interaction and react accordingly. If the preexisting phenomena stimulated by a given interaction are negative, the likelihood of a negative or dysfunctional interaction is increased. For example, unresolved distress from childhood sexual abuse constitutes a negative context variable and may significantly account for a dysfunctional interaction between spouses where the actual interaction appears benign. In this case, treatment would focus on both a context variable—the unresolved issues of the spouse's childhood sexual abuse (either individual, conjoint treatment, or both)—and a process variable—the dynamics of the immediate interaction that stimulated thoughts, emotions, and other behavioral responses associated with the sexual abuse.

The manner in which couples mediate their interaction has critical bearing on their outcomes. A variety of interrelated cognitive phenomena has been identified by various theorists.

Discrepancy between Intention and Impact.

Gottman (1979) has noted that a dysfunctional exchange may take place between spouses when a verbal message or behavior is received and given a significantly different meaning than was intended. In short, a discrepancy between intention and impact may account for ineffective communication or dysfunctional interaction. The intention resides in the mind of the sender. The meaning attached is a function of the receiver's cognitive processing. The discrepancy may result from various cognitive factors. First, the receiver may be generally predisposed to perceive negativity where it does not clearly exist (for example, hearing a negative voice tone when it is not objectively present). Second, a negative emotional overlay may promote a negative meaning irrespective of the objective message sent. Third, hypervigilance and supersensitivity to negative aspects of predominantly positive behavior or communication may be operative. And fourth, although the receiver's subjective appraisal of *what* is

occurring may be error-free, a negative causal inference (attribution) may account for the discrepancy ("You are being nice to me now only because your parents are present"). Attributional statements have great potential for error due to their inferential nature. In addition to the four explanations delineated for discrepancy between intention and impact, many more probably exist, for as Weiss (1984a) has noted, there is much more to be learned about the ways couples encode their interaction.

Baucom and Epstein (1990) have identified five interrelated cognitive phenomena that contribute to the development and maintenance of marital dysfunction: "*perceptions* (about *what* events occur), *attributions* (about *why* events occur), *expectancies* (predictions of what *will* occur), *assumptions* (about the nature of the world and correlations among events), and *beliefs* or *standards* (about what 'should' be)" (p. 47). These cognitive processes operate to promote either well-being and satisfaction between spouses or dysfunction and disregard.

Perception.

Several perceptual factors may account for distress. Significant positive behavior may be screened out or given minimal meaning. Beck and his colleagues have identified selective abstraction as an information processing disorder in which a negative aspect of an interchange is focused on while salient positive features of the interaction are ignored or minimally weighted in the overall appraisal of the experience (Beck, Rush, Shaw, & Emery, 1979). Conflict between spouses may be traced to a disagreement regarding what actually took place or what was said. Several studies have exposed low rates of agreement between spouses concerning the occurrence of specific events (Christensen, Sullaway, & King, 1983; Elwood & Jacobson, 1982; Floyd & Markman, 1983; Jacobson & Moore, 1981; Margolin, Hattem, John, & Yost, 1985). Baucom and Epstein (1990) also identify fatigue and emotional arousal as factors contributing to perceptual distortion.

Attributions.   Attributions are explanations regarding the cause or motivation for a given behavior or condition. As couples come to "know" each other, they form hypotheses about the spouse that serve to explain why he or she behaves a certain way in a given situation. There is a tendency to form both simple and singular causal explanations for complex transactions. Because attributions are inferential, there is much room for cognitive distortion and error. Drawing on the learned-helplessness model, attributions have been categorized into stable-unstable, internal-external, and specific-global (Abramson, Seligman, & Teasdale, 1978; Doherty, 1981a, 1981b). A spouse may attribute a behavior to a fixed trait (stable) and view it as highly unchangeable ("He's an angry person," rather than "He's angry because he's having a bad day"). Stable negative attributions are more likely to be associated with a sense of hopelessness with regard to change, whereas unstable attributions would more likely be associated with a sense of optimism. The attribution of an outcome to oneself (internal) would promote a greater sense of responsibility for and control over the outcome, whereas attributing an outcome to another person or to the environment (external) would not. Blaming one's mate for marital problems is an example of an external attribution. A global attribution is a causal explanation that is viewed as broadly representative of the person or relationship, as opposed to a specific, more narrowly confined conclusion. For example, a failure to record a check in the check register is viewed as the consequence of general irresponsibility (global). Among the findings of studies focused on the three patterns of attributions described above, one of the most salient is as follows:

> Distressed spouses tend to rate the causes of negative behaviors by their partners as more

global and stable than do nondistressed spouses, and nondistressed spouses tend to rate the causes of positive partner behavior as more global and stable than do distressed individuals. (Baucom & Epstein, 1990, p. 71)

The following forms of negative attributions are abstracted from Granvold (1988):

A. *Blaming:* "You make me so mad" (responsibility for anger is displaced to the mate).
B. *Terminal hypotheses* (Hurvitz, 1975): behavior, meanings, or feelings are interpreted such that change cannot take place.
   1. *Psychological classifications:* "You're a manic depressive."
   2. *Pseudoscientific labels:* "You're a Virgo, and that's why you act the way you do."
   3. *Inappropriate generalizations about innate qualities or traits that cannot be changed:* "He has no willpower and was born that way; that's why he's so fat."
C. Coercion or impression management (Epstein, 1982): "He's taking me out more often because he's afraid I'll leave him if he doesn't." In response to therapist-assigned behaviors: "You only commented on my appearance because the therapist suggested that you be more complimentary."
D. Malevolent intent (Epstein, 1982): "You purposely came home late to make me worry about you." "You took your secretary to lunch just to make me jealous."

Expectancies.   A spouse's belief in his or her ability to bring about a particular outcome is considered to have a great bearing on attributional conclusions reached and subsequent actions taken to minimize conflict and other relationship problems. Bandura (1977a) has identified two types of expectancies, outcome expectancies and efficacy expectancies. An outcome expectancy is a person's belief that a given behavior will lead to a certain consequence; an efficacy expectancy is the belief that one has the ability to behave in a way to produce the desired consequences. To differentiate these expectancies, a spouse's view that marital problems are insurmountable even if significant personal efforts to change are achieved represents a low outcome expectancy, whereas the spouse's belief that he or she does not have the ability to make the necessary changes to solve the marital problems represents a low efficacy expectation. Other formulations that can be drawn on in identifying and treating expectancies is the learned helplessness model (Abramson et al., 1978), briefly discussed in relation to attribution, and locus of control (Rotter, 1966). Recent findings indicate that efficacy expectations relate positively to marital satisfaction (Bradbury, 1989; Fincham & Bradbury, 1989; Notarius & Vanzetti, 1983; Weiss, 1984b). Consistent with these findings, expectations are considered to be significant active ingredients in cognitive processing leading to effective marital problem solving and change. Weiss (1984b) encourages therapists to assess spouses' potential "belief barriers" in developing an understanding of the attributional conclusions about themselves, their partners, and their relationships.

Assumptions and Standards. Marital partners have beliefs and expectations regarding human functioning, including the meaning of marriage; the roles that mates are to assume; the nature of the relationship that married people are to have with each other, with others, and with the world; the meaning of various objects (house, job, title); and so forth. It is through these cognitive structures that meaning is attached to objects, events, and experiences and that current life experience is integrated with existing awareness. Objects, conditions, and events are viewed as having certain qualities and as being related to one another in certain ways. These expectations, referred to as *assumptions* by Baucom and Epstein (1990), function as

scripts for human behavior and the human experience. In contrast to assumptions, people exist with *standards* against which life is evaluated. If a mate's standard is similar to his or her assumption regarding a given aspect of marriage, he or she can expect to be comfortable with that aspect of the relationship. Conversely, if there is dissimilarity between assumption and standard, the result is distress. Baucom and Epstein (1990) give a clarifying example: "Whereas an individual may have an assumption that the more time a couple spends together the more happy they will be, he or she also may have a standard that spouses *should* spend as much time together as possible in order to have a good marriage" (pp. 57–58). The mate's behavior would be evaluated through the use of the standard in the context of the assumption held in that area. It is readily apparent that much room exists for disagreement between spouses on both dimensions. Marital distress may be the product, in part, of unrealistic or extreme standards. Baucom and Epstein (1990) note that "standards tend to be dysfunctional when they are inflexible, unattainable, or so extreme that meeting them takes a significant toll on a person" (p. 59). The cognitive restructuring of ill-founded assumptions or of faulty, exaggerated, or unrealistic standards may be indicated to reduce marital conflict or distress.

ASSESSMENT

Assessment and intervention have been described as flowing imperceptibly into each other (Weiss & Margolin, 1977). To this we would simply add, only if done correctly! Assessment methods described in this section are based on empirical practice and the view that assessment data should be of direct clinical use. The purpose of assessment in marital counseling has been identified as providing information necessary to (1) describe problems in the relationship, (2) identify variables that control the problem behaviors, (3) select appropriate therapeutic interventions, and (4) recognize when the intervention has been effective (Jacobson & Margolin, 1979; Weiss & Margolin, 1977). Problem description should include cognitive, behavioral, affective, and environmental factors. A thorough assessment of marital functioning should be "comprehensive and specific, historic and contemporary, initial and on-going, interactional and individual problem oriented, and couple-relationship as well as therapy-process oriented" (Granvold, 1988, p. 72). Box 9.1 provides an overview of the content of initial assessment.

There are benefits to both comprehensive and specific assessment information. Global information regarding such factors as satisfaction level, commitment, and relevant affective variables (such as depression) provide important baseline information and a broad, overall view of the relationship. Specific, op-erationalized data regarding the couple's unique problems as well as their personal and relationship skills expose treatment goals and produce implications for the selection of intervention methods.

Data collected should be focused on current cognitive, behavioral, affective, and environmental factors contributing to the marital distress, as well as on individual prerelationship history and the couple's developmental history. Combining current and historical data may expose well-established patterns of negative interaction. Understanding the developmental bases of such phenomena as expectations, reinforcers, patterns of behavior exchange, emotional episodes, and methods of interpersonal control may provide valuable insight into the context of such factors, including antecedent conditions and relationship-specific as well as extraneous controlling factors.

Although the predominant focus of assessment is on couple interaction, individual be-

---

BOX 9.1   *Initial Assessment Content*

Satisfaction level (global and specific)
    Communication
    Conflict management
    Sex
    Finances
    Support
    Decision making
    Trust
    Affection
    Household responsibilities
    Time spent together
    Time spent apart
    Child management
What prompted the couple to seek therapy at this time
Presenting problem(s)—target problems
Early relationship attractions
Personal history—information about family of origin

Client therapy goals
Commitment to staying married
Relationship developmental history
Information processing skills and errors
Expectations
Behavioral excesses and deficits
Emotional disorders
Communication patterns and properties
Relationship strengths—cognitive and behavioral skills relevant to coupling
Individual psychopathology
Environmental factors—stressors on the relationship (for example, interference from extended family)

NOTE: Adapted from "Treating Marital Couples in Conflict and Transition" by D. K. Granvold. In *Innovations in Health Care Practice,* by J. S. McNeil and S. E. Weinstein (Eds.). copyright © 1988 by the National Association of Social Workers.

havioral and emotional maladjustment and psychopathology may be evident. In such cases, assessment methods should be introduced that are tailored to both the individual and the couple. For example, the treatment of a couple in which one partner is clinically depressed would ideally incorporate an assessment and intervention procedure sensitive both to the individual symptoms of depression as well as the role of depression in the couple's interaction. Couple-interaction variables would include the behaviors of the nondepressed spouse that serve to stimulate and reinforce the depression and the benefits the nondepressed spouse receives from the mate's depression.

In addition to assessing interpersonal and intrapersonal factors related to the spouses and their relationship, assessment should also focus on the couple's response to therapy and to the therapist (for example, openness to disclosing relevant content and feelings in therapy, to completing homework assignments, and so forth). Discussion of treatment goals and procedures, clients' commitment to stated process and goals, and evolving expectations of clients regarding the therapist's role provides an opportunity for valuable feedback, clarification, and the enhancement of change expectancies and commitment.

Assessment methods include both conjoint and individual clinical interviews, self-report indexes and questionnaires, daily data-collection measures, and structured procedures to evaluate such factors as problem behaviors, communication, problem solving, and information processing. Effective assessment requires the use of measurement instruments (Jordan & Cobb, 1992). As noted above, both global and specific data have importance in a comprehensive assessment. Suggested global instruments include:

Marital Pre-Counseling Inventory (Stuart, 1974)
Family Pre-Counseling Inventory (Stuart & Stuart, 1975b)

Sexual Adjustment Inventory (Stuart, Stuart, Maurice, & Szasz, 1975)
Pre-Marital Counseling Inventory (Stuart & Stuart, 1975a)
Multi-Problem Screening Inventory (Hudson, 1990)
Multimodal Life History Questionnaire (Lazarus, 1980).

Others have developed questionnaires designed to measure more specific aspects of the marital relationship. Fredman and Sherman (1987) report instruments for measuring such factors as communication, intimacy, and jealousy. The authors also review projective tests, as well as observational schemes to measure problem behaviors directly. Sheafor, Horejsi, and Horejsi (1988) review assessment techniques, including self-report indexes and questionnaires, daily data-collection measures, and other structured procedures.

Corcoran and Fischer (1987) present rapid-assessment instruments for use with both individuals and couples and families, to determine both interpersonal and intrapersonal problems. Scales measure married couples' problems, including overall marital satisfaction, sexual satisfaction, satisfaction with the parenting role, and more specific marital problems such as jealousy and communication. These scales are designed to be used not only for assessment but also for the evaluation of treatment effectiveness.

Baucom and Epstein (1990) recommend the use of various self-report inventories for the assessment of behavior, attribution, and other cognitive variables. Included are the following:

Behavioral Measures

Areas-of-Change Questionnaire (Weiss, Hops, & Patterson, 1973)
Dyadic Adjustment Scale (Spanier, 1976)
Marital Satisfaction Inventory (Snyder, 1979)
Spouse Observation Checklist (Weiss et al., 1973)

Attribution Inventories

Dyadic Attributional Inventory (Baucom, Sayers, & Duhe, 1987)

Attribution Questionnaire (Fincham & O'Leary, 1983)

Partner Observational/Attributional Questionnaire (Baucom, Wheeler, & Bell, 1984)

Daily Record of Dysfunctional Thoughts (Beck et al., 1979)

Cognitive Inventories

Marital Agendas Protocol (Notarius & Vanzetti, 1983)

Irrational Beliefs Test (Jones, 1968)

Relationship Beliefs Inventory (Eidelson & Epstein, 1982)

THERAPEUTIC GUIDELINES

The therapist has several responsibilities in applying cognitive-behavioral marital therapy. The following procedures are recommended for shaping the couple's expectations regarding the process of therapy and for promoting the development of knowledge necessary to engage in effective treatment (Granvold, 1988):

- *Control of the treatment process:* Although it is important to be attentive to the specific expectations of the couple regarding the therapeutic process, the goals of therapy, and the therapist's role, it is the therapist's responsibility to take control and guide the couple in treatment. The therapist should control the tempo of the sessions, decide on the ratio of enjoyment to pain, manage conflict, and provide strategic reinforcement to the couple. The productivity of the session is in some measure contingent on the skill of the therapist in managing these responsibilities.
- *Explication of the overall goals of therapy:* This responsibility is somewhat variable, specifically dependent on the status of the

couple. For those who are fully committed to remaining married, the goal is to promote constructive change to (1) reduce the frequency, intensity, and duration of conflict and unhappiness; (2) increase positively rewarding interchanges in the relationship; and (3) enhance the satisfaction level of each partner. For those couples who are contemplating divorce or are undecided, the goal is to interrupt dysfunctional marital interaction and to promote optimal functioning as a couple to facilitate decision making to either maintain the marriage or divorce. If the couple is separated, an altered intervention plan is required to meet the unique needs inherent in separation (Granvold, 1983; Granvold & Tarrant, 1983).

- *Explanation of the assessment process:* The therapist provides the couple with an understanding of the importance of developing a treatment plan based on a comprehensive yet specific understanding of their functioning. The therapist sets the expectation with the couple that they participate actively in the assessment process (although they may consider it laborious and too time consuming at times) in order to make a responsible treatment plan and evaluate it for effectiveness.
- *Fostering collaborative set:* Acceptance by each partner that their marital problems are interactional is necessary for effective engagement in couple treatment. The therapist promotes the view that each partner has contributed both knowingly and unintentionally to the distress and that each must change to achieve effective outcomes.
- *Promoting "collaborative empiricism":* This procedure involves engaging the couple as participants and collaborators in formulating the treatment plan, a plan that "tests out" hypotheses regarding specific cognitive, behavioral, or affective changes and relationship satisfaction. The concept of collaborative empiricism, introduced by Beck and his colleagues in their treatment of de-

pression, calls on the therapist to use inge- nuity and resourcefulness to stimulate the active participation of the clients in the de- sign, implementation, and evaluation of the intervention (Beck et al., 1979).

- *Promoting positive expectancies:* The effort is to alter the typical negative-biased perspec- tive of the couple and to instill confidence that the therapist can guide them in construc- tive change. With regard to negative bias, Jacobson and Margolin (1979) and Stuart (1975, 1980) suggest a focus on the strengths of the relationship and a sensitivity to posi- tive behavior as a means to dilute the nega- tive bias. Beginning with the initial inter- view, the couple are encouraged to track the positives in the relationship. This focus on positive interchanges between spouses, both within and outside sessions, is emphasized throughout the course of treatment.

- *Explanation of the complexity of relation- ship interaction:* The therapist explains the concept of social exchange theory as it re- lates to the couple's relationship, social learning theory and marital interaction, the role of cognitive factors in human function- ing and spouse interaction, and behavioral excesses and deficits relevant to marital interaction and therapeutic change.

- *Contracting:* The couple are asked to com- mit to a minimum of eight weeks of marital treatment, meeting with the therapist con- jointly approximately weekly (in one-hour sessions) and for one session individually during each of the first three weeks. The couple are expected to continue therapy as prescribed for the duration of the eight weeks, to take no definitive legal action to dissolve the marriage during that time, and, consistent with Stuart's (1975) long-stand- ing recommendation, to act "as if" the mar- riage is successful and will be maintained. The latter contract term is particularly im- portant in shaping the couple's expectations and perceptions. At the end of the eight- week period, the course of treatment will be evaluated, and, if therapy is continued, new

treatment goals and time limits will be de- fined. If treatment termination takes place at that time, follow-up and relevant subse- quent individual treatment should be scheduled.

- *Homework:* The couple are informed that specific homework assignments will be made at each session and reviewed at the subsequent session. These assignments may be assessment-focused or change-focused; individual or couple; cognitive, behavioral, or affective; shared or private; and specifi- cally or vaguely defined.

INTERVENTION

Cognitive-behavioral marital therapy is an educational model. Couples are taught to un- derstand the causal link between cognitions and behavior, and ultimately, through in- session application, they learn to identify and modify the negative cognitions affecting their marital interaction. They are instructed con- comitantly in the principles of social learning and social exchange theory as background knowledge for learning methods to change be- havior. Imparting this knowledge along with a rationale for its importance is designed to more effectively enlist the cooperation of the couple in the assessment process and in stra- tegic intervention.

Behavioral Treatment

Techniques to change specific behavior or to enhance social competency can be taught to clients in a step-by-step process (Cormier & Cormier, 1985). The first step is instruction. The practitioner explains the technique or skill and gives a rationale. Second is model- ing; the practitioner models or demonstrates the technique. Third, the practitioner encour- ages the couple to practice the technique. In the fourth step the practitioner gives the couple feedback about their performance. Then the couple practice the technique once again. Finally, they are given an assignment to practice what they have learned at home.

The procedures reviewed below include behavior-change techniques and social-skills methods. The intervention procedures addressed are representative of the areas of intervention common to behavioral marital therapy. Many other procedures in these and other categories exist, however, and only space limitations prevent their inclusion. The reader is directed to the following sources for additional information on behavioral marital treatment: Baucom and Epstein (1990), Bornstein and Bornstein (1986), Jacobson (1984), Jacobson and Margolin (1979), Margolin (1987), Markman, Floyd, Stanley, and Jamieson (1984), Paolino and McCrady (1978), and Stuart (1980).

Positive Tracking and Positive Control. Couples in marital distress often overfocus on the negative aspects of their relationship, to the exclusion of the positives. Positive tracking and control help refocus couples on the positive aspects of the relationship (Jacobson & Dallas, 1981). Positive tracking is a way of helping spouses become aware of their partner's positive contributions by looking for and recording these positives. The Spouse Observation Checklist (Weiss et al., 1973) and Caring Days Procedure (Stuart, 1980) are two examples of useful tracking procedures. Positive control involves the use of positive reinforcement to encourage a positive change in the partner. The attention spouses give to the positive behavior of their mate through recording or verbal feedback serves to positively reinforce the desired behaviors. Teaching couples to positively reinforce each other sets the stage for increasing their skills in areas where they may have deficiencies.

Communication-Skills Training.   Training in communication skills focuses on teaching couples how to communicate better both verbally and nonverbally. Specific training elements include teaching them how to listen and empathize with their spouse's point of view; how to level, or communicate their intended message directly; and how to edit information that is not necessary and may, in effect, be counterproductive (Gottman, Notarius, Gonso, & Markman, 1976).

To listen and empathize, couples are taught to recognize and call a halt to faulty interactions or miscommunications using behavioral techniques, and to ask for clarification and feedback. Couples learn to make nonconfrontive requests, make direct requests for feedback from the spouse, and respond to requests using active listening techniques. They also learn to respond to the content and feeling of what their partner is saying. For example, the wife may make a nonconfrontive request: "I'm worried about the household chores, and I'd like to set a time with you so we can talk about it. When is a good time for you?" The husband responds with a direct request for feedback, "Do you feel that we need to talk about the chores getting done?" The wife responds, "Yes, I'm worried that I can't get all the jobs done at home when I start my new job next week." The husband responds, using active listening, "You're feeling overwhelmed thinking about keeping up the housework and working outside the home?" This allows the wife either to confirm that her husband has heard her message correctly or to clarify content that her husband has distorted or failed to include. Finally, the listener validates the spouse, even if he or she is not in agreement with what has been said. In the example, the husband may say: "I understand that you're worried about the housework. If it's convenient with you, I can talk about it after dinner tonight."

Leveling, or communicating openly with one's spouse, is a technique for couples who typically avoid conflict. Many factors influence a reluctance to openly communicate, including a fear of disapproval from the mate, a low tolerance threshold for conflict, and a lack of problem-solving skills. The first step in leveling is to help partners address their fears about sharing their feelings with their mate. Some fears may be irrational and can be discussed by asking the client, "What is the worst that could happen, and what is the best that could happen, if you opened up to your spouse?" Secondly, spouses who do not share their feelings in marriage may not have learned a language for communicating feelings. Lists of feeling words can be used to help them put their emotions into words. Third, spouses are instructed to write their feelings on a piece of paper to give to their partner. This gives the partner time to think about an appropriate, caring response to validate the spouse's expression of feelings. Fourth, partners may need help in distinguishing between assertiveness and aggressiveness. Partners who have not been able to express their needs and feelings may fear that asking for what they want is too aggressive or selfish. The discussion may center on the right of each partner to have his or her needs met in the relationship. Finally, partners are taught to give signals to the spouse to indicate whether they are in the mood to "level." For example, if the husband says, "The boss was a tyrant today," the wife would be "warned" to wait to level until a more opportune time when her partner would probably be more receptive.

Other couples fight over issues, rather than avoiding them. These arguments may begin with a specific problem but escalate rapidly. Dragging up old unresolved issues and calling names may be a part of the scenario. A useful technique for these couples is called editing; couples are taught to edit out information that is irrelevant, unproductive, or impolite. Guidelines for editing include these: first, say what you can do for your partner, not what you cannot or will not do. For example, "I'll help you shop for a present for your mother for an hour tonight"; edit out "I don't want to go shopping for your mother. It's a waste of time, since she won't like what we pick out anyway." Second, give sincere compliments

or praise. The husband might say, "Thanks for cooking dinner tonight," editing out "One night out of seven isn't so bad!" Third, be considerate. Fourth, listen to your spouse, and act interested in what is important to your partner. Fifth, avoid interrupting your partner. Sixth, do not put your partner down. Seventh, accept responsibility when you make a mistake. Eighth, stay in the present, avoiding bringing up past grievances or unpleasant events. And ninth, try to think not only of yourself and what you want but also of what your partner would like.

Gambrill and Richey (1988) suggest that practitioners give feedback about clients' voice qualities, which may affect the message being sent. For example, voice tone may be monotonous, voice level may be too loud or too soft, and the pace of speaking may be too slow or too fast. These are important qualities in conveying a spoken message. Practitioners can watch to see if one partner monopolizes the conversation at the expense of the other, if conversation is too superficial, or if it gets bogged down by too much detail.

Nonverbal communication also is a very powerful aspect of communication between spouses. Elements of nonverbal communication that can be taught to couples include facial expression; for example, spouses should make eye contact, have a warm expression, smile when it is appropriate, and respond expressively to their partner. Posture should be relaxed, with the body turned to the partner, and gestures should be appropriate (Hepworth & Larsen, 1986).

Training in Problem-Solving Skills. Problem-solving training is designed to help couples resolve their areas of conflict (Gottman, 1979; Thorpe & Olson, 1990; Weiss & Wieder, 1982). Problem-solving techniques (Sheafor et al., 1988) help couples learn how to clearly define the problem, look at each partner's investment in the problem, brainstorm and write down all possible solutions or options without evaluating them, throw out those options that are totally unacceptable to either spouse, evaluate and rank the remaining solutions, select and put into effect the most promising solution, and make adjustments as necessary or select another alternative. Feindler and Ecton (1986) specify guidelines to help in the problem-solving process, including being specific when defining problems; focusing on present problems, not past ones; focusing on one problem at a time; listening when others are sharing their problem; and sharing problems in a positive and constructive way.

Contingency Contracting. The use of behavioral-exchange contracts has been found to be effective in increasing the display of desirable behavior between spouses. The most common method of contracting in marital treatment is contingency contracting, a procedure that specifies the consequences for compliance with the terms of the contract. There are two types of contingency contracts: quid pro quo (QPQ) and good faith.

A QPQ contract is tit for tat. The agreement between the spouses is to "exchange" a behavior desired by the mate: "I, Mary, agree to rub your back for 15 minutes, three times per week, in exchange for your talking with me uninterruptedly three times per week for 15 minutes each." Compliance on the part of one partner prompts compliance on the part of the other. If a mate fails to honor his or her side of the contract, the other is not obligated to perform. Contract terms should be clearly stated, with time lengths, frequency rates, and number of items or repetitions specified. A significant limitation of this form of contingency contracting is that one mate can sabotage the change effort by withholding the contract behavior.

The good faith contract also involves a behavior change considered pleasing and desirable by the spouse. The contingencies for compliance with the contract terms, however, are placed independently of the mate. The reward for compliance should be strong enough in value to motivate performance, and the specified reward for mate A should not be displeasing, undesirable, or punishing to mate B. An example of a good-faith contract is as follows: "I, Joe, agree to talk uninterruptedly with you for 15 minutes three times per week in exchange for golfing 18 holes on Saturday morning." Failure to comply results in Joe's being ineligible to go golfing on Saturday. A response-cost term could also be added to the contract, as follows: "I agree to wash the kitchen windows inside and outside on Saturday morning if I fail to honor the terms of the contract." The mate would write a separate contract in a desired area of behavior change, and likewise, the contingencies would be independent of the spouse. Both types of contracts can be useful in increasing positive behavior in the relationship. Written contracts are highly preferable early in treatment and may give way to verbal contracts as the couple's relationship improves and they become more adept at exchanging behaviors.

Cognitive Restructuring

The goal of cognitive restructuring is the identification and modification of cognitive processes that contribute to individual psychological distress and dysfunctional interpersonal behavior. The intervention may be focused on information processing distortions and other cognitive errors or on beliefs that underlie an individual's appraisals and conclusions reached regarding his or her own behavior and the behavior of others. Terms used to describe this latter phenomenon include personal constructs (Kelly, 1955); irrational beliefs (Ellis, 1973, 1977a); automatic thoughts and schemata (Beck, 1976; Beck et al., 1979); and deep structures (Guidano & Liotti, 1983). The term *schemata* will be used here as representative of a personal philosophy that promotes a distortion in thought processing and leads to behavioral, emotional, and interpersonal dysfunction. Schemata are further defined as inflexible, general rules or silent assumptions (beliefs, attitudes, concepts) that (1) develop as enduring concepts from past (early) experiences; (2) form the basis for screening, discriminating, weighing, and coding stimuli; and (3) form the basis for categorizing, evaluating experiences and making judgments, and distorting reality situations (Rush & Beck, 1978).

Once the couple has been taught the role of cognitions in human functioning and in marital distress specifically, cognitive restructuring is presented as a treatment procedure. The application of the model involves the identification of cognitive processes considered potentially accountable for dysfunctional interaction or individual distress. The spouses develop awareness of cognitive distortion and are instructed in monitoring and validating their cognitions. Faulty or counterproductive cognitions are targeted for modification. Cognitive restructuring skills are taught in session, and homework assignments are given that promote the transfer of learning to the natural environment.

Modifying Information Processing Errors and Other Cognitive Distortions.
Information processing errors have been described by Beck and his colleagues (Beck et al., 1979) in relation to depression, and they have been applied directly to the treatment of marital distress by several researcher/practitioners (Baucom & Epstein, 1990; Beck, 1988; Epstein, Schlesinger, & Dryden, 1988; Granvold, 1988, 1992). These errors distort the client's view of self, others, and the world and result in maladaptive emotions, negatively biased expectations, and overt and verbal behaviors that promote negative responses from others. The following, adapted from Granvold (1988), is a description of common information processing errors:

Absolutistic and dichotomous thinking: This disorder is the tendency to view experiences, objects, and situations in a polarized manner: good/bad, right/wrong, strong/weak. Mary, upset with her husband, John, because he failed to assert himself in collecting a delinquent payment from their renters, refers to John as a "spineless, weak man." In response to her characterization, he likewise views himself as spineless and weak, feels ashamed and depressed, and has a strong sense of worthlessness and self-loathing. Absolutistic thinking simplifies and distorts the meaning of life events. It is illogical because a given condition or experience can rarely be rated objectively as at one extreme or the other.

Overgeneralization: Reaching a conclusion or drawing a general rule on the basis of minimal evidence and applying the concept across the board to all related and unrelated situations is the act of overgeneralization (Beck et al., 1979). Susie is typically not sexually provocative. One evening she dons a skimpy negligee, and her husband, Joe, who is usually attentive to her, responds in an otherwise preoccupied, inattentive, and sexually uninterested manner. Susie thinks: "I can't turn Joe on; I'm just not a lover. I'm not going to wear any more sexy clothes because it just doesn't work."

Selective abstraction: This error involves focusing on the negative in a situation, ignoring other positive (sometimes more salient) features, and viewing the entire experience as negative, based on the selective view. For example, Tom and Janet spend an enjoyable Saturday night together, during which they have a disagreement that lasts about ten minutes before being satisfactorily resolved. Tom later refers to the Saturday night with Janet as "fight night." In this manner, the meaning he attaches to the night is drawn from the comparatively brief conflict, and the remainder of the night is ignored.

Arbitrary inference involves reaching a negative conclusion on the basis of minimal supportive evidence or in light of evidence to the contrary. Two types of arbitrary inference are mind reading and negative prediction (Freeman, 1983):

1. *Mind reading.* Paul says to Cathy, "The children were sure unruly in church this morning." Cathy thinks that Paul thinks she is a bad mother. Paul actually considers Cathy a great mother even though he rarely tells her so. Bedrosian (1983) identifies the tendency of mates to "infer one another's inferences" (p. 101): "You think I'm angry, but I'm not." "Your look tells me that you think I'm kidding, but I couldn't be more serious."

2. *Negative prediction:* This type of arbitrary inference involves imagining or anticipating that something bad or unpleasant is going to happen without adequate or realistic support for the prediction. A functionally orgasmic woman has failed to reach an orgasm during the previous four sexual encounters with her husband (each encounter experienced while she was very fatigued). She thinks, "I'm never going to have an orgasm again; when you lose it (the ability), it's gone forever." She becomes uninterested in sexual contact with her mate and becomes cold and aloof.

Magnification and minimization: An individual may catastrophize an action, issue, or event and display a concomitant extremely negative reaction. The distortion is the magnification of the meaning and perceived consequence of the stimulus. For example, a husband displays an extreme reaction to his wife's "failure" to immediately ask him about an important conference with his boss that day. An opposite distortion is the minimization of the significance of a behavior, event, or condition. A relatively unassertive mate approaches her spouse with a difficult request and dismisses her action as meaningless in her effort to become more assertive with her partner.

Personalization involves making a causal connection between a negative event or situation and oneself without adequate supportive evidence. This is a form of attribution, a process that will receive more attention later.

There are two forms of personalization. In the first instance an arbitrary conclusion is reached in which a negative event is viewed as caused by the subject. To illustrate, Larry does not eat lunch because his wife failed to put his lunch by his briefcase that morning. Linda thinks, "I'm responsible for Larry's missing lunch" (although he could either have eaten out or remembered the lunch even though it was not in its usual place by his briefcase). She further thinks of herself as an uncaring wife for her action. In an alternative form of personalization, the individual views himself or herself as the object of a negative event. Kay encounters a traffic jam on the way to meet Roger for lunch and concludes, "If I didn't have a lunch date with Roger, there wouldn't be a traffic jam!" She failed to allow adequate time for the typical heavy midday traffic.

Faulty interpretation is the interpretation of a message inconsistent with the intention—a discrepancy between intent and impact (Gottman, 1979). Louis makes the following statement to his wife about a colleague at work: "I don't care much for Arthur." His wife, Arlene, thinks, "Louis doesn't like his job." Such an interpretation may go unvalidated and give rise to an emotive and possibly overt behavioral response followed by a stream of evaluative, interpretive, and problem-solving, action-oriented thoughts. This covert activity may largely account for the subsequent behavior. Arlene becomes physically tense and says, "I wish we hadn't bought this house and taken on such a high house payment." Her thought process has flowed from "Louis doesn't like his job" to "He may quit or take another job, perhaps for less money" to "If he does that, I'm worried that we won't be able to make the house payment." Arlene's concomitant emotional response is anxiety, coupled with some mounting hostility toward Louis over his putting them in such a financial bind (were he to act in accordance with her chain of thoughts). Louis, unaware of Arlene's chain of thoughts (because she does not verbalize them), covertly responds with curiosity over the connection between his comment about Arthur and Arlene's comment about the purchase of their house. In sum, the discrepancy between intent and impact is the product of a faulty premise followed by an unvalidated stream of thought.

Once the practitioner has an awareness that an information processing error is actively contributing to the couple's dysfunctional interaction, a series of questions can be asked that exposes the erroneous thinking to the client. These questions guide the client through a process of reasoning in which clear, logical evidence is sought to support the conclusions reached. The process serves to expose flaws in thinking, and, in turn, the faulty cognitions are replaced by logical and verifiable conclusions. Untoward emotions experienced by the client in connection with his or her faulty thinking can be expected to modify concomitantly with the cognitive change. Change in emotions is, however, a more gradual process than cognitive change. In the following case example, Tom's selective abstraction regarding a recent night out with Janet is the focus of intervention. Janet brings the issue to therapy because she feels upset over Tom's negative characterization of their night out, which she considers to have been very enjoyable overall:

Therapist: Tom, you say that the fight you had Saturday night is what captured your attention about the evening and resulted in your referring to the evening as "fight night." How do you feel when you think that?

Tom: I feel bothered, sort of disheartened . . . sad. And Janet was bothered Sunday when I referred to Saturday night as "fight night." She told me I was being negative again.

Therapist: So focusing on the fight results in some negative feelings in this case for both you and Janet. Do you think the fight was representative of the evening?

Tom: No, not really. It was a very enjoyable evening overall.

Therapist: Then what could you think that would put the fight in proper perspective?

Tom: The evening was really a nice evening together. The argument was only a brief part of the night. We resolved it, and we didn't allow it to ruin our night.

Therapist: How do you feel as you consider Saturday night in this manner?

Tom: Much better, not nearly so bad . . . actually kind of good. Janet, I really did enjoy Saturday night.

Perceptions, attributions, expectations, assumptions, and standards can be the focus of change. Following an explanation of these concepts, the couple are guided in the identification of these cognitive processes in their own functioning, and connections are made between these phenomena and marital distress. In some cases the actual description of one of the five cognitive distortions may be stimulated by a specific problem. For example, a negative attribution may be central to a distressing interchange and provide the therapist an opportunity to explain this type of cognitive distortion. Following the explanation, the client is guided through the process of restructuring his or her thinking and thereby achieving some degree of problem resolution:

Therapist: Tim, you say that Ann left for the office early Tuesday morning before you awakened just to avoid having contact with you.

Tim: Yes, her schedule is flexible, so she could have gone in at the regular time. And Ann always withdraws from me when we aren't getting along very well.

Ann: I told you that I had a meeting with the company vice president at 9:00 A.M. that I had to prepare for! *That's* why I went in early!

Therapist: Tim, how do you feel toward Ann when you think that she's intentionally withdrawing from you?

Tim: I feel resentment and distrust. I think, "Why can't you hang in there and work at building a positive relationship instead of walling yourself off?"

Therapist: Do you like having those feelings—resentment and distrust?

Tim: Of course not.

Therapist: That's good thinking. I agree that having those feelings is not very pleasant. Tim, the belief a person holds regarding *why* his mate behaves in a certain way is called an *attribution*. A simple definition of attribution is implied causality. Negative attributions like the one you made are often the result of distorted thinking. What evidence do you have to support your view that Ann left for work early to avoid you?

Tim: Just that she withdraws from me and gets distant when we're on the outs. We had a disagreement about the kids Monday night. I just figured that she was still upset and decided to avoid me.

Therapist: Can you think of any other explanation for Ann's behavior?

Tim: Yes, that she had work to do.

Therapist: Yes, that's a plausible explanation, particularly in light of what Ann has said about her need to prepare for the 9:00 A.M. business meeting with the VP. How do you feel when you conclude that rather than withdrawing from you, Ann was satisfying a job responsibility by leaving early for work?

Tim: Well, I don't feel resentment. Put that way, I feel sort of pleased and proud that I'm married to such a successful businesswoman and conscientious person.

Therapist: Now, can you think of any evidence to support your initial conclusion, aside from Ann's tendency in the past to withdraw from you after conflict?

Tim: No. I really can't. I guess that I was just extra ready to find fault with Ann, and her leaving early for work seemed like a good opportunity.

Therapist: So shifting from the negative explanation, "She's withdrawing from me by leaving for work early," to the positive explanation, "Ann left for work early to prepare for her meeting with the VP," results in a change in your feelings toward her from such negative feelings as hostility and distrust to positive feelings of pride and perhaps appreciation?

Tim: Yes, that's the shift in feelings that results. I really am proud of Ann, and I do appreciate her in many ways, work included. I guess I've gotten in the habit of looking for negatives.

Tim would be guided in monitoring his negative attributions, to seek evidence to support them and to think of competing explanations for the causal conclusions he has reached in specific instances. The practitioner would be obligated to determine if Ann shares Tim's view that she withdraws emotionally or physically after conflict. If she does actually tend to withdraw after conflict, that behavior and the supporting cognitions would become the targets of intervention.

Modifying Faulty Beliefs.   Marital discord and emotional distress may be the products of dysfunctional cognitive structures (schemata). Several initial efforts have been made to treat marital distress through applying cognitive restructuring methods to dysfunctional schemata (Abrahms, 1983; Baucom & Epstein, 1990; Beck, 1988; Bedrosian, 1983; DiGiuseppe & Zeeve, 1985; Ellis, 1969a, 1969b, 1977b; Ellis & Dryden, 1987; Ellis, Sichel, Yeager, DiMattia, & DiGiuseppe, 1989; Epstein, 1982; Epstein & Eidelson, 1981; Epstein, Schlesinger, & Dryden, 1988; Granvold, 1988; Huber & Baruth, 1989; Jacobson, 1984; Margolin, 1987; McClellan & Steiper, 1977; Revenstorf, 1984; Schindler & Vollmer, 1984; Weiss, 1984b). "Common among the procedures outlined by these authors is the identification of unrealistic, demanding expectations of self and the marital partner, specification of faulty attributions and a deliberate effort on the part of the therapist to foster the client's disengagement from maladaptive beliefs and judgements" (Granvold, 1988, p. 83). Through interviewing procedures or paper/pencil assessment methods the practitioner seeks evidence of causal theories, basic assumptions, or irrational beliefs. The practitioner and client collaborate in the development of strategies to validate those schemata identified as potentially accountable for individual and marital dysfunction. The assumption of many researchers is that dysfunctional schemata cannot be so much eliminated as altered or changed (Kendall & Ingram, 1987). The practitioner can also expect the modification of longstanding basic beliefs operative in personal, marital, and family functioning to require considerable evidence (Epstein et al., 1988).

The approach to validating schemata is similar to the methods used in modifying information processing errors. Socratic methods of inquiry are used to achieve logical examination of schemata and to strategically search for supportive evidence. Epstein and his colleagues note that unrealistic beliefs may be reinforced by feedback and consensus within the family (Epstein et al., 1988). As a consequence, the practitioner may guide the client outside the family system to invalidate faulty schemata.

Couples present for therapy with highly idiosyncratic dysfunctional schemata. Despite these variations, DiGiuseppe and Zeeve (1985) offer a useful categorization of irrational beliefs relevant to relationship problems: "These include (1) dire needs for love and approval; (2) perfectionistic demands of self, mate, and relationships in general; (3) a philosophy of blame and punishment; (4) beliefs that frustration and/or discomfort are catastrophic; and (5) beliefs that emotions are externally caused and therefore uncontrollable (Ellis & Harper, 1961)."

Even though a given belief is faulty, a client may strongly believe it and suffer marital dysfunction and emotional distress as a consequence. The steps of cognitive restructuring recommended to modify the faulty belief involve guiding the client to (1) commit to altering the belief on the basis that it is destructive, (2) test out the validity of the belief by looking for logical evidence to support or negate it, (3) allow the strength of the belief to erode on the basis of the evidence—to repeatedly rate and rerate the *degree* to which the belief is held, and (4) allow the concomitant negative feelings to reduce in intensity and duration as the strength of the belief erodes.

The following excerpt illustrates the initial application of cognitive restructuring to a client who demands approval from his wife and reacts with hurt and anger when she is critical of his behavior. Behaviors that accompany these emotions include raising his voice, using sarcasm, and throwing objects. There is no history of physical abuse. In a recent interchange his wife was critical of him for not showing much interest in her work. After determining that her expectations in this area were reasonable (not excessive) and that, from the perspectives of both husband and wife, he had shown little interest in her work, the practitioner addressed the husband's demand for approval. (The desirability of paying more attention to the wife's work was addressed later in the session.) The transcript is picked up at the point the therapist is paraphrasing information just expressed by the couple (H = husband; T = therapist):

T: Joe, it's my understanding, then, that when Sandy is critical of you, as she was in asking that you show more interest in her work, you feel anger and hurt. You express your feelings by raising your voice, sounding sarcastic, and, at times, throwing things. Do you *like* feeling and acting in this manner?

H: No, I don't. I feel embarrassed, even as we talk about it.

T: Not liking the way you act and doing something about it are two different things. Do you *want* to change the way you feel?

H: Yes, I really do want to get a handle on this.

T: I'm pleased that you're committed to change, Joe. You'll recall from our earlier discussions that I've indicated that feelings often come from thoughts or beliefs that we hold. I'm interested in your beliefs about criticism. Do you think Sandy shouldn't criticize you?

H: Well, yes, kind of . . . I've never been good at accepting criticism . . . from anybody . . . and it seems to really sting coming from Sandy.

T: So, you're demanding that you be free of criticism, is that correct?

H: Yes, I suppose so.

T: Joe, do you think it's reasonable to expect to go through life free of criticism?

H: No, not really.

T: So the belief that "I must never receive criticism from Sandy" is a faulty belief.

H: Yes, it is . . . although I'd like to have her approve of the way I act.

T: *Wanting* her approval is acceptable, Joe. It's the *demand* that she *never* be critical of you at all, your *intolerance* of it, and your inappropriate reactions when she *is* critical that are the problems. In order to shift from the demand for Sandy's approval to only wanting it, what could you tell yourself, think, when she's critical of your behavior?

H: I'm not really sure . . . I guess I could think something like "It's OK that Sandy wants me to act differently." I suppose I'm not as perfect as I wish I were.

T: Joe, that's excellent thinking! By saying that it's OK for Sandy to criticize your behavior, you shift away from the *demand* for constant approval to merely wanting her approval and accepting her occasional disapproval of your attitudes or behavior.

As with Tim in an earlier example, Joe would be guided in monitoring his *demand* for approval from Sandy and others as well. Within the session, Joe and Sandy can be in-structed to engage in a communication exercise in which she provides negatively critical feedback to him while he practices active listening. This activity could both produce the benefit of improving the couple's communication skills and serve to begin the process of shaping his tolerance of her criticism. His homework may be the assignment of "shame-attacking exercises" (Ellis, 1969a, 1969b; Ellis & Becker, 1982) in which he is to act in a manner ("shamefully") to deliberately gain attention from others and practice tolerating the ensuing discomfort in relation to the "disapproval" from those around him. By developing a greater tolerance for disapproval from others, he may likewise become more tolerant of his wife's disapproval. Often intolerance of disapproval is associated with a sense of conditional self-regard. This possibility would be explored with Joe, and if he were found to function with conditional self-regard, the restructuring of that view to healthy self-acceptance would be sought. In subsequent sessions he would be guided in the repeated bombardment of the faulty belief that Sandy must *only* be approving of him. Self-statements reflecting coping ("I can handle Sandy's occasional criticism") and self-affirmation ("I'm handling my feelings much better") would be identified and rehearsed.

CONCLUSION

The efficacy of behavioral marital therapy (BMT) has been challenged, and clinicians have been charged to address cognitive factors in marital distress and treatment (Bennum, 1986; Jacobson, 1984; Schindler & Vollmer, 1984; Weiss, 1984b). This encouragement to include cognition as well as affect is not necessarily to be viewed as an expansion of BMT, for as Holtzworth-Munroe and Jacobson (1991) note, "behaviorism never excluded them in the first place" (p. 98). Despite their inclusion in the behavioral perspective, cognitive factors have only recently become the focus of attention. Although a body of assessment and intervention knowledge has begun to be developed regarding the role of cognitions in marital interaction and the treatment of marital distress, this knowledge should be viewed as preliminary. There is need for the creative, empirically based development of marital assessment and treatment methods that effectively combine cognitive with behavioral factors.

Although the need for additional research is substantial, existing research can offer direction for the application of current methods of practice and the expansion and development of new methods. For example, Holtzworth-Munroe and Jacobson (1991) report adaptability, flexibility, and the capacity to change as key ingredient in the long-term success of marital relationships. Means of assessing these qualities in couples and methods of intervention designed to teach couples the skills of adaptability, flexibility, and change should be incorporated (and further developed) in marital treatment efforts to produce desired long-term effects. It is through the responsible application of this process that the outcomes that therapists seek and the methods they select, hopefully from an array of tempting alternatives, can be expected to more closely and efficaciously meet the treatment needs of the couples with whom they work.

REFERENCES

Abrahms, J. L. (1983). Cognitive-behavioral strategies to induce and enhance a collaborative set in distressed couples. In A. Freeman (Ed.), *Cognitive therapy with couples and groups.* New York: Plenum.

Abramson, L. Y., Seligman, M. E. P., & Teasdale, J. D. (1978). Learned helplessness in humans: Critique and reformulation. *Journal of Abnormal Psychology, 87,* 49–74.

Alberts, J. K. (1988). An analysis of couples' conversational complaints. *Communication Monographs, 55,* 184–197.

Baars, B. J. (1986). *The cognitive revolution in psychology.* New York: Guilford Press.

Bandura, A. (1969). *Principles of behavior modification.* New York: Holt, Rinehart & Winston.

Bandura, A. (1977a). Self-efficacy: Toward a unifying theory of behavioral change. *Psychological Review, 84,* 191–215.

Bandura, A. (1977b). *Social learning theory.* Englewood Cliffs, NJ: Prentice-Hall.

Bandura, A. (1985). Model of causality in social learning theory. In M. J. Mahoney & A. Freeman (Eds.), *Cognition and psychotherapy.* New York: Plenum.

Baucom, D. H., & Epstein, N. (1990). *Cognitive-behavioral marital therapy.* New York: Brunner/Mazel.

Baucom, D. H., Epstein, N., Sayers, S., & Sher, T. G. (1989). The role of cognitions in marital relationships: Definitional, methodological and conceptual issues. *Journal of Consulting and Clinical Psychology, 57,* 31–38.

Baucom, D. H., Sayers, S. L., & Duhe, A. D. (1987, November). *Attributional style and attributional pattern among married couples.* Paper presented at the annual meeting of the Association for Advancement of Behavior Therapy, Boston.

Baucom, D. H., Wheeler, C. M., & Bell, G. (1984, November). *Assessing the role of attributions in marital distress.* Paper presented at the annual meeting of the Association for Advancement of Behavior Therapy, Philadelphia.

Beck, A. T. (1976). *Cognitive therapy and the emotional disorders.* New York: International Universities Press.

Beck, A. T. (1988). *Love is never enough.* New York: Harper & Row.

Beck, A. T., Rush, A. J., Shaw, B. F., & Emery, G. (1979). *Cognitive therapy of depression.* New York: Guilford Press.

Bedrosian, R. C. (1983). Cognitive therapy in the family system. In A. Freeman (Ed.), *Cognitive therapy with couples and groups.* New York: Plenum.

Bennum, I. (1986). Cognitive components of marital conflict. *Behavioral Psychotherapy, 14,* 302–309.

Birchler, G. R., Weiss, R. L., & Vincent, J. P. (1975). A multimethod analysis of social reinforcement exchange between maritally distressed and nondistressed spouse and stranger dyads. *Journal of Personality and Social Psychology, 31,* 349–360.

Bornstein, P. H., & Bornstein, M. T. (1986). *Marital therapy: A behavioral-communications approach.* New York: Pergamon Press.

Bradbury, T. N. (1989). *Cognition, emotion, and interaction in distressed and nondistressed couples.* Unpublished doctoral dissertation, University of Illinois, Urbana.

Christensen, A., Sullaway, M., & King, C. (1983). Systematic error in behavioral reports of dyadic interaction: Egocentric bias and content effects. *Behavioral Assessment, 5,* 131–142.

Corcoran, K., & Fischer, J. (1987). *Measures for clinical practice: A sourcebook.* New York: Free Press.

Cormier, W. H., & Cormier, L. S. (1985). *Interviewing strategies for helpers.* Pacific Grove, CA: Brooks/Cole.

DiGiuseppe, R., & Zeeve, C. (1985). Marriage: Rational-emotive couples counseling. In A. Ellis & M. E. Bernard (Eds.), *Clinical applications of rational-emotive therapy.* New York: Plenum.

Doherty, W. J. (1981a). Cognitive process in intimate conflict: I. Extending attribution theory. *American Journal of Family Therapy, 9*(1), 5–13.

Doherty, W. J. (1981b). Cognitive processes in intimate conflict: II. Efficacy and learned helplessness. *American Journal of Family Therapy, 9*(2), 35–44.

Eidelson, R. J., & Epstein, N. (1982). Cognition and relationship maladjustment: Development of a measure of dysfunctional relationship beliefs. *Journal of Consulting and Clinical Psychology, 50,* 715–720.

Ellis, A. (1962). *Reason and emotion in psychotherapy.* New York: Lyle Stuart.

Ellis, A. (1969a). Neurotic interaction between marital partners. In B. N. Ard & C. C. Ard (Eds.), *Handbook of marriage counseling.* Palo Alto, CA: Science and Behavior Books.

Ellis, A. (1969b). A weekend of rational encounter. *Rational Living, 4*(2), 1–8.

Ellis, A. (1973). *Humanistic psychotherapy.* New York: McGraw-Hill.

Ellis, A. (1977a). The basic clinical theory of rational-emotive therapy. In A. Ellis & R. Grieger (Eds.), *Handbook of rational-emotive therapy.* New York: Springer.

Ellis, A. (1977b). The nature of disturbed marital interactions. In A. Ellis & R. Grieger (Eds.), *Handbook of rational-emotive therapy.* New York: Springer.

Ellis, A., & Becker, I. (1982). *A guide to personal happiness.* North Hollywood, CA: Wilshire Books.

Ellis, A., & Dryden, W. (1987). *The practice of rational-emotive therapy (RET).* New York: Springer.

Ellis, A., & Harper, R. A. (1961). *A guide to successful marriage.* North Hollywood, CA: Wilshire Books.

Ellis, A., Sichel, J. L., Yeager, R. J., DiMattia, D. J., & DiGiuseppe, R. (1989). *Rational-emotive couples therapy.* New York: Pergamon Press.

Elwood, R. W., & Jacobson, N. S. (1982). Spouses' agreement in reporting their behavioral interactions: A clinical replication. *Journal of Consulting and Clinical Psychology, 50,* 783–784.

Epstein, N. (1982). Cognitive therapy with couples. *American Journal of Family Therapy, 10,* 5–16.

Epstein, N., & Baucom, D. H. (1989). Cognitive-behavioral marital therapy. In A. Freeman, K. M. Simon, L. E. Beutler, & H. Arkowitz (Eds.), *Comprehensive handbook of cognitive therapy.* New York: Plenum.

Epstein, N., & Eidelson, R. J. (1981). Unrealistic beliefs of clinical couples: Their relationship to expectations, goals, and satisfaction. *American Journal of Family Therapy, 9,* 13–22.

Epstein, N., Schlesinger, S. E., & Dryden, W. (1988). Concepts and methods of cognitive-behavioral family therapy. In N. Epstein, S. E. Schlesinger, & W. Dryden (Eds.), *Cognitive behavioral therapy with families.* New York: Brunner/Mazel.

Feindler, E., & Ecton, R. (1986). *Adolescent anger control: Cognitive-behavioral techniques.* New York: Pergamon Press.

Fincham, F. D., & Bradbury, T. N. (1989, November). *Cognition and marital dysfunction: The role of efficacy expectations.* Paper presented at the 23rd annual convention of the Association for Advancement of Behavior Therapy, Washington, DC.

Fincham, F. D., & O'Leary, K. D. (1983). Causal inferences for spouse behavior in maritally distressed and nondistressed couples. *Journal of Social and Clinical Psychology, 1,* 42–57.

Floyd, F. J., & Markman, H. J. (1983). Observational biases in spouse observation: Toward a cognitive/behavioral model of marriage. *Journal of Consulting and Clinical Psychology, 5,* 450–457.

Fredman, N., & Sherman, R. (1987). *Handbook of measurements for marriage and family therapy.* New York: Brunner/Mazel.

Freeman, A. (1983). Cognitive therapy: An overview. In A. Freeman (Ed.), *Cognitive therapy with couples and groups.* New York: Plenum.

Gambrill, E., & Richey, C. (1988). *Taking charge of your social life.* Belmont, CA: Behavioral Options.

Gottman, J. M. (1979). *Marital interaction: Experimental investigations.* New York: Academic Press.

Gottman, J., Notarius, C., Gonso, J., & Markman, H. (1976). *A couple's guide to communication.* Champaign, IL: Research Press.

Gottman, J., Notarius, C., Markman, H., Bank, S., Yoppi, B., & Rubin, M. E. (1976). Behavior exchange theory and marital decision making. *Journal of Personality and Social Psychology, 34,* 14–23.

Granvold, D. K. (1983). Structured separation for marital treatment and decision-making. *Journal of Marital and Family Therapy, 9,* 403–412.

Granvold, D. K. (1988). Treating marital couples in conflict and transition. In J. S. McNeil & S. E. Weinstein (Eds.), *Innovations in health care practice.* Silver Spring, MD: National Association of Social Workers.

Granvold, D. K. (1992). Treating information processing errors. In T. S. Nelson & T. S. Trepper (Eds.), *101 interventions in family therapy.* New York: Haworth Press.

Granvold, D. K., & Tarrant, R. (1983). Structured marital separation as a marital treatment method. *Journal of Marital and Family Therapy, 9,* 189–198.

Guidano, V. F., & Liotti, G. (1983). *Cognitive processes and emotional disorders.* New York: Guilford Press.

Hepworth, D., & Larsen, J. (1986). *Direct social work practice.* Chicago: Dorsey Press.

Holtzworth-Munroe, A., & Jacobson, N. S. (1991). Behavioral marital therapy. In A. S. Gurman & D. P. Kniskern (Eds.), *Handbook of family therapy* (Vol. 2). New York: Brunner/Mazel.

Homans, G. C. (1958). Social behavior as exchange. *American Journal of Sociology, 62,* 597–606.

Homans, G. C. (1974). *Social behavior: Its elementary forms.* New York: Harcourt Brace Jovanovich.

Hooley, J. M., & Hahlweg, K. (1989). Marital satisfaction and marital communication in German and English couples. *Behavioral Assessment, 11,* 119–133.

Huber, C. H., & Baruth, L. G. (1989). *Rational-emotive family therapy: Systems perspective.* New York: Springer.

Hudson, W. W. (1990). *The multi-problem screening inventory.* Tempe, AZ: Walmyr.

Hurvitz, N. (1975). Interaction hypotheses in marriage counseling. In A. S. Gurman & D. G. Rice (Eds.), *Couples in conflict.* New York: Aronson.

Jacobson, N. S. (1984). The modification of cognitive processes in behavioral marital therapy: Integrating cognitive and behavioral intervention strategies. In K. Hahlweg & N. S. Jacobson (Eds.), *Marital interaction.* New York: Guilford Press.

Jacobson, N. S., & Dallas, M. (1981). Helping married couples improve their relationships. In W. E. Craighead, A. E. Kazdin, & M. J. Mahoney (Eds.), *Behavior modification.* Boston: Houghton Mifflin.

Jacobson, N. S., Follette, W. C., & McDonald, D. W. (1982). Reactivity to positive and negative behavior in distressed and nondistressed married couples. *Journal of Consulting and Clinical Psychology, 50,* 706–714.

Jacobson, N. S., & Holtzworth-Munroe, A. (1986). Marital therapy: A social learning-cognitive perspective. In N. S. Jacobson & A. S. Gurman (Eds.), *Clinical handbook of marital therapy.* New York: Guilford Press.

Jacobson, N. S., & Margolin, G. (1979). *Marital therapy.* New York: Brunner/Mazel.

Jacobson, N. S., & Moore, D. (1981). Spouses as observers of the events in the relationship. *Journal of Consulting and Clinical Psychology, 49,* 269–277.

Jones, R. G. (1968). *A factored measure of Ellis' irrational belief system, with personality and maladjustment correlates.* Unpublished doctoral dissertation, Texas Technological College, Lubbock.

Jordan, C., & Cobb, N. (1992). Competency-based treatment of marital discord. In K. Corcoran (Ed.), *Structuring change.* Chicago: Lyceum.

Kelley, H. H. (1979). *Personal relationships: Their structures and processes.* Hillsdale, NJ: Erlbaum.

Kelly, G. (1955). *The psychology of personal constructs* (Vols. 1 & 2). New York: Norton.

Kendall, P. C., & Ingram, R. (1987). The future for cognitive assessment of anxiety: Let's get specific. In L. Michelson & L. M. Ascher (Eds.), *Anxiety and stress disorders.* New York: Guilford Press.

Kierkegaard, S. (1959). *Either/Or* (Vol. 1) (D. F. Swenson & L. M. Swenson, Trans.). Princeton, NJ: Princeton University Press.

Lazarus, A. (1980). *Multimodal life history questionnaire.* Champaign, IL: Research Press.

Lazarus, R. S. (1989). Constructs of the mind in mental health and psychotherapy. In A. Freeman, K. M. Simon, L. E. Beutler, & H. Arkowitz (Eds.), *Comprehensive handbook of cognitive therapy.* New York: Plenum.

Mahoney, M. J. (1974). *Cognition and behavior modification.* Cambridge, MA: Ballinger.

Mahoney, M. J. (1985). Psychotherapy and human change processes. In M. J. Mahoney & A. Freeman (Eds.), *Cognition and psychotherapy.* New York: Plenum.

Margolin, G. (1981). Behavioral exchange in happy and unhappy marriages: A family cycle perspective. *Behavior Therapy, 12,* 329–343.

Margolin, G. (1987). Marital therapy: A cognitive-behavioral-affective approach. In N. S. Jacobson (Ed.), *Psychotherapists in clinical practice.* New York: Guilford Press.

Margolin, G., Hatten, D. John, R. S., & Yost, K. (1985). Perceptual agreement between spouses and outside observers when coding themselves and a stranger dyad. *Behavior Assessment, 7,* 235–247.

Margolin, G., & Wampold, B. E. (1981). Sequential analysis of conflict and accord in distressed and nondistressed marital partners. *Journal of Consulting and Clinical Psychology, 49,* 554–567.

Markman, H. J., Floyd, F. J., Stanley, S. M., & Jamieson, K. (1984). A cognitive-behavioral program for the prevention of marital and family distress: Issues in program development and delivery. In K. Hahlweg & N. S. Jacobson (Eds.), *Marital interaction.* New York: Guilford Press.

McClellan, T. A., & Stieper, D. R. (1977). A struc-

tured approach to group marriage counseling. In A. Ellis & R. Grieger, *Handbook of rational-emotive therapy.* New York: Springer.

Meichenbaum, D. (1977). Cognitive-behavior modification. New York: Plenum.

Merluzzi, T. V., Glass, C. R., & Genest, M. (1981). *Cognitive assessment.* New York: Guilford Press.

Notarius, C. I., & Vanzetti, N. A. (1983). The marital agendas protocol. In E. E. Filsinger (Ed.), *Marriage and family assessment: A sourcebook for family therapy.* Beverly Hills, CA: Sage.

Paolino, T. J., & McCrady, B. S. (Eds.). (1978). *Marriage and marital therapy: Psychoanalytic, behavioral and systems theory perspectives.* New York: Brunner/Mazel.

Revenstorf, D. (1984). The role of attribution of marital distress in therapy. In K. Hahlweg & N. S. Jacobson (Eds.), *Marital interaction.* New York: Guilford Press.

Rosenbaum, A., & O'Leary, K. D. (1981). Marital violence: Characteristics of abusive couples. *Journal of Consulting and Clinical Psychology, 49,* 63–71.

Rotter, J. B. (1966). Generalized expectancies for internal versus external control of reinforcement. *Psychological Monographs, 80*(1, whole No. 609).

Rush, A. J., & Beck, A. T. (1978). Adults with affective disorders. In M. Hersen & A. S. Bellack (Eds.), *Behavioral therapy in the psychiatric setting.* Baltimore: Williams & Wilkins.

Schaap, C. (1984). A comparison of the interaction of distressed and nondistressed married couples in a laboratory situation: Literature survey, methodological issues, and an empirical investigation. In K. Hahlweg & N. S. Jacobson (Eds.), *Marital interaction: Analysis and modification.* New York: Guilford Press.

Schindler, L., & Vollmer, M. (1984). Cognitive perspectives in behavioral marital therapy: Some proposals for bridging theory, research, and practice. In K. Hahlweg & N. S. Jacobson (Eds.), *Marital interaction: Analysis and modification.* New York: Guilford Press.

Sheafor, B., Horejsi, C., & Horejsi, G. (1988). *Techniques and guidelines for social work practice.* Boston: Allyn & Bacon.

Snyder, D. K. (1979). Multidimensional assessment of marital satisfaction. *Journal of Marriage and the Family, 41,* 813–823.

Spanier, B. G. (1976). Measuring dyadic adjustment: New scales for assessing the quality of marriage and similar dyads. *Journal of Marriage and the Family, 38,* 15–28.

Straus, M. A., Gelles, R., & Steinmetz, S. (1980). *Behind closed doors: Violence in the American family.* New York: Doubleday.

Stuart, R. B. (1974). *Marital pre-counseling inventory: Counselor's guide* (rev. ed.). Champaign, IL: Research Press.

Stuart, R. B. (1975). Behavioral remedies for marital ills: A guide to the use of operant-interpersonal techniques. In A. S. Gurman & D. G. Rice (Eds.), *Couples in conflict.* New York: Aronson.

Stuart, R. B. (1980). *Helping couples change: A social learning approach to marital therapy.* New York: Guilford Press.

Stuart, R. B., & Stuart, F. (1975a). *Counselor's guide: Pre-marital counseling inventory.* Champaign, IL: Research Press.

Stuart, R. B., & Stuart, F. (1975b). *Guide to family pre-counseling inventory program.* Champaign, IL: Research Press.

Stuart, F., Stuart, R. B., Maurice, W., & Szasz, G. (1975). *Counselor's guide: Sexual adjustment inventory.* Champaign, IL: Research Press.

Thibaut, J. W., & Kelley, H. H. (1959). *The social psychology of groups.* New York: Wiley.

Thorpe, G., & Olson, S. (1990). *Behavior therapy: Concepts, procedures, and applications.* Needham Heights, MA: Allyn & Bacon.

Ting-Toomey, S. (1983). An analysis of verbal communication patterns in high and low marital adjustment groups. *Human Communication Research, 9,* 306–319.

Vincent, J. P., Friedman, L. C., Nugent, J., & Messerly, L. (1979). Demand characteristics in observations of marital interaction. *Journal of Consulting and Clinical Psychology, 47,* 557–566.

Weiss, R. L. (1978). The conceptualization of marriage from a behavioral perspective. In T. J. Paolino & B. S. McCrady (Eds.), *Marriage and marital therapy.* New York: Brunner/Mazel.

Weiss, R. L. (1980). Strategic behavioral marital therapy: Toward a model for assessment and intervention. In J. P. Vincent (Ed.), *Advances in family intervention* (Vol. 1). Greenwich, CT: JAI Press.

Weiss, R. L. (1984a). Cognitive and behavioral measures of marital interaction. In K. Hahlweg & N. S. Jacobson (Eds.), *Marital interaction: Analysis and modification.* New York: Guilford Press.

Weiss, R. L. (1984b). Cognitive and strategic interventions in behavioral marital therapy. In K. Hahlweg & N. S. Jacobson (Eds.), *Marital interaction: Analysis and modification.* New York: Guilford Press.

Weiss, R. L., & Heyman, R. E. (1990). Observation of marital interaction. In F. D. Fincham & T. N. Bradbury (Eds.), *The psychology of marriage.* New York: Guilford Press.

Weiss, R. L., Hops, H., & Patterson, G. R. (1973). A framework for conceptualizing marital conflict, a technology for altering it, some data for evaluating it. In L. A. Hamerlynck, L. C. Handy, & E. J. Mash (Eds.), *Behavior change: Methodology, concepts and practice.* Champaign, IL: Research Press.

Weiss, R. L., & Margolin, G. (1977). Assessment of marital conflict and accord. In A. R. Ciminero, K. S. Calhoun, & H. E. Adams (Eds.), *Handbook of behavioral assessment.* New York: Wiley.

Weiss, R. L., & Wieder, G. B. (1982). Marital distress. In A. S. Bellack, M. Hersen, & A. E. Kazdin (Eds.), *International handbook of behavior modification and therapy.* New York: Plenum.

10

C H A P T E R

Cognitive Family Therapy

Carlton E. Munson

There are at least 18 subtypes of cognitive therapy practiced by various disciplines using numerous modalities in a wide range of practice settings with diverse populations (Vallis, 1991). It would be impossible to discuss cognitive family therapy in a comprehensive manner in a single chapter. I will focus on an overview of cognitive therapy that includes diverse schools of cognitive thought but will emphasize concepts that are fairly common to all the schools.

The material is organized around the idea that the process of intervention is as important as the techniques of intervention, and the primary orientation is to integrate cognitive concepts with a process model I have developed. A core of concepts transcends the different theories of family therapy, and these ideas have been used to ground the discussion of family therapy from the cognitive perspective.

THE FAMILY IN TRANSITION

The family as a societal institution is constantly discarding and taking on functions to satisfy cultural needs and expectations. In this process there is always a lag between family functioning and these needs and expectations, causing the family to constantly play a game of catch-up as culture evolves (Munson, 1980a). From a cognitive perspective this can lead to confusion and distortion for individual families, as vague and conflicting expectations become part of cognitive development. The family has undergone significant change in the last three decades that rivals the massive changes that accompanied the industrial revolution. The events of the last 30 years parallel the industrial revolution in what has been labeled the "technological revolution." An individual's response to society and a therapist's interventions are shaped by the times (Wachtel & Wachtel, 1986). A paradox of our age shapes the beliefs, assumptions, expectations, and distortions that people bring to therapy. There is a social and political emphasis on expanding individual freedom and choice, but economic and political institutions have produced a system requiring intense interdependence that has led to a great sense of individual economic slavery. This clashing paradox gives rise to complex cognitive dilemmas that people bring to treatment.

Most of the family changes have been induced by economic changes. In 1960 the traditional nuclear, male-headed family accounted for 61% of households. In 1990 this form of the family represented only 22% of the total households. Female members of married households participating in the work force grew from 34% in the 1960s to 68% in 1989. Males have been gradually unable to solely support families. This trend has led to more divorce and more single-parent households (Riche, 1991). Households headed by women increased from 11% in 1970 to 17% in

1990. For black families the rates were 28% in 1970 and 44% in 1990. Single-parent households have grown more dramatically. In 1970, single-parent families made up 28% of the total families, and in 1990 the figure had reached 43% (U.S. Department of Commerce, 1990). While single-parent and female-headed households have been increasing, the size of households has begun to rise (Exter, 1991). Fathers' departure from the household is counteracted by adult children returning home because of economic hardship, newly married couples residing in the parental home, single teenagers delaying leaving home, and a rising birthrate. The birthrate is highest among minority families, and projections are that in the year 2001 33% of children will be minorities (Waldrop & Exter, 1991).

These changes are occurring in the context of dramatic increases in work-force participation by females, albeit at average wages lower than those of males. Increased economic independence for women has led to increased marital dissatisfaction and higher divorce rates (Riche, 1991). There have been significant increases in the number of "latchkey" children, with estimates that four times as many children were home alone in the 1980s than in the 1970s (Robinson, Rowland, & Coleman, 1986). Although the research is limited, there are indications that larger numbers of these children undergo changes in perceptual and cognitive processes that cause disturbance in the form of increased management problems and high levels of fear while home alone. Use of day care has increased significantly at a time when estimates are that 40% of these programs do not meet federal standards of operation. Dramatic increases in alcohol and other drug abuse in all age groups, dramatic increases in teenage pregnancy, and increased violence committed by adults and children in households have all combined to place tremendous stresses on the family, and these are the people who present themselves for treatment.

HISTORICAL OVERVIEW

To understand the issues in the development of a cognitive approach to family therapy, it is necessary to understand the history of the family-therapy movement as well as its standing in the professional community. In this section I will also discuss the history of cognitive theory and take a look into the future.

History of Family Therapy

Family therapy is one of the youngest of the treatment modalities in use. Its evolution has been rather haphazard when compared with that of other modalities. The diverse nature of family therapy theory evolved during the information explosion of the 1960s. Before a solid base of concepts and schools of thought could be developed, this explosion had produced a vast amount of speculative family theory and research.

The evolution of the theory can be described and ordered historically (see Figure 10.1). What is essential to understand from the figure is that all family therapy theory evolved from three primary sources: (1) schizophrenia research, (2) the child-guidance movement, and (3) marriage counseling practice. Also, from an evolutionary perspective, family therapy originated from psychoanalytic theory (Guerin, 1976). This has presented some problems for more recent theorists, such as feminist theorists and cognitive theorists, as they have tried to build on the traditions of the field but at the same time pioneer new methods and techniques. The difficulties in this struggle are highlighted throughout this chapter.

The evolution of theory has been hampered because family therapy has been and continues to be viewed with skepticism by the traditional mental health community. Psychiatry has been slow to embrace family therapy, and the major diagnostic system, *Diagnostic*

FIGURE 10.1   Brief History of Family Therapy

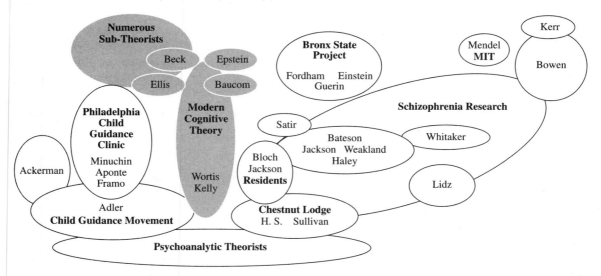

Indicates cognitive theory association

and Statistical Manual of Mental Disorders (DSM-III-R) (American Psychiatric Association, 1987), does not contain a family-classification system. This has resulted in more diffuse and uncoordinated development of theory and research. It is from this vague and multifaceted content that cognitive theorists must attempt to develop a coherent set of practice concepts and techniques appropriate to family therapy.

History of Cognitive Theory

The roots of cognitive therapy can be traced to the Freudians. Some have argued that cognitive ideas predated Freudian conceptions (Ellis, 1989). For the brief review necessary in this chapter, the modern origins are traced to the Freudian era. Alfred Adler has been described as the first to articulate the basic tenets of cognitive therapy when he split with Freud and developed "individual psychology." Harry Stack Sullivan's interpersonal psychotherapy became the route for the introduction of cognitive concepts in the United States (Safran, 1984). In the 1950s a group of psychoanalytically trained therapists moved away from Freudian thought and began modern formulations of cognitive therapy. Joseph Wortis introduced the term *rational psychotherapy,* Albert Ellis further expanded this orientation with the development of rational-emotive therapy (RET), and William Glasser formulated reality therapy. Kelly (1955) developed the notion of psychological constructs (discussed later in this chapter), which became the classic organizing principles for modern cognitive theory.

Aaron Beck (1976), trained initially as a psychoanalyst, integrated the work of many others to develop the first unified conceptualization of cognitive therapy (Werner, 1982). Lazarus (1976, 1985), during the same period, developed multimodal therapy. He has indicated that his approach is not associated with a theoretical school, but many cognitively oriented theorists draw heavily on his work. The writings of Ellis, Beck, and Lazarus have spawned much research and writing on the cognitive approach, leading to expansion, refinement, and depth.

It was not until the 1980s that literature regarding the cognitive treatment of couples and families began to appear. This delay was probably due to cognitive therapy having been developed from approaches focused on treating individuals. As mental health research evolved and as the nature of relationships in societal institutions changed, it became apparent that many of the problems of the individual were rooted in and connected to relationships (Epstein & Baucom, 1989).

Two historically important cognitive concepts are core constructs and peripheral constructs. *Core constructs* are cognitive patterns based in the self and developmental history, and *peripheral constructs* are cognitive responses emerging from interaction (Kelly, 1955). Others have developed various terms for these two concepts, but the basic ideas remain intact and can serve the clinician today. For example, Persons (1989) has labeled these two concepts "underlying psychological mechanisms" and "overt difficulties."

Core and peripheral constructs require different intervention strategies, and some theorists question whether core constructs can be reached by therapy. The nature of family therapy necessitates that therapists work primarily in the realm of peripheral constructs, but there is a trend to integrate work on peripheral and core concepts. Language and behavior are the processes that reflect these concepts, and the therapist can observe and confront them. At the same time, the therapist's core and peripheral constructs are subject to the same forces and influences as the client's constructs. Literature regarding the functioning of the therapist's cognitive construct system is emerging (Childress & Burns, 1983; Persons, 1989; Ryle, 1990).

The Future

In the last two decades cognitive theory has undergone a dramatic expansion in the advancement of theory, in research into practice, and in use by practitioners. The theory has a bright future, but additional progress is necessary for it to enjoy much broader acceptance and utilization. Theorists will have to develop a set of concepts with standardized meaning and application. There are few universal concepts that cognitive theorists and therapists use as standard reference points. Research will have to clarify differential use of cognitive therapy. With which client groups it works efficaciously is a key question, but more significant is the question of which client groups it does not work with. For example, there is limited research on the use of cognitive therapy with children, adolescents, alcoholics, and other substance abusers. There is debate about the use of cognitive therapy with schizophrenics and borderline patients (Schuyler, 1991). Regarding family therapy, the majority of cognitive theory and research has evolved in the area of marital therapy. There is very limited application of cognitive theory to family therapy. Some hold that the future of cognitive theory hinges on the development of a theory of family therapy (Efran, Lukens, & Lukens, 1990). The definitive work on both family therapy and cognitive therapy lies ahead of us. Cognitive therapy will continue to evolve, but the major challenge is developing integrated models that take into account the individual while at the same time defining concepts that allow multiple individuals to be helped in single treatment processes.

Historically, theories of behavior or intervention have emerged as models of individual therapy and have then evolved group models and, much later, family therapy models. This is true of cognitive therapy, which has not yet evolved a substantial base of family-therapy theory. In part, cognitive theory has the same difficulty as psychoanalytic theory in that theorists cannot directly observe the cognitive processes that are the focus of their research. This has led cognitive theorists and researchers to recognize the relatedness of cognition, affect, behavior, and environment (Merluzzi, Glass, & Myles, 1981).

This chapter is written primarily from the perspective of the therapist operating from a cognitive model. The emphasis is on the cognitive shifts and approaches that promote and facilitate change in family functioning. Specific cognitive guidelines are provided within the context of traditional and accepted generic aspects of family intervention.

THEORY AND TECHNIQUE

Pine (1990) has observed that "clinical work is often more widely varying than our theories reflect" (p. 7). This is the problem we face when attempting to describe how we use theory to guide intervention techniques and strategies. There is much disagreement among family therapists regarding the use of theory versus technique in family treatment. This debate is not confined to family therapists and has been a factor in the evolution of other forms of therapy. Bowen believed that theory is important to family intervention (Haley, 1971). Whitaker believes that the use of theory isolates the therapist, dichotomizes the treatment, makes the therapist an observer, and stifles practitioner creativity (Guerin, 1976). There has been little systematic study of how theory is actually used in family intervention and how it affects what is said and what gets done.

There appears to be little conscious use of theory in the actual practice of family therapy. Beginning practitioners struggle with the intensity of the family situation and may have little energy to invest in the skilled use of theory. The experienced practitioner may focus on the interaction and issues to be explored without conscious consideration of the theoretical implications of his or her own activity. This does not mean that theory is not important in family intervention. What practitioners have been taught about family therapy does show up in their work, but it is seldom consciously recognized. For the pur-

poses of developing a cognitive style of intervention, this becomes an important point. A cognitive approach to family therapy requires that the therapist consciously choose appropriate intervention techniques and strategies at any given point in the treatment process.

In order for practitioners to develop the technical skill to know how to deal with therapy content, they must have some cognitive way to organize and analyze content during sessions, as well as in postsession review. Even though the practitioner may not always be aware of the use of theory in the practice situation, effective evaluation of practice must be theoretically based.

Therapist Cognitive Style and Process

Many practitioners assume that family therapy is not significantly different from individual therapy. This belief usually grows out of a lack of experience in the conduct of family therapy and a tendency to rely on generic skills. This is especially problematic in cognitive therapy because individual therapy allows the therapist to orchestrate the cognitive restructuring. The family therapist must rely on the family members to do a significant amount of restructuring, and they will have a variety and range of cognitive orientations and styles that may not be consistent with the therapist's perspective. There is a tendency to rely heavily on the family member who is the most like the therapist in style and orientation, which can create problems for the therapist and the chosen person. In settings where family intervention is utilized, it is important to guard against using staff members to do family therapy without training, supervision, and consultation. This is essential in settings where practitioners have the responsibility of doing individual, group, and family therapy.

Theoretical grounding alone is not sufficient to guarantee effective family therapy. Although generic skills are necessary to any practice situation, they are not sufficient. For example, because more people are involved, family therapy automatically decreases the practitioner's control as compared with individual treatment. The interactional combinations that can occur increase exponentially as the number of participants in the treatment group is increased (Munson, 1980b). In order to make the treatment manageable, the practitioner must make important decisions about how many family members and how many therapists to involve in the treatment. No amount of generic skills will help the therapist cope with a treatment group of unmanageable size. Bowen theoretically conceptualized the complexity of adding participants to the treatment situation (Haley, 1971). It was his view that when therapists who think in terms of individual therapy are presented clinically with families, they cannot "hear family concepts." The cognitive therapist should heed his observation, because the majority of current cognitive diagnostic and treatment concepts are based on an individual model, and much of the work of adapting these concepts must be integrated and applied to family therapy by the individual family therapist.

To do family therapy effectively, the practitioner has to develop the ability to integrate multiple, complex interactions involving clients with diverse cognitive styles. Individual treatment from a cognitive perspective confronts the therapist with a single deficit and distortion structure in client cognition. In cognitive family therapy the therapist is faced with multiple cognitive structures that compete, conflict, distort, and reinforce.

Within the context of family therapy, each individual in treatment gives rise to expanded interactional and cognitive systems that are incompatible with individual treatment models. Bowen (1978) identifies one difference for the practitioner as that of identifying family patterns that do not emerge in individual treatment. For example, a common pattern is for the family to put one member in the "sick" role, or the "patient" role.

The SEES Model

Discovering the process of treatment and its relationship to technique is as important as diagnosis and theory in learning family therapy. The effective practitioner develops a style that integrates process and technique. During the last ten years, I have devised a conceptual scheme that is fairly simple to master and at the same time conveys how successful family therapists integrate theory and practice. Content analysis was applied to master family therapists' videotaped sessions with a focus on identifying the purpose and function of intervention strategies. This analysis yielded four activities that are core cognitive techniques of interaction. The therapist generally uses these activities in a flexible sequence that constitutes a repeated process of intervention.

In the first part of the session, the practitioner analyzes the family's *style* of relating. The therapist then moves to adjusting or adapting his or her own natural style of intervention to the family's style, which allows the practitioner to enter the family, join the family, or form an alliance with the family. This sets the stage for the therapist to *enable* individual family members to express themselves and be protected from other family members or to help the entire family mobilize its resources to accomplish a task. Once this is done, the therapist then *encounters* the family by clarifying family patterns of relating and behaving. This is a form of confrontation without anger and is done in a caring way. Once the encounter has occurred, the practitioner then guides the family in the development of more effective ways of relating. This procedure is referred to as *shifting the dysfunction*. In shifting the dysfunction, the therapist goes through the steps of initiating the shift, implementing the shift, and implanting the shift. This involves setting up the situation as it would normally occur and then altering the pattern of interacting and working to have the alterations so powerful that family

FIGURE 10.2   SEES Model for Analyzing Interactional Sequences in Family Therapy

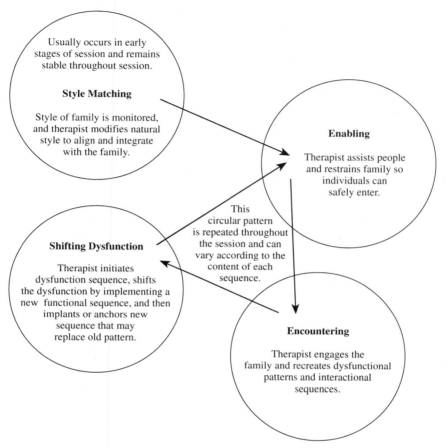

members are disinclined to return to the old pattern of thinking and relating. There are numerous ways of achieving a shift. It can be through the whole family participating or through one family member being encouraged to alter his or her usual response.

This process of style matching, enabling, encountering, and shifting dysfunction occurs repeatedly in master therapists' work (see Figure 10.2). The effective therapist uses these four techniques in a sequence that identifies problems, promotes change, and supports family members. The SEES techniques are evident in some of the earliest tapes of sessions done by pioneering family therapists in the 1960s, as well as in the latest models of

family therapy (see, for example, Brendler, Silver, Haber, & Sargent, 1991).

CONCEPTS AND TECHNIQUES OF COGNITIVE FAMILY THERAPY

Table 10.1 lists the major general techniques that have been developed in association with cognitive therapy. The techniques have been grouped according to the SEES model discussed above. This table can aid in orienting therapists to the major techniques, as well as assisting in the development of an understanding of treatment techniques in the context of

TABLE 10.1   The SEES Model and Cognitive Therapy Techniques

Style Matching	Collaborative empiricism (Beck & Weishaar, 1989)
	Briar patch syndrome analysis (Freeman, 1987)
	Cognitive assessment
	In vivo interviewing (Freeman, 1990)
	Thought record (Persons, 1989)
	Reciprocal-interaction model (Beck, 1987)
Enabling	Decatastrophizing (Beck & Weishaar, 1989)
	Role playing (Beck & Weishaar, 1989)
	Redefining (Beck & Weishaar, 1989)
	Behavior contracting (Baucom & Epstein, 1990)
	Problem list (Persons, 1989)
	Partner reports (Baucom & Epstein, 1990)
	Rewards (Persons, 1989)
	Reinforcement (Persons, 1989)
	Relaxation exercises
Encountering	Socratic dialogue (Beck & Weishaar, 1989)
	Hypothesis testing (Beck & Weishaar, 1989)
	Decentering (Beck & Weishaar, 1989)
	Reattribution (Beck & Weishaar, 1989)
	Balancing (Abrahms, 1983)
	Behavior exploration (Munson, 1992)
	Flooding
	Interaction analysis (Munson, 1992)
	Scheduling
Shifting Dysfunction	Guided discovery (Beck & Weishaar, 1989)
	Guided imagery
	Connecting beliefs and behaviors (Persons, 1989)
	Cognitive restructuring (Baucom & Epstein, 1990)
	Homework
	Punishments (Persons, 1989)
	Reframing
	Shaping (Persons, 1989)

NOTE: Techniques that have a known source are indicated with a citation. General techniques in common use have no source cited.

the SEES model. These are not all the cognitive techniques, but they represent the more common ones that have emerged in the literature.

Although the SEES model can be used to create an organizing framework for understanding intervention, there are conceptual aspects of cognitive theory that should be kept in mind when approaching family therapy. The concepts are classified below in three areas: basic concepts, therapy concepts, and techniques. Most of these concepts were developed in work with individuals but have relevance to family treatment. Each concept is discussed in relation to family treatment, and in some cases, application of the concepts in individual treatment has been modified for use with families.

Basic Concepts

Perception.   Perception is the gateway to cognition. It is the way in which visual and other stimuli are processed (Bruce, 1988). There are basic spatial components and boundaries in pattern recognition that allow for object recognition. When energy is received by the eye, sensations occur that are transmitted to the brain as nerve impulses. In the brain the nerve impulses from the sensation are integrated with other brain processes that make the sensation meaningful. This is the process of perception (Block & Yuker, 1989). The thoughts we have about these meanings constitute the process of cognition, and language is the representation, or symbol, we assign to these cognitions. In addition, there are many nuances of perception that permit diversity in objects and relationships but also produce much disagreement, confusion, and faulty communication. Cognition is more than a process that takes place in our minds. It has been observed that "rather than just examining the cortex of individuals in our attempts to understand human cognition, we must look elsewhere—on the battlefield and the playing field, in the boardroom and the classroom, at the dinner table and the TV nook—the arenas in which life's games are pursued" (Efran et al., 1990, p. 30). This is a compelling statement supporting the logic and need for a cognitive theory of family therapy.

The relationship of perception, cognition, and environmental forces (in our case, the family) has not been extensively researched by cognitive theorists or therapists. Much more work is needed in this area. The role of perception is important to cognitive therapy. The therapist, as part of any family-evaluation process, should evaluate each person's perceptual skills. Gross distortions in perception may require more intense treatment. In children and adolescents and in alcohol-related disorders, other substance abuse, and certain mental disorders, perception is often temporarily or permanently distorted to the point that cognitive family therapy is not efficacious. Individual treatment, drug therapy, or hospitalization may be required before cognitive family therapy can be initiated.

Language.   Language is the primary vehicle of intervention. It is a complex vehicle of communication that is constantly evolving in individual, family, and cultural contexts. Each culture has a language system with nuances of usage and meaning, and each family, within the cultural context, has its own unique language system that gives rise to the individual's unique language system. This complex of language systems is the reason that style is given much importance in the SEES model of family therapy. Until the therapist calibrates his or her unique language system to that of the family, much miscommunication can occur. Cognitive interventions must be placed in the context of family language if the therapist is to be successful.

Behavior and Emotions.   Dysfunctional families experience confusion, chaos, and diminished capacity for understanding, memory, and recall. This requires the therapist to progress deliberately and repetitively and to be cognitively specific. A primary aspect of this process is to help the family differentiate emotions and behavior and rebuild an understanding of how to separate emotions from the behaviors that grow out of them. In some families, people need to learn how to separate emotions and behavior, and in others the need is to learn to connect emotions and behavior.

Anxiety.   Anxiety may be a part of one or more family members' functioning, and the therapist can address the anxiety early in the treatment using the SEES model. Anxiety is not caused by the cognitive processes alone (Beck & Emery, 1985) but is generated in the context of the family situation. New anxiety will be generated as a result of the application of the therapy process, and this should be related to the ongoing family anxiety in order to be used as a catalyst for intervention-induced change. The basis of anxiety is a sense of vulnerability (Beck & Emery, 1985), and the strategy to shift dysfunction is for family members to promote and support anxiety reduction. If the anxiety is life threatening, the more secure family members should be encouraged to exercise greater responsibility for the vulnerable member (see Brendler et al., 1991).

Conflict. Conflict develops from differing and competing assumptions, standards, and expectancies. Interactional conflict in family therapy is similar to internal conflicts in individual therapy. The major difference is that in individual therapy the therapist needs to focus on only a single conflict situation ("I'm not sure I'll be any happier if I get a divorce"). In family therapy, the therapist must make choices regarding multiple views that contribute to the conflict (Husband: "I'm not sure I'll be happier if I get a divorce." Wife: "I can't stand to go on living if he divorces me. He's only thinking of himself." Children: "Why do adults have to fight all the time and blame everything on us?"). The family therapist must reconcile and shift competing distortions and reinforce realistic perceptions at the same time.

Conflict will be replicated in the treatment and often erupts in the treatment. The therapist will need an individually developed cognitive model for dealing with conflict to promote change. The SEES concept of style becomes important in relation to family conflict. The therapist must determine the style and pattern of the conflict to make effective interventions. Beck (1987) has identified a "reciprocal-interactional model" (p. 25) that incorporates the cognitive theoretical formulations of intrapsychic factors and social forces. In this model the emphasis is not on who or what started the depressive behavior that produces the conflict but on the mutually reinforcing behavior that promotes conflict and fuels the depression.

Therapists can become anxious in dealing with conflict, especially when several competing distortions and realities are articulated. It takes time and experience to become comfortable with conflict and to be able to manage it for therapeutic gain. The most anxious

family member usually becomes more anxious and more dysfunctional as the conflict increases during therapy. The therapist needs to be aware of this when inducing encounters with the family. Any increase in anxiety should be considered in relation to long-term therapeutic aims. Expressions of pain by one family member associated with conflict can be a key signal for initiating a specific intervention that focuses on a given reality that is problematic for all family members. In the example given above, the mother has expressed pain associated with the idea of divorce. The therapist could focus on this potential event by having all family members express what divorce would mean for them.

Assumptions. Assumptions are a part of the cognitive structure that determine an individual's present view of a situation based on past experience. People come to believe that certain objects and events have particular qualities and are associated in certain ways (Baucom & Epstein, 1990). They make assumptions about the roles of husbands, wives, and children. For example, a mother might make the assumption that "I could manage the children better if he stayed at home at night and laid down the law to the kids rather than going out to some bar." Assumptions are made by each family member regarding other family members, almost all events that confront the family, and the family therapist. To make effective interventions, the therapist should learn the general and specific assumptions held by each member and identify the discrepancies that clash and block logical and reasonable functioning. Assumptions are in contrast to standards, which are discussed below.

Standards. Assumptions deal with how relationships are, whereas standards deal with perceptions of how relationships should be (Baucom & Epstein, 1990). There are numerous past role models for present standards. A wife may base standards for how her husband should be on the way her father or grandfather acted in her family, how an ideal husband was portrayed in a movie or novel, how an older sister's husband acted, or a combination of all these models. Standards are usually stated as generalizations. For example, the woman above whose husband went out to drink instead of helping her with the disciplining of the children says: "That's what a marriage is all about, working together and helping each other out. It's important to present a united front to the kids, or else they'll run all over you." The degree of internal inconsistency of the assumptions and standards held by an individual family member can be as problematic as competing and conflicting assumptions and standards among a set of members. A crucial task for the family therapist is to clarify what type and combination of incongruity between assumptions and standards exists before making interventions. To fail to do this can lead to confusion and lack of focus in the treatment.

Attributions.   Attributions are the explanations that people develop for the causative factors leading to certain events (Baucom & Epstein, 1990). For example, a husband makes the following comment about his chaotic marriage: "I did a lot of terrible things in the past, and I guess God is punishing me. He sure is doing a good job of getting even." Attributions can be historical, preconceived, or spontaneous. Negative attributions held by family members toward others in the family may result in distorted meanings of behavior and events, promote negative attitudes between family members, and lead to such interactional problems as conflict, lack of cooperation, and withdrawal.

Cognitive Distortion.   People distort events, relationships, and time sequences for various deliberate and unrealized reasons. The family therapist is concerned with distinguishing distortions and accuracies in events

and relations. There is not space to cover all the types of distortions, but the primary distortions are identified below (see Baucom and Epstein, 1990, for more detailed explanations):

An *arbitrary inference* is an inference regarding unobserved behavior that is based on observed behavior without evidence of a connection between the two behaviors. A daughter discussing her parents' relationship comments: "See how he's talking to her now; well, wait until we leave here. As soon as she asks him to do something, he'll blow up." This is not the case, but it is the typical response of the daughter to draw negative conclusions that she expects to occur.

Emotional reasoning is an inferential error in which subjective experiences, such as emotions and facts, are equated. A husband makes the following statement about his relationship with his wife: "I guess it's over. I don't feel the same anymore. The old spark just isn't there."

Dichotomous thinking is a view of the world in which events are an all-or-nothing proposition. This concept is illustrated by a teenage son's statement about his parents: "If they can't accept all the things I do and believe, there's no use trying to deal with them. I'll just have to move out."

Illusory correlation is drawing the conclusion that two events are causally linked when they are not related. A stepfather's comment about the disciplining of his wife's daughter illustrates this concept: "I never get involved in disciplining Mary, because I think my wife will think I'm sticking up for Mary or siding with her."

Magnification is overestimation of the significance of an event or behavior. A wife accurately describes her husband's magnification: "He worries about every little thing—his health, his job, his bank account. He doesn't think about anything else. He's driving himself crazy."

Minimization is underestimation of the significance of an event or behavior. A husband says to his wife: "I don't know what the big deal is. You think I'm spoiling Karen [his daughter], but there's nothing wrong with doing things for *your* daughter." In fact, the husband is spending an inordinate amount of money on his daughter to the detriment of the family financially.

Overgeneralization is reaching a broad conclusion based on a limited number of incidents. A wife says: "Men, you can't depend on them for anything. I've given up on all men."

Personalization is an overestimation of the degree to which events or behaviors are related to oneself. This distortion is illustrated by a mother observing about the relationship between her daughter and her husband: "I get sick of the way he treats her. He knows it makes me mad, and he does it just to make me jealous."

Selective abstraction is giving attention only to part of the available information and drawing conclusions based on that limited information. A husband says about his wife: "I saw how she was looking at this guy I work with. Next she'll be trying to make out with him. That's why I don't trust her."

Expectancies: People have expectations of what would be the likely outcome of potential situations and interactions were they actually to occur. Rotter distinguished between "specific" and "generalized expectancies" (Baucom & Epstein, 1990). For example, a specific expectancy is illustrated by a wife who says in a family therapy session: "He thinks it's OK for him to go out every night and not tell me where he is or when he'll come home, but if I went out one night by myself, he would go into a rage when I came in and want to know where I had been and who I had been with, and he wouldn't believe me but accuse me of seeing another man." A generalized expectancy is illustrated by a quiet adolescent in response to a therapist's question about his silence: "It's useless for me to say anything, because no one around here believes what I say anyway."

Therapy Concepts

Collaborative Empiricism. The therapist and family form an alliance in which they agree to explore individual cognitions, family patterns, and dysfunctional behavior that results in creative change strategies. The therapist "joins" the family and engages with the members in a mutual process of development of understanding, sharing of information, efforts to produce change, and evaluation of behavior and beliefs. This process is documented and articulated in a verbal and written contract (treatment plan) between the therapist and family. In the SEES model, collaborative empiricism closely parallels style and enabling.

Socratic Dialogue. Language is the basic structure of intervention, and questioning is the primary tool the cognitive family therapist uses to assist the family in altering the structure. Questioning has special meaning in cognitive therapy in that the therapist plans sequences of questions that are designed to promote a specific outcome. The purposes of the questions are to (1) identify and clarify problems; (2) identify thoughts, images, and assumptions; (3) explore meanings of events; and (4) examine the consequences of dysfunctional thoughts and behavior (Beck & Weishaar, 1989). In the SEES model, Socratic dialogue is equivalent to encountering.

Interactional Sequences. The therapist must keep in mind the treatment process, but the majority of early-stage treatment based on cognitive intervention should occur in the context of a series of brief, related sequences of interaction. These sequences focus on identifying specific problems and promoting small increments of change. After the family has shifted to new perceptions and has developed new interactional strategies, the newly developed skills can be used in the later stages of treatment to integrate more comprehensive cognitive associations. In cognitive therapy this is referred to as "guided discovery." The therapist uses this process to help the family use information, facts, and probabilities to gain a realistic perspective (Beck & Weishaar, 1989).

Outcomes.   The family members should be asked to specify the outcomes they expect from the interventions. Outcomes can be specified in a contract as well as being specific verbalizations that occur as part of interactional sequences at any given point in the treatment. All family members should participate in the contractual process of specifying outcomes. This will lead to a mutually agreed-on treatment plan that can be put into writing, reviewed, and signed by family members. The development and review of the treatment plan and the signing ceremony can be of therapeutic meaning itself and promote compliance with change strategies.

Contractual and interactional specification of outcomes is illustrated by the Walters family. In the contract phase of the treatment the family identified many conflict issues and complained that Mr. Walters's mother was constantly intruding by trying to manipulate and control family members. Therapist inquiries revealed that each member agreed with this view of her. The children said that their grandmother was mean and controlling even though they benefited from her role in the family through gifts, money, and transportation to and from school and other events. The treatment contract included improving the relationships with Mr. Walters's mother. During a therapy session, Mrs. Walters mentioned that Mr. Walters's mother had disrupted the family by offering to pay for the children to take a summer vacation with another family. This led to a heated exchange between the husband and wife about his mother's general intrusion. The therapist asked the couple to specify the expected outcome by asking, "How would you know when she was no longer interfering in your family?" This led to a series of indicators that were added to the treatment plan.

Power and Control.   In any family therapy, power and control will be key issues in treatment even though they are not stated directly. These issues will emerge from family life as well as from the context of the treatment as the family relates to the therapist. Power and control often lead to distortions that can be the entry point for the family therapist. Common power and control issues center on the disciplining of children, financial matters, and sexual problems.

Reciprocity.   In family and marital therapy, reciprocity is a key concept in evaluation and treatment. Reciprocity refers to the extent to which members feel that they are getting satisfaction out of the family fairly equal to what they are putting into the family (Baucom & Epstein, 1990). It also applies to the therapeutic relationship with the family therapist. The therapist will have to give and take in the sessions just as the family members are expected to do if a genuine alliance is to develop. The therapist will need to become involved in exploring and adjusting family reciprocity issues, as well as monitoring family members' views of the reciprocity balance in the treatment process.

Trust.   The therapist must have a trusting relationship with the majority of the family members to accomplish therapeutic change. Trust occurs in stages in the therapy, and individual family members develop it at different intervals. The more common indicators are openness, absence of deception, expressions of acceptance of the therapist, and positive utilization of therapist directives and interpretations.

Techniques

Decatastrophizing.   The "what-if" technique is used to decrease fear surrounding possible events, real or imagined. Use of decatastrophizing with family members can lead to planning for who will deal with particular problems or tasks as the "dreaded" event approaches. A therapist used this technique with parents who were overwhelmed by the thought of appearing in court to testify along with their 14-year-old retarded daughter, who had been sexually assaulted by a neighbor. The therapist reviewed their fears and explained to them how courts work. The therapist put the family in touch with the state's attorney who was representing the child. The attorney did a pretrial conference with the entire family. As the trial date approached, the therapist used the "what-if" technique to prepare the family for events that were anticipated.

Reattribution. The technique of reattribution allows the therapist to test assumptions and thoughts when the entire family or a family member has reached an inaccurate causal conclusion about an event. The therapist explores alternative explanations with the family. A husband and wife believed that school officials were pushing them to allow their 10-year-old child to be placed on medication for hyperactivity because he had an older brother who had gone through the school several years before and had been a management problem for the teachers. The parents refused medication for the child and disagreed with school officials regarding strategies for managing the boy. The therapist systematically went through the child's behavior record and showed the parents that none of the school officials involved had known the older child. The parents were able to alter their belief that the child was being punished for the actions of the older brother. The family's altered view led to acceptance that the boy had a behavioral disorder independent of his brother's experience. This altered attribution allowed the family to enter a more reasonable negotiation with the school officials regarding management of the child and use of medication.

Redefining. Redefinition is used to help families who believe that problems are beyond the ability of members to control. A mother and her two children were living with a man the mother had recently met. The cou-

ple had many arguments, which usually occurred when the man was drinking and focused on how he treated the children. The man participated in the therapy, and it was the therapist's opinion that he might harm the children. The woman believed that she could not tell the man to leave because she was fearful he would report her to the social services as an unfit mother. The therapist reviewed with her the risk of his possibly harming the children. She was able to develop an understanding that she was not at risk of losing her children because of accusations by this man. The therapist reviewed with her all the people who knew she was a competent mother. She eventually was able to redefine her view of her mothering abilities as evaluated by friends and relatives instead of basing her views on the statements of her dysfunctional companion. This redefinition was a significant factor in her decision to separate from the man.

Decentering. In some cases individual family members inaccurately believe that they are the center of everyone's attention. Decentering is the process of assisting a person in realizing that he or she is not the focus of the actions of others. One 14-year-old boy observed in a family therapy session that "they're always picking on me." The therapist explored with the boy whom precisely he viewed as picking on him, the reasons they would want to do this, and specifically how he knew this was "picking" behavior. With exploration the boy was able to change his view of others' actions toward him as well as to see more accurately how other family members reacted to one another.

Hypothesis Testing. Family members often make statements that need to be tested by getting input from other members or outsiders. Some examples of common statements that need hypothesis testing are "These people don't love me." "If I left, everyone would be happier." "None of the kids at school like me." The client is guided in establishing evidence to support or negate the conclusion reached.

Role Playing.   Family members sometimes cannot articulate what they think or feel. When this is the case, the people often have explosive encounters with others, or they withdraw. The therapist can use role playing to clarify issues and focus problems. In one family the parents were scheduled to meet with school officials about their child's performance. They were anxious about the meeting because, in a previous meeting, they had gotten into a shouting match with the school principal. The therapist role-played the meeting with the family. The parents became better prepared for the second meeting, and the results were more positive than their earlier experience.

Diversion.   When family members become focused on a single issue or event in a distorted or obsessive manner, the therapist can use diversion to get them to focus on other events, other activities, or other people. Diversion was used with a family that had a small child who almost constantly demanded attention from the mother during the family therapy session. The therapist used diversion to get the child to cuddle a large doll. The therapist then encouraged the mother to use diversion in the therapy and at home. Seeing the positive effects of the technique gave the mother confidence in the method. The therapy proceeded more rapidly because there were fewer interruptions from the child.

Homework.   The use of homework is widespread among cognitive therapists. For homework to be effective, it must be thoroughly planned and cautiously implemented. Homework assignments should be relatively simple and within the capabilities of the family. Assignments that are unreasonable and unrealistic cause the family to undergo an increased sense of failure and produce erosion of confidence in the therapy and the thera-

pist. The therapist must give specific instructions for the homework, including when it is to be completed and reported back. If someone is to be in charge of the homework activity, it is best to decide in advance whether the context and nature of the family operations require a powerful or weaker person to be placed in charge. Homework without follow-up by the therapist should be avoided. The therapist should have a plan for what will be done if the family does not complete the assignment. In reviewing failure to complete homework, it is best not to judge the client and to acknowledge human weakness (Dryden & DiGiuseppe, 1990) before moving to what prevented the family from completing the assignment, and to develop a revised homework plan that circumvents identified obstacles. A family member who is not committed to or is hostile to the treatment can sabotage the treatment process by not cooperating with the homework. The behavior of the uncooperative family member should be addressed by the therapist as a means of maintaining therapist control and promoting effective treatment outcomes.

CASE EXAMPLE: THE SLAYTON FAMILY

The Slayton family will be used to illustrate the concepts and techniques presented in the last section. (*Specific concepts and techniques from the discussion above are highlighted in italics.*) This family has been referred to the outpatient division of a private psychiatric hospital by a school counselor. The Slaytons are a middle-class couple with two children. Barbara is 16 years old and a sophomore in high school. Her grades have fallen dramatically during the past year in spite of superior intelligence (IQ 139). The second child, Kenny, is a 12-year-old junior high student. The family was referred because Barbara had started dating an older boy who introduced her to drugs. She began missing school. The parents had just learned that she was pregnant. The treatment began with outpatient family therapy.

The pregnancy precipitated the family entering treatment because it raised *power and control issues* to new heights in the family and increased *anxiety* over a number of issues. The parents want Barbara to have an abortion, but she wants to have the baby and marry the father of the unborn child. She has made certain *assumptions* about her situation based on her own parents' past experience, which they have forgotten. The parents had much upheaval in their adolescent years. Mrs. Slayton's parents prevented her from marrying Mr. Slayton when she was 16 years old. Her father arranged for his employer to transfer him to another city. The family moved, and several years later the Slaytons renewed the relationship and married. This history comes out in the therapy, and the parents are able to connect their past with some of the elements of Barbara's situation.

The daughter has difficulty expressing her *assumptions* and *standards*. She handles her frustration by exploding at the parents. The therapist tries to alter this situation by *shifting the dysfunction* after observing the *family stylistic pattern* and *encountering* the family through confronting the interactional process that has been repeatedly occurring. The therapist begins with issues less volatile than the pregnancy as a way to enable members of this family to develop new patterns of interaction before engaging in decision making regarding the pregnancy.

During the first session, the parents attempt to give social history and family history information, which from Barbara's perspective contains many *attributions* and *cognitive distortions*. Barbara keeps interrupting and telling her parents that they have events, dates, and reflections about events wrong. This leads to intense *conflict* that ends in a shouting match. The therapist *enables* Barbara to tell her story by having her recount her version of the family history. This process includes *interactional sequences, Socratic dialogue, guided discovery,* and *collaborative empiricism.* A segment of the family therapy session that occurred after the therapist stopped the conflict over the family history illustrates this process:

Mother: Barbara will not listen to reason. Nothing like this has ever happened in our family. It would kill her grandmother to find this out.

Barbara [in a loud voice]: That's bullshit. You people don't know what you're talking about. You're blind, and you're stupid. I don't know why I agreed to come here. You don't care about me [*cognitive distortion based on emotional reasoning*].

Therapist: How do you know that, Barbara [*Socratic dialogue*]?

Barbara: Because they're old. They're ancient [*assumption*].

Therapist: Old people can't understand or care for young people?

Barbara: No, because we're a totally different generation. The world has changed completely since they were young. This is the 1990s, not the 1960s. Kids are smarter today. We're a lot smarter than them. That's the whole problem [*overgeneralization based on an attribution*].

Father [pleading]: Honey, we do care, and we're trying to understand, but you won't listen. You have to have an abortion. We know what will happen to your life if you don't stop seeing this boy and stay away from drugs. We're trying to reach you.

Barbara [to therapist]: They're just trying to break me and Tony up. God, I'm not *stupid* [*illusory correlation*].

Therapist: I know you're not stupid. In fact, you're very bright. I've seen your school records. You even got straight A's in history [*enabling*]. Which makes me wonder, some things are very different, but maybe some things are the same. Can you think of any things that are the same today as in the past [*Socratic dialogue* and *decentering*]?

Barbara: Well, I don't know, love and hate, I guess. Some people go on loving, and some go on hating. That never changes.

Therapist: That's true, so some things don't change. How about in your family? Are there some things that haven't changed from your parents' generation to your generation, just like love and hate [*hypothesis testing*]?

Barbara: Sure, that's what I was just trying to tell you about how my parents are trying to stop me just like their parents tried to break them up. Any idiot could see that.

Therapist: I'm a little slow and dumb at times, so help me with this. What is the connection [*enabling through modified partner report, in this case, a child report*]?

Barbara then gives a detailed narrative of the family history. It is a thorough, accurate, chronological account of events, which includes how her mother's parents attempted to keep her from marrying Mr. Slayton. Mrs. Slayton's father arranged for his company to transfer him to another city to break up the relationship. This led to much conflict in the family, and Mrs. Slayton became so depressed that she thought of suicide. In college Mr. and Mrs. Slayton got back together, and there was much conflict with Mrs. Slayton's parents until Barbara was born. The parents are amazed that Barbara knows all these events and ask her how she knew the history. Barbara responds, "Grandma told me."

Therapist: So, you all do have a lot in common, and it sounds as if some things have not changed at all since the 1960s. I want you to do something for me. We will meet again later this week. Would you have a family meeting and come to agreement on all the details of the historical events, since there are some differences here about what happened when. This will help me determine how some of these events are connected to what is going on now. Also, I

would like you to discuss and then to list for me how Barbara's situation is different and how it is like what you two went through [*homework based on guided discovery*].

Mr. Slayton: I can tell you one difference right off. We were not pregnant.

Therapist: OK, perhaps you could start the list with that. I want to make sure everyone agrees to do this and to participate.

All the family members nod agreement. The therapist asks each person to express agreement, and all do.

At the next session the therapist asks the family to report on the homework assignment. The family members have completed the assignment and report a list of significant events that they believe have contributed to the family functioning. While doing the homework, Barbara reminded her parents of an incident when she and Kenny were in child care and he was sexually fondled by one of the child-care workers. This occurred when he was 3. This outcome of the homework assignment adds a new dimension to the treatment (*homework follow-up*). The family members have a positive response to the homework and are elated that they were able to do it without erupting into conflict.

Mother: I know these things are important, but we have an immediate thing we have to deal with, and I think you know what I'm talking about.

Therapist: I'm not sure what you're referring to.

Mother: Barbara's pregnancy.

Therapist: Well, you're getting ahead of me here, and that's good [*reinforcement*]. You did so well with the family meeting assignment [*reinforcement*] that I want you to do another one for me for the next session. I want you to discuss what, as a family, you think should be done about Barbara's pregnancy. I'd like you to arrive at a tentative decision about the pregnancy and bring it here next session. OK [*outcome specification*]?

Mother: What about Kenny. Does he need to be in on this?

Therapist: Kenny has known about this from the beginning, if I remember correctly.

Mother: Yes.

Therapist: He is a member of the family, right?

Mother: Yes.

Therapist: How could you find out if he needs to be there?

Mother: I don't know.

Therapist: Does anyone know?

Father: We could talk to him?

Therapist: Could you do that right now?

Father: Yes.

Therapist: Then do it [*encounter*].

Father: Kenny, do you want to talk with us about this, or would you rather stay out of it?

Kenny: I don't care.

Therapist: I think when you call the family meeting you should discuss this again with Kenny and decide if he should be there. He may have given this some thought by the time of the meeting, and perhaps the rest of you will have more ideas. The first item for the meeting will be a decision about Kenny participating. [*Scheduling an outcome. The therapist deliberately sets the decision about Kenny as the first agenda item so the family can experience success on a relatively simple decision before moving to the momentous decision regarding Barbara's pregnancy.*] Also, Barbara, I would like you to jot down your thoughts as you have them about what you want to bring up in the meeting. This might make it easier for you. I would like you to bring whatever you write down to the next therapy session [*thought record*]. OK? [The family nods approval.]

The family reports at the next session that the meeting went well even though there was some conflict. The initial agenda item regard-ing Kenny's participation resulted in the decision that he would not participate because he preferred to go skateboarding. The decision was for Barbara to have an abortion.

Barbara shares her thoughts that she has written down. Her thoughts focus on having to give up her friends at school; having to give up attending college, which she has been planning for some time; reactions of her boyfriend that surprised and upset her; and even feelings that she might hurt her family (*redefining*). The therapist reviews the meeting, and the family finalizes the decision.

This brief analysis is from a complex and extensive treatment process. Only a limited number of concepts and techniques could be demonstrated. The key features are that the therapist established a *trusting relationship* with the family and engaged in an initial treatment process that required the family to do cognitive tasks that reestablished a more functional family interactional system. The therapist sequenced assignments so that the family could move from simple to more difficult tasks. By doing this, the members could experience success and develop confidence in their ability to interact and make decisions before attempting the more complex decisions that could have enormous effects on the family.

The skills learned early in the treatment became an important foundation for the many problems that came later for this family. Several weeks after her abortion, Barbara refused to stop seeing her boyfriend and attempted to jump out of the family car at 50 miles per hour when the father was returning her from the boy's home. Later in the evening, she went into a rage, threatened her parents, and threw a knife at her mother. The therapist assisted the family in arranging a hospital admission for Barbara. The family was able to use the skills of family interaction learned early in family therapy to make this important decision. Barbara participated in the session and eventually agreed to the hospitalization. After two weeks, she manipulated her father into checking her out of the hospital before treatment was completed (promising to be a model teenager). She began acting out sexually with several boys and had to be treated for a sexually transmitted disease. This event resulted in the family returning to treatment. A series of family sessions and separate individual therapy for Barbara led to a positive outcome in which all the family members made significant changes. The father changed jobs to be home in the evenings to participate in the management of the children (he had worked nights previously). Barbara and her mother began doing more activities together. They developed a close relationship in which they shared many feelings and thoughts in a way they had never done before. Barbara ended the relationship with her older boyfriend and began dating a boy her own age. She and Kenny fought less and became closer, although he continued to be a marginal participant in the family. Follow-up with the family two years after the therapy ended revealed that the family was doing well. Barbara was enrolled in college and doing high-quality work. She was working part time for the same company that employed her mother.

CONCLUSION

Cognitive mediation plays a significant role not only in individual psychological distress but in family dysfunction as well. Knowledge gained from the application of cognitive intervention strategies to treat individual problems can be extended to address cognitive factors considered significant in their contributions to maladaptive interactions within the family. These procedures are suitable for the treatment of individual problems within the context of the family and for family therapy designed to ameliorate dysfunctional interaction patterns. Although cognitive treatment procedures have shown great promise in family treatment, their employment in combination with behavioral methods and other problem-focused strategies is strongly recommended.

REFERENCES

Abrahms, J. L. (1983). Cognitive behavioral strategies to induce and enhance a collaborative set in disturbed couples. In A. M. Freeman (Ed.), *Cognitive therapy with couples and groups.* New York: Plenum.

American Psychiatric Association. (1987). *Diagnostic and statistical manual of mental disorders* (3rd ed. rev.). Washington, DC: Author.

Baucom, D. H., & Epstein, N. (1990). *Cognitive-behavioral marital therapy.* New York: Brunner/Mazel.

Beck, A. T. (1976). *Cognitive therapy and emotional disorders.* New York: International Universities Press.

Beck, A. T. (1987). Cognitive models of depression. *Journal of Cognitive Psychotherapy, 1,* 5–37.

Beck, A. T., & Emery, G. (1985). *Anxiety disorders and phobias: A cognitive perspective.* New York: Basic Books.

Beck, A. T., & Weishaar, M. E. (1989). Cognitive therapy. In R. J. Corsini & D. Wedding (Eds.), *Current psychotherapies.* Itasca, IL: F. E. Peacock.

Block, J. R., & Yuker, H. E. (1989). *Can you believe your eyes?* New York: Gardner Press.

Bowen, M. (1978). *Family therapy in clinical practice.* New York: Aronson.

Brendler, J., Silver, M., Haber, M., & Sargent, J. (1991). *Madness, chaos, and violence: Therapy with families at the brink.* New York: Basic Books.

Bruce, V. (1988). Perceiving. In G. Claxton (Ed.), *Growth points in cognition.* New York: Routledge & Kegan Paul.

Childress, A. R., & Burns, D. D. (1983). The group supervision model in cognitive therapy training. In A. Freeman (Ed.), *Cognitive therapy with couples and groups.* New York: Plenum.

Dryden, W., & DiGiuseppe, R. (1990). *A primer on

rational-emotive therapy. Champaign, IL: Research Press.

Efran, J. S., Lukens, M. D., & Lukens, R. J. (1990). *Language, structure, and change.* New York: Norton.

Ellis, A. (1989). The history of cognition in psychotherapy. In A. Freeman, K. M. Simon, L. E. Beutler, & H. Arkowitz (Eds.), *Comprehensive handbook of cognitive therapy.* New York: Plenum.

Epstein, N., & Baucom, D. H. (1989). Cognitive-behavioral marital therapy. In A. Freeman, K. M. Simon, L. E. Beutler, & H. Arkowitz (Eds.), *Comprehensive handbook of cognitive therapy.* New York: Plenum.

Exter, T. (1991, January). Average household size up for first time in seven years. *American Demographics,* p. 10.

Freeman, A. (1987). Understanding personal, cultural and religious schema in psychotherapy. In A. Freeman, N. Epstein, & K. M. Simon (Eds.), *Depression in the family.* New York: Haworth Press.

Freeman, A. M. (1990). *Clinical applications of cognitive therapy.* New York: Plenum.

Guerin, P. J. (1976). *Family therapy: Theory and practice.* New York: Gardner Press.

Haley, J. (1971). *Changing families: A family therapy reader.* New York: Grune & Stratton.

Kelly, G. A. (1955). *The psychology of personal constructs.* New York: Norton.

Lazarus, A. A. (1976). *Multimodal behavior therapy.* New York: Springer.

Lazarus, A. A. (1985). *Casebook of multimodal therapy.* New York: Springer.

Merluzzi, T. V., Glass, C. R., & Myles, G. (1981). *Cognitive assessment.* New York: New York University Press.

Munson, C. E. (1980a). *Social work with families: Theory and practice.* New York: Free Press.

Munson, C. E. (1980b). Supervising the family therapist. *Social Casework, 61* (March), 131–137.

Munson, C. E. (1992). *Clinical social work supervision.* New York: Haworth Press.

Persons, J. B. (1989). *Cognitive therapy in practice: A case formulation approach.* New York: Norton.

Pine, F. (1990). *Drive, ego, object, and self.* New York: Basic Books.

Riche, M. F. (1991, March). The future of the family. *American Demographics,* pp. 44–47.

Robinson, B. E., Rowland, B. H., & Coleman, M. (1986). *Latchkey kids: Unlocking doors for children and families.* Lexington, MA: Lexington Books.

Ryle, A. (1990). *Cognitive-analytic therapy: Active participation in change.* New York: Wiley.

Safran, J. D. (1984). Some implications of Sullivan's interpersonal theory for cognitive therapy. In M. A. Reda & M. J. Mahoney (Eds.), *Cognitive psychotherapies: Recent developments in theory, research, and practice.* Cambridge, MA: Ballinger.

Schuyler, D. (1991). *A practical guide to cognitive therapy.* New York: Norton.

U.S. Department of Commerce. (1990). *Household and family characteristics: March 1990 and 1989.* Washington, DC: U.S. Bureau of the Census.

Vallis, T. M. (1991). Theoretical and conceptual bases of cognitive therapy. In T. M. Vallis, J. L. Howes, & P. C. Miller (Eds.), *The challenges of cognitive therapy: Applications to nontraditional populations.* New York: Plenum.

Wachtel, E. F., & Wachtel, P. L. (1986). *Family dynamics in individual psychotherapy: A guide to clinical strategies.* New York: Guilford Press.

Waldrop, J., & Exter, T. (1991, March). The legacy of the 1980s. *American Demographics,* pp. 32–38.

Werner, H. D. (1982). *Cognitive therapy: A humanistic approach.* New York: Free Press.

11

C H A P T E R

Cognitive-Behavioral Divorce Therapy*

Donald K. Granvold

The U.S. divorce rate spiraled upward during the 1960s and 1970s, reaching a record high in 1981 when 1.21 million people divorced, affecting some 3 million men, women, and children (National Center for Health Statistics, 1986). (The crude divorce rate rose to 5.3 per 1,000 population.) Although there has been a decline in the divorce rate since 1981, the failure rate of marriage in the United States continues at about 50% (Glick, 1989). And second marriages appear to be more likely to end in divorce than first marriages (Bumpass & Sweet, 1972; Cherlin, 1977; Glick & Norton, 1971, 1977).

A variety of factors has been identified as influential in the burgeoning failure rate of marriage over the past three decades, including the liberalization of divorce laws (no-fault divorce); the desacralization of marriage (Weiss, 1975); the shifting role of women, including their greater economic independence; the greater social acceptance of divorce concomitant with the increasing frequency rate (divorce begets divorce); a shift away from the traditional view of the intrinsic permanence of marriage to a more "pragmatic" view based on internal and external reward/cost factors (Scanzoni, 1972); and, perhaps most important, the trend toward greater satisfaction of personal goals, interests, and desires along with higher expectations for

marital happiness (Weitzman, 1985). From the perspective of social exchange theory, the cost/benefit ratio of divorce has assumed a far more competitive stance in relation to that of long-term marriage. The perceived potential and readily realizable rewards of divorce pose a formidable challenge to marriage. This challenge is so great that "the enduring married couple has been identified as somewhat of an endangered species" (Reissman, 1990, p. 4).

Divorce is a pervasive phenomenon in contemporary society, and it wields extreme consequences for the families who experience it and those around them as well. The consequences extend across categories including psychological, interpersonal, social, economic, legal, and religious. This chapter is focused on the psychological and interpersonal consequences of divorce and on intervention to ameliorate its debilitating cognitive, emotional, and behavioral effects. However, sensitivity to the context of divorce is encouraged, including knowledge and awareness of the various social systems that impinge on the divorced, both during the transition and well after the divorce is a legal and psychological reality (for example, the church, the courts, and the business community).

The prevalence of divorce is so great that practitioners in a broad range of settings are highly likely to be called on to treat those experiencing it and its effects. This population includes children and members of the extended family as well as the former spouse. In the helping professions divorce therapy has

*Part of this material also appears in "Postdivorce Treatment" by D. K. Granvold in *The Divorce and Divorce Therapy Handbook,* edited by M. R. Textor, 1989, Northvale, NJ: Aronson.

emerged as a new subspecialty, with its development spanning more than two decades to date (Olson, Russell, & Sprenkle, 1980). Everett and Volgy (1991) encourage a shift from viewing "divorce therapy" as a discrete or independent clinical discipline (considered to be lacking in a clear body of clinical knowledge or specific techniques) to viewing it as the treatment of the outcomes of the divorce process within the context of systemic family therapy. Although I agree with the treatment of divorce in the context of the multigenerational family, there is tremendous need to develop far greater understanding of the intricacies of the divorce process and to generate, apply, and empirically validate specific interventions to effectively treat people at any point in the process. The treatment format should be matched to client need and may take the form of individual, couple, group, family, or multigenerational-family treatment. It is likely that as clients progress through the divorce process, their therapeutic needs will change, creating a corresponding requirement to alter the treatment format. As an example, Kaslow recommends a post-divorce "therapeutic/healing divorce ceremony" to promote closure on the marriage, to be held at least two years after legal divorce and to involve the divorced couple, their children, and a male and female witness/participant as representatives of their male and female friends (Kaslow, 1991; Kaslow & Schwartz, 1987). Siblings and parents may attend as well, based on the preferences of the ex-mates.

THE DIVORCE PROCESS

Divorce is not an event but is, rather, a process with broad universal characteristics, uniquely experienced by the many who go through it. In recognition of this uniqueness, Baker (1981) notes that it is a myth that "a divorce is a divorce is a divorce." Historical-

ly, divorce was viewed as a negative event and was considered to represent psychological instability. More recently, divorce has come to be considered a viable option for the psychologically healthy, and it has been found to comprise both positive and negative experiences (Buehler & Langenbrunner, 1987; Chiriboga, 1978; Chiriboga & Cutler, 1977; Diedrick, 1991; Spanier & Thompson, 1983, 1984). Divorce can be considered damaging yet growth-producing; fear-provoking yet stimulating self-assurance; dependency-prompting while promoting independence; identity shattering yet inducing ego differentiation and individuation; and relieving yet distressing. Divorce, it appears, is a series of contravening processes involving personal, interpersonal, and environmental conditions producing cognitive, emotive, and behavioral change.

Many authors have described sequential task patterns in an attempt to clarify the process (Bohannon, 1971; Brown, 1976; DeFazio & Klenbort, 1975; Fisher, 1973; Froiland & Hozman, 1977; Kessler, 1975; Kressel, 1980; Storm & Sprenkle, 1982; Weiss, 1975). These "stage theorists" collapse generally common divorce-related experiences into categories. J. K. Rice and D. G. Rice (1986) provide an excellent comparative presentation of an array of stage theorists. Ponzetti and Cate (1988) write that "the postulation of stages of divorce offers a useful conceptualization of the experience of dissolving marital relationships, but these stages fail to highlight the complexity of the processes involved in marital dissolution" (p. 3). Although I agree with this view, there is facility in broadly subdividing the divorce process to specify common objectives and tasks associated with a given period in the process. Kaslow (1984) and Storm and Sprenkle (1982) consider the divorce process as comprising three overlapping stages, *decision making, transition,* and *postdivorce recovery.* Each stage has its unique challenges, demands, discomforts, and opportunities.

Decision Making

Although it takes the mutual consent of two people to marry, the decision to divorce takes only one. Despite there being no requirement for agreement, the decision to divorce is not an easy one. The decision-making phase of the divorce process is an agonizing experience for most, characterized by ambivalence, confusion, extreme frustration, anticipatory fear of the unknown (should divorce be the decision), and protracted uncertainty. The decision-making period, based on lengthy clinical experience and extensive review of the literature, is the most difficult stage in which to intervene, probably due to the fact that the methods for facilitating a decision of this nature and magnitude are significantly less developed than the methods for treatment in subsequent stages of divorce. It is inappropriate to tell the couple what decision to make (despite this being an all-too-frequent request from clients) or to bias the decision making due to a personal preference toward either marriage or divorce or as a result of one's clinical impressions and judgment. To think and subtly communicate that "this couple would be happier apart" is a temptation to be resolutely resisted, as is the view that people "must stay married, for marriage is forever." Sprenkle (1989) cautions that treatment during decision making can be highly frustrating to the practitioner due to the above-mentioned lack of clinical tools and the high potential for spouses to function with differing agendas and preferred procedures.

Turner (1985) has identified the risk that due to the extreme stress associated with marital unhappiness, an individual may make a premature decision to divorce to avoid unpleasant feelings such as anxiety, worry, and anger. Janis (1982) notes that the decision maker under high levels of stress is likely to display *premature closure* on the decisional dilemma, thereby preventing the generation of all the alternatives and an appraisal of their projected outcomes. Janis and Mann (1977,

1982) present a decision-making model that can be applied to divorce in which premature closure is avoided and a more rational, balanced decision is sought.

During the decision-making stage it is desirable to see the couple conjointly in order to treat systemic issues (D. G. Rice, 1989) and to avoid a divorce bias. Whitaker and Miller (1971) note that the exclusion of a mate from treatment may constitute "an intervention in favor of divorce" (p. 254). In working conjointly with the couple, Salts (1985) recommends a "marital evaluation contract" to facilitate the decision-making process, involving seven steps as follows:

1. identification and definition of needs and problems of the individuals and couple
2. development of alternative solutions to meet these needs and to solve the problems
3. consideration of the potential outcome of each alternative solution
4. choice of the best and most fair solutions
5. implementation of the choices
6. evaluation of the outcome
7. further identification of needs and problems if the evaluation is not satisfactory

The result of the implementation of this procedure is the determination of whether to proceed with marital therapy or divorce therapy.

Imber-Black (1988) has suggested a procedure in which clients are encouraged to ritualize the alternatives of either staying married or divorcing. On "odd days" of the week they act as if they have decided to remain married, and on the even days they act as if the decision has been made to divorce. In the clinical implementation of this flip-flop procedure, I have found that clients generally prefer two or more days in any one mode before shifting to live out the alternative stance.

Structured Marital Separation.   During the decision-making stage it may be desirable for the couple to gain distance from each other through physical separation. It is recommended that the couple receive guidance in the implementation of a structured marital separation (SMS) in which ground rules are delineated to avoid misunderstandings and "violations" that may effectively drive them apart (Granvold, 1983; Granvold & Tarrant, 1983; Green, Lee, & Lustig, 1973; Hight, 1977; Phillips, 1979; Toomim, 1975). High levels of conflict (including the threat of physical harm), low commitment to the relationship, and extreme ambivalence regarding the decision to divorce or remain married are common factors prompting distressed couples to exercise the option to separate. Granvold and Tarrant (1983) discuss factors that would support the couple's decision to separate and describe the potential benefits of the procedure:

> The purpose of structured separation is to interrupt dysfunctional marital interaction as a means of facilitating the decision to either divorce or maintain the marriage. It affords the couple respite from the intensity of interaction characteristic of maritally distressed spouses and provides time for careful consideration of the marriage and its alternatives prior to committing to a plan of action [p. 197].

The practitioner's role in facilitating an SMS is to assess the couple to determine the degree to which their needs fit the potential benefits of the procedure; explain the procedure, including a rationale for each aspect of it; delineate the risks and potential benefits; and guide the couple in their deliberation and determination of its suitability for them. SMS should *not* be recommended to the couple as the most appropriate option for them (that is their decision to make), with the exception of those relationships in which physical violence and personal injury are risks.

Several models of marital separation have been suggested. Features common among most approaches are the use of a written contract; the continuation of conjoint, and perhaps concurrent individual, therapy; a mora-torium on the initiation of legal action; a time-limited initial separation period of three months or less; and structured rules for spouse contact and interaction during the separation. (See Granvold, 1983, for a comparative review of several separation models and guidelines for developing a separation contract and its implementation.) Separation provides the couple with an opportunity to approximate life apart before making a firm and final decision to divorce. They may continue to work at improving their relationship while being relieved of daily contact. A primary objective is to strike a balance between "out of sight, out of mind" and "absence makes the heart grow fonder" as a context within which to make their decision (Granvold, 1983, p. 407). It should be noted that the risks of marital separation are rather high (information that should be discussed with the couple as they consider separation). Research findings reveal that approximately one-half to two-thirds of all couples who separate, divorce (Granvold & Tarrant, 1983; Toomim, 1975). D. G. Rice and J. K. Rice (1986) identify other limitations of SMS, including the demand for spouses to continue to cooperate and collaborate at a time of such high vulnerability, psychological upheaval, and stress; the negative effects of reduced time spent together on efforts to change behavior; and the potential for the two mates to be at different stages in their decision making. Risks and limitations notwithstanding, SMS may be useful both in facilitating the decision-making process and in promoting greater amicability in couples who ultimately decide to divorce.

Transition

The decision to divorce, whether bilateral or unilateral, thrusts the spouses into a transition from married to single life involving physical separation (unless they have already separated); redefinition of self and object-loss trauma; role loss, disorientation, and restructuring; and lifestyle adjustment. The crisis of divorce becomes a reality with the decision to terminate the marriage, and the stress associated with this crisis is extreme, the second most severe that one can undergo (Holmes & Rahe, 1967). Conjoint treatment may continue, albeit with a focused change in goals from sustaining and improving the marriage to dissolving the marriage, promoting and effecting as smooth and conflict-free a transition as can be managed, and improving the couple's relationship in the context of the divorce process. Although divorce ends marriage, the relationship of the two individuals may continue, albeit dramatically changed. Intervention during this stage is oriented to the cognitive, emotional, and behavioral responses of the divorcing mates to rejection, the experience of loss (family dissolution), anticipation of the unknown inherent in life apart, the challenges and demands of extensive change, and the like. Hutchinson and Spangler-Hirsch (1989) identify divorce as a major disruptive experience requiring integrative changes within the following categories: "(1) primary psychological or emotional responses with accompanying behavioral manifestations; (2) geographic changes influencing and/or compounding adjustment processes; (3) systemic alterations; and (4) economic issues affecting phenomenological adjustment" (pp. 8–9).

A major objective during this stage of divorce therapy is to avoid the adversarial divorce process by way of promoting more healthy family restructuring. To this end the practitioner may assume a role as mediator at this time, although it has been my experience that the shift from marital therapist to mediator is difficult with some couples and inadvisable with highly conflicted couples. (Highly conflicted couples should be referred for mediation services.) A cornerstone of formal divorce mediation is the empowerment of disputing parties by a *neutral* third party to settle differences in a mutually agreeable fashion (Neville, 1989). Although the established

therapeutic alliance developed during conjoint marital treatment or divorce decision-making intervention is presumably objective and neutral to a degree, the neutrality required during mediation may be confounded by the existing therapeutic relationship. If the practitioner has seen only one mate in treatment, the therapeutic relationship with that partner would contraindicate the assumption of a neutral mediational role with the couple. It may be most appropriate to refer these couples for mediation services through the family court system or private mediators. Mediation is a divorce-intervention method in its own right and involves special skills in managing interpersonal conflict, aiding decision making about marital dissolution, arbitration, contracting, economics, therapy, and law (although a mediator is not to give legal advice). The reader is referred to the following sources for information and guidelines on the process and procedures of divorce mediation: Cohen (1985), Coogler (1978), Haynes (1981), Irving (1981), Milne (1986), Neville (1989), and Ricci (1985).

The psychological and emotional responses of the divorcing couple and their children and the behavioral manifestations of these responses during the transition phase may be extreme. Sprenkle (1989) recommends conjoint therapy with family therapy to treat children's issues during this stage. He notes that "including children at least at some point during this stage is crucial. Often children are neglected emotionally during this period because, as Wallerstein and Kelly (1980) have noted, parents are overwhelmed by their own needs" (p. 184). The emotional adjustment of parents is a significant factor in the adjustment of children to divorce. Children may be enlisted by their parents in a variety of divisive and emotionally damaging activities from this stage forward. Practitioners are cautioned to be highly sensitive to the role children play in the parents' dissolution process and the ways in which the parents can support, nurture, and promote the healthy adjustment of their children to the divorce.

The treatment of the couple during this stage is focused on their immediate reactions to the divorce decision and to the initiation of the dissolution process. The extreme stress of divorce is well documented (Buehler & Langenbrunner, 1987; Chester, 1971; Chiriboga & Cutler, 1977; Chiriboga, Roberts, & Stein, 1978; Ensel, 1986; Holmes & Rahe, 1967; Kaslow & Schwartz, 1987). Extreme depression, excessive drinking and drug use, suicide, and homicide are manifestations of the stress and emotional injury associated with divorce. Wallerstein and Kelly (1980) found significant depression among both men and women, with women reporting greater severity. Hunt (1966) found the suicide rate for divorced women to be three times that of married women and the suicide rate of divorced men to be four times that of married men. Crisis intervention and stress management methods are appropriate considerations for intervention at this time, along with focused treatment of other psychological and emotional responses, including anxiety; fear (particularly of the unknown); hostility and anger; guilt; regret; hurt; grief, sorrow, and love loss; disappointment; self-loathing; insecurity; and the maladaptive behavioral manifestations of these responses, including psychosomatic disorders.

Postdivorce Recovery

A client's postdivorce recovery is subject to influence by many factors, including length of marriage, length of separation before divorce, age of the individual, whether the person initiated the action, level of conflict during decision making and transition, precipitating event(s) leading to divorce, psychosocial adjustment leading up to divorce, level of personal independence, financial preparation for single life, and per-sonality characteristics such as self-efficacy (locus of control), self-assuredness, assertiveness, social-skill level, and the like (J. K. Rice & D. G. Rice, 1986). Although it is difficult to place a time limit on the post-divorce recovery period due to extreme variability among people regarding the nature of the divorce itself and in their coping and adjustment capacities, adjustment can be expected to take from 12 to 24 months—far longer than that for many, shorter for others. Therapeutic efforts during the recovery phase may address issues of object-loss trauma; self-esteem and redefinition of self as a single entity rather than as a part of a dyad; lingering maladaptive emotional responses; ill-founded behavior patterns established within the marriage or in earlier stages of divorce (for example, alcohol abuse, obsessive/compulsive behaviors); performance of social roles as a single person (single parenting); and the establishment of new social relationships. Sutton and Sprenkle (1985) provide a useful delineation of the goals of divorce therapy as guidelines for the practitioner. Most of these caveats relate to the postdivorce recovery phase of intervention:

- acceptance of the end of the marriage
- functional postdivorce relationship with the ex-spouse
- emotional adjustment
- cognitive adjustment (development of realistic understanding)
- social support and adjustment
- parental adjustment
- children's adjustment
- use of opportunities for learning and personal growth
- process and outcome of a legal settlement
- general life adjustment and physical well-being

Sprenkle (1989) notes that this is not a comprehensive or exhaustive list, and it may fail, for example, to cover more complex issues related to second and third divorces.

ASSESSMENT

A primary ingredient in the treatment of postdivorce adjustment problems—or any clinical problem—is effective assessment. Consistent with Jacobson and Margolin's (1979) approach to assessing marital dysfunction, the purpose of assessment in divorce therapy is to (1) identify problems in the individual's adjustment, (2) identify variables that control the problem behaviors, (3) select appropriate therapeutic interventions, and (4) determine when the intervention has been effective. A thorough assessment is comprehensive and specific, historic and contemporary, initial and ongoing, and oriented to the therapeutic process.

Identification of postdivorce adjustment problems requires a functional analysis of the client's target problematic behavior, including antecedents and consequences. Emphasis is placed on the interrelationship of thoughts, actions, and emotions. As the practitioner gains an understanding of overt behavior and emotions in their environmental/situational context, assessment shifts to cognitive processes, including information processing and schemata (beliefs, self-view, and rules).

The multiple aspects of postdivorce adjustment obligate the practitioner to make a comprehensive assessment. Although no consistent agreement exists regarding successful postdivorce adjustment, variables generally include emotional response, self-image, social role and lifestyle changes, modification of interpersonal relationships, and practical changes. Although knowledge of the client's overall adjustment is important, it is only as the practitioner identifies and analyzes specific target problems that intervention can be facilitated.

Although a rationale can be built for making the primary focus of assessment the client's current cognitive functioning and the behavioral excesses and deficits that are contributing to his or her postdivorce maladjust-

ment, gathering information on past history is also advisable. Gaining an understanding and appraisal of the developmental bases of such phenomena as self-view, coping skills, chronic and situational emotional distress, cognitive distortions and behavior problems will provide valuable insight into (1) patterns of dysfunction; (2) contextual variables, including antecedent conditions and extraneous controlling variables; and (3) historic frequency, magnitude, and duration of adjustment problems. This information, combined with current data, may expose repetitive, inflexible patterns of maladjustment reinforced over time. Haley (1976) asserts that the discovery of repetitive sequences of behavior that maintain dysfunctional behavior is potentially of greatest significance to the practitioner.

Assessment that is ongoing satisfies the responsibilities of the practitioner to (1) track progress or other change throughout treatment, rather than only before and after therapy; (2) identify and appraise evolving adjustment dilemmas as they arise; and (3) plan the course of intervention efficaciously. Close monitoring of change in the target areas in which treatment goals have been set will provide the practitioner and the client with valuable feedback. Feedback on positive change is reinforcing to both and may shape the development of the client's efficacy expectations. Data that fail to support constructive change serve to promote exploration of the barriers to effective treatment outcome. The complexity of postdivorce adjustment in terms of breadth of impact and the continuous and expansive adjustment demands placed on the individual by others and environmental circumstances make ongoing assessment imperative. It is highly unlikely that narrowly defined problem-focused intervention will satisfy the demands of postdivorce therapy. Hence, the treatment plan will require continuous modification.

In addition to identification of client problems and progress in relation to therapeutic efforts, it is important to assess the client's response to therapy and to the practitioner. Assessment includes appraising the client's openness to express content and feelings in therapy; active participation and collaboration with the practitioner in various therapeutic operations (design, implementation, and evaluation of the change effort); willingness to complete homework; and acceptance of explanation, interpretation, and feedback. The practitioner should also assess the client's commitment to the ongoing process of therapy and its goals as well as his or her expectations regarding the practitioner's role.

A vital assessment responsibility of the practitioner is to evaluate treatment efficacy. The clinical interview serves the practitioner well in achieving other assessment responsibilities, but it is inadequate in performing the outcome measurement requisite for practice accountability. There are a number of ways to measure client change, including behavioral observations, paper/pencil measures (standardized measures, self-anchored scales, and client logs), unobtrusive measures, and electromechanical measures. An array of standardized instruments exists to assess and measure emotion, self-concept, behavior, and cognitive variables, including beliefs, satisfaction, and expectancy. The reader is directed to Corcoran and Fischer's (1987) *Measures for Clinical Practice: A Sourcebook* for a comprehensive compilation of measures and publishing sources.

COGNITIVE INTERVENTION

Cognitive-behavioral treatment of divorce problems is based on social learning theory and cognitive psychology, in which cognition, behavior, emotion and physical/physiological factors are considered interactive within a social/environmental context. Any of the above variables can be targeted for intervention with the expectation that change in one variable will promote change in all other interactive dimensions. The treatment strategy selected may seek (1) emotional or behavioral change through modification of thoughts, perception, beliefs, expectations, or information processing; (2) emotional or behavioral change through the development of new verbal or behavioral skills or through the increased performance of adaptive verbal or behavioral skills infrequently used; (3) emotional or behavioral change through reduction of maladaptive behavioral excesses; and (4) environmental modification. Each intervention method noted has a relevant role to fulfill in the comprehensive treatment of postdivorce adjustment. My approach to divorce therapy relies heavily on each method.

Cognitive methods of intervention have been used by a number of practitioners to treat postdivorce adjustment problems (Broder, 1985; Ellis, 1986; Graff, Whitehead, & LeCompte, 1986; Granvold, 1989, 1992; Granvold & Welch, 1977, 1979; Huber, 1983, 1993; Johnson, 1977; Walen & Bass, 1986; Walen, DiGiuseppe, & Wessler, 1980). The crisis of divorce and the ensuing adjustment demands provide ample opportunity for clients to display errors in cognitive functioning. The focus of cognitive intervention may be on perceptual errors, self-expectancies, information processing errors, or schemata. Preceding the development of an intervention strategy, as noted in the previous section, a functional assessment must be completed in which cognitive, behavioral, emotional, physical/physiological, and social/environmental factors are delineated and their interactive relationships preliminarily identified. Targets of intervention are specified collaboratively by the client and practitioner, and interactional effects of the change effort are hypothesized. For example, a behavior or cognition may be targeted for change with the explicitly stated expectation that such change will effectively produce a change in a given cognitive, emotional, and/ or behavioral response. Evaluation of the change effort is performed to determine the treatment's effectiveness, and adjustments to the intervention strategy are made accordingly.

Presentation of the Model

Early in treatment the client is instructed in the interactive nature of cognitive, emotional, behavioral, physical/physiological, and social/environmental factors and their contributions to psychological disturbance and associated maladaptive behavior. A significant aspect of this didactic presentation is the application of the model to the client's unique symptoms to promote understanding and relevance. The course of treatment should be described, with the roles of the client and practitioner delineated. Collaboration of the client and practitioner is promoted in the formulation, implementation, and evaluation of intervention strategies. Subsequent to the presentation and discussion of the model, the client is instructed in monitoring and validating his or her cognitions. Faulty cognitions are identified in relation to the client's postdivorce adjustment problems, and specific cognitions are targeted for change. Initial change efforts should be focused on two or three information processing errors or faulty schemata considered most meaningful in the client's maladjustment. Caution should be taken to limit the number of targeted cognitive errors in order to avoid overwhelming the client. Early success in cognitive change may establish a pattern of learning that can be generalized to other cognitive errors. Methods of cognitive restructuring are taught in the session, and homework is assigned to further implement the treatment effort.

Faulty Information Processing

The following information processing errors distort the client's view of self, others, and the world. The result is a negative, pessimistic view that carries with it maladaptive emotion; negatively biased expectations of self, others, and life; and overt and verbal behaviors that promote negative responses from others. In Chapter 1, information processing errors are identified and defined. Following are examples of distortions expressed by divorcing clients:

Absolutistic and Dichotomous Thinking.
The first distortion involves viewing events, actions, and objects in a polarized manner: Alice views herself as *totally* weak because she typically fails to "stand up" to her ex-husband when he violates preset agreements regarding their child-visitation schedule. After avoiding opportunities to confront him, she is extremely self-critical and feels angry, guilty, disappointed, loathsome, and depressed.

The intervention focuses on Alice's evaluation of her assertive abilities in degrees rather than dichotomously and the identification of situations where she has been assertive. This evidence is used to modify her self-assessment. Cognitive methods are joined with behavioral strategies to coach, rehearse, implement, and evaluate greater assertiveness with her ex-spouse.

Overgeneralization.
Donna's husband of 12 years filed for a divorce after having fallen in love with another woman. Donna's view is that all men are no good, faithless, and uncaring when it comes to the feelings of women.

The intervention focuses initially on the emotion associated with Donna's views. The hurt and anger she feels are refocused from men generally to her ex-spouse and his wrongdoing. Cognitive restructuring procedures (to be discussed later) are applied to those feelings. The validity of her generalized statement is tested out against her knowledge of men in her world whose behavior is incompatible with her generalization. She learns the dangers of generalization in fostering negative expectations and perceptual errors.

Selective Abstraction. Another distortion involves focusing on the negative and filtering out positive factors in a situation or life experience. Arthur and his wife had both wanted the divorce they secured during 1987. Arthur views that year as a terrible, wasted year. He focuses his appraisal of the year only on the divorce and does not consider the promotion he received, his daughter's successful graduation from college, and the birth of his first grandchild.

The practitioner guides Arthur in seeing that screening out positive data and focusing on one or two negative factors (no matter what their magnitude might be) may account for his negativism regarding 1987 and his corresponding negative feelings. Arthur learns that, for him, selective abstraction is a rather pervasive cognitive error leading to faulty appraisals of himself, others, and life experiences. He finds further that by changing this information processing error, he feels less emotionally burdened.

Arbitrary Inference. One form of arbitrary inference is "mind reading": "People at work think of me as a loser now that I'm divorced." "My ex-husband feels guilty when he sees me depressed." A second form is negative prediction: "I'm going to grow old as a lonely, unloved person." "This date I'm going on is going to work out as badly as the last one."

The client is guided in searching for evidence to support such inferential statements. Where statements cannot be validated, more accurate, rational statements are devised to replace the faulty ones. With regard to negative predictive statements, the client is engaged in a discussion of self-fulfilling prophecy and the role that each individual plays in shaping his or her future. Together the practitioner and client delineate various actions that the client could take to minimize the likelihood that the undesirable prediction will come true.

Magnification and Minimization.
Freeman (1983) refers to the "binocular trick," in which the individual either blows up the meaning of behavior, conditions, or events or shrinks them. Problems, flaws in oneself, and obstacles in life are viewed as bigger than they realistically are, and successes, personal strengths and attributes, and life opportunities are minimized.

To illustrate, a divorced man magnifies the effect of his child-support payments by saying, "I pay so much money to my ex-wife, I don't have a cent left for myself!" The emotions he feels associated with this thought are anger, resentment, and dislike toward his ex-mate. Interactions with his ex-wife while thinking this thought are punctuated by anger, sarcasm, and unkindness. The modification of this thought to more closely reflect the realistic consequences of the child-support payments carries with it concomitant changes in the client's emotional responses, and subsequent interactions with his ex-mate become less negatively charged and less unpleasant.

Personalization. There are two forms of personalization. In the first form clients view themselves as the cause of a negative outcome. To illustrate, Mary, divorced for two years, is informed that her 6-year-old daughter behaved poorly in Sunday school. Her conclusion is that "I'm really a poor mother" and, hence, the cause of her daughter's poor behavior. In the second form of personalization clients conclude that they are the object of a negative event although no objective evidence exists to substantiate this arbitrary conclusion. Kay seeks to enroll her child in a day-care program near her home. Upon learning that the last available opening was awarded to another child earlier in the day, she concludes, "If I didn't need day care for my child, there would be plenty of openings at this center." She has made a causal connection between her need and the lack of availability, a connection for which there is no logical support.

Negative Attribution.   Another distortion is the view that a given behavior is produced out of a negative motivation. Mahoney (1974) defines attribution as implied causality. Attributions are often simplistic statements that are perceived as accounting for a given behavior. The tendency is to attribute single causation to complex patterns of behavior. Negative attributions can take the form of blaming—"You make me so mad"— in which the responsibility for the anger is displaced to the ex-mate. Epstein (1982) identifies behavior changes that are attributed to coercion or impression management: "He treats my children extra kindly because he's afraid I won't make love with him if he doesn't." The implications are that (1) the only reason behind the kindness is sexual desire and (2) being kind is actually misrepresentative of the individual's feelings and preferences in relation to the children. Another form of negative attribution is malevolent intent: "She bought the children season passes to the amusement park just to make me look bad in my current financial situation." Many other forms of attribution exist in addition to those identified above. The practitioner is encouraged to be sensitive to faulty causal statements and their emotional consequences. Such attributions should be identified, challenged, and restructured to produce more rational causal conclusions.

Faulty Interpretation.   A final distortion involves an interpretation of a message that is inconsistent with the intention, a discrepancy between intent and impact (Gottman, 1979). To illustrate, Joe and Mary negotiated an amicable divorce and have had minimal subsequent interactional problems. Mary informs Joe that she has opened and is building a college fund for their child with a portion of each child-support payment. She intends merely to keep him informed and to promote his view of her as being responsible with the child-support money. But he concludes: "She doubts my commitment to paying for our child's ed-ucation. She doesn't think I'll have the money when it's needed." He feels sad that she doesn't think more of him and feels some resentment regarding the account. He behaves uncharacteristically coolly toward her in their next interaction.

The ease of making faulty interpretations is evident as one considers the variable meanings that can be attached to a given message. It is only as information is shared and clarification received that the discrepancy between intended and ascribed meaning can be minimized.

The procedure common to the treatment of all information processing errors is the identification of adequate, logical evidence to support the conclusions reached. It is for this reason that the process of "collaborative empiricism" is so important (Beck, Rush, Shaw, & Emery, 1979). For as the client and practitioner begin to generate possible hypotheses related to the conclusions reached, the illogic in the thinking will surface with the deliberate and focused guidance of the practitioner. The client's initial lack of awareness of the self-sustained cognitive distortions and the emotional overlay associated with such thinking will evolve into an organized evaluation of the validity of the hypotheses that have heretofore operated automatically and invalidly. As a result, change can be expected in the client's view of self and significant others and in the negative emotional episodes that have been associated with cognitive distortions.

Irrational Beliefs and Faulty Expectations

Cognitive distortions emerge from and are governed by an underlying set of rules, including such elements as cognitive organization, structural causal theories, attitudes toward oneself and toward reality, and belief system. Terminology used to identify an individual's underlying set of rules varies as follows: personal constructs (Kelly, 1955), irrational beliefs (Ellis, 1973, 1977), automatic thoughts and schemata (Beck, 1976; Beck et al., 1979), and deep structures (Guidano & Liotti, 1983). I will use the term *irrational beliefs* as representative of a personal philosophy that promotes a distortion in thought processes and leads to emotional, behavioral, and interpersonal dysfunction.

Ellis (1962) has identified 11 irrational beliefs that serve as the basis for dysfunctional thinking and faulty expectations. These beliefs incorporate such imperatives as (1) the demand (as opposed to the desire) for love and approval, perfection, and control over one's world; (2) freedom from responsibility for one's own emotions; (3) extreme dependency on others; (4) the irrefutable right to blame others for one's own and others' imperfections and shortcomings; and (5) the indelible effect of history on current behavior and emotions. Following is a discussion of these imperatives in relation to postdivorce adjustment.

Demandingness. It is common for the divorced individual to fail to detach his or her identity and sense of worth from the ex-mate. *Love and approval* from the former spouse are considered imperative for a positive sense of self and of overall worthiness. The negative view toward self has corresponding negative emotions such as depression, self-loathing, hurt, guilt, and despair. Often, there is a negative view of the ex-mate with corresponding negative feelings, including anger, resentment, disappointment, disgust, and fear.

The belief that the love of another is a need rather than a desire or preference promotes prolonged emotional disturbance when the love is withdrawn. A shift in belief reflecting lost love as only a desire rather than a need contingent for survival with happiness is necessary for the divorced individual to develop or recapture a positive sense of self and constructively adjust to the divorce.

Irrational Beliefs
"I am nothing without him."

"I must have her love; I can't stand life without it."
"I'll never be happy again."
"I'm a total failure."

The failed marriage may represent imperfection and a lack of control over one's life and the world. The *demand for perfection* may translate into the view of divorce as the ultimate in marital "imperfection." The client's theology and personal philosophy regarding the permanence of marriage may be inherent in the demand for perfection. Sustained marriage becomes, in a sense, compliance with a higher-order law or rule, the violation of which leaves the individual feeling deeply flawed and powerless.

The *demand for control* may be an expression of narcissism and hedonism. Consistent with the views of Rice (1977), divorcing represents narcissistic injury. Furthermore, the rewards of controlling others and maintaining the order in one's world may be central to the expectation of extreme or total control. The divorce, then, becomes a threat to the individual's stability and pleasure in life.

The assumption of a central omnipotent position in the world produces demandingness. Clients set up artificial, self-declared imperatives that they consider necessary for their emotional well-being. Judgments regarding life's injustices, imperatives, and impositions made from a lofty, all-controlling position produce intolerance. The practitioner should aid clients in realizing that although they know they are not the center of the universe, they are judging certain life experiences and conditions as if they were. The client's expectations require expansion to include tolerance and acceptance in light of personal dislike, disregard, and disapproval. Frustrated desires and incomplete control over life's demands are to be considered properties inherent in the human social condition.

Irrational Beliefs
"I'm no good [imperfect] because I'm divorced."

"Life's a bitch."

"My life is totally ruined because my marriage failed."

"I should have prevented the divorce."

"It's Your Fault."   The placement of responsibility for one's emotions on another is a denial that human emotions exist under one's self-control. Although ex-spouses can be held responsible for their behavior (the activating event), the emotions one experiences in response to those actions are, in the last analysis, one's own responsibility. It is reasonable to expect the client to experience a "normal" expression of human emotion in relation to divorce recovery in which a fluctuation in mood is healthy and adaptive. However, extreme, highly consistent negative emotion viewed by the client as both the fault of the ex-spouse and as nonresponsive to self-control requires cognitive restructuring. Acceptance of responsibility for one's own emotions and the development of the cognitive skill of emotional self-control represent appropriate treatment goals in response to blaming and a lack of emotional self-efficacy.

The client may further blame the ex-spouse for the divorce and the ensuing problems and accommodation demands. This placement of total responsibility on the ex-spouse is in violation of the collaborative view of couple interaction as set forth in social exchange theory (Homans, 1958, 1974; Thibaut & Kelley, 1959). Divorce is considered to result when one or both spouses find the relative "costs" of the relationship to be greater than the relative "rewards" available in the relationship, and when one or both view single life (comparison level for alternatives) as potentially more rewarding than the marriage. Each partner contributes to the exchange, and hence, any action or decision in the relationship cannot be logically considered to be independent of each mate's influence. Such action or decision may, however, be directly contrary to the wishes or expectations of one party. Blaming the ex-spouse for past and current problems

prevents clients from (1) acknowledging their contribution to past and current problems, (2) accepting self-responsibility to cope and adjust to the current situation, (3) solving problems effectively, and (4) changing.

Irrational Beliefs

"It's his fault that I'm having all this trouble with these children."

"I can't be a father because of her."

"I've been depressed for two years because of him."

"She taught me how to hate."

"I was kind and sweet before him."

"I Need Another on Whom to Rely"—Dependency.   The strength of attachment to the ex-spouse may be so strong as to constitute a perceived "need" on the part of the client. Similar to the demand for love from the ex-spouse, the belief that one needs another on whom to rely for the satisfaction of practical and emotional demands is faulty. Such "needs" and dependency represent an erosion of clients' sense of self (lack of self-confidence, self-reliance) and prevent them from developing and exercising mastery over their world.

It is highly likely that the client has not been totally dependent on the ex-spouse. Identification of long-standing skills of self-reliance and newly developed abilities to meet personal, interpersonal, and environmental demands may serve to begin restructuring the client's stance of extreme dependency. Graduated assignments promoting acts of independence may further enhance the client's recognition of the potential for greater self-reliance.

Irrational Beliefs

"I *need* another [ex-spouse] in my life to help me."

"I'm too insecure to make it alone."

"I can't make decisions by myself."

"My Ex-Spouse Deserves Punishment."   The ex-spouse may be considered a villainous character with despicable qualities—one who has created disagreeable, offensive, and un-healthy attributes in the client. The ex-spouse is believed to deserve punishment for his or her unsavory behavior and "indelible" nega-tive influence on the client. Clients may be preoccupied with punishing thoughts and wishes or may actually be planning or admin-istering consequences hurtful to the ex-mate. Similar to their placing of responsibility for their own emotions and problems on their ex-mate, clients hold their former spouse ac-countable for feelings of distrust, hate, cold-ness, vindictiveness, and the like. The nega-tive ideation focused on the punishment of the former spouse typically has concomitant negative emotions—anger, resentment, hate. This preoccupation prevents clients from making healthy, positive efforts to recover. The practitioner should guide clients in shift-ing attention from the counterproductive ir-rational thoughts related to their ex-spouse to their own current goals, realized and poten-tial joys in life, and, perhaps, alternative con-structive relationships.

Irrational Beliefs
"I'll never be able to trust again; she took that with her."
"I hope he rots in hell."

"I Can't Change—This Is the Way I Am."

Although divorce presents an opportunity for pervasive change, many individuals consider themselves highly unchangeable. Beliefs, emotions, and behavior typical of the client's past functioning are considered to be all-im-portant determiners of present behavior. Such committed intractability violates the learning potential in us all. The practitioner is challenged to guide the client to the realiza-tion that change is a possibility, although not without commitment, hard work, and sus-tained effort. In uncovering clients' beliefs in their unchangeability, the practitioner should also seek the identification of extraneous con-trolling variables that reinforce their beliefs and behaviors. The use of cognitive restruc-turing along with the assignment and comple-tion of easily achievable tasks that invalidate the client's views, the removal of environ-mental reinforcers, and the practitioner's strategic encouragement and reinforcement can be expected to alter clients' views that they are unchangeable.

Irrational Beliefs
"I'm shy and always will be."
"I've always had a problem with anger [de-pression, worry]."
"I'm a failure—all divorced people are losers."

Even though a given belief is irrational, a client (or practitioner, for that matter) may strongly believe it and suffer the concomitant emotional distress. It is the responsibility of the practitioner, through the use of the So-cratic method, to guide the client to (1) a commitment to altering the belief on the basis that it is a destructive belief to hold, (2) test out the validity of the belief by looking for logical evidence to support or negate it, and (3) allow the strength of the belief to erode on the basis of the evidence—to repeatedly rate and rerate the *degree* to which the belief is held with an expectation of reduced commit-ment to the thought.

Case Illustration

The following excerpt illustrates the initial application of cognitive restructuring meth-ods to a divorced client who is suffering nega-tive feelings over his failures while married. James entered therapy with me six months af-ter his divorce was final. He and his wife, Nancy, jointly decided to end their ten-year marriage. In looking back over his experience in marital therapy with another practitioner, he concluded that he had neither put a fo-cused effort into the marital therapy nor made a legitimate attempt to make his mar-riage work from the beginning. He was de-pressed and "upset" with himself. At some point, it would be appropriate to determine the factors that might have contributed to his lack of effort in his marriage and to strategize ways to invest more effectively in future relationships. At this time, however, the targets of change are his views regarding his past behavior and the negative emotions he is currently experiencing.

James: I really miss Nancy and what we could have had together. But I didn't put any effort in . . . I blew it.

Practitioner: And how do you feel in relation to that?

James: Depressed . . . a bit angry with myself.

Practitioner: I see, not very comfortable feelings . . . And these feelings are associated with the view that you didn't put any effort into your marriage, is that correct?

James: Yes, that's what I think.

Practitioner: While it's very likely that you *did* put effort into your marriage, let's *assume* that you didn't put *any* effort in at all. What's so bad about that?

James: Well, for crying out loud, a person should put effort into his marriage, if he's any kind of person at all.

Practitioner: So you're no good as a person for not putting more effort into your marriage, is that what you're concluding?

James: That's it, all right.

Practitioner: How does not putting effort into your marriage make you no good?

James: It just does.

Practitioner: Must you behave "right" to feel OK as a person?

James: Not in everything, just some things.

Practitioner: So in certain select areas, defined by you, you *must* behave "right" in order to feel OK. Given the fact that we are all fallible, screwed-up, error-prone humans, do you see any problems with this demand to have really worked at your marriage?

James: I think I see what you're getting at. I'm operating with what you earlier called

"conditional self-regard," that I'm only OK if I behave in such and such a way.

Practitioner: That's right, James. You appear to be concluding total no-goodness, based on not having tried to make your marriage work. To further explore the point, earlier you said that you *must* behave "right" in certain areas—in this case, working on your marriage. Where is the evidence that you *must* behave right?

James: You just should. There really isn't any evidence to support it.

Practitioner: That's right, there is no evidence to support it. There is actually evidence to the contrary—that people characteristically fail to behave "right" consistently. It is your *expectation* that you do right that is the basis of your negative judgment of yourself. What kind of person would you have to be to *always* do the "right" thing— to meet all your expectations?

James: I guess I'd have to be pretty flawless and more self-disciplined than I am.

Practitioner: Yes, you'd have to be perfect to always do right. Are you perfect?

James: Of course not!

Practitioner: And I agree, you're not. But you're judging yourself as if you were.

James: I guess I am. I've really never thought of it that way.

Practitioner: In response to your demand that you behave "right" and put effort into your marriage, you've been feeling depressed and somewhat angry with yourself. What could you think to reduce the intensity of these feelings?

James: I guess I could think that I prefer to have tried harder at my marriage but I just didn't. I'm an error-prone person, as you said, and I behaved less than perfectly.

Practitioner: That's sound thinking, James. Now, on the basis of this revised thinking, is there any change in the intensity of your feelings of depression and anger with yourself?

James: Perhaps some reduction . . . but not much.

Practitioner: It will take practice and repeated bombardment of your faulty thinking to change the intensity of your feelings. Based on the past few minutes, do you recognize the possibility of changing your views and ultimately how you feel?

James: Yes, I think so. I feel some sense of hope. I do want to get over these feelings, and I'm resigned to not being able to change the past or to reconcile with Nancy. I first want to be able to have a better attitude about the past and to feel better.

Practitioner: To summarize, James, you appear to have two flaws in your thinking in relation to trying harder in your marriage. First, you concluded that you weren't an OK person because you didn't put effort into your marriage—conditional self-regard. Second, you realized that you were exercising a perfection demand, expecting to behave more perfectly than you humanly happen to be.

James was given the assignment to record his thoughts about his failure to have tried harder at his marriage. He was instructed to record his thoughts as they emerged. When he found himself mired in feelings of depression and anger at himself, he was instructed to begin the process of deductive reasoning to determine the faulty thoughts behind his feelings and to dispute them. He was instructed to record his thoughts and feelings on Ellis's RET Self-Help Form (Ellis & Dryden, 1987). A useful alternative form is Beck's Daily Record of Dysfunctional Thoughts (Beck et al., 1979). This homework was reviewed at each subsequent session with the following objectives: (1) to reinforce the cognitive restructuring process, (2) to oversee the effective implementation of the procedure, (3) to revise the intervention as new beliefs and thought processing errors became identified, and (4) to promote the generalization of the method to other stimulus conditions and corresponding maladaptive emotional and behavioral consequences.

OTHER COGNITIVE METHODS

Many other cognitive methods are worthy of consideration in the treatment of the array of problems associated with divorce. Meichenbaum's (1977) self-instruction training and stress-inoculation training have widespread facility. Covert modeling and positive imagery (Cautela, 1971; Mahoney, 1974) may be useful in developing skills and in preparing to perform infrequently used or newly developed skills. Extreme anxiety arising out of specific circumstances (state anxiety) can be effectively treated through the use of systematic desensitization (Wolpe, 1958). Thought stopping is a useful adjunctive technique to limit or terminate unwanted ruminations and undesirable urges (Wolpe, 1958, 1969; Wolpe & Lazarus, 1966). Problem solving can be useful as an adaptive means of strategizing actions to resolve divorce-related problems and to cope with problems left in the wake of divorce (D'Zurilla, 1988; D'Zurilla & Goldfried, 1971).

BEHAVIORAL METHODS

Although changes in cognitive functioning can promote and bring about change emotionally and behaviorally, behavior change likewise has facility in the promotion and creation of cognitive and affective change. The coordinated use of cognitive and behavioral methods for change is recommended for efficient and effective outcomes.

Homework

Homework is an integral component of effective treatment for many reasons, including (1) the promotion of skill development through repetitive practice, (2) the application of methods rehearsed in the sessions to natural environmental conditions, (3) the generalization of change from one stimulus condition to other stimulus conditions, and (4) relapse prevention. Shelton and Ackerman (1974) note that the use of homework "increases the client's ability for self-evaluation and self-regulation long after therapy has ended" (p. 3). Homework assignments may focus on cognitive factors (for example, recording such variables as urges to behave in undesirable ways that are held in check, ruminations, or self-affirmative thoughts); emotions (for example, maintaining a daily mood scale or charting loneliness); or behavior (for example, pleasant activities performed or assertive behavior displayed). Identifiable, measurable, and sustained cognitive, emotional, and behavioral changes mark treatment effectiveness. The assignment of homework significantly raises the likelihood that such change will be achieved, in addition to the therapeutic benefits of catharsis, therapist empathy and support, and insight.

Stress Management Procedures

As mentioned earlier, the stress associated with the divorce process is extreme. Responsible treatment of divorce obligates the practitioner to incorporate stress management procedures in the intervention plan. Training in deep-muscle relaxation is a well-established procedure and should be given strong consideration as one component of effective stress management. Training in deep-muscle relaxation and the audiotape recording of an in-session training provides portability to the client's practice and ultimate habituation of a greater state of physical relaxation. Other viable stress-management procedures include the use of biofeedback and the assignment of aerobic, physically demanding recreational activities and "low-demand" leisure activities. It is recommended that the practitioner be sensitive to the following: (1) inappropriate stress management methods such as routine and excessive use of alcohol and other

drugs and extremely physically demanding exercise regimens, (2) nutrition, (3) sleep behavior, and (4) cognitive and emotive factors, including extreme demandingness, excessive focus on tasks, drivenness, low frustration threshold, perfectionism, proneness to agitation, and hurriedness.

Modeling, Coaching, and Behavior Rehearsal

Observation is one of the primary means by which behavior is learned. Not only do models teach novel ways of thinking and behaving, Bandura (1971, 1977) notes that the influence of modeling can weaken or strengthen inhibitions over behavior the client has previously learned. Given the strength of influence associated with the therapeutic alliance, practitioner modeling can serve as an important intervention procedure in its own right. For this reason, it is critical that practitioners proceed with constant vigilance and purpose in their expression of appropriate and adaptive thoughts, thought patterns, beliefs, emotional expressions, and overt behavior. Inadvertent modeling of maladaptive overt or covert behavior may have as great an influence on the client as purposeful modeling. Although modeling is taking place constantly during treatment, the practitioner may engage in role playing with the client in which specific thoughts and beliefs, information processing procedures, problem solving, and overt behaviors are strategically modeled.

The practitioner may function as coach in guiding clients' development of a specific skill. As part of behavior rehearsal, clients may receive prompting in their communication content or expression or in their overt behavior. Prompting may focus on cognitive or behavioral responses to specific stimulus conditions. Coached responses are those considered to promote adaptation and effective behavioral performance. The coaching effort may be applied to coping strategies (statements of self-control and tolerance), self-corrective thoughts and actions, and self-affirmative statements.

Role playing can be designed for the client to rehearse infrequently used behaviors or to develop novel skills. Role rehearsal provides "safe" opportunities for skill development. The practitioner offers feedback to facilitate the modification and shaping of client skill. As an example, although most divorced people were skilled at dating earlier in life, many find themselves in need of practice to display the array of skills that is integral to effective dating. Behavioral rehearsal affords an opportunity to practice the behavior and, in the process, to limit negative emotional responses and their undesirable effects on performance. Gottman and Leiblum (1974) report other benefits of role playing, including the opportunity for self-correction, the anticipation of difficult or problematic encounters and the rehearsal of ways of handling them, and appreciation for the feelings and experiences of others.

Recording and Charting

Self-observation methods can be employed to promote cognitive and behavioral change. Recording behavior may effectively raise the client's level of awareness, and it provides for the systematic evaluation of the occurrence of the behavior. Greater self-awareness may operate to more effectively interrupt a habituated stimulus-response pattern, and through systematic evaluation, insights can be gained into discriminative stimuli, contextual variables, and reinforcing consequences that promote maladaptive responses or retard the performance of adaptive responses. A variety of devices can be used for counting, including notebooks, wrist counters, pocket counters, and note cards. Wrist counters, developed for golfing and adapted originally by Lindsley (1968), are highly useful both in their novelty and relative unobtrusiveness. Recording and *charting* provide opportunities for (1) visual-

izing the change effort more clearly; (2) public awareness, which, in turn, affords support, encouragement, and social reinforcement; and (3) self-reinforcement for the achievement of preset levels of success in the desired change.

Skill Training

Divorced clients may be functioning with skill deficiencies that prevent them from greater adaptation to being divorced or inhibit their progressive change in new roles and relationships. In response to these deficiencies the practitioner may provide individually designed skill training to promote the development of verbal and communication skills (for example, active listening, expressions of feeling, and voice tone); assertiveness to protect individual rights and to promote healthy self-interest (Alberti & Emmons, 1970a, 1970b; Bach & Goldberg, 1974; Bower & Bower, 1976; Cotler & Guerra, 1976; Dawley & Wenrich, 1976; Smith, 1976); and behavioral skills in such areas as sexual functioning (for example, noncoital sensate pleasuring techniques), parenting (Bavolek, 1984; Dangel & Polster, 1980, 1984a, 1984b; Dinkmeyer & McKay, 1982; Gordon, 1970; Patterson, 1971; Popkin, 1983), and dating and interpersonal skills (Bach & Deutsch, 1970; Johnson, 1977). Skill acquisition can be achieved through in-session instruction, modeling, coaching, and behavioral rehearsal; *in vivo* application of developing skills; and group treatment. It is recommended that strong consideration be given to the use of group methods in assertion training, social-skills training, and parent training.

Stimulus-Control Methods

Stimulus-control methods involve the rearrangement of environmental conditions that have been determined to influence target behaviors. For example, if specific cues such as memorabilia, pictures, and gifts stimulate depression and an overwhelming sense of loss in the divorced client, they can be removed, thereby preventing the undesirable emotional responses or reducing the frequency and intensity of such responses. Wanderer and Cabot (1978) recommend that all such memorabilia be placed in a box and stored until later in the recovery process, when the individual will floodingly expose himself or herself to the contents of the box and the memories associated with them ("Implosion Day"). Clients may consider putting new pictures on the wall, replacing furniture, purchasing new sheets with a different pattern or color, and remodeling if it is feasible. They may be instructed in changing their routine and avoiding exposure to circumstances and conditions that prompt undesirable responses (staying away from a favorite restaurant or nightclub; tuning the radio away from love songs; changing health clubs). During periods of the greatest feelings of loss and discomfort, clients are instructed to devote time, attention, and energy to an activity that will have the strength to displace the maladaptive response pattern. For example, a client who before the divorce had driven to and from work with his wife, suffered a great sense of loss while commuting. To compete with these feelings, he played French-language tapes on his way to and from work in preparation for a trip to France the following summer. He found that his focused attention on the French lessons significantly displaced his sense of loss in relation to his ex-wife. It has been found that "the probability of a response is dramatically influenced by the presence or absence of stimulus cues previously associated with that response" (Thoresen & Mahoney, 1974, p. 17). Stimulus-control methods have great facility in the amelioration of postdivorce emotional problems.

Behavior Change through Self-Reinforcement

Bandura (1977) has noted that behavior is largely regulated by its consequences and that reinforcement for behavior can be derived externally, vicariously, or from oneself. Efforts to change behavior can be enhanced through the design of self-administered reinforcement procedures. It has been said that motivation is simply the proper arrangement of contingencies. Although this concise statement is so true, the operationalization of it poses great challenges. In the design of a self-reinforcement program to alter target behavior, an early task is the instruction of the client in various self-reinforcement procedures. Thoresen and Mahoney (1974) note that "self reward is comprised of presenting oneself with a positive stimulus or removing some negative stimulus contingent on a desired performance" (p. 88). They caution that clients may present themselves with an aversive stimulus condition in order to later remove it to receive the self-regulated reward. So, for example, a client could endure depression for a time and earn a reward through the effective reduction or termination of the depression. Dependent on the strength of meaning of the reward, an individual may be "willing" to suffer depression subsequently as a negative stimulus condition for ultimate removal and contingent reward. A maladaptive cycle would thereby become established. The practitioner may guide the client in the modification of the self-reinforcement procedure to prevent such outcomes; for example, rewards can be established for the length of time spent depression-free or minimally depressed.

A highly useful self-reward procedure described by Premack (1965, 1971) and termed the *Premack Principle* involves the employment of behaviors frequently engaged in by the client as reinforcers contingent on the performance of less frequently displayed behavior. Stated alternatively, the Premack Principle is the placement of a high-frequency/high-reward behavior or activity contingent on the performance of a low-frequency/low-reward behavior or activity. A more familiar form of this principle is "Clean up your room and you can go out and play!" Thoresen and Mahoney (1974) note that effective self-reinforcement requires a state of partial self-deprivation. Hence, implementation of the Premack Principle may require categorical deprivation to promote effective outcomes. For example, if watching *L.A. Law* is established as contingent on the client's doing 30 minutes of aerobic exercises on three occasions a week while the client is eligible to engage in all other TV watching, the deprivation of *L.A. Law* alone may not have sufficient reinforcement strength to promote consistent behavior change. Substantial reduction in all TV watching would be required to promote reinforcer effectiveness. I have found the Premack Principle to be highly useful in the promotion of behavior change in divorcing or divorced clients.

An alternative self-reinforcement program involves the design of a reward system for behavior compliance or the achievement of particular outcomes. The use of response-cost consequences for failure to comply with behavior-change objectives may provide additional strength to the procedure. A client may contract with herself to change behavior X in a measurable way (either to increase or decrease it in frequency, intensity, or duration) followed by a reward for compliance. For example, Mary, functioning as a single parent, felt overwhelmed by the demands of parenting. She recognized the importance of reading to her preschool daughter but failed to do so at a rate that she considered to be minimally acceptable. Repeated commitments to increase the behavior had failed to produce compliance with her objectives. The practitioner aided her in the development of a contingency contract as follows: "I agree to read to my daughter three times per week for 15 minutes each. Reward: Movie out with a friend."

It was determined that, for Mary, going out to a movie was highly rewarding and she agreed that she was ineligible to see any movies unless she earned the "right" to attend through reading to her daughter for the designated time. A response cost could also be specified for noncompliance. Should Mary fail to honor the commitment, she would not only be ineligible to attend a movie but also could require herself to engage in an activity she considered to be aversive in nature, such as donating a meaningful amount of money to a cause she disagreed with, scrubbing and waxing the kitchen and dining room floors even though they did not need it, or calling her ex-mother-in-law long distance and talking for 20 minutes! As noted above, the reward program can be applied to process variables as well as outcome variables. For example, if the contracted change relates to an overall objective to lose weight, compliance with a structured eating program could earn a reward irrespective of weight loss; alternatively, the reward could be made contingent on weight loss irrespective of eating behavior. Thoresen and Mahoney (1974) have noted that self-regulatory efforts are far more effectively maintained when they receive environmental support. Hence, it is desirable to build in social approval for behavioral compliance through practitioner reinforcement or reinforcement from significant others in the client's environment.

Flooding, or Implosive Therapy

Flooding is designed to reduce maladaptive avoidant behavior and involves the repeated exposure to a stimulus situation heretofore avoided due to subjective emotional consequences (Gottman & Leiblum, 1974; Hogan & Kirchner, 1967; Stampfl & Levis, 1967). "Flooding is based on a classical extinction paradigm which states that in the absence of reinforcement, a response will decrease in frequency" (Gottman & Leiblum, 1974, p. 73). Clients are continuously and extensively exposed to the stimulus condition that they have been avoiding. The exposure to the unpleasant stimuli is continued despite the negative emotional consequences. Ultimately the discomfort will reach a peak, and because the response is not reinforced (by termination of the exposure), there will be a decrease in the discomfort. In effect, the client becomes desensitized to the stimulus condition. Flooding may be implemented in the form of Implosion Day (Wanderer & Cabot, 1978), in which the client devotes an entire day to grieving and crying over the box of memorabilia and other love objects that have been previously packed away. The client is directed to go through the entire contents of the box, to incessantly play the music that was shared with the ex-mate, and to eat "their" favorite foods. It is critical that the *timing* of the flooding procedure be consistent with the client's readiness to accommodate the loss of the mate in this fashion. It is recommended that the practitioner use conservatism in judging clients' readiness. The objective is for clients to rid themselves of the pain—to become desensitized to the loss. In order to effectively accomplish this objective, several iterations may be necessary.

CONCLUSION

The treatment of divorce poses great challenges to the practitioner. As noted by Sprenkle (1989), there is far more information about the phenomenon of divorce than there is about how to effectively treat it. This chapter has provided multiple procedures for use in the treatment of problems associated with the divorce process. Although the procedures presented have a substantial body of empirical support, there is need for further refinement and creative application of these methods to children, ex-spouses, and members of the extended family.

REFERENCES

Alberti, R. E., & Emmons, M. L. (1970a). *Stand up, speak out, talk back.* San Luis Obispo, CA: Impact.

Alberti, R. E., & Emmons, M. L. (1970b). *Your perfect right.* San Luis Obispo, CA: Impact.

Bach, G. R., & Deutsch, R. M. (1970). *Pairing: How to achieve genuine intimacy.* New York: Avon.

Bach, G. R., & Goldberg, H. (1974). *Creative aggression: The art of assertive living.* New York: Avon.

Baker, L. (1981). *The transition to divorce: Discrepancies between husbands and wives.* Unpublished doctoral dissertation, Purdue University, West Lafayette, IN.

Bandura, A. (1971). Vicarious and self-reinforcement processes. In R. Glaser (Ed.), *The nature of reinforcement.* New York: Academic Press.

Bandura, A. (1977). *Social learning theory.* Englewood Cliffs, NJ: Prentice-Hall.

Bavolek, S. J. (1984). *Handbook for the adult-adolescent parenting inventory.* Eau Claire, WI: Family Development Resources.

Beck, A. T. (1976). *Cognitive therapy and the emotional disorders.* New York: International Universities Press.

Beck, A. T., Rush, A. J., Shaw, B. F., & Emery, G. (1979). *Cognitive therapy of depression.* New York: Guilford Press.

Bohannan, P. (1971). The six stations of divorce. In P. Bohannan (Ed.), *Divorce and after.* New York: Doubleday/Anchor.

Bower, S. A., & Bower, G. H. (1976). *Asserting yourself: A practical guide for positive change.* Reading, MA: Addison-Wesley.

Broder, M. S. (1985). Divorce and separation. In A. Ellis & M. E. Bernard (Eds.), *Clinical applications of rational-emotive therapy.* New York: Plenum.

Brown, E. (1976). Divorce counseling. In D. H. Olson (Ed.), *Treating relationships.* Lake Mills, IA: Graphic.

Buehler, C., & Langenbrunner, M. (1987). Divorce-related stressors: Occurrence, disruptiveness, and area of life change. *Journal of Divorce, 11,* 25–50.

Bumpass, L. L., & Sweet, J. A. (1972). Differentials in marital stability: 1970. *American Sociological Review, 37,* 754–766.

Cautela, J. R. (1971). *Covert modeling.* Paper presented to the Association for Advancement of Behavior Therapy, Washington, DC.

Cherlin, A. (1977). The effects of children on marital dissolution. *Demography, 14,* 265–272.

Chester, R. (1971). Health and marriage breakdown: Experience of a sample of divorced women. *British Journal of Preventive and Social Medicine, 25,* 231–235.

Chiriboga, D. A. (1978). Life event weighting systems: A comparative analysis. *Journal of Psychosomatic Research, 21,* 415–422.

Chiriboga, D. A., & Cutler, L. (1977). Stress responses among divorcing men and women. *Journal of Divorce, 1,* 95–106.

Chiriboga, D. A., Roberts, J., & Stein, J. A. (1978). Psychological well-being during marital separation. *Journal of Divorce, 2,* 21–35.

Cohen, S. N. (1985). Divorce mediation: An introduction. In D. H. Sprenkle (Ed.), *Divorce therapy.* New York: Haworth Press.

Coogler, O. J. (1978). *Structured mediation in divorce settlement.* Lexington, MA: D. C. Heath.

Corcoran, K., & Fischer, J. (1987). *Measures for clinical practice: A sourcebook.* New York: Free Press.

Cotler, S. B., & Guerra, J. J. (1976). *Assertion training.* Champaign, IL: Research Press.

Dangel, R. F., & Polster, R. A. (1980). *Winning!* Arlington, TX: Authors.

Dangel, R. F., & Polster, R. A. (Eds.). (1984a). *Parent training: Foundations of research and practice.* New York: Guilford Press.

Dangel, R. F., & Polster, R. A. (1984b). Winning!: A systematic, empirical approach to parent training. In R. F. Dangel & R. A. Polster (Eds.), *Parent training: Foundations of research and practice.* New York: Guilford Press.

Dawley, H. H., & Wenrich, W. W. (1976). *Achieving assertive behavior: A guide to assertive training.* Pacific Grove, CA: Brooks/Cole.

DeFazio, V. J., & Klenbort, I. (1975). A note on the dynamics of psychotherapy during marital dissolution. *Psychotherapy: Theory Research and Practice, 12,* 101–104.

Diedrick, P. (1991). Gender differences in divorce adjustment. *Journal of Divorce and Remarriage, 14,* 33–45.

Dinkmeyer, D., & McKay, G. (1982). *The parents handbook.* Circle Pines, MN: American Guidance Service.

D'Zurilla, T. J. (1988). Problem-solving therapies. In K. S. Dobson (Ed.), *Handbook of cognitive-behavioral therapies.* New York: Guilford Press.

D'Zurilla, T. J., & Goldfried, M. R. (1971). Problem solving and behavior modification. *Journal of Abnormal Psychology, 78,* 107–126.

Ellis, A. (1962). *Reason and emotion in psychotherapy.* New York: Stuart.

Ellis, A. (1973). *Humanistic psychotherapy.* New York: McGraw-Hill.

Ellis, A. (1977). The basic clinical theory of rational-emotive therapy. In A. Ellis & R. Grieger (Eds.), *Handbook of rational-emotive therapy.* New York: Springer.

Ellis, A. (1986). Application of rational-emotive therapy to love problems. In A. Ellis & R. Grieger (Eds.), *Handbook of rational-emotive therapy* (Vol. 2). New York: Springer.

Ellis, A., & Dryden, W. (1987). *The practice of rational-emotive therapy.* New York: Springer.

Ensel, W. M. (1986). Sex, marital status, and depression: The role of life events and social support. In N. Lin, A. Dean, & W. M. Ensel (Eds.), *Social support, life events, and depression.* Montreal: Academic.

Epstein, N. (1982). Cognitive therapy with couples. *American Journal of Family Therapy, 10,* 5–16.

Everett, C. A., & Volgy, S. S. (1989). Mediating child custody disputes. In M. R. Textor (Ed.), *The divorce and divorce therapy handbook.* Northvale, NJ: Aronson.

Everett, C. A., & Volgy, S. S. (1991). Treating divorce in family-therapy practice. In A. S. Gurman & D. P. Kniskern (Eds.), *Handbook of family therapy* (Vol. 2). New York: Brunner/Mazel.

Fisher, E. O. (1973). A guide to divorce counseling. *The Family Coordinator, 22,* 56–61.

Freeman, A. (1983). Cognitive therapy: An overview. In A. Freeman (Ed.), *Cognitive therapy with couples and groups.* New York: Plenum.

Froiland, D. J., & Hozman, T. L. (1977). Counseling for constructive divorce. *Personnel and Guidance Journal, 55,* 525–529.

Glick, P. C. (1989). Remarried families, stepfamilies and stepchildren: A brief demographic profile. *Family Relations, 38,* 24–27.

Glick, P. C., & Norton, A. J. (1971). Frequency, duration, and probability of marriage and divorce. *Journal of Marriage and the Family, 33*(2), 307–317.

Glick, P. C., & Norton, A. J. (1977). *Marrying, divorcing and living together today* (Population Bulletin, Vol. 32, No. 5). Washington, DC: Population Reference Bureau.

Gordon, T. (1970). *PET: Parent effectiveness training*. New York: Peter A. Wyden.

Gottman, J. M. (1979). *Marital interaction*. New York: Academic Press.

Gottman, J. M., & Leiblum, S. R. (1974). *How to do psychotherapy and how to evaluate it: A manual for beginners*. New York: Holt, Rinehart & Winston.

Graff, R. W., Whitehead, G. I., & LeCompte, M. (1986). Group treatment with divorced women using cognitive-behavioral and supportive-insight methods. *Journal of Counseling Psychology, 33,* 276–281.

Granvold, D. K. (1983). Structured separation for marital treatment and decision-making. *Journal of Marital and Family Therapy, 9,* 403–412.

Granvold, D. K. (1989). Postdivorce treatment. In M. R. Textor (Ed.), *The divorce and divorce therapy handbook*. Northvale, NJ: Aronson.

Granvold, D. K. (1992). The treatment of postdivorce adjustment problems through cognitive restructuring. In T. S. Nelson & T. S. Trepper (Eds.), *101 interventions in family therapy*. New York: Haworth Press.

Granvold, D. K., & Tarrant, R. (1983). Structured marital separation as a marital treatment method. *Journal of Marital and Family Therapy, 9,* 189–198.

Granvold, D. K., & Welch, G. J. (1977). Intervention for postdivorce adjustment problems: The treatment seminar. *Journal of Divorce, 1,* 81–92.

Granvold, D. K., & Welch, G. J. (1979). Structured, short-term group treatment of postdivorce adjustment. *International Journal of Group Psychotherapy, 29,* 347–358.

Green, B. L., Lee, R. R., & Lustig, N. (1973). Transient structured distance as a maneuver in marital therapy. *The Family Coordinator, 22,* 15–22.

Guidano, V. F., & Liotti, G. (1983). *Cognitive processes and emotional disorders: A structural approach to psychotherapy*. New York: Guilford Press.

Haley, J. (1976). *Problem-solving therapy: New strategies for effective family therapy*. San Francisco: Jossey-Bass.

Haynes, J. (1981). *Divorce mediation: A practical guide for therapists and counselors*. New York: Springer.

Hight, E. S. (1977). A contractual, working separation: A step between resumption and/or divorce. *Journal of Divorce, 1,* 21–30.

Hogan, R., & Kirchner, J. (1967). Preliminary report of the extinction of learned fear in a short-term implosive therapy. *Journal of Abnormal Psychology, 72,* 106–109.

Holmes, T. H., & Rahe, R. H. (1967). Social readjustment rating scale. *Journal of Psychosomatic Research, 11,* 213–218.

Homans, G. C. (1958). Social behavior as exchange. *American Journal of Sociology, 62,* 597–606.

Homans, G. C. (1974). *Social behavior: Its elementary forms*. New York: Harcourt Brace Jovanovich.

Huber, C. H. (1983). Feelings of loss in response to divorce: Assessment and intervention. *Personnel and Guidance Journal, 61,* 357–361.

Huber, C. H. (1993). RET and divorce adjustment. In W. Aryden & L. K. Hill (Eds.), *Innovations in rational-emotive therapy*. Newbury Park, CA: Sage.

Hunt, M. (1966). *The world of the formerly married*. New York: McGraw-Hill.

Hutchinson, R. L., & Spangler-Hirsch, S. L. (1989). Children of divorce and single-parent lifestyles: Facilitating well-being. *Journal of Divorce, 12,* 5–24.

Imber-Black, E. (1988). Normative and therapeutic rituals in couples therapy. In E. Imber-Black, J. Roberts, & R. A. Whiting (Eds.), *Rituals in families and family therapy*. New York: Norton.

Irving, H. H. (1981). *Divorce mediation: A rational alternative to the adversary system*. New York: Universe.

Jacobson, N. S., & Margolin, G. (1979). *Marital therapy: Strategies based on social learning and behavior exchange principles*. New York: Brunner/Mazel.

Janis, I. L. (1982). Decisionmaking under stress. In L. Goldberger & S. Breznitz (Eds.), *Handbook of stress: Theoretical and clinical aspects*. New York: Free Press.

Janis, I. L., & Mann, L. (1977). *Decision making: A psychological analysis of conflict, choice and commitment*. New York: Free Press.

Johnson, S. M. (1977). *First person singular: Living the good life alone*. New York: Signet.

Kaslow, F. W. (1984). Divorce: An evolutionary process of change in the family system. *Journal of Divorce, 7,* 21–39.

Kaslow, F. W. (1991, November). *Dilemmas of divorce: Coping with the pains of parting.* Presentation at the annual convention of the American Association for Marriage and Family Therapy, Dallas.

Kaslow, F. W., & Schwartz, L. L. (1987). *The dynamics of divorce: A life cycle perspective.* New York: Brunner/Mazel.

Kelly, G. (1955). *The psychology of personal constructs* (Vols. 1 & 2). New York: Norton.

Kessler, S. (1975). *The American way of divorce: Prescriptions for change.* Chicago: Nelson-Hall.

Kressel, K. (1980). Patterns of coping in divorce and some implications for clinical practice. *Family Relations, 29,* 234–240.

Lindsley, O. R. (1968). A reliable wrist counter for recording behavior rates. *Journal of Applied Behavior Analysis, 1,* 77–78.

Mahoney, M. J. (1974). *Cognition and behavior modification.* Cambridge, MA: Ballinger.

Meichenbaum, D. (1977). *Cognitive-behavior modification.* New York: Plenum.

Milne, A. L. (1986). Divorce mediation: A process of self-definition and self-determination. In N. S. Jacobson & A. S. Gurman (Eds.), *Clinical handbook of marital therapy.* New York: Guilford Press.

National Center for Health Statistics. (1986, September 25). Advance report of final divorce statistics. In *1984 Monthly Vital Statistics Report, 35*(6) (Supp. DHS Pub. No. PHS 86-1120). Hyattsville, MD: U.S. Public Health Service.

Neville, W. G. (1989). Mediation. In M. R. Textor (Ed.), *The divorce and divorce therapy handbook.* Northvale, NJ: Aronson.

Olson, D. H., Russell, C. S., & Sprenkle, D. H. (1980). Marital and family therapy: A decade review. *Journal of Marriage and the Family, 42,* 973–993.

Patterson, G. R. (1971). *Families: Applications of social learning theory to family life.* Champaign, IL: Research Press.

Phillips, C. E. (1979). *Successful separation counseling.* Unpublished manuscript, California Family Study Center, Burbank, CA.

Ponzetti, J. J., & Cate, R. M. (1988). The divorce process: Toward a typology of marital dissolution. *Journal of Divorce, 11,* 1–20.

Popkin, M. H. (1983). *Active parenting handbook.* Atlanta: Active Parenting.

Premack, D. (1965). Reinforcement theory. In D.

Levine (Ed.), *Nebraska symposium on motivation.* Lincoln: University of Nebraska Press.

Premack, D. (1971). Catching up with common sense or two sides of a generalization: Reinforcement and punishment. In R. Glaser (Ed.), *The nature of reinforcement.* New York: Academic Press.

Reissman, C. K. (1990). *Divorce talk: Women and men make sense of personal relationships.* New Brunswick, NJ: Rutgers University Press.

Ricci, I. (1985). Mediator's notebook: Reflections on promoting equal empowerment and entitlements for women. *Journal of Divorce, 8,* 49–61.

Rice, D. G. (1977). Psychotherapeutic treatment of narcissistic injury in marital separation and divorce. *Journal of Divorce, 1,* 119–128.

Rice, D. G. (1989). Marital therapy and the divorcing family. In M. R. Textor (Ed.), *The divorce and divorce therapy handbook.* Northvale, NJ: Aronson.

Rice, D. G., & Rice, J. K. (1986). Separation and divorce therapy. In N. S. Jacobson & A. S. Gurman (Eds.), *Clinical handbook of marital therapy.* New York: Guilford Press.

Rice, J. K., & Rice, D. G. (1986). *Living through divorce: A developmental approach in divorce therapy.* New York: Guilford Press.

Salts, C. J. (1985). Divorce stage theory and therapy: Therapeutic implications throughout the divorcing process. In D. H. Sprenkle (Ed.), *Divorce therapy.* New York: Haworth Press.

Scanzoni, J. (1972). *Sexual bargaining.* Englewood Cliffs, NJ: Prentice-Hall.

Shelton, J. L., & Ackerman, J. M. (1974). *Homework in counseling and psychotherapy.* Springfield, IL: Charles C Thomas.

Smith, M. J. (1976). *When I say no I feel guilty.* New York: Bantam Books.

Spanier, G. B., & Thompson, L. (1983). Relief and distress after marital separation. *Journal of Divorce, 7,* 31–49.

Spanier, G. B., & Thompson, L. (1984). *Parting: The aftermath of separation and divorce.* Beverly Hills, CA: Sage.

Sprenkle, D. H. (1989). The clinical practice of divorce therapy. In M. R. Textor (Ed.), *The divorce and divorce therapy handbook.* Northvale, NJ: Aronson.

Stampfl, T. G., & Levis, D. J. (1967). Essentials of implosive therapy: A learning theory based on psychodynamic behavioral therapy. *Journal of Abnormal Psychology, 72,* 496–503.

Storm, C. L., & Sprenkle, D. H. (1982). Individual treatment in divorce therapy: A critique of an assumption. *Journal of Divorce, 6,* 87–98.

Sutton, P. M., & Sprenkle, D. H. (1985). Criteria for a constructive divorce: Theory and research to guide the practitioner. In D. H. Sprenkle (Ed.), *Divorce therapy.* New York: Haworth Press.

Thibaut, J. W., & Kelley, H. H. (1959). *The social psychology of groups.* New York: Wiley.

Thoresen, C. E., & Mahoney, M. J. (1974). *Behavioral self-control.* New York: Holt, Rinehart & Winston.

Toomim, M. K. (1975). Structured separation for couples in conflict. In A. S. Gurman & D. G. Rice (Eds.), *Couples in conflict.* New York: Aronson.

Turner, N. W. (1985). Divorce: Dynamics of decision therapy. In D. H. Sprenkle (Ed.), *Divorce therapy.* New York: Haworth Press.

Walen, S. R., & Bass, B. A. (1986). Rational divorce counseling. *Journal of Rational-Emotive Therapy, 4,* 95–109.

Walen, S. R., DiGiuseppe, R., & Wessler, R. L. (1980). *A practitioner's guide to rational-emotive therapy.* New York: Oxford University Press.

Wallerstein, J. S., & Kelly, J. B. (1980). *Surviving the breakup: How children and parents cope with divorce.* New York: Basic Books.

Wanderer, Z., & Cabot, T. (1978). *Letting go.* New York: Warner Books.

Weiss, R. S. (1975). *Marital separation.* New York: Basic Books.

Weitzman, L. J. (1985). *The divorce revolution: The unexpected social and economic consequences for women and children in America.* New York: Free Press.

Whitaker, C. A., & Miller, M. S. (1971). Evaluation of "psychiatric" help when divorce impends. In J. Haley (Ed.), *Changing families: A family therapy reader.* New York: Grune & Stratton.

Wolpe, J. (1958). *Psychotherapy by reciprocal inhibition.* Stanford, CA: Stanford University Press.

Wolpe, J. (1969). *The practice of behavior therapy.* New York: Pergamon Press.

Wolpe, J., & Lazarus, A. A. (1966). *Behavior therapy techniques.* New York: Pergamon Press.

PROBLEM-FOCUSED INTERVENTIONS

12 CHAPTER

Treatment of Negative Self-Concept and Depression

Paula S. Nurius
Sharon B. Berlin

Take a moment to envision who comes to mind when you think of individuals struggling with a shaky personal identity or a wounded sense of self-worth and with the unhappiness and depression that stem from such injury. Were we to compare images that come to mind, we would notably see a remarkable diversity—reflecting, for example, the spectrum of populations and specific problem areas addressed in this book and more. The point in this exercise is to underscore that issues of self-concept are fundamental factors in social functioning and psychological adjustment. Self-concepts constitute a cornerstone in the foundation of individual well-being. At the same time, different self-concepts also accompany many different types of personal adversity and problems in living.

In this chapter we will examine the problem of depression, especially the contributions of self-concepts to depression. It is important to note at the outset that depression is not a unitary phenomenon. It can be experienced as a variation of normal mood, a symptom, or a cluster of cognitive, emotional, behavioral, and biological symptoms. Similarly, the causes of depression are varied and multiple (Beckham & Leber, 1985). Nonetheless, we assume that self-concept is implicated in all of the forms of depression as a cause, a consequence, or a contributing factor. Even in more severe disorders, which require pharmacologic treatment as the primary approach, self-concept is often a focus of accompanying psychotherapeutic intervention (Elkin, Parloff, Hadley, & Autry, 1989).

If we are to understand the issues of self-concept and depression, it is essential to look at both personal and environmental factors and at normative aspects of social life as well as what happens "when things go wrong." We will draw on recent theory and evidence about how human perception and reasoning relate to the development of the self-concept as a linchpin of social functioning in both adaptive ways (such as optimism) and maladaptive ways (such as depression). Focusing on notions of cognitive mediation, we will describe the information processing steps that people undertake in constructing an understanding about themselves and their world.

Because of the disproportionate representation of females within depressed populations, we will briefly examine the role of gender-related social messages in the evolution of a depressive self. Finally, we will identify the implications of these factors for assessment, intervention, and maintenance activities with problems of damaged self-concept and depression. Although we are focusing here on the role of self-concept in depression, we urge practitioners to take a broader view. Because distorted self-concepts interact with a variety of other factors in making up an individual's experience of depression, it is important to recognize that intervention may need to differentially focus on a range of biological, family, and social resources, as well as personal targets.

THE MEDIATIONAL MODEL: WHAT DOES IT REALLY MEAN?

So much has been written using the notion of "mediation" that it is not always clear exactly what it means or why a seemingly esoteric theoretical point may be important to the practitioner. Essentially, cognitive-emotional mediation refers to the influence of individuals' ways of attending, storing, interpreting, and remembering information on how they understand themselves and the world. As Heller and Swindle (1983) suggest, both distant experiences (childhood memories) and current experiences (work or school achievement) can be filtered through the "lens" of people's unique way of constructing concepts about themselves and their personal assets, deficits, and options.

This filtering is at the heart of the concept of mediation. As one kind of lens, or filtering mechanism, our self-conceptions tend to bias us in the direction of reconfirming what we already believe to be true about ourselves. Although the *content* of adaptive and maladaptive information processing responses varies widely, in most cases the very same cognitive and emotional *processes* govern both types of responses. To effectively assist clients in moving from a negative to a positive direction in their perception, reasoning, and reaction patterns, the practitioner must understand the relationships among cognitive-emotional content and processes and the experience of well-being.

What makes mediation more than a handy metaphor is the detailed (although by no means complete) level of understanding we now have about how information that is pulled together to make up the self-concept is structured and the processes through which this information operates. One key component in these operations is knowledge structures referred to as schemata. The term *schema* connotes a framework or diagram, and it conveys that the function of these structures is to guide the individual in searching for and collecting information consistent with existing specifications and then in constructing interpretations and responses, much as with a mental blueprint (Nurius, 1991; Taylor & Crocker, 1981).

Schemata about the self, therefore, serve as the frameworks within which attributes, images, feelings, and evaluations related to personal identity are recorded in memory and are then drawn on as individuals define, evaluate, and generate predictions about themselves as part of their ongoing functioning in the social world. As carriers of personalized knowledge, self-schemata have become an important link in research into both depression and optimism. Essentially, in both scenarios, different subsets of an individual's repertoire of self-schemata become dominant, and they subsequently fuel negative or positive information processing styles, respectively (Beck, Rush, Shaw, & Emery, 1979; Brown, 1986; Kuiper, Olinger, MacDonald, & Shaw, 1985).

Three major self-concept factors have been found to differentiate depressed from nondepressed persons (Segal, 1988). First is the availability of self-schemata—for example, the number and range of personal constructs stored in memory. Depressed people appear to amass numerous schemata biased in the direction of negativity that incline them to seek out information consistent with negative "knowns." The second factor is the accessibility of self-schemata—for example, the ease with which negative or positive self-schemata can be activated. A depressed mood tends to make negative schemata more likely to be activated, and they in turn reinforce the depressed mood, contributing to a vicious cycle. Third is the notion of a superordinate "depressed self" schema. This idea suggests that, for some, depression or devaluation becomes a core organizing feature of self-definition. In the case of the seriously depressed, many attributes of the self are linked to this core structure in memory and carry similarly negative self-appraisals ("I'm a bad mother." "I'm spineless." "No one could ever love me." "I'm fated to end up alone."). Because of the associative interconnections among these negative knowledge structures, once one of them is activated, associations to the whole network of negative self-schemata are increasingly likely.

DIFFERENT FACES OF DEPRESSION

At this point, let us contrast some examples of depression-inducing situations to illustrate how very differently these and related self-concept factors may look and operate across people and situations:

Tom was laid off from his job at the factory a year ago. Since then he has searched in vain for another job, occasionally finding a few days' work washing dishes, and now he is at risk of being evicted. He feels ashamed that he has had to turn to public assistance, and he believes that he has failed his family as a provider. He feels desperate that his financial situation is virtually out of control, and he is developing sleep and health problems.

Six months ago, Maria's mother, to whom she was very close, died rather suddenly. Then her oldest son was involved in a disabling accident, and she learned that her youngest child's problems in school are due to a learning disability. The special needs of her family have taken a toll on the family budget, and although they are not in serious trouble, it hurts Maria to see the many things her husband and children must do without.

Seven years ago, Brigit married and moved from her rural hometown. Her husband became increasingly abusive over the years, and as the abuse increased, her self-concept and self-esteem eroded. What began as doubts about her ability to be a good wife spread to doubts about her capacity to be a good mother, attractive to others, talented in the art work she cherishes, employable, or independent, and she now feels paralyzed.

Angela came from a poor family of color, but she was able to win a college scholarship based on her good grades. Her family had always encouraged her to pursue her goals and clearly accepted and was proud of her. Angela encountered financial and discriminatory barriers along the way. Yet she sustained an optimism that most problems could be dealt with, sought out mentors and assistance when needed, and persisted toward achieving the first college degree in her family as well as a fellowship for graduate school.

With assessment, we find that Tom's self-concept injury is relatively domain-specific; that is, he has experienced a serious challenge to his self-concept in the domain of work-related achievement. At this point, however, he retains positive self-conceptions in other domains: he sees himself as a caring father, a good athlete, and a contributor to his community (he continues his involvement with his church and the youth center). He has a rather large repertoire of positive self-schemata available to him overall. But one life domain (related to his employment and provider roles) has become negatively skewed in what tends to be activated and thereby dominant in that aspect of social functioning.

We find that Maria's challenges are also delimited, but in a different fashion. Her self-definition is buffeted by the experience of loss—loss of some of her own valued relationships and roles and empathic pain for others' losses. She is experiencing extreme sadness and can no longer access much of the sense of optimism and control over life events that she relied on in the past. Although she is having difficulty adjusting to the changes, she has not labeled these events personal failings and thus is not experiencing a direct erosion of positive self-conceptions. However, despite having a large repertoire of positive schemata that are potentially available, her current mood is biasing what is most accessible and what gets activated across several life domains in the thematic direction of loss and sadness. The result is that current and past experiences of loss and associated feelings of sadness dominate her awareness.

Brigit's self-concept injury has spread from the domain of marriage to virtually all other life domains. Her self-concept is overwhelmed by negativity. She has incorporated social messages that she is unworthy in multiple ways, that she is incapable of making significant changes alone, and that she has no real resources or alternatives. She shows signs of a superordinate depressive self-schema that operates across situations. This set of devaluing self-definitions and expectations serves to further elicit and reinforce negative social input and to further fuel negative self-evaluations.

Angela was also greatly influenced by social messages. She, too, increasingly incorporated these messages and progressively built on them—as did Brigit—but with very different outcomes. Here we can see how the *same* cognitive-emotional processes play a role in both adaptive and maladaptive outcomes. The *content* of social messages that Angela was receiving was very different from Brigit's. As did Brigit, Angela became increasingly resistant to messages that challenged her evolving self-concept and increasingly behaved in ways that communicated her expectations of herself and others, thus contributing to outcomes that confirmed her beliefs and expectations. Again, however, due to the differences in the *content* of Angela's self-schemata (abstracted from the messages she received) and subsequent beliefs and expectations, she was able to reject subsequent denigrating messages and to gravitate toward the more positive.

These examples illustrate a few of the varying ways that the self-concept mediates life events to influence mood and outlook—in both positive and negative directions.

The terms *self-concept* and *depression* are often applied in an overly general and ill-defined manner. In particular, clinicians refer to low self-concept as if it were a uniform phenomenon. This lack of clarity places the practitioner at risk of applying intervention techniques that are insufficiently tailored to the needs and goals of the particular client. We will be returning to Tom, Maria, Brigit, and Angela later in this chapter to illustrate practice implications of their respective self-concept functioning.

EVOLUTION OF A DEPRESSIVE SELF: THE SELF/SOCIAL INTERFACE

In this section we will first take a closer look at some of the key mechanisms through which personal variables and the social environment influence the self-concept and at how the self-concept subsequently influences response patterns and mental health outcomes. We will then examine gender as a vulnerability factor and the broader issue of social constraints on self-development and well-being.

The Self as Social Product but Also Social Force

Both as growing children and as evolving adults, we largely acquire, revise, and sustain a sense of self by looking at ourselves through the perspectives of those around us. These are the social messages we get regarding who we are, who we should be, and the relative "goodness" or "badness" of our attributes. The self-definitions that emerge from this input have to do with the selves we once were (for example, the fat kid who was never invited to play with the other kids), the selves we can and cannot become (for example, the developmentally disabled child who is urged not to reach very far because he can never be what others are), as well as the self we and others see ourselves as being at the moment.

This social shaping of self-definition, however, is far from a passive or one-way process. The individual is actively involved in the selection, recollection, interpretation, and evaluation of incoming messages. For most people, one characteristic of this filtering is a markedly self-enhancing bias, or an "illusory glow" that prompts us to see ourselves in better terms than others see us or than the circumstances may warrant and thus to maintain optimistic expectations (Greenwald, 1980; Lewinsohn, Mischel, Chaplin, & Barton, 1980). Specifically, considerable evidence suggests that overly positive self-evaluations, exaggerated perceptions of control or mastery, and unrealistic optimism are characteristic of normal human thought. These appear to promote other dimensions of mental health, including the ability to care about others, the ability to be happy or contented, and the ability to engage in productive and creative work (Taylor & Brown, 1988). In contrast, when depressed, we lose these illusions and become more "coldly realistic" in assessing our immediate capacities and others' views of us (Alloy & Abramson, 1982).

As the cognitive building blocks of the self-concept (Kihlstrom & Cantor, 1984), self-schemata are tenaciously resistant to altering what is "known" by the self. At times, as with being depressed or living in abusive relationships, the resistance involves prioritizing information that confirms a "known reality" at the expense of happiness and self-enhancement. If one has a very impoverished or limited set of ways to self-define, each self-schema becomes particularly precious for retaining a sense of self and of predictability in the world. Any identity, even a devalued one, provides existential security, behavioral guidance, and a form of linkage to the social environment. Given few identity options, commitment to each should be high despite its relative cultural worth (Thoits, 1983).

We now begin to see some very specific, powerful forces at work within the self-concept not only *reflecting* individuals' images of themselves but also vigilantly *protecting* that image (even if negative) and *projecting* it into the future by anticipating, seeking out, and eliciting from others information consistent with expectations. This self-confirmatory tendency also extends backward in time so that we *reconstruct* our recall and memories to be consistent with current beliefs (Riskind & Rholes, 1984).

Consider then how these normative features of the relationship between the self and the social environment may quite naturally (albeit maladaptively) contribute to the development and maintenance of a negative self-concept and depression once a "depressive set" has germinated. To explore further this risk, we will next address a number of gender-related factors as a vehicle for considering how relatively vulnerable, less societally powerful groups may become entrapped in vicious cycles.

Gender as a Vulnerability Factor

To date, women have been consistently found to report higher rates of depression than men (Weissman, 1987; Weissman & Klerman, 1977).* In cognitive-emotional terms, women and men reflect differences in *how* they go about defining a sense of self and what they

*There appears to be a variety of potentially interactive contributing factors to gender differences in depression. Some data suggest that women's higher rates of depression do not occur along the whole continuum of depression, but rather at the extreme, severe end of the spectrum (Golding, 1988) and at the mild, or simply sad, other end (Craig & Van Natta, 1979; Hammen, 1982; Newmann, 1987). Reviews of research exploring potential physiological bases of these differences have suggested that genetic transmission is unlikely to account for overrepresentation of women but that hormonal fluctuations that occur during postpartum recovery or the premenstrual period or as a result of oral contraception may contribute to women's higher rates (Hammen, 1982; Weissman & Klerman, 1977).

Sociodemographic factors—for example, younger age (18–44), single status, unemployment, and low levels of education and income are associated with higher rates of depression among both men and women. Most studies (Kaplan et al., 1987; Mirowsky & Ross, 1989) suggest that African-American racial status is not related to depression when socioeconomic status is controlled. However, Holzer and associates (1986) report that when age and socioeconomic status are controlled, women are still more than two times more likely to be depressed than men. Employed women are less depressed than women who work in the home (Mirowsky & Ross, 1989), but employed women are still more depressed than employed men. Depression levels are reduced among women whose husbands help with child care and housework (Kessler & McRae, 1982), but decision-making patterns remain a key factor. Using data obtained from 680 married couples, Mirowsky (1985) found that each spouse in the couple was the least depressed when decision making was more or less shared.

prioritize as self-relevant, rendering women more inherently at risk of a diminished sense of self and depression. We will address (1) the relative tendency of women to define themselves in terms of relationships *to and through others* and (2) the nature of social forces that *restrict* women's range of self-definitional *possibilities.*

Research related to societally held gender norms demonstrates that these social influences profoundly affect schema development and ongoing information processing. Similarly, socialization into a socially devalued female role contributes to women's greater vulnerability to depression (Bem, 1981; Cox & Radloff, 1984; Deaux & Major, 1987). Indeed, Kaplan (1986) suggests that depression among women may be an exaggeration of the normative state of being female in Western society.

Social ties have been found to be important to mental health for both men and women. Yet there is also evidence that *aspects* of social connectedness (or its loss) place women at greater risk. Because women tend to be more in touch with their feelings and to absorb the sadness of others' losses, they are likely to both feel and articulate sadness more than men. Although this level of sensitivity to feelings may be a risk factor for serious depression, it is not the same as depression and may be misconstrued by others (Newmann, 1987).

Stiver and Miller (1988) note that although sad feelings may be painful, they are much more adaptive than the sense of numbness, emptiness, and paralysis that often accompany depression. Moreover, Lerner (1983) reminds us that men and women both have dependency needs—needs for comfort, nurturing, and encouragement. But because women are often better at taking care of men than the converse, it sometimes seems that women are excessively dependent. If women are expressing more dependency needs than their male partners, it may simply be because their needs are not adequately met (Berlin, 1980).

Significant gender differences in role opportunities and experiences point to a "double whammy" for many women. That is, married women who do not work must typically draw on a smaller, less complex (less distinctly different), and less socially valued (low-status, socially isolated) set of roles in establishing personal identity and meaning. On the other hand, women who do work often experience gender-related stress and discrimination in the workplace, as well as more stress from role overload as they continue primary responsibility in the domestic sphere and often curtail career goals to accommodate domestic obligations (Gove, 1979; Thoits, 1986).

To sum up, for women and for all of us, social messages are manifest via "reflected appraisals" (images and evaluations of who we are and the worth of these characteristics reflected back to us from others) *and* the nature of social structures. As a final example, Ogilvie (1987) found that the amount of time actually spent in favored identities by late-middle-aged people accounted for three times as much variance in life satisfaction as that explained by health. This finding suggests that people whose options for living out key identities are restricted by ageism, racism, heterosexism, or other forms of role closure face a significant life-satisfaction risk. Clearly, then, the target of change does not reside in the heads and hearts of our clients alone.

ASSESSMENT: THE MULTIFACETED SELF VERSUS THE "TRUE" SELF

For purposes of assessment, we need to make a crucial set of distinctions regarding "the" self-concept. Frequently our vagueness in defining self-conceptions has handicapped our understanding of exactly *how* they influence people's psychological well-being and their efforts to cope and strive. This fuzzy understanding has also limited our effectiveness in intervening therapeutically.

In this section, we differentiate between the notion of a single, "true" self and self-image and the notion of a multifaceted self and multiple self-images that are variously activated according to the situation at hand. Although self-schemata resist change, their *relative* accessibility or momentary salience is quite fluid. Metaphorically, the self-concept is like a kaleidoscope in that the actual elements are not easily replaced but the interrelations among elements continuously reflect different patterns in response to turns of events.

There is an interesting paradox in self-concept functioning. We seldom truly "purge" schemata from our memory system (suggesting that we have a continuously growing set of self-conceptions amassed over a lifetime). Yet we are able to maintain only a few chunks of information in working memory at any one time (Anderson, 1983). How then can "the" self-concept, some enormous collection of separable pieces of information about oneself, concretely come into play in any given moment?

Essentially, it cannot. At any one point, only a partial set of self-schemata can be "on" in an information processing and social-functioning sense. This is not a random or haphazard set but one that reflects meaningful links between the demands of the situation and self-conceptions related to those cues. It is this subset that generates our phenomenological sense of self and influences mood, judgments, and behaviors in the moment (Markus & Kunda, 1986; Nurius & Markus, 1990).

The subset of selves that is active at any given moment is the working self-concept. In situations where we are interacting with our children, self-schemata that have to do with parenting, nurturance, and the topic of the moment are likely to be active. (When we are helping our 8-year-old with her math homework, we will be drawing on different specific aspects of parenting and topical knowledge than when we are talking with our aloof 16-year-old about drug use.) In situations where we are interacting with work colleagues, self-schemata that have to do with ourselves as competent (or incompetent), with ourselves as members of the organization or profession, and with the topic of the moment are likely to be active. (Participating in a clinical consultation will draw on different professional skills and topical knowledge than will an interorganization meeting to evaluate regional services.)

We may well "see" very different working self-concepts and self-presentations of the same individuals under these differing situations. One is not necessarily more "true" or real than the other. They simply reflect different facets of the individual's totality of social roles and attributes. This person-in-situation variability is illustrated in Figure 12.1. Consider Tom, the unemployed father we introduced earlier. We see a shift in the qualitative nature of his working self-concept related to work over time, but we can also see that working self-concepts associated with other life domains (as parent, athlete, and community member) do not reflect the depressive content of his work-related self-concept.

Contrast Tom's profile to that of Brigit. Over the course of seven years, negative self-schemata and associations among them have increasingly permeated multiple life domains for Brigit. To a large extent, her *repertoire* of self-conceptions in memory has become revised in a negative direction. She has a more fully elaborated depressive self. This means that depressive self-schemata are more likely to be activated in working memory, and she is consequently more likely to experience chronically negative self-evaluations, feelings, and expectations.

Maria also reports a near-pervasive sense of sadness. Yet her repertoire of self-conceptions contrasts markedly with that of Brigit. Maria has considerable self-concept resources

FIGURE 12.1   *Illustrations of Self-Concept Repertoires and Working Self-Concept Profiles of Two Clients*

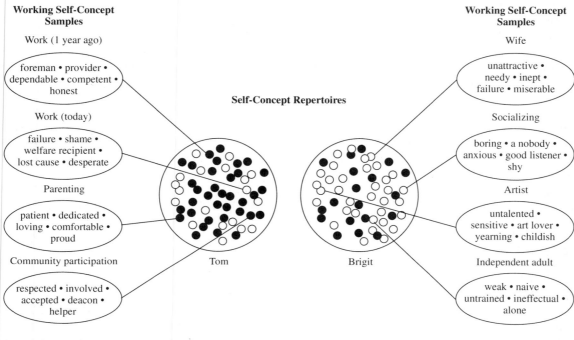

= Positive schemata

= Negative schemata

that are presently being underutilized. Because of the events in her and her family's lives, she is experiencing frequent activation of self-conceptions that are associated with sadness. Thus, a vicious circle ensues wherein her sad feelings activate sadness-related self-schemata that carry with them further symbols and memories of sadness. These, in turn, sustain the sad mood and make it difficult to activate alternatives that encompass other feelings and attributes (Brown & Taylor, 1986).

As we discussed earlier, sadness is certainly a component of depression. But people often experience sadness, even profound sadness, without necessarily developing the self-denigration, loss of perceived self-efficacy, and sense of hopelessness that tend to characterize depression. It may be that in these instances sadness is not linked to a sense of isolation and weakness. For most people, sadness is followed by mood-repairing thoughts and behaviors that help return them to their initial affective equilibrium (Isen, 1984; Salovey & Rodin, 1985). Moods, such as sadness, initially limit responses by making mood-*incongruent* schemata difficult to access. However, individuals with high self-complexity will probably experience less extreme swings in affect and self-esteem and more quickly regain equilibrium.

Many factors trigger memory and thus changes in the working self-concept. Things we hear, see, taste, smell, and feel (tactilely and emotionally) as well as our own thoughts trigger key memory nodes that then fan out, activating memory structures closely linked to them. Figure 12.2 depicts a simplified graphic of this effect. Recall the times that an "oldies" tune on the radio or a smell like

FIGURE 12.2   Triggering Memory Structures and Their Spreading Activation across Networks

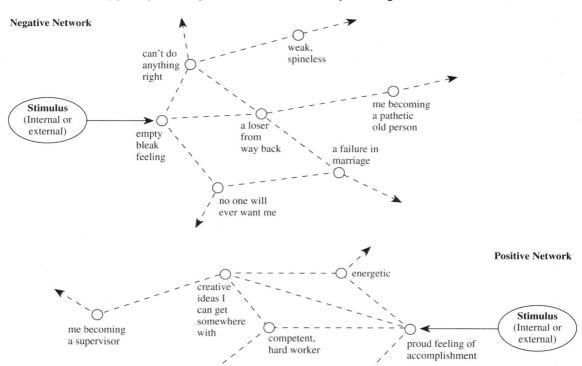

one's grandmother's house or the taste of a favorite childhood treat brought back a rush of nostalgia. Even among these more dormant memory structures, associations remain intact and automatically spread with extraordinary speed. So, too, as we see in Figure 12.2, do more current associations function in both positive and negative networks.

In this regard, feeling states do not influence social behaviors directly so much as they are linked to behaviors through cognitions about the self. For example, pronounced feeling states cause increased self-focus of attention and corresponding changes in cognitions about self that are most salient (working self-concept), which in turn influence social behaviors. These behaviors elicit covert and overt responses by oneself and others that

feed back to the prevailing feeling state and so forth in a cycle of functioning (Salovey & Rodin, 1985). We will discuss later in this chapter ways to interrupt maladaptive cycles and ways to introduce and strengthen adaptive cycles. At this point, let us consider assessment implications.

For assessment purposes we need information about several specific features of self-concept. Specifically, we need to know (1) what *kinds* of self-schemata constitute the working self-concepts that are most closely associated with the presenting problem, (2) what schemata are and are not available in the individual's larger self-concept *repertoire,* (3) what cues tend to *habitually* trigger certain sets of self-schemata from long-term memory into working memory, and (4) what cues are needed to recruit *alternative* self-conceptions in the circumstances when they are most needed yet are most difficult to access.

For example, we often see evidence that individuals may indeed have the necessary skills for effective performance and even have a schema of themselves as efficacious in a particular area of functioning ("I'm an assertive person in my work world"). Yet within certain high-risk situations, such as the presence of threatening people or tasks, the individual is unable to activate these self-conceptions, or recruit them into working memory. (Perhaps the person can work well except with certain individuals who closely resemble aggressors in a past trauma.) Thus, in terms of functioning in the moment, the images of themselves as efficacious and the skill guides for how to behave are not a part of the here-and-now working self-concept.

As we can begin to see, both cognitive-content factors (for example, range of self-schemata available and deficiencies or imbalances) and cognitive-process factors (for example, automatic triggering of certain schemata and associative networks that further reinforce schemata initially triggered) play important roles in individuals' prevailing self-concept and vulnerability to depression. Different combinations of these factors will be operating for different individuals, and different combinations raise implications for how we go about planning interventions. Is there a lack of certain types of self-schemata in the individual's available repertoire? Are certain self-schemata available from earlier history but underdeveloped due to limited or distant use? Are certain self-schemata available and used in some situations but not in problematic situations; for example, are they conceived as not being relevant to the problematic situations, or are they blocked by incongruent mood? Are the self-concept problems relatively limited in scope (for example, related to work achievement or to sexuality), or do they appear to have spread across many life domains?

Answers to questions such as these help determine which types and which sequence of interventions will be best suited to a client. We will discuss intervention methods later in the chapter. First, let us explore more fully some of the assessment factors noted above.

Qualitative Form of Self-Schemata

Schemata contain information in a variety of forms. Some information is semantic; it is stored in the form of language and word-based constructs (for example, descriptors such as "weak," "incompetent," "worthless," and "pathetic" or, conversely, "strong," "resilient," "confident," and "proud"). Other information in schemata includes images and other sensory input (aural, olfactory, tactile), emotions, kinesthetic representations and if/then procedural knowledge. The latter depicts the how-tos of manifesting or actualizing a given construct (for example, "*If* I see someone looking at me and smiling, I *then* interpret this as a constrained form of laughing at me *and* feel badly about their derisive judgments of me").

Clinically relevant maladaptive schemata tend to be well developed, typically in a negative direction, having become elaborated over a period of time. Due to the various forms that information can take, however, clients may have initial difficulty in putting words to the self-conceptions that make up their problematic working self-concepts. Therefore, various forms of assessment should be considered, such as describing or drawing an image or sensation, experiencing or expressing feelings, role playing and reverse role playing, and use of self-monitoring aids in relevant life situations.

There is a caution here. Whatever approaches to assessment we take, we run a considerable risk of imposing our own preconceptions on what we elicit from the client and what we make of the information the client gives us. By using multiple assessment tools and looking for convergence of data as well as data that may *disconfirm* our hunches, we are more likely to help the client learn to catch and change automatic assumptions and images of the self, and we are less likely to impose our own theoretical or social biases on the client.

Mindlessness and Self-Observation

The automatic nature of our typical information processing patterns is both a benefit and a bane. The expectation, assumption, and interpretation shortcuts on which we generally rely free us from the fatigue of constant vigilance. Yet for the person with problems of negative self-concept and depression, this "mindless," or relatively unaware, approach to perception, reasoning, and judgment contributes to the problems. Langer and her colleagues point out the difficulty of change when one is unaware of one's own cognitive and emotional processing patterns and the importance of "mindfulness," or greater awareness and deliberate choice, in changing patterns that have become ingrained (Langer, 1989; Langer & Piper, 1987). Thus, assessment is not something the clinician does to the client. Ideally, the client is fully involved in trying to identify her own patterns of self-definition—for example, when she's feeling depressed, when she's feeling hopeful, when she's working, when her husband says "You look terrific," when her child says "You don't know anything, Mom."

In attaining this goal, self-observation and monitoring tools, in a variety of forms, are useful. Here, the practitioner has multiple aims. The most obvious is to gain a more detailed and accurate picture of the social, cognitive, emotional, and behavioral interactions that characterize the client's typical or high-risk problem scenarios. Some of this picture can be captured in treatment sessions through efforts to reinstate these scenarios via enactment techniques such as role playing.

Because very different information (schemata) is activated in working memory at different times and situations, it is important to re-create as closely as possible the working self-concepts and subsequent interpretations and actions that are active during both problematic and well-functioning situations.

An additional aim is to aid clients in gaining better self-observational abilities. One of the biggest barriers to changing one's self-concept and to ending depression is loss of perspective. Thus, aids to support greater awareness of both vicious cycles and productive cycles (like the positive cycles we saw in Angela earlier in the chapter) go beyond serving assessment functions to serving intervention and maintenance functions. Particularly with serious and long-standing self-concept dysfunction, durable change takes considerable effort outside the boundaries of formal treatment sessions (Berlin, 1985). As Safran and Segal (1990) suggest, one of the basic steps in altering negative self-assessment patterns is catching oneself in the act of a negative, dysfunctional appraisal and realizing that it is more of a habit than a true assessment of who one is or has to be.

For purposes of assessment, self-observation tasks should initially be very specific. For example, rather than continuously or for arbitrary periods, clients should self-monitor during contexts or situations likely to fill important information gaps. In the case of Tom, this might mean contrasting thoughts and feelings in work-related contexts and in community-involvement contexts. Practitioners need to be aware that when they seek the most accurate statement of events possible, they should ask the client to *describe* what occurs. If practitioners seek a sample of biasing perception and interpretation processes, they should ask the client to *evaluate* or summarize what occurs (Hollon & Garber, 1988). In the first instance, we are asking clients to stay evidence- or data-driven. In the second, we are asking clients to be concept-driven, drawing on beliefs and understandings embedded within their schemata to generate meaning in what they observe.

Self-observation and monitoring assignments may ask clients to keep track of the antecedents, experiences, and results of operating out of one of several selves. The resultant data can then form the basis for future explorations between the practitioner and client about how the old self can be weakened and the new one strengthened. In the case of Brigit, a self-observation recording form might look something like this:

October 17, 1991

Weak, Incapable Self

Car broke down on the expressway as I was driving to the grocery store. Sat in the car for about an hour just staring into space and feeling totally defeated. Tried not to think. Wanted to keep my mind blank. But I had a few thoughts: "This is too much for me, the last straw." "What the hell am I supposed to do now?" "Big Jake's right. I just can't handle things on my own." "Why can other people handle their lives, but not me?" When I finally looked around I saw a phone a few yards ahead. I almost didn't want to see it because it meant I had to figure out something else—who to call. I finally figured out to call Margaret. She was sympathetic and looked in her phone book for numbers of gas stations and gave me some numbers.

"Why Me?" Self

Whenever any trouble comes up—like with the car or something going wrong in the apartment or with Jake—I feel overburdened and cheated. I find myself asking "Why do these things always happen to me?" and feel like I am the only one who has to face this stuff. I spend a lot of time asking "Why?" and never really figure out the answer.

Evolving "I Can Do It" Self

Followed your advice to talk with Little Jake's teacher about his school problems. Had to push and pull myself all the way to the school. Kept saying all the way "You can do

this." We had a good conversation. I was nervous but felt proud of myself anyway. Feeling lasted about 20 minutes until Big Jake came home in a nasty, critical mood. Then I got caught up in a spell of "Why me?" thinking.

With respect to the working self-concept, it is particularly important to know what stimuli serve as the key cues, or triggers, for activating some self-schemata rather than others. What are the patterns? What appear to be the associations among the schemata? (When one self-schema is activated, other schemata closely associated with it will have a higher likelihood of being activated than more distant conceptions.) What "sets" of self-schemata appear to clump together, and what is repeatedly absent? Knowing the cues and patterns of association is useful in three major ways. First, such knowledge allows clients to view their negative processing as a predictable pattern and thereby distance their conscious sense of self from it. Second, it allows them to analyze their response patterns, considering their original and current function. And finally, this knowledge allows them to plan for alternate ways to respond to the cues and alternative associative pathways to mindfully employ.

Underused Schema Resources in Memory

Earlier we distinguished between schemata that are available (that exist and are stored in long-term memory) but may be difficult to access and those that are highly accessible (that can be readily reached and drawn into working memory). Assessment needs to include discovering whether preferred, but currently inaccessible, schemata may exist as untapped resources. For instance, Tom and Maria have more underutilized self-schema resources than does Brigit. Although Brigit is unlikely to be totally without positive, healthy self-schemata, these may well be less developed and less influential than the presently more powerful negative schemata.

A variety of common assessment techniques can be used to locate schema resources. For example, a review of past roles, relationships, and activities, as well as dreams and goals, provides a basis for determining if alternative identities and self-conceptions were present in the past and may be available to build on. So a practitioner might ask: "What was it like for you then?" "Describe it for me." "What were the best times you had?" "What was your dream for yourself?" Reverse role playing or asking clients to brainstorm what another person could do in situations similar to theirs is another avenue. These methods may help tap general schemata about attributes or options that the person has considerable knowledge of but has not encoded as being *self*-descriptive. The practitioner might wonder, for example, "How was your best friend able to turn things around for herself—how did she do it?" Again, the presence of such schemata provides a potential foundation on which to build.

Ongoing Monitoring of Incremental Change

An additional form of assessment is more ongoing in nature. That is, over the course of treatment, we need to know how clients are progressing in light of specific changes that constitute their goals. We can observe this progress in terms of cognitive "products" such as their level of self-esteem, self-efficacy, initiative, response patterns, and persistence. These are important litmus tests of underlying change in the self-concept and depressive syndrome. However, they often do not reveal incremental shifts in underlying cognitive content (for example, changes in specific attributes and feelings making up key working self-concepts) or in the patterns of cognitive processes (for example, shifting from a more

mindless form of concept-driven processing to a more mindful form of evidence-driven processing).

Thus, it will be useful for the practitioner to help the client monitor these incremental content and process changes. A client might keep a journal in which to record shifts in her cognitive-emotional state: "Now I feel angry and cheated and I want to go my own way without the help of anyone." "Now I feel as if we all have to look out for one another and be more accepting of our feelings. If I expect to be looked after or cared about perfectly, I'll always be disappointed. I think I often wait for that to happen, instead of shaping things to go the way I want. I could do more shaping." As should be evident, monitoring change in self-concept is highly related to defining and pursing alternatives.

This monitoring goes hand in hand with intervention. In fact, it *is* intervention. In monitoring/constructing desired changes, it is important to consider and explicitly record several aspects of change. For example, do newer schemata include procedural information as well as semantic information? That is, can the client demonstrate an understanding of and an ability to carry out the "how-to" steps of actualizing the concept. (For example, a client may be able to describe the concepts of independence, self-respect, and strength, but does she have the know-how and capacity for manifesting these in her relationships and daily life?)

A related question is how routinized newer schemata appear to be. In other words, how easily can a client draw them into awareness (working memory)? Does the client appear to be developing more automatic response patterns based on the new, preferred schemata? When the client is feeling ambivalent, confused, or emotionally overwhelmed, does he appear able to shift into a mindful processing mode and either seek assistance or "talk himself" through more effective responding?

INTERVENTION: REVISING POSSIBILITIES, PATTERNS, AND PRODUCTS

At the beginning of this chapter we discussed the importance of understanding *normative* self-concept functioning as a base for understanding what is happening in *maladaptive* functioning. If, for example, we make a judgment that a co-worker is rather aggressively competitive and arrogant, we are likely to expect the person to try to "one-up" us in our next encounter. Moreover we are likely to fortify ourselves against him or her (perhaps taking offense as a best defense), thereby biasing the situation to *elicit* the very characteristics that we do not particularly care for but that would confirm our interpretation of this individual.

Depressed people will behave in a parallel fashion. For example, operating out of their "inept" and "boring" selves, they tend to limit efforts and to withdraw interest in others. They make more mistakes at work, miss more deadlines, and are more remote with friends. And, in fact, friends may begin to feel that it is a bit of a burden to spend time with them. Behaving in ways consistent with these perceptions, they elicit feedback suggesting that the perceptions are true. Such outcomes, even though possibly distorted, avoidable, or amenable to change, serve to confirm to them the reality base of their negative self-view, world view, and future view (Beck et al., 1979).

It is important to note here that the self-confirmatory nature of information processing is not only normal but also essential. Intervention needs to build on these normative processes. Three central targets of change are: (1) the scope of self-conceptions accessible for use—the goal being to broaden the repertoire, (2) the qualitative nature of the schemata that are active in key working self-concepts—the goal being to add ones that are self-enhancing, and (3) the regularity with which preferred schemata are activated and used in interpretation and responding—the goal being to promote use of the most constructive schemata and thereby to elaborate them and to make their retrieval automatic when needed (that is, to take advantage of self-confirmatory biases in positive directions). A number of other important targets are embedded within these three, such as influencing the role of the social environment in prompting and reinforcing preferred over problematic self-schemata and reducing opportunity barriers to the client's realistically pursuing preferred self-goals.

Obviously, the treatment of self-concept problems and depression is a complex and broad topic. Full-length books on the topic have been written for practitioners. Our goal here will not be to summarize what other sources adequately provide but to highlight some of the principle extensions that recent work on changing self-concept provides (see also Nurius, in press). For further reading in the treatment of depression and the self-concept, see Beck's now classic book (Beck et al., 1979) as well as Alloy (1989), Beckham and Leber (1985), Coyne et al. (1987), Goldfried and Robins (1983), Guidano and Liotti (1983), Hollon and Garber (1988), Ingram (1986), Mahoney (1991), Safran and Greenberg (1986), and Safran and Segal (1990).

Enhancing Scope through Developing Possibilities

In the assessment section, we discussed some means by which to assess self-schemata resources—for example, preferred identity structures that have remained relatively undeveloped or have languished as stronger maladaptive schemata outcompeted them for influence. We also discussed the inherent conservatism of the self-system, or the resistance of established self-schemata to change. Thus, the task of introducing and developing alternative self-conceptions must often be undertaken within an ambivalent psychological environment. Although clients desire alternative self-conceptions in line with their goals for change, realizing this desire often involves challenging long-standing sources of personal definition and a great deal of work to change equally long-standing habits of perception and response.

One aid in this process is the use of "possible selves" as a base on which to build. Possible selves are the selves we envision when we contemplate future directions—both those we wish for and strive toward and those we fear becoming and strive to move away from (Markus & Nurius, 1986; Nurius, 1991). Some possible selves are linked to present roles and events, such as Angela's future conceptions of finishing her degree, getting a good job, and serving as a mentor to younger women of color. Other possible selves are less extensions of the present than they are reflections of our personal hopes, fears, and symbols (the image of oneself "really making it big" or "becoming an abandoned and embittered bag lady").

Possible selves are powerful, in part because they are not refutable in the same ways that past and present selves are. Even if not "realistic," they remain as possibilities, as symbols of threat and hope. Consider for yourself the loss you would feel if you were absolutely forced to face the vast improbability of some privately cherished dream. Thus, positive possible selves can serve as powerful allies, and negative possible selves can operate as formidable barriers in the work of changing the self-concept.

There are two advantages to making clinical use of possible selves. One is that this technique provides a means of sidestepping some of the natural resistance to change within the self-concept. Clients have reported, for instance, finding the notion of a working self-concept useful in understanding how they could have such variations in self-image and still be "normal." They have found the notion of possible selves useful in accepting that something could be possible for them even though at an early point in treatment they could not "really see it" (Nurius, Lovell, & Edgar, 1988; Nurius & Majerus, 1988).

A second advantage is that possible selves are a part of the natural evolution of self-conceptions. That is, we typically begin new self-schemata in the form not of what already "is" but of something that we could become or are becoming. Thus, development of preferred self-schemata can be framed within the context of learning and normal development. In other words, imagining a desired state can be the first step in making it "true." The mental structures that are developed or accessed form at least a rudimentary alternative self-schema that can then be further established. For Tom, this type of imagining may involve constructing alternative images of what "being a good provider" could look like, depending on what work alternatives his environment and abilities support, perhaps building on existing strengths such as his athletic ability, teaching skills with youths, and community ties.

Particular care needs to be taken to at least begin to develop emotional associations and social supports for the emerging new schemata. This step allows us not only to envision and reflect on a new possibility but also to "feel" it—feel excited about it, enticed by the prospect, and proud of our first awkward steps toward it. Our own emotional investment in an evolving self is at least partly generated by the responses of significant other people. For example, it will matter to Tom—and his sense of possibility—whether his family sees and encourages his new vision of himself as a worker. It goes without saying that the response he receives from training programs and from the job market will also have a powerful influence on his sense of "I can do this."

Again, it is important to note the critical need for what we have called procedural information as a component of alternative self-schemata. Part of the problem is that some selves become richly elaborated with symbols, images, and affective and sensory associations but not with how-to, behavioral guidance. The net effect is that they flood the perceiver with powerful affect and motivation in the moment but do not provide the means/ends information about how to act—how to manifest that attribute or how to accomplish that activity (Linville & Clark, 1989; Markus, Cross, & Wurf, 1990).

For example, Brigit may have a powerful desire to be proud and independent. She may have encoded these goals with strong feelings, a definition of what these terms mean, images of other women who have these attributes, and a sense of an enormous gulf between them and herself. Even if she were able to adopt a greater belief in her ability to achieve these goals, unless she has encoded how-to, procedural information of *herself enacting* these goals, she will have few to no internally generated guides for how to manifest or achieve them. She is then vulnerable to having her response patterns governed more by other schemata (self as weak or ineffectual) or by external input (social messages and directives from others).

We will discuss some of the techniques for strengthening possible self-schemata in subsequent sections. An initial step to expanding the scope of possibility is to translate client goals into specific attributes, actions, and circumstances that are essential to accomplishing these goals. This step serves as a beginning point for elaborating the informational, evaluative, and emotional content needed to build up preferred self-schemata to be effectively competitive with more familiar but maladaptive schemata. Three factors must be stressed in this translation process:

1. For a schema to effectively influence habitual response patterns, it must be *self*-referent (specific images of *oneself* as competent rather than the general notion of what it means to be competent).
2. The broader the network of associations of the target schemata with other schemata,

the more likely it is that the target will be activated as part of an associative link. Thus, associating the target self-schema of competence with thoughts about core values such as responsibility, with affective states such as anxiety or pride, and with frequent events such as looking at one's watch will help to activate and integrate it with other aspects of the self.

3. Self-conceptions are social products, meaning that development of possible self-schemata must include their incorporation into the client's natural social transactions. Making new patterns competitive with older, more established patterns requires that changes initiated in the treatment session be progressively incorporated into daily life and be supported by ongoing interpersonal interactions and events.

At this point, let us turn our attention to what changes related to the above factors would look like within the working self-concept. Specifically, what qualitative changes would we be seeking in working self-concepts associated with *high-risk* or *high-need* circumstances?

Configurations in Key Working Self-Concepts

Given that working memory is extremely limited compared with long-term memory, it is essential that treatment work to bias the composition of currently active self-schemata in a positive direction. This work, of course, must be accompanied by efforts of the client and others to provide clear feedback and to reinforce this preferred configuration of schemata.

This need has long been understood, as reflected in clinical efforts to generate more positive self-statements, or "internal dialogue" (Arnkoff & Glass, 1982; Berlin, 1980). It is becoming clear, however, that a dual approach is needed wherein both the activation of positive schemata and the suppression or reconstruction of negative schemata are undertaken. Long-standing negative schemata for depressed people have become so "chunked," or condensed, that a far greater amount of information can be contained within a smaller cognitive work space than is the case with new, more rudimentary positive schemata. This means that of the "seven plus or minus two" bits of information that can be held in working memory, a very few long-standing negative self-schemata can threaten to overwhelm newer, more rudimentary positive self-schemata in part because of their relative density of information (autobiographical memories, feelings and evaluations, how-to procedural knowledge).

Even when clients have achieved a certain measure of success in consciously recruiting preferred schemata (for example, of themselves as worthy or as assertive), the practitioner should be aware that habitual, competing negative schemata may also be active within the same working self-concept of the moment. This results in a mixed, or ambiguous, working self-concept, which can contribute to an experiential sense of confusion or inauthenticity in the moment—for example, "I know it intellectually, but not emotionally." Thus, it is important to forewarn clients both of the natural resistance to change that they may experience (even to change they greatly desire), and of the importance of persevering through periods of change that feel unnatural and contrived.

It is important to note that changing the self-concept is rarely a clean, linear progression. In an intensive analysis of how depressed women accomplished cognitive-emotional change in therapy, Berlin, Mann, and Grossman (1991) found that a recycling back through the steps of change was typical. For example, getting and *keeping* distance from dysfunctional appraisals was an ongoing struggle, and the ability to step back and "disembody" appeared to be a distinguishing attribute of those with successful outcomes.

The buildup of cleaner and more elaborated alternative appraisals was gradual and was facilitated when slips or setbacks were used as opportunities to analyze existing pulls and to generate more vivid alternative appraisals that took these obstacles to change into account. One aid to weakening the dominance of negative schemata is simply to "witness" them without following the procedural guides or investing in them as true (Marlott & Gordon, 1985). "Just because you hear the music doesn't mean you have to get up and dance."

An additional important technique for revising working self-concept compositions is an extension of the tool of self-monitoring that we introduced under assessment. Rather than merely observing and articulating observed patterns, we would now aid the client to consciously *activate* and operationalize preferred schemata. The use of memory aids like mnemonics will help to activate clusters of information. For example, Brigit may develop a mnemonic using a symbolic term like *strong* to encapsulate the self-conception cluster of "Self-sufficient, Tenacious, Resilient, Open to change, Now-focused, and Gutsy." During treatment, each of these self-conceptions would be defined in terms of their instrumental value for her goals; would be elaborated in terms of what they mean and look like and how they are attained; and would be analyzed in terms of how her relevant social environment poses resources or barriers to change.

In essence, restructuring of schemata requires (1) recognition of the pitfalls inherent in the old self-identities and their associated emotions and action implications, (2) formulation of more constructive possible selves, and (3) repeated encounters with information that possible selves really are possible and information that fills out and elaborates these alternative conceptualizations. The information that strengthens and develops the new perspectives comes from multiple sources: experiences of emotions, reflections, behavioral feedback, and the reactions of others. It is the practitioner's job to arrange encounters with new information—for example, to mobilize family support; to teach skills that will make effective behavior possible; to focus clients on experiencing, tolerating, and reframing uncomfortable emotions; and to encourage them to look for, find, and use opportunities to "exercise" the new self.

Even though we started out by saying that similar cognitive processes can support both negative and positive conceptions of oneself, what we are beginning to see here is revision of habitual cognitive *processes* as a vehicle for revision of habitual cognitive structures or content. Such self-concept revisions generally require taking clients through a period of mindful awareness of their processing habits and options, with greater reliance on therapeutic questioning of the accuracy and utility of the ways in which they are sizing things up and experimenting with alternative constructions or actions. For example, we might ask Brigit to use the well-known technique of pairing negative arousal (body tension, anxiety) or stimulus (interactions with people who undermine her) with active coping. Part of this coping could include a set of self-questions to help challenge negative inferential leaps and to reorient attention and interpretation ("What is the evidence for this interpretation?" "If I were advising my friend Susan, in what other ways would I suggest she look at it?" "Even if this interpretation is true, are the implications necessarily what they seem to be?") (Hollon & Garber, 1988, p. 236). Eventually, Brigit may view her negative self-concepts as "ways I sometimes think" but not as "the core of who I am."

In summary, we are describing means by which to revise the repertoire of self-knowledge that is available to draw on, to improve the accessibility and activation of preferred self-schemata, and to revise the questions that one poses to oneself and others in "making sense" of oneself in the moment. This process pertains particularly to those conditions assessed as being high risks for negative working self-concepts and for those situations most likely to support desired change. The next set of concerns involves making these fledgling self-schemata more routinized (more automatic and natural) as well as more competitive in a meaning-making sense. We address these concerns next.

Frequency and Practice as Linchpins

As we will emphasize again in our discussion of maintenance, *durable* change in one's self-concept is difficult to accomplish. We emphasize the word *durable* because too often efforts to change self-concept have suffered from being relatively ill-defined and focusing on temporary self-*esteem* relief. These changes tend to erode quickly once the supports of treatment are withdrawn, leaving the client with little to no real change in *self-concept* or diminishment of vulnerability to depression.

Although such change is by no means simple, two factors appear absolutely pivotal. These are *frequent* activation of preferred or possible self-schemata and *focus* within these practice efforts (Ashcroft, 1989; Linville & Clark, 1989). The power of frequent and focused practice involves both direct and indirect effects. For example, increased frequency of activation directly strengthens neurological pathways, making them far more likely to be used than less frequently activated cognitive structures. In fact, *lack* of use is one way in which self-schemata can become more remote in memory and become more difficult to access even though they still exist. Indirect effects of frequency of activation come through the greater degree of elaboration (for example, more numerous and more detailed autobiographical memories and how-to understandings) that result when new experiences are assimilated into existing schemata.

In short, to be functionally effective, self-conceptions must move beyond the level of general values, goals, and philosophy to take concrete and detailed form and be used as a moment-to-moment guide in the individual's daily life. Once again, we see the crucial role of the social environment in augmenting the individual's own efforts to cue, elaborate, and validate alternative, preferred self-schemata. In this regard, group therapy or support groups are often beneficial, serving as a social microcosm to provide needed feedback and validation as well as the opportunity to try out and to practice possible selves. Because feedback from the environment is often vague, subtle, or delayed, potentially supportive people (family members, friends, co-workers, group members) should be advised and helped to provide focused feedback that is immediate, specific, visible, and constructive.

A key to fostering focus in practice is to make rehearsal efforts as relevant as possible. That is, rather than merely memorizing information related to a new schema through simple repetition (as one might a new phone number), the client needs several conditions to enhance relevance. These include (1) simulating the conditions that characterize the target situations under which the preferred self-schemata are most needed (for example, when feeling angry or confronted with challenge); (2) self-reflection during the process of practice (for example, drawing meaning associations, noticing what forms resistance to change take, or developing personal mnemonics); and (3) deliberate use of multiple mediums of representation (for example, the use of visualization and modeling to create vivid pictures and symbols of possible selves, or attention to bodily states to encode sensory states to provide new concepts with emotional meaning).

An additional function of frequent and focused practice is building up the if/then interpretation and action chains of preferred self-schemata. Some find it odd to think of a self-*image* in terms of a skill. Yet, without an understanding of how to incorporate an image or conception into one's "real life" and both the perceived and actual ability to go about being or doing what is envisioned, these images amount to little more than wishes. In building these if/then links, the practitioner should remember that specific chains tend to be more readily activated than are abstract, broad ones. Thus, new procedural rules to support a change in the self-concept will be most effective if, initially, they are limited in scope and undertaken as task- or domain-specific. For example, rather than "*If* I feel threatened, *then* I'll be assertive," a chain such as "*If* I feel anxious about my ability to make it as a returning student, *then* I'll use that feeling as a reminder to recall my '*strong*' mnemonic *and* visualize myself contending with the task or challenge using each of these attributes *and* consult a trusted support person or my journal to help me feel positive and confident" will be more likely to be recalled and to provide the kind of cognitive, emotional, behavioral, and social supports needed in the moment.

Finally, we would like to revisit the importance of what has been referred to as self-complexity. This trait has to do both with the number of distinct self-conceptions one has available within a readily accessible repertoire and the variety of types of self-conceptions. For example, Pietromonaco (1985) argues that depressed people are highly attuned to the affective nature of information and rely heavily on it to understand and organize thoughts of themselves. Thus, relative to nondepressed people, they are hindered in making distinctions among messages about themselves or of producing a varied or multiaspect self-structure. Further, Linville (1985) found self-complexity to be a significant moderating variable of depression and a buffer against the affective consequences of failure and of life crisis. That is, people with high self-complexity or numerous ways of defining the self were found more likely to be able to contain the negative impact and to maintain positive affect stemming from aspects of their life not directly associated with the crisis.

In summary, a limited range of present and positive selves places the individual at risk.

This is not to say that more is necessarily better. One can spread oneself too thin with numerous and conflicting role and relationship obligations. However, social forces often serve to define and constrain role options along lines that benefit the existing social structure. Therefore, although goals for changing self-concept in the context of clinical practice must typically begin with a focus on remediating the client's social and psychological problems in living, an overarching goal of social work is fostering options and well-being in broader terms. Thus, we will turn next to maintenance and support of client empowerment via self-help.

MAINTAINING AND EXTENDING THERAPEUTIC GAINS

We have been explicit about a collaborative orientation in work with clients. For people like Brigit, stable, durable changes will take some time to solidify. Due to constraints on cost, time, and resources, much of this work will probably need to take place outside of a formal helping arrangement. Consequently, within the context of community-based groups and ongoing self-help efforts, client understanding and training in self-concept management and change are important components of treatment.

The self-monitoring aids that had their initial role in assessment continue to play an important role in the ongoing self-observational and self-management needs of maintaining gains and contending with slips and setbacks (Marlatt & Gordon, 1985). A long-term challenge for the seriously depressed is to resist impulses toward persistent self-focus (chronic thinking about and evaluation of oneself) and orientation toward affective information to the near exclusion of other aspects of information (for example, focusing on good/bad self-judgments and not on the relative diffi-

culty of the task, impediments, one's degree of preparation, or the experiences of others). Self-monitoring aids, self-management skills (for example, using "slips" as cues to invoke self-corrective routines and mindfulness of neglected information), and proactive efforts toward environmental intervention (for example, negotiating for specific kinds of feedback, support, or change) will be important in sustaining change efforts and gains.

We have focused on means by which to influence the self-concept as one clinical target within this interactive model. In addition to this coping and adjustment framework, we also need to look at change within the context of contributing problems. Part of the educational orientation we have prescribed includes efforts to help individuals not simply adapt to or accommodate a flawed environment but recognize the connections between social messages and self-definition, between damaged self-definition and depression, and between depression and passive reinforcement of the social conditions that were at the core of this set of chain reactions.

CONCLUSION

Hobfoll and Walfisch (1984) have referred to self-concept and social support as "first lines of defense" against the negative psychological and health consequences of life stressors. Thus, these keys to well-being and social functioning are likely to be relevant to a wide sweep of specific presenting problems that the practitioner will encounter. Our focus has been on cognitive-emotional analysis of interaction between the self-concept and social forces and on the relationship of self-concept functioning to depression. Our goal has been to supplement existing approaches to treatment of depression, with explicit attention to specifying person/environment links to one's self-concept and to examining empowerment-oriented treatment approaches, both of which typify the perspective of social work and other helping professions.

In conclusion, the self-concept can be thought of as the lens through which virtually all our information processing about matters of personal significance is construed. This is not to minimize the multiplicity of factors that greatly influence people's lives. Nor is it to say that we are necessarily "correct" in our self-perceptions. The central point is that accurate or not, rational or not, the self-concept serves as an important arbiter and interpreter of these personal and environmental factors, thus shaping our construction of reality and our perceived place and options within it.

Depression is supported by particular ways of constructing reality—of finding personal meaning. In intervening with depression, it is important to move from an overly general focus on improving "the" self-concept to assessing a range of schema resources and then differentially intervening to augment positive possible selves (with practice and focus) at the expense of negative counterparts. We have argued that our evolving knowledge base affords us increasingly clear and well-supported definitions and directives regarding "the self"—how it evolves, how it functions both positively and negatively, and how to bring about constructive change. Part of the challenge for today's practitioner is to energize and engage clients in their own process of self-change. For all of us, but particularly for the seriously depressed, revising the bedrock of self-concept is both dismaying and yet exciting, both an arduous and yet a potentially revitalizing undertaking.

REFERENCES

Alloy, L. B. (Ed.). (1989). *Cognitive processes in depression.* New York: Guilford Press.

Alloy, L. B., & Abramson, L. Y. (1982). Learned helplessness, depression, and the illusion of control. *Journal of Personality and Social Psychology, 42,* 1114–1126.

Anderson, J. R. (1983). *The architecture of cognition.* Cambridge, MA: Harvard University Press.

Arnkoff, D. B., & Glass, C. R. (1982). Clinical cognitive constructs: Examination, evaluation, and elaboration. In P. C. Kendall (Ed.), *Advances in cognitive-behavioral research and therapy* (Vol. 1). New York: Academic Press.

Ashcroft, M. H. (1989). *Human memory and cognition.* Glenview, IL: Scott, Foresman.

Beck, A. T., Rush, A. J., Shaw, B. F., & Emery, G. (1979). *Cognitive therapy of depression.* New York: Guilford Press.

Beckham, E. E., & Leber, W. R. (Eds.). (1985). *Handbook of depression: Treatment, assessment, and research.* Pacific Grove, CA: Brooks/Cole.

Bem, S. (1981). Gender schema theory: A cognitive account of sex typing. *Psychological Review, 88,* 354–364.

Berlin, S. B. (1980). Cognitive-behavior intervention for problems of self-criticism among women. *Social Work Research and Abstracts, 16,* 19–28.

Berlin, S. B. (1985). Maintaining reduced levels of self-criticism through relapse prevention treatment. *Social Work Research and Abstracts, 21,* 21–33.

Berlin, S. B., Mann, K. B., & Grossman, S. F. (1991). Task analysis of cognitive therapy for depression. *Social Work Research and Abstracts, 27,* 3–11.

Brown, J. D. (1986). Evaluations of self and others: Self-enhancement biases in social judgments. *Social Cognition, 4,* 353–376.

Brown, J. D., & Taylor, S. E. (1986). Affect and the processing of personal information: Evidence for mood-activated self-schemata. *Journal of Experimental Social Psychology, 22,* 436–452.

Cox, S., & Radloff, L. S. (1984). Depression in relation to sex roles: Learned susceptibility and precipitating factors. In C. S. Widom (Ed.), *Sex roles and psychopathology.* New York: Plenum.

Coyne, J. C., Kessler, R. C., Tal, M., Turnbull, J., Wortman, C. B., & Greden, J. F. (1987). Living with a depressed person. *Journal of Consulting and Clinical Psychology, 55,* 347–352.

Craig, T. J., & Van Natta, P. A. (1979). Influence of demographic characteristics on two measures of depressive symptoms: The relation of prevalence and persistence of symptoms with sex, age, education and marital status. *Archives of General Psychiatry, 36,* 149–154.

Deaux, K., & Major, B. (1987). Putting gender into context: An interactive model of gender-related behavior. *Psychological Review, 94,* 369–389.

Elkin, I., Parloff, M. B., Hadley, S. W., & Autry, J. H. (1989). NIMH treatment of depression collaborative research program: Background and research plan. *Archives of General Psychiatry, 42,* 305–316.

Goldfried, M. R., & Robins, D. (1983). Self-schemata, cognitive bias, and the processing of therapeutic experiences. In P. C. Kendall (Ed.), *Advances in cognitive-behavioral research and therapy.* New York: Academic Press.

Golding, J. M. (1988). Gender differences in depressive symptoms: Statistical considerations. *Psychology of Women Quarterly, 12,* 61–74.

Gove, W. (1979). Sex differences in the epidemiology of mental disorder: Evidence and explanations. In E. Bumberg & V. Franks (Eds.), *Gender and disordered behavior: Sex differences in psychopathology.* New York: Brunner/Mazel.

Greenwald, A. G. (1980). The totalitarian ego: Fabrication and revision of personal history. *American Psychologist, 35,* 603–618.

Guidano, V. F., & Liotti, G. (1983). *Cognitive processes and emotional disorders: A structural approach to psychotherapy.* New York: Guilford Press.

Hammen, C. L. (1982). Gender and depression. In I. Al Issa (Ed.), *Gender and psychopathology.* New York: Academic Press.

Heller, K., & Swindle, R. W. (1983). Social networks, perceived social support, and coping with stress. In R. D. Felner, L. A. Jason, J. N. Moritsugu, & S. S. Farber (Eds.), *Prevention psychology: Theory, research, and practice.* New York: Pergamon Press.

Hobfoll, S. E., & Walfisch, S. (1984). Coping with a threat to life: A longitudinal study of self-concept, social support, and psychological distress. *American Journal of Community Psychology, 12,* 87–100.

Hollon, S. D., & Garber, J. (1988). Cognitive therapy. In L. Y. Abramson (Ed.), *Social cognition and clinical psychology.* New York: Guilford Press.

Holzer, C. E., Shea, B. M., Swanson, J. W., Leaf, P. J., Myers, J. K., George, L., Weissman, M. M., & Bednarski, P. (1986). The increased risk for specific psychiatric disorders among persons of low socioeconomic status. *American Journal of Social Psychiatry, 6,* 259–271.

Ingram, R. E. (Ed.). (1986). *Information processing approaches to clinical psychology.* New York: Academic Press.

Isen, A. M. (1984). Toward understanding the role of affect in cognition. In R. S. Wyer & T. K. Srull (Eds.), *Handbook of social cognition* (Vol. 3). Hillsdale, NJ: Erlbaum.

Kaplan, A. G. (1986). The "self-in-relation": Implications for depression in women. *Psychotherapy, 23,* 234–242.

Kaplan, A. G., Roberts, R. E., Camacho, T. C., & Coyne, J. C. (1987). Psychosocial predictors of depression: Prospective evidence from the Human Population Laboratory Studies. *American Journal of Epidemiology, 125,* 206–220.

Kessler, R. C., & McCrae, J. A. (1982). The effect of wives' employment on the mental health of married men and women. *American Sociological Review, 47,* 216–227.

Kihlstrom, J. F., & Cantor, N. (1984). Mental representations of the self. In L. Berkowitz (Ed.), *Advances in experimental social psychology* (Vol. 17). New York: Academic Press.

Kuiper, N. A., Olinger, L. J., MacDonald, M. R., & Shaw, B. F. (1985). Self-schema processing of depressed and nondepressed content: The effects of vulnerability to depression. *Social Cognition, 3,* 77–93.

Langer, E. J. (1989). *Mindfulness.* Reading, MA: Addison-Wesley.

Langer, E. J., & Piper, A. I. (1987). The prevention of mindlessness. *Journal of Personality and Social Psychology, 53,* 280–287.

Lerner, H. E. (1983). Female dependency in context: Some theoretical and technical considerations. *American Journal of Orthopsychiatry, 53,* 697–705.

Lewinsohn, P. M., Mischel, W., Chaplin, W., & Barton, R. (1980). Social competence and depression: The role of illusory self-perceptions. *Journal of Abnormal Psychology, 90,* 213–219.

Linville, P. W. (1985). Self-complexity and affective extremity: Don't put all of your eggs in one cognitive basket. *Social Cognition, 3,* 94–120.

Linville, P. W., & Clark, L. F. (1989). Can production systems cope with coping? *Social Cognition, 7,* 195–236.

Mahoney, M. J. (1991). *Human change processes: The scientific foundations of psychotherapy.* New York: Basic Books.

Markus, H., Cross, S., & Wurf, E. (1990). The role of the self-system in competence. In R. J. Steinberg & J. Kolligian, Jr. (Eds.), *Competence considered.* New Haven, CT: Yale University Press.

Markus, H., & Kunda, Z. (1986). Stability and malleability of the self-concept. *Journal of Personality and Social Psychology, 51,* 858–866.

Markus, H., & Nurius, P. S. (1986). Possible selves. *American Psychologist, 41,* 954–969.

Marlatt, G. A., & Gordon, J. R. (1985). *Relapse prevention: Maintenance strategies in the treatment of addictive behaviors.* New York: Guilford Press.

Mirowsky, J. (1985). Depression and marital power: An equity model. *American Journal of Sociology, 91,* 557–592.

Mirowsky, J., & Ross, C. E. (Eds.). (1989). *Social causes of psychological distress.* New York: Aldine de Gruyter.

Newmann, J. P. (1987). Gender differences in vulnerability to depression. *Social Service Review, 61,* 447–468.

Nurius, P. S. (1991). Possible selves and social support: Social cognitive resources for coping and striving. In J. Howard & P. Collero (Eds.), *The self-society dynamic: Cognition, emotion, and action.* New York: Cambridge University Press.

Nurius, P. S. (in press). Guidelines from the memory system. *Social Work.*

Nurius, P. S., Lovell, M., & Edgar, M. (1988). Self-appraisals of abusive parents: A contextual approach to study and treatment. *Journal of Interpersonal Violence, 3,* 458–470.

Nurius, P. S., & Majerus, D. (1988). Rethinking the self in self-talk: A theoretical note and case example. *Journal of Social and Clinical Psychology, 6,* 335–345.

Nurius, P. S., & Markus, H. (1990). Situational variability in the self-concept: Appraisals, expectancies, and asymmetries. *Journal of Social and Clinical Psychology, 9,* 316–333.

Ogilvie, D. M. (1987). Life satisfaction and identity structure in late middle-aged men and women. *Psychology and Aging, 2,* 217–224.

Pietromonaco, P. R. (1985). The influence of affect on self-perception in depression. *Social Cognition, 3,* 121–134.

Riskind, J. H., & Rholes, W. S. (1984). Cognitive accessibility and the capacity of cognitions to predict future depression: A theoretical note. *Cognitive Therapy and Research, 8,* 1–12.

Safran, J. D., & Greenberg, L. S. (1986). Hot cognition and psychotherapy process: An information processing/ecological approach. In P. C. Kendall (Ed.), *Advances in cognitive-behavioral research and therapy.* New York: Academic Press.

Safran, J. D., & Segal, Z. V. (Eds.). (1990). *Interpersonal process in cognitive therapy.* New York: Basic Books.

Salovey, L., & Rodin, J. (1985). Cognitions about the self: Connecting feeling states to social behavior. In P. Shaver (Ed.), *Self, situations, and social behavior: Review of personality and social psychology* (Vol. 6). Beverly Hills, CA: Sage.

Segal, Z. V. (1988). Appraisal of the self-schema construct in cognitive models of depression. *Psychological Bulletin, 103,* 147–162.

Stiver, I. P., & Miller, J. B. (1988). *From depression to sadness in women's psychotherapy.* Work in progress, Stone Center of Developmental Services and Studies, Wellesley College, Wellesley, MA.

Taylor, S. E., & Brown, J. D. (1988). Illusion and well-being: A social psychological perspective on mental health. *Psychological Bulletin, 103,* 193–210.

Taylor, S. E., & Crocker, J. (1981). Schematic bases of social information processing. In E. P. Higgins, P. Herman, & M. Zanna (Eds.), *Social cognition.* Hillsdale, NJ: Erlbaum.

Thoits, P. A. (1983). Multiple identities and psychological well-being: A reformulation and test of the social isolation hypothesis. *American Sociological Review, 48,* 174–187.

Thoits, P. A. (1986). Multiple identities: Examining gender and marital status differences in distress. *American Sociological Review, 51,* 259–272.

Weissman, M. M. (1987). Advances in psychiatric epidemiology: Risks and rates for major depression. *American Journal of Public Health, 77,* 445–451.

Weissman, M. M., & Klerman, G. L. (1977). Sex differences and the epidemiology of depression. *Archives of General Psychiatry, 34,* 98–111.

Treatment of Clients with Anxiety Disorders

Bruce A. Thyer
Pamela Birsinger

It is torture to fear what you cannot overcome.

—Anacharsis

This chapter contains an overview of the behavioral treatment of clients suffering from one or more of the anxiety disorders, as defined in the *Diagnostic and Statistical Manual of Mental Disorders* (DSM-III-R) (American Psychiatric Association, 1987). This is a highly significant area of clinical practice, inasmuch as the general category of anxiety disorders is the most prevalent class of so-called mental illnesses in the United States (Robins & Regier, 1991). It is more common than either alcohol abuse or depression, two conditions once thought to occur more frequently. The anxiety disorders should thus not be considered a "minor" problem. Recent studies have shown that certain of these conditions can lead to virtually complete incapacitation (for example, obsessive/compulsive disorder, agoraphobia) and that others, such as panic disorder, are strongly associated with suicide (Coryell, Noyes, & House, 1986). Clearly these are not trivial disorders.

The diagnostic terminology employed in this chapter, such as referring to specific anxiety disorders, does not imply acceptance of the hypothesis that the clinical phenomena being referred to have an existence as independent disease states or disorders that clients "have." It is recognized that "anxiety" itself has not been shown to exist, apart from the bodily states and client reports from which the existence of anxiousness is inferred, and any implication of reification is not intended by the authors and should be avoided by the reader. As noted in the DSM-III-R itself, we should state that clients meet the criteria for panic disorder (and so on) rather than saying that clients have or suffer from panic disorder. Nevertheless, it is the conventional practice to refer to these labels as things, and as long as we keep in mind that what are being referred to are hypothetical constructs rather than actual illnesses in a biological sense, scientific rigor will not be compromised in the service of facile communication.

At present the DSM-III-R outlines diagnostic criteria for 16 distinct anxiety disorders, only 3 of which are said to primarily occur among children or adolescents (see Table 13.1). This level of specificity in delineating among the anxiety disorders is remarkable, considering that the DSM-II (published in 1968) contained criteria for only three such disorders, anxiety neurosis, phobic neurosis, and obsessive/compulsive neurosis. Of course, the clinical phenomenology of the anxiety disorders has not appreciably changed, and the actual numbers of truly differing conditions is not growing larger. Rather, what we are seeing is the result of increasingly detailed empirical inquiry, which enables clinicians and researchers to distinguish among heretofore undifferentiated conditions based (at least partially) on *data,* as opposed to informal observations or theoretical speculations.

A few further changes appear likely for the

TABLE 13.1 DSM-III-R Categories for the Anxiety Disorders*

Anxiety Disorders

Panic disorder with agoraphobia (Barlow & Cerny, 1988)

Panic disorder without agoraphobia (Barlow & Cerny, 1988)

Agoraphobia without history of panic disorder (Marks, 1987)

Social phobia (Leitenberg, 1990; Mattick et al., 1989)

Simple phobia (Marks, 1987; Thyer, 1987)

Obsessive/compulsive disorder (Steketee, 1992)

Posttraumatic stress disorder (Keane et al., 1989)

Generalized anxiety disorder (Power et al., 1989)

Anxiety disorder not otherwise specified

Anxiety Disorders of Childhood or Adolescence

Separation anxiety disorder (Thyer & Sowers-Hoag, 1988)

Avoidant disorder of childhood or adolescence (Prinz, 1990)

Overanxious disorder (Kane & Kendall, 1989; Strauss, 1988)

Other Anxiety Disorders

Dream anxiety disorder (Kellerman, 1980)

Sleep terror disorder (Lask, 1988)

Organic anxiety disorder

Psychoactive substance anxiety disorder

---

*NOTE: From *Diagnostic and Statistical Manual of Mental Disorders* (3rd ed. rev.) by the American Psychiatric Association, 1987, Washington, DC: Author.

forthcoming DSM-IV, and these are noted in Table 13.2. The condition of simple phobia is proposed to be changed to *specific phobia,* dream anxiety disorder is proposed to be called *nightmare disorder,* and organic anxiety disorder is proposed to be called *substance-induced anxiety disorder,* all being more descriptively accurate phrases. Two new diagnoses have been proposed for the DSM-IV, *mixed anxiety-depressive disorder* and *sec-*

TABLE 13.2 Proposed Changes in the DSM-IV Anxiety Disorder Categories*

Anxiety Disorders

Specific phobia (formerly simple phobia)

Mixed anxiety-depressive disorder (new)

Secondary anxiety disorder due to a nonpsychiatric medical condition (new)

Substance-induced (intoxication/withdrawal) anxiety disorder (formerly organic anxiety disorder)

Nightmare disorder (formerly dream anxiety disorder)

---

*NOTE: From *DSM-IV Options Book: Work in Progress* by the Task Force on DSM-IV, 1991, Washington, DC: American Psychiatric Association.

ondary anxiety disorder due to a nonpsychiatric medication condition (see Task Force on DSM-IV, 1991). The former is intended to fill the clinically observed gap of an appropriate diagnosis for persons presenting with features of both depression and anxiety concurrently but who seem subthreshold for either disorder in isolation. The latter is to take into account persons with a biological condition (for example, hyperthyroidism, pheochromocytoma) that has a significant symptom profile characterized by anxious feelings.

Space does not permit a detailed description of these conditions, but the reader is referred to a number of books that contain rich clinical material in additional to competent presentations of the formal diagnostic criteria for each of the anxiety disorders (Babior & Goldman, 1990; Spitzer, Gibbon, Skodol, Williams, & First, 1989; Steketee, 1992; Steketee & White, 1990; Thyer, 1987b).

THERAPEUTIC GUIDELINES AND KEY METHODS

The clinician working with persons who meet the criteria for one or more of the anxiety disorders should be aware of the following facts:

- Behavioral and cognitive-behavioral therapies have been shown to be treatments of choice for virtually all of the anxiety disorders.
- Virtually no empirical evidence supports the use of psychodynamic therapy and its variants in the treatment of clinically anxious clients.

It is incumbent upon each practitioner practicing with clinically anxious clients to acquire expertise in providing behavioral and cognitive-behavioral therapy. In our opinion, not to do so or to provide clinical services that lack evidence of effectiveness represents an evasion of professional responsibility and may constitute a violation of the principles of ethical practice.

A thorough review of the diverse approaches to behavioral practice appropriate to each of the 16 anxiety disorders listed in Table 13.1 is clearly not a feasible undertaking in a chapter. In fact, a complete book devoted to the subject would be an inadequate treatment, and we are now seeing the emergence of entire books devoted to a review of behavioral treatment methods for single disorders. Among some of the finer examples of this trend are the recent texts by Steketee (1992), Barlow and Cerny (1988), and Leitenberg (1990), respectively dealing with obsessive/compulsive disorder, panic disorder, and social phobia.

What we have done is to provide the interested reader with citations to one or more recent, clinically relevant, and empirically oriented articles that describe the use of various behavioral methods to treat the specific conditions listed in Table 13.1. These citations are found in parentheses next to most of the listed disorders and can be followed up by the reader interested in learning about the treatment of various conditions in greater detail than can be provided in this chapter. In the final section we also provide information about organizations that focus on clinical research and training in this area.

A number of highly specific intervention techniques have been shown to be useful in the treatment of clients with one or more of the anxiety disorders. We will review several of these in the next section, followed by the presentation of a case history describing the treatment of a woman with agoraphobia and of a practitioner's efforts to evaluate the results of the treatment program.

APPLICATION OF TECHNIQUES

In the 1950s some preliminary analyses suggested that the technique called systematic desensitization (SD), developed by a South African psychiatrist, Joseph Wolpe, was extremely effective in helping clients with pathological anxiety and in treating some other selected problems (see Wolpe, 1958, 1973, for reviews of this literature). During the 1960s, a growing number of increasingly sophisticated and well-controlled studies replicated the findings of Wolpe's preliminary analyses, essentially confirming that SD was a very useful treatment. In fact, SD became the first psychosocial treatment subjected to well-controlled clinical trials that produced favorable outcomes. This wonderful news was followed by further searching inquiry into the precise therapeutic mechanisms responsible for the effectiveness of SD. Was it the relaxation training component? Was it having the client compose a hierarchy of fear-evoking situations and imagining confronting these situations? Was it the graded hierarchy of increasingly frightening scenarios? Was it the pairing of being deeply relaxed while imagining these scenes? Was it the real-life homework that Wolpe assigned clients after they had successfully confronted feared stimuli in imagination? To make a very long story short, it transpired that the critical ingredient to the success of SD was the ability of the procedure to persuade the client to confront phobic situations in real life and to remain there (with support) until calm (Sherman, 1972). Thus, during the 1970s and 1980s the focus of behavior therapy for clients with an anxiety disorder shifted from SD to the more parsimonious approach labeled exposure therapy (ET), described below. (The following section is taken from Thyer, 1987b, p. 41–46.)

Exposure Therapy

During the initial evaluation sessions, the practitioner should ensure that the client meets the prerequisites for exposure therapy listed in Box 13.1. Time should be spent engaging the client in a therapeutic alliance characterized by the usual conditions associated with all good clinical practice, such as empathy, warmth, and genuineness. Before embarking on a program of behavior therapy, it is often helpful to make available a number of self-help books for the client to read. Highly recommended ones include Marks (1978), Babior and Goldman (1990), and Steketee and White (1990). Such "bibliotherapy" serves several useful purposes. First, it provides reassurance to clients, above and beyond the clinician's own efforts, that they are not alone in suffering from "crazy" fears. Second, such books contain numerous true examples of people who have successfully overcome similar fears. Third, such books go into greater detail regarding the rationale for ET than the practitioner with a heavy caseload may have time to initially explain. Such books should *not* be construed as an adequate substitute for a thorough review and discussion of ET with a client but as a useful adjunct for the client to review at leisure, away from the consulting room. Fourth, clients can share the information and case histories provided in these self-help books with their spouses, friends, and other loved ones, saying, in effect, "See, I am not the only one with this problem, and since these people overcame it, with your help I can too!"

Next the practitioner engages the client in stimulus mapping, isolating the critical ingredients of the client's unique anxiety-evoking stimuli (AES). This is essential for planning the actual steps of therapeutic exposure. People are individuals, and not all phobics are alike. One dog phobic is terrified of being bitten, whereas another abhors the sensation of

---

BOX 13.1 Prerequisites for the Use of Exposure Therapy

1. The client meets the DSM-III-R criteria for one or more anxiety disorders.
2. Specific anxiety-evoking stimuli or situations can be clearly identified, and it is possible to recreate these in some manner (direct exposure, audio or videotapes, pictures, books, physical sensations, saying or doing certain things).
3. The client is committed to working hard to overcome the anxiety disorder.
4. The practitioner and client can jointly plan a projected program of graduated exposure to the identified anxiety-evoking stimuli, working from lesser to more frightening situations.
5. Exposure to the client's anxiety-evoking stimuli does not involve any appreciable element of realistic danger.
6. The client is willing, with or without a support person, to confront mildly anxiety-evoking situations and to maintain this contact until anxiety subsides.
7. The client is not under the influence of alcohol or other psychoactive drugs during treatment sessions. (Selected antipanic medications may be an exception to this rule.)
8. The client does not have any medical condition that precludes experiencing moderate levels of anxiety.

being licked, and yet a third shudders at the sound of a dog's bark. The so-called speech phobic may be found to be quite comfortable when addressing children or inferiors at work, whereas another may do best with large audiences and not small, intimate ones. The clinician needs to approach each client as an individual, without preconceived notions of how treatment should proceed. Clients should be asked about any circumstances in which they are *less* afraid and about those situations that provoke maximum panic. Through a series of skillful questions the practitioner can eventually construct, in writing, a hierarchy of graduated tasks or circumstances involving potential exposure to the client's AES. You should review this list with the client to ascertain that your understanding of the specific things your client is afraid of is indeed accurate and that the situations are listed in the correct order of their fear-evoking potential.

The next step is for the clinician and client to agree where, on this list of AES, treatment should begin. Traditional systematic desensitization began with the lowest item on the client's hierarchy of fear-evoking cues. In ET it is best to allow the clients to make this choice, suggesting that they try to challenge themselves moderately at the onset of treatment. Clients should never be expected or forced to approach or to encounter AES at a level of demand or at a rate faster than they consent to. Note, however, that clients need *not* be comfortable and relaxed, only that they give their consent to a more difficult level of encounter. It is not atypical for well-motivated clients, with tears in their eyes, to move resolutely closer to a frightening AES (dog, snake, and the like). In general, the more anxiety clients are willing to tolerate during treatment sessions, the faster they will overcome their fears. Tedious plodding through a hierarchy of AES, either in fantasy or in real life, *will* eventually produce a satisfactory result in that the client's fears will dissipate, but the financial cost to the client will be correspond-

ingly greater, not to mention the additional expense in time and energy.

One should proceed in a step-by-step manner in order to arrive at an agreement on where to begin with the first treatment session. The following dialogue is reconstructed from a preliminary session with a woman suffering from a severe fear of snakes:

Therapist: Would you be willing to begin next week by looking at a caged foot-long snake from 15 feet away?

Client: No!

T: How about from 30 feet away?

C: No! I don't want to look at any snakes!

T: Would you be willing to look at a toy rubber snake from 15 feet away?

C: No! No rubber snakes either!

T: All right, how about a small photograph of a snake?

C: No, I can't stand to look at pictures of snakes either. I make my husband cut them out of our magazines before I read them.

T: OK, would you be willing to look at a realistic drawing of a snake?

C: No, I still think that would be too difficult for me to begin with.

T: How about if we used a cartoon of a snake, one from the Sunday comics?

C: No, that would be too frightening too.

T: Suppose I covered up the cartoon of the snake with a piece of cardboard, so that you could only see one-eighth of an inch of the snake's tail? I could cover it all up then if you asked me to.

C: Well . . . I suppose I could try that, but only if you promise me not to make me look at the whole thing all at once.

Bingo! That is where we began treatment. After prolonged exposure to increasing bits of snake cartoon, we moved to more realistic drawings of snakes, photographs, nature movies of snakes (at first greatly blurred and then brought slowly into focus), toy snakes, and then the real things borrowed from a cooperative pet store owner. At the end of 12 sessions of about 90 minutes each, she was comfortably catching live snakes I had hidden in the grass for her to find.

Obviously, clients may be somewhat dubious at embarking on a course of exposure therapy. The following reassurances are often helpful:

- "There will be no tricks or surprises. I will always ask for and obtain your permission before introducing a new level of exposure."
- "At any time you may ask me to temporarily remove the anxiety-evoking stimulus (or for us to leave the situation). I *will do so immediately* upon your firm request."
- "You can terminate our session anytime you wish."

After giving these reassurances, point out to clients that in actuality *they* have control over the treatment session and that they do not have to do anything they strongly do not wish to attempt. At this point, most clients will be willing to attempt at least a single session with you.

Here are two other points to take into account when planning these initial treatment sessions: First, *long sessions are better than short ones.* By long we mean sessions on the order of two or more hours. As a general rule one makes more progress the longer one engages in prolonged exposure; hence, clients have a greater sense of progress and satisfaction after a long session than after a short one. Because their improvements are quite marked from session to session, their motivation to continue is increased. Second, if ET is likely to be of benefit to a client, *marked improvements are usually noted within the first few sessions.* Thus, the skeptical client is quickly won over. There are few things that the anxious person finds as satisfying as comfortably encountering an animal, object, or situation that filled him or her with dread only a session or two before. If little progress is evident after three or four sessions, however, this is a sign for the practitioner to reconsider the adequacy of the stimulus-mapping

procedure or to consider employing an alternative approach.

The above is but a brief sketch of beginning a program of exposure therapy with an anxious client. More detailed accounts can be found in a number of other publications (Himle & Thyer, 1989; Marks, 1978, 1987; Thyer, 1981, 1983, 1984, 1985, 1987b; Thyer & Curtis, 1983; Thyer & Stocks, 1986). As summarized in Marks (1987), real-life therapeutic exposure is a treatment technique of proven efficacy for patients meeting the criteria for panic disorder (with or without agoraphobia), agoraphobia without panic disorder, simple or social phobia, obsessive/compulsive disorder, and posttraumatic stress disorder (including rape victims and combat veterans). Preliminary studies also suggest its useful role in the treatment of separation anxiety disorder, dream anxiety disorder, and avoidant disorder. Clearly, this is an extremely important treatment procedure for the clinician to become familiar with and to acquire some expertise in conducting. A supervised clinical experience under the tutelage of a mental health professional skilled in the conduct of exposure therapy would be an appropriate vehicle for this training. The annual convention of the Association for Advancement of Behavior Therapy usually provides at least one day-long didactic workshop on various aspects of the technique.

It is important that therapeutic exposure be carried out not only in real life but also within the natural contexts of phobic situations (Thyer, 1984). After all, most clients are not afraid of *imaginary* snakes, dogs, panic attacks, or contamination but of their real-life counterparts. Accordingly, treatment conducted in naturalistic contexts is more likely to result in improvements that will be maintained and generalized by the client in actual phobic circumstances. As a general rule, therapeutic exposure to anxiety-evoking stimuli in *fantasy* or through *visualization* is primarily indicated if it is not possible to reproduce the client's AES in real life, if time constraints preclude arranging such sessions, or if the client is simply unwilling to tolerate initial exposure sessions in real life. Other clinical examples of AES that may be impossible to reproduce in real life include thunderstorms, lightning, panic attacks, speeches before large gatherings, professional musical performances, or transatlantic flights.

Breathing Training

An approach that has been shown to be effective in treating clients experiencing panic attacks is training in proper breathing techniques. Barlow and Cerny (1988) have produced an excellent clinician's manual detailing a comprehensive treatment program for the panic-stricken patient, which includes detailed instructions on this procedure. Babior and Goldman (1990) provide a corresponding self-help manual intended for client use, which we believe would also be quite helpful in its portrayal of breathing techniques (Birsinger, 1991). Breathing training has become increasingly evident as an important component of treatment for persons with panic disorder, because it now appears that chronic hyperventilation may account for the experience of spontaneous panic attacks (Ley, 1985).

Relaxation Training

Structured training in various aspects of relaxation appears to be a useful treatment approach for clients meeting the criteria for generalized anxiety disorder (Power, Jerrom, Simpson, Mitchell, & Swanson, 1989), but its role in the treatment of persons with other anxiety disorders remains largely unproven. This is a difficult finding for many clinicians to accept, given the apparently natural match between an anxious client and the technique of relaxation training. Nevertheless, contemporary empirical research suggests that relaxation training is a treatment of choice for GAD but that it is *not* a first-choice treatment for persons meeting the criteria for other disorders. To provide relaxation training alone or as an initial treatment for persons meeting the criteria for agoraphobia, panic disorder, simple or social phobia, obsessive/compulsive disorder, or posttraumatic stress disorder would not appear to constitute appropriate care in most instances. Counterintuitive though it may seem, relaxation training does *not* seem to add to the efficacy of exposure therapy. Barlow and Cerny (1988) do include this approach as a component of a comprehensive program for panic disorder, involving patient education, ET, breathing training, so-called cognitive restructuring, and relaxation training, and it may well have a useful role in such circumstances.

In the following section we describe the initial two months of treatment provided to a middle-aged woman with agoraphobia, along with the therapist's attempts at evaluating the treatment program provided to this client.

CASE EXAMPLE

Mrs. Dorsett, at age 44, met the DSM-III-R criteria for panic disorder with agoraphobia. Her panic attacks began when she was 24 years old, and avoidance behaviors related to her fears of having a panic attack and of ultimately going crazy had progressed to the point at which she had quit her job. She was able to leave her house and to travel short distances from home but experienced severe anticipatory anxiety when doing so. She had learned that if she became severely anxious while away from home, these feelings would often abate if she returned to the comforts of her familiar dwelling. She was referred to one of the authors (Pam Birsinger) by a psychiatrist who felt that the client would benefit from some therapist-assisted exposure therapy.

During the initial assessment visits, Mrs. Dorsett completed the Clinical Anxiety Scale (CAS) (Westhuis & Thyer, 1989), a rapid assessment instrument that is both reliable and valid in ascertaining severe anxiousness. Her score on her first administration of the CAS was 37, well above the recommended cutting score of 30 as reflective of a problem with clinical anxiety. She was also asked to begin keeping daily records of the frequency, circumstances, and duration of her panic attacks and was taught to distinguish among phobic anxiety, panic attacks, anticipatory anxiety, and generalized anxiety. This was accomplished didactically with the therapist and through the reading assignments completed by the client. The CAS was administered about every other week.

Treatment had two components. First, a psychoeducational aspect was conducted in the consulting room over two sessions. It concerned the nature of panic attacks, how agoraphobia develops, and the use of diaphragmatic breathing techniques to prevent or abort actual panic attacks. Mrs. Dorsett was asked to read two self-help books, *Living with Fear* (Marks, 1978) and *Overcoming Panic Attacks* (Babior & Goldman, 1990), between sessions, and she discussed the books' contents with the therapist. These sessions also covered the planned program of exposure therapy. The second element of treatment involved nine weekly sessions during which Mrs. Dorsett accompanied the therapist to anxiety-evoking situations, in this case, a large department store. After entering the store with the therapist, she was asked to rate her level of anxiety using a 10-point subjective scale, with 10 being severe panic and 0 being completely relaxed. She was asked to go to those parts of the store that were most frightening (for example, in the back away from the exit) and while accompanied by the therapist to remain in that setting until she was calm. The therapist assisted her through verbal reassurance, prompting in breathing techniques, general support and praise, the selective use of humor, and (initially) the use of distraction techniques to divert her attention from feelings of panic. She was, of course, fully aware that she could terminate these individual sessions at any time, and no other methods besides those outlined above were employed to get her to remain in the store.

During these exposure sessions Mrs. Dorsett was asked to periodically report her anxiety levels (1–10 scale), and the therapist noted the length of time it took for her reported level of fear to decline to a relatively tolerable point (defined by the client as a rating of 4 or lower). Her weekly CAS scores and the length of time it took for her anxiety to be appreciably reduced during each session of exposure therapy served as the outcome measures for the purposes of evaluating the effects of treatment.

These two measures are depicted in Figures 13.1 and 13.2. As can be seen in Figure 13.1, during the first session it took Mrs. Dorsett approximately 55 minutes to become comfortable. Ordinarily, of course, she would have left the store immediately upon becoming highly anxious. It took her about 45 minutes in session 2, 36 minutes in session 3, almost no time in session 4, and about 20 minutes in session 5. Four sessions followed in which she became comfortable immediately. Not only did it seem that she was experiencing less fear during these sessions, but clinically it was evident that she was indeed learning that fear can be mastered and overcome, rather than letting it dominate her actions.

Mrs. Dorsett completed the CAS twice before beginning exposure therapy and four times during the succeeding seven weeks. Her baseline scores were 37 and 35 (Figure 13.2), well above the 30 reflective of clinical anxiety. After exposure therapy began, her scores declined to below 30 and remained there for four consecutive sessions.

These structured client reports, the lengths of time it took for her to become comfortable, and her CAS scores corroborated the thera-

FIGURE 13.1   Length of Time it Took Mrs. Dorsett to Become Comfortable in the Phobic Situation

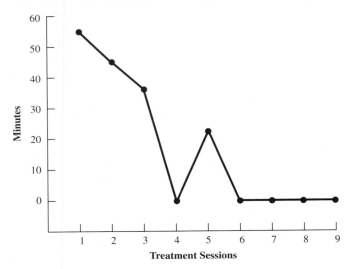

pist's clinical impressions of the obvious improvements achieved by Mrs. Dorsett. These data indicated that the treatment approach was indeed a useful one, and they provided both the therapist and the client with useful feedback throughout the course of treatment.

In between therapist-assisted exposure sessions Mrs. Dorsett was asked to revisit the site of these sessions and practice her newly developing skills in overcoming fear on her own. Her husband was also recruited to provide some assistance in such sessions, and he proved to be of great help. He read the self-help books and accompanied his wife and the therapist during several treatment sessions so that he could subsequently provide similar help in circumstances without the therapist's presence. This case study illustrates the benefits of utilizing empirically supported research findings in the selection of a program of treatment and the subsequent use of single-subject research designs in the self-evaluation

FIGURE 13.2   Mrs. Dorsett's Clinical Anxiety Scale Score Before and During Exposure Therapy

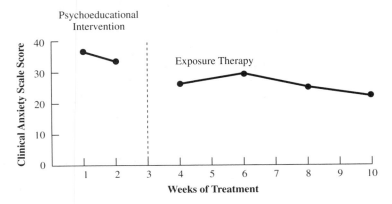

BOX 13.2   *Organizations Focusing on Clinical Research, Practice, and Training in the Field of Anxiety Disorders*

Association for Advancement of Behavior Therapy
15 West 36th Street
New York, NY 10018
(212) 279-7970

Activities: journals, newsletter, annual bibliography of articles on anxiety disorders, membership directory of therapists focusing on the anxiety disorders, informational brochures, annual convention

Obsessive Compulsive Foundation, Inc.
P.O. Box 9573
New Haven, CT 06535
(203) 772-0565
Activities: newsletter, therapist directory, informational brochures

Anxiety Disorders Association of America
6000 Executive Boulevard, Suite 200
Rockville, MD 20852-4004
(301) 231-9350
Activities: newsletter, informational brochures, therapist directory, annual convention

of one's own clinical practice. This example of empirical self-evaluation is becoming increasingly accepted as a component of responsible and ethical practice within the helping professions. See Thyer (1992a) for a further discussion of this methodology.

SOME FURTHER CONSIDERATIONS

A number of professional associations and professional journals have been established that specialize in the field of anxiety disorders. The three major organizations in this area are listed in Box 13.2, and the three major journals are presented in Box 13.3. The Anxiety Disorders Association of America is composed of both professional members and persons who suffer from an anxiety disorder. At the annual ADAA convention, practitioners, researchers, and persons with anxiety disorders give presentations covering a wide array of topics, ranging from behavioral or medical research on the nature of anxiety to workshops on promoting self-help groups for agoraphobics. The ADAA sponsors the *Journal of Anxiety Disorders,* a quarterly publica-

BOX 13.3   *Journals Specializing in the Field of Anxiety Disorders*

Journal of Anxiety Disorders
Cynthia G. Last, Co-Editor
Nova University, Department of Psychology
3111 University Drive, Suite 307
Coral Springs, FL 33065

Anxiety Research
Irwin G. Sarason, Co-Editor
Department of Psychology

University of Washington
Seattle, WA 98195

Behaviour Research and Therapy
S. Rachman, Editor
Department of Psychology
University of British Columbia
Vancouver, B.C.
Canada

tion that primarily publishes empirical clinical research with an applied focus.

The Obsessive Compulsive Foundation (OCF) is a national, nonprofit group composed of persons with obsessive/compulsive disorder, their families and friends, and professionals active in the field. The OCF promotes educational activities related to this disorder, provides information and referral services, and publishes an excellent newsletter.

The Association for Advancement of Behavior Therapy (AABT) is an interdisciplinary professional group of behavioral and cognitive-behavioral therapists, most of whom possess doctorates in psychology, social work, education, or medicine. The AABT has a phobia special-interest group that produces an annual bibliography (with abstracts) of articles related to the anxiety disorders and published in professional journals. It conducts an annual convention that serves as the forum for many papers and clinical training workshops related to helping anxious persons, and it publishes *Behavior Therapy* and *Behavioral Assessment,* journals that frequently contain articles pertaining to the anxiety disorders.

Practitioners treating clinically anxious persons should consider joining one or more of these professional associations and reading these journals on a regular basis in order to remain abreast of developments in the field.

CONCLUSION

Although the focus in this chapter has been on individual therapy provided one-on-one with an anxious client, the therapeutic value of support and treatment groups should not be overlooked (Thyer, 1987a). Each of the authors has had experience in facilitating such groups, and we have found them to be of immense value. In keeping with the general theme of behavioral practice—namely, empiricism—we are pleased to note that such group-therapy programs have been shown in well-controlled studies to be of significant benefit (Watson, Mullett, & Pillay, 1973). Couples therapy has also been shown to be helpful where the focus is on patient and spousal education and exposure therapy, but not directly on any presumed marital pathology per se (Cerny, Barlow, Craske, & Himadi, 1987). There is no evidence to suggest that marital dysfunction can be construed as *generally* responsible for a client's experience of any anxiety disorder, although in selected cases assessment may reveal that such is the case.

The distinction is often made in our field between so-called cognitive or cognitive-behavioral therapy and conventional behavior therapy. We believe that this distinction is of little value and actually divisive (Thyer, 1992b). According to contemporary formulations, including those of B. F. Skinner since 1938, the term *behavior* refers to what a person *does,* regardless of whether the behavior is publicly observable or not. In Skinner's radical behaviorism, everything the person does is considered to be behavior, amenable to scientific analysis, empirical inquiry, and clinical intervention, whether the issue is overt action; subjective feelings; or thoughts, cognitions, or self-statements. To separate cognitive-behavioral therapy from behavior therapy implies, erroneously, that behavior therapy does not encompass efforts at intervention with cognitive variables. (See Thyer, 1991, for a further discussion.) We support the terms *behavior therapy* or *applied behavior analysis* as the more comprehensive and descriptively accurate labels for all those approaches to treatment derived from social learning theory.

REFERENCES

American Psychiatric Association. (1987). *Diagnostic and statistical manual of mental disorders* (3rd ed. rev.). Washington, DC: Author.

Babior, S., & Goldman, C. (1990). *Overcoming panic attacks.* Minneapolis: CompCare.

Barlow, D. H., & Cerny, J. A. (1988). *Psychological treatment of panic.* New York: Guilford Press.

Birsinger, P. (1991). A review of *Overcoming panic attacks. Research on Social Work Practice, 1,* 441–442.

Cerny, J. A., Barlow, D. H., Craske, M. G., & Himadi, W. G. (1987). Couples treatment of agoraphobia: A two-year follow-up. *Behavior Therapy, 18,* 401–415.

Coryell, W., Noyes, R., & House, J. D. (1986). Mortality among outpatients with anxiety disorders. *American Journal of Psychiatry, 143,* 508–510.

Himle, J., & Thyer, B. A. (1989). Clinical social work and obsessive compulsive disorder: A single-subject investigation. *Behavior Modification, 13,* 459–470.

Kane, M. T., & Kendall, P. C. (1989). Anxiety disorders in children: A multiple-baseline evaluation of a cognitive-behavioral treatment. *Behavior Therapy, 20,* 499–508.

Keane, T. M., Fairbank, J. A., Caddell, J. M., & Zimering, R. T. (1989). Implosive (flooding) therapy reduces symptoms of PTSD in Vietnam combat veterans. *Behavior Therapy, 20,* 245–260.

Kellerman, J. (1980). Rapid treatment of nocturnal anxiety in children. *Journal of Behavior Therapy and Experimental Psychiatry, 11,* 9–11.

Lask, B. (1988). Novel and non-toxic treatment for night terrors (letter). *British Medical Journal, 297,* 592.

Leitenberg, H. (Ed.). (1990). *Handbook of social and evaluative anxiety.* New York: Plenum.

Ley, R. (1985). Blood, breath, and fears: A hyperventilation theory of panic attacks and agoraphobia. *Clinical Psychology Review, 5,* 271–285.

Marks, I. M. (1978). *Living with fear.* New York: McGraw-Hill.

Marks, I. M. (1987). *Fears, phobias, and rituals.* New York: Oxford University Press.

Mattick, R. P., Peters, L., & Clarke, J. C. (1989). Exposure and cognitive restructuring for social phobia: A controlled study. *Behavior Therapy, 20,* 3–23.

Power, K. G., Jerrom, D. W. A., Simpson, R. J., Mitchell, M. J., & Swanson, V. (1989). A controlled comparison of cognitive-behaviour therapy, diazepam and placebo in the management of generalized anxiety. *Behavioural Psychotherapy, 17,* 1–14.

Prinz, R. J. (1990). Socially withdrawn and isolated children. In H. Leitenberg (Ed.), *Handbook of social and evaluation anxiety.* New York: Plenum.

Robins, L. N., & Regier, D. A. (Eds.). (1991). *Psychiatric disorders in America: The epidemiologic catchment area study.* New York: Free Press.

Sherman, A. R. (1972). Real-life exposure as a primary therapeutic factor in the desensitization treatment of fear. *Journal of Abnormal Psychology, 79,* 19–28.

Spitzer, R. L., Gibbon, M., Skodol, A. E., Williams, J. B. W., & First, W. B. (Eds.). (1989). *DSM-III-R casebook.* Washington, DC: American Psychiatric Press.

Steketee, G. S. (1992). *Treatment of obsessive-compulsive disorder.* New York: Guilford Press.

Steketee, G. S., & White, K. (1990). *When once is not enough: Help for obsessions and compulsions.* Oakland, CA: New Harbinger.

Strauss, C. C. (1988). Behavioral assessment and treatment of overanxious disorder in children and adolescents. *Behavior Modification, 12,* 234–251.

Task Force on DSM-IV. (1991). *DSM-IV options book: Work in progress.* Washington, DC: American Psychiatric Association.

Thyer, B. A. (1981). Prolonged *in vivo* exposure therapy with a 70-year-woman. *Journal of Behavior Therapy and Experimental Psychiatry, 12,* 69–71.

Thyer, B. A. (1983). Treating anxiety disorders with exposure therapy. *Social Casework, 64,* 77–82.

Thyer, B. A. (1984). The treatment of phobias in their natural contexts. *Journal of Applied Social Sciences, 9*(1), 73–83.

Thyer, B. A. (1985). Audio-taped exposure therapy in a case of obsessional neurosis. *Journal of Behavior Therapy and Experimental Psychiatry, 16,* 271–273.

Thyer, B. A. (1987a). Community-based self-help groups in the treatment of agoraphobia. *Journal of Sociology and Social Welfare, 14,* 135–141.

Thyer, B. A. (1987b). *Treating anxiety disorders: A guide for human service professionals.* Newbury Park, CA: Sage.

Thyer, B. A. (1991). Behavioral social work: It is not what you think. *Arete, 16*(2), 1–16.

Thyer, B. A. (1992a). Single system designs. In R. M. Grinnell (Ed.), *Social work research and evaluation* (4th ed.). Itasca, IL: F. E. Peacock.

Thyer, B. A. (1992b). The term "cognitive-behavior" therapy is redundant (letter). *The Behavior Therapist, 15*(5), 112, 128.

Thyer, B. A., & Curtis, G. C. (1983). The repeated pretest-posttest single-subject experiment: A new design for empirical clinical practice. *Journal of Behavior Therapy and Experimental Psychiatry, 14,* 311–315.

Thyer, B. A., & Sowers-Hoag, K. M. (1988). Behavior therapy for separation anxiety disorder. *Behavior Modification, 12,* 205–233.

Thyer, B. A., & Stocks, J. T. (1986). Exposure therapy in the treatment of a phobic blind person. *Journal of Visual Impairment and Blindness, 80,* 1001–1003.

Watson, J. P., Mullett, G. E., & Pillay, H. (1973). The effects of prolonged exposure to phobic situations upon agoraphobic patients treated in groups. *Behaviour Research and Therapy, 11,* 531–545.

Westhuis, D., & Thyer, B. A. (1989). Development and validation of the Clinical Anxiety Scale. *Educational and Psychological Measurement, 49,* 153–163.

Wolpe, J. (1958). *Psychotherapy by reciprocal inhibition.* Stanford, CA: Stanford University Press.

Wolpe, J. (1973). *The practice of behavior therapy* (2nd ed.). New York: Pergamon Press.

Prevention of Health-Care Problems*

Steven P. Schinke
Beverly R. Singer

This chapter describes our work in the prevention of health-care problems among minority youths—specifically, Native American adolescents. Working from the premise that a major cause of adult chronic diseases such as some types of cancer is positively connected with lifestyle factors, such as poor diet and the use of smoked or smokeless tobacco, and working from psychosocial behavioral theory, we have developed a number of prevention interventions designed to reduce the risk of cancer by modifying lifestyle and dietary habits and reducing the prevalence of tobacco use among Native Americans. First we will discuss the issues of psychosocially oriented preventive medicine, and then we will describe a theory-based and culturally sensitive intervention based on our past and current research.

BACKGROUND: PREVENTING DISEASE

In the 19th century, public-health officials were primarily concerned with communicable diseases and the germs that caused them, and medical scientists focused on the discovery of microbiologic agents of disease and ways to control them. The discovery that certain aspects of the environment were associated with disease led to the establishment of sanitation facilities and services such as refuse collection, plumbing systems, and food preservation for entire communities.

In the 20th century, public-health officials have been primarily concerned with chronic disease and the behavior that causes it. In the 1970s, medical specialists found that the average life expectancy of a middle-aged American man was only slightly greater than that at the turn of the century (Lew & Seltzer, 1970). The current major causes of illness and death are the chronic diseases of middle and old age such as cardiovascular disease and cancer, often brought on by prolonged unhealthy lifestyle factors such as poor diet and habitual use of tobacco.

Cardiovascular disease and cancer are particularly expensive and difficult to treat once contracted. Health officials are recognizing the superior cost efficiency and effectiveness of prevention over treatment. Prevention has become a priority for government health agencies, because it promises to reduce the need for medical care.

Preventive medicine focuses on ways of altering a patient's or a population's "risk," or probability for future illness. Many prevention strategies now in use are concerned with reducing the prevalence of unhealthy behavior in the general population and thereby reducing the risk of disease. The training in social and personal skills that we have used in our own work with adolescents and adults in preventing the use of tobacco and other sub-

*Research reported in this chapter was supported by the National Cancer Institute (CA S2251).

stances has proved effective in reducing risk (Botvin & Eng, 1982; Botvin, Renick, & Baker, 1983; Botvin & Wills, 1985; Schinke & Gilchrist, 1983). Lately we have been concerned with tailoring that approach, which is otherwise a broad-based approach to the *syndrome* of risk-taking behavior, to specific problems among minority groups. One group-specific problem is tobacco use and poor dietary habits among Native Americans.

LIFESTYLE, DISEASE, AND HEALTH RISK

A growing body of health-care professionals, Native American and non–Native American, is recognizing the important role of tobacco use and other lifestyle factors in the risk of cancer.

Tobacco Use

Cigarette smoking has a proven association with cardiovascular disease (U.S. Department of Health and Human Services [USDHHS], 1983), cancer (USDHHS, 1982), and chronic obstructive lung disease (USDHHS, 1984). Ingestion of tobacco through the lungs, when smoked, or through buccal and oral mucosa tissue, when chewed or sniffed, is dangerous to those tissues in addition to being addictive. Habitual cigarette use, especially, contributes to cancers of the lung, larynx, oral cavity, esophagus, bladder, kidney, pancreas, stomach, and uterus (U.S. Office on Smoking and Health, 1982, 1983, 1984).

Users of smokeless tobacco experience gingival recession, leukoplakia, and soft-tissue dysplasia (Christen, 1985; Greer & Poulson, 1983; Squier, 1984). Snuff use, in particular, is linked with verrucous and squamous cell carcinomas (Hoffman, Harley, Fisenne, Adams, & Brunnemann, 1986; Levy, 1983; Marwick,

1984; Shah, Sarode, & Bhide, 1985). Also, the nicotine delivered by snuff and chewing tobacco may antecede hypertension, elevated heart rate, and concentrated blood lipids and catecholamines (McPhaul et al., 1984; Schroeder & Chen, 1985). Sodium, sweeteners, and flavoring constituents in smokeless tobacco may also interfere with blood pressure and glucose control (Hampson, 1985; Poulson, Lindenmuth, & Greer, 1984).

Added problems from tobacco use are implied in data showing a progression of substance use as children move through the teenage years and into young adulthood. Research with adolescents has shown a predictable sequence of experimentation that begins with the use of tobacco and alcohol and is followed by marijuana and perhaps eventually other substances such as depressants, amphetamines, and opiates. Early researchers considered tobacco (nicotine) and alcohol "gateway" substances that greatly increase the probability of habitual or excessive use of other substances (Hamburg, Braemer, & Jahnke, 1975; Kandel, 1978). Other data linked tobacco use in adolescence with delinquent, promiscuous, and aggressive behavior in young adulthood (Brunswick & Messeri, 1984a, 1984b; Jessor, 1984; Kellam, Ensminger, Branch, Brown, & Fleming, 1984; Red Horse, 1982). Newer research, however, seeks to directly address substance abuse within the immediate context of the user rather than emphasizing predictors for abuse.

In general, lifestyle habits such as cigarette smoking and consumption of alcohol, as well as diet and levels of physical activity, are often established in adolescence (Hetzel & Berenson, 1987). According to the Advocacy Institute, of the nearly 435,000 Americans killed by smoking-induced diseases in 1988 alone, about half had started smoking by age 13. Once acquired, the tobacco habit is hard to break. A recent disclosure of the Imperial Tobacco Company's market research shows that this dynamic of early addiction is in fact what tobacco companies rely on. In a study the company found that most beginning smokers were 12 or 13 but that by the age of 16 or 17 they already regretted it (Mintz, 1991).

Nicotine addiction is in part responsible for the recalcitrance of the tobacco use habit. Evidence cited in the 1988 *Report on Smoking and Health* produced by the U.S. Surgeon General's office further substantiates the role of physiological addiction as a factor in the maintenance of tobacco use once the habit is learned. According to Robins (1984), tobacco is a longer-lasting addiction than marijuana.

On the addictive nature of smokeless tobacco, the National Institutes of Health Office of Medical Applications of Research has reported that its use causes blood levels similar to those of cigarette smoking and that addicted users increase their dosage until it levels off at one that fulfills their need. Such users need nicotine continually (Bernstein, 1986).

Adolescence, Behavior, and Health

A psychosocially based prevention intervention designed to prevent unhealthy behavior in adolescents must address a complex array of factors. Health is not a major concern for many adolescents, who tend to feel invulnerable to long-term health risks and think "it won't happen to me" (Urberg & Robbins, 1983). Interventions such as the Stanford Three-Community Study (Farquhar, 1983; Maccoby & Alexander, 1979) and the North Karelia project in Finland (Puska, Nissinen, Salnonen, & Tuomilehto, 1983), known for having effectively reduced the risk of cardiovascular disease in whole communities using a psychosocial approach, have targeted mainly adults who are concerned about their risk for heart disease. Engaging adolescents in preventing future health-care problems requires special skill and commitment to working with young people.

First, adolescence is a time of experimentation. As adolescents gain more independence and curiosity about the adult world, they begin trying new activities and new perspectives. The spirit of experimentation itself is often the reason for initiation of substance use, and the long-term health risks involved are often peripheral to an adolescent's decision to try or not to try a substance that endangers their health.

Second, adolescent experimentation with tobacco and alcohol entails legal as well as health risks. This and other risk-taking behavior such as sexual precociousness is, during adolescence, "problem behavior" (illegal, antisocial, or morally prohibited). The fact that certain behaviors are not just unhealthy but are also crucially connected to problems of self-esteem, self-control, and social competence makes prevention interventions designed to curtail these behaviors more complex, requiring strategies that take into account the complex mixture of social and psychological factors involved in adolescent experimentation with and later dependency on alcohol, tobacco, and other drugs.

Cancer Risk
Prevention for Native Americans

Native Americans suffer from cancers associated with behavioral and lifestyle patterns (Beauvais, Oetting, Wolf, & Edwards, 1989; Mao, Morrison, Semenciw, & Wigle, 1986; National Cancer Institute, 1986). Continued higher rates of those cancers are especially disturbing in light of extensive cancer research and highly visible public-information campaigns for cancer prevention through abstinence from tobacco, decreased consumption of alcohol and dietary fat, and increased consumption of foods rich in fiber, carotenes, and other nutrients (Hiatt, Klatsky, & Armstrong, 1988; Shoenborn & Benson, 1988; Wallace, Watson, & Watson, 1988). Clearly, cancer-prevention wisdom has not found its way into the lives of most Native American people; culturally sensitive and empirically tested strategies for reducing cancer in Native Americans simply do not exist (Greenwald, Cullen, & McKenna, 1987).

INTERVENTION: PREVENTION AMONG ADOLESCENTS

Our research concerning tobacco use and dietary modification among Native American adolescents grew out of and is interlinked with our work on substance-abuse prevention, and our tobacco-use prevention intervention is also designed to provide adolescents with the social and personal skills to avoid all other unsafe substances and behaviors. The approach involving training in personal and social skills is more flexible than situation-specific, because it approaches problem behavior as a syndrome that has a variety of symptoms: smoking, drug use, drinking, truancy, and sexual risk taking (Botvin & Wills, 1985). Alcohol and drug use often overlaps in incidence and in cause with the use of smoked and smokeless tobacco, especially in adolescence when substance use is frequently a social or experimental activity. As a result, our research into preventive intervention has frequently targeted these twin behaviors of substance use and tobacco use. The following describes the intervention development and procedures.

Intervention Staff

Our preventive intervention curriculum can be delivered by graduate-level practitioners or by workers with less than graduate degrees if they are directly supervised by master's level or similarly advanced clinicians. With the appropriate level of supervision, cancer-prevention intervention on an Indian reservation can be delivered by paraprofessionals from human services agencies, by undergraduate or graduate assistants from a college or university, by teachers (Botvin et al., 1983), and by older peer leaders (Botvin & Eng, 1982; Botvin et al., 1984; McAlister, Perry, & Maccoby, 1979).

A crucial component of the intervention teams are indigenous Native American people and members of the research staff, at least 20 years old and with one or more years of relevant experience, who are recruited on site and paid for their participation. These indigenous researchers ensure the credibility and integrity of each independent variable, help gain the confidence and attention of subjects for personal intervention, and open up communication and access to the Native American community on a broader level.

Curriculum Development

To design a curriculum responsive to the needs and preferences of Indian youths, we begin by reviewing past prevention research, as found in the literature on scientific and social work practice. The growing literature on psychosocial approaches to prevention intervention and our own work with Native Americans, smoking cessation, and weight-reduction programs all contribute to the first stage of curriculum design.

Next we gather and analyze the base-rate information, in order to empirically portray the nature and scope of cancer risk factors among the Indian children and youths who live on a reservation. At the same time, we are trying to identify, early on, deficits in youths' abilities to avoid tobacco use or make healthy lifestyle choices, which focuses our efforts to improve those abilities.

Base-Rate Data Gathering

The first step of a cancer-prevention intervention among Indian and other high-risk youths involves accurately determining the prevalence (current rate) of poor dietary habits and use of smoked and smokeless tobacco among the sample. This step involves developing and administering assessment instruments to validly quantify youths' tobacco use and dietary habits. Then we analyze the collected data to determine the psychological and behavioral correlates of cancer-related dietary habits and use of smoked and smokeless tobacco.

The measurements we use have been developed through field testing and revision in the course of our and others' research with Native American adolescents (Cvetkovich, Earle, Schinke, Gilchrist, & Trimble, 1987; Gilchrist, Schinke, Trimble, & Cvetkovich, 1987; Oetting et al., 1983; Schinke et al., 1988; Schinke, Schilling, & Gilchrist, 1986). These measurements aim to determine prevalence and psychosocial causes of tobacco use.

To obtain valid estimates of the prevalence of tobacco use among subjects, investigators rely on a combination of self-report and biochemical sampling procedures.

Self-Report Procedures. Self-report measures simply ask youths to respond to multiple-choice questions about the incidence and number of cigarettes, smokeless tobacco products, alcohol, and other drugs consumed during the index reporting period (usually the most recent past day and week). Other questions asked on the self-report measure aim to determine subjects' demographic profile, knowledge and attitudes about tobacco and diet, education level, self-esteem, communication skills, problem-solving skills, and other psychosocial determinants of tobacco use and diet.

Biochemical Sampling. At the same time that subjects are completing the self-report measures, researchers obtain from each youth a small amount of biochemical material (saliva and expired lung air are most often used due to their relative ease of collection) from which laboratory technicians can later isolate tobacco-use byproducts: nicotine, carbon monoxide, thiocyanate, or cotinine. Biochemical sampling is often used in conjunc-

tion with self-report procedures to convince subjects that their tobacco use will be physiologically evident, which often corrects their tendency to underreport or overreport their recent tobacco use (Murray, O'Connell, Schmid, & Perry, 1987).

Analysis of Base-Rate Data. In the age group targeted for this intervention, few subjects smoke regularly enough to produce significant biochemical evidence of tobacco use. Base-rate information on psychological and behavioral correlates of youths' substance use is more critical data for predicting the *risk* that an adolescent will use or not use tobacco in the future. Fortunately, information about these nonphysiological parameters are relatively simple to obtain. Psychological and behavioral factors relevant to cancer risk prevention with Native American youths are their knowledge, attitudes, and preferences about tobacco use and diet, factors that their answers to the self-reporting measures readily reveal. In addition, investigators can administer various standard psychometric measures of other crucially related variables such as youths' sense of self-efficacy, locus of control, degree of sensation seeking and risk taking, social networks, and interpersonal skills.

Adapting the Study to the Subject Population

Because this particular intervention is concerned specifically with the reduction of the risk of cancer, the target substances and lifestyle factors are tobacco and consumption of alcohol and dietary fat. Data on youths' knowledge, attitudes, and beliefs about substance use help shape the program by guiding the level and complexity of instruction for beginning intervention. For instance, the number of youths in a subject population who have experimented with smoking helps us determine the general level of familiarity that the subjects have with the social pressures and health risks involved. At this point in the study we aim for a clear picture of the cultural and lifestyle aspects of tobacco use and dietary habits among the target population, as well as the relevant social skills the adolescents have or lack: interpersonal communication skills, strategies for coping with peer pressure, problem-solving skills, and the ability to analyze and resist media influences to use and abuse alcohol.

Another element of the base-rate information germane to adapting the study to the subject population is information about youths' orientation to the Indian way of life. Knowing the level of Native American youths' awareness of their cultural background and its influence on their lives helps us shape the amount and nature of cultural information included in the preventive program.

Intervention Design

The intervention design isolates the effects of two interventions, prevention of tobacco use and dietary modification, separately and combined. We were interested in determining the synergistic effects of efforts to prevent tobacco use and modify diet. We hope to determine which is more effective: an integrated approach to promoting overall health and well-being, treating two behaviors at once, or focused and specialized interventions treating each behavior separately.

IMPLEMENTING THE INTERVENTION

This intervention actually involves delivering three interventions: one concerns preventing tobacco use, one concerns modifying diet, and the third combines the two interventions. The procedural structure for all three interventions is the same.

Procedure

Prospective subjects are recruited through presentations, posters, and local broadcast media. After the subjects learn of the study's purposes and requirements and the researchers obtain passive consent from parents, random samples are drawn from the pool of eligible subjects, who are then divided into groups of 8 to 12 youths. These groups are meant to provide a secure outlet in which youths can discuss their personal dilemmas and ask questions of their peers and intervention leaders. The youths are assured of the confidentiality of everything they share with the group; they are reminded that all study data are anonymously coded and that confidentiality oaths are signed by everyone involved.

Working in teams of two, research staff members and indigenous leaders deliver personal intervention in 15 group sessions of 50 minutes each. Group sessions are held during the school day or concurrent with regularly scheduled recreational activities at a community center.

Format

When the additional pretesting and posttesting sessions are included, study subjects in fact participate in 17 sessions (plus biannual booster sessions for two years afterwards). Intervention teams have the option of scheduling the 50-minute sessions weekly, semiweekly, or three times a week, depending on the availability of subjects, space, and transportation. A reservation-based intervention may require weekly sessions after school or on the weekend.

Content

The personal intervention sessions incorporate themes and situations attuned to youths' cultural values, and they aim to integrate normative and learning theory components. In this section we will describe session themes that pervade both the tobacco-use intervention and the dietary-modification program.

Our strategy for tobacco-use intervention grew out of our studies involving substance use and alcohol abuse, and it has its roots in social learning theory (Bandura, 1977), persuasive-communications theory (McGuire, 1964), and problem-behavior theory (Jessor & Jessor, 1977), which have changed the face of prevention interventions by showing how behavior is learned from and promoted by the social and family environment. The intervention we have developed and found effective uses the Life Skills Training (LST) approach, which teaches subjects pressure-resistance tactics within the framework of a program designed to enhance general personal and social competence (Botvin & Wills, 1985).

The dietary-modification intervention parallels tobacco-use prevention by incorporating similar theoretical and conceptual principles and stressing similar concepts: health, communication, peer pressure, problem solving, and the media. The content of the diet-specific modification explores eating less fat and fewer fatty foods, eating more high-fiber foods, and maintaining a desirable weight.

Both intervention curricula draw on concepts of *bicultural competence* to show youths how they can improve their eating patterns and avoid using tobacco by using both Native American and mainstream knowledge and resources. Research has shown that Native Americans who have learned bicultural competence are better adjusted and have a lower rate of tobacco and substance use than either "acculturated" Native Americans (who adopted the mainstream culture) or "traditional" Native Americans (who remain tied to Native American traditions) (LaFramboise, 1982; LaFramboise & Rowe, 1983; Oetting, Goldstein, Beauvais, Edwards, & Velarde, 1980).

Ethnic Pride and Values.   Integral to each session is content on ethnic pride and values that is regionally and tribally specific. Con-

tent responsive to acculturation and spiritual variables that affect Native American youths' tobacco use is woven throughout personal intervention. Group leaders use tribally specific folk tales, legends, and myths to promote healthy development and to devalue smoking, drinking, and the intake of unhealthy, cancer-related food. In the dietary-modification interventions, the meaning and importance of food and tradition in Native American culture and in the family are discussed.

Ethnic pride is made manifest in posters of Native American leaders, athletes, performers, artists, and craftspersons, as well as pictures of Indian art and excerpts from Indian poetry. Leaders also involve Native American youths in drumming, singing, and dancing during group meetings to elicit active personal involvement from each subject.

Values content emphasizes the strengths and positive attributes of native people. In each instance, personal, familial, and community values are related to Indian youths' decisions about tobacco use. For instance, leaders explain to young Native Americans that the Indian traditional use of peyote during religious ceremonies has always severely excluded the secular and habitual use of those substances (Beauvais & La Boueff, 1985).

Additional exercises during these sessions designed to actively infuse cultural values into the subjects' everyday lives involve getting the youths to observe and report on instances where Native American values did or could beneficially serve them in everyday tasks. By the infusion of ethnic identity, intervention encourages Native American adolescents to apply their cultural heritage along with prevention skills to promote their health and avoid unhealthy behavior. Group members are asked to view habitual abstinence from tobacco use as an expression of traditional values. Leaders note that although values are subjective, the consequences of value-oriented decisions are sometimes objective and predictable.

In homework assignments, subjects observe how the values of both Native Americans and the majority culture manifest themselves in everyday decisions. One assignment asks subjects to specify a forthcoming situation—whether or not tobacco use is involved—and to note a range of possible choices for action. At the next group session, subjects discuss the Indian and majority cultural values inherent in those choices. Reports on homework assignments provide additional opportunities to discuss the use of smoked and smokeless tobacco in the context of traditional values.

Health Information. Via films, games, and peer testimonials, youths learn facts about using smokeless and smoked tobacco. Age-relevant films about both types of tobacco use are viewed and discussed. Games are patterned after Native American games that are both entertaining and skill-building. The diet-modification program teaches subjects how the body absorbs food and the role that food, sleep, exercise, and hygiene play in good health. Subjects are encouraged to weigh and measure themselves and to rate their current level of health.

Role Models. Homework reports focus on Native American people who abstain from tobacco and who project independence, autonomy, and sophistication. Additionally, subjects observe in their everyday lives respected Indian people who avoid tobacco. Group members describe the qualities that characterize these people as responsible, owing to a purity of mind, body, and spirit. Toward this end, leaders draw attention to abstainers who have obviously and successfully resisted media, advertising, and peer pressure to use tobacco.

In the dietary-modification program, subjects learn how others influence their behavior, and they are asked to describe someone they like or admire, including the person's diet and activities. Role models might be athletes or dancers whose health is evident and who represent tobacco abstinence in a positive way.

Positive Self-Image. Positive self-image content addresses the role of smoking or chewing tobacco in Native Americans' images of themselves as young adults. Leaders solicit from subjects a discussion of lifestyle image and of stereotypes of Native American people using or abstaining from tobacco use. Subjects are asked to contrast stereotypes of Native Americans with Euro-American images of attractiveness, popularity, sophistication, and success. With examples, leaders initiate discussions on how film and the other mass media create positive images of people who use tobacco, and subjects are encouraged to give their opinions of people portrayed in the media with such descriptors as rich, poor, happy, sad, popular, unpopular, independent, and dependent.

Likewise, group members together generate images of cigarette smokers and users of smokeless tobacco in their own lives and experience. Subjects are provided with suggestions, as needed, and reminders of smokeless and smoked tobacco's unpleasant cosmetic features, disharmony with the Native American respect for life, and negative health and lifestyle consequences. Through such exercises, in which youths participate imaginatively in changing their own attitudes, subjects learn to actively associate tobacco use with negative images and negative stereotypes of native people.

Advertisements. For the session focused on advertising and its influence, subjects are asked in advance to collect newspaper and magazine advertisements for both smokeless and smoked tobacco and also for food. During the session, group members critique the advertisements for their accuracy, realism, and motivational purposes in order to discover what kind of lifestyle is being sold.

Also, Native American subjects investigate the stereotypes of Indian life conveyed in advertisements, on television, in pop culture, in books, and in films. This investigation takes several sessions, as youths learn to uncover the messages being sent to them through the media. The final activity has subjects designing their own food advertisement, relevant to Native Americans.

Problem-Solving Skills. In line with the concept of bicultural competence, problem-solving skills enable subjects to discriminate among their options and to make reasoned decisions when faced with urges, temptations, and pressures involving food, alcohol, tobacco, other drugs, or any other problem situation. Through posters or videotapes of Native American youths in difficult situations, group leaders teach five steps to problem solving. The steps, represented by the memorable acronym SODAS, are stop, options, decide, act, and self-praise. Each step is explained by group leaders and then practiced by subjects.

The first step, *stop,* advises subjects to remember to pause and think, rather than reacting automatically, when confronted with situations involving tobacco use or a choice of food. Pausing helps subjects realize how unconscious their decisions often are and, in turn, allows them to define the problem and their role in solving it.

The second step, *options,* asks youths to consider several different solutions to tobacco-use problems. Through examples, group members discuss the relative merits of various options to specific situations. They learn to eliminate less viable options and see how to narrow their range of solution alternatives.

The third step, *decide,* is introduced with age- and culture-relevant examples of decisions made by others in various situations. The process of decision making is practiced to competence by subjects. Initially, youths apply this step to rank their options on costs, benefits, and feasibility. Based on these criteria, group members choose options for problem situations around tobacco use.

Throughout, leaders impress upon subjects that they alone can decide what options are best for them. Group members are assured that they can modify, discard, and replace their chosen option as circumstances dictate.

Act, the fourth step, involves planning and rehearsal. Leaders ask subjects to visualize themselves in problem situations, in which they are acting on a decision they have made through the above steps. By actually acting out the behavior or the expression of feelings necessary to taking that action, subjects learn what works best and feels most comfortable, and they learn how to plan thoughts, words, and gestures appropriate to the situations. With these plans in mind, subjects verbalize their preferred strategies for handling tobacco-use problems. Once they receive feedback from other group members on their plans, subjects rehearse as if they were in the situations. Role-playing rehearsals in groups of two or three are accompanied by feedback, coaching, and encouragement from group leaders and from other subjects.

Self-praise, the final problem-solving step, is practiced in subgroup rehearsals. Group members learn how to reward their own behavior, contingent on simply using problem-solving steps.

Coping Skills. Also part of bicultural competence, coping skills equip Native American subjects with strategies to manage personal stress. Leaders introduce coping skills by helping subjects recognize situational, social, and emotional cues that trigger tobacco use (Biglan & Ary, 1985) and also poor dietary choices. Situational cues include personal and interpersonal physical settings and events associated with tobacco use. Social cues include personal and interpersonal actions that could precipitate tobacco use—for example, listening to the radio or seeing friends use smokeless tobacco. Emotional cues, in concert with or separate from situational and social cues, include urges and temptations to use smokeless and smoked tobacco. With practice, Native American youths will regard these cues as signaling the need for coping skills.

Instruction in cognitive coping skills begins as leaders ask subjects for examples of thoughts, feelings, and words that helped them manage their behavior in past stressful situations. Modeling and practice follow. Special attention is given to coping statements that help subjects focus on their own and others' emotions, such as the following: "I don't have to feel bad if I don't go along with Patricia when she wants me to use Skoal. I can be friends with her without using it. After a while, Patricia will get over her hurt feelings." Behavioral skills, also modeled by leaders and practiced by subjects, include overt steps that are covertly rehearsed. Illustrative are: "Since I didn't use snuff when Patricia did, I deserve a special treat later. Maybe I'll stop at the store on the way home and buy myself something."

Through graduated homework assignments, subjects learn to cope during a variety of tasks—when alone and when with others. At first, leaders ask subjects to use cognitive and behavioral coping skills in routine situations. The subjects progressively apply the skills to increasingly difficult situations.

Interpersonal Communication Skills.
A third bicultural-competence skill covered by personal intervention is interpersonal communication. Leaders begin by asking how Native American young people communicate ineffectively and effectively. Group leaders discuss cultural, gender, and individual differences in interpersonal communication. Next, they demonstrate and suggest ways for Indian youths to communicate toward (1) achieving an objective, (2) maintaining an interpersonal relationship, and (3) gaining self-respect. In role playing, subjects model these communication styles for one another. Subject pairs then try out the three communication styles for avoiding use of smokeless and smoked tobacco.

Subject pairs take turns as protagonists and antagonists as they practice communicating to achieve an objective—that is, avoiding tobacco

use at all costs or resisting the food a friend's mother is offering you. In the same situation, subjects practice communicating to maintain an interpersonal relationship—for example, preserving a friendship at all costs or avoiding offending an adult. Last, subjects use the situation to communicate the need for self-respect—that is, preserving personal dignity at all costs. Once each subject has practiced and experienced the three purposes of communication, group leaders add two more communication techniques: embellishment and redirection. Embellishments include humor, empathy, explanation, and flattery to help antagonists hear and accept refusals of tobacco use.

A youth might offset peer pressure by saying: "Jenna, it's OK for you to do what you want. If you want to smoke, that's your decision. My decision is not to smoke. Because you're smart and because you know how I think, you know why I don't want to smoke. That's why you're my friend. You let me do what I want." Redirection includes messages that let subjects avoid confrontation. For instance, a youth may say: "Do I want a dip of snuff? Gee, I don't think so. Let's do something else. Want to go to the store?" In pairs, subjects practice embellishment and redirection.

Finally, communication skills can be introduced by videotapes of Native American youths who are shy at first and then learn skills to competently interact with peers. Group members can model for one another effective use of eye contact, posture, gestures, intonation, and words. They can break into dyads for experiential practice while group leaders offer feedback and coaching. Scripted interactions ease subjects into these practices.

CONCLUSION

What we have described and illustrated in this chapter is an approach to working with younger Native Americans to reduce their risk of cancer. Working from the premise that a major cause of adult chronic diseases such as some types of cancer is positively connected with lifestyle factors such as poor diet and the use of smoked or smokeless tobacco, we have developed a series of interventions based on psychosocial behavioral theory and designed to reduce the risk of cancer by modifying lifestyle and dietary habits and reducing the prevalence of tobacco use among Native Americans. We have discussed the proven relationship between lifestyle and risk of disease, the need for prevention intervention during adolescence rather than late in life, and the skills-training approach we use in our preventive interventions. We hope that our description of this process will generate similar studies, especially studies sensitive to the psychosocial environment of cultural minorities whose needs have so far been under-researched.

Our descriptions of the intervention development and session content illustrate the way in which psychosocial Life Skills Training strategies encourage youths to participate actively in increasing their own ethnic pride, learning about the use of tobacco and about their dietary habits, and understanding their susceptibility to role models, peer influence, and the media. We also describe an active approach to improving subjects' problem-solving, communication, and general coping skills through practice. The premise of our approach is that acquisition of these skills reduces the susceptibility of adolescents to psychosocial and environmental factors that provoke them to smoke, to chew, or to eat unhealthy foods.

Preventive medicine is becoming increasingly important, as cancer and cardiovascular disease remain two of the highest causes of death in the country. Information dissemination and psychosocial skills for gaining control over lifestyle are survival tools that should be provided to minority as well as majority cultures. Our work with Native American youths constitutes a step in the direction of further developing psychosocial behavioral strategies for reducing the risk of disease among our culturally diverse population in the United States by taking positive cultural characteristics and values into account.

REFERENCES

Bandura, A. (1977). *Social learning theory.* Englewood Cliffs, NJ: Prentice-Hall.

Beauvais, F., & La Boueff, S. (1985). Drug and alcohol abuse intervention in American Indian communities. *International Journal of the Addictions, 20*(1), 139–171.

Beauvais, F., Oetting, E. R., Wolf, W., & Edwards, R. W. (1989). American Indian youth and drugs, 1976–87: A continuing problem. *American Journal of Public Health, 79,* 634–636.

Bernstein, M. J. (1986). Health applications of smokeless tobacco use. *Journal of the American Medical Association, 255,* 1045–1048.

Biglan, A., & Ary, D. V. (1985). Current methodological issues in research on smoking prevention. In E. S. Bell & R. Battjes (Eds.), *Prevention research on deterring drug abuse among children and adolescents* (NIDA Research Monograph Series). Washington, DC: U.S. Government Printing Office.

Botvin, G. J., & Eng, A. (1982). The efficacy of a multicomponent approach to the prevention of cigarette smoking. *Preventive Medicine, 11,* 199–211.

Botvin, G. J., Renick, N., & Baker, E. (1983). The effects of scheduling format and booster sessions on a broad-spectrum psychosocial approach to smoking prevention. *Journal of Behavioral Medicine, 6*(4), 359–379.

Botvin, G. J., & Wills, T. A. (1985). Personal and social skills training: Cognitive-behavioral approaches to substance abuse prevention. In C. Bell & R. Battjes (Eds.), *Prevention research: Deterring drug abuse among children and adolescents* (NIDA Research Monograph Series). Washington, DC: U.S. Government Printing Office.

Brunswick, A. G., & Messeri, P. (1984a). Causal factors in onset of adolescents' cigarette smoking: A prospective study of urban black youth.

Advances in Alcohol and Substance Abuse, 3, 35–52.

Brunswick, A. G., & Messeri, P. (1984b). Gender differences in the processes leading to cigarette smoking. *Journal of Psychosocial Oncology, 2,* 49–69.

Christen, A. G. (1985). The four most common alterations of the teeth, periodontium, and oral soft tissues observed in smokeless tobacco users: A literature review. *Journal of the Indiana Dental Association, 64,* 15–18.

Cvetkovich, G., Earle, T. C., Schinke, S. P., Gilchrist, L. D., & Trimble, J. E. (1987). Child and adolescent drug use: A judgment and information processing perspective to health-behavior interventions. *Journal of Drug Education, 17,* 295–313.

Farquhar, J. (1983). Community approaches to risk factor reduction: The Stanford project. In J. Herd & S. Weiss (Eds.), *Behavior and antisclerosis.* New York: Plenum.

Gilchrist, L. D., Schinke, S. P., Trimble, J. E., & Cvetkovich, G. T. (1987). Skills enhancement to prevent substance abuse among American Indian adolescents. *International Journal of the Addictions, 22,* 869–879.

Greenwald, P., Cullen, J. W., & McKenna, J. W. (1987). Cancer prevention and control: From research through applications. *Journal of the National Cancer Institute, 79,* 389–400.

Greer, R. O., Jr., & Poulson, T. C. (1983). Oral tissue alterations associated with the use of smokeless tobacco by teenagers. *Oral Surgery, 56,* 275–284.

Hamburg, B. A., Braemer, H. C., & Jahnke, W. A. (1975). Hierarchy of drug use in adolescence: Behavioral and attitudinal correlates of substantial drug use. *American Journal of Psychiatry, 132,* 1155–1167.

Hampson, N. B. (1985). Smokeless is not saltless. *New England Journal of Medicine, 312,* 919–920.

Hetzel, B., & Berenson, G. (Eds.). (1987). *Cardiovascular risk factors in childhood: Epidemiology and prevention.* New York: Elsevier.

Hiatt, R. A., Klatsky, A. L., & Armstrong, M. A. (1988). Alcohol consumption and the risk of breast cancer in a prepaid health plan. *Cancer Research, 48,* 2284–2287.

Hoffman, D., Harley, N. H., Fisenne, I., Adams, J. D., & Brunnemann, K. D. (1986). Carcinogenic agents in snuff. *Journal of the National Cancer Institute, 76,* 435–446.

Jessor, R. (1984). Adolescent development and behavioral health. In J. D. Matarazzo, S. M. Weiss, J. A. Herd, & N. E. Miller. (Eds.), *Behavioral health: A handbook of health enhancement and disease prevention.* New York: Wiley.

Jessor, R., & Jessor, S. L. (1977). *Problem behavior and psychosocial development: A longitudinal study of youth.* New York: Academic Press.

Kandel, D. B. (1978). Convergences in perspective longitudinal surveys of drug use in normal populations. In D. B. Kandel (Ed.), *Longitudinal research on drug use: Empirical findings and methodological issues.* New York: Wiley.

Kellam, S. G., Ensminger, M. E., Branch, J., Brown, C. H., & Fleming, J. P. (1984). The Woodlawn mental health longitudinal community epidemiological project. In S. A. Mednick, M. Harway, & K. M. Finello (Eds.), *Handbook of longitudinal research* (Vol. 2). New York: Praeger.

LaFramboise, T. D. (1982). *Assertion training with American Indians: Cultural/behavioral issues for trainers.* Las Cruces: Educational Resources Information Center Clearinghouse on Rural Education and Small Schools, New Mexico State University.

LaFramboise, T. D., & Rowe, W. (1983). Skills training for bicultural competence: Rationale and application. *Journal of Consulting Psychology, 30,* 589–595.

Levy, S. M. (1983). Host differences in neoplastic risk: Behavioral and social contributors to disease. *Health Psychology, 2,* 21–44.

Lew, E. A., & Seltzer, F. (1970). Uses of the life tables in public health. *Milbank Memorial Fund Quarterly, 48,* 15.

Maccoby, N., & Alexander, J. (1979). Reducing heart disease risk using the mass media: Comparing the effects on three communities. In R. F. Munoz, L. F. Snowden, & J. G. Kelly (Eds.), *Social and psychological research in community settings.* San Francisco: Jossey-Bass.

Mao, Y., Morrison, H., Semenciw, R., & Wigle, D. (1986). Mortality on Canadian Indian reserves: 1977–1982. *Canadian Journal of Public Health, 77,* 263–268.

Marwick, C. (1984). Medical news. *Journal of the American Medical Association, 252,* 2797–2799.

McAlister, A., Perry, C., & Maccoby, N. (1979). Adolescent smoking: Onset and prevention. *Pediatrics, 63,* 650–658.

McGuire, W. J. (1964). Inducing resistance to persuasion: Some contemporary approaches. In L. Berkowitz (Ed.), *Advances in experimental social psychology* (Vol. 1). New York: Academic Press.

McPhaul, M., Punzi, H. A., Sandy, A., Borganelli, M., Rude, R., & Kaplan, N. (1984). Snuff-induced hypertension in pheochromocytoma. *Journal of the American Medical Association, 252,* 2860–2862.

Mintz, M. (1991, May 6). Marketing tobacco to children. *The Nation,* pp. 590–610.

Murray, D. M., O'Connell, T. S., Schmid, L. A., & Perry, C. L. (1987). The validity of smoking self-reports by adolescents: A reexamination of the bogus pipeline procedure. *Addictive Behaviors, 12,* 7–15.

National Cancer Institute. (1986). Cancer in minorities: Report of the subcommittee on cancer, Part I. *Report of the Secretary's Task Force on Black and Minority Health.* Washington, DC: U.S. Department of Health and Human Services.

Oetting, E. R., Beauvais, F., Edwards, R., Waters, M. R., Velarde, J., & Goldstein, G. S. (1983). *Drug use among Native American youth: Summary of findings (1975–1981).* Fort Collins: Colorado State University.

Oetting, E. R., Goldstein, G. S., Beauvais, F., Edwards, R., & Velarde, J. (1980). *Drug abuse among Indian children.* Fort Collins: Colorado State University.

Poulson, T. C., Lindenmuth, J. E., & Greer, R. O. (1984). A comparison of the use of smokeless tobacco in rural and urban teenagers. *CA-A Cancer Journal for Clinicians, 34,* 11–24.

Puska, P., Nissinen, A., Salnonen, J., & Tuomilehto, J. (1983). Ten years of the North Karelia project: Results with community-based prevention of coronary heart disease. *Scandinavian Journal of Social Medicine, 11,* 565–571.

Red Horse, Y. (1982). A cultural network model: Perspectives for adolescent services and paraprofessional training. In S. M. Manson (Ed.), *New directions in prevention among American Indian and Alaska Native communities.* Portland: Oregon Health Sciences University.

Robins, L. N. (1984). The natural history of adolescent drug use. *American Journal of Public Health, 74,* 656–657.

Schinke, S. P., & Gilchrist, L. D. (1983). Primary prevention of tobacco smoking. *Journal of School Health, 53,* 416–419.

Schinke, S. P., Orlandi, M. A., Botvin, G. J., Gilchrist, L. D., Trimble, J. E., & Locklear, V. S. (1988). Preventing substance abuse among American Indian adolescents: A bicultural competence skills approach. *Journal of Counseling Psychology, 35,* 87–90.

Schinke, S. P., Schilling, R. F., & Gilchrist, L. D. (1986). Prevention of drug and alcohol abuse in American Indian youths. *Social Work Research and Abstracts, 22*(4), 18–19.

Schoenborn, C. A., & Benson, V. (1988). Relationships between smoking and other unhealthy habits: United States, 1985. *Advance Data, No. 154, Vital Statistics.* Hyattsville, MD: National Center for Health Statistics.

Schroeder, K. L., & Chen, M. S. (1985). Smokeless tobacco and blood pressure. *New England Journal of Medicine, 312,* 919.

Shah, A. S., Sarode, A. V., & Bhide, S. V. (1985). Experimental studies on mutagenic and carcinogenic effects of tobacco chewing. *Journal of Cancer Research and Clinical Oncology, 109,* 203–207.

Squier, C. A. (1984). Smokeless tobacco and oral cancer: A cause for concern? *CA-A Cancer Journal for Clinicians, 34,* 242–247.

U.S. Department of Health and Human Services. (1982). *The health consequences of smoking: Cancer* (Public Health Service Publication [OSH] No. 82-50179). Washington, DC: U.S. Government Printing Office.

U.S. Department of Health and Human Services. (1983). *The health consequences of smoking: Cardiovascular disease.* (Public Health Service [OSH] Publication No. 82-50179). Washington, DC: U.S. Government Printing Office.

U.S. Department of Health and Human Services. (1984). *The health consequences of smoking: Chronic obstructive lung disease.* (Public Health Service [OSH] Publication No. 84-50205). Washington, DC: U.S. Government Printing Office.

U.S. Department of Health and Human Services. (1985). *Report of the Secretary's Task Force on Black and Minority Health: Vol. 2. Crosscutting issues in minority health.* Washington, DC: U.S. Government Printing Office.

U.S. Office on Smoking and Health. (1982). *The health consequences of smoking: Cancer: A report of the surgeon general.* Washington, DC: U.S. Government Printing Office.

U.S. Office on Smoking and Health. (1983). *The health consequences of smoking: Cardiovascular disease: A report of the surgeon general.* Washington, DC: U.S. Government Printing Office.

U.S. Office on Smoking and Health. (1984). *The health consequences of smoking: Chronic obstructive lung disease: A report of the surgeon general.* Washington, DC: U.S. Government Printing Office.

Urberg, K., & Robbins, R. (1983). *Adolescent invulnerability: Developmental course, antecedents, and relationship to risk-taking behavior.* Unpublished manuscript, Wayne State University.

Wallace, C. L., Watson, R. R., & Watson, A. A. (1988). Reducing cancer risk with vitamins C, E, and selenium. *American Journal of Health Promotion, 3,* 5–16.

15

Social Support Skill Training

Cheryl A. Richey

Mrs. Williams has been referred to a support group for women with breast cancer. She attends her first meeting at the clinic and finds that everyone seems much more at ease than she is in talking about personal issues and feelings. She waits, but no one inquires about her situation. She listens, asks one question during the meeting, and leaves as soon as it is over. She decides not to go back the next week because "it's too much trouble, people don't seem interested in me, and basically I'm a shy person anyway."

Roland and his wife are having a lot of conflict about how to handle their adolescent son, who has problems at home and at school. Roland learns that one of his co-workers at the plant, Sam, has had similar family problems. He keeps hoping that the right moment will come when he can bring up the topic of his son with Sam, and ask for some advice. However, he feels awkward about doing this because they have never talked about anything other than the job. He has tried dropping a few hints—for example, "Yeah, I'm slow today. Had another rough weekend"—but Sam doesn't pursue these, and Roland changes the topic.

Evelyn, a single parent, begins a conversation with another mother, Leslie, at the Head Start program where they both bring their children. Evelyn wants to get more involved with other mothers who have similar life struggles. She'd also like to arrange to share with another parent some baby-sitting during the week.

After a little small talk, Evelyn tells Leslie all about how her man left her and the kids, her son's bed-wetting problem, and her own feelings of being overwhelmed. During most of the interaction, Leslie is polite but quiet, and soon after Evelyn stops talking, Leslie excuses herself and leaves.

These vignettes illustrate how opportunities for the exchange of social support—in the form of emotional support, practical assistance, socializing, and advice or guidance—can be compromised or lost if important skills in social interaction are inadequate. In this chapter I will focus on social skill training to help adults enhance the amount and quality of social support they experience in their day-to-day lives, including times of individual and family stress. I will describe and illustrate specific cognitive-behavioral strategies that can be implemented in various settings to help people develop and expand the interpersonal competencies needed to identify, mobilize, use, and reciprocate various forms of help from other people, including emotional and instrumental support and problem-solving assistance. Social skill training has been identified by those working with at-risk populations as a possible intervention to assist individuals in developing and maintaining more supportive relationships (Booth, Mitchell, Barnard, & Spieker, 1989; Gaudin, Wodarski, Arkinson, & Avery, 1990–1991; Kirkham, Schinke, Schilling, Meltzer, & Norelius, 1986; Oates & Forrest, 1985; Polansky, Gaudin, Ammons, & Davis, 1985; Richey, Lovell, & Reid, 1991; Robinson, 1988).

The chapter is divided into four sections. The first section is an overview of two distinct but related bodies of literature: one addresses cognitive-behavioral training in social skills and its effects, and the other focuses on the types, theories, and consequences of social support. In the second section I summarize and illustrate important assessment questions that practitioners should consider before implementing training in social-support skills. For example, how adequate or satisfactory are the social supports of a particular client; what are the possible explanations for inadequate social support, in addition to or instead of social skills deficiencies; if inadequate social skills are identified as central to low social support, what specific cognitive and behavioral competencies should be targeted for intervention? In the third section of the chapter I describe core social skills training procedures utilized in treatment groups with several different client populations, including shy women and parents at risk for child maltreatment. The chapter concludes with a fourth section in which I explore implications for intervention development and research.

SOCIAL SKILL AND SOCIAL SUPPORT

Social Skill Training

The term *social skill* training reflects my adoption of a process model rather than a component model of social behavior (Gambrill & Richey, 1986). A process, or systems, model of social behavior emphasizes the interaction of verbal and nonverbal behaviors; cognitions, including personal values, attributions, and feelings; and situational cues and consequences. *Social skills* are the discrete verbal and nonverbal behavioral

components that are viewed as socially appropriate in everyday interactions—facial expression, eye contact, vocal qualities, and speech content (Bellack & Morrison, 1982). The term *social skill,* along with such related terms as *social competence* and *social performance,* emphasizes generating or producing socially skilled behavior, which is goal directed (Trower, 1982). Thus, social skill training can be viewed as an intervention to help people develop, strengthen, and emit social behaviors in specific situations that enable them to more effectively achieve short- and long-term personal and social goals (Gambrill & Richey, 1986).

In much of the intervention literature, spanning decades and disciplines, development of social skills has been viewed as a means to an end, or an instrumental (Rosen & Proctor, 1978) or proximal (Garbarino, 1986) goal. Instrumental outcomes are those that are believed or known to result automatically in the attainment of ultimate outcomes—the reasons for which intervention was initially mobilized (Rosen & Proctor, 1978). Thus, building specific social competencies is often viewed as a way to enable clients to behave more successfully in important life domains so that they can achieve ultimate outcomes. For example, studies of social skill training have demonstrated that becoming more interpersonally competent, or skillful, can enhance postdivorce adjustment (Joanning, 1985); improve couple communication and marital satisfaction (Jacobson, 1985; Wackman & Wampler 1985); reduce unipolar and chronic depressions (deJong, Treiber, & Gerhard, 1986; Hersen, Bellack, Himmelhoch, & Thase, 1984; Libet & Lewinsohn, 1973); reduce relapse and rehospitalization and enhance successful community living among the chronic mentally ill (Christoff & Kelly, 1985; Dispenza & Nigro, 1989; Gordon & Gordon, 1985; Wallace, 1982); among persons with mental retardation, expand verbal problem solving (Foxx, Kyle, Faw, & Bittle, 1989) and independent living capability (Andrasik & Matson, 1985) and reduce vulnerability to sexual exploitation and sexual abuse (Haseltine & Miltenberger, 1990); increase prosocial interaction and decrease self-stimulatory responses with deaf/blind severely handicapped individuals (Van Hasselt, Hersen, Egan, McKelvey, & Sisson, 1989); increase resistance to social pressure to engage in unsafe or unhealthy behavior—for example, using drugs and alcohol (Monti, Abrams, Binkoff, & Zwick, 1986); reduce interpersonally aggressive, abusive, and violent behavior (Deffenbacher, Story, Stark, Hogg, & Brandon, 1987; Goldstein & Keller, 1987); among the elderly, enhance communication with healthcare providers and adjustment to nursing home and community living, and reduce depression (Gambrill, 1986); improve job-interview skills and employment options and opportunities (Heimberg, Cunningham, Heimberg, & Blankenberg, 1982; Hood, Lindsay, & Brooks, 1982); enhance supervisory and managerial effectiveness in business and industry (Komaki & Zlotnick, 1985; Metcalfe & Wright, 1986); increase the ability of welfare mothers to negotiate more effectively with social service providers (Galinsky, Schopler, Satier, & Gambrill, 1978); and facilitate parenting effectiveness (Brock & Coufal, 1985).

As the preceding list suggests, a broad spectrum of multidisciplinary research supports the conclusion that cognitive-behavioral interventions to enhance interpersonal competence enable individuals to achieve their goals. Further, the goals targeted for intervention—be they independent living, performing well in a job interview, getting adequate medical information about one's condition from health-care providers, or handling intrusive/aggressive individuals more successfully—span the prevention/rehabilitation continuum (Bloom, 1991) and represent many disciplines, including social work, psychology, nursing, rehabilitation, special education, public health, and business.

In contrast to these goals, the application of social skill training to the development of social support is a relatively recent and untested innovation. In part, this is due to the recency of interest in the phenomenon of social support. Some have called the growing emphasis on social support a "quiet revolution" in the human services field (Whittaker & Garbarino, 1983). This "revolution" could have wide-reaching implications for many practice arenas, including health and mental health services and services to children, adolescents, families, and the elderly. In the next section I define social support; discuss its dimensions, forms, and functions; and review the theoretical formulations that undergird it.

Social Support

The term *social support* has multiple meanings. Most researchers agree that the concept is not unitary but, rather, multifaceted, including an individual's integration into and interconnectedness with a group of people, the resources or supports received from others, perceptions of the need for and availability of support, and satisfaction with the support received (Sarason, Sarason, & Pierce, 1990). Typically, social support refers to various forms of help offered to a distressed individual by family and friends, co-workers, or neighbors (Thoits, 1986). This type of support, frequently called *informal support* or *mutual aid*, is offered by lay helpers and is distinguished from *formal support,* or services offered by trained professionals (Whittaker & Garbarino, 1983).

Social networks are the relational structures and communication links through which people offer and receive support (Garbarino, 1983). Social networks provide the *social architecture* for the person-to-person exchange of tangible and intangible resources (Albrecht & Adelman, 1987b). Personal networks often comprise individuals who are immediate and extended family members, neighbors, friends, co-workers, and others. Network members who know one another form a web of interrelationships, which can be diagrammatically represented by lines, reflecting relationships between individuals within a particular network (Sharkey, 1989).

Dimensions of Social Support.

Researchers have distinguished the structural, or quantitative, dimensions of social support from the more functional, or qualitative, dimensions (Fiore, Coppel, Becker, & Cox, 1986). *Structural dimensions* include the total number of important people in a person's life; the areas of life or domains represented by these individuals—for example, family, friends, and neighbors; frequency and duration of interaction; length or history of the relationship; geographic distance; and number of people in the network who know one another. For example, social-network analysts describe as *dense* those networks containing a high proportion of acquaintances. The presence and characteristics of structural resources are often assessed graphically and mathematically via social-network analysis, which originated in the field of social anthropology (Sharkey, 1989). Social-network analysis can address such questions as whether potentially supportive people are available to the individual, nearby, and accessible. Several procedures for assessing a person's individual social network will be presented later in this section.

The *functional dimensions* of support include subjective appraisals of the availability or accessibility of different types of support, one's satisfaction with support received, and perceptions of reciprocity or fairness in the exchange of resources. Another subjective property of social support is level of intimacy, a person's appraisal of the degree of emotional closeness in relationships (Pilisuk & Parks, 1988). Social relationships that are judged to be more intimate or close are often referred to as *strong ties,* whereas relationships that are

more distant or casual are termed *weak ties* (Zippay, 1990–1991).

Types of Social Support.

The literature on social support delineates various forms of support resources exchanged by individuals and their network systems. Similar to the distinction between the quantitative and qualitative dimensions of support, most types of support can be roughly divided into (1) concrete, tangible, or instrumental support and (2) emotional, or verbal, support. Examples of concrete, or practical, assistance include the provision of food, child care, transportation, help with a household repair, or a loan of money. Emotional, or verbal, support includes active, nonjudgmental listening; expressing appreciation, understanding, or empathy; and offering information or advice to help solve a problem. As these examples suggest and as others have pointed out, support may not always be the provision of unconditional positive regard. For example, Pines and Aronson (1981) describe six types of support, one of which is *nonjudgmental listening* and another of which is *unconditional emotional support.* The remaining four types of support expand our understanding of what may constitute socioemotional resources. These are *emotional challenge,* or questioning someone's excuses and attributions; *technical support,* or an expert affirming someone's technical competence; *technical challenge* by an expert who offers questions, reservations, or critical feedback; and *social reality testing and sharing*, which provide external validation of one's perceptions and interpretations. Other potential support resources have been identified in an examination of reciprocal relationships between mentors and protégés (Richey, Gambrill, & Blythe, 1988). For example, mentors can offer access to opportunities and resources, advocate for protégés, and provide role models for behavior, attitudes, and values. Potential supports offered by protégés include increased visibility and public approval of the mentor, access to different channels of communication, and replication of ideas and projects.

Thus, in addition to the many ways in which people help one another in concrete or practical ways, there appears to be a myriad of interpersonal or communication pathways for the exchange of information, perspectives, and models for living, coping, and striving. Further, successful mobilization, utilization, and reciprocity of these diverse socioemotional resources require adeptness in a variety of interpersonal competencies, including knowledge of the prevailing norms and rules (etiquette) of such exchanges; skills to elicit needed supports and terminate unhelpful forms of assistance; and the ability to identify whom to approach for help, when, and under what conditions. Developing and refining the competencies necessary to successfully generate and negotiate person-to-person exchanges of support is the purview of social skill training.

Social Support Effects. The functions, or effects, of social support have been documented by research in many fields, including child and family services, mental health, health care, and gerontology. Although most studies document positive effects of support, others report neutral or negative effects. A brief review of these findings will be summarized here. The reader is referred to other, more extensive reviews of the research on the effects of social support (Cohen & Syme, 1985; Gottlieb, 1988; Whittaker & Garbarino, 1983).

In most studies, social support is viewed as an instrumental goal to other ultimate goals. For example, evidence from various fields suggests that social support is associated with better service outcomes among at-risk families (Maluccio & Whittaker, 1988); a reduced burden on those who care for the elderly (Robinson, 1988); finding and securing income and employment resources (Granovetter, 1974; Zippay, 1990–1991); better adjustment to pregnancy and better outcomes

(Cronenwett, 1985; Nuckolls, Cassel, & Kaplan, 1972), more successful cross-cultural adaptation among Southeast Asian refugees (Matsuoka & Ryujin, 1989; Rumbaut, 1986); reduced morbidity and mortality rates (Berkman, 1985); the onset (Blumenthal et al., 1987) and experience (Berkman & Seeman, 1986) of coronary disease; enhanced coping in women who are treated for breast cancer (Brandt, 1987; Cooper, Cooper, & Faragher, 1986); better mental health adjustment, or emotional well-being (Abbey, Abramis, & Caplan, 1985; Cohen, Teresi, Holmes, 1985); better posttraumatic adjustment (Murphy, 1987); reduced feelings of loneliness (Christen, 1986; Eisemann, 1984; Jones & Moore, 1987); enhanced resiliency in coping with stress and increased positive self-concept among employed African-American women (Allen & Britt, 1983); greater life satisfaction and reduced role conflict among dual-earner Mexican-American families (Holtzman & Gilbert, 1987); improved mental health and well-being among elderly women (Israel & Antonucci, 1987); and better self-concepts among black adolescents (Coates, 1985).

Despite the persuasive evidence documenting the facilitative effects of social support, not all correlates or consequences of support appear to be positive. For example, research suggests that social isolation, or the absence of social resources, may be associated with the existence of some problems but not with others. A recent critical review of evidence for the relationship between parental isolation and child maltreatment concluded that existing research clearly supported this relationship among neglectful parents but was equivocal among physically abusive parents (Seagull, 1987). The benefits of support may also vary greatly across individuals who differ on such characteristics as gender, age, socioeconomic status, and cultural background. For example, Dressler (1985) found in a study of 285 households in a predominantly African-American community that social support from extended kin had buffering effects on depression for men (age 17 to 65) and women over 35 but not for younger women, 17 to 34.

Closely knit network structures may not be helpful to some people in times of trouble because they can impede or postpone the seeking of help from formal service providers. For example, in one study of 1,224 people over 60 years of age, the presence of a large extended family and the availability of kin confidants appeared to inhibit awareness of services and seeking of help (Chapleski, 1989). Similarly, among Southeast Asian refugees, the presence of dense (well-interconnected) networks of social support along with a general unfamiliarity with and distrust of formal service systems can drastically inhibit seeking timely assistance for a family crisis or conflict (Duong-Tran, 1992). For example, a husband and wife who are involved in a serious, potentially violent, marital conflict may insist on getting help from family members and kin rather than seeking more formal help from providers outside their ethnic community.

Furthermore, information, feedback, or advice from disturbed or deviant network members may be of questionable quality or value in terms of promoting effective problem solutions. For instance, among parents who have been identified as abusive to their children, frequent or extended contact with their family of origin and extended kin may be contraindicated. Often, abusive parents report a family history of abuse, including being maltreated themselves as children. Frequently, these adult children, who are now parents themselves, continue to experience members of the extended family as intrusive, critical, or coersive rather than as supportive (Richey, Lovell, & Reid, 1991).

Because developing and maintaining large networks may require extraordinary time and attention, the added stress of network upkeep may counteract or outweigh the potential stress-buffering effects of available resources (Schilling, 1987). For example, in a comparative study of Samoan immigrants and New Zealanders of European backgrounds and their adjustment to a major industrial city, social support systems appeared to provide no positive effect in buffering stress, particularly among Samoan immigrants (Graves & Graves, 1985). These authors suggest that the psychic costs of maintaining multiple kinship ties exceeded the benefits of kin support.

Finally, sociocultural norms can encourage rigid helper roles within extended families. For instance, women are often expected to assume greater caretaking responsibility than men in maintaining contact and reciprocity of support with members of the family network. One consequence of these role-bound expectations of caregiving can be a *support gap* between what providers give to others and what they, in turn, receive (Belle, 1982).

Theoretical Formulations. The voluminous empirical literature documenting the association between social support and an array of (mostly) positive outcomes far outweighs comparable advances in theoretical development. Some scholars predict that the growth of theory will be the next major advance in the field of social support (Sarason, Sarason, & Pierce, 1990). Although explanations for how social connectedness advances health and well-being require further specification and refinement, a number of theoretical formulations have been postulated for conceptualizing the observed health-protective effects of social support. These formulations are multidisciplinary and include the psychological theory of attachment, which views social support as a personality characteristic developed in early childhood (Bowlby, 1988); stress and coping theory, which conceptualizes support as a process for coping with, or buffering, negative life events and chronic life strains (Thoits, 1986); and anthropological concepts of kinship (Matsuoka & Ryujin, 1989). Among these formulations are several social science theories that conceptualize social support as interpersonal transactions (Heller, Swindel, & Dusenbury, 1986; Kahn & Antonucci, 1980; Shinn, Lehmann, &

Wong, 1984; Shumaker & Brownell, 1984; Wortman, 1984). These theories, specifically social exchange, equity, and communication theories, will be highlighted here because they bolster the selection of social skills training as an intervention to enhance interpersonal relations and the activation of supportive transactions.

Social exchange theory provides an overarching framework for understanding social support. This sociological theory posits that social interaction is influenced in large part by the giving and receiving of resources and the principles of reciprocity (Homans, 1974). Within this framework, social support processes are characterized as bidirectional exchanges of benefits, costs, and influences, rather than as the unidirectional receipt or provision of support (Bandura, 1977). Further, the exchange of resources may not reflect a *quid pro quo*—or something for something—arrangement. More likely, the principles of social exchange embody a "bank-account" model in which interactants offer or invest resources at one time, expecting that at a later time the exchange will balance out (Gottman, Markman, & Notarius, 1977). Social exchange theory is compatible with social learning or operant-conditioning principles. In fact, proponents of social exchange theories are often referred to as "behavioral sociologists" (Burgess & Bushell, 1969).

Equity theory adds to our understanding of the reciprocal nature of social support. Specifically, greater relationship satisfaction is experienced if interactants view their exchange of resources as "fair." Conversely, individuals who perceive themselves as either "overbenefitted" or "underbenefitted" (receiving too much or too little) will perceive the relationship as less satisfactory than if they feel equitably treated (Hatfield & Traupmann, 1981).

Efforts to understand and eventually to influence social support are also bolstered by *communication theory* (Albrecht & Adelman, 1987a). Recent efforts to more precisely conceptualize social support have recommended distinguishing the cognitive, or perceptual, forms of social support from the behavioral aspects (Dunkel-Schetter & Bennett, 1990). The behavioral forms of support consist of the actual interpersonal exchanges and specific behaviors of providers and recipients of support. Formulating social support as an interpersonal, or communication, process focuses interventive attention on the verbal and nonverbal transactions between or among people in network structures. For example, messages may be perceived as more supportive if they encourage a shift in attribution, help break down an overwhelming task into smaller steps, and encourage independence (Albrecht & Adelman, 1987b). Thus, communication theory facilitates a "micro" analysis of social support in person-to-person exchanges (Albrecht & Adelman, 1987b), which in turn can inform micro-level intervention efforts with individuals, families, and small groups.

Given that much attention in the human services is devoted to helping people prevent, overcome, or solve life problems, regain personal and familial equilibrium after a crisis, or develop new patterns of living to cope with personal disability or limitation, the accumulating research on social support provides compelling evidence that the professional helper can expand or intensify intervention efforts by attending to the number and quality of important relationships the client has with family and extended kin, friends, coworkers, and neighbors at different life stages. Given the extent to which problems in social support mobilization, satisfaction, or reciprocity are influenced by interpersonal or communication-skill deficiencies, social skill training may be an important strategy to include with other methods to help clients connect with and activate informal support resources. The next section contains guidelines for assessing (1) the existence, characteristics, and quality of clients' social support re-

FIGURE 15.1   Examples of Social-Network Schemata

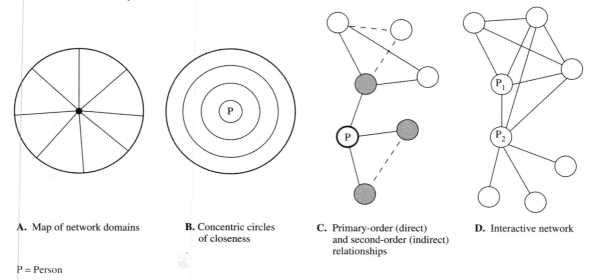

A. Map of network domains

B. Concentric circles
of closeness

C. Primary-order (direct)
and second-order (indirect)
relationships

D. Interactive network

P = Person

sources, (2) possible reasons or explanations for inadequate supports, and (3) the appropriateness and focus of social skill training as a support-enhancement intervention.

ASSESSMENT OF SOCIAL SUPPORT

Assessment of social support requires an examination of both the *structural* and *functional* dimensions of support. Features of *structural* support include such variables as the total number of people in the client's social network, the distribution of these members across network domains (household, extended family, friends), and the frequency and duration of daily social contacts. Features of *functional* support include perceptions of support availability, satisfaction with support received and provided, and feelings of closeness, or intimacy, with others.

If assessing structural and functional support suggests deficiencies or imbalances in support resources, utilization, or satisfaction, the next assessment step is to consider alter-

native explanations for low support in addition to inadequate social skills—for example, situational/environmental, psychological, and physiological factors. Finally, if interpersonal or social inadequacies are identified as major contributors to low social support, the practitioner's final assessment activity is to identify the particular competencies to be targeted for intervention with a particular client. These four assessment activities, along with specific guidelines and examples for each, are discussed in this section.

Assessing Structural Support

Social-Network Analysis.   A variety of social-network characteristics can be appraised using any number of available strategies. Frequently, some sort of symbolic or graphic schema is constructed that represents important individuals in a person's life and their relationships. In addition to simply identifying or naming people, respondents are asked to distribute or arrange network members. For example, as illustrated in Figure 15.1, respondents may be asked to:

1. Distribute people across various network domains (household members, extended family, friends, co-workers) as shown in Diagram A (Lovell & Hawkins, 1988; Richey, Lovell, & Reid, 1991; Tracy, 1990).
2. Place network members in concentric circles representing degrees of closeness, or intimacy, as shown in Diagram B (Antonucci, 1986).
3. Draw lines between oneself and network members who are known directly ("primary-order" relationships) and those known indirectly, or through others ("second-order" relationships). Solid lines can also illustrate "strong," or "high-intensity," ties, and broken lines can represent "weak," or "low-intensity," ties, as shown in Diagram C (Mitchell, 1969; Uehara, in press).
4. Illustrate the "interactive network" they share with their spouse or partner by connecting with lines persons known by one or both individuals, as shown in Diagram D (Surra, 1988).

Building on the work of network analysts at the University of Washington and others (Fiore et al., 1986; Hawkins & Fraser, 1985; Lovell & Hawkins, 1988; Resnick, 1985; Rook, 1984), I have utilized, with clinical and nonclinical populations, network-mapping procedures similar to the model in Diagram A that emphasize domain distribution of individual members (Richey, Hodges, & Agbayani-Siewert, 1991; Richey, Lovell, & Reid, 1991). This procedure invites the respondent to list the names of all the people who are *important,* or *significant,* to them with whom they have had contact during the *previous month.* Box 15.1 provides a sample text of these network-assessment instructions. Although instructions for assessing network characteristics can vary (Wood, 1984)—for example, some researchers place a limit on the number of people who can be named (such as 10 to 15) or ask that only those persons who are supportive be listed—these net-work-assessment guidelines were selected for several reasons. First, given the wide variability in total network size reported by both clinical populations (from 9 to 33 network members for mothers at risk for child maltreatment—Richey, Lovell, and Reid, 1991) and nonclinical populations (from 8 to 86 network members for African-American and Filipino-American parents—Richey, Hodges, & Agbayani-Siewert, 1991), much information would be lost if an arbitrary limit was placed on how many network members could be named. Second, enforcing a maximum network size could limit the addition of "less intense," or "weaker," ties. These less emotionally close or resource-specific contacts (such as a co-worker) have been shown to be more effective than closer ties in providing certain types of support—for example, employment-related information (Zippay, 1990–1991). Finally, limiting network members to only those who provide positive forms of support may eliminate significant or influential people in the person's life who are sources of both support and stress (Rook, 1984). Thus, the advantages of the network-assessment strategy proposed here include the calculation of *total* network size, distribution of network members across life domains, and "connections" among individual network members.

Amount of Social Interaction. Another dimension of structural support is the frequency and duration of contact with network members and others. Even though the size and distribution of a client's network may appear adequate, infrequent or brief and superficial contacts with network members or high-frequency contacts with others may compromise the availability and exchange of meaningful supports. Information on the amount of social interaction with network members can be gleaned during assessment from client estimates of contact frequencies—for example, do they have contact with this person once a year, a few times a year, monthly, weekly, or daily (Tracy, 1990)? More

BOX 15.1   Sample Instructions for Identifying Members of a Client's Social Network in Several Life Domains

I would like to know about the kinds of relationships you have with your family and friends. I am not interested in knowing specific details about people, but I would like to know whether the individuals you consider important in your life give you and your family help and support. Please think back to people you had contact with during the last month who were important to you. Important or significant people are those who (1) can make you feel good or bad, (2) are involved or play a part in your life, (3) influence decisions you and your family make, or (4) perform necessary or vital roles or services for you and your family. Think of the people you talked to on the phone, as well as those you saw face to face or wrote a letter to. The number and types of important people that individuals identify varies a lot from family to family. There is no right or wrong number.

First, think of the important people in your household. Whom does that include?

What about other family members you identify as important, significant, or influential?

Think of people you know at work, at school, or in social activities who are important to you. Don't forget to include people who give you practical help like transportation or baby-sitting. Did you include them in your list? What about neighbors?

What people from church, clubs, or organizations would you include? What about friends who haven't been listed in the other domains?

Sometimes we may remember and list only those people whom we have positive interactions with. Think of significant or influential people you had contact with where the interaction was negative or unpleasant. If they are important in your life, please include them. Now review your list of important people. Is anyone missing? Do you want to remove any names? Would you say that these people make up your social network?

accurate tallies of daily contact frequencies can be obtained using client diaries. Several "checklist" formats have been used successfully with clinical (Richey, Lovell, & Reid, 1991) and nonclinical individuals (Richey, Hodges, & Agbayani-Siewert, 1991). For example, American (Richey, Lovell, & Reid, 1991) and Canadian (Lovell & Richey, 1991) parents identified by Child Protective Services as at risk for child maltreatment completed daily records of their in-person and telephone contacts on a modified version of Wahler's Community Interaction Checklist (Wahler, Leske, & Rogers, 1979). For each contact, respondents identified their role or relationship with the person (friend, employee), who had initiated the contact, and the

content (topics), duration, and enjoyment level or valence of the interaction. Other studies have reported collecting similar information on social activity (Jones, 1981; Welbourn & Mazuryk, 1980).

Examining the structural features of a client's social support system can alert the practitioner to a number of characteristics or patterns that may suggest intervention directions. For example, small network size (eight or fewer), low frequency and duration of weekly contacts with network members, high concentrations of contact with network members in only a few domains (family, extended kin, and formal service providers), or high proportions of uninitiated (uninvited) contacts with certain network members (a critical parent, angry teacher, or depressed neighbor) may suggest the importance of helping the person develop a wider circle of supportive contacts in nonkin and nonprofessional domains—for example, co-workers, acquaintances in community clubs, and neighbors.

On the other hand, the size or characteristics of the network are only a part of the assessment profile. People with small networks may have no need for additional support persons if the existing members are perceived as trustworthy, dependable, helpful confidants. Similarly, persons with large networks may not perceive these as supportive but, rather, as obligatory, restrictive, or offering too little of the wrong thing too late. Hence, the client's subjective appraisal of the degree or quality of support is as important as the more objective documentation of the "presence" and "availability" of support resources. Suggestions for assessing the functional dimensions of support are reviewed in the next section.

Assessing Functional Support

Many standardized questionnaires and client- or problem-specific rating scales are available to assess a client's perceptions of and satisfaction with the amount and quality of companionship, social connectedness, or support from others. Because a thorough account of all the available assessment tools is beyond the scope of this chapter, the reader is referred to other reviews of potentially useful measures (Sarason, Shearin, Pierce, & Sarason, 1987; Tardy, 1985; Wood, 1984).

Based on comprehensive literature reviews of social support measures and on field research in which these measures were utilized with culturally diverse clinical and nonclinical populations, I have selected a number of measures that can provide useful information on the qualitative, or subjective, dimensions of support. Most of the measures listed below are included in a recent study (called the Family and Friends Study) of nonclinical Af-

rican-American and Filipino-American parents (Richey, Hodges, & Agbayani-Siewert, 1991).*

The Revised UCLA Loneliness Scale. This 20-item scale assesses subjective perceptions of the amount and quality of companionship, personal satisfaction with social relationships, and the experience of loneliness (Russell, Peplau, & Cutrona, 1980). Respondents rate on a 4-point scale (1 = never, 4 = often) how often they feel the way described in each statement—for example, "No one really knows me well." There is evidence of discriminant validity and concurrent validity between loneliness scores and self-report measures of social activities and relationships (amount of time spent alone each day; number of close friends). Russell and colleagues also report evidence of discriminant validity. A 4-item "short form" is also available.

Perceived Social Support from Family and Friends. This 20-item scale, one for families (PSS-Fa) and one for friends (PSS-Fr), measures the extent to which individuals perceive that their needs for emotional support, information, and feedback are fulfilled by friends and family (Procidano & Heller, 1983). Sample items explore the provision of support ("My friends come to me for emotional support") and the receipt of support ("I get good ideas about how to do things or make things from my family)." Procidano and Heller report high internal consistency, high test/retest reliability, and significant correlations between perceived support and measures of psychopathology and distress, conversational behavior, and trait anxiety.

Index of Family Relations (IFR). This 25-item instrument measures the degree, severity, or magnitude of problems that family

*A copy of the Family and Friends measurement packet, which contains slight alterations in questionnaire wording and scaling to enhance cultural appropriateness, is available from the author, Cheryl A. Richey, Professor, School of Social Work, University of Washington, 4101 15th Avenue N.E. (JH-30), Seattle, WA 98195.

members have in their relationships (Hudson, 1982). The IFR can be used as a measure of intrafamilial stress and as a rough index of relationship quality among family members and perceptions of family-mediated supports. This instrument, along with others that are a part of the Hudson Clinical Measurement Package, has high internal consistency and test/retest reliabilities and high face, concurrent, and construct validity (Hudson, 1982).

Index of Self-Esteem (ISE). Although not a measure of social support per se, this Hudson scale elicits one's evaluation of self as a social being. For example, "I feel that people really like to talk with me," "I think my friends find me interesting," and "When I am with strangers, I am very nervous" are representative items. The number of items, scaling format, instructions for scoring and interpretation, and data on reliability and validity are similar to those for the other measures in the Clinical Measurement Package (Hudson, 1982).

Network Orientation Scale. This 20-item instrument assesses a person's beliefs about relying on others and willingness to utilize social support resources, or seek help (Vaux, Burda, & Stewart, 1986). Sample items include: "You can never trust people to keep a secret," "Friends often have good advice to give," and "It's OK to ask favors of other people." Vaux and colleagues report good internal consistency and convergent validity. Because the Network Orientation Scale lacked published instructions for applied use, including guides for scoring and interpretation, scoring procedures were developed for specific use in several clinical studies (Lovell & Richey, 1991; Richey, Lovell, & Reid, 1991).

Satisfaction with Social Support. Visual analogue (10-cm line) scales have been developed to measure satisfaction with available social support from family and friends (Richey, Hodges, & Agbayani-Siewert, 1991; Richey, Lovell, & Reid, 1991). Different types of support are included—for example, financial assistance, socializing, problem solving, practical help, emotional support, physical comfort, and opportunity to help others (Tardy, 1985). For each type of support with both family and friends, respondents mark the place on a 10-cm line between "not satisfied at all" and "very satisfied" that corresponds to their current perceptions.

Quality of Social Support from Core Network Members. Additional questions can be asked of respondents about the nature of the supports exchanged and the relationships with the "15 most important" people in their networks (Lovell, 1986; Tracy, 1990). For example, what types of supports are exchanged with these "stronger" ties, how satisfied is the person with the supports provided, and how reciprocal does the person perceive the exchange of resources to be?

Quality of daily social interactions. In addition to information on frequency and duration of social contacts collected by clients on daily checklists, other information can be noted about the nature and quality of the interaction, including the valence rating of each contact as either positive, neutral, or negative and the topic(s) of conversation. For example, a small pilot study of social support skill training of abusive mothers found at pretraining that participants rated a large percentage of their daily contacts as negative (44%) (Richey, Lovell, & Reid, 1991). At posttraining this fell to 18% negative, and at follow-up, to 11% negative. Others have also reported that the social interaction patterns of at-risk parents are marked by negatively perceived coercive relationships (Wahler, Leske, & Rogers, 1979).

Examining the range of topics discussed in daily contacts can also shed light on the extent to which interactions focus on trading "war stories" or on solving problems (Wahler & Hann, 1984). High rates of sharing others' misfortunes can result in greater stress through vicarious or contagion reactions (Belle, 1987).

Exploring Alternative Explanations for Low Social Support

If assessing dimensions of functional as well as structural support suggests that a client feels lonely, has few or unsatisfactory friendships, has little contact with network members, cannot depend on family and friends for support, is wary of seeking support or asking for help or advice from others, and has few meaningful or conflict-free interactions with people, he or she probably has deficiencies or imbalances in support resources as well as skill difficulties in identifying, mobilizing, utilizing, and reciprocating support. However, the specific role of interpersonal skills as a cause, correlate, and consequence of low social support must be determined if social skills training is to be a viable option. Other factors may, in fact, account for some or most of the "interference" that limits the exchange and personal experience of social support. By carefully considering and eliminating these alternative explanations, the practitioner will be able to more confidently select social skills training as the intervention of choice.

Situational/Environmental Factors. A number of external obstacles can interfere with a person's establishing and maintaining supportive relationships. Some of these are constricted physical mobility, limited concrete resources, prejudice and discrimination, and restricted personal freedom. For example, *mobility* should be considered as a possible contributing factor to low support levels. Geographic isolation; absence of safe, affordable, reliable transportation; and structural barriers to access for those with disabilities can contribute to social isolation independently of the person's level of social competence.

The availability of such basic *resources* as time, income, and housing is also a fundamental consideration when assessing support obstacles. Does the person have the time to pursue personal relationships? For low-income single parents with young children, time and energy are at a premium. Working double or night shifts or having additional caretaking responsibilities for frail or elderly family members can leave very little time in the day or on weekends for supportive social contacts. Financial status is also a consideration. Does the person have money for transporation, child care or respite care, telephone service, or a movie or meal out with a friend? Finally, the quality of one's housing situation can also influence social relationships. For example, if housing is crowded or uncomfortable, there may be little space for private or relaxed conversations. Living in an unsafe area may limit a person's willingness to venture out for very long, as well as others' willingness to visit.

Another situational barrier to a client's getting support may be the *presence of a significant other* in the social network who controls the person's interactions with others. For example, in abusive relationships the male partner often demands that the woman stay at home and responds with excessive surveillance, possessiveness, and jealousy if she attempts to establish other relationships (Mitchell & Hodson, 1983). In such cases, efforts to increase a woman's friendships and contacts beyond the immediate or extended family may meet with resistance and even violence from others in the family system. In these instances, goals of network expansion and redistribution of support resources would require very careful thought and planning to minimize adverse consequences for the woman and possibly for other family members, including children. Because the mother is often the target for family-focused interventions or is the only one in the family to attend parenting classes or support groups, the temptation is to intervene with her unilaterally. However, overlooking the systemic implications of this narrow intervention focus could result in weakened effects, at the least, or unintended ramifications, at the most. Greater consideration often needs to be given to how to induct male partners and other significant family members into procedures to enhance social support, including social skill training. In contrast to what is known about women, little is known about the social-network characteristics of men in violent or neglectful family systems, and few efforts have been documented for intervening with them (Martin, 1984).

Cognitive/Psychological Factors.   Another cluster of variables associated with social support use and satisfaction that may not be directly connected with levels of social skill per se includes attitudes about help-seeking (Eckenrode, 1983), attributional and coping styles, and the presence of mental and personality disorders. As mentioned above, the Network Orientation Scale is a tool for assessing one's *attitudes about seeking help* from others—whether people are trustworthy or offer good advice (Vaux et al., 1986). Network orientation may reflect a relatively stable "world view" based on prior learning experiences that may not be amenable to relatively short-term, skills-focused intervention. Multiproblem mothers, for example, even after a 12-week group for social support skill training and subsequent changes in some social support indexes, continued to report a fairly equal mix of beliefs that people can and cannot be trusted to help (Richey, Lovell, & Reid, 1991).

An *internal attributional style,* or a preference for *nonaffiliative coping strategies,* may also compromise the effects of interventions aimed at increasing social support resources and utilization (Sandler & Lakey, 1982). Clients who take personal responsibility for solving most problems will probably select coping or problem-solving strategies that do not rely on reaching out to or depending on others. Thus, social supports may be underutilized not because of deficiencies in social skill but because of a preference for independent coping alternatives. Further, the literature on coping suggests that many different reactions can be helpful in reducing stress and managing the problems of living—for example, taking a break or a vacation, thinking through a problem covertly, taking direct action, listening to music, or praying (Astor-Dubin & Hammen, 1984; Billings & Moos, 1982; Folkman & Lazarus, 1980).

The presence of *mental or personality disorders* can also exacerbate an individual's ability to reach out effectively to others and to reciprocate support. Likewise, major psychiatric impairment can affect how others react and respond to requests for support. For example, depression would certainly affect a person's motivation and ability to interact with others, as well as influencing perceptions of and satisfaction with support. Recent evidence also suggests that a diagnosis of avoidant personality disorder, which is characterized by early onset of social withdrawal, low self-esteem, and heightened sensitivity to social criticism, may often be associated with "extreme shyness," social isolation, poor-quality interactions, and a variety of psychiatric conditions (Alden, 1989; Alden & Cappe, 1988).

Physiological Factors.   A comprehensive assessment of alternative explanations for inadequate social support must also consider the potential influence of excessive autonomic arousal, alcohol and other drug addiction, and sensory and physical limitations. For example, *high levels of arousal or anxiety,* which may include fears of being observed or negatively judged (social phobia) or fears of being away from home or in a crowded place (agoraphobia), may seriously interfere with a person's ability to perform skillfully in social situations, even when the requisite skills are available. Some research suggests that individuals with "pure" social phobias tend not to have social skill deficits; rather, they are characterized by extreme discomfort and accompanying somatic symptoms in social situations (Turner, Beidel, & Townsley, 1990).

Often, social contacts take place in the presence of *substance use or abuse*. The excessive use of alcohol or other drugs can compromise successful social interaction in a number of ways. For example, substance abuse can reduce accurate perception and interpretation of social cues, sensitivity to taking turns and conversational reciprocity, and appropriate timing and depth of emotional expressiveness.

Finally, social interaction can be significantly influenced by an individual's *sensory or other physical limitations*. For example, differences in vision, hearing, memory, and stamina can directly affect the quality of social relationships and contribute to social isolation. Limitations of this kind may be especially problematic for the frail elderly (Gambrill, 1986).

In summary, there may be many other explanations for low levels of social support in addition to inadequate social skills. Although these alternative explanations do not necessarily eliminate social skill training as an intervention strategy, their viability in any case suggests the consideration of additional, perhaps more primary, strategies for addressing core environmental, cognitive, and physiological factors that may interfere with the social exchange of supportive resources. On the other hand, if assessment suggests that social isolation and poor-quality social interactions are related to low levels of interpersonal skill—for example, the person is unable to initiate or maintain a meaningful conversation, is shy or awkward with people, fails to listen to or acknowledge others' contributions, is abrupt or rude, gives premature or inappropriate advice, is unable to offer positive feedback or praise, or is unable to develop new or close relationships—then social-skill training may be the intervention of choice (Lovell, 1991; Lovell & Richey, 1991). Before training in social support skills commences, a final assessment activity is pursued that involves identifying the specific interpersonal competencies that will be selected or targeted for intervention with a particular client or client group.

Targeting Specific Interpersonal Competencies

A number of knowledge and skill competencies have been associated with success in interpersonal relationships, including abilities in initiating, maintaining, deepening, altering, and ending relationships (Gambrill & Richey, 1988). Despite a growing interest in social skill training to enhance social support, however, there is little empirical evidence suggesting which specific competencies or components should be the focus of intervention efforts. Clearly, the nature of the client population (for example, adolescents or older adults) and the parameters of the problem (for example, an abusive parent's insularity or a widow's loneliness) will influence the content or focus of social skills training. I have participated in the development or delivery of social skill training with shy or socially inactive women of various ages and with parents at risk for child abuse and neglect. Based on these experiences, on consultation with other professionals engaged in social support intervention, and on related professional literature, four cognitive and five behavioral competencies are offered as important topics for social support skill training:

A. Cognitive competencies
   1. *Basic knowledge about relationships:* what they are, why they are important, how they develop, and the social norms about what behaviors are more or less appropriate in different situations
   2. *Perceptual skills:* the ability to identify and accurately interpret (decode) the meaning communicated by others verbally and nonverbally
   3. *Decision-making skills:* the ability to determine if and when to approach

someone for conversation, to assess whether a person is receptive to social interaction or requests for support

4. *Cognitive-restructuring or cognitive-replacement skills:* the ability to consider alternative explanations for or meanings of one's own and others' behavior and reactions; the ability to alter and replace unproductive or distorted thoughts and beliefs that interfere with satisfying or comfortable social relationships

B. Behavioral competencies
   1. *Self-presentation skills:* the ability to present oneself in socially appropriate ways to increase the likelihood of positive expectations and reactions from others
   2. *Social initiation skills:* the ability to take the initiative in approaching people, starting conversations, and offering suggestions
   3. *Basic conversational skills:* the ability to talk with and listen to others, including the ability to maintain turn-taking or reciprocity
   4. *Maintenance skills:* the ability to pursue conversations and contacts over time, including the ability to establish deeper or closer relationships
   5. *Conflict-resolution skills:* the ability to handle disagreement, disappointment, or lack of rewards in relationships

Although not an exhaustive list, these specific competency areas can provide a comprehensive base for intervention. The particular mix of skills targeted will depend in part on the nature of the clients and their presenting concerns and goals, as well as the structural and time limitations placed on treatment configurations by agency sponsors.

Further assessment and goal setting with clients can facilitate the selection and prioritization of competencies for training. For example, written instruments, like the 30-item

Social Situations Questionnaire (Trower, Bryant, & Argyle, 1978) and the 40-item Assertion Inventory (Gambrill & Richey, 1975), can provide information on specific interpersonal activities and interactions that are more or less challenging or important to clients. The Social Situations Questionnaire asks respondents to rate how difficult it is for them to go to parties, meet strangers, get to know people in depth, or take the initiative in keeping a conversation going (0 = no difficulty, 4 = avoid if possible).

With the Assertion Inventory, respondents rate how much discomfort or anxiety they would experience in each situation (1 = none, 5 = very much), and the probability or likelihood of displaying the behavior if actually presented or confronted with the situation (1 = always do it, 5 = never do it). Situations include initiating a conversation with a stranger, requesting a meeting or a date with someone, asking personal questions, expressing a difference of opinion, giving and receiving compliments, and giving and receiving negative feedback. In an experimental study of social skill training with 21 shy or socially inactive women, age 23 to 59, mean total discomfort and probability scores before training were above normative levels, with 118.25 for discomfort (normative score total = 96) and 119.44 for response probability (normative score total = 104) (Richey, 1979). Further, items identified by members as those they would like to handle more effectively can shape session-by-session training content, and mean discomfort scores on selected items can influence the order or sequence of topic presentation. For instance, disagreeing may be rated as less anxiety-provoking than handling criticism and thus would be introduced earlier in training.

Information on clients' social contacts can also provide useful parameters for pinpointing and structuring training content. For example, shy women reported on checklists that despite having weekly social contacts, they initiated few of the contacts, the contacts were fairly brief, and the women often rated them as uncomfortable and unenjoyable (Richey, 1979). Moreover, client ratings of others' reactions to the contacts revealed that fewer than half were judged positive (47%), half were rated as neutral (51%), and 2% were rated as negative.

Based on these baseline data and on descriptions of themselves as "shy" by 81% of the clients, the focus of training became social-initiation skills, being more active in conversations, and having more enjoyable conversations (Richey, 1979). The specific topics selected for the five- to six-week, 12.5-hour training groups included information about relationships; self-assessment and goal setting; where to go to meet people; initiating, maintaining, and ending conversations; and having more comfortable and enjoyable social experiences (Gambrill & Richey, 1988).

In contrast to the content areas targeted for shy women, the training topics targeted for parents identified by Child Protective Services (CPS) as at risk for child abuse and neglect emphasized more basic information about relationship development, self-protection skills, and assertiveness. As with the shy groups, the general goal of training with the at-risk parents was increasing positive social interaction and friendships. However, network-assessment data and clinical observations suggested that many of the parents were relying heavily on support from immediate and extended family members and professional service providers and that few identified important people in other network domains, such as friends or neighbors (Lovell, 1986; Tracy, 1990). Before social support skill training, for example, at-risk parents reported that 29% of their daily contacts were with immediate and extended family members, 25% with professional service or care providers, and fewer than 13% with friends (Richey, Lovell, & Reid, 1991).

Early in the development of training with at-risk parents in social support skills, I conducted an informal survey of Homebuilders therapists, who provide intensive services to multiple-problem families on the verge of disruption (Kinney, Haapala, & Booth, 1991). Many of these families are referred to Homebuilders by CPS officials. Often these families are viewed as socially isolated or lacking in adequate social support resources (Tracy, 1990). Twenty-seven Homebuilders therapists were asked to list the 5 most important skills they believed would help the families they worked with develop more supportive social contacts. Table 15.1 summarizes the 17 general skill areas identified and the number of therapists selecting each area. The top 5 skill areas identified—assertiveness, listening, positive about self and others, self-presentation and social etiquette, and emotion management—were consistent with clinical observations of other agency staff members working with similar populations of parents in treatment for child abuse and neglect (Lovell & Richey, 1990; Richey, Lovell, & Reid, 1991). For example, when mothers interacted with other clients and agency employees, they were often inappropriate in their comments, making rude remarks about others' behavior and dress without apparent awareness of the embarrassment they were causing. Client self-report data on daily social contacts revealed that mothers experienced 44% of their interactions as negative, 32% as neutral, and only 24% as positive (Richey, Lovell, & Reid, 1991). Many of the mothers also had difficulty being assertive. They were either too passive and were taken advantage of or were very aggressive. Many alternated between the extremes. A number of the mothers also reported being frightened of friendship. For example, when asked to rate perceived satisfaction with social support from friends, several initially refused, saying that they wanted nothing to do with friends. Friends were the people who hurt you, stole your money or your partner, or reported you to the authorities. Many of these women had a personal history of exploitation and punishment in close relationships. Consequently,

TABLE 15.1   Skill Areas Identified by Homebuilders Therapists as Important for Multiproblem Families to Mobilize Social Support

Rank	Skill Area	Frequency	Example
1	Assertiveness	25	Giving constructive feedback, setting personal limits
2	Listening	24	Showing interest, reflection
3	Positive about self and others	17	Giving and receiving positive feedback
4	Basic self-presentation, social etiquette	16	Engaging in small talk
5	Emotion management	13	Modulating angry or sad feelings
6	Active in conversations	10	Asking questions, introducing topics
6	Reciprocity and balance	10	Employing give and take in conversations, returning favors
8	Initiating contacts	8	Suggesting activities
8	Identifying and using support resources	8	Asking who is available and willing to help
10	Interpreting others' reactions	7	Noticing others' nonverbals
11	Topic diversity	6	Having the ability to talk about a number of topics in conversations
12	Decision making	5	Knowing whom to approach, when, how
13	Starting conversations	3	Talking to strangers, greeting people
13	Being open minded	3	Accepting differences
15	Problem solving	2	Considering alternative solutions
15	Self-esteem and self-care	2	Having positive self-regard
17	Time management	1	Organizing time better so you can follow through with social agreements

$n=27$

they had little trust in others and were often in situations or relationships that were exploitative or unsafe.

Building on observations and suggestions of both American and Canadian professionals who provide services to severely troubled, often involuntary parents and families and on pretraining information collected from clients themselves, a cluster of cognitive and behavioral competencies was selected and organized into a 16-week curriculum (Lovell, 1991; Lovell & Richey, 1991). Table 15.2 presents a summary of session content or competency themes. Noteworthy is the relative emphasis on "self-protection skills." The focus early in training on strategies for feeling

safer was viewed as a necessary precursor to helping these parents reach out to people in new, prosocial ways.

Targeting client-specific competencies for intervention establishes the content foci for social support skill training and moves the practitioner from assessment to intervention. The unique combination and sequence of targeted skill areas address the *what* of treatment—what topics and skills will be covered in training. The next consideration is *how*—how identified content or skill areas will be taught. What *methods* will be employed to enhance behavioral and attitudinal changes? In the third section of this chapter I describe and illustrate the core cognitive-behavioral proce-

TABLE 15.2   *Session Content for Social Support Skill Training with At-Risk Parents*

Sessions	Content
1 and 2	*Stages of relationships:* identifying the phases of friendship, the positive and negative aspects of having a friend
3 and 4	*Danger signs in relationships:* identifying fears and personal vulnerabilities associated with friendship; identifying characteristics or behaviors of others that signal caution in developing a relationship
5 and 6	*Self-protection skills:* exploring personal values and beliefs that define boundaries in relationships; identifying unsafe situations
7	*Prosocial activities:* qualities to look for in a friend; meeting and making friends
8–10	*Basic conversational skills:* starting conversations, developing listening skills, changing the topic, ending conversations
11–14	*Assertive skills:* giving and receiving compliments, discussing negative concerns with others, handling criticism, refusing and making requests
15	*Community support resources:* identifying organizations and activities that can help members increase the number of supportive people in their social networks
16	*Endings and new beginnings:* acknowledging social support goals achieved; identifying ongoing and future relationship goals and steps for achieving these

NOTE: Adapted from *The Friendship Group: Learning the Skills to Create Social Support. A Manual for Group Leaders* by M. L. Lovell. Copyright © 1991 by the University of British Columbia, School of Social Work.

dures for group social support skill training. The discussion includes specific examples of training innovations and modifications developed for use with diverse and hard-to-reach clients.

CORE PROCEDURES FOR SOCIAL SUPPORT SKILL TRAINING

Social skill training typically includes information on social relationships and socially effective behavior; development of training goals; modeling or demonstrations; behavior rehearsal or role playing; feedback or social reinforcement; anxiety management; training in self-reinforcement and cognitive restructuring; and homework assignments. Working with people in small groups has many advantages, especially when the training focus is enhanced interpersonal or relationship skills. Some of these advantages are reducing feel-ings of isolation and hopelessness that may come from being the "only person" with problems; increasing opportunities for mutual reinforcement, multiple modeling, and group brainstorming of problem solutions and alternatives; exchanging feedback and suggestions; and observing how others react to patterns of self-presentation (Rose, 1989). Within the context of a group of 6 to 12 members that meets regularly for a designated period (weekly 2-hour sessions for 12 weeks), the core procedures presented in this section are recommended.

Transmitting Relevant Information on Social Relationships

It is important to expose clients to the many relevant findings from the social sciences on the stages and processes of relationship formation, the different functions of friendships (Duck, 1977, 1983; Duck & Gilmore, 1981); the criteria for social perceptions or judgments of appropriate behavior (Knapp, 1978); and the social norms for nonverbal behavior and how these can communicate and maintain interpersonal power relationships (Henley, 1977). For example, research suggests that some forms of self-disclosure are appropriate during brief conversations (less than 15 minutes), whereas information of a more personal nature is apppropriate only if offered during extended contacts (Knapp, 1978). A low-intimacy topic might be talking about how often your relatives and family get together, whereas a high-intimacy topic might be disclosing problems of alcoholism or drug abuse in your family. Having information of this kind can reduce trial-and-error learning, which can be punishing and can discourage the performance of new skills.

In training groups with shy women, information on relationships was often made available in the form of between-session readings. For example, several chapters in *Taking Charge of Your Social Life* (Gambrill & Richey, 1988) were assigned during the week, and the topic—for instance, initiating conversations—was discussed and practiced at the next session.* In training groups with American and Canadian at-risk parents, assigning reading material was not viewed as appropriate or facilitative of learning because these parents had marginal literacy skills and often associated educational or training activities with criticism and embarrassment. Therefore, several innovations based on visual aids were developed specifically to convey complex information on social relationships. For example, unique to these groups was the Relationship Roadmap, a visual metaphor that illustrates key concepts about relationship development (Lovell, 1991; Lovell & Richey, 1991; Richey, Lovell, & Reid, 1991).† Meta-

phor has been found to facilitate rapport, enable people to shift or reframe their perspective, communicate new information in ways that are less threatening, and promote generalization of learning to new situations (Bagarozzi & Anderson, 1988; Lankton & Lankton, 1989; Marlatt & Fromme, 1987; Marlatt & Gordon, 1985).

Figure 15.2 presents a simplified version of the Relationship Roadmap, which illustrates the journey to friendship and intimacy through five normative stages of relationship development. These five stages, depicted as towns along the road, are Acquaintanceville, Buddyborough, Friendly City, Personal Friendsville, and Partnersburg. Each town describes central behavioral referents for that stage in a relationship; for example, a "buddy" (a resident of Buddyborough) is described as a person with whom you might share one activity such as bowling but with whom you would be unlikely to disclose intensely personal information. Guidelines suggesting the time needed to move between towns, as well as warning signs, dead ends, and the skills needed to handle them, are also drawn on the map at points along the road.

The Relationship Roadmap provided a central theme for training and a structure for the weekly group sessions. This elaborate allegorical framework, which was less threatening and less tedious than traditional instructional methods, appeared to accelerate parents' personal involvement with the material and promoted discussion of common relationship difficulties among group members. Parents identified their own relationship patterns, problems, and goals in road-map terms, such as the "freeway" approach to sexual intimacy. Thus, the map provided a symbolic representation of relationship development as well

---

*Copies of *Taking Charge of Your Social Life* are available from Behavioral Options, P.O. Box 8118, Berkeley, CA 94707.

†A detailed poster-size copy of the Relationship Roadmap is included with *The Friendship Group* training manual (Lovell, 1991). The manual provides a session-

by-session guide and suggestions for group-member selection, leader training, and facilitating a cohesive group climate. Requests for the manual can be sent directly to Madeline L. Lovell, Assistant Professor, Department of Sociology, Seattle University, Seattle, WA 98122-4460. The cost for the manual, including mailing, is $25.

FIGURE 15.2 A Simplified Representation of the Relationship Roadmap

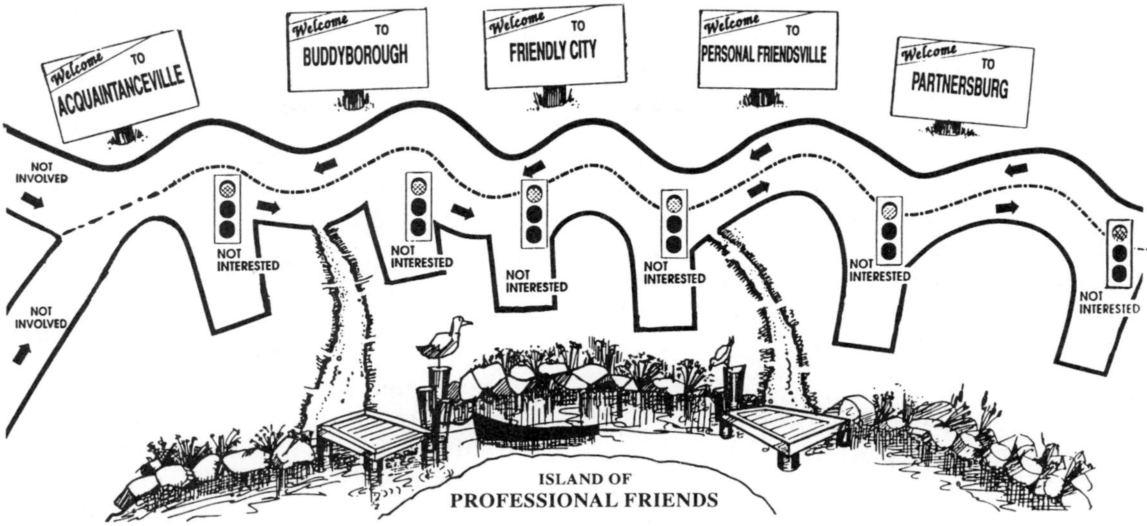

Relationship Roadmap © 1991 by Madeline L. Lovell, Ph.D.

as a stimulus for self-disclosure and empathic sharing.

Over the course of training, participants enthusiastically elaborated map details—for example, relegating "professional friends" such as counselors and social workers to an island that was served only by ferries. Early in training (session 2) each group member was given an individual copy of the Relationship Roadmap to use as a tool for personal assessment and goal setting. For example, parents were asked to list their network members on the map in the appropriate towns. This exercise provided a basis for establishing goals for network change—for instance, expanding the "population" of Buddyborough, or moving someone from Friendly City to Personal Friendsville.

Modeling and Rehearsal

In most training sessions a "modeling sequence" was employed to build and strengthen specific verbal and nonverbal communication skills (Rose, 1989). The modeling sequence combined overt demonstration, behavioral role playing, positive feedback, and coaching. Because the training groups with at-risk parents were conducted at a number of different community agencies, demonstration videotapes were produced to ensure consistency of modeled responses across groups (Lovell & Richey, 1991).* The videotapes displayed levels of effective responses by a variety of models with whom parent trainees could identify (Bandura, 1977). A number of social situations were portrayed from less difficult scenarios (changing the topic during a conversation with a friend) to more challenging ones (initiating a conversation with a stranger and handling criticism in a group meeting). The modeling tapes presented a number of possible alternatives for handling each situation, some more effective than others. The videotapes promoted lively group interaction, including spirited role playing among members. In one group, parents decid-

---

*Information about purchasing a copy of the demonstration videotape can be obtained from Madeline L. Lovell, Assistant Professor, Department of Sociology, Seattle University, Seattle, WA 98122-4460.

ed that they could make a more effective modeling tape and produced their own demonstration of ways to engage a new parent at the agency and to maintain a conversation with a very shy acquaintance.

In contrast to groups with multiproblem parents, groups with shy women did not emphasize live modeling during sessions (Richey, 1979). It was assumed that these women, although self-described as "shy," probably had requisite social-interactional skills (Turner, Beidel, & Townsley, 1990) and that symbolic representations of specific skills, in the form of examples in the training manual, would be sufficient to guide behavior during role playing. For example, *Taking Charge of Your Social Life* (Gambrill & Richey, 1988) includes numerous samples of dialogue that illustrate different ways to initiate conversations, bring up new topics, handle difficult situations, and create a more personal atmosphere. Other social skill researchers have suggested that overt modeling may add little to training effects with individuals who have basic skills but are socially anxious, whereas among individuals who are socially inadequate or lack social competence, overt modeling may be essential for successful performance (Eisler, Hersen, & Miller, 1973; McFall & Twentyman, 1973; Trower, Yardley, Bryant, & Shaw, 1978).

Behavior rehearsal, or role playing, in social skill training groups provides opportunities to practice new behaviors in a relatively structured and safe environment. Rehearsal allows clients to experiment with different ways of responding to realistic situations and to get feedback from others on the appropriateness and impact of these responses. Shy women and at-risk parents uniformly identified behavior rehearsal as one of the most helpful aspects of training. For rehearsal to have maximum benefits, situations for practice should be specifically described and realistic for participants. To minimize performance anxiety and feelings of personal inadequacy, shaping principles should be incorporated into the development and presentation of situations. For example, it may be easier for group members to practice standard or scripted scenes rather than to have to practice a real or personal situation. Thus, initial role playing exercises may offer participants a menu of possible situations from which to select. Sample exercises for initiating conversations and arranging future meetings are listed below:

During a coffee break at work, you go up to a new employee and ask him or her to join you for lunch that afternoon (Gambrill & Richey, 1988, p. 109).

You are riding a bicycle and at a signal another cyclist pulls up alongside. You want to find out the shortest route to the park (Gambrill & Richey, 1988, p. 110).

New neighbors just moved into the house beside yours last week. You don't know anything about them, but they look like nice people. The husband is out in his yard playing ball with his son. You are in your yard and decide to start a conversation with him (Lovell, 1991, p. 46).

You meet an interesting single father at the library where you have both taken your children to hear stories. You exchange good ideas of possible books for the children to read. You have to leave now, but you'd like to continue this conversation (Lovell, 1991, p. 52).

You have been helping your neighbor clean up her backyard. All the children have been playing at her house. You'd like to see her again sometime soon for a more adult-oriented talk (Lovell, 1991, p. 52).

Structured exercises performed in small groups can also result in members viewing practice as an enjoyable, safe activity. For example, members in groups of three or four can be given the assignment to (1) each express, in turn, one opinion on a preselected topic of conversation, (2) enter an ongoing conversation among the other members in their small group without interrupting, (3) talk to their group on a topic of their choice for one minute, or (4) reflect the feeling message or emotional tone of their neighbor's comments by selecting possible words from a "feelings list" (Gambrill & Richey, 1988; Richey, 1981). These exercises, like games, engage all members in small-group practice of component skills in ways that are often fun and energizing.

Additional procedures can ease performance anxiety of members who may be frightened to role play in front of a group. For example, participants can remain in their seats, as part of the circle, instead of going to the front and "being on stage" (Lovell, 1991). Groups with at-risk parents found a team approach to role playing helpful in allaying initial anxiety. Each two-person team would consult before acting out the dialogue with another dyad.

Attention to personal levels of anxiety when discussing or rehearsing difficult situations can also help members manage or cope with interpersonal arousal. For instance, at-risk parents practiced identifying different levels of anxiety and corresponding physiological responses with the aid of the Anxiety Thermometer (Lovell, 1991). This graphic drawing of a thermometer was enlarged and posted or provided to members as an individual handout. Gradations of anxiety are depicted on the vertical scale along with descriptive phrases for each level; for example, "calm, peaceful, contented" is at the bottom, "edgy, dry throat, trouble swallowing, can't concentrate" is near the middle, and "terrified, panicky, want to run away or defend self" is at the top. During role playing segments, members were asked to use the Anxiety Thermometer to identify and communicate their level of anxiety. When reported levels got unduly elevated, the leader reminded members to institute strategies for reducing anxiety or perceived risk, including having someone else play the role while the person observed, taking a time-out relaxation break, or pacing practice of tough situations by selecting another situation for rehearsal that was less challenging.

When role-playing challenging or real situations, a structured procedure for taking turns and providing feedback has proved to foster active involvement by group members, peer modeling of alternative responses, and mutual reinforcement and support of successive improvements in performance (Richey, 1977). Members in small groups of three or four are encouraged to follow the following steps:

• If the situation is a real one, *briefly describe* it to others, giving a *current* example for illustration.
• Indicate what you want to accomplish in the role play. *What are your goals*?
• *Reverse roles.* You play the *other* person, acting out the situation with another member who plays you.
• Encourage *constructive feedback*, first from the person who played you and then from other group members, about the effectiveness of the alternative responses displayed by the person playing you.
• *Observe* other members of your small group playing both roles in the situation, you and the other person.
• Encourage *additional feedback* and suggestions.
• *Role-play yourself* in the situation while someone else plays the part of the other person. Incorporate the group's suggestions for improvement.
• *Appraise your own behavior*, including what you liked as well as what could be improved, and encourage group feedback; repeat the role play as necessary.
• *Discuss how and when you will try out the new reactions* in a similar situation during the next week.

Social Reinforcement and Self-Reinforcement

Consistent with fundamental shaping principles for developing and strengthening new behavior, it is important that clients get generous amounts of positive reinforcement for small improvements that approximate desired skill outcomes. In group social skill training, reinforcement can come from the leader, other members, and the participants themselves in the form of self-reinforcement. The leader is an important role model for delivering constructive, positive feedback to individual members and to the group as a whole. For example, positive feedback is frequently offered following member rehearsal of a difficult situation in small groups. As the small practice groups are rehearsing, the leader circulates, observes the role playing, and offers acknowledgment or praise of specific verbal and nonverbal behaviors. Positive feedback is more meaningful if it is descriptive and individualized. For example, the comment "That was good" does not specify the behaviors that were helpful, nor does it relate to a particular individual or situation. A more powerful reinforcing comment might be "Brenda, your question connected well with her earlier comment. It showed you were really listening. You also showed your interest in what she had to say by looking at her and nodding, so much so that she wanted to keep talking! Well done!"

With some client groups, corrective feedback and suggestions for improvement may be postponed until later sessions to allow members to develop a greater sense of competence. For instance, with at-risk parents, group leaders provided only positive feedback and ignored inappropriate client responses until the sixth session. Even at this time, when suggestions for improvement were introduced, feedback stressed the improvements that could be made rather than the errors that were observed (Lovell & Richey, 1991).

Corrective feedback is often more palatable and more helpful if the positive aspects of performance are articulated first—"Your initiating remark was just fine. It related to the situation and you shared something about yourself"—followed by specific suggestions for improvement—"Perhaps if you smiled and looked at her more, she would be even more interested in talking with you." Corrective feedback can also be softened if it focuses on discrimination learning, acknowledging that a client's behavior may be appropriate in one situation but not in another. Thus, the message is not that the client has inadequate skills but, rather, that there may be a lack of fit between the client's repertoire and the particular situation being rehearsed. For instance, in training groups with Canadian parents, 36% of whom were Native Indian, the leader's feedback often focused on helping participants better discriminate between contexts in the application of skills, such as direct eye contact (Lovell, Richey, & Newman, 1990). Thus, learning goals for these parents were often context- or culture-specific.

In addition to directly modeling positive reinforcement, the leader can also encourage members to provide specific and constructive feedback to each other during role playing and group discussions by incorporating helpful norms or prompts. For instance, the leader can set a group rule that the positive aspects of a role play are stated first, followed by one specific suggestion for improvement. This rule could apply to social feedback as well as to self-feedback. Once group norms of this kind are established, the leader and other members can remind one another. For example, if one member begins reacting to another after a role play with "You were too pushy that time," the leader or another member could prompt the person to specify first a positive aspect of the performer's behavior and then to name the behavior that could be increased or decreased:

> You were direct in letting the person know your situation and what you needed. I think Jean's reaction might have been more positive if you had given her more time to think about it and to respond. For example, I noticed you interrupted her twice when she started to ask for clarification.

Positive reinforcement can be provided by the leader and other members during structured group segments devoted to "testimonials" (Richey, 1981) or "brags" (NiCarthy, Merriam, & Coffman, 1984; Robinson, 1988). In social skill groups, this segment is often the first activity of the session. Group testimonials can serve several functions:

- to provide social reinforcement to each member in the form of group praise and specific positive feedback from the leader and other participants for "successes"
- to provide opportunities for positive talk about oneself, to encourage overt self-praise for attempts to change one's interpersonal patterns, and to discourage self-criticism for perceived "failures"
- to provide group members with experience in talking about themselves in a group or public-speaking situation, and to decrease anxiety over social performance and self-presentation
- to provide continuity from one session to the next by encouraging members to think about and acknowledge the cumulative effect of small improvements over time
- to provide a positive, supportive atmosphere for the remainder of the group session

Testimonial guidelines encourage participants to share one of their accomplishments or successes between sessions that relates to their goals. To discourage long narrations that bore other members or elaborations of failures that result in group reinforcement of a member's self-criticism, guidelines also encourage stories that are brief and focus on positive aspects of performance. In groups for shy women, participants developed a specific action goal at the end of each session that they agreed to carry out during the week. During the testimonial period, individual members reported on their progress to complete their assignment. When individual members share successes with the group, it is important that the leader display a rich repertoire of reinforcing reactions so that feedback is varied and individualized. For instance, leaders can expand their reinforcement vocabulary by systematically incorporating in each session different words and phrases that replace "very good." For years, I have distributed to social workers and group leaders a list of "97 Ways to Say 'Very Good.' " Examples are:

> "You did it that time! That's really nice. Much better. Super! You make it look easy. I knew you could do it. Terrific! Way to go! That's it! You're really learning a lot. Well look at you go! That's the best ever. Congratulations! You must have been practicing."

In addition to the leader modeling positive verbal and nonverbal reactions, members can also be encouraged to give one another attention and praise through testimonials. Initially, the leader may need to invite other members to respond or relate to a person's testimonial. After training is well under way, applause often spontaneously erupts as members report back on situations that were worked on in small groups or were first reported in a testimonial session as less than successful. In groups where members may have difficulty giving and receiving compliments, specific attention may need to be given to the exchange of positive comments among members. For example, the leader could help members explore why giving compliments is important and address personal barriers to giving and receiving compliments, including such beliefs as "I don't deserve compliments. Accepting compliments means that I'm conceited. If I compliment people, they'll think I'm phony or want something in return" (Lovell, 1991).

Self-reinforcement is encouraged in group social skill training in several ways. First, as mentioned earlier, the sequence of role playing and feedback for small-group practice encourages members performing new behaviors to first comment on the positive aspects of their own performance before other members respond (Richey, 1981). If self-reinforcement comes first, social evaluation does not become the sole criterion for self-praise. To encourage clients to acknowledge their accomplishments, it is important to have them consider criteria for self-praise, in addition to social outcomes. This is especially important at the beginning of training, when social reactions to developing skills may not be very positive. In addition to the response of others, for example, clients are encouraged to base their self-reinforcement on how much effort they made, their degree of discomfort or anxiety, and whether they were responding in a new way for the first time (Gambrill & Richey, 1988).

In groups with shy women, overt self-praise has been paired with giving oneself points on a wrist counter or points on a rating scale (Richey, 1981). The points represent the client's evaluation of her behavior in a particular situation and provide visible evidence that self-reinforcement is occurring. In the event that the person "forgets" to praise herself or award points for her performance, other members can remind her or support her for rewarding herself. Self-reinforcement in the form of points awarded and personal satisfaction ratings are also elicited on weekly record sheets of social contacts, which are maintained by clients throughout training (Gambrill & Richey, 1988). With shy, socially anxious, or socially inhibited women, improving conversational skills is often less challenging than increasing clients' personal acknowledgment of their own accomplishments. For this reason, overt attention to the self-reinforcement component in training is especially important, given the empirical connections between self-reinforcement and the maintenance and generalization of behavior change (Jackson & VanZoost, 1972; Jeffrey, 1974; Kanfer, Duerfeldt, & LePage, 1969; Richey, 1974).

Cognitive Restructuring

Helping clients increase their awareness of negative self-statements, irrational beliefs, or automatic thoughts and learn ways to challenge and replace these with more helpful internal dialogue or positive self-statements can accelerate and expand the development of interpersonal competence (Glass, Gottman, & Shmurak, 1976; Mandel & Schrauger, 1980; Young, 1982). Many of the competencies identified as facilitative of social support—for example, emotion management, positive self-presentation, and taking the initiative in contacts and conversations—appear related to and influenced by an individual's cognitive environment. Excessive self-criticism, fear of negative social evaluation, and unrealistic beliefs about or expections of self and others can inhibit or interfere with the performance of effective social behavior.

Social support skill training can influence clients' thinking directly and indirectly. Negative self-labels and expectancies can be *indirectly* challenged and modified by successful behavioral performance. For instance, beliefs that one is not very likable or interesting can be eroded when others respond positively to expanded or novel displays of self in and between training sessions. For example, after group training, 20 shy women reported significant increases over baseline levels in general social confidence and in personal satisfaction with their responses to behavioral role-playing skill tests (Richey, 1979). These self-evaluative changes were in accord with noted improvements in such behavioral indicators as content of verbal responses to role-playing tests and percentage of contacts initiated with people between sessions. Moreover, at one-year follow-up, the percentage of subjects who described themselves as shy decreased from 81% before training to 56%, suggesting that training effects included changes in basic self-description for many of the women. Those who continued to label themselves as shy may have been a more severely impaired group similar in some ways to socially phobic individuals who are characterized by more chronic patterns of interpersonal impairment (Turner et al., 1990).

Direct attention to client cognitions can be readily integrated into weekly sessions. For instance, in groups with at-risk parents, session 5 introduces exercises designed to encourage participants to explore their values and beliefs about personal boundaries in relationships (Lovell, 1991). Leaders create vignettes that reflect the daily realities of their clients' lives and are associated with feeling angry or upset. The leader helps members identify how their negative or intense feelings may connect with their beliefs about "right" and "wrong." Several sample vignettes are presented, and members are asked to rank them based on how hurt, angry, or upset they would feel if the situation happened to them:

> Alice called her buddy to ask her to come for a visit because she was feeling depressed and lonely. She had just had a very hard week that included a fight with her boyfriend and money troubles. Her friend replied that she didn't have time and that Alice should stop feeling sorry for herself [Lovell, 1991, p. 26].

Possible values or beliefs might include: "Friends are supposed to help each other out. It's always important to be polite. If I ask for help, I must be a weak person. I shouldn't let these little troubles get me down. People are either for you or against you." After the vignettes are read and rated, the leader reviews each story and invites members who rated it as *most upsetting* to identify which of their values or beliefs were violated or compromised in the story and thus contributed to their feeling upset.

In social skill training with shy women, a more structured cognitive identification and replacement exercise has been introduced in the final sessions. This exercise follows one described in some detail by Gambrill and Richey (1988). The exercise, Challenging Irrational Beliefs and Cognitive Distortions (p. 262), can be a powerful group experience, whether done by members privately or in small groups. The leader passes out index cards, and members are asked to list examples of negative thoughts they have in a particular situation. It is often helpful to have cli-

ents imagine themselves in an uncomfortable situation, perhaps one with a very low satisfaction or enjoyment level, and then to identify what they were probably saying to themselves—their thoughts, images, or self-talk—during this unpleasant encounter. After members have the situation in mind and can begin to recall their internal dialogue, they are asked to list these negative words and phrases on the card. Next, they are encouraged to develop and list positive counterparts or comebacks to the negative statements and to write these on the reverse side of the card. The positive statements will be more powerful if they are reasonable and convincing. Members have developed positive counterparts for their negative thoughts while working independently or in small groups. Support can be offered for both approaches. Very shy or socially anxious members may find sharing their negative thoughts with others too embarrassing or threatening. On the other hand, discussing one's dysfunctional thoughts with others can "normalize" them, given the similarity in such ruminations. Further, members can assist one another in creating more helpful or reasonable self-talk, perhaps sharing their own thoughts in similar situations. Box 15.2 lists examples of negative thoughts in difficult social situations and positive, or "rational," replacements developed by group members.

Another useful strategy to assist clients in identifying and counteracting distorted thought patterns is presented by McKay, Davis, and Fanning (1981) in their step-by-step workbook. They first describe 15 styles of distorted thinking:

filtering	blaming
polarized thinking	shoulds
overgeneralization	emotional reasoning
mind reading	fallacy of change
catastrophizing	global labeling
personalization	being right
control fallacies	heaven's reward fallacy
fallacy of fairness	

After practice exercises that help the reader identify particular distorted thinking patterns, a four-step procedure is presented for combating cognitive distortions associated with an unpleasant interpersonal conflict. A homework sheet allows the reader to follow each step:

1. Name your emotion.

2. Describe the situation or event (as if you were talking to a close friend), including what you were thinking.
3. Review your narrative and identify which of the 15 distortions are represented.
4. For each distortion identified write out the sentence, first including the distortion and then again without the distortion.

BOX 15.2   *Client Examples of Negative Thoughts and Positive Replacements*

Situation: Social anxiety when interacting with co-workers.

Negative thoughts: "I'm not as sharp, as smart as the others here. People are thinking I'm not as competent as I look. How did I get myself into this mess? How do I get myself out without losing face, making excuses? Why can't I perform better, be more articulate, be perceptive, assert and risk more?"

Positive replacement: "I'm at a beginning level and doing quite nicely given my previous experience and educational focus. With enough practice, my skills will sharpen, and I'll like my performance even more."

Situation: Anger toward an acquaintance.

Negative thoughts: "That guy doesn't think any more of me than the waste basket. I'm worthless. I wish he'd fall down the stairs for making me feel so bad. I was enjoying myself until he came. The others seemed interested in what I was saying; now all they can listen to is him. If I ever get the chance, I'll do the same to him."

Positive replacement: "Sure you feel put down. He really did totally ignore you. That's the kind of guy he is. He's probably always been that way. He probably doesn't even realize how offensive his behavior is. Next time he

does that, you should let him know. Heck, if it really bothers me that much, I should tell him now. No, I don't want to tell him now. It's not that important. I won't worry about it now. It's really more his problem than mine."

Situation: Feeling awkward at a social gathering.

Negative thoughts: "They all know each other so well already. I'm at such a disadvantage. They're comfortable with each other. They don't care if I stay out. They don't want me to enter the group. If they wanted me in, they would have made some friendly gesture. They didn't, so they don't. It's easier to wait than to act. It's up to them."

Positive replacement: "It's true you're are at a disadvantage. But you make friends easily. You can talk to a group of complete strangers. Their knowing each other doesn't change the fact that you're a good listener and an interesting person. You're scared—admit it. Then do something so you don't have to stay scared. They don't know you want to join them. You have to break in. Maybe they'll be glad to meet you! After all, it's up to me!"

The authors provide a useful summary of possible "rational comebacks" for each of the 15 distorted thought styles. These examples offer clients models for building their own positive counterparts. For example, clients have found it helpful to counteract "catastrophizing" ("What if I invite her over and we have nothing to say to each other?!") by assessing the "realistic odds"—the likelihood or probability of the catastrophe occurring—for example, 1%, 10%, or 25% probability. By considering the odds, a person is not asked to eliminate the worry altogether (which often meets with resistance) but, rather, to realistically evaluate the probability that the feared outcome will occur.

To assist members in replacing negative cognitions with positive counterparts, the group exercise can incorporate imagery and active thought substitution. For example, once members develop their positive counterparts and list these on the card, invite them as a group to close their eyes and imagine the situation again, repeating the negative self-statements to themselves. Ask them to reiterate the negative thoughts to themselves while remaining in the visualized situation until they begin to experience some of their unpleasant feelings. After several minutes, ask members to stop the negative thoughts (a thought-stopping strategy can be incorporated at this time) and replace them with positive counterparts. Continue to coach members to remain in the imagined scene while saying to themselves the positive statements they have developed. Invite them to notice any changes in feelings associated with thought replacement. After the exercise, encourage members to share their experiences—for example, difficulty in stopping well-learned negative thought patterns and feelings of relief when the positive thoughts were repeated.

Practice Assignments

Practicing new social skills in real-life situations between sessions is one of the most im-portant ingredients of training programs. These practice opportunities allow each client to progress comfortably toward his or her goals in small steps. Since people learn by doing, assignments that require real-life practice enhance learning. Group members are helped to develop and carry out assignments tailored to their individualized goals. Often, people will need help in deciding where to begin. In groups with at-risk parents, goal setting was difficult because few had experienced prior success in establishing, striving for, and achieving personal goals (Lovell & Richey, 1991). During the course of training, leaders reinforced parents' attempts to set and pursue specific and realistic goals for changing social networks and increasing social support. Several parents needed ongoing assistance in breaking down and operationalizing such global goals as "making friends" or "getting along better."

Discussing and selecting among possible sample assignments and listening to what others plan to do between sessions can facilitate individual decision making about "where to begin." Some sample assignments are listed below (Gambrill & Richey, 1988):

Go to a familiar neighborhood bookstore on a week night and stay for 15 minutes (p. 101).

Attend a co-ed volleyball game at the local community center on a Friday night with a friend. After you observe one game, join in for the second (p. 102).

In your next three conversations, encourage others to speak most of the time (p. 143).

Increase the frequency with which you change the topic of conversation if the topic bores or upsets you (p. 143).

Compliment someone once during each conversation you have over the next week (p. 183).

Find out why people have certain beliefs. Remember, the reasons behind people's beliefs are often more interesting than the beliefs themselves (p. 184).

Increase the number of times you share your feelings with others during the next week (p. 184).

Increase the number of open-ended questions you ask others about their feelings, opinions, or experiences (p. 184).

Telephone someone soon after a meeting (if it went well), and arrange another (p. 152).

In *The Friendship Group* training manual, leaders are encouraged to provide general parameters for practice activities to be carried out by at-risk parents (Lovell, 1991). For example, after session 7, leaders are asked to have members consider their own favorite activities and daily habits and then to identify five places or ways they could meet new people. After session 9, members are asked to prepare a topic for conversation with a person they know and to talk with the person for at least five minutes on the topic during the following week.

Sample assignments are helpful insofar as they give group members ideas for creating personalized practice opportunities that advance them toward their individual social support goals. For example, one member, James, may want to increase his contacts with acquaintances (increase the number of people in Acquaintanceville). He could begin by developing tasks to perform between sessions that would help him gradually increase such contacts from a baseline level of two per week to ten per week. He could select assignments that would place him in situations providing opportunities to meet new people as well as assignments that allow him to initiate more exchanges with acquaintances. Another group member, Theresa, may want to increase the duration and enjoyment of her social exchanges, to "move" people she already knows from Buddyborough to Friendly City. To accomplish this goal, she may select assignments that encourage her to introduce topics of interest to her, be more self-disclosing in conversations, and arrange enjoyable activities to share with her buddies. Thus, each

group member's individualized goals will influence the selection of practice tasks between sessions.

Initial skill levels will also influence practice assignment selection. For example, if James's two baseline contacts were uninitiated conversations with old friends, an assignment of initiating conversations with ten new people in one week may be too difficult. Developing a number of intermediate steps toward this goal would make successful completion more likely. Practice assignments are often not completed because they are too challenging or not specific enough with respect to where, when, and how the assignment will be completed. Selecting assignments that are too vague or too difficult is often associated with avoidance, self-criticism, and feelings of hopelessness. Leaders can assist clients in breaking goals down into manageable proportions. For example, a reasonable first assignment for James might be to invite a new co-worker out for coffee at work. If this step still seems too big, a first assignment might be calling to get information about a community organization or club that he might be interested in joining. Additional steps could be attending one club meeting and staying for 30 minutes, going to a second meeting and staying for 45 minutes and initiating one conversation, and so on. All goals, even very complex ones, can be broken down into a series of intermediate tasks that have a high probability of successful completion.

Verbal or written agreements to carry out assignments can increase member adherence to following through between training sessions (Shelton & Levy, 1981). Agreements can be made among participants, between the leader and group members, or with oneself. With shy women, time was taken at the end of every session for small groups to help each member craft an individualized assignment, which was summarized on her weekly record sheet and reported to the leader and entire group before the session ended. Many members reported that these agreements with the group provided powerful incentives during the week when fatigue, apprehension, or other priorities tempted the person to abandon her assignment. One member reported that she would visualize the group applauding her success at the next group meeting and that this gave her the extra "push" to carry out an assignment.

In groups with at-risk parents, assignments were often articulated early in the session (Lovell & Richey, 1991). For example, one client identified joining a community self-help group as a social support goal, and then members discussed with her the realistic steps to accomplish this goal. Members might also rehearse with the person the specific skills needed to carry out the assignment—for example, how to initiate conversations with strangers at the first meeting of a self-help group. Finally, members would verbalize to the group what they had agreed to do and would report back on their progress the following week. Occasionally, group members agreed to carry out an assignment as a team. For instance, two mothers who lived near each other decided to meet during the week and take their children swimming at the community center.

CONCLUSION

I have stressed the importance of case-by-case assessment in order to determine the appropriateness and specific focus of social support skill training. That is, the training goals and procedures outlined here may not always be the intervention of choice for all clients. In addition to *tailoring* the intervention to particular clients and problems, practitioners should devote attention to the agency or service setting in which the training will be offered. For instance, if it is to be offered to clients as an adjunct to an existing program, a number of considerations need to be ad-

dressed. These include (1) recruitment and screening of participants, with specification of inclusion and exclusion criteria; (2) selection, training, and supervision of social skill trainers; and (3) integration and coordination of the training with an agency's ongoing service program (Lovell & Richey, 1991). For example, implementation of training groups in several Canadian family service agencies highlighted the importance of ongoing attention to and clarification of the roles and responsibilities of group leaders vis-à-vis regular agency staff members.

Additional considerations include programming for maintenance and generalization of desired changes. For example, Stokes and Osnes (1989) outline specific principles and tactics that can enhance the comprehensiveness and durability of training outcomes. These include (1) teaching behaviors that are likely to result in naturally reinforcing consequences—for example, encouraging clients to initiate topics of conversation and suggest social activities that individuals in their social environments are more likely to reinforce; (2) using multiple and diverse stimulus situations and response exemplars for modeling and rehearsal procedures; and (3) varying the consequences of the target behavior so clients practice in the presence of more realistic (intermittent) reinforcement schedules. These strategies can be incorporated into role-playing sequences in training sessions and into practice assignments between sessions.

With multiproblem, at-risk clients who participate as part of their involvement in a more comprehensive agency program, the addition of posttraining case management may further enhance their follow-through and goal attainment. For example, a unique and important component of the training project with Canadian family service agencies was the posttraining role of group leaders who functioned as case managers (Lovell & Richey, 1991). They assisted parents in achieving and maintaining their individual social-network and social-relationship goals during the three-month follow-up period.

Future efforts to enhance client social support via interpersonal skill training would benefit from a greater understanding of the adaptive and culturally and developmentally relevant features of support. For example, we need to know more about the specific cognitive and behavioral processes that enable individuals to successfully exchange a variety of supports or resources with different network members, at different times, in different situations, for different reasons. In the literature, for instance, much attention has focused on the social support characteristics of troubled families, mainly mothers of abused and neglected children (Polansky, Gaudin, Ammons, & Davis, 1985; Salzinger, Kaflan, & Artemyeff, 1983). With some notable exceptions (Crittenden, 1985; Hanson, 1986; Lindblad-Goldberg & Dukes, 1985) few parameters are available in the literature for judging which network configurations and patterns of interaction are more or less "adaptive" or "problematic" for families with young children. Without normative guidelines, the validity or desirability of certain social support outcomes, such as increases in network size, increases in contacts with members of the extended family, or increases in the number of confidants or "close" ties, remains unverified.

It is also important that we learn more about the optimal proportions of strong and weak ties and of "primary" and "secondary" relationships in social networks that provide effective support. People with larger and more diverse networks—which include a number of less intimate acquaintances with connections to different social worlds, as well as friends and family members—may be more successful in mobilizing financial, material, and employment supports or resources in times of crisis and hardship (Uehara, in press; Zippay, 1990–1991). Moreover, the interpersonal competencies needed to locate and mobilize weak ties or secondary-zone contacts may be quite different from those competencies identified as important for maintaining social exchange relationships with close network members.

The goal of social skill training pursued in this chapter—to enhance social support as a buffer against adversity and as a correlate of health and well-being—while appealing, should not be exempt from critical analysis. For example, current conceptualizations of social support may harbor subtle class and gender biases and may promote devaluation of more solitary forms of coping. Much of the literature on social support focuses on *vulnerable*, *at-risk*, or *underserved* populations (Gottlieb, 1988). These are often women and people of color who are educationally and economically disadvantaged and occupy lower socioeconomic strata (single parents, widows, the home-bound elderly, family caregivers of chronically mentally ill or disabled family members). The informal support that is mobilized for these individuals may be in the form of emotional support; practical help, such as offers to baby-sit or to provide respite care or transportation; a loan of money; or helpful advice to solve a family problem. In contrast, for people with adequate incomes, many of these "supports" can be purchased. With an adequate income, people can hire a baby-sitter or take a child to day care; own, insure, and maintain a car; consult with a therapist or an attorney about a personal or family problem; and go to a cash machine for a short-term loan. Thus, having an adequate income may diminish the need for informal social supports in some areas, whereas having an inadequate income makes "getting by" with a little help from friends, family, and neighbors, more imperative.

Finally, the ever-expanding appeal of social support as a coping strategy may deflect attention from other, equally effective approaches for solving problems, reducing stress, and regaining a sense of equilibrium in times of uncertainty or crises. For instance, research on stress and coping patterns suggests that adults activate a variety of strategies, in addition to or instead of social support, to manage family, health, and employment problems and transitions (Folkman & Lazarus, 1980; Ilfeld, 1980). With some types of stressors, other strategies, which may not be interaction-oriented, may be more frequently utilized than social support. For example, I asked 105 British and American social workers to list the strategies they used to cope with job dissatisfaction and burnout. Although social support was among the strategies listed most often, the most frequently mentioned coping responses included *taking time off, taking a break, going on vacation,* and *getting away on holiday.* Further, coping strategies that are frequently utilized may not be the most effective. For instance, a sample of middle-aged adults who were members of a religious group reported that although social support was one of the most frequently used coping strategies, it was not as helpful as prayer when dealing with a variety of stressors (Davis, 1985).

Thus, the prominence of social support, or social connectedness, as the avenue for reducing stress, regaining one's perspective, and coping with adversity may be overstated. Given the nature of particular stressors or problems and people's resources and coping styles, social support may be one of a number of coping options available. Other viable options include "creative solitude" (Storr, 1988), "aloneness" (Peplau & Perlman, 1982), or "flow" (Csikszentmikalyi, 1975), which comes from complete and non-self-conscious involvement in an activity.

Finally, social support interventions, including those that target interpersonal skill, like all clinical interventions, will benefit from greater consideration of the interaction among specific stressors or problems, individual client proclivities, and available or potential personal and collective resources. By attending to these multidimensional factors, we can continue to hone practice strategies that enable people to more effectively relate to and influence their social environments.

REFERENCES

Abbey, A., Abramis, D. J., & Caplan, R. D. (1985). Effects of different sources of social support and social conflict on emotional well-being. *Basic and Applied Social Psychology*, 6(2), 111–130.

Albrecht, T. L., & Adelman, M. B. (1987a). Communicating social support: A theoretical perspective. In T. L. Albrecht & M. B. Adelman (Eds.), *Communicating social support*. Newbury Park, CA: Sage.

Albrecht, T. L., & Adelman, M. B. (1987b). Communication networks as structures of social support. In T. L. Albrecht & M. B. Adelman, (Eds.), *Communicating social support*. Newbury Park, CA: Sage.

Alden, L. (1989). Short-term structured treatment for avoidant personality disorder. *Journal of Consulting and Clinical Psychology*, 57, 756–764.

Alden, L., & Cappe, R. (1988). Characteristics predicting social functioning and treatment response in clients impaired by extreme shyness: Age of onset and the public/private shyness distinction. *Canadian Journal of Behavioral Science*, 20, 40–49.

Allen, L., & Britt, D. W. (1983). Black women in American society: A resource development perspective. *Issues in Mental Health Nursing*, 5(1–4), 61–79.

Andrasik, F., & Matson, J. L. (1985). Social skills training for the mentally retarded. In L. L'Abate & M. A. Milan (Eds.), *Handbook of social skills training and research*. New York: Wiley.

Antonucci, T. C. (1986). Hierarchical mapping technique. *Generations*, 10, 10–12.

Astor-Dubin, L., & Hammen, C. (1984). Cognitive versus behavioral coping responses of men and women: A brief report. *Cognitive Therapy and Research*, 8, 35–90.

Bagarozzi, D. A., & Anderson, S. A. (1988). *Personal, marital, and family myths: Theoretical formulations and clinical strategies*. New York: Norton.

Bandura, A. (1977). *Social learning theory*. Englewood Cliffs, NJ: Prentice-Hall.

Bellack, A. S., & Morrison, R. L. (1982). Interpersonal dysfunction. In A. S. Bellack, M. Hersen, & A. E. Kazdin (Eds.), *International handbook of behavior modification and behavior therapy.* New York: Plenum.

Belle, D. (1982). The stress of caring: Women as providers of social support. In L. Goldberger & S. Breznitz (Eds.), *Handbook of stress: Theoretical and clinical aspects.* New York: Free Press.

Belle, D. (1987). Gender differences in the social moderators of stress. In R. C. Barnett, L. Biener, & G. K. Baruch (Eds.), *Gender and stress.* New York: Free Press.

Berkman, L. F. (1985). The relationship of social networks and social support to morbidity and mortality. In S. Cohen & S. L. Syme (Eds.), *Social support and health.* Orlando, FL: Academic Press.

Berkman, L. F., & Seeman, T. (1986). The influence of social relationships on aging and the development of cardiovascular disease—a review. *Postgraduate Medical Journal, 62,* 805–807.

Billings, A. G., & Moos, R. H. (1982). Stressful life events and symptoms: A longitudinal model. *Health Psychology, 1,* 99–118.

Bloom, M. (1991). Primary prevention: Theory, issues, methods, and programs. In A. R. Roberts (Ed.), *Contemporary perspectives in crisis intervention and prevention.* Englewood Cliffs, NJ: Prentice-Hall.

Blumenthal, J. A., Burg, M. M., Barefoot, J., Williams, R. B., Haney, T., & Zimet, G. (1987). Social support, type A behavior, and coronary artery disease. *Psychosomatic Medicine, 49*(4), 331–334.

Booth, C. L., Mitchell, S. K., Barnard, K., & Spieker, S. (1989). Development of maternal social skills in multiproblem families: Effects in the mother-child relationship. *Developmental Psychology, 25*(3), 403–412.

Bowlby, J. (1988). Developmental psychiatry comes of age. *American Journal of Psychiatry, 145,* 1–10.

Brandt, B. T. (1987). The relationship between hopelessness and selected variables in women receiving chemotherapy for breast cancer. *Oncology Nursing Forum, 14*(2), 35–39.

Brock, G., & Coufal, J. D. (1985). Parent education as skills training. In L. L'Abate & M. A. Milan (Eds.), *Handbook of social skills training and research.* New York: Wiley.

Burgess, R. L., & Bushell, D. (Eds.). (1969). *Behav-ioral sociology: The experimental analysis of social process.* New York: Columbia University Press.

Chapleski, E. (1989). Determinants of knowledge of services to the elderly: Are strong ties enabling or inhibiting? *Gerontologist, 29*(4), 239–245.

Christen, A. G. (1986). Developing a social support network system to enhance mental and physical health. *Dental Clinics of North America, 30*(4), 79–92.

Christoff, K. A., & Kelly, J. A. (1985). A behavioral approach to social skills training with psychiatric patients. In L. L'Abate & M. A. Milan (Eds.), *Handbook of social skills training and research.* New York: Wiley.

Coates, D. L. (1985). Relationships between self-concept measures and social network characteristics for black adolescents. *Journal of Early Adolescence, 5*(3), 319–338.

Cohen, C. I., Teresi, J., & Holmes, D. (1985). Social networks and adaptation. *Gerontologist, 25*(3), 297–304.

Cohen, S., & Syme, S. L. (Eds.). (1985). *Social support and health.* Orlando, FL: Academic Press.

Cooper, C. L., Cooper, R. F. D., & Faragher, E. B. (1986). A prospective study of the relationship between breast cancer and life events, type-A behavior, social support and coping skills. *Stress Medicine, 2*(3), 271.

Crittenden, P. (1985). Social networks, quality of child rearing, and child development. *Child Development, 56,* 1299–1313.

Cronenwett, L. R. (1985). Network structure, social support, and psychological outcomes of pregnancy. *Nursing Research, 34*(2), 93–99.

Csikszentmikalyi, M. (1975). *Beyond boredom and anxiety: The experience of play in work and games.* San Francisco: Jossey-Bass.

Davis, G. R. (1985). *Developmental patterns of stress and coping: Middle age and older adulthood.* Unpublished dissertation, University of Washington, Seattle.

Deffenbacher, J. L., Story, D. A., Stark, R. S., Hogg, J. A., & Brandon, A. D. (1987). Cognitive relaxation and social skills interventions in the treatment of general anger. *Journal of Counseling Psychology, 34,* 171–176.

deJong, R., Treiber, R., & Gerhard, H. (1986). Effectiveness of two psychological treatments for inpatients with severe and chronic depressions. *Cognitive Therapy and Research, 10,* 645–663.

Dispenza, D. A., & Nigro, A. G. (1989). Life skills for the mentally ill: A program description. *Journal of Applied Rehabilitation Counseling, 20*(1), 47–49.

Dressler, W. W. (1985, March). Extended family relationships, social support, and mental health in a southern black community. *Journal of Health and Social Behavior, 26,* 39–48.

Duck, S. (Ed.). (1977). *Theory and practice of interpersonal attraction.* New York: Academic Press.

Duck, S. (1983). *Friends for life: The psychology of close relationships.* Brighton, England: Harvester Press.

Duck, S., & Gilmore, R. (Eds.). (1981). *Personal relationships 2: Developing personal relationships.* New York: Academic Press.

Dunkel-Schetter, C., & Bennett, T. L. (1990). Differentiating the cognitive and behavioral aspects of social support. In B. R. Sarason, I. G. Sarason, & G. R. Pierce (Eds.), *Social support: An interactional view.* New York: Wiley.

Duong-Tran, Q. (1992). *The influence of family functioning and social support on Southeast Asian adolescents' psychosocial well-being.* Unpublished manuscript, University of Washington, Seattle.

Eckenrode, J. (1983). The mobilization of social supports: Some individual constraints. *American Journal of Community Psychology, 11,* 509–528.

Eisemann, M. (1984). The relationship of personality to social network aspects and loneliness in depressed patients. *Acta Psychiatrica Scandinavica, 70*(4), 337–341.

Eisler, R. M., Hersen, M., & Miller, P. M. (1973). Effects of modeling on components of assertive behavior. *Journal of Behavior Therapy and Experimental Psychiatry, 4,* 1–6.

Fiore, J., Coppel, D. B., Becker, J., & Cox, G. B. (1986). Social support as a multifaceted concept: Examination of important dimensions for adjustment. *American Journal of Community Psychology, 14,* 93–111.

Folkman, S., & Lazarus, R. S. (1980). An analysis of coping in a middle-aged community sample. *Journal of Health and Social Behavior, 21,* 219–239.

Foxx, R. M., Kyle, M. S., Faw, G. D., & Bittle, R. G. (1989). Problem-solving skills training:

Social validation and generalization. *Behavioral Residential Treatment, 4*(4), 269–288.

Galinsky, M. J., Schopler, J. H., Satier, E. J., & Gambrill, E. D. (1978). Assertion training for public welfare clients. *Social Work with Groups, 1*(4), 365–379.

Gambrill, E. (1986). Social skills training with the elderly. In C. R. Hollin & P. Trower (Eds.), *Handbook of social skills training Vol. 1: Applications across the life span.* New York: Pergamon Press.

Gambrill, E. D., & Richey, C. A. (1975). An assertion inventory for use in assessment and research. *Behavior Therapy, 6,* 550–561.

Gambrill, E. D., & Richey, C. A. (1986). Criteria used to define and evaluate social competent behavior among women. *Psychology of Women Quarterly, 10,* 183–196.

Gambrill, E. D., & Richey, C. A. (1988). *Taking charge of your social life.* Berkeley, CA: Behavioral Options.

Garbarino, J. (1983). Social support networks: Rx for the helping professionals. In J. K. Whittaker & J. Garbarino (Eds.), *Social support networks: Informal helping in the human services.* New York: Aldine.

Garbarino, J. (1986). Can we measure success in preventing child abuse? Issues in policy, programming and research. *Child Abuse and Neglect, 10,* 143–156.

Gaudin, J. M., Wodarski, J. S., Arkinson, M. K., & Avery, L. S. (1990–1991). Remedying child neglect: Effectiveness of social network interventions. *Journal of Applied Social Sciences, 15*(1), 97–123.

Glass, C., Gottman, J., & Shmurak, S. (1976). Response acquisition and cognitive self-statement modification approaches to dating skills training. *Journal of Counseling Psychology, 23,* 520–526.

Goldstein, A. P., & Keller, H. (1987). *Aggressive behavior: Assessment and intervention.* New York: Pergamon Press.

Gordon, R. E., & Gordon, K. K. (1985). A program of modular psychoeducational skills training for chronic mental patients. In L. L'Abate & M. A. Milan (Eds.), *Handbook of social skills training and research.* New York: Wiley.

Gottlieb, B. H. (Ed.). (1988). *Marshaling social support: Formats, processes, and effects.* Newbury Park, CA: Sage.

Gottman, J., Markman, H., & Notarius, C. (1977). The typography of marital conflict: A sequential analysis of verbal and nonverbal behavior. *Journal of Marriage and the Family, 39,* 461–477.

Granovetter, M. (1974). *Getting a job: A study of contacts and careers.* Cambridge, MA: Harvard University Press.

Graves, T. U., & Graves, N. B. (1985). Stress and health among Polynesian migrants to New Zealand. *Journal of Behavioral Medicine, 8*(1), 1–19.

Hanson, S. (1986). Healthy single parent families. *Family Relations, 35,* 125–132.

Haseltine, B., & Miltenberger, R. G. (1990). Teaching self-protection skills to person with mental retardation. *American Journal on Mental Retardation, 25*(2), 188–197.

Hatfield, E., & Traupmann, J. (1981). Intimate relationships: A perspective from equity theory. In S. Duck & R. Gilmore (Eds.), *Personal Relationships 1: Studying Personal Relationships.* New York: Academic Press.

Hawkins, J. D., & Fraser, M. W. (1985). Social networks of street drug users: A comparison of two theories. *Social Work Research and Abstracts, 21*(1), 3–12.

Heimberg, R. G., Cunningham, J., Heimberg, J. S., & Blankenberg, R. (1982). Preparing unemployed youth for job interviews: A controlled evaluation. *Behavior Modification, 6,* 299–322.

Heller, K., Swindle, R. W., Jr., & Dusenbury, L. (1986). Component social support processes: Comments and integration. *Journal of Consulting and Clinical Psychology, 54,* 466–470.

Henley, N. (1977). *Body politics: Power, sex and nonverbal communication.* Englewood Cliffs, NJ: Prentice-Hall.

Hersen, M., Bellack, A. S., Himmelhoch, J. M., & Thase, M. E. (1984). Effects of social skills training, amitriptyline, and psychotherapy in unipolar depressed women. *Behavior Therapy, 15,* 21–40.

Holtzman, E. H., & Gilbert, L. A. (1987, April). Social support networks for parenting and psychological well-being among dual-earner Mexican-American families. *Journal of Community Psychology, 15*(2), 176–186.

Homans, G. C. (1974). *Social behavior: Its elementary forms* (2nd ed.). New York: Harcourt Brace Jovanovich.

Hood, E. M., Lindsay, W., & Brooks, N. (1982). Interview with adolescents: A controlled group study incorporating generalization and social validation. *Behavior Research and Therapy, 20,* 581–592.

Hudson, W. W. (1982). *The clinical measurement package: A field manual.* Pacific Grove, CA: Brooks/Cole.

Ilfeld, F. W., Jr. (1980). Coping styles of Chicago adults: Description. *Journal of Human Stress, 6,* 2–10.

Israel, B. A., & Antonucci, T. C. (1987). Social network characteristics and psychological well-being: A replication and extension. *Health Education Quarterly, 14*(4), 461–481.

Jackson, B., & VanZoost, B. (1972). Changing study behaviors through reinforcement contingencies. *Journal of Counseling Psychology, 19,* 192–195.

Jacobson, N. S. (1985). A component analysis of behavioral marital therapy. *Journal of Consulting and Clinical Psychology, 52,* 295–305.

Jeffrey, D. B. (1974). A comparison of the effects of external control and self-control on the modification and maintenance of weight. *Journal of Abnormal Psychology, 83,* 404–410.

Joanning, H. (1985). Social skills training for divorced individuals. In L. L'Abate & M. A. Milan (Eds.), *Handbook of social skills training and research.* New York: Wiley.

Jones, W. H. (1981). Loneliness and social contact. *Journal of Social Psychology, 113,* 295–296.

Jones, W. H., & Moore, T. L. (1987). Loneliness and social support. *Journal of Social Behavior and Personality, 2*(2), 145–156.

Kahn, T. L., Antonucci, T. C. (1980). Convoys over the life course: Attachment, roles, and social support. *Life Span Development and Behavior, 3,* 253–286.

Kanfer, F. H., Duerfeldt, P., & LePage, A. (1969). Stability of patterns of self-reinforcement. *Psychological Reports, 24,* 663–670.

Kinney, J., Haapala, D., & Booth, C. (1991). *Keeping families together: The Homebuilders model.* New York: Aldine de Gruyter.

Kirkham, M. A., Schilling, R. F., Norelius, K., & Schinke, S. P. (1986). Developing coping styles and social support networks: An intervention outcome study with mothers of handicapped children. *Child Care, Health and Development, 12,* 313–323.

Kirkham, M. A., Schinke, S. P., Schilling, R. F., Meltzer, N. J., & Norelius, K. L. (1986). Cognitive-behavioral skills, social supports, and child abuse potential among mothers of handicapped children. *Journal of Family Violence, 1*, 235–245.

Knapp, M. L. (1978). *Social intercourse: From greeting to good-bye.* Newton, MA: Allyn & Bacon.

Komaki, J. L., & Zlotnick, S. (1985). Toward effective supervision in business and industry. In L. L'Abate & M. A. Milan (Eds.), *Handbook of social skills training and research.* New York: Wiley.

Lankton, C. H., & Lankton, S. R. (1989). *Tales of enchantment: Goal-oriented metaphors for adults and children in therapy.* New York: Brunner/Mazel.

Libet, J., & Lewinsohn, P. M. (1973). The concept of social skills with special reference to the behavior of depressed persons. *Journal of Consulting and Clinical Psychology, 40*, 304–312.

Lindblad-Goldberg, M., & Dukes, J. L. (1985). Social support in black, low income, single-parent families: Normative and dysfunctional patterns. *American Journal of Orthopsychiatry, 55*(1), 42–58.

Lovell, M. L. (1986). *An evaluation of a parent training and social support group for mothers at risk to maltreat their children.* Unpublished dissertation, University of Washington, Seattle.

Lovell, M. L. (1991). *The Friendship Group: Learning the skills to create social support. A manual for group leaders.* Vancouver: University of British Columbia, School of Social Work.

Lovell, M. L., & Hawkins, D. J. (1988). An evaluation of a group intervention to increase the personal networks of abusive parents. *Children and Youth Services Review, 10*, 175–188.

Lovell, M. L., & Richey, C. A. (1991). Implementing agency-based social-support skill training. *Families in Society, 72*(9), 563–571.

Lovell, M. L., Richey, C. A., & Newman, J. A. (1990, November). *Group social support training for parents at risk for child maltreatment.* Paper presented at the annual conference of the National Association of Social Workers, Boston.

Maluccio, A. N., & Whittaker, J. K. (1988). Helping the biological families of children in out-of-home placement. In E. W. Nunnally, C. S. Chilman, & F. M. Cox (Eds.), *Families in trouble series: Vol. 3. Troubled relationships.* Beverly Hills, CA: Sage.

Mandel, N. M., & Schrauger, J. S. (1980). The effects of self-evaluation statements on heterosexual approach in shy and nonshy men. *Cognitive Therapy and Research, 4*, 369–381.

Marlatt, G. A., & Fromme, K. (1987). Metaphors for addiction. *Journal of Drug Issues, 17*, 9–28.

Marlatt, G. A., & Gordon, J. R. (Eds.). (1985). *Relapse prevention: Maintenance strategies in the treatment of addictive behaviors.* New York: Guilford Press.

Martin, J. A. (1984). Neglected fathers: Limitations in diagnostic and treatment resources for violent men. *Child Abuse and Neglect, 8*(4), 387–392.

Matsuoka, J. K., & Ryujin, D. H. (1989). Vietnamese refugees: An analysis of contemporary adjustment issues. *Journal of Applied Social Sciences, 14*(1), 20–39.

McFall, R. M., Twentyman, C. T. (1973). Four experiments on the relative contribution of rehearsal, modeling, and coaching to assertive training. *Journal of Abnormal Psychology, 81*, 199–218.

McKay, M., Davis, M., & Fanning, P. (1981). *Thoughts and feelings: The art of cognitive stress intervention.* Richmond, CA: New Harbinger.

Metcalfe, B. M. A., & Wright, P. (1986). Social skills training for managers. In C. R. Hollin & P. Trower (Eds.), *Handbook of social skills training: Vol. 1. Applications across the life span.* New York: Pergamon Press.

Mitchell, J. C. (Ed.). (1969). *Social networks in urban situations.* Manchester, England: University of Manchester Press.

Mitchell, R. E., Hodson, C. A. (1983). Coping with domestic violence: Social support and the psychological health among battered women. *American Journal of Community Psychology, 11*, 629–654.

Monti, P. M., Abrams, D. B., Binkoff, J. A., & Zwick, W. R. (1986). Social skills training and substance abuse. In C. R. Hollin & P. Trower (Eds.), *Handbook of social skills training: Vol. 2. Clinical applications and new directions.* New York: Pergamon Press.

Murphy, S. A. (1987). Self-efficacy and social support: Mediators of stress on mental health following a natural disaster. *Western Journal of Nursing Research, 9*(1), 58–86.

NiCarthy, G., Merriam, K., & Coffman, S. (1984). *Talking it out: A guide to groups for abused women.* Seattle, WA: Seal Press.

Nuckolls, K. B., Cassel, J., & Kaplan, B. H. (1972). Psychosocial assets, life crises, and the prognosis of pregnancy. *American Journal of Epidemiology, 95,* 431–441.

Oates, R. K., & Forrest D. (1985). Self-esteem and early background of abusive mothers. *Child Abuse and Neglect, 9,* 89–93.

Peplau, L. A., & Perlman, D. (Eds.). (1982). *Loneliness: A sourcebook of current theory, research and therapy.* New York: Wiley.

Pilisuk, M., & Parks, S. H. (1988). Caregiving: Where families need help. *Social Work, 33,* 436–440.

Pines, A., & Aronson, E. (1981). *Burnout: From tedium to personal growth.* New York: Free Press.

Polansky, N. A., Gaudin, J. M., Ammons, P. W., & Davis, K. B. (1985). The psychological ecology of the neglectful mother. *Child Abuse and Neglect, 9,* 265–275.

Procidano, M. E., & Heller, K. (1983). Measures of perceived social support from friends and from family: Three validation studies. *American Journal of Community Psychology, 11,* 1–24.

Resnick, G. (1985). Enhancing parental competencies for high risk mothers: An evaluation of prevention effects. *Child Abuse and Neglect, 9,* 479–489.

Richey, C. A. (1974). *Increased female assertiveness through self-reinforcement.* Unpublished dissertation, University of California, Berkeley.

Richey, C. A. (1977). *How to conduct an assertion training group: A workshop manual for trainers.* Unpublished manuscript, University of Washington, Seattle.

Richey, C. A. (1979, September). *A program to increase social skills among shy women.* Paper presented at the 87th annual convention of the American Psychological Association, New York.

Richey, C. A. (1981). Assertiveness training for women. In S. P. Schinke (Ed.), *Behavioral methods in social welfare.* New York: Aldine.

Richey, C. A., Gambrill, E. D., & Blythe, B. J. (1988). Mentor relationships among women in academe. *Affilia, 3*(1), 34–47.

Richey, C. A., Hodges, V. G., & Agbayani-Siewert, P. (1991, March). *Supportive family ties: Identifying adaptive social support network characteristics among culturally diverse families.* Paper presented at the annual program meeting of the Council on Social Work Education, New Orleans.

Richey, C. A., Lovell, M., & Reid, K. (1991). Interpersonal skill training to enhance social support among women at risk for child maltreatment. *Children and Youth Services Review, 13*(1 & 2), 41–59.

Robinson, K. M. (1988). A social skills training program for adult caregivers. *Advances in Nursing Science, 10*(2), 59–72.

Rook, K. S. (1984). The negative side of social interaction: Impact on psychological well-being. *Journal of Personality and Social Psychology, 46,* 1097–1108.

Rose, S. D. (1989). *Working with adults in groups: Integrating cognitive-behavioral and small group strategies.* San Francisco: Jossey-Bass.

Rosen, A., & Proctor, E. K. (1978). Specifying the treatment process: The basis for effectiveness research. *Journal of Social Service Research, 2,* 25–43.

Rumbaut, R. G. (1986). Mental health and the refugee experience: A comparative study of Southeast Asian refugees. In T. C. Owan (Ed.), *Southeast Asian mental health: Treatment, prevention, services, training, and research.* Washington, DC: National Institute of Mental Health.

Russell, D., Peplau, L. A., & Cutrona, C. E. (1980). The revised UCLA Loneliness Scale: Concurrent and discriminant validity evidence. *Journal of Personality and Social Psychology, 39*(3), 472–480.

Salzinger, S., Kaflan, S., & Artemyeff, C. (1983). Mothers' personal social networks and child maltreatment. *Journal of Abnormal Psychology, 92,* 68–76.

Sandler, I. N., & Lakey, B. (1982). Locus of control as a stress moderator: The role of control perceptions and social support. *American Journal of Community Psychology, 10,* 65–80.

Sarason, B. R., Sarason, I. G., & Pierce, G. R. (1990). Traditional views of social support and their impact on assessment. In B. R. Sarason, I. G. Sarason, & G. R. Pierce (Eds.), *Social support: An interactional view.* New York: Wiley.

Sarason, B. R., Shearin, E. N., Pierce, G. R., & Sarason, I. G. (1987). Interrelationships among social support measures: Theoretical and practical implications. *Journal of Personality and Social Psychology, 52,* 813–832.

Schilling, R. F. (1987). Limitations of social support. *Social Service Review, 61,* 19–31.

Seagull, E. A. (1987). Social support and child maltreatment: A review of the evidence. *Child Abuse and Neglect, 11,* 41–52.

Sharkey, P. (1989). Social networks and social service workers. *British Journal of Social Work, 19,* 387–405.

Shelton, J. L., & Levy, R. L. (1981). *Behavioral assignments and treatment compliance: A handbook of clinical strategies.* Champaign, IL: Research Press.

Shinn, M., Lehmann, S., & Wong, N. W. (1984). Social interaction and social support. *Journal of Social Issues, 40,* 55–76.

Shumaker, S. A., & Brownell, A. (1984). Toward a theory of social support: Closing conceptual gaps. *Journal of Social Issues, 40,* 11–36.

Stokes, T. F., & Osnes, P. G. (1989). An operant pursuit of generalization. *Behavior Therapy, 20,* 337–355.

Storr, A. (1988). *Solitude: A return to the self.* New York: Free Press.

Surra, C. A. (1988). The influence of interactive network on developing relationships. In R. M. Milardo (Ed.), *Families and social networks.* Beverly Hills, CA: Sage.

Tardy, C. (1985). Social support measurement. *American Journal of Community Psychology, 13,* 187–202.

Thoits, P. A. (1986). Social support as coping assistance. *Journal of Consulting and Clinical Psychology, 54*(4), 416–423.

Tracy, E. M. (1990). Identifying social support resources of at-risk families. *Social Work, 35*(3), 252–258.

Trower, P. (1982). Toward a generative model of social skills: A critique and synthesis. In J. P. Curran & P. M. Monti (Eds.), *Social skill training: A practice handbook for assessment and treatment.* New York: Guilford Press.

Trower, P., Bryant, B., & Argyle, M. (1978). *Social skills and mental health.* London: Methuen.

Trower, P., Yardley, K., Bryant, G. M., & Shaw, P. (1978). The treatment of social failure. *Behavior Modification, 2,* 41–60.

Turner, S. M., Beidel, D. C., & Townsley, R. M. (1990). Social phobia: Relationship to shyness. *Behavior Research and Therapy, 28*(6), 497–505.

Uehara, E. (in press). The influence of the social network's "second-order zone" on social support mobilization: A case example. *Journal of Personal and Social Relations.*

Van Hasselt, V. B., Hersen, M., Egan, B. S., McKelvey, J. L., & Sisson, L. A. (1989). Increasing social interactions in deaf-blind severely handicapped young adults. *Behavior Modification, 13*(2), 257–272.

Vaux, A., Burda, P., & Stewart, D. (1986). Orientation toward utilization of support resources. *Journal of Community Psychology, 14,* 159–170.

Wackman, D. D., & Wampler, K. S. (1985). The couple communication program. In L. L'Abate & M. A. Milan (Eds.), *Handbook of social skills training and research.* New York: Wiley.

Wahler, R. G., & Hann, D. M. (1984). The communication patterns of troubled mothers: In search of a keystone in the generalization of parenting skills. *Education and Treatment of Children, 7,* 335–350.

Wahler, R. G., Leske, G., & Rogers, E. (1979). The insular family: A deviance support system for oppositional children. In L. A. Hamerlynch (Ed.), *Behavior systems for the developmentally disabled: Vol. 1. School and family environments.* New York: Brunner/Mazel.

Wallace, C. J. (1982). The social skills training project of the Mental Health Clinical Research Center for the Study of Schizophrenia. In J. P. Curran & P. M. Monti (Eds.), *Social skills training: A practical handbook for assessment and treatment.* New York: Guilford Press.

Welbourn, A. M., & Mazuryk, G. F. (1980). Interagency intervention: An innovative therapeutic program for abuse prone mothers. *Child Abuse and Neglect, 4,* 199–203.

Whittaker, J. K., & Garbarino, J. (1983). *Social support networks: Informal helping in the human services.* New York: Aldine.

Wood, Y. P. (1984). Social support and social networks: Nature and measurement. In P. McReynolds & G. J. Chelvne (Eds.), *Advances in psychological assessment* (Vol. 6). San Francisco: Jossey-Bass.

Wortman, C. B. (1984). Social support and the cancer patient: Conceptual and methodologic issues. *Cancer, 53,* 2339–2360.

Young, J. E. (1982). Loneliness, depression and cognitive therapy: Theory and applications. In L. A. Peplau and D. Perlman (Eds.), *Loneliness: A sourcebook of current theory, research and therapy*. New York: Wiley.

Zippay, A. (1990–1991). The limits of intimates: Social networks and economic status among displaced industrial workers. *Journal of Applied Social Sciences, 15*(1), 75–95.

16

Stress Management

Coleen Shannon

Although cognitive therapy is not usually viewed as a single intervention method in the treatment of stress, it is certainly one of the major components in an effective, comprehensive approach to the problem. It is useful not only as a component of intervention but also as a way to understand the basic phenomenon. Given that numerous books are devoted to the subject of stress and stress management, it would be impossible to cover the entire subject in one chapter. Consequently, an overview of stress, stress management, and the role of cognitive therapy will be given.

This chapter is based on the theory of stress posited by Hans Selye. Attention is given to physiological changes related to the stress response, the role of cognition in stress, and stress management interventions, with emphasis on cognitive intervention. Because cognitive therapy is usually a part of a holistic approach to problems resulting from stress, I will describe other interventions in order to establish a complete context for therapeutic intervention. I will use the term *stress management* to include relaxation, biofeedback, nutrition, physical fitness, social support, and cognitive therapy.

THEORETICAL FOUNDATIONS

Stress is an extremely popular term. In our everyday lives we often hear complaints about someone being "stressed out" or suffer-

ing from stress. In fact, stress is blamed for everything from poor job performance to life-threatening illnesses. The term, though important to understanding the problems that clients face, is certainly a complex and confusing concept. There is general agreement, however, that stress is unavoidable in that we all have it and that it does not have to be detrimental to our health and well-being.

The significance of stress as a problem stems from the great extent to which it contributes to ill health for so many people. Some estimates are that at least 25% of all Americans suffer from the effects of excessive stress and that anywhere from 50% to 80% of patients seen in general medical practice have stress-related problems (Manuso, 1978). In fact, according to Everly (1989), as of 1960 the primary causes of death in the United States were no longer germ-related. It is this phenomenon of being sick without having a specific germ involved that attracted the attention of the founder of stress research, Hans Selye.

While he was a medical student, Selye became curious about patients he saw who were ill with a wide range of conditions that could not be attributed to the traditional disease model. As a result, he referred to them as having the syndrome of "just being sick" (Selye, 1956). As he continued to study these patients, Selye developed the concept of stress, which he introduced in 1926. His early use of the term referred to the rate of wear and tear in the body resulting from the sum of a person's nonspecific physical responses. Eventually, he moved to a definition of stress as "the nonspecific response of the body to any demand made on it" (Selye, 1974, p.14).

Selye was influenced in his theory development by the fields of physics and engineering and the idea of stress, or pressure, on a structural system. In this original sense, however, stress was defined as the load, or demand, placed on a metal surface, with strain as the result (Cox, 1978). As Selye said later, he should have called his theory "strain" rather than "stress," because he meant to refer to the response and not the stimulus. Consequently, confusion arose over whether the term *stress* referred to the demand or the effect of the demand. Selye's solution to this confused state was to suggest that the term *stressor* applied to the demand and that stress was the result. However, confusion has remained, and the term is still commonly used in reference to both an event and the effect.

According to Selye (1956, 1974), stress is not necessarily negative. In actuality, we need stress to challenge us, keep us alive, and push us to achieve at our peak performance level. This positive stress is referred to as *eustress* and the term for excessive, destructive stress is *distress.* Each of us has an optimal level of performance that is reached when we are under an optimal level of stress. As the level of stress continues to increase beyond this optimal level, however, our performance begins to decrease (Everly, 1989; Everly & Rosenfeld, 1981). This apex of our tolerance for stress as a positive, productive force is influenced by genetics and by physiological and behavioral factors, and it is highly individual. Consequently, one person's level of eustress may be distress for another.

Although stress has this positive aspect, which Selye referred to as the "spice of life," obviously stress can become too much and thus negative for many people. We can consider stress as having "gone bad" when the consistent elicitation of the response breaks down the body's equilibrium, or balance. If the response is elicited too frequently over a

long period, the person's body and mind begin to break down, resulting in illness, depression, and a sense of helplessness (Curtis & Detert, 1981). This process, which can eventually lead to serious illness and even death, is described by Selye as the general adaptation syndrome (GAS).

Selye presented his GAS model as a unified explanation of the stress response and its ultimate result of end-organ pathologies such as hypertension, migraine headaches, or ulcers. His model consists of three phases. The first, the alarm phase, can be characterized as the "call to arms," or "fight-or-flight" response. The physiological changes seen in this stage prepare the body for quick action so that the individual can defend against the event or threat. Within a fraction of a second our bodies have made the hundreds of neurological and chemical changes necessary to handle whatever threat is confronting us. This emergency stage gives us astounding energy and power, which, of course are vital if we are facing a clear and present danger. In our modern world, however, we are not often faced with the need for such extreme action, and most frequently we are faced with stressors that continue unresolved over a period of time. The physical and emotional call to arms in the alarm state is so profound that we cannot live long in such a state of arousal without resolution. Consequently, we often find ourselves in Selye's second stage, resistance.

During the resistance stage, the body attempts to adapt to the stressor and return to balance, or homeostasis. It reduces the neurological and chemical activity from the earlier alarm reaction while maintaining a degree of elevation so that it has some help to resolve the stressor. Ideally, some resolution can be reached, and the body can return to its basic level of balance. We all go through stages 1 and 2 regularly without harm.

If we continue to activate the stress response over and over without resolution and without returning to homeostasis, however, we will eventually enter the third stage, exhaustion. After extended arousal our resistance begins to break down so that wear and tear on end-organs begins to take place. As the individual moves from stage 2 to 3, the body becomes susceptible to symptoms, disease, and eventually death. According to Selye, if the person continues in a state of disrupted homeostasis, the result is a depletion in the adaptive energy reserve issued at birth, which ultimately leads to disease.

Although Selye in his writing is unclear about the nature of adaptive energy, he hypothesizes that it is finite and that it is used up through exposure to stressors. Stress studies using animals as well as autopsies of humans have indicated that repeated exposure to stress does leave lasting physical scars, giving support to Selye's theory (Greenspoon & Olson, 1986).

In addition, as we use more and more of this energy, we begin to age and ultimately die. Selye contends that we do not die from old age, but rather from the wear and tear of stress. If we were to die of old age, our bodies would wear out all at once instead of one part at a time. The implication is that how we react to stress can influence our rate of aging, illness, and death (Curtis & Detert, 1981; Danskin & Crow, 1981; Everly, 1989; Selye, 1974). Although other theorists and researchers have explored aspects of stress and expanded the scientific concepts, Selye's theoretical foundation remains highly regarded.

THE PHYSIOLOGY OF STRESS

As Selye developed his theory of stress, he drew on the work of Walter Cannon, who found that when an organism was faced with a threat, it mobilized the physical arousal referred to as the fight-or-flight response. Thus, Selye incorporated the fight-or-flight response into his first, or alarm, stage of GAS (Kabat-Zinn, 1990; Nurenberger, 1981). Physiologically, this first stage of stress begins with the central nervous system. The stressor is first received by the brain through some form of sensory input. In other words, we are presented with threatening stimuli, leading us to notify our bodies through our nervous system to get ready for action. As the brain sends the signal through the spinal cord, the autonomic nervous system is called into play through its sympathetic and parasympathetic branches. At that point, a large number of nerve firings and chemical changes are initiated, creating Cannon's fight-or-flight reaction.

We are quite aware of the result of these massive physical and emotional changes when they occur. Our hands become cool and sweaty and our heart races, creating hyperalertness. Along with the heart rate increase there is an increase in blood pressure, so that more blood is delivered to large muscles required for action. At the same time, less blood is sent to the stomach and other parts of the digestive system, which slows down, accounting for those "butterfly" feelings you may have experienced under stress. Other physiological changes include dilation of the eyes, thickening of saliva, pilorerection causing your hair to "stand on end," and the release of stress hormones, particularly the familiar adrenaline. Our emotions also undergo changes, leading to strong feelings of anxiety, fear, anger, or even rage (Everly & Rosenfeld, 1981; Kabat-Zinn, 1990).

If the stressor (stressful event) is immediately resolved, the body returns to homeostasis, and deactivation of the response occurs. However, if no resolution is achieved and the stress response continues, the body remains activated. With the release of the two adrenal medullary catecholamines, epinephrine and norepinephrine, 20 to 30 seconds after the activation of the autonomic nervous system there is a resulting increase in the physiological effect and a tenfold increase in duration of the response (Everly, 1989). The body not only continues to react because the stressor is still present but will also require more time to return to homeostasis, because the released hormones increase the time needed to deactivate the process.

In the event that the stress response continues beyond the introduction of hormones, the body responds by calling for the release of even more chemicals through the endocrine system. This third part of the process, referred to as the endocrine axes, is the most chronic and prolonged somatic responses to stress (Everly, 1989). Effects of these hormones, such as the adrenocorticotropic hormone (ACTH) released by the anterior pituitary, are seen through the body on the cell level. These effects not only give us an understanding of the way stress is involved in the wear and tear process but also lead us to consider the profound influence we can have on the cells of our bodies. According to Asterita (1985), data support the idea that stress can be influential at the "cellular level (liver cells, various blood cells, etc.), molecular level (glucose in the blood, cholesterol, etc.), tissue level (muscular, coronary, etc.), the organ level (skin, heart, etc.) and the systems level (cardiovascular, immune, gastrointestinal, neuroendocrine, etc.)" (p. 195).

It seems clear that this hyperaroused state is vital to surviving threats representing clear and present danger. However, it also seems clear that some of us get stuck in hyperarousal and that the stress response becomes chronic, so that we adapt to it as a way of life. Certainly the human body can endure the effects of stress for a time, but eventually it begins to suffer the wear and tear described by Selye. As people begin to develop physical, behavioral, and emotional symptoms, the work of health-care professionals begins.

THE ROLE OF COGNITIONS IN STRESS

When stress is defined as a response to a demand, we assume that the demand is an actual real-life event that causes an automatic reaction. However, all of us can think of examples of different people responding differently to the same event. One person may be relieved to be laid off from a job, for example, whereas another may view it as a personal failure and feel devastated. Obviously, some type of cognitive process is involved in the elicitation of the stress response and all of its physical processes.

Although Selye and other early theorists commented on the fact that people tend to react with varying degrees of intensity to a stressor, Lazarus was the first to develop theoretical concepts to explain the cognitive processes involved. According to Lazarus, our appraisal of an event influences how we respond. In other words, stress is in the eye of the beholder. Lazarus (1977) writes that cognitive appraisal is the cornerstone of his analysis of emotions. In his criticism of Selye's theory of stress as an automatic response, Lazarus maintains that Selye's general adaptation syndrome can be physiologically mediated by cognitive appraisal. The stress response is not an automatic reaction. This initial appraisal of threat is not merely a perception of the elements of the situation but also includes data that are interpreted, leading to a judgment concerning the seriousness of the threat (Lazarus, 1966).

The process of appraisal has been expanded by Leventhal and Nerenz (1983) in their work concerning the way patients respond to serious illness. They note that part of the appraisal process can be automatic and nonconscious. In other words, on some occasions we appraise an event to be threatening without a conscious judgment. This is particularly true when we react emotionally.

In order to reach a cognitive appraisal of an event stimulus, we first capture input through a sensory organ, and this information is sent to the brain for processing. The stimulus is then integrated with various relevant past memories, leading to a perceptual representation (Leventhal & Nerenz, 1983). Once

FIGURE 16.1   The Role of Appraisal in the Stress Response

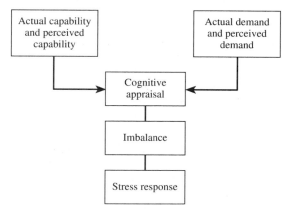

the brain has the representation, cortical processes become involved, and if a judgment is made that a current situation is indeed threatening, the stress response is on its way, complete with nerve firings and chemical releases.

The dramatic involvement of cognition in the stress response has led some authors to assert that stress is a perceptual phenomenon (Cox, 1978). According to Cox, "Stress may be said to arise when there is an imbalance between the perceived demand and the person's perception of his capability to meet that demand" (p. 18). He emphasizes that the creation of stress is not the result of an imbalance between a demand and our capability to handle it but between the *perception* of the demand and the perception of our capability to meet the demand. As Figure 16.1 illustrates, in order to experience stress, a person must perceive that the situation is too big or too overwhelming to handle using available resources. Stress is not an external condition in our environment waiting for us. The definition of a situation as stressful is the result of a cognitive process in which an environmental condition is appraised as threatening or demanding.

Although our perception of an event influences our stress response, we as humans have the unique ability to create stress even when we have no stimulus in our environment (Woolfolk & Lehrer, 1984, p. 227). Humans,

in fact, can internally generate a full-blown stress response by the process of merely thinking. By recalling a past event or anticipating a future happening, we can send the stress response physically on its way through our bodies. Surely you can remember a time when you observed either yourself or someone else in a typical stress response with no external condition to account for it. For example, every year I see students who worry so much over an anticipated failure of a test that a stress response is stimulated. The result is that the student has difficulty both preparing for and taking the examination. The result is poor performance and the increased likelihood of failure. It is this ability to internally generate primary stressors that leads to an activation of the stress response. This stress response is a major factor in the development of a chronic stress habit out of which serious health consequences develop. Stress habits can be changed and the stress response mediated through a number of intervention approaches, which have been loosely grouped together and referred to as "stress management."

STRESS MANAGEMENT INTERVENTIONS

Physicians are called on to treat the target-organ effects of diseases resulting from chronically repeated or intensely activated stress responses. Although most stress-related conditions such as headaches, ulcers, back pain, and the like can be highly successfully treated medically, many patients have recurring problems because they have not learned to modify the manner in which they elicit the stress response. It is at this point that we, as nonmedical practitioners, may become involved (by request of the physician or the patient) to guide the person in the development of stress management skills. Stress management comprises several components.

In order to adequately address stress management, the intervention needs to be based on an assessment of the person's problem, symptoms, and coping strategies. Effectiveness will be increased if we offer a comprehensive approach that integrates both the mind and body. Stress management can be delivered in either a group or individual format that includes basic stress-reduction components. These major components include instruction in the nature of stress and the development of healthy coping strategies. By providing information about stress and a rationale for stress management, we can help the individual begin to feel a sense of control early in the process. Knowledge is power in the case of learning to manage stress. After the practitioner has an understanding of stress based on an individualized assessment, appropriate, healthy coping strategies can be taught. The strategies most often covered are relaxation, biofeedback, cognitive intervention, nutrition, physical fitness, and support systems. A brief summary of each will be presented here, with emphasis given in a later section to cognitive stress management.

Relaxation and Biofeedback

Relaxation is a physiological state that is the opposite of the stress response. In other words, it is impossible to be relaxed and to simultaneously emit a stress response with its many physiological and physical components. Deep-muscle relaxation is an excellent way to counteract the negative effects of stress on the body and to cultivate a state of lowered arousal. Through relaxation, a person can learn to relatively quickly return to homeostasis after experiencing a stressful event. People who practice relaxation skills regularly are likely to be more psychologically and physiologically stable, less anxious, and in greater control of their lives than people who do not (Shannon, 1990). For example, Herbert Benson's (1975) investigations of his

relaxation method, the relaxation response, revealed profound physical changes in participating subjects.

Although relaxation can be quite helpful to people who need to decrease a chronic hyperarousal state, many of those who could benefit are unable to relax because they have habituated to a hyperaroused state and cannot learn by simply trying to relax. Such a person, for example, may have tension headaches that originate in tense shoulder or neck muscles. If muscle tension is chronic for an extended period, the person no longer notices it and is unaware of developing problems until the muscles of the head become involved, resulting in a headache. In this case, teaching relaxation may be not only difficult but also frustrating to the client. The person may require more specific information regarding the physiology involved. Biofeedback can give the type of specific information needed by many people suffering from stress-related disorders.

Biofeedback refers to the use of electronic equipment to assess and provide information to people about internal physiological events, both normal and abnormal, so that they can learn to voluntarily control these events (Basmajian, 1989; Olton & Noonberg, 1980). In other words, if you can see your physiology and the way in which you respond under stress, you can more quickly and more effectively learn to gain control over processes that you previously considered involuntary. The end result is not merely relaxation but the development of new ways to assume physical states that, in turn, can have an impact on the target-organ symptom. In addition, in a study reported by Shellenberger, Turner, Green, and Cooney (1986), individuals in a stress management and biofeedback program significantly reduced stress indicators on three dimensions. Results indicated that the treatment group had fewer visits to physicians, improved their perceptions of both physical and mental health, and reduced 17 physical symptoms. Biofeedback is helpful in treating headaches, various types of chronic pain, anxiety, digestive disorders, and cardiovascular disorders as well as in teaching relaxation.

Nutrition, Physical Fitness, and Social Support

In addition to using relaxation and biofeedback to decrease the physical arousal level, it is important to direct our attention to ways to prevent the wear and tear that can occur through prolonged stress. The first method is to ensure that the body is getting proper nutrition. Responsible weight control and proper nutrition are essential elements in stress management, because the nutritional needs of the body increase dramatically during periods of stress. The body can become depleted of essential vitamins and minerals. As this occurs, its ability to resist the impact of stressors diminishes. Increased stress and decreased resistance can result in illness and eventually complete exhaustion. Substances such as caffeine, sugar, and salt contribute further to this problem by increasing the production of stress chemicals and further depleting the body of nutrients (Shannon, 1990).

Another method of stress management that can be utilized to both diminish the effects of stress and to prepare for future stressful times is physical fitness. A regular fitness program can help moderate both physical and psychological responses to stress. People who are physically fit have lower resting levels of catecholamines in their blood, hormones that are important to the stress response (Quick, Shannon, & Quick, 1983). In addition, exercise lowers heart rate and blood pressure, increases endurance, raises metabolism, decreases appetite, burns up calories, and can dissipate excess stress chemicals that build up during a stress response. Psychologically, it can help relieve depression, tension, and anxiety and can increase a person's energy level and sense of self-control (Shannon, 1990).

A final concept receiving increased attention in stress management is social support.

In fact, social support may play a major role as a mediating factor in the stress response. Researchers are hypothesizing that individuals with strong support systems develop fewer stress-related disorders than those without social support (House & Kahn, 1985). Support relates to both the amount and the quality of involvement with other people. Recent studies indicate that strong social relationships are related to lower death rates. Relationships that have a positive effect on health include those with a spouse, other family members, friends, pets, religious groups, and other organizations. In addition, it has been found that disease rates are significantly higher for people who are widowed and divorced (Neidhardt, Weinstein, & Conry, 1985).

COGNITIVE STRESS MANAGEMENT

The stress response is an interactive process involving the environment, cognitive processing, and physiological responses. As these elements interact over time, cognitive habits develop that can lead us to appraise our environment as overly threatening and to a chronically hyperaroused physical state with possible negative health consequences. Because thinking occupies such an important link in the activation of the stress response, it stands to reason that for a stress management program to be comprehensive and effective, the cognitive processes are important to investigate and change. In stress management we can change any of the three elements, environment, thinking, or physical/physiological response. In some situations it is necessary for the person to change either the environment (quit a job or leave a battering spouse) or the physiology (learn hand warming to prevent the onset of migraine headaches). In cognitive stress management, however, we help clients understand and change what and how they think in order to modify the unnecessary activation of their stress response. As a consequence, they evidence less reactivity to the environment and more control of themselves.

Appraisal and Coping

Appraisal, according to Lazarus (1977), is a transactional process consisting of two parts. First, we engage in a primary appraisal directed at determining the degree of threat (if any) in a situation. If a stimulus is appraised as a threat or challenge, we make a secondary appraisal in which we determine the extent to which we have the personal resources to meet the demand of the threat. If, after the secondary appraisal, we believe that we do not have adequate resources available to meet the demand, a stress response results. Stress continues through an ongoing series of appraisals as we attempt to meet the demand (Leventhal & Nerenz, 1983). It is the secondary appraisal that is involved in the concept of coping. For example, if you are met with a challenge or threat from your environment such as a commitment to make a speech to a large number of very important people, your primary appraisal is the determination of the degree to which the situation is dangerous or a threat. After you decide that you may indeed be in danger (in this case, emotionally), you will then conduct a secondary appraisal concerning the resources you have to meet the danger. During your secondary appraisal, you will remember other speeches to get guidance on coping, determine what you know about making speeches, think about the audience and how friendly you expect it to be, and decide what other resources would be available to you. Through this secondary appraisal, you determine how well you can cope with the threat. After you make your speech, you will again appraise the situation to see if your resources were capable of meeting the demand. If your appraisal indicates that you can make a speech to a large number of very important people, then future invitations will probably be appraised as less threatening. If your ap-

praisal leads you to believe that your attempt to cope was not successful, however, you may view the next opportunity to make a speech as a major threat.

Because our cognitive processes, including memories and belief systems, are highly influential in both primary and secondary appraisals, it is clear that cognitive stress management is an important aspect in the process. Two major methods of cognitive change, stress inoculation and cognitive restructuring, are frequently used to alter the appraisal and coping aspects of stress.

Stress Inoculation

Donald Meichenbaum (1977) originated the term *stress inoculation.* His idea was to develop a skills-based approach that would offer protection from stress in the sense that people receive protection from disease through inoculation. Because the idea is to prepare for stress before a stressful event occurs, it is a fitting analogy. Although stress inoculation was originally used for treatment of phobias, it has been applied to a large number of problem areas such as anxiety, pain, anger, rape trauma, and alcohol abuse. The general stress-inoculation paradigm consists of three phases: education, rehearsal, and application. As these phases have been researched, refined, and relabeled, new phases have been labeled conceptualization, skills acquisition and rehearsal, and application and follow-through (Meichenbaum & Cameron, 1983). Each phase is designed to build on the previous one, with each having tasks to be accomplished.

Phase 1. The objective of the conceptualization phase, as in other intervention methods, includes providing a rationale to the client. It is important for the client to understand the nature of the stress response and to begin to view the problem as having a cognitive component. As the practitioner collects data and provides a conceptualization for the process, a mutual understanding and collaborative relationship develop with the client. Meichenbaum (1983) considers the questions asked, the assessment instruments used, and the rationale given as interacting to contribute to the training process and providing a model for clients.

Data collection can be accomplished through the use of several methods. The primary source of data is the client, who can give valuable information concerning the frequency, intensity, and duration of their problem along with circumstances under which it occurs. Also, it is important to know what they have done in the past to try to solve the problem. If they can describe a situation in detail, the practitioner has the opportunity to clarify terms such as "overwhelmed," "anxious," or "stressed" in order to prevent misunderstandings later in treatment.

In addition to discussion and questions in an interview, Meichenbaum suggests that image-based reconstruction can be used. The practitioner may use imagery in which clients mentally place themselves back in the situation in order to more effectively retrieve specific images, feelings, and thoughts.

Other noninterview methods can also be effective in data collection. For example, a way to obtain current information is to have a client engage in self-monitoring. Recording sheets are useful for some, whereas for others a more flexible diary approach may be more effective in gathering information. This may be particularly helpful in understanding subtle cues to the onset of the stress response. Many people referred for stress problems are unaware of physical sensations or thoughts prior to the symptom onset (pain, anxiety). However, a caution is that when we ask our clients to do homework such as self-monitoring, we need to be sensitive to the complexity of the task and the amount of time required. The practitioner is cautioned against placing overly laborious assessment demands on clients in light of the many demands on their lives outside the counseling office.

As we review the collected data with our clients, we have a natural opportunity to offer a reconceptualization, or new way of looking at the problem. Meichenbaum suggests that by the way we explore information and ask questions, we begin to shape a different viewpoint and encourage self-exploration.

Phase 2. The second phase, skills acquisition and rehearsal, is the time to train clients in the basic skills they will need when confronting stressors in the real world. Clients will have different skill deficits, exposed through assessment, and therefore specific training needs. Meichenbaum divides coping skills into instrumental and palliative. Instrumental skills are related to the type of situation confronted and include problem solving, parenting, study, communication, and assertion. Palliative skills, on the other hand, are useful when the stressor cannot be changed and the person must confront it. Examples of palliative skills are perspective taking, attention diversion, use of social supports, appropriate expression of affect, and relaxation.

After learning skills, the client engages in rehearsal in order to gain confidence and to begin the process of habituation. Rehearsals can be carried out through role playing with the practitioner, other group members, or staff members. If videotaping is possible, the practitioner and client can analyze role-playing interaction together, which allows for coaching of new behaviors. An alternative to live rehearsal is to have clients use imagery to rehearse a situation.

Another aspect of rehearsal, self-instruction training, involves a predetermined set of self-statements designed to aid clients when they are faced with an identified stressor. Self-generated statements are divided into four categories: preparing for a stressor, confronting and handling a stressor, coping with the feelings of being overwhelmed, and reinforcing self-statements. Clients are helped to develop appropriate statements in each category and to rehearse them. Meichenbaum emphasizes that it is important that these statements be meaningful to the client and not merely catch phrases to be repeated mindlessly. They should be personally relevant, and the intention is that they will ultimately be used during a stressful event.

Phase 3. The final phase of stress inoculation is referred to as application and follow-through. Its purpose is to implement these newly learned coping responses through day-to-day situations and, by generalizing, to ensure long-term effects of the change effort. Often a first step is to have clients rehearse their skills under stress-inducing circumstances. This process can be initiated in the office by role-playing increasingly difficult situations. You may want to alternate roles with clients in order to model behavior as well as to serve as an antagonist. Another closely related strategy is to use imagery rehearsal in which the client considers a series of increasingly stress-provoking images.

Once clients are comfortable with the various types of rehearsals, it is time for *in vivo* experiences. As in other aspects of the training, it is important in this phase to engage clients in graded behavior. At first you may accompany a client through the first few experiences so that you can both model and coach new coping skills. An example of this method with a client whose manifestation of stress is fear involves the practitioner accompanying the phobic client up two floors on an elevator. As the client develops coping skills and gains confidence, he or she is expected to implement skills independently.

This self-initiated practice brings a wealth of information and learning. During this time clients may experience both success and failure, either of which can be used in subsequent counseling sessions to help them refine skills. When they learn how to analyze unsuccessful coping and make changes based on their learning, they are taking another step toward self-sufficiency. Once a person has a successful ex-

perience, self-reinforcement can be emphasized, which leads to increased self-efficacy.

According to Meichenbaum, greater self-efficacy and confidence lead to better generalization and long-term change. Consequently, it is important to prepare clients for the possibility of a temporary relapse so that it is not seen as a failure of the training. In addition, training should not be stopped abruptly or too soon. Give your clients continued support by fading the training through a decreased frequency of sessions. If possible, offer prearranged booster, or follow-up, sessions several months after termination. These structural supports can be pivotal in facilitating lasting change.

Stress-inoculation training has been useful in treating many types of stress-related problems. Its effectiveness is due in part to its comprehensiveness, which includes not only cognitive changes but also problem solving, coping skills, rehearsal, and *in vivo* experiences. Additional key elements are the practitioner's ability to build a collaborative relationship with the client and to understand the problem from the client's perspective.

Cognitive Restructuring

A second major approach to cognitive stress management is cognitive restructuring. The model originates with Ellis and his rational-emotive therapy approach to treatment, which has been further operationalized and developed by Beck (1984) and others. It assumes that people have idiosyncratic cognitive patterns that are hyperactive and lead to a chronically activated autonomic nervous system and a continuing stress state. These patterns become involved in the primary appraisal of threat as well as the secondary appraisal of resources to meet the demand. Indeed, distorted thinking patterns allow the person to generate stress without an external stressor.

Distorted patterns are usually identified as irrational beliefs or distorted thinking because they are illogical and automatic and lead us to maladaptive emotional and behavioral responses. They can be grouped into various categories such as overgeneralization, mind reading, and personalization, which are observed to be operational in people who declare themselves to be "stressed out." Several authors (Eliot & Breo, 1984; McKay, Davis, & Fanning, 1981) have identified specific patterns that seem to be prevalent in people who are suffering from stress-related problems. Pearsall (1987) offers an even more specific categorization of distorted thinking styles and relates them to personality types designated as "hot" and "cold" running people.

Because these distorted patterns are responsible for elicitation of the stress response, restructuring of patterns is considered an important intervention. According to Beck's model (Everly, 1989), three strategies are used to facilitate restructuring. The first is to ask clients for evidence to support the conclusions they have reached. For example, faulty logic is often the basis for the distortions habitually used in a person's cognitive process. During this questioning, the therapist not only helps clients understand more clearly how faulty logic leads to unrealistic conclusions but also models the type of thinking process that can lessen distorted thinking. A second strategy is to ask if there is another way to look at the situation. Many times clients get fixated on one interpretation. By offering different interpretations of an event, the practitioner can teach clients that alternatives are possible and can be tested in the real world. An advantage of this type of question is that clients can, at a minimum, begin to have a broader perspective on the event(s). The third part of the restructuring process involves the question "So what if this happens?" The implication is that even if a situation is stressful, clients can use coping strategies and problem-solving methods to meet the demands. Through a collaborative relationship the client and therapist together develop new ways of responding to stressors. By

following this process of inquiry and exploration, clients gain objectivity and the capacity to examine their thinking, motivations, and behavior with more distance. They also gain perspective through an expanded frame of reference (Beck, 1984).

Vital to the process of changing cognitive patterns is an examination of self-talk. Many clients do not realize that what they say to themselves makes a difference in how they view the world and how they respond to stressors. Hence, one of the early tasks for clients is to become aware of self-statements and then to learn new statements designed to bring an alternative, more adaptive perspective to the situation.

After learning to pinpoint destructive cognitive patterns and to change those patterns, clients can be expected to find a significant difference in their feelings and a sense of relief from stress. Although it may take months to fully integrate the new patterns as habits, many people can quickly experience a positive change.

CASE ILLUSTRATION

An effective approach to stress management is a comprehensive approach. As we have seen, stress is a complex phenomenon that cannot be adequately addressed with a simplistic answer such as suggesting to clients to enroll in an exercise class. Although fitness and exercise can be quite helpful, they are not an adequate answer. A far more effective method is to address the problem in a comprehensive manner using interventions more broadly suited to the person and the problem. The following discussion illustrates the use of several methods of stress management with the emphasis on cognitive change methods.

Louis, age 37, was referred for stress management by his physician. The primary stress-related problem was his uncontrolled hypertension. Other symptoms included a high cholesterol level, insomnia, irritability, and fatigue. The client's major concern was to get control over his hypertension because he disliked the side effects of the prescribed medication. When he took enough medication to lower his blood pressure, he was too lethargic and drowsy to function. Identified stressors included a job with too much time spent on the telephone, a great deal of travel, and conflict among management. In addition, he was unhappy with his job because his college degree was in music and he wanted to teach and perform. But he could not pursue his desired career because he could not support his family on the income he would earn through teaching.

Assessment

A psychophysiological stress profile carried out with biofeedback equipment indicated that Louis's autonomic nervous system was highly reactive to stress. He showed a marked peripheral vasoconstriction, an increase in heart rate under stress, with an extended recovery time. As we discussed the implication of this situation, he agreed that after he experienced a stressful event, he continued to ruminate about it for quite some time. These results indicated that his increase in heart rate and vasoconstriction were contributing to his hypertension problem.

An assessment of his lifestyle showed that Louis had already made health-promoting changes in diet and exercise. His doctor and a nutritionist were providing guidance on ways to decrease fat and cholesterol, and he was walking two or three miles at least three times per week to increase his fitness level.

When asked about his support system, Louis indicated that his wife, daughter, and mother were strong sources of support for him. However, he also viewed them as stressors, because he felt financial responsibility for them. He listed no friends or work colleagues as a part of his support system.

An analysis of Louis's thinking patterns revealed several destructive areas. He used polarized thinking in management meetings when his supervisor disagreed with him. Other distortions included "shoulds," personalization, and negative filtering.

Treatment

The treatment plan for Louis was an integrated approach using biofeedback to promote self-regulation of his physiological response to stress, cognitive restructuring of dysfunctional thought patterns so that his primary and secondary appraisal could be affected, stress inoculation for management meetings, and problem solving to increase his support system and life satisfaction.

Cognitive restructuring consisted of identifying self-statements leading to distorted thinking patterns. For example, Louis found that he was making self-statements before management meetings that created anger. Consequently, he was angry at the beginning of meetings and became angrier through interactions during them. Once he understood that he was responsible for his anger, he was able to change the self-statements and his belief about management conflict.

In addition to cognitive restructuring, stress inoculation was implemented to handle the large number of (mostly negative) telephone calls he received each day. He learned diaphragmatic breathing to interrupt the stress response, rehearsed new skills for communication, and used reinforcing self-talk to give himself credit for good performance.

This integrated, multimethod approach to stress management was quite effective for Louis. Within six months his blood pressure was under control with less medication, and the negative side effects were correspondingly reduced. In addition, his cholesterol was in a range considered healthy. He explored career options so that he no longer felt trapped in his job, and he joined a community choir where he could enjoy being around music. All of these changes contributed to a higher life satisfaction.

Although it is not possible to say which component of the stress-management program made the greatest contribution to Louis's changes, it is certain that cognitive intervention was pivotal to the outcome. By changing the way he thought about the stressors he confronted, he found that he could be in charge of his life, a process that was then validated by the changes in physiology related to his blood pressure and changes in his emotions. He completed treatment after six months with an attitude of well-being both physically and emotionally. During a follow-up session after one year, he demonstrated physiological control through skill in hand warming (vasodilation) and reported that his cognitive skills had contributed to a much less pressured lifestyle.

CONCLUSION

Stress is a part of all of our lives. We need it for the challenge that pushes us to peak performance. However, since stress is a reaction to demands made on us, we can, over time, wear down the systems called into play by pushing too hard and too often. Selye's model of stress, which he refers to as the general adaptation syndrome (GAS), provides a way of understanding this ongoing process of wear and tear on the body. Once a person progresses through the first two stages, alarm and resistance, the third stage brings on illness and even the possibility of death. According to Selye, when we have used all of the adaptive energy issued at birth, the result is death. In fact, according to Selye's theory, we do not die of old age but of worn-out parts due to stress.

Stress management is a complex process involving both physical and affective processes. In order to be effective, stress management must be comprehensive and inclusive of all components. Through thorough assessment of the client's lifestyle, physiology, cognitions, and behavior, an individualized treatment plan can be developed with the client. Changing the way in which a person manages stress will most certainly lead to a more comfortable life with decreased emotional and physical symptoms and possibly increased longevity.

REFERENCES

Asterita, M. F. (1985). *The physiology of stress.* New York: Human Sciences Press.

Basmajian, J. V. (1989). *Biofeedback: Principles and practice for clinicians.* Baltimore: Williams & Wilkins.

Beck, A. T. (1984). Cognitive approaches to stress. In R. Woolfolk & P. Lehrer (Eds.), *Principles and practice of stress management.* New York: Guilford Press.

Benson, H. (1975). *The relaxation response.* New York: Morrow.

Cox, T. (1978). *Stress.* London: Macmillan.

Curtis, J. D., & Detert, R. A. (1981). *How to relax: A holistic approach to stress management.* Palo Alto, CA: Mayfield.

Danskin, D. G., & Crow, M. A. (1981). *Biofeedback: An introduction and guide.* Palo Alto, CA: Mayfield.

Eliot, R. S., & Breo, D. L. (1984). *Is it worth dying for?* New York: Bantam Books.

Everly, G. S. (1989). *A clinical guide to the treatment of the human stress response.* New York: Plenum.

Everly, G. S., & Rosenfeld, R. R. (1981). *The nature and the treatment of the stress response: A practical guide for clinicians.* New York: Plenum.

Greenspoon, J., & Olson, J. (1986). Stress management and biofeedback. *Clinical Biofeedback and Health, 9,* 65–80.

House, J. S., & Kahn, R. L. (1985). Measures and concepts of social support. In S. Cohen & S. L. Syme (Eds.), *Social support and health.* Orlando, FL: Academic Press.

Kabat-Zinn, J. (1990). *Full catastrophe living: Using the wisdom of your body and mind to face stress, pain, and illness.* New York: Delacorte.

Lazarus, R. S. (1966). *Psychological stress and the coping process.* New York: McGraw-Hill.

Lazarus, R. S. (1977). Cognitive and coping processes in emotion. In A. Monat & R. Lazarus (Eds.), *Stress and coping: An anthology.* New York: Columbia University Press.

Leventhal, H., & Nerenz, D. R. (1983). A model for stress research with some implications for the control of stress disorders. In D. Meichenbaum & M. E. Jaremko (Eds.), *Stress reduction and prevention.* New York: Plenum.

Manuso, J. (1978). Testimony to the President's Commission on Mental Health. In *Report of the President's Commission on Mental Health: Vol. 2. Appendix.* Washington, DC: U.S. Government Printing Office.

McGrath, J. E. (1977). Settings, measures, and themes: An integrative review of some research on socialpsychological factors in stress. In A. Monat & R. Lazarus (Eds.). *Stress and coping: An anthology.* New York: Columbia University Press.

McKay, M., Davis, M., & Fanning, P. (1981). *Thoughts and feelings: The art of cognitive stress intervention.* Oakland, CA: New Harbinger Publications.

Meichenbaum, D. (1977). *Cognitive-behavior modification: An integrative approach.* New York: Plenum.

Meichenbaum, D. (1983). *Coping with stress.* New York: Facts on File Publications.

Meichenbaum, D., & Cameron, R. (1983). Stress inoculation training: Toward a general paradigm for training coping skills. In D. Meichenbaum & M. E. Jarenko (Eds.), *Stress reduction and prevention.* New York: Plenum.

Neidhardt, E. J., Weinstein, M. S., & Conry, R. F. (1985). *No-gimmick guide to managing stress.* North Vancouver, British Columbia: International Self-Counsel Press.

Nurenberger, P. (1981). *Freedom from stress.* Honesdale, PA: Himalayan International Institute of Yoga Science and Philosophy.

Olton, D. S., & Noonberg, A. R. (1980). *Biofeedback: Clinical applications in behavioral medicine.* Englewood Cliffs, NJ: Prentice-Hall.

Pearsall, P. (1987). *Superimmunity: Master your emotions and improve your health.* New York: Ballantine.

Quick, J. C., Shannon, C., & Quick, J. D. (1983). Managing stress in the Air Force: An ounce of prevention. *Air Force University Review, 34,* 76–83.

Selye, H. (1956). *The stress of life.* New York: McGraw-Hill.

Selye, H. (1974). *Stress without distress.* Philadelphia: Lippincott.

Shannon, C. (1990). *Stress management services guide.* Irving, TX: Employee Assistance Plus.

Shellenberger, R., Turner, J., Green, J., & Cooney, J. (1986). Health changes in a biofeedback and stress management program. *Clinical Biofeedback and Health, 9,* 23–34.

Woolfolk, R. L., & Lehrer, P. (1984). *Principles and practice of stress management.* New York: Guilford Press.

Cognitive and Behavioral Treatment: Clinical Issues, Transfer of Training, and Relapse Prevention

Donald K. Granvold
John S. Wodarski

The integration of cognitive and behavioral treatment methods has gradually developed from early acknowledgment by behaviorists of the concept of cognition to the combined application of mediational factors and behavioral principles in the formulation of treatment methods. Understandably, the efforts have evidenced bias toward either cognitive or behavioral variables. These biases continue today as reflected in many of the chapters in this volume, in which the treatment programs described are more strongly cognitive or behavioral. The development of the mediational model has produced varied and increasingly elaborate procedures for accessing cognitive phenomena and producing change cognitively and behaviorally. The integration of cognitive methods with behavioral change procedures has not been free of evolutionary growing pains. And the current lack of integration of the two perspectives remains a valid criticism (Berlin, Mann, & Grossman, 1991). Despite the limitations, the infusion of mediational content in treatment is of critical importance and makes up a body of knowledge that critics of behavioral practice contend will have to be dealt with before behavior modification becomes a viable treatment technology (Littrell & Magel, 1991).

Chapters 1 and 2 reviewed basic concepts of cognitivism and behaviorism, respectively. In this chapter several clinical issues are addressed, and strategies are presented for effectively transferring treatment effects into the client's natural environment and maintaining changes.

CLINICAL ISSUES

As evidenced in this and many other volumes, cognitive-behavioral methods have been used effectively to treat a broad range of psychological, interpersonal, and social problems across diverse populations. Although these techniques are highly promising, many issues require further extensive and focused exploration to determine their impact on treatment effects and stability of change. The ingredients of the treatment process selected for consideration are among the most salient, although many other factors are worthy of consideration as well.

Therapeutic Relationship

The relationship between the practitioner and the client has long been recognized as a highly significant ingredient in effective treatment. Cognitive-behavioral therapy is a collaborative approach in which the practitioner and client *together* specify and define problems, assess problems and contextual variables, set short- and long-term goals of treatment, design and evaluate the change effort (collaborative empiricism), determine when termination of ongoing treatment is appropriate, and establish relapse prevention methods and follow-up procedures. Mahoney (1991) writes that "the optimal therapeutic relationship creates a special and intimate human context—a context in and from which the client can safely experiment with and explore familiar and novel ways of experiencing self, world (especially the interpersonal), and possible relationships" (p. 267). The therapeutic relationship is one of intimacy, involving disclosure of the most closely held thoughts, emotions, contemplations, aspirations, and judgments. The evolution of intimacy is promoted by the client's trust in the therapist's confidentiality, expertise, and genuine caring. It may involve testing the therapist to determine the boundaries of treatment. Just what can the client safely disclose? What tends to promote the therapist's interest and enthusiasm? What can the client "get away with"? (For example, are all aspects of homework evaluated; is relatively superficial discussion tolerated for extended periods?) The practitioner is responsible for providing a safe environment in which the therapeutic relationship can develop and treatment outcomes can be responsibly sought. In this relationship the practitioner seeks to know and understand the uniqueness of the individual and displays respect for that uniqueness. The focus of attention is on the client's life. Far greater time is spent on the client, and the breadth, degree, and nature of disclosure is far greater from the client to the practitioner than vice versa.

Within the context of client input and influence, it is the practitioner who is ultimately responsible for the course of treatment and issues such as timing; establishing realistic yet challenging change objectives; providing support, encouragement, and reinforcement of client behaviors relevant to the change effort; sensitive and caring confrontation of the client's minimal compliance or noncompliance with the agreed-on treatment process (for example, homework, staying focused in session); and determination and removal of barriers (psychological, environmental, and social) that prevent effective treatment outcomes. The practitioner is cautioned against

labeling the client resistant and is urged, rather, to seek a clear understanding of the client's unique orientation to change, self-efficacy, and extraneous factors that may be operating to confound the change effort. Furthermore, the practitioner should continually reevaluate (1) the clarity of change objectives and actions designed to meet those objectives; (2) the degree of challenge the current change effort poses (too small or too great); (3) the timeliness of the change being expected (are other issues more pressing; is the client ready psychologically to proceed?); and (4) the skill deficiencies (cognitive and behavioral) that may account for a lack of change.

Another responsibility of the practitioner is the conscious, purposeful, and strategic modeling of adaptive cognitions, emotions, and behaviors (Safran & Segal, 1990). The accurate display of information processing skill through verbal modeling is presumed to be therapeutically influential on the client. Statements by the practitioner reflecting faulty attributions, dichotomous thinking, personalization, and the like may effectively move the client away from the development and practice of adaptive cognitive functioning. The modeling of error-free cognitive behavior, appropriate verbal skills (for example, not interrupting and reflecting content and feelings), and other behaviors capitalizes on the potential of observational learning. Humor is also a useful tool if used judiciously. It is of particular facility when practitioners model acceptance of themselves with their flaws, foibles, and proneness to error. One of the authors spilled coffee during a treatment session (more than once!) and used laughter and statements of personal error-proneness without overtones of self-castigation or denigration by way of modeling a desirable response to human error.

The therapeutic relationship provides a privileged opportunity for the practitioner to operate with the sanction to influence the client. It presents the practitioner with challenge, the opportunity for creativity, the joys of intimacy, and the rewards that come with seeing clients rejuvenate themselves, develop life skills, attain their personal goals, resolve problems, and increase their happiness.

Clinical Judgment

Practitioners' theoretical orientation and past training and clinical experience shape their expectations in making clinical decisions. These expectancies have a critical bearing on practitioners' perception, the data they seek, the meaning they attach to the information they ascertain, the content they store and retrieve from memory, the conclusions they reach, their appraisals of client behavior and that of clients' significant others, their views of clients' potential for change, and the like. The potential for bias is extreme. Turk and Salovey (1986) note the tendency of practitioners to observe what they expect to observe, and they go on to say that "not only must clinicians be concerned with the influence of *a priori* hypotheses on the attention to and interpretation of data, but they should also be concerned about the impact of their behavior on the *creation* of confirming data, so-called self-fulfilling prophecies" (p. 307). The data that practitioners seek through specific questions and the subtle reinforcement they give to client disclosures in specific areas may effectively generate supportive "evidence" for their preliminary views and judgments. The resulting bias may significantly influence practitioners' problem definition, diagnosis, prognosis, perception of client efficacy expectations, and perception of relationship formulation, treatment compliance, and other treatment variables. In effect, clinical bias jeopardizes both the validity and efficacy of treatment.

To combat bias in information processing, clinical judgment, and decision making, Turk and Salovey (1986) suggest the following procedures:

- Explicitly generate and evaluate competing hypotheses.
- Determine how the evidence fits the hypotheses with the one specified.
- "Deautomatize" decision making (Nisbett, Krantz, Jepson, & Kunda, 1983; Nisbett & Ross, 1980).
- Use feedback regarding successes and failures in making future predictions.
- Determine and evaluate evidence both for and against a given hypothesis (complete a Ben Franklin sheet listing advantages and disadvantages).
- Develop an awareness of your own unique metacognition, and monitor your own processing (memory, comprehension, knowledge).
- Students and novices should seek supervision in which the supervisor models the process of making clinical judgments. They should use supervision as a forum for generating alternative decisional hypotheses as noted above.

The reduction of clinical bias is an important aspect of responsible professional behavior. The development of a personal awareness of clinical bias and the incorporation of procedures to limit it will enhance practitioner performance and treatment effects.

Cognitive Assessment

Cogito, ergo sum—in this brief statement Descartes established thinking as the essence of human existence. Agreed, but then what are we specifically as thinkers? Practitioners and researchers have continued to be intrigued and challenged by both the content and process of cognition in relation to adaptive and maladaptive behavior. Efforts have been made to classify cognitive phenomena and to categorize and evaluate cognitive content on such dimensions as accessibility, complexity, depth, breadth, and stability. These and other efforts represent the domain of cognitive assessment.

Conceptual Framework. The cognitive taxonomic system of Ingram (Ingram, 1983; Ingram & Kendall, 1986; Kendall & Ingram, 1987), outlined in Chapter 1 is a useful framework for cognitive assessment methods. The four domains identified are (1) cognitive structure (*organization* of information stored in memory for retrieval), (2) cognitive propositions (*content* stored in cognitive structure), (3) cognitive operations (*processes* by which information is encoded, stored, and retrieved), and (4) cognitive *products* (thoughts, self-verbalizations, beliefs, judgments, and feelings). Cognitive structure and content combine to form schemata, resulting in a complex construct encompassing both the process and content dimensions of cognition. To clarify, Neisser (1976) writes that schemata are "not only the plan, but also the executor of the plan" (p. 56). For more information on definition and assessment of schemata, the reader is referred to the following: Kendall and Ingram (1987), Kihlstrom and Nasby (1981), Landau and Goldfried (1981), Markus and Wurf (1987), and Winfrey and Goldfried (1986).

Merluzzi and Boltwood (1989) note that research in the domain of cognitive operations, based on the information-processing paradigm, includes exploration of selective attention, perceptual distortion, and selective encoding and retrieval. Cognitive products and the content dimensions of schemata are the cognitive variables most frequently assessed by clinical practitioners.

Avoiding Isolationism. The study of cognition is not to be done in isolation. Cognition is one of several variables (cognition, affect, behavior, physical and physiological factors, and environmental factors) that interact reciprocally, and as Meichenbaum and Cameron (1981) note, "cognitive processes are probably at once both causes and effects" (p. 9). Despite these realities, independent assessment techniques and procedures need to be developed for each variable. Although cog-

nitive assessment methods exist in relatively early stages of development, proven behavioral methods of assessment should not be abandoned but, rather, should be incorporated in a comprehensive assessment package whenever appropriate and feasible.

Self-Reports. The major problem with cognitive assessment is the obvious fact that the information sought is not directly observable. This leaves the practitioner with several methodological problems, including accessibility, definition, measurement, accuracy in terms of both validity and veridicality, and temporal factors. These concerns notwithstanding, it is necessary to assess cognitive phenomena because of the impact that such factors have on behavior. And how shall we go about assessing cognitive functioning? Mischel (1981) aptly writes that "the most direct way to find out what a person thinks, values, knows, or believes (about himself or herself or about other people) is to ask directly" (p. 479). The alternative is for the practitioner to infer cognitive processes on the basis of nonverbal behaviors and performance.

There is a history of skepticism among practitioners and researchers regarding the use of self-report assessment methods. In this regard, Mischel (1981) notes that for years "psychologists who were heavily influenced by Freudian theory, tended to assume automatically . . . that what a person said about himself or herself in response to direct questions was likely to be either superficial or defensively distorted and misleading" (p. 480). Assuming that the cognitive-behavioral practitioner is beyond this form of interpretation, other opportunities for error in the use of self-report remain. Potential client self-report error exists in such areas as (1) retrieval from short- and long-term memory; (2) perception—screening data in and screening data out; (3) weighting data; (4) data-sequencing recall; (5) emotional overlays influencing information processing; (6) attributional conclusions; and (7) temporal factors. Nisbett and Wilson (1977) raised early issue with the validity of client self-reports based on the inability of clients to accurately report causal explanations of their behavior. This influential article was met with extensive rebuttal contending that errors in clients' causal explanations should not be taken as evidence to invalidate all verbal report data (Bainbridge, 1979; Cantor, Mischel, & Schwartz, 1981; Genest & Turk, 1981; Meichenbaum & Butler, 1980; Smith & Miller, 1978; White, 1980).

Although discomfort continues regarding the use of self-report measures, long-standing evidence exists that self-report is a relatively accurate predictor of behavior (Mischel, 1968, 1972, 1977). Thus, clients can be useful sources of information about themselves. In order to increase the quality and credibility of cognitive self-report data, Meichenbaum and Cameron (1981) suggest the following guidelines:

- The inquiry should be conducted as soon as possible following the cognitive events of interest, assessing directly for information in short-term memory whenever possible.
- The amount of probing should be minimized in order to decrease the likelihood that the client or subject will engage in inferential processes about his or her own cognitive experience or about the expectancies of the clinician or experimenter.
- Analysis of the internal consistency of such reports should be included in order to assess the validity of the verbal report.
- Clients or subjects should be asked to describe their cognitive experience. They should not be asked to explain why they behaved as they did or provide motives for their behavior.
- Clients or subjects should be given a set that motivates them to provide honest and full accounts. In providing such a set, the assessor might emphasize that his or her ability to study the target experience depends entirely on honest, careful reporting.

- It may be helpful to provide a set that legitimizes disclosure of cognitions. For example, clients or subjects might be asked to provide their "impressions" or descriptions of their experience during the experimental task, as opposed to being asked to "recollect" what occurred or to tell what they "did."
- Providing the client or subject with retrieval cues immediately after performance may also foster full and veridical reporting.*

Although there are inherent problems in the use of self-report data, support exists for the viability of self-report as an assessment procedure. The guidelines presented above offer suggestions that can significantly enhance the quality of the data collected.

Assessment of Self-Talk. A variety of procedures has been developed for the assessment of cognitive phenomena. The most frequently used procedure is the therapeutic interview, in which the practitioner seeks to determine the client's self-talk: internal dialogues, automatic thoughts, self-statements, and internal sentences. Sutton-Simon (1981) notes that interviews designed to assess belief systems require that the practitioner and client share a similar cognitive view of psychological problems and speak in terms familiar to both participants. This requires an initial educational process in which clients are encouraged to recognize the role of cognitive factors in their problems.

Interviews may be more or less structured and comprise various assessment approaches. In a structured interview, for example, clients may be presented with specific statements, thoughts, or beliefs and asked to report how frequently they might think the thought or how strongly they might hold a belief. Glass and Merluzzi (1981) describe this procedure as a "recognition method" of self-statement assess-

*From "Issues in Cognitive Assessment: An Overview," by D. Meichenbaum and R. Cameron. In *Cognitive Assessment*, by T. V. Merluzzi, C. R. Glass, and M. Genest (Eds.). Copyright © 1981 by Guilford Press.

ment. They provide a five-class taxonomy of methods of self-statement assessment: (1) recognition methods, (2) recall methods, (3) prompted-recall methods, (4) expressive methods, and (5) projective methods. Recall procedures involve a review of past circumstances and a listing of thoughts associated with the time or circumstance. This thought listing procedure (Cacioppo & Petty, 1981) may involve imaging as a means of enhancing recall. Prompted recall involves using a videotape of client performance as a cue to elicit self-statements. Expressive procedures, considered to be the best overall method, involve the client "thinking aloud" while performing a task. Projective procedures involve the client's consideration of a picture or vignette and a report of the thoughts or beliefs of the character depicted.

In Vivo Assessment.   The practitioner may devise methods to achieve *in vivo* assessment based on the evidence that what a person believes (or even attends to) may vary as a function of place (cues) and time (Hollon & Kendall, 1981). Contextual and temporal factors are considered to be influential on the stream of cognition, particularly with regard to recall. *In vivo* observations present a viable means for limiting these effects. Various *in vivo* monitoring methods have been used to assess a variety of targets. Thought sampling in the natural environment has been achieved through the use of a "beeper" set to randomly prompt the client to record thoughts and corresponding behaviors (Hurlburt, 1979; Kendall & Hollon, 1981). Daily records have also been used in which the client spot-checks or, at designated intervals, records emotions, behaviors, and associated thoughts, *In vivo* monitoring procedures should be considered a means of addressing the transient nature of cognitive functioning.

Assessment Inventories.   A variety of inventories has been developed for the assessment of cognitive behavior. The following is a sampling of such inventories: the Automatic Thoughts Questionnaire (ATQ), developed by Hollon and Kendall (1980) to determine negative cognitions associated with depression; the Dysfunctional Attitude Scale (DAS) (Weissman, 1978; Weissman & Beck, 1978), developed to assess negative attitudes (schemata) associated with depression; the Attributional Style Questionnaire (ASQ) (Peterson et al., 1982), designed to measure attributional style on internal/external, stable/unstable, and global/specific dimensions; the Irrational Beliefs Test (IBT) (Jones, 1969), designed to measure the degree to which subjects maintain beliefs associated with Ellis's (1962) list of irrational beliefs; the Rational Behavior Inventory (RBI), developed by Shorkey and Whiteman (1977), also designed to measure irrational beliefs; and the Assertion Self-Statement Test (ASST), developed by Schwartz and Gottman (1976) to assess the role of self-statements in individuals' ability to complete assertive tasks. Inventories such as these are of use for assessment purposes and also for outcome evaluation.

Concluding Comments on Cognitive Assessment.   The practitioner is encouraged to design a comprehensive assessment package covering the relevant interacting variables considered most important in the treatment of a specific client. Assessment of cognitive functioning through methods such as those identified above should be part of that package. Finally, once information processing errors, irrational beliefs, or other cognitive dysfunctions are identified, intervention should closely follow. A major strength of cognitive-behavioral intervention is the continuity between assessment and treatment.

TRANSFER OF TRAINING AND RELAPSE PREVENTION

The impact of treatment on clients' functioning in their natural environment and the achievement of long-term, sustained change are two major concerns of helping professionals. While in the treatment environment clients may gain awareness and understanding of their problems and treatment methods, observe and practice cognitive and behavioral skills for resolving problems, and strategize the implementation of change *in vivo,* it is only as the transfer of changes is made to their natural environment and the treatment effects extend past termination that treatment can be considered to be successful. Clients' natural environmental circumstances (family, work, church, social and recreational groups, and organizations) make up the context within which their problems have ultimate meaning and importance. For example, although depressed clients' symptoms are of particular discomfort to them, their family and friends, their work performance and interpersonal relations in the workplace, and their avocational and leisure activities also suffer the ill effects of the depression. The practitioner is obligated to promote the transfer of clients' changes into these contexts in order to effect pervasive, socially relevant, and resilient change. Evidence of the change effort in the natural environment may also produce the benefit of reinforcement from significant others for changes in the client's behavior. Such reinforcement is a valuable factor in establishing and maintaining new behavior patterns.

Transfer of Training Methods

There are many strategies for promoting transfer of training. Although the selection of procedures may vary, it is widely held that fostering generalization should be an active undertaking by the practitioner and should be initiated early in treatment rather than just prior to termination (Stokes & Baer, 1977). A number of procedures are designed for implementation in the therapeutic environment, and other procedures are for *in vivo* implementation. Some procedures are appropriate for use across settings.

Simulation and Behavior Rehearsal.

Treatment in the office should simulate real-life situations as the context in which behavior rehearsal is accomplished. The practitioner should seek detailed descriptions of the environmental circumstances in which problem behaviors are evidenced. This involves engaging the client in a collaborative effort in describing the circumstances in which problem behaviors occur; specification of discriminative stimuli; and identification of the client's cognitions, emotional responses, and behaviors in identified contexts. The use of relaxation methods and guided imagery may facilitate and enhance the simulation process. Whether simulated or *in vivo,* training should provide sufficient exemplars of stimulus conditions or responses (Stokes & Baer, 1977). As skills are developed through repetitive behavior rehearsal, the practitioner should vary response options and introduce diverse situations in which targeted behavior change is desired. For example, if the client is developing assertiveness skills, develop several different simulated circumstances in which to rehearse variable assertive responses. To promote greater transfer of interpersonal skills development, Gottman and Leiblum (1974) recommend the use of co-therapists and group treatment. Both are viable considerations for enhancing the client's ability to display improved social skills in a variety of social contexts and relationships. These intervention formats would be useful in generalization programming for the treatment of many problems in addition to deficiencies in social skills. The treatment setting can also be altered to more closely represent the environmental context to which the transfer of training is desired. For example, Schaefer, Sobell, and Mills (1971) placed a portable bar in the treatment setting in their aversive treatment of alcohol abuse.

Mastery of Skills and Longer Treatment.

Cognitive and behavioral change require the mastery of relevant skills through extended practice until the desired performance level is achieved. This requires redundancy and persistence on the part of both the client and practitioner. Furthermore, it has been recommended that overlearning be accomplished to maximize transfer (Baer, 1981; Gottman & Leiblum, 1974; Miller, 1984). Sensitivity to individual differences in clients' rates of acquiring skills is encouraged. The establishment of time limits of treatment for given problems is likely to violate client variability in rates of both skill development and generalization. Not only may clients display variable overall learning rates, a given client's rate of skill acquisition in treatment may vary significantly from his or her rate of transfer of learning. Some clients may rapidly become rather accomplished at skills in the office and have great difficulty in performing in the natural setting, and others may take much longer to learn the skill and find it easy to transfer their learning to other contexts once they have gained proficiency in the treatment setting.

The time requirements for the development of mastery and transfer to the natural environment are of particular concern given the current trend toward brief treatment in response to managed health-care treatment limitations. Despite these limitations, longer term treatment may be required to adequately accomplish the performance level necessary for effective and durable change and transfer to the client's natural environment.

Training in Broad Change.   A narrowly designed treatment program focused on discrete cognitive events (as opposed to the changing of underlying cognitive structures) and tightly controlled stimulus conditions with opportunity for only a few behavioral responses may function to restrict generalization (Stokes & Baer, 1977). Ellis (1973) promotes profound philosophic change as a means of producing both generalizable and long-term change. A change in a faulty underlying belief may have applicability across a broad range of maladaptive emotional and behavioral responses and stimulus conditions. Behavior training that incorporates the presentation of a broad range of stimulus conditions (for example, settings, populations, tasks, demands), response options, and consequences (for example, approval, ridicule) may produce greater transfer of training across natural environmental situations, settings, and populations.

Training in Metacognition.   Rosen (1989) recommends training in metacognition, or thinking about one's own thinking—types of errors, reasoning strategies, associations among cognitive errors, faulty beliefs, and the like—as a means of enhancing the transfer of change across contexts and after treatment has been terminated. Skills in metacognizing are presumed to take the individual to a higher level of cognitive ability. These skills of self-monitoring one's own cognitive activity are valuable in checking cognitive errors and effecting the cognitive restructuring of faulty beliefs in the context of daily living.

Training in Self-Management.   Self-management refers to a set of cognitive-behavioral processes through which the individual consciously and diligently promotes the likelihood of engaging in desirable behavior. It is a *generalization* strategy designed to extend new behaviors into the client's home and daily life under his or her own direction and control (Rehm & Rokke, 1988). Antecedent conditions, mediation, and consequences of behaviors are all points of modification in individuals' development of greater control over their behavior. Before proceeding with a discussion of self-management methods, a word of clarification is in order regarding the terms *self-management, self-control,* and *self-regulation.* Despite significant differences, these terms have been used somewhat interchangeably in the literature. This may be due in part to their overlapping procedures. Self-control, initially most frequently used, has lost favor due to "its connotations of will power and containment of the expression of emotion" (Rehm & Rokke, 1988, p. 136). Self-regulation relates to the incorporation of methods to gain voluntary control over psychological, behavioral, and physiological processes (for example, biofeedback). We prefer the term *self-management* rather than self-control due to its semantic clarity.

Despite this terminological preference, traditional self-control definitions and descriptions are relevant to the explication of self-management procedures. Goldfried and Merbaum (1973) define self-control as "a process through which an individual becomes the principal agent in guiding, directing, and regulating those features of his own behavior that might eventually lead to desired positive consequences" (p. 11). It is assumed that human beings possess the potential to develop knowledge and skills to promote and regulate their own behavior. To exercise self-management, the individual must understand the factors that influence behavior and how these factors can be altered to produce desired changes. Thoresen and Mahoney (1974) propose the following definition: "A person displays self-control when in the relative absence of immediate external constraints, he engages in bahavior whose previous probability has been less than that of alternatively available behaviors (involving lesser or delayed reward, greater exertion or aversive properties, and so on)" (p. 12). Hence, a central objective of self-management is the client's acquisition of cognitive and behavioral skills for use in resisting immediate reinforcement in exchange for delayed positive reinforcement, which is more compatible with current objectives for behavior change and the attainment of long-term goals. Self-management procedures involve arranging environmental conditions, developing cognitive aids or supports, and modifying the consequences of actions in order to maximize the probability of eliciting appropriate behavior. Environmental planning (stimulus control) may involve decreasing or removing environmental cues or opportunities to respond. For

example, a person on a snack-free, regimented eating program may keep no snacks in the home or carry no cash for snack purchases while at work. Cognitive procedures may include altering self-efficacy (Bandura, 1977a, 1977b), self-instruction (Meichenbaum, 1977), imagery (Edwards, 1989), covert modeling (Cautela, 1971), coping skills training (Kazdin, 1973, 1974; Meichenbaum, 1977), and covert self-reinforcement (Cautela, 1970). Contingent self-reinforcement procedures may include methods of self-monitoring (counting, tracking, charting) and self-imposed contingencies (rewards, response costs). Of particular facility as a self-reinforcement strategy is the utilization of high-probability (high-reward) behaviors already in the client's repertoire as contingent reinforcers for the performance of low-probability behaviors (Premack, 1965, 1971). A client's preferred activities can thus be utilized as deferred consequences for the performance of tasks that, although of some meaning and importance to the client, have been avoided. This principle of self-management was learned by most of us years ago in the form of "Clean up your room, and you can go out and play!"

The value of self-management as a technique is not in applying learning principles to clients but in teaching the principles to clients for their application to themselves (Rehm & Rokke, 1988). There are ample data to support the contention that when clients participate in the choice of therapeutic procedures and their implementation, their motivation and commitment to change is increased, a condition indicated by research to be necessary for behavioral change (Brehm, 1976; Feldman & Wodarski, 1975). It is this focus on client self-application that makes self-management such a powerful generalization strategy (Kazdin, 1975).

Use of Homework. The use of clearly defined homework assignments has been found to be an effective means of transferring gains from the therapeutic environment into the client's natural environment. The purpose and anticipated benefits of homework should be explained by the practitioner as a rationale for the assignments and to promote both the client's expectancy of a constructive outcome for completing homework and to increase the likelihood of compliance. Homework should be strategically formulated and tailored to the client rather than being routinely assigned from a "standard" treatment package. The demands of the homework should be graduated and based on a principle of being challenging, yet achievable. It is of utmost importance that homework assignments be biased toward success in order to avoid the negative self-judgments and other deleterious treatment effects that may accompany failure. To this end, care should be taken to ensure that the client possesses the knowledge and cognitive and behavioral skills necessary to successfully complete assigned tasks. Inasmuch as homework is an extratherapy extension of treatment, it should also be closely aligned with the course of treatment being carried out in the therapy environment. As a measure of promoting homework compliance and success in the treatment of anxiety disorders, Greenwald (1987) recommends that client understanding

> be tested *before* clients leave the session, so that the therapist is assured that they know their assignments and exactly when and where the assignments will take place. Following rationale, review and description of assignments, it is sometimes helpful to model or have clients enact the behavior. Some clinicians suggest that homework not be assigned until a patient completes a form of the assignment in session [p. 600].

In this manner the practitioner has the opportunity to appraise the client's skill level, to further coach and rehearse the skill, to provide reinforcing statements regarding performance, and to instruct the client in coping and self-reinforcement statements.

In order to effectively transfer skills to the natural environment, homework assignments should involve repetitive practice trials graduated in demand and complexity and carried out across several environmental contexts. Such multiple practice trials result in greater learning and enlarge the number of discriminative stimuli that control the behavior, thereby increasing the probability of the client's actually exhibiting the behavior in the desired context (Staats, 1975).

Homework should be checked when the client returns for treatment. This establishes with the client the importance that the practitioner places on assignments, which, in turn, may have a positive effect on compliance with homework. It provides valuable feedback to the practitioner useful in further assessment and in the advancement of the intervention strategy.

Inclusion of Family and Significant Others in Treatment. Involvement of significant others from the client's natural environment is another means of enhancing generalization. Kanfer and Schefft (1988) note the involvement of family as an essential feature in the transfer of gains into the natural environment for chronically ill patients in rehabilitation, children below the age of adolescence, and clients with partnership problems. These and other populations are subject to significant influence by important family and community members. The client's social system has great potential either for reinforcing adaptive changes or for producing barriers that functionally prevent the display of treatment gains.

Family therapy emerged in recognition that problem behavior is not merely a product of intrapsychic phenomena but develops in the family and that treatment effects can be enhanced by treatment in the family. Family therapy should be carefully considered for problems that are predominantly evident within the family (for example, parent/child conflict, sibling conflict) and for acting-out behaviors on the part of children and adolescents that may be amenable to family treatment.

Employee assistance programs and human resource departments in work settings have produced treatment programs within the workplace to address work-related problems. Substance abuse, depression, and interpersonal conflict are examples of problems that have been the focus of treatment in such treatment programs involving workers and, at times, supervisors and supervisees together.

Providing Treatment in the Natural Environment. The enhancement of generalization is one of the many benefits of providing treatment in the client's natural environment. Treatment in the client's home, school, workplace, or other relevant social/environmental context allows the practitioner the opportunity to access and treat the maladaptive behavior in the actual situation(s) in which the behavior was learned and is being maintained. The potential to assess the current social/environmental contingencies on behavior is significantly enhanced. For example, the practitioner can more effectively determine the role played by significant others in the client's problem behavior and maladaptive interactional patterns. Exposure to environmental conditions may result in environmental-modification procedures as part of the comprehensive treatment package. Treating clients in the natural environment and targeting environmental factors for change has been a tradition in social work. Mental health professionals from other disciplines have also been encouraging a shift in treatment from the office to natural settings and the broadening of treatment focus to include the environment as a viable point of intervention. The reader is referred to the classic volume by Tharp and Wetzel, *Behavior Modification in the Natural Environment* (1969), for a discussion of the rationale, clinical implications, and application of behavioral methods *in vivo*.

The school has frequently been used as the setting in which to treat children's behavior problems. This trend can be attributed to the success of applied behavior analysis in changing behavior and the enthusiasm with which educators embraced the methodology (Hughes, 1988). A broad range of academic problems and social and behavioral problems has been effectively treated in schools involving outside practitioners, school counselors, teachers, and other school personnel. Frequently, a consulting practitioner instructs teachers, aids, school counselors, and others in cognitive-behavioral treatment principles and their application to targeted problems; designs an intervention tailored to the specific problem consistent with child age, teacher capabilities, and other school environmental variables; and actively trains and supervises staff members in carrying out the procedures. Treatment in the school of many academic and school-related problems may effectively minimize the problem of generalization. However, generalization programming will still be required to promote the effective transfer of training from the school to the home and community for such problems as poor study habits, impulsivity, hyperactivity, and aggressive behavior.

A more recent noteworthy trend in providing treatment in the natural environment is the in-home treatment of child and family problems (Bryce & Lloyd, 1981; Maybanks & Bryce, 1979; Tracy, Haapala, Kinney, & Pecora, 1991). These home-based treatment programs were initially designed for treatment of acting-out and delinquent children as an alternative to institutionalization, which was considered to be comparatively costly and of questionable long-term effect. Home-based treatment has been favorably received, particularly for treating child behavior problems and teaching parenting skills. (See Chapter 4 for a discussion of in-home treatment.)

Success in transferring treatment effects from the practice setting to the natural environment has also been reported in the treatment of anxiety and fears in which the practitioner accompanies the client to the actual situation in which the anxiety, fear, or avoidance responses have been experienced (Barlow, 1988; Barlow & Waddell, 1985; Barlow & Wolfe, 1981; Mathews, Gelder, & Johnston, 1981; Sacco, 1981). Practitioner-aided exposure treatment may involve graduated procedures or "prolonged *in vivo* exposure" (Barlow, 1988) in which the practitioner or a trained assistant remains with the client in the difficult situation until the anxiety or fear diminishes. The contention of Stokes and Baer (1977) that effective generalization programming can be enhanced by the determination of natural environmental contingencies operating to reinforce clients' behavior change supports the importance of the practitioner's accompanying the client into the natural environment for the purposes of assessment, treatment planning, and implementation.

Use of the foregoing procedures is recommended in the design and implementation of treatment in order to increase the probability that the client will generalize gains from the treatment environment to extratherapeutic circumstances. Although the procedures identified are those most frequently cited in the literature, other generalization strategies exist. The reader is referred to Baer (1981), Greenwald (1987), Meichenbaum (1984), Olson and Dowd (1984), Stokes and Baer (1977), and Wodarski (1980) for additional information on transfer of training methods.

Relapse Prevention Methods

The maintenance of treatment effects well after termination continues to be a major challenge to mental health practitioners. Special attention to the development of strategies to prevent the deterioration of treatment gains has only recently been undertaken. The problem of relapse is a significant one. For example, the relapse rate for people suffering from addictive disorders has been reported as ranging from 50% to 90% depending on various factors, including the type of addiction and individual characteristics (Brownell, Marlatt, Lichtenstein, & Wilson, 1986). It has been found that between 20% and 40% of patients suffering from various forms of depression experienced at least one episode of relapse during the year following treatment (Baker & Wilson, 1985; Keller et al., 1984). These findings along with empirical data from many other researchers and widespread clinical impressions regarding the problem of relapse provide ample support for the importance of incorporating relapse prevention methods in treatment. The remainder of this section describes procedures aimed at maintenance and relapse prevention.

Self-Efficacy. An individual's conviction that he or she can sustain treatment gains is a critical component of relapse prevention. Bandura (1977a) has defined two expectancy systems that, he postulates, operate as different sources of futility: "An outcome expectation is defined as a person's estimate that a given behavior will lead to certain outcomes. An efficacy expectation is the conviction that one can successfully execute the behavior required to produce the outcomes" (p. 193). A sense of doubt in one's abilities to reach a required level of performance (efficacy expectancy) or, alternatively, confidence in one's capabilities but an expectation that the desired results will not be forthcoming in an unresponsive or punishing environment (outcome expectation) will, in either case, result in a sense of futility. The strength of people's efficacy expectations is considered to affect whether they will even try to cope and the degree of coping—"how much effort people will expend and how long they will persist in the face of obstacles and aversive experiences" (Bandura, 1977a, p. 194). Furthermore, perceived self-efficacy will influence the choice of behavioral settings. Avoidance of a threatening condition or, alternatively, self-initiated exposure to the condition is considered to be a product of efficacy expectations. To strengthen the individual's perceived efficacy requires the development of competencies and a sense of personal effectiveness. Competencies are developed through effective treatment coupled with adequate training in the implementation of relapse prevention measures. The sense of personal effectiveness may evolve along with mastery but is likely to require the application of self-instruction or other cognitive restructuring procedures and practitioner support.

There has been much exploration into the role of self-efficacy in the prevention of relapse (Baer et al., 1989; Burling, Reilly, Moltzen, & Ziff, 1989; Devins, 1992; Haaga & Stewart, 1992; Hall, Havassy, & Wasserman, 1990; O'Leary & Wilson, 1987; Stevens & Hollis, 1989). The perception of self-efficacy has been found to be associated with both cessation and maintenance. However, it is interesting to note that extreme strength of self-efficacy may result in an "optimistic cognitive bias" (usually considered adaptive) "leading to inappropriate complacency about the adequacy of one's skill for coping with difficult situations" (Haaga & Stewart, 1992, p. 27). It has been proposed that moderate levels of self-efficacy may be optimal in preventing relapse (Devin, 1992; Haaga & Stewart, 1992).

Coping Skills Training. Because it is reasonable to expect that clients will be confronted with future problematical situations similar to past circumstances in which they evidenced maladaptive responses and will encounter other highly stressful circumstances with a marked potential to stimulate relapse, the practitioner is encouraged to train them in coping skills. Coping has been defined as "adjusting, adapting, successfully meeting a challenge. Coping mechanisms are all the ways . . . that a person uses in adjusting to environmental demands without altering his

(or her) goals or purposes" (Campbell, 1989, p. 158). Support for the use of coping strategies to prevent relapse has been advanced by several researchers (Baer et al., 1989; Kanfer & Schefft, 1988; Kirschenbaum & Tomarken, 1982; Marlatt & Parks, 1982). Furthermore, the use of multiple coping strategies has been found to be associated with the increased likelihood of abstinence (Bliss, Garvey, Heinold, & Hitchcock, 1989). Hence, it is important that the client's view of future demands and the threat of situational relapse reflect a mind set of coping capabilities. This coping stance, as opposed to an expectation of constant mastery (free of anxiety, fear, insecurity, or self-doubt and consistently flawlessly competent) is a superior cognitive set and increases the likelihood that the client will effectively perform (that is, adaptively respond to the demand).

The coping skills training procedures delineated below are largely composed of common treatment components from various coping skills programs as outlined by Meichenbaum (1977). First, if it has not already been established, it is necessary to instruct the client in the role of cognition in the problem behavior and in how cognitive methods can be employed in the prevention of relapse. Next, high-risk situations that are anticipated to be challenging are identified. Situation-specific coping responses and corresponding overt behaviors are generated for each high-risk situation identified. The practitioner can model self-statements for the client in the context of simulated conditions, followed by coaching the client in the rehearsal of coping, self-evaluative, and self-reinforcing statements. Using vivid projected imagery, the client then rehearses (without coaching) positive self-evaluation and coping statements. A broad range of imaginal stimulus conditions is rehearsed to promote generalization (for example, settings, populations, tasks, demands). Optional behavioral responses are generated through the use of problem-solving procedures and can be incorporated in the imaginal rehearsals. Relaxation training and graduated *in vivo* behavioral assignments in which to rehearse coping can also be utilized. The reader is referred to the following researcher/practitioners for information on alternative coping-skills training programs: Goldfried, Decenteceo, and Weinberg (1974); Langer, Janis, and Wolfer (1975); Lazarus (1977, 1981); Meichenbaum and Turk (1976); Meichenbaum, Turk, and Burstein (1975); and Suinn and Richardson (1971).

Establishing an Understanding of Relapse and Inoculating against Future Relapse.
Clients should be educated regarding their role in maintaining treatment gains and in implementing relapse prevention measures (Greenwald, 1987). The practitioner should instill in them the expectancy that they will not be problem-free in the future regardless of the problem. Rather than being "cured" of such problems as anxiety, depression, urges toward substance abuse, and marital distress, they have learned strategies for both coping with a level of discomfort and improving the undesirable responses or conditions. A worthy treatment outcome is, in effect, their development of the capacity to be their own therapist (Cautela, 1969; Kazdin, 1975; Selmi, Klein, Greist, Sorrell, & Erdman, 1990; Watson & Tharp, 1972). The methods learned in treatment can repeatedly be drawn on by the client to address future personal challenges.

Inoculation against future relapse, initiated well in advance of termination, involves clients' actively contemplating future problematic situations—with anticipated accompanying cognitive, emotional, and behavioral responses—for the purpose of rehearsing self-administered coping strategies and other forms of intervention. In discussing inoculation against future relapse with a client with an anxiety disorder, Freeman and Simon (1989) say that "in point of fact, the return of the anxiety will be an opportunity to demonstrate the success of the therapy" (p. 360). Instructing clients in reframing the meaning of future problems in this manner and repetitively practicing the implementation of skills that they have learned will further prepare them to effectively react to relapse opportunities. Freeman and Simon further recommend that clients, with the aid of the practitioner, generate a list of anticipated crises with a corresponding list of techniques to support effective coping. In this manner, the actual meaning of future crises is modified, and clients are strategically prepared for them.

Environmental Planning.
Environmental planning involves the strategic arrangement of stimulus conditions to promote the likelihood of maintenance and relapse prevention. This is a self-management procedure discussed earlier in relation to transfer of training. To promote the maintenance of gains through environmental planning, the practitioner should engage the client in the collaborative determination of environmental factors that function to support the maintenance of gains or, alternatively, operate with great potential to stimulate relapse. In this manner, the practitioner and client can develop strategies for modifying the environment to minimize the likelihood of relapse. For example, clients may consciously avoid participating in activities that they associate with the problem behavior or avoid certain situations and people that contribute to an increased opportunity for and likelihood of relapse. Alternatively, clients are encouraged to seek out conditions, situations, and people anticipated to be supportive of the therapeutic gain, thus reducing the likelihood of relapse. In short, environmental conditions are managed in a way to increase the likelihood of producing the desired outcomes.

An alternative means of stimulus control in which the practitioner should instruct the client is removing from the environment those resources that are perceived as potential contributors to relapse and introducing other resources perceived as potential contributors to maintenance. For example, the graduate student with marginal grades may sell her television set and replace it with a computer to promote the maintenance of responsible study habits; the post-heart-attack patient may purchase a treadmill to promote compliance with the conditioning regimen to which he is committed.

Training clients to exercise greater control over environmental factors for the benefit of satisfying their goals results in empowerment. The technique requires the conscious evaluation of environmental factors with regard to their perceived influence on a client's behavior—the strength of the environmental cue in affecting the probability of performing the associated behavior—followed by a self-managed strategy to arrange those environmental factors in a way that significantly increases the probability of self-control. This procedure is of particular facility in the prevention of relapse of behaviors that are highly stimulus-controlled.

Self-Monitoring. Systematic self-monitoring is useful in raising clients' awareness of high-risk situations and the thoughts, feelings, and behaviors experienced under those circumstances. Clients can be taught various self-monitoring methods for use after treatment is terminated in order to promote their greater awareness of both risk and response factors. The use of a journal or a more structured behavioral record allows them to more closely track such phenomena as the degree of demand associated with specific situations, the degree of temptation to relapse, and the coping statements and behaviors that were implemented. For example, a client who has been treated for social anxiety may attend a singles group for the first time and, using a 10-point scale, rate the demand as an 8 and the temptation to leave a 6. She may record coping and self-affirmation statements such as "I'm feeling anxious, but I'm sure I can stay a bit longer" and "I'm doing just fine, even though this is not the most friendly

group I've been around"; and she may record her behaviors: "I went to the snack table and got some punch, relaxing myself along the way." "I initiated a conversation with someone who appeared a little uneasy too." Another form of self-monitoring is counting behavior. A wrist counter or other mechanism can be used to count relapse urges or adaptive responses in high-risk situations. Counting behavior has been found to be reinforcing, raising the likelihood of performing the behavior more or less frequently as desired. The awareness-raising and reinforcement potential of recording, counting, and other self-monitoring methods makes them worthy of consideration for inclusion in a relapse prevention strategy.

Lifestyle Change. Lifestyle change may provide greater support and reinforcement of the client's change effort and thereby promote maintenance and the prevention of relapse. The practitioner can participate in determining ways in which clients can (1) improve their quality of life; (2) limit certain stressors and acquire better stress management abilities (including health-maintenance measures); (3) more effectively pursue mastery and pleasure activities (Beck, Rush, Shaw, & Emery, 1979); and (4) promote relationships with significant others that are relatively conflict-free, personally enriching, and psychologically beneficial (pleasurable, reinforcing of desirable traits, provocative, stimulating of creativity). Lifestyle change may result in the reduction in frequency of problem behavior or its displacement by more adaptive, competitively rewarding behavior and, in so doing, enhance response maintenance. Increased interest in health and exercise, development of sports and hobby interests, attention to creative and other mastery activities, involvement in civic or charitable endeavors, and work, spiritual, and avocational self-improvement are examples of activities that have high reward potential and, therefore, are worthy of consideration in the design and implementation of lifestyle change.

As with all change efforts, an assessment is necessary to determine the desirability and viability of lifestyle change. Assessment of lifestyle should be conducted to expose those factors that are supportive of constructive change; those that function to limit, prevent, or undermine the maintenance of gains; undeveloped and underdeveloped areas of potential self-actualization; and those factors that, although not directly related to the maintenance of the current change, function to the disadvantage of the client. Although all are important, the primary focus of intervention should be on lifestyle changes that can further enhance the maintenance of client gains and those lifestyle factors considered likely to promote relapse. Marlatt and his colleagues provide valuable information on lifestyle assessment and modification in relation to relapse prevention (Marlatt & Gordon, 1980, 1985; Marlatt & Parks, 1982).

Social System Support. Consistent with their facility in the promotion of transfer of training, significant people from the client's social environment can likewise participate in furthering relapse prevention. Family members can be enlisted or may volunteer to participate in the client's maintenance of gains through such measures as (1) cuing newly acquired behaviors and relapse prevention responses; (2) governing contingencies under which the client operates, thus affording opportunities to provide ongoing reinforcement to desired responses; (3) participating with the client in behaviors and activities that provide opportunities to exercise the behavior change; (4) taking active steps to remove barriers that may interfere with or prevent the maintenance of change; (5) supporting and encouraging the client to use social and other resources that increase the likelihood of successful relapse prevention (for example, encouraging attending Alcoholics Anonymous meetings or participating in Al Anon); and (6)

enhancing the client's quality of life as a context in which to maintain behavior change (for example, sustaining a satisfying marital relationship).

Prior to termination, family members and others should meet with the practitioner to determine the various ways in which they can support treatment gains. It is important to ensure that the manner in which others behave in relation to the maintenance of the client's changes are palatable to the client. Clarification should be gained regarding both the acceptable roles for significant others to assume and means of communicating support. Coercion, threat, nagging, criticism, and the like may promote relapse rather than preventing it. The practitioner should instruct significant others in communicating their support and encouragement through modeling, rehearsal, and behavioral assignments.

Other means of gaining social support are through the client's participation in various groups and organizations such as problem-focused self-help groups (Alcoholics Anonymous, Rational Recovery, Overeaters Anonymous, Bereaved Parents); self-improvement classes and groups (Toastmasters); social or interest groups (singles Sunday School classes, the Sierra Club); and sports and arts and crafts group activities (Sporting Life, organized sports leagues and tournaments, chess clubs, art associations, quilting groups). These group activities should be considered in the development of a comprehensive relapse prevention strategy given the findings that participation in such groups after treatment has enhanced treatment maintenance (Brownell et al., 1986; Daley, 1987; Iodice & Wodarski, 1987; Sheeren, 1987).

Fading. Fading procedures are for the purpose of displacing the reinforcement for change and maintenance of change from practitioner-held contingencies to client-maintained and natural environmental consequences. Fading involves the gradual reduction in frequency of treatment sessions.

Extending the time between sessions allows clients an opportunity to function increasingly more independently and to gain a greater sense of self-confidence in the changes they have made and continue to make. It also provides greater opportunity for problem situations to develop between sessions and for clients to intervene on their own behalf. Fading treatment, as opposed to sharp termination, also allows clients to exercise increasingly more self-control and independence from the practitioner with the psychological comfort of a continuing, albeit less frequently active, therapeutic relationship.

Early Detection of Relapse Cues. The prevention of relapse may also be facilitated through the detection of early signs of relapse vulnerability. Relapse may evolve partly due to the client's failure to adequately read the cues of relapse. Failing to perceive the "signs" of relapse or denying them despite awareness may be early elements of relapse. Therefore, during the latter stage of therapy when relapse prevention is being addressed, the practitioner and client should develop a list of relapse cues or indicators and discuss corresponding self-intervention strategies suitable for the client to implement in response to the cues. The client is then instructed in a "cue alert" procedure for independent use. Once treatment has terminated or during the fading of practitioner contact, clients are occasionally to put themselves on cue alert, during which they search their recent past for early indicators of relapse. They are to refer to the list of cues developed during therapy against which to check their behavior but also should carefully evaluate their cognitive and behavioral activities for relapse indicators not included on the list. For example, a client treated for pedophilia has recently approached a playground and watched children play from "a safe distance." During cue alert he is to identify and label this behavior as a potential relapse cue. Following the identification of an indicator of potential relapse through the cue alert proce-

dure, he is ready to implement such measures as coping strategies, problem-solving procedures, self-management methods, or perhaps the initiation of booster sessions or other social system support. Failure to initiate relapse preventive self-intervention early on may result in protracted relapse responses and possibly complete loss of control over the behavior. The client should be informed that early detection of relapse indicators and immediate intervention provide the greatest likelihood of relapse prevention.

Follow-up Contacts and Booster Sessions. Although fading procedures can be effective in the gradual withdrawal of therapist-maintained contingencies and the promotion of greater client independence, sustained practitioner involvement through follow-up contact and booster sessions can be instrumental in the maintenance of treatment gains. Follow-up visits can be conducted in the treatment environment, the natural environment, by telephone, or by mail and should address the client's level of maintenance along with a discussion of relapse prevention procedures being implemented. Evaluation of the degree of effectiveness of specific methods to prevent relapse and knowledge of maintenance success provide the practitioner valuable feedback. Based on this information, the practitioner can gain reassurance of the client's successful maintenance of treatment gains or, alternatively, find it appropriate to suggest modifications to the relapse prevention strategy or recommend booster sessions. Greenwald (1987) encourages practitioners to be sensitive to the possible reluctance of the client to report difficulty and suggests that, where a significant other has been involved, his or her report on the client's follow-up status may be helpful.

Prior to termination it should be established with clients that booster sessions are readily available if situation-specific crises arise or a gradual decline in treatment gains is experienced. Under the latter circumstance clients are expected to have attempted various relapse prevention procedures to retard or stop the decline. It is when self-initiated relapse prevention efforts prove inadequate that booster sessions should be sought.

There is inadequate empirical research to guide practitioners in the selection of measures to strategize relapse prevention for a specific population or problem. Without such guidance, practitioners are left to select those measures with which they are most familiar and those most feasible. In addition, however, it may be helpful to know what others are doing. To determine the comparative use of various strategies, Krantz, Hill, Foster-Rawlings, and Zeeve (1984) surveyed cognitive-behavioral researchers and practitioners and compiled the following list (ranked from most to least frequently used strategy):

- Promote internal attributions of change.
- Train general strategies.
- Identify barriers to maintenance.
- Transfer directiveness from the therapist to the client.
- Discuss the need for continuing change efforts.
- Plan for high-risk situations.
- Fade the frequency of sessions.
- Work on a variety of targets.
- Involve the client in planning transfer and maintenance.
- Plan for recovery from a setback.
- Discuss the application of skills to untreated situations.
- Schedule booster contacts.
- Change the environment to support new behaviors.
- Address problems for others stemming from client gains.
- Enlist significant others to help maintain gains.
- Practice beyond the criterion (overlearning).
- Train in natural settings.

For treatment to be truly effective, it must be resilient and long lasting. In order to accomplish this maintenance objective, practitioners are obligated to program for it in their treatment strategies through incorporating procedures such as those identified and discussed above.

CONCLUSION

Many factors contribute to effective psychotherapeutic treatment. In this chapter we have identified the therapeutic relationship, clinical judgment, and cognitive assessment as highly important ingredients in the treatment process. In performing a cognitive assessment, the practitioner has been encouraged to incorporate several methods to collect data and to combine cognitive assessment with a comprehensive assessment package covering other relevant aspects of client functioning.

In recognition of the challenge to the practitioner to develop treatment strategies designed to promote clients' change in their natural environment and to increase the likelihood of long-term, sustained change, many suggestions and procedures have been presented. Although lacking in convincing empirical support, these procedures are representative of current clinical practice. Attention to the issues raised in this chapter and integration of the methods and procedures identified can enhance the effectiveness of the cognitive-behavioral practitioner.

REFERENCES

Baer, D. M. (1981). *How to plan for generalization.* Lawrence, KS: H & H Enterprises.

Baer, J. S., Kamarck, T., Lichtenstein, E., & Ransom, C. C., Jr. (1989). Prediction of smoking relapse: Analyses of temptations and transgressions after initial cessation. *Journal of Consulting and Clinical Psychology, 57,* 623–627.

Bainbridge, L. (1979). Verbal reports as evidence of the process operator's knowledge. *International Journal of Man-Machine Studies, 11,* 411–436.

Baker, A. L., & Wilson, P. H. (1985). Cognitive-behavior therapy for depression: The effects of booster sessions on relapse. *Behavior Therapy, 16,* 335–344.

Bandura, A. (1977a). Self-efficacy: Toward a unifying theory of behavioral change. *Psychological Review, 84,* 191–215.

Bandura, A. (1977b). *Social learning theory.* Englewood Cliffs, NJ: Prentice-Hall.

Barlow, D. H. (1988). *Anxiety and its disorders: The nature and treatment of anxiety and panic.* New York: Guilford Press.

Barlow, D. H., & Waddell, M. T. (1985). Agoraphobia. In D. H. Barlow (Ed.), *Clinical handbook of psychological disorders: A step-by-step treatment manual.* New York: Guilford Press.

Barlow, D. H., & Wolfe, B. (1981). Behavioral approaches to anxiety disorders: A report on the NIMH-SUNY Albany Research Conference. *Journal of Consulting and Clinical Psychology, 49,* 448–454.

Beck, A. T., Rush, A. J., Shaw, B. F., & Emery, G. (1979). *Cognitive therapy of depression.* New York: Guilford Press.

Berlin, S. B., Mann, K. B., & Grossman, S. F. (1991). Task analysis of cognitive therapy for depression. *Social Work Research and Abstracts, 27*(2), 3–11.

Bliss, R. E., Garvey, A. J., Heinold, J. W., & Hitchcock, J. L. (1989). The influence of situation and coping on relapse crisis outcomes after smoking cessation. *Journal of Consulting and Clinical Psychology, 57,* 443–449.

Brehm, S. S. (1976). *The application of social psychology to clinical practice.* New York: Wiley.

Brownell, K. D., Marlatt, A. G., Lichtenstein, E., & Wilson, T. G. (1986). Understanding and preventing relapse. *American Psychologist, 41*(7), 765–782.

Bryce, M., & Lloyd, J. C. (1981). *Treating families in the home.* Springfield, IL: Charles C Thomas.

Burling, T. A., Reilly, P. M., Moltzen, J. O., & Ziff, D. C. (1989). Self-efficacy and relapse among inpatient drug and alcohol abusers: A predictor of outcome. *Journal of Studies on Alcohol, 50*(4), 354–360.

Cacioppo, J. T., & Petty, R. E. (1981). Social psychological procedures for cognitive response analysis: The thought-listing technique. In T. V. Merluzzi, C. R. Glass, & M. Genest (Eds.), *Cognitive assessment.* New York: Guilford Press.

Campbell, R. J. (1989). *Psychiatric dictionary* (6th ed.). New York: Oxford University Press.

Cantor, N., Mischel, W., & Schwartz, J. (1981). Social knowledge: Structure, content, use and abuse. In A. Hastorf & A. Isen (Eds.), *Cognitive social psychology.* New York: Elsevier North-Holland.

Cautela, J. R. (1969). Behavior therapy and self-control: Techniques and implications. In C. F. Franks (Ed.), *Behavior therapy: Appraisal and status.* New York: McGraw-Hill.

Cautela, J. R. (1970). Covert reinforcement. *Behavior Therapy, 1,* 33–50.

Cautela, J. R. (1971). *Covert modeling.* Paper presented to the Association for Advancement of Behavior Therapy, Washington, DC.

Daley, D. C. (1987). Relapse prevention with substance abusers: Clinical issues and myths. *Social Work, 32*(2) 138–142.

Devins, G. M. (1992). Social cognitive analysis of recovery from a lapse after smoking cessation: Comment on Haaga and Stewart (1992). *Journal of Consulting and Clinical Psychology, 60*(1), 29–31.

Edwards, D. J. A. (1989). Cognitive restructuring through guided imagery: Lessons from Gestalt therapy. In A. Freeman, K. M. Simon, L. E. Beutler, & H. Arkowitz (Eds.), *Comprehensive handbook of cognitive therapy.* New York: Plenum.

Ellis, A. (1962). *Reason and emotion in psychotherapy.* New York: Stuart.

Ellis, A. (1973). *Humanistic psychotherapy.* New York: McGraw-Hill.

Feldman, R. A., & Wodarski, J. S. (1975). *Contemporary approaches to group treatment.* San Francisco: Jossey-Bass.

Freeman, A., & Simon, K. M. (1989). Cognitive therapy of anxiety. In A. Freeman, K. M. Simon, L. E. Beutler, & H. Arkowitz (Eds.), *Comprehensive handbook of cognitive therapy.* New York: Plenum.

Genest, M., & Turk, D. C. (1981). Think-aloud approaches to cognitive assessment. In T.V.

Merluzzi, C. R. Glass, & M. Genest (Eds.), *Cognitive assessment*. New York: Guilford Press.

Glass, C. R., & Merluzzi, T. V. (1981). Cognitive assessment of social-evaluative anxiety. In T. V. Merluzzi, C. R. Glass, & M. Genest (Eds.), *Cognitive assessment*. New York: Guilford Press.

Goldfried, M. R., Decenteceo, E. T., & Weinberg, L. (1974). Systematic rational restructuring as a self-control technique. *Behavior Therapy, 5,* 247–254.

Goldfried, M. R., & Merbaum, M. (Eds.). (1973). *Behavior change through self control.* New York: Holt, Rinehart & Winston.

Gottman, J. M., & Leiblum, S. R. (1974). *How to do psychotherapy and how to evaluate it: A manual for beginners.* New York: Holt, Rinehart & Winston.

Greenwald, M. A. (1987). Programming treatment generalization. In L. Michelson & L. M. Ascher (Eds.), *Anxiety and stress disorders.* New York: Guilford Press.

Haaga, D. A. F., & Stewart, B. L. (1992). Self-efficacy for recovery from a lapse after smoking cessation. *Journal of Consulting and Clinical Psychology, 60*(1), 24–28.

Hall, S. M., Havassy, B. E., & Wasserman, D. A. (1990). Commitment to abstinence and acute stress in relapse to alcohol, opiates, and nicotine. *Journal of Consulting and Clinical Psychology, 58*(2), 175–181.

Hollon, S. D., & Kendall, P. C. (1980). Cognitive self-statements in depression: Development of an automatic thoughts questionnaire. *Cognitive Therapy and Research, 4,* 109–143.

Hollon, S. D., & Kendall, P. C. (1981). *In vivo* assessment techniques for cognitive-behavioral processes. In P. C. Kendall & S. D. Hollon (Eds.), *Assessment strategies for cognitive-behavioral interventions.* New York: Academic Press.

Hughes, J. N. (1988). *Cognitive behavior therapy with children in schools.* New York: Pergamon Press.

Hurlburt, R. T. (1979). Random sampling of cognitions and behaviors. *Journal of Research in Personality, 13,* 103–111.

Ingram, R. E. (1983). Content and process distinctions in depressive self-schemata. In L. B. Alloy (Chair), *Depression and schemata.* Symposium presented at the meeting of the American Psychological Association, Anaheim, CA.

Ingram, R. E., & Kendall, P. C. (1986). Cognitive clinical psychology: Implications of an information processing perspective. In R. E. Ingram (Ed.), *Information processing approaches to clinical psychology.* New York: Academic Press.

Iodice, J. D., & Wodarski, J. S. (1987). Aftercare treatment for schizophrenics living at home. *Social Work, 32*(2), 122–127.

Jones, R. G. (1969). A factored measure of Ellis' Irrational Belief System (Doctoral dissertation, Texas Technological College, 1968). *Dissertation Abstracts International, 29,* 4379B-4380B.

Kanfer, F. H., & Schefft, B. K. (1988). *Guiding the process of therapeutic change.* Champaign, IL: Research Press.

Kazdin, A. E. (1973). Covert modeling and the reduction of avoidance behavior. *Journal of Abnormal Psychology, 81,* 87–95.

Kazdin, A. E. (1974). Covert modeling, model similarity, and reduction of avoidance behavior. *Behavior Therapy, 5,* 325–340.

Kazdin, A. E. (1975). *Behavior modification in applied settings.* Homewood, IL: Dorsey Press.

Keller, M. B., Klerman, G. L., Lavori, P. W., Coryell, W., Endicott, J., & Taylor, J. (1984). Long-term outcome of episodes of major depression: Clinical and public health significance. *Journal of the American Medical Association, 252*(6), 788–792.

Kendall, P. C., & Hollon, S. D. (1981). Assessing self-referent speech: Methods in the measurement of self-statements. In P. C. Kendall & S. D. Hollon (Eds.), *Assessment strategies for cognitive-behavioral interventions.* New York: Academic Press.

Kendall, P. C., & Ingram, R. (1987). The future for cognitive assessment of anxiety: Let's get specific. In L. Michelson & L. M. Ascher (Eds.), *Anxiety and stress disorders: Cognitive-behavioral assessment and treatment.* New York: Guilford Press.

Kihlstrom, J. F., & Nasby, W. (1981). Cognitive tasks in clinical assessment: An exercise in applied psychology. In P. C. Kendall & S. D. Hollon (Eds.), *Assessment strategies for cognitive-behavioral interventions.* New York: Academic Press.

Kirschenbaum, D. S., & Tomarken, A. J. (1982). On facing the generalization problem: The study of self-regulatory failure. In P. C. Kendall (Ed.), *Advances in cognitive-behavioral research and therapy* (Vol. 1). New York: Academic Press.

Krantz, S. E., Hill, R. D., Foster-Rawlings, S., & Zeeve, C. (1984). Therapists' use of and perceptions of strategies for maintenance and generalization. *The Cognitive Behaviorist, 6,*19–22.

Landau, R. J., & Goldfried, M. R. (1981). The assessment of schemata: A unifying framework for cognitive, behavioral and traditional assessment. In P. C. Kendall & S. D. Hollon (Eds.), *Assessment strategies for cognitive-behavioral interventions.* New York: Academic Press.

Langer, E. J., Janis, I., & Wolfer, J. (1975). Reduction of psychological stress in surgical patients. *Journal of Experimental Social Psychology, 1,* 155–166.

Lazarus, R. S. (1977). Psychological stress and the coping process. In Z. S. Lipowski, D. R. Lipsitt, & P. C. Whybrow (Eds.), *Psychosomatic medicine: Current trends and clinical applications.* New York: Oxford University Press.

Lazarus, R. S. (1981). The stress and coping paradigm. In C. Eisdorfer, D. Cohen, A. Kleinman, & P. Maxim (Eds.), *Models for clinical psychopathology.* New York: Spectrum.

Littrell, J., & Magel, D. (1991). The influence of self-concept on change in client behaviors: A review. *Research on Social Work Practice, 1*(1), 46–67.

Mahoney, M. J. (1991). *Human change processes: The scientific foundations of psychotherapy.* New York: Basic Books.

Markus, H., & Wurf, E. (1987). The dynamic self concept: A social psychological perspective. *Annual Review of Psychology, 38,* 299–377.

Marlatt, G. A., & Gordon, S. G. (1980). Determinants of relapse: Implications for the maintenance of behavior change. In P. O. Davison & S. M. Davison (Eds.), *Behavioral medicine: Changing health lifestyles.* New York: Brunner/Mazel.

Marlatt, G. A., & Gordon, S. G. (Eds.). (1985). *Relapse prevention: Maintenance strategies in addictive behavior change.* New York: Guilford Press.

Marlatt, G. A., & Parks, G. A. (1982). Self-management of addictive behaviors. In P. E. Karoly & F. H. Kanfer (Eds.), *Self-management and behavior change.* New York: Pergamon Press.

Mathews, A. M., Gelder, M. G., & Johnston, D. W. (1981). *Agoraphobia: Nature and treatment.* New York: Guilford Press.

Maybanks, S., & Bryce, M. (1979). *Home-based services for children and families.* Springfield, IL: Charles C Thomas.

Meichenbaum, D. (1977). *Cognitive-behavior modification: An integrative approach.* New York: Plenum.

Meichenbaum, D. (1984). Fostering generalization: A cognitive-behavioral approach. *The Cognitive Behaviorist, 6,* 9–10.

Meichenbaum, D., & Butler, L. (1980). Cognitive ethology: Assessing the streams of cognition and emotion. In K. B. Blankstein, P. Pliner, & J. Polivy (Eds.), *Advances in the study of communication and affect: Assessment and modification of emotional behavior* (Vol. 6). New York: Plenum.

Meichenbaum, D., & Cameron, R. (1981). Issues in cognitive assessment: An overview. In T. V. Merluzzi, C. R. Glass, & M. Genest (Eds.), *Cognitive assessment.* New York: Guilford Press.

Meichenbaum, D., & Turk, D. (1976). The cognitive-behavioral management of anxiety, anger, and pain. In P. O. Davidson (Ed.), *The behavioral management of anxiety, depression, and pain.* New York: Brunner/Mazel.

Meichenbaum, D., Turk, D., & Burstein, S. (1975). The nature of coping with stress. In I. G. Sarason & C. D. Spielberger (Eds.), *Stress and anxiety* (Vol. 2). New York: Wiley.

Merluzzi, T. V., & Boltwood, M. D. (1989). Cognitive assessment. In A. Freeman, K. M. Simon, L. E. Beutler, & H. Arkowitz (Eds.), *Comprehensive handbook of cognitive therapy.* New York: Plenum.

Miller, I. W. (1984). Strategies for maintenance of treatment gains for depressed patients. *The Cognitive Behaviorist, 6,* 10–13.

Mischel, W. (1968). *Personality and assessment.* New York: Wiley.

Mischel, W. (1972). Direct versus indirect personality assessment: Evidence and implications. *Journal of Consulting and Clinical Psychology, 38,* 319–324.

Mischel, W. (1977). On the future of personality measurement. *American Psychologist, 32,* 246–254.

Mischel, W. (1981). A cognitive–social learning approach to assessment. In T. V. Merluzzi, C. R. Glass, & M. Genest (Eds.), *Cognitive assessment.* New York: Guilford Press.

Neisser, U. (1976). *Cognition and reality.* San Francisco: W. H. Freeman.

Nisbett, R. E., Krantz, D. H., Jepson, C., & Kunda, Z. (1983). The use of statistical heuristics in everyday inductive reasoning. *Psychological Review, 90*, 339–363.

Nisbett, R. E., & Ross, L. (1980). *Human inference: Strategies and shortcomings of social judgment.* Englewood Cliffs, NJ: Prentice-Hall.

Nisbett, R. E., & Wilson, T. P. (1977). Telling more than we know: Verbal reports on mental processes. *Psychological Review, 84*, 231–259.

O'Leary, K. D., & Wilson, G. T. (1987). *Behavior therapy: Application and outcome.* Englewood Cliffs, NJ: Prentice Hall.

Olson, D. H., & Dowd, E. G. (1984). Generalization and maintenance of therapeutic change. *The Cognitive Behaviorist, 6*, 13–19.

Peterson, C., Semmel, A., von Baeyer, C., Abramson, L. Y., Metalsky, G. I., & Seligman, M. E. P. (1982). The Attributional Style Questionnaire. *Cognitive Therapy and Research, 6*, 287–299.

Premack, D. (1965). Reinforcement theory. In D. Levine (Ed.), *Nebraska Symposium on Motivation.* Lincoln, NE: University of Nebraska Press.

Premack, D. (1971). Catching up with common sense or two sides of a generalization: Reinforcement and punishment. In R. Glaser (Ed.), *The nature of reinforcement.* New York: Academic Press.

Rehm, L. P., & Rokke, P. (1988). Self-management therapies. In K. S. Dobson (Ed.), *Handbook of cognitive-behavioral therapies.* New York: Guilford Press.

Rosen, H. (1989). Piagetian theory and cognitive therapy. In A. Freeman, K. M. Simon, L. E. Beutler, & H. Arkowitz (Eds.), *Comprehensive handbook of cognitive therapy.* New York: Plenum.

Sacco, W. P. (1981). Cognitive therapy *in vivo.* In G. Emery, S. D. Holon, & R. C. Bedrosian (Eds.), *New directions in cognitive therapy: A casebook.* New York: Guilford Press.

Safran, J. D., & Segal, Z. V. (1990). *Interpersonal process in cognitive therapy.* New York: Basic Books.

Schaefer, H., Sobell, M., & Mills, K. (1971). Baseline drinking behaviors in alcoholics and social drinkers' kinds of drinks and sip magnitudes. *Behavior Research and Therapy, 9*, 23–27.

Schwartz, R. M., & Gottman, J. M. (1976). Toward a task analysis of assertive behavior. *Journal of Consulting and Clinical Psychology, 44*, 910–920.

Selmi, P. M., Klein, M. H., Greist, J. H., Sorrell, S. P., & Erdman, H. P. (1990). Computer-administered cognitive-behavioral therapy for depression. *American Journal of Psychiatry, 147*(1), 51–56.

Sheeren, M. (1987). The relationships between relapse and involvement in Alcoholics Anonymous. *Journal of Studies on Alcohol, 49*(1), 104–106.

Shorkey, C., & Whiteman, V. (1977). Development of the Rational Behavior Inventory: Initial validity and reliability. *Educational and Psychological Measurement, 37*, 527–534.

Smith, E. R., & Miller, E. R. (1978). Limits on perception of cognitive processes: A reply to Nisbett and Wilson. *Psychological Review, 85*, 355–362.

Staats, A. W. (1975). *Social behaviorism.* Pacific Grove, CA: Brooks/Cole.

Stevens, V. J., & Hollis, J. F. (1989). Preventing smoking relapse, using an individually tailored skills-training technique. *Journal of Consulting and Clinical Psychology, 57*(3), 420–424.

Stokes, T. F., & Baer, D. M. (1977). An implicit technology of generalization. *Journal of Applied Behavior Analysis, 10*, 345–367.

Suinn, R. M., & Richardson, F. (1971). Anxiety management training: A nonspecific behavior therapy program for anxiety control. *Behavior Therapy, 2*, 498–510.

Sutton-Simon, K. (1981). Assessing belief systems: Concepts and strategies. In P. C. Kendall & S. D. Hollon (Eds.), *Assessment strategies for cognitive-behavioral interventions.* New York: Academic Press.

Tharp, R. G., & Wetzel, R. J. (1969). *Behavior modification in the natural environment.* New York: Academic Press.

Thoresen, C. E., & Mahoney, M. J. (1974). *Behavioral self-control.* New York: Holt, Rinehart & Winston.

Tracy, E., Haapala, D., Kinney, J., & Pecora, P. (Eds.). (1991). *Intensive family preservation services: An instructional sourcebook.* Cleveland: Case Western Reserve University, Mandel School of Applied Social Sciences.

Turk, D. C., & Salovey, P. (1986). Clinical information processing: Bias inoculation. In R. E. Ingram (Ed.), *Information processing approach-*

es to clinical psychology. Orlando, FL: Academic Press.

Watson, D. L., & Tharp, R. G. (1972). *Self-directed behavior: Self-modification for personal adjustment*. Pacific Grove, CA: Brooks/Cole.

Weissman, A. N. (1978). *Development and validation of the Dysfunctional Attitudes Scale*. Paper presented at the annual meeting of the Association for Advancement of Behavior Therapy, Chicago.

Weissman, A. N., & Beck, A. T. (1978). *Development and validation of the Dysfunctional Attitudes Scale: A preliminary investigation*. Paper presented at the annual meeting of the American Education Association, Toronto.

White, P. (1980). Limitations on verbal reports on internal events: A refutation of Nisbett and Wilson and of Bem. *Psychological Review, 87*, 105–112.

Winfrey, L. L., & Goldfried, M. R. (1986). Information processing and the human change process. In R. E. Ingram (Ed.), *Information processing approaches to clinical psychology*. New York: Academic Press.

Wodarski, J. S. (1980). Procedures for the maintenance and generalization of achieved behavioral change. *Journal of Sociology and Social Welfare, 7*(2), 298–311.

Author Index

Subject Index

TO THE OWNER OF THIS BOOK:

I hope that you have enjoyed *Cognitive and Behavioral Treatment: Methods and Applications*. I'd like to know as much about your experiences with the book as you care to offer. Only through your comments and the comments of others can I learn how to make a better book for future readers.

School: _____

Address: _____

Department: _____

Instructor's name: _____

1. What did you like most about the book? _____

_____

_____

2. What did you like least about the book? _____

_____

_____

3. Were all of the chapters of the book assigned for you to read? _____

_____

   If not, which ones weren't? _____

4. In the space below, or on a separate sheet of paper, please let me know what other comments about the book you'd like to make. (For example, were any chapters or concepts particularly difficult?) I'd be delighted to hear from you!

_____

_____

_____

_____

_____

_____

_____

Optional:

Your name: _____ Date: _____

May Brooks/Cole quote you, either in promotion for *Cognitive and Behavioral Treatment: Methods and Applications* or in future publishing ventures?

Yes: _____ No: _____

Sincerely,
Donald K. Granvold

FOLD HERE

FOLD HERE